SOFTWARE

Yogesh Singh

CAMBRIDGE
UNIVERSITY PRESS

4843/24, 2nd Floor, Ansari Road, Daryaganj, Delhi - 110002, India

Cambridge University Press is part of the University of Cambridge.

It furthers the University's mission by disseminating knowledge in the pursuit of education, learning and research at the highest international levels of excellence.

www.cambridge.org
Information on this title: www.cambridge.org/9781107012967

© Yogesh Singh 2012

This publication is in copyright. Subject to statutory exception and to the provisions of relevant collective licensing agreements, no reproduction of any part may take place without the written permission of Cambridge University Press.

First paperback edition 2012
Reprint 2015, 2016 (twice)

Printed in India by Shree Maitrey Printech Pvt. Ltd., Noida

A catalogue record for this publication is available from the British Library

Library of Congress Cataloguing in Publication data
Singh, Yogesh, 1966-
Software testing / Yogesh Singh.
p. cm.
Includes bibliographical references.
Summary: "Discusses the concept of Software Testing with real-life case studies and solved examples"-- Provided by publisher.
ISBN 978-1-107-01296-7 (hardback)
1. Computer software--Testing. 2. Computer software--Quality control. I. Title
QA76.76.T48S56 2011
005.1'4–dc22 2011012053

ISBN 978-1-107-01296-7 Hardback
ISBN 978-1-107-65278-1 Paperback

Cambridge University Press has no responsibility for the persistence or accuracy of URLs for external or third-party internet websites referred to in this publication, and does not guarantee that any content on such websites is, or will remain, accurate or appropriate.

Contents

List of Figures   *xi*
List of Tables   *xv*
Preface   *xxi*
Acknowledgements   *xxiii*

1. Introduction   1

- 1.1 Some Software Failures   1
  - 1.1.1 The Explosion of the Ariane 5 Rocket   1
  - 1.1.2 The Y2K Problem   2
  - 1.1.3 The USA Star-Wars Program   3
  - 1.1.4 Failure of London Ambulance System   3
  - 1.1.5 USS Yorktown Incident   3
  - 1.1.6 Accounting Software Failures   3
  - 1.1.7 Experience of Windows XP   4
- 1.2 Testing Process   4
  - 1.2.1 What is Software Testing?   5
  - 1.2.2 Why Should We Test?   14
  - 1.2.3 Who Should We Do the Testing?   15
  - 1.2.4 What Should We Test?   16
- 1.3 Some Terminologies   19
  - 1.3.1 Program and Software   19
  - 1.3.2 Verification and Validation   20
  - 1.3.3 Fault, Error, Bug and Failure   21
  - 1.3.4 Test, Test Case and Test Suite   21
  - 1.3.5 Deliverables and Milestones   22
  - 1.3.6 Alpha, Beta and Acceptance Testing   22
  - 1.3.7 Quality and Reliability   23

	1.3.8	Testing, Quality Assurance and Quality Control	23
	1.3.9	Static and Dynamic Testing	23
	1.3.10	Testing and Debugging	24
1.4	Limitations of Testing		24
	1.4.1	Errors in the Software Requirement and Specification Document	24
	1.4.2	Logical Bugs	24
	1.4.3	Difficult to Measure the Progress of Testing	26
1.5	The V Shaped Software Life Cycle Model		26
	1.5.1	Graphical Representation	27
	1.5.2	Relationship of Development and Testing Parts	27

Multiple Choice Questions — *28*

Exercises — *34*

Further Reading — *35*

2. Functional Testing — 37

2.1	Boundary Value Analysis		38
	2.1.1	Robustness Testing	43
	2.1.2	Worst-Case Testing	44
	2.1.3	Robust Worst-Case Testing	46
	2.1.4	Applicability	48
2.2	Equivalence Class Testing		63
	2.2.1	Creation of Equivalence Classes	63
	2.2.2	Applicability	65
2.3	Decision Table Based Testing		81
	2.3.1	Parts of the Decision Table	81
	2.3.2	Limited Entry and Extended Entry Decision Tables	82
	2.3.3	'Do Not Care' Conditions and Rule Count	82
	2.3.4	Impossible Conditions	83
	2.3.5	Applicability	83
2.4	Cause-Effect Graphing Technique		96
	2.4.1	Identification of Causes and Effects	97
	2.4.2	Design of Cause-Effect Graph	97
	2.4.3	Use of Constraints in Cause-Effect Graph	97
	2.4.4	Design of Limited Entry Decision Table	99
	2.4.5	Writing of Test Cases	99
	2.4.6	Applicability	99

Multiple Choice Questions — *102*

Exercises — *105*

Further Reading — *108*

3. Essentials of Graph Theory — 110

3.1	What is a Graph?		110
	3.1.1	Degree of a Node	112
	3.1.2	Regular Graph	113

3.2	Matrix Representation of Graphs		113
	3.2.1	Incidence Matrix	114
	3.2.2	Adjacency Matrix	114
3.3	Paths and Independent Paths		116
	3.3.1	Cycles	117
	3.3.2	Connectedness of a Graph	117
3.4	Generation of a Graph from Program		123
	3.4.1	Program Graphs	124
	3.4.2	DD Path Graphs	127
3.5	Identification of Independent Paths		144
	3.5.1	Cyclomatic Complexity	144
	3.5.2	Graph Matrices	150

Multiple Choice Questions   *159*

Exercises   *161*

Further Reading   *163*

4. Structural Testing   **165**

4.1	Control Flow Testing		165
	4.1.1	Statement Coverage	166
	4.1.2	Branch Coverage	167
	4.1.3	Condition Coverage	167
	4.1.4	Path Coverage	167
4.2	Data Flow Testing		173
	4.2.1	Define/Reference Anomalies	174
	4.2.2	Definitions	174
	4.2.3	Identification of du and dc Paths	175
	4.2.4	Testing Strategies Using du-Paths	175
	4.2.5	Generation of Test Cases	176
4.3	Slice Based Testing		197
	4.3.1	Guidelines for Slicing	197
	4.3.2	Creation of Program Slices	198
	4.3.3	Generation of Test Cases	202
4.4	Mutation Testing		212
	4.4.1	Mutation and Mutants	212
	4.4.2	Mutation Operators	216
	4.4.3	Mutation Score	216

Multiple Choice Questions   *223*

Exercises   *226*

Further Reading   *228*

5. Software Verification   **230**

5.1	Verification Methods		230
	5.1.1	Peer Reviews	231

		5.1.2	Walkthroughs	231
		5.1.3	Inspections	231
		5.1.4	Applications	232
	5.2	Software Requirements Specification (SRS) Document Verification		233
		5.2.1	Nature of the SRS Document	233
		5.2.2	Characteristics and Organization of the SRS Document	233
		5.2.3	SRS Document Checklist	235
	5.3	Software Design Description (SDD) Document Verification		238
		5.3.1	Organization of the SDD Document	239
		5.3.2	The SDD Document Checklist	239
	5.4	Source Code Reviews		241
		5.4.1	Issues Related to Source Code Reviews	241
		5.4.2	Checklist of Source Code Reviews	242
	5.5	User Documentation Verification		243
		5.5.1	Review Process Issues	244
		5.5.2	User Documentation Checklist	244
	5.6	Software Project Audit		245
		5.6.1	Relevance Scale	246
		5.6.2	Theory and Practice Scale	246
		5.6.3	Project Audit and Review Checklist	246
	5.7	Case Study		257
	Multiple Choice Questions			*279*
	Exercises			*282*
	Further Reading			*283*

6. Creating Test Cases from Requirements and Use Cases — 285

	6.1	Use Case Diagram and Use Cases		285
		6.1.1	Identification of Actors	286
		6.1.2	Identification of Use Cases	287
		6.1.3	Drawing of Use Case Diagram	288
		6.1.4	Writing of Use Case Description	290
	6.2	Generation of Test Cases from Use Cases		292
		6.2.1	Generation of Scenario Diagrams	293
		6.2.2	Creation of Use Case Scenario Matrix	294
		6.2.3	Identification of Variables in a Use Case	295
		6.2.4	Identification of Different Input States of a Variable	296
		6.2.5	Design of Test Case Matrix	296
		6.2.6	Assigning Actual Values to Variables	296
	6.3	Guidelines for generating validity checks		316
		6.3.1	Data Type	316
		6.3.2	Data Range	316
		6.3.3	Special Data Conditions	316
		6.3.4	Mandatory Data Inputs	316
		6.3.5	Domain Specific Checks	316
	6.4	Strategies for Data Validity		317
		6.4.1	Accept Only Known Valid Data	317

	6.4.2	Reject Known Bad Data	322
	6.4.3	Sanitize All Data	322
6.5	Database Testing		326

Multiple Choice Questions — *331*
Exercises — *333*
Further Reading — *334*

7. Selection, Minimization and Prioritization of Test Cases for Regression Testing — **335**

7.1	What is Regression Testing?		335
	7.1.1	Regression Testing Process	336
	7.1.2	Selection of Test Cases	337
7.2	Regression Test Cases Selection		339
	7.2.1	Select All Test Cases	339
	7.2.2	Select Test Cases Randomly	339
	7.2.3	Select Modification Traversing Test Cases	339
7.3	Reducing the Number of Test Cases		340
	7.3.1	Minimization of Test Cases	340
	7.3.2	Prioritization of Test Cases	341
7.4	Risk Analysis		342
	7.4.1	What is Risk?	342
	7.4.2	Risk Matrix	343
7.5	Code Coverage Prioritization Technique		346
	7.5.1	Test Cases Selection Criteria	347
	7.5.2	Modification Algorithm	347
	7.5.3	Deletion Algorithm	352

Multiple Choice Questions — *363*
Exercises — *364*
Further Reading — *365*

8. Software Testing Activities — **368**

8.1	Levels of Testing		368
	8.1.1	Unit Testing	369
	8.1.2	Integration Testing	370
	8.1.3	System Testing	373
	8.1.4	Acceptance Testing	373
8.2	Debugging		374
	8.2.1	Why Debugging is so Difficult?	374
	8.2.2	Debugging Process	375
	8.2.3	Debugging Approaches	377
	8.2.4	Debugging Tools	378
8.3	Software Testing Tools		379
	8.3.1	Static Software Testing Tools	379

viii Contents

	8.3.2 Dynamic Software Testing Tools	381
	8.3.3 Process Management Tools	382
8.4	Software Test Plan	382
Multiple Choice Questions		*383*
Exercises		*386*
Further Reading		*387*

9. Object Oriented Testing 389

9.1	What is Object Orientation?	389
	9.1.1 Classes and Objects	390
	9.1.2 Inheritance	391
	9.1.3 Messages, Methods, Responsibility, Abstraction	393
	9.1.4 Polymorphism	394
	9.1.5 Encapsulation	394
9.2	What is Object Oriented Testing?	395
	9.2.1 What is a Unit?	395
	9.2.2 Levels of Testing	395
9.3	Path Testing	396
	9.3.1 Activity Diagram	396
	9.3.2 Calculation of Cyclomatic Complexity	400
	9.3.3 Generation of Test Cases	401
9.4	State Based Testing	404
	9.4.1 What is a State Machine?	404
	9.4.2 State Chart Diagram	406
	9.4.3 State Transition Tables	407
	9.4.4 Generation of Test Cases	408
9.5	Class Testing	411
	9.5.1 How Should We Test a Class?	412
	9.5.2 Issues Related to Class Testing	412
	9.5.3 Generating Test Cases	412
Multiple Choice Questions		*415*
Exercises		*417*
Further Reading		*418*

10. Metrics and Models in Software Testing 420

10.1	Software Metrics	420
	10.1.1 Measure, Measurement and Metrics	420
	10.1.2 Applications	421
10.2	Categories of Metrics	422
	10.2.1 Product Metrics for Testing	422
	10.2.2 Process Metrics for Testing	423
10.3	Object Oriented Metrics Used in Testing	423

Contents ix

10.3.1 Coupling Metrics	424
10.3.2 Cohesion Metrics	424
10.3.3 Inheritance Metrics	425
10.3.4 Size Metrics	426
10.4 What Should We Measure During Testing?	427
10.4.1 Time	427
10.4.2 Quality of Source Code	428
10.4.3 Source Code Coverage	429
10.4.4 Test Case Defect Density	429
10.4.5 Review Efficiency	429
10.5 Software Quality Attributes Prediction Models	430
10.5.1 Reliability Models	430
10.5.2 An Example of Fault Prediction Model in Practice	437
10.5.3 Maintenance Effort Prediction Model	442
Multiple Choice Questions	*446*
Exercises	*449*
Further Reading	*451*

11. Testing Web Applications — 453

11.1 What is Web Testing?	453
11.1.1 Web Application versus Client Server Application	453
11.1.2 Key Areas in Testing Web Applications	455
11.2 Functional Testing	456
11.3 User Interface Testing	458
11.3.1 Navigation Testing	458
11.3.2 Form Based Testing	459
11.3.3 User Interface Testing Checklist	461
11.4 Usability Testing	463
11.4.1 What is Usability and Usability Testing?	463
11.4.2 Identification of Participants	464
11.4.3 Development of Usability Testing Questionnaire	465
11.4.4 Setting up Environment for Conducting Test	468
11.4.5 Conducting the Test	469
11.4.6 Analyze the Results and Observations	469
11.5 Configuration and Compatibility Testing	469
11.5.1 Browser Testing	470
11.5.2 Guidelines and Checklist for Configuration and Compatibility Testing	470
11.6 Security Testing	471
11.7 Performance Testing	476
11.7.1 Load Testing	476
11.7.2 Stress Testing	479
11.7.3 Performance Testing Checklist	479
11.8 Database Testing	480
11.9 Post-Deployment Testing	482

x Contents

11.10 Web Metrics	485
Multiple Choice Questions	*486*
Exercises	*490*
Further Reading	*492*

12. Automated Test Data Generation — 494

12.1 What is Automated Test Data Generation?	494
12.1.1 Test Adequacy Criteria	495
12.1.2 Static and Dynamic Test Data Generation	495
12.2 Approaches to Test Data Generation	496
12.2.1 Random Testing	496
12.2.2 Symbolic Execution	496
12.2.3 Dynamic Test Data Generation	501
12.3 Test Data Generation using Genetic Algorithm	502
12.3.1 Initial Population	503
12.3.2 Crossover and Mutation	503
12.3.3 Fitness Function	504
12.3.4 Selection	505
12.3.5 Algorithm for Generating Test Data	505
12.4 Test Data Generation Tools	511
Multiple Choice Questions	*512*
Exercises	*513*
Further Reading	*514*
Appendix I	*517*
Appendix II	*541*
Appendix III	*594*
References	*612*
Answers to Multiple Choice Questions	*617*
Index	*621*

List of Figures

1.1	Program 'Minimum' to find the smallest integer out of a set of integers	5
1.2	Modified program 'Minimum' to find the smallest integer out of a set of integers	11
1.3	Final program 'Minimum' to find the smallest integer out of a set of integers	13
1.4	Phase wise cost of fixing an error	15
1.5	Control flow graph of a 10 to 20 statement program [MYER04]	18
1.6	Components of the software	19
1.7	Documentation manuals	19
1.8	Operating system manuals	20
1.9	A typical example	25
1.10	V shaped software development life cycle model	27
2.1	Functional (Black Box) testing	37
2.2	Five values for input 'x' of 'Square' program	38
2.3	Selected values for input values x and y	39
2.4	Valid input domain for the program 'Addition'	39
2.5	Graphical representation of inputs	40
2.6	Graphical representation of inputs	44
2.7	Graphical representation of inputs	45
2.8	Graphical representation of inputs	46
2.9	Graphical representation of inputs	64
2.10	Equivalence classes of input domain	65
2.11	Steps for the generation of test cases	96
2.12	Basic notations used in cause-effect graph	97
2.13	Constraint symbols for any cause-effect graph	98
2.14	Example of cause-effect graph with exclusive (constraint) and requires constraint	99
2.15	Cause-effect graph of rental car problem	100
2.16	Cause-effect graph of triangle classification problem	101
3.1	Undirected and directed graphs	111
3.2	Graphs with loop and parallel edges	111
3.3	Types of graphs	112
3.4	Regular graphs	113
3.5	Cyclic graph	117
3.6	Disconnected graphs	118
3.7	Strongly connected graph	118
3.8	Weakly connected graph	119

xii List of Figures

3.9	Basic constructs of a program graph	124
3.10	Program 'Square' and its program graph	125
3.11	Program to find the largest among three numbers	126
3.12	Program graph to find the largest number amongst three numbers as given in Figure 3.11	126
3.13	DD path graph and mapping table of program graph in Figure 3.10	127
3.14	DD path graph of the program to find the largest among three numbers	128
3.15	Source code of determination of division of a student problem	130
3.16	Program graph	130
3.17	DD path graph of program to find division of a student	132
3.18	Source code for classification of triangle problem	134
3.19	Program graph of classification of triangle problem	134
3.20	DD path graph of the program to classify a triangle	136
3.21	Source code for determination of day of the week	139
3.22	Program graph for determination of day of the week	140
3.23	DD path graph for determination of day of the week	143
3.24	Program graph	145
3.25	Program graph with 3 connected components	146
3.26	Program graphs and graph matrices	151
3.27	Connection matrix for program graph shown in Figure 3.26(b)	152
3.28	Various paths of program graph given in Figure 3.26(a)	153
3.29	Program graph	154
3.30	DD path graph for determination of division problem	155
3.31	Graph matrix for determination of division problem	156
3.32	Connection matrix for determination of division problem	156
3.33	DD path graph for classification of triangle problem	157
3.34	Graph matrix for classification of triangle problem	158
3.35	Connection matrix for classification of triangle problem	158
4.1	Source code with program graph	166
4.2	Portion of a program	198
4.3	Two slices for variable 'c'	199
4.4	Example program	199
4.5	Some slices of program in Figure 3.11	202
4.6	Slices of program for determination of division of a student	207
4.7	Mutant$_1$ (M$_1$) of program to find the largest among three numbers	214
4.8	Mutant$_2$ (M$_2$) of program to find the largest among three numbers	214
4.9	Mutant$_3$ (M$_3$) of program to find the largest among three numbers	215
6.1	Components of use case diagram	288
6.2	Use case diagram of the URS	289
6.3	Basic and alternative flows with pre-and post-conditions	293
6.4	Basic and alternative flows for login use case (a) Login (b) Change password	294
6.5	Basic and alternative flows for 'maintain school', 'programme', 'scheme', 'paper', or 'student details' use cases (a) Add details (b) Edit details (c) Delete details (d) View details	301
6.6	Login form	318
	6.7 Change password form	320

6.8	Maintain school details form	322
6.9	Maintain program details form	324
7.1	Steps of regression testing process	337
7.2	Program for printing value of z	338
7.3	Threshold by quadrant	343
7.4	Alternate threshold by quadrant	344
7.5	Threshold by diagonal quadrant	345
7.6	Threshold based on high 'Impact of Problem' value	345
7.7	Threshold based on high 'probability of occurrence of problem' value	346
8.1	Levels of testing	369
8.2	Unit under test with stubs and driver	370
8.3	Coupling amongst units	371
8.4	Integration approaches	372
9.1	Class and its objects	390
9.2	Class courier	391
9.3	The categories around fast track courier	392
9.4	A class hierarchy	393
9.5	An example of an activity diagram	397
9.6	Program to determine division of a student	399
9.7	Activity diagram of function validate()	400
9.8	Activity diagram of function calculate()	400
9.9	Program to determine largest among three numbers	403
9.10	Activity diagram for function validate()	403
9.11	Activity diagram for function maximum()	404
9.12	A typical state machine diagram	405
9.13	Typical life cycle of a process	406
9.14	State chart diagram for class stack	407
9.15	State chart diagram of withdrawal from ATM	410
9.16	Specification for the class stack	413
9.17	Class ATM withdrawal	414
10.1	λ as a function of μ	431
10.2	Relationship between τ and μ	431
10.3	Relationship between λ and τ	432
10.4	ROC curve for (a) Model I (b) Model II (c) Model III (d) Model IV using LR method	442
10.5	Comparison between actual and predicted values for maintenance effort	446
11.1	Two-tier architecture of client-server application	454
11.2	Three-tier architecture of web based applications	454
11.3	Web application process	455
11.4	Homepage of online shopping web application	456
11.5	Sample online registration form	460
11.6	Usability testing steps	464
11.7	Participant characteristics for online shopping website	464
11.8	Usability testing questionnaire	468
11.9	Sample questions for online shopping website	468

11.10	Security threats	472
11.11	Working of a firewall	473
11.12	Post deployment testing questionnaire	484
11.13	Typical post deployment testing procedure of a web application	484
12.1	Program for determination of nature of roots of a quadratic equation	497
12.2	Program graph of program given in Figure 12.1	498
12.3	A typical program	501
12.4	Flow chart of various steps of genetic algorithm	506
12.5	Program to divide two numbers	507
II-1	Basic and alternative flows for maintain faculty details use case (a) Add a faculty (b) Edit a faculty (c) Delete a faculty (d) View a faculty	577
II-2	Basic and alternative flows for maintain registration details use case (a) Add student registration details (b) Edit student registration details	587
III-1	Validity checks for scheme form	595
III-2	Test case with actual data values for the scheme form	597
III-3	Validity checks for paper form	598
III-4	Test case with actual data values for paper form	600
III-5	Validity checks for student form	601
III-6	Test case with actual data values for the student form	603
III-7	Validity checks for faculty form	604
III-8	Test case with actual data values for the faculty form	605
III-9	Validity checks for maintain registration details	607
III-10	Test case with actual data values for the student registration form	611

List of Tables

1.1	Inputs and outputs of the program 'Minimum'	6
1.2	Some critical/typical situations of the program 'Minimum'	7
1.3	Possible reasons of failures for all nine cases	8
1.4	Reasons for observed output	9
1.5	Results of the modified program 'Minimum'	12
1.6	Persons and their roles during development and testing	16
1.7	Test case template	21
1.8	Test cases for function of Figure 1.9	25
1.9	Typical test cases where outputs are different	26
2.1	Test cases for the 'Square' program	38
2.2	Test cases for the program 'Addition'	40
2.3	Boundary value test cases to find the largest among three numbers	41
2.4	Boundary value test cases for the program determining the division of a student	41
2.5	Boundary value test cases for triangle classification program	42
2.6	Boundary value test cases for the program determining the day of the week	43
2.7	Robustness test cases for two input values x and y	44
2.8	Worst test cases for the program 'Addition'	45
2.9	Robust worst test cases for the program 'Addition'	47
2.10	Robust test cases for the program to find the largest among three numbers	48
2.11	Worst case test cases for the program to find the largest among three numbers	48
2.12	Robust test cases for the program determining the division of a student	51
2.13	Worst case test cases for the program for determining the division of a student	52
2.14	Robust test cases for the triangle classification program	55
2.15	Worst case test cases for the triangle classification program	55
2.16	Robust test cases for program for determining the day of the week	59
2.17	Worst case test cases for the program determining day of the week	59
2.18	Test cases for program 'Square' based on input domain	63
2.19	Test cases for the program 'Addition'	64
2.20	Test cases for program 'Square' based on output domain	65
2.21	Test cases for program 'Addition' based on output domain	65
2.22	Output domain test cases to find the largest among three numbers	66
2.23	Input domain test case	67
2.24	Output domain test cases	68
2.25	Input domain test cases	70

2.26	Output domain test cases for triangle classification program	71
2.27	Input domain test cases	73
2.28	Output domain equivalence class test cases	74
2.29	Input domain equivalence class test cases	78
2.30	Decision table	81
2.31	Typical structure of a decision table	82
2.32	Decision table for triangle problem	82
2.33	Decision table	84
2.34	Test cases of the given problem	84
2.35	Limited entry decision table	85
2.36	Test cases of the given problem	86
2.37	Extended entry decision table	87
2.38	Test cases of the problem	88
2.39	Decision table	89
2.40	Test cases	90
2.41	Modified decision table	90
2.42	Test cases of the decision table given in table 2.41	92
2.43	Decision table	94
2.44	Test cases of the program day of the week	95
2.45	Decision table of rental car problem	100
2.46	Test cases of the given decision table	100
2.47	Decision table	101
3.1	Paths of undirected graph in Figure 3.1(a)	116
3.2	Paths of directed graph in Figure 3.1(b)	117
3.3	Mapping of program graph nodes and DD graph nodes	127
3.4	Mapping of program graph nodes and DD graph nodes	131
3.5	Mapping of program graph nodes and DD graph nodes	135
3.6	Mapping of program graph nodes to DD graph nodes	141
4.1	Test cases	168
4.2	Test cases for statement coverage	170
4.3	Test cases for path coverage	171
4.4	Test cases for statement coverage	172
4.5	Test cases for path coverage	173
4.6	Test cases for all du-paths and all uses	180
4.7	Test cases for all definitions	180
4.8	All du-paths	182
4.9	Test cases for all du-paths	183
4.10	All uses paths for triangle classification problem	184
4.11	Test cases for all uses paths	185
4.12	All definitions paths for triangle classification problem	185
4.13	Test cases for all definitions paths	186
4.14	All uses paths for determination of the day of week problem	189
4.15	Test cases for all uses	192
4.16	All-definitions paths for determination of the day of week problem	195
4.17	Test cases for all-definitions	196

4.18	Test cases using program slices of program to find the largest among three numbers	203
4.19	Test cases using program slices	207
4.20	Test cases using program slices	209
4.21	Test cases using program slices	211
4.22	Mutated statements	217
4.23	Actual output of mutant M_1	217
4.24	Actual output of mutant M_2	217
4.25	Actual output of mutant M_3	218
4.26	Actual output of mutant M_4	218
4.27	Actual output of mutant M_5	218
4.28	Additional test case	218
4.29	Output of added test case	218
4.30	Revised test suite	219
4.31	Test suite A	219
4.32	Test suite B	219
4.33	Mutated lines	219
4.34	Actual output of $M_1(A)$	220
4.35	Actual output of $M_2(A)$	220
4.36	Actual output of $M_3(A)$	220
4.37	Actual output of $M_4(A)$	220
4.38	Actual output of $M_5(A)$	221
4.39	Actual output of $M_1(B)$	221
4.40	Actual output of $M_2(B)$	221
4.41	Actual output of $M_3(B)$	222
4.42	Actual output of $M_4(B)$	222
4.43	Actual output of $M_5(B)$	222
4.44	Additional test case	222
4.45	Revised test suite B	223
5.1	Comparison of verification methods	232
5.2	Organization of the SRS [IEEE98a]	234
5.3	Checklist for the SRS document	236
5.4	Checklist for the SDD Document	239
5.5	Source code reviews checklist	242
5.6	User Documentation checklist	244
6.1	Jacobson's use case template	290
6.2	Alternative use case template	291
6.3	Scenario matrix for the flow of events shown in Figure 6.3	294
6.4	Scenario matrix for the login use case	295
6.5	A typical test case matrix	296
6.6	Test case matrix for the login use case	297
6.7	Test case matrix with actual data values for the login use case	298
6.8	Scenario matrix for the 'maintain school details' use case	302
6.9	Test case matrix for the 'maintain school details' use case	303
6.10	Test case matrix with actual data values for the 'maintain school' use case	305
6.11	Scenario matrix for the 'maintain programme details' use case	308

6.12	Test case matrix for the 'maintain programme details' use case	309
6.13	Test case matrix with actual data values for the programme use case	313
6.14	Validity checks for login form	318
6.15	Test case with actual data values for the login form	319
6.16	Validity checks for change password form	320
6.17	Test case with actual data values for the 'Change Password' form	321
6.18	Validity checks for school form	323
6.19	Test case with actual data values for the school form	323
6.20	Validity checks for program form	324
6.21	Test case with actual data values for the program form	325
6.22	Operations of 'school details' form	326
7.1	Comparison of regression and development testing	336
7.2	Test suite for program given in Figure 7.2	338
7.3	Risk analysis table	342
7.4	Risk analysis table of 'University Registration System'	343
7.5	Variables used by 'modification' algorithm	347
7.6	Test cases with execution history	348
7.7	Test cases with number of matches found	349
7.8	Test cases in decreasing order of number of modified lines covered	350
7.9	Test cases in descending order of number of matches found (iteration 2)	350
7.10	Test cases in descending order of number of matches found (iteration 3)	351
7.11	Test cases in descending order of number of matches found (iteration 4)	351
7.12	Test cases in descending order of number of matches found (iteration 5)	351
7.13	Variables used by 'deletion' algorithm	352
7.14	Test cases with execution history	352
7.15	Modified execution history after deleting line numbers 4, 7 and 15	353
7.16	Redundant test cases	354
7.17	Modified table after removing T1 and T5	355
7.18	Test cases with modified lines	355
7.19	Test cases in descending order of number of modified lines covered	355
7.20	Test cases in descending order of number of modified lines covered (iteration 2)	355
9.1	Symbols of an activity diagram	398
9.2	Test cases for validate function	401
9.3	Test cases for calculate function	402
9.4	Test cases of activity diagram in Figure 9.10	403
9.5	Test cases of activity diagram in Figure 9.11	404
9.6	Terminologies used in state chart diagram	405
9.7	State transition table for stack class	408
9.8	Test cases for class stack	409
9.9	Illegal test case for class stack	409
9.10	Test cases of withdrawal from ATM	411
9.11	Test cases of function push()	413
9.12	Test cases of function pop()	414
9.13	Test cases for function withdraw()	414
10.1	Coupling metrics	424

10.2	Cohesion metrics	425
10.3	Inheritance metrics	425
10.4	Size metrics	426
10.5	Time-based failure specification	427
10.6	Failure-based failure specification	428
10.7	Distribution of faults and faulty classes at high, medium and low severity levels	438
10.8	Descriptive statistics for metrics	438
10.9	Correlations among metrics	439
10.10	High severity faults model statistics	439
10.11	Medium severity faults model statistics	440
10.12	Low severity faults model statistics	440
10.13	Ungraded severity faults model statistics	440
10.14	Confusion matrix	440
10.15	Results of 10-cross validation of models	441
10.16	ANN summary	443
10.17	Rotated principal components	444
10.18	Validation results of ANN model	445
10.19	Analysis of model evaluation accuracy	445
11.1	Comparison of client/server and web based applications	454
11.2	Sample functional test cases of order process of an online shopping web application	457
11.3	Navigation testing test cases for online shopping website	459
11.4	Test cases of registration form of an online shopping web application	460
11.5	Checklist for testing user interfaces	461
11.6	Web application usability attributes	463
11.7	Browser's compatibility matrix	470
11.8	Configuration and compatibility testing checklist	471
11.9	Security testing checklist	474
11.10	Load testing metrics	477
11.11	Performance testing checklist	479
11.12	Sample database test cases	481
11.13	Web metrics	485
12.1	Constraints and values of paths (feasible/not feasible) of program given in Figure 12.1	499
12.2	Examples of one point crossover operator	503
12.3	Examples of two point crossover operator	504
12.4	Chromosomes with fitness values for initial population	505
12.5	Automated test data generation tools	511
II-1	Scenario matrix for the maintain scheme details use case	544
II-2	Test case matrix for the maintain scheme details use case	545
II-3	Test case matrix with actual data values for the maintain scheme details use case	549
II-4	Scenario matrix for the maintain paper details use case	555
II-5	Test case matrix for the maintain paper details use case	556

II-6	Test case matrix with actual data values for the maintain paper details use case	560
II-7	Scenario matrix for the maintain student details use case	566
II-8	Test case matrix for the maintain student details use case	567
II-9	Test case matrix with actual data values for the maintain student details use case	571
II-10	Scenario matrix for the maintain faculty details use case	578
II-11	Test case matrix for the maintain faculty details use case	579
II-12	Test case matrix with actual data values for the maintain faculty details use case	582
II-13	Scenario matrix for the maintain registration details use case	587
II-14	Test case matrix for the maintain registration details use case	588
II-15	Test case matrix with actual data values for the maintain registration details use case	591

Preface

There is a worldwide awareness of realizing the importance of software testing. Many universities now offer a course in software testing for undergraduate and graduate studies in Computer Science and Engineering, Computer Applications, Information Technology, Software Engineering and Electronics and Communication Engineering.

The book discusses software testing in the context of testing concepts and methods that can be implemented in practice. It has been designed as a main textbook for a course in software testing and as a useful resource for teachers and software practitioners.

The main features of this book are:

- It focuses on the importance, significance and limitations of software testing.
- It presents functional testing techniques that may help to design test cases without considering internal structure of the program.
- It presents structural testing techniques and introduces some fundamental structural testing techniques like control flow testing, dataflow testing, slice based testing and mutation testing.
- It promotes verification testing as an integral to modern software testing practices, equally as important as validation testing. Verification activities such as walkthroughs and inspections can be carried out at early phases of software development. Use case testing has also been introduced.
- It addresses important issues of selection, minimization and prioritization of test cases for regression testing. Complementary approaches for achieving adequate number of test cases during regression testing is also discussed in the book to show how to reduce maintenance cost.
- It presents software testing activities, debugging approaches and testing tools along with their commercial applications.
- It signifies the importance of object oriented testing. It also presents metrics used in software testing with their practical application in predicting models using commercial data sets.
- It emphasizes on testing web applications covering key areas such as functional testing, usability testing, user interface testing, security testing, performance testing, configuration and compatibility testing.
- It introduces the concepts of automated test data generation using static and dynamic test data generation techniques. Genetic algorithm is used for the generation of test data along with suitable examples.

The work for this book was primarily collected from the author's several years of teaching. Therefore, the text has been thoroughly tested in classroom and revised accordingly in the form of this textbook. The book contains numerous solved examples and each chapter ends with multiple choice questions and self-assessment Exercises. The answers to multiple choice questions have also been provided for verification. An Instructor Manual for teachers is also available on the website to provide guidance in teaching software testing.

I do realize the importance of feedback of our readers for continuous improvement in the contents of the book. I shall appreciate the constructive criticism about anything and also about any omission due to my ignorance. It is expected that the book will be a useful addition in the literature on software testing. Any suggestion about the book would gratefully be received.

Yogesh Singh

Acknowledgements

This book is the result of hardwork of Dr Ruchika Malhotra, Assistant Professor, Department of Software Engineering, Delhi Technological University, Delhi. The book would not have been completed without her kind support.

Thanks to my undergraduate and postgraduate students of the University School of Information Technology, Guru Gobind Singh Indraprastha University for motivating me to write this book. Their expectations, discussions and enthusiasm always become my strength for continuous improvement in academic pursuit. I would also like to thank all researchers, practitioners, software developers, testers and teachers whose views, ideas and techniques find a place in this book. I am also grateful to Sandeep Kumar, Stenographer of Examination Division of the University for typing the draft of the manuscript.

Lastly, I am thankful to Dr Pravin Chandra, Associate Professor, Delhi University, Dr Jitendra Chabra, Associate Professor, National Institute of Technology, Kurukshetra, Dr Arvinder Kaur, Associate Professor, Guru Gobind Singh Indraprastha University for their valuable suggestions. My thanks are also due to Dr Chetna Tiwari, Assistant Professor, University School of Humanities and Social Sciences, Guru Gobind Singh Indraprastha University for reading a few chapters of the manuscript.

1

Introduction

What is software testing? Why do we need to test software? Can we live without testing? How do we handle software bugs reported by the customers? Who should work hard to avoid frustrations of software failures?

Such questions are endless. But we need to find answers to such burning questions. Software organizations are regularly getting failure reports of their products and this number is increasing day by day. All of us would appreciate that it is extremely disappointing for the developers to receive such failure reports. The developers normally ask: how did these bugs escape unnoticed? It is a fact that software developers are experiencing failures in testing their coded programs and such situations are becoming threats to modern automated civilization. We cannot imagine a day without using cell phones, logging on to the internet, sending e-mails, watching television and so on. All these activities are dependent on software, and software is not reliable. The world has seen many software failures and some were even fatal to human life.

1.1 SOME SOFTWARE FAILURES

A major problem of the software industry is its inability to develop error-free software. Had software developers ever been asked to certify that the software developed is error-free, no software would have ever been released. Hence 'software crises' has become a fixture of everyday life with many well-publicized failures that have had not only major economic impact but also have become the cause of loss of life. Some of the failures are discussed in subsequent sections.

1.1.1 The Explosion of the Ariane 5 Rocket

The Ariane 5 rocket was designed by European Space Agency and it was launched on June 4, 1996. It was an unmanned rocket and unfortunately exploded only after 40 seconds of its take off from Kourou, French Guiana. The design and development took ten long years with a cost of $7 billion. An enquiry board was constituted to find the reasons of the explosion. The board identified the cause and mentioned in its report that [LION96]: "The failure of the Ariane 5 was caused by the complete loss of guidance and altitude information, 37 seconds after start of the main engine ignition sequence (30 seconds after lift-off). This loss of information was due to specification and design errors in the software of the inertial reference system. The extensive reviews and tests carried out during the Ariane 5 development programme did not include adequate analysis and testing of the inertial reference system or of the complete flight control system, which could have detected the potential failure". A software fault in the inertial reference system was identified as a reason for the explosion by the enquiry committee. The inertial reference system of the rocket had tried to convert 64 bit floating point number of horizontal velocity to a 16 bit signed integer. However, the number was greater than 32,767 (beyond the permissible limit of 16 bit machine) and the conversion process failed.

Unfortunately, the navigation system of Ariane 4 was used in Ariane 5 without proper testing and analysis. The Ariane 5 was a high speed rocket with higher value of an internal alignment function, known as horizontal bias. This value is for the calculation of horizontal velocity. On the day of the explosion, this value was more than expectations due to different trajectory of this rocket as compared to the Ariane 4. Therefore, the main technical reason was the conversion problem at the time of converting the horizontal bias variable, and this resulted into the shutdown of the computer of the inertial reference system. When the computer shut down, it passed control to an identical, redundant unit, which was there to provide backup in case of such a failure. But the second unit had failed in the identical manner before a few milliseconds. Why wouldn't it be? It was running the same software.

The designers never thought that the particular velocity value would ever be large enough to cause trouble. After all, it never had been before. Unfortunately Ariane 5 was a faster rocket than Ariane 4. Moreover, the calculation containing the error, which shut down the computer system, actually served no purpose, once the rocket was in the air. Its only function was to align the system before launch. So it should have been turned off. But designers chose long ago, in an earlier version of the Ariane 4, to leave this function running for the first forty seconds of flight – a 'special feature' meant to make the restart of the system easy in the event of a brief hold in the countdown. Such design decisions and poor testing resulted in the explosion of Ariane 5.

1.1.2 The Y2K Problem

The Y2K problem was the most critical problem of the last century. The whole world was expecting something drastic on January 1, 2000. Significant sums of money were spent by software companies to get rid of this problem. What was the problem? It was simply the case of using two digits for the year instead of four digits. For instance, 1965 was considered as 65. The developers could not imagine the problem of year 2000. What would happen on January 1, 2000? The last two digits i.e. 00 may belong to any century like 1800, 1900, 2000, 2100, etc. The simple ignorance or a faulty design decision to use only the last two digits for the year resulted into the serious Y2K problem. Most of the software was re-tested and modified or discarded, depending on the situation.

1.1.3 The USA Star-Wars Program

'Patriot missile' was the result of the USA 'Star Wars' program. This missile was used for the first time in the Gulf war against the Scud missile of Iraq. Surprisingly, 'Patriot missiles' failed many times to hit the targeted Scud missile. One of the failures killed 28 American soldiers in Dhahran, Saudi Arabia. An investigation team was constituted to identify the cause of failure. The team re-looked at every dimension of the product and found the reason for the failure. The cause of the failure was a software fault. There was a slight timing error in the system's clock after 14 hours of its operation. Hence, the tracking system was not accurate after 14 hours of operations and at the time of the Dhahran attack, the system had already operated for more than 100 hours.

1.1.4 Failure of London Ambulance System

The software controlling the ambulance dispatch system of London collapsed on October 26-27, 1992 and also on November 4, 1992 due to software failures. The system was introduced on October 26, 1992. The London Ambulance Service was a challenging task that used to cover an area of 600 square miles and handled 1500 emergency calls per day. Due to such a failure, there was a partial or no ambulance cover for many hours. The position of the vehicles was incorrectly recorded and multiple vehicles were sent to the same location. Everywhere people were searching for an ambulance and nobody knew the reason for non-arrival of ambulances at the desired sites. The repair cost was estimated to be £9m, but it is believed that twenty lives could have been saved if this failure had not occurred. The enquiry committee clearly pointed out the administrative negligence and over-reliance on 'cosy assurances' of the software company. The administration was allowed to use this system without proper alternative systems in case of any failure. The committee also termed the possible cause of failure as [ANDE98, FINK93]: "When the system went live, it could not cope with the volume of calls and broke under the strain. The transition to a back-up computer system had not been properly rehearsed and also failed."

1.1.5 USS Yorktown Incident

The USS Yorktown - a guided missile cruiser was in the water for several hours due to the software failure in 1998. A user wrongly gave a zero value as an input which caused a division by zero error. This fault further failed the propulsion system of the ship and it did not move in the water for many hours. The reason behind this failure was that the program did not check for any valid input.

1.1.6 Accounting Software Failures

Financial software is an essential part of any company's IT infrastructure. However, many companies have suffered failures in the accounting system due to errors in the financial software. The failures range from producing the wrong information to the complete system failure. There is widespread dissatisfaction over the quality of financial software. If a system gives information in the incorrect format, it may have an adverse impact on customer satisfaction.

1.1.7 Experience of Windows XP

Charles C. Mann shared his views about Windows XP through his article in technology review [MANN02] as: "Microsoft released Windows XP on October 25, 2001. That same day, what may be a record, the company posted 18 megabyte of patches on its website for bug fixes, compatibility updates, and enhancements. Two patches fixed important security holes. Or rather, one of them did; the other patch did not work. Microsoft advised (still advises) users to back up critical files before installing patches." This situation is quite embarrassing and clearly explains the sad situation of the software companies. The developers were either too careless or in a great hurry to fix such obvious faults.

We may endlessly continue discussing the history of software failures. Is there any light at the end of the tunnel? Or will the same scenario continue for many years to come? When automobile engineers give their views about cars, they do not say that the quality of today's cars is not better than the cars produced in the last decade. Similarly aeronautical engineers do not say that Boeing or Airbus makes poor quality planes as compared to the planes manufactured in the previous decade. Civil engineers also do not show their anxieties over the quality of today's structures over the structures of the last decade. Everyone feels that things are improving day by day. But software, alas, seems different. Most of the software developers are confused about the quality of their software products. If they are asked about the quality of software being produced by companies, they generally say, "It is getting worse day by day." It is as if we say that Boeing's planes produced in 2009 are less reliable than those produced in 1980. The blame for software bugs belongs to nearly everyone. It belongs to the software companies that rush products to market without adequately testing them. It belongs to the software developers who do not understand the importance of detecting and removing faults before customers experience them as failures. It belongs to a legal system that has given the software developers a free pass on error-related damages. The blame also belongs to universities that stress more on software development than testing.

1.2 TESTING PROCESS

Testing is an important aspect of the software development life cycle. It is basically the process of testing the newly developed software, prior to its actual use. The program is executed with desired input(s) and the output(s) is/are observed accordingly. The observed output(s) is/are compared with expected output(s). If both are same, then the program is said to be correct as per specifications, otherwise there is something wrong somewhere in the program. Testing is a very expensive process and consumes one-third to one-half of the cost of a typical development project. It is largely a systematic process but partly intuitive too. Hence, good testing process entails much more than just executing a program a few times to see its correctness.

1.2.1 What is Software Testing?

Good testing entails more than just executing a program with desired input(s). Let's consider a program termed as 'Minimum' (see Figure 1.1) that reads a set of integers and prints the smallest integer. We may execute this program using Turbo C complier with a number of inputs and compare the expected output with the observed output as given in Table 1.1.

```
LINE NUMBER    /*SOURCE CODE*/
               #include<stdio.h>
               #include<limits.h>
               #include<conio.h>
1.             void Minimum();
2.             void main()
3.             {
4.                     Minimum();
5.             }
6.             void Minimum()
7.             {
8.                     int array[100];
9.                     int Number;
10.                    int i;
11.                    int tmpData;
12.                    int Minimum=INT_MAX;
13.                    clrscr();
14.                    "printf("Enter the size of the array:");
15.                    scanf("%d",&Number);
16.                    for(i=0;i<Number;i++) {
17.                            printf("Enter A[%d]=",i+1);
18.                            scanf("%d",&tmpData);
19.                            tmpData=(tmpData<0)?-tmpData:tmpData;
20.                            array[i]=tmpData;
21.                    }
22.                    i=1;
23.                    while(i<Number-1) {
24.                            if(Minimum>array[i])
25.                            {
26.                                    Minimum=array[i];
27.                            }
28.                            i++;
29.                    }
30.                    printf("Minimum = %d\n", Minimum);
31.                    getch();
32.            }
```

Figure 1.1. Program 'Minimum' to find the smallest integer out of a set of integers

Table 1.1. Inputs and outputs of the program 'Minimum'

Test Case	Inputs Size	Inputs Set of Integers	Expected Output	Observed Output	Match?
1.	5	6, 9, 2, 16, 19	2	2	Yes
2.	7	96, 11, 32, 9, 39, 99, 91	9	9	Yes
3.	7	31, 36, 42, 16, 65, 76, 81	16	16	Yes
4.	6	28, 21, 36, 31, 30, 38	21	21	Yes
5.	6	106, 109, 88, 111, 114, 116	88	88	Yes
6.	6	61, 69, 99, 31, 21, 69	21	21	Yes
7.	4	6, 2, 9, 5	2	2	Yes
8.	4	99, 21, 7, 49	7	7	Yes

There are 8 sets of inputs in Table 1.1. We may feel that these 8 test cases are sufficient for such a trivial program. In all these test cases, the observed output is the same as the expected output. We may also design similar test cases to show that the observed output is matched with the expected output. There are many definitions of testing. A few of them are given below:

(i) Testing is the process of demonstrating that errors are not present.
(ii) The purpose of testing is to show that a program performs its intended functions correctly.
(iii) Testing is the process of establishing confidence that a program does what it is supposed to do.

The philosophy of all three definitions is to demonstrate that the given program behaves as per specifications. We may write 100 sets of inputs for the program 'Minimum' and show that this program behaves as per specifications. However, all three definitions are not correct. They describe almost the opposite of what testing should be viewed as. Forgetting the definitions for the moment, whenever we want to test a program, we want to establish confidence about the correctness of the program. Hence, our objective should not be to show that the program works as per specifications. But, we should do testing with the assumption that there are faults and our aim should be to remove these faults at the earliest. Thus, a more appropriate definition is [MYER04]: **"Testing is the process of executing a program with the intent of finding faults."** Human beings are normally goal oriented. Thus, establishment of a proper objective is essential for the success of any project. If our objective is to show that a program has no errors, then we shall sub-consciously work towards this objective. We shall intend to choose those inputs that have a low probability of making a program fail as we have seen in Table 1.1, where all inputs are purposely selected to show that the program is absolutely correct. On the contrary, if our objective is to show that a program has errors, we may select those test cases which have a higher probability of finding errors. We shall focus on weak and critical portions of the program to find more errors. This type of testing will be more useful and meaningful.

We again consider the program 'Minimum' (given in Figure 1.1) and concentrate on some typical and critical situations as discussed below:

(i) A very short list (of inputs) with the size of 1, 2, or 3 elements.
(ii) An empty list i.e. of size 0.

(iii) A list where the minimum element is the first or last element.
(iv) A list where the minimum element is negative.
(v) A list where all elements are negative.
(vi) A list where some elements are real numbers.
(vii) A list where some elements are alphabetic characters.
(viii) A list with duplicate elements.
(ix) A list where one element has a value greater than the maximum permissible limit of an integer.

We may find many similar situations which may be very challenging and risky for this program and each such situation should be tested separately. In Table 1.1, we have selected elements in every list to cover essentially the same situation: a list of moderate length, containing all positive integers, where the minimum is somewhere in the middle. Table 1.2 gives us another view of the same program 'Minimum' and the results are astonishing to everyone. It is clear from the outputs that the program has many failures.

Table 1.2. Some critical/typical situations of the program 'Minimum'

S. No.		Size	Inputs Set of Integers	Expected Output	Observed Output	Match?
Case 1 A very short list with size 1, 2 or 3	A	1	90	90	2147483647	No
	B	2	12, 10	10	2147483647	No
	C	2	10, 12	10	2147483647	No
	D	3	12, 14, 36	12	14	No
	E	3	36, 14, 12	12	14	No
	F	3	14, 12, 36	12	12	Yes
Case 2 An empty list, i.e. of size 0	A	0	–	Error message	2147483647	No
Case 3 A list where the minimum element is the first or last element	A	5	10, 23, 34, 81, 97	10	23	No
	B	5	97, 81, 34, 23, 10	10	23	No
Case 4 A list where the minimum element is negative	A	4	10, –2, 5, 23	–2	2	No
	B	4	5, –25, 20, 36	–25	20	No
Case 5 A list where all elements are negative	A	5	–23, –31, –45, –56, –78	–78	31	No
	B	5	–6, –203, –56, –78, –2	–203	56	No
Case 6 A list where some elements are real numbers	A	5	12, 34.56, 6.9, 62.14, 19	6.9	34 (The program does not take values for index 3,4 and 5)	No
	B	5.4	2, 3, 5, 6, 9	2	858993460 (The program does not take any array value)	No

(Contd.)

8 Software Testing

(Contd.)

S. No.	Inputs		Expected Output	Observed Output	Match?
	Size	Set of Integers			
Case 7 A list where some elements are characters	A	5	23, 2I, 26, 6, 9	6	2 (The program does not take any other index value for 3, 4 and 5)	No
	B	1I	2, 3, 4, 9, 6, 5, 11, 12, 14, 21, 22	2	2147483647 (Program does not take any other index value)	No
Case 8 A list with duplicate elements	A	5	3, 4, 6, 9, 6	3	4	No
	B	5	13, 6, 6, 9, 15	6	6	Yes
Case 9 A list where one element has a value greater than the maximum permissible limit of an integer	A	5	530, 4294967297, 23, 46, 59	23	1	No

What are the possible reasons for so many failures shown in Table 1.3? We should read our program 'Minimum' (given in Figure 1.1) very carefully to find reasons for so many failures. The possible reasons of failures for all nine cases discussed in Table 1.2 are given in Table 1.3. It is clear from Table 1.3 that this program suffers from serious design problems. Many important issues are not handled properly and therefore, we get strange observed outputs. The causes of getting these particular values of observed outputs are given in Table 1.4.

Table 1.3. Possible reasons of failures for all nine cases

S. No.	Possible Reasons
Case 1 A very short list with size 1, 2 or 3	While finding the minimum, the base value of the index and/or end value of the index of the usable array has not been handled properly (see line numbers 22 and 23).
Case 2 An empty list i.e. of size 0	The program proceeds without checking the size of the array (see line numbers 15 and 16).
Case 3 A list where the minimum element is the first or last element	Same as for Case 1.
Case 4 A list where the minimum element is negative	The program converts all negative integers into positive integers (see line number 19).
Case 5 A list where all elements are negative	Same as for Case 4.

(Contd.)

(Contd.)

S. No.	Possible Reasons
Case 6 A list where some elements are real numbers	The program uses scanf() function to read the values. The scanf() has unpredictable behaviour for inputs not according to the specified format. (See line numbers 15 and 18).
Case 7 A list where some elements are alphabetic characters	Same as for Case 6.
Case 8 A list with duplicate elements	(a) Same as for Case 1. (b) We are getting the correct result because the minimum value is in the middle of the list and all values are positive.
Case 9 A list with one value greater than the maximum permissible limit of an integer	This is a hardware dependent problem. This is the case of the overflow of maximum permissible value of the integer. In this example, 32 bits integers are used.

Table 1.4. Reasons for observed output

Cases	Observed Output	Remarks
1 (a)	2147483647	The program has ignored the first and last values of the list. This is the maximum value of a 32 bit integer to which a variable minimum is initialized.
1 (b)	2147483647	
1 (c)	2147483647	
1 (d)	14	The program has ignored the first and last values of the list. The middle value is 14.
1 (e)	14	
1 (f)	12	The program has ignored the first and last value of the list. Fortunately, the middle value is the minimum value and thus the result is correct.
2 (a)	2147483647	The maximum value of a 32 bit integer to which a variable minimum is initialized.
3 (a)	23	The program has ignored the first and last values of the list. The value 23 is the minimum value in the remaining list.
3 (b)	23	
4 (a)	2	The program has ignored the first and last values. It has also converted negative integer(s) to positive integer(s).
4 (b)	20	
5 (a)	31	Same as Case 4.
5 (b)	56	
6 (a)	34	After getting '.' of 34.56, the program was terminated and 34 was displayed. However, the program has also ignored 12, being the first index value.
6 (b)	858993460	Garbage value.
7 (a)	2	After getting 'l' in the second index value '2l', the program terminated abruptly and displayed 2.
7 (b)	2147483647	The input has a non digit value. The program displays the value to which variable 'minimum' is initialized.
8 (a)	4	The program has ignored the first and last index values. 4 is the minimum in the remaining list.
8 (b)	6	Fortunately the result is correct although the first and last index values are ignored.
9 (a)	1	The program displays this value due to the overflow of the 32 bit signed integer data type used in the program.

10 Software Testing

Modifications in the program 'Minimum'

Table 1.4 has given many reasons for undesired outputs. These reasons help us to identify the causes of such failures. Some important reasons are given below:

(i) **The program has ignored the first and last values of the list**

The program is not handling the first and last values of the list properly. If we see the line numbers 22 and 23 of the program, we will identify the causes. There are two faults. Line number 22 "i = 1;" should be changed to "i = 0;" in order to handle the first value of the list. Line number 23 "while (i<Number -1)" should be changed to "while (i<=Number-1)" in order to handle the last value of the list.

(ii) **The program proceeds without checking the size of the array**

If we see line numbers 14 and 15 of the program, we will come to know that the program is not checking the size of the array / list before searching for the minimum value. A list cannot be of zero or negative size. If the user enters a negative or zero value of size or value greater than the size of the array, an appropriate message should be displayed. Hence after line number 15, the value of the size should be checked as under:

```
if (Number < = 0||Number>100)
{
        printf ("Invalid size specified");
}
```

If the size is greater than zero and lesser than 101, then the program should proceed further, otherwise it should be terminated.

(iii) **Program has converted negative values to positive values**

Line number 19 is converting all negative values to positive values. That is why the program is not able to handle negative values. We should delete this line to remove this fault.

The modified program, based on the above three points is given in Figure 1.2. The nine cases of Table 1.2 are executed on this modified program and the results are given in Table 1.5.

```
LINE NUMBER    /*SOURCE CODE*/
               #include<stdio.h>
               #include<limits.h>
               #include<conio.h>
1.             void Minimum();
2.             void main()
3.             {
4.                    Minimum();
5.             }
6.             void Minimum()
7.             {
8.                    int array[100];
9.                    int Number;
```

(Contd.)

(Contd.)

```
10.         int i;
11.         int tmpData;
12.         int Minimum=INT_MAX;
13.         clrscr();
14.         printf("Enter the size of the array:");
15.         scanf("%d",&Number);
16.         if(Number<=0||Number>100) {
17.             printf("Invalid size specified");
18.         }
19.         else {
20.             for(i=0;i<Number;i++) {
21.                 printf("Enter A[%d]=",i+1);
22.                 scanf("%d",&tmpData);
23.                 /*tmpData=(tmpData<0)?-tmpData:tmpData;*/
24.                 array[i]=tmpData;
25.             }
26.             i=0;
27.             while(i<=Number-1) {
28.                 if(Minimum>array[i])
29.                 {
30.                     Minimum=array[i];
31.                 }
32.                 i++;
33.             }
34.             printf("Minimum = %d\n", Minimum);
35.         }
36.         getch();
37.     }
```

Figure 1.2. Modified program 'Minimum' to find the smallest integer out of a set of integers

Table 1.5 gives us some encouraging results. Out of 9 cases, only 3 cases are not matched. Six cases have been handled successfully by the modified program given in Figure 1.2. The cases 6 and 7 are failed due to the scanf() function parsing problem. There are many ways to handle this problem. We may design a program without using scanf() function at all. However, scanf() is a very common function and all of us use it frequently. Whenever any value is given using scanf() which is not as per specified format, scanf() behaves very notoriously and gives strange results. It is advisable to display a warning message for the user before using the scanf() function. The warning message may compel the user to enter values in the specified format only. If the user does not do so, he/she may have to suffer the consequences accordingly. The case 9 problem is due to the fixed maximal size of the integers in the machine and the language used. This also has to be handled through a warning message to the user. The further modified program based on these observations is given in the Figure 1.3.

Software Testing

Table 1.5. Results of the modified program 'Minimum'

Sr. No.		Inputs Size	Set of Integers	Expected Output	Observed Output	Match?
Case 1						
A very short list with size 1, 2 or 3	A	1	90	90	90	Yes
	B	2	12, 10	10	10	Yes
	C	2	10, 12	10	10	Yes
	D	3	12, 14, 36	12	12	Yes
	E	3	36, 14, 12	12	12	Yes
	F	3	14, 12, 36	12	12	Yes
Case 2						
An empty list, i.e. of size 0	A	0	–	Error message	Error message	Yes
Case 3						
A list where the minimum element is the first or last element	A	5	10, 23, 34, 81, 97	10	10	Yes
	B	5	97, 81, 34, 23, 10	10	10	Yes
Case 4						
A list where the minimum element is negative	A	4	10, –2, 5, 23	–2	–2	Yes
	B	4	5, –25, 20, 36	–25	–25	Yes
Case 5						
A list where all elements are negative	A	5	–23, –31, –45, –56, –78	–78	–78	Yes
	B	5	–6, –203, –56, –78, –2	–203	–203	Yes
Case 6						
A list where some elements are real numbers	A	5	12, 34.56, 6.9, 62.14, 19	6.9	34	**No**
	B	5.4	2, 3, 5, 6, 9	2	858993460	**No**
Case 7						
A list where some elements are alphabetic characters	A	5	23, 2I, 26, 6, 9	6	2	**No**
	B	1I	2, 3, 4, 9, 6, 5, 11, 12, 14, 21, 22	2	858993460	**No**
Case 8						
A list with duplicate elements	A	5	3, 4, 6, 9, 6	3	3	Yes
	B	5	13, 6, 6, 9, 15	6	6	Yes
Case 9						
A list where one element has a value greater than the maximum permissible limit of an integer	A	5	530, 42949672 97, 23, 46, 59	23	1	**No**

LINE NUMBER	/*SOURCE CODE*/
	#include<stdio.h>
	#include<limits.h>
	#include<conio.h>
1.	void Minimum();
2.	void main()
3.	{
4.	Minimum();
5.	}
6.	void Minimum()
7.	{
8.	int array[100];
9.	int Number;
10.	int i;
11.	int tmpData;
12.	int Minimum=INT_MAX;
13.	clrscr();
14.	printf("Enter the size of the array:");
15.	scanf("%d",&Number);
16.	if(Number<=0||Number>100) {
17.	printf("Invalid size specified");
18.	}
19.	else {
20.	printf("Warning: The data entered must be a valid integer and must be between %d to %d, INT_MIN, INT_MAX\n");
21.	for(i=0;i<Number;i++) {
22.	printf("Enter A[%d]=",i+1);
23.	scanf("%d",&tmpData);
24.	/*tmpData=(tmpData<0)?-tmpData:tmpData;*/
25.	array[i]=tmpData;
26.	}
27.	i=0;
28.	while(i<=Number-1) {
29.	if(Minimum>array[i])
30.	{
31.	Minimum=array[i];
32.	}
33.	i++;
34.	}
35.	printf("Minimum = %d\n", Minimum);
36.	}
37.	getch();
38.	}

Figure 1.3. Final program 'Minimum' to find the smallest integer out of a set of integers

14 Software Testing

Our goal is to find critical situations of any program. Test cases shall be designed for every critical situation in order to make the program fail in such situations. If it is not possible to remove a fault then proper warning messages shall be given at proper places in the program. The aim of the best testing person should be to fix most of the faults. This is possible only if our intention is to show that the program does not work as per specifications. Hence, as given earlier, the most appropriate definition is **"Testing is the process of executing a program with the intent of finding faults."** Testing never shows the absence of faults, but it shows that the faults are present in the program.

1.2.2 Why Should We Test?

Software testing is a very expensive and critical activity; but releasing the software without testing is definitely more expensive and dangerous. No one would like to do it. It is like running a car without brakes. Hence testing is essential; but how much testing is required? Do we have methods to measure it? Do we have techniques to quantify it? The answer is not easy. All projects are different in nature and functionalities and a single yardstick may not be helpful in all situations. It is a unique area with altogether different problems.

The programs are growing in size and complexity. The most common approach is 'code and fix' which is against the fundamental principles of software engineering. Watts S. Humphrey, of Carnegie Mellon University [HUMP02] conducted a multiyear study of 13000 programs and concluded that "On average professional coders make 100 to 150 errors in every thousand lines of code they write." The C. Mann [MANN02] used Humphrey's figures on the business operating system Windows NT 4 and gave some interesting observations: "Windows NT 4 code size is of 16 million lines. Thus, this would have been written with about two million mistakes. Most would have been too small to have any effect, but some thousands would have caused serious problems. Naturally, Microsoft exhaustively tested Windows NT 4 before release, but in almost any phase of tests, they would have found less than half the defects. If Microsoft had gone through four rounds of testing, an expensive and time consuming procedure, the company would have found at least 15 out of 16 bugs. This means five defects per thousand lines of code are still remaining. This is very low. But the software would still have (as per study) as many as 80,000 defects."

The basic issue of this discussion is that we cannot release a software system without adequate testing. The study results may not be universally applicable but, at least, they give us some idea about the depth and seriousness of the problem. When to release the software is a very important decision. Economics generally plays an important role. We shall try to find more errors in the early phases of software development. The cost of removal of such errors will be very reasonable as compared to those errors which we may find in the later phases of software development. The cost to fix errors increases drastically from the specification phase to the test phase and finally to the maintenance phase as shown in Figure 1.4.

If an error is found and fixed in the specification and analysis phase, it hardly costs anything. We may term this as '1 unit of cost' for fixing an error during specifications and analysis phase. The same error, if propagated to design, may cost 10 units and if, further propagated to coding, may cost 100 units. If it is detected and fixed during the testing phase, it may lead to 1000 units of cost. If it could not be detected even during testing and is found by the customer after release, the cost becomes very high. We may not be able to predict the cost of failure for a life critical system's software. The world has seen many failures and these failures have been costly to the software companies.

The fact is that we are releasing software that is full of errors, even after doing sufficient testing. No software would ever be released by its developers if they are asked to certify that the software is free of errors. Testing, therefore, continues to the point where it is considered that the cost of testing processes significantly outweighs the returns.

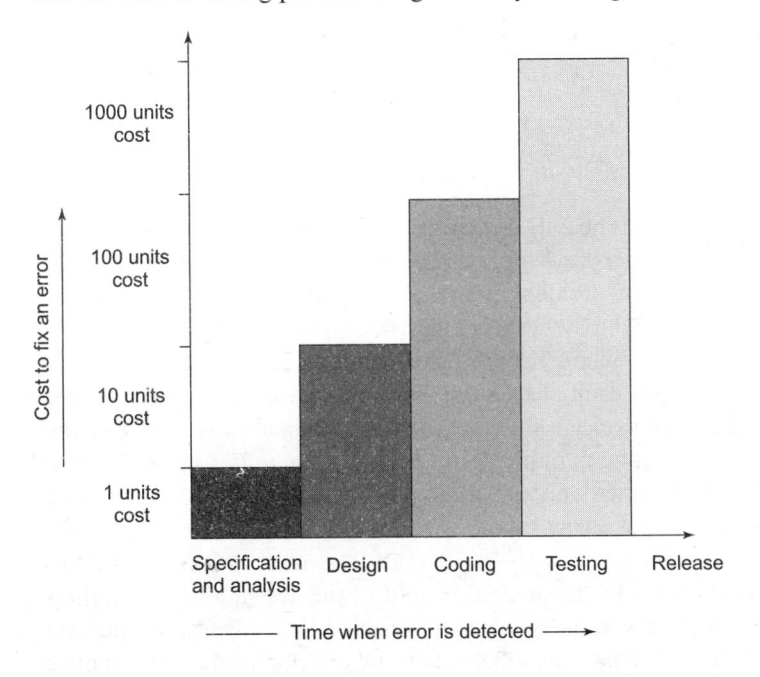

Figure 1.4. Phase wise cost of fixing an error

1.2.3 Who Should We Do the Testing?

Testing a software system may not be the responsibility of a single person. Actually, it is a team work and the size of the team is dependent on the complexity, criticality and functionality of the software under test. The software developers should have a reduced role in testing, if possible. The concern here is that the developers are intimately involved with the development of the software and thus it is very difficult for them to point out errors from their own creations. Beizer [BE1Z90] explains this situation effectively when he states, "There is a myth that if we were really good at programming, there would be no bugs to catch. If we could really concentrate; if everyone used structured programming, top down design, decision figures; if programs were written in SQUISH; if we had the right silver bullets, then there would be no bugs. So goes the myth. There are bugs, the myth says because we are bad at what we do; and if we are bad at it, we should feel guilty about it. Therefore, testing and test design amount to an admission of failures, which instils a goodly dose of guilt. The tedium of testing is just punishment for our errors. Punishment for what? For being human? Guilt for what? For not achieving human perfection? For not being able to distinguish between what another developer thinks and what he says? For not being telepathic? For not solving human communication problems that have been kicked around by philosophers and theologians for 40 centuries."

The testing persons must be cautious, curious, critical but non-judgmental and good communicators. One part of their job is to ask questions that the developers might not be able to ask themselves or are awkward, irritating, insulting or even threatening to the developers. Some of the questions are [BENT04]:

(i) How is the software?
(ii) How good is it?
(iii) How do you know that it works? What evidence do you have?
(iv) What are the critical areas?
(v) What are the weak areas and why?
(vi) What are serious design issues?
(vii) What do you feel about the complexity of the source code?

The testing persons use the software as heavily as an expert user on the customer side. User testing almost invariably recruits too many novice users because they are available and the software must be usable by them. The problem is that the novices do not have domain knowledge that the expert users have and may not recognize that something is wrong.

Many companies have made a distinction between development and testing phases by making different people responsible for each phase. This has an additional advantage. Faced with the opportunity of testing someone else's software, our professional pride will demand that we achieve success. Success in testing is finding errors. We will therefore strive to reveal any errors present in the software. In other words, our ego would have been harnessed to the testing process, in a very positive way, in a way, which would be virtually impossible, had we been testing our own software [NORM89]. Therefore, most of the times, the testing persons are different from development persons for the overall benefit of the system. The developers provide guidelines during testing; however, the overall responsibility is owned by the persons who are involved in testing. Roles of the persons involved during development and testing are given in Table 1.6.

Table 1.6. Persons and their roles during development and testing

S. No.	Persons	Roles
1.	Customer	Provides funding, gives requirements, approves changes and some test results.
2.	Project Manager	Plans and manages the project.
3.	Software Developer(s)	Designs, codes and builds the software; participates in source code reviews and testing; fixes bugs, defects and shortcomings.
4.	Testing co-ordinator(s)	Creates test plans and test specifications based on the requirements and functional and technical documents.
5.	Testing person(s)	Executes the tests and documents results.

1.2.4 What Should We Test?

Is it possible to test the program for all possible valid and invalid inputs? The answer is always negative due to a large number of inputs. We consider a simple example where a program has two 8 bit integers as inputs. Total combinations of inputs are $2^8 \times 2^8$. If only one second is required (possible only with automated testing) to execute one set of inputs, it may take 18 hours to test all possible combinations of inputs. Here, invalid test cases are not considered which may also require a substantial amount of time. In practice, inputs are more than two and the size is also more than 8 bits. What will happen when inputs are real and imaginary numbers? We may wish to go for complete testing of the program, which is neither feasible nor possible. This situation has made this area very challenging where the million dollar question is, "How to choose a reasonable number of test cases out of a large pool of test cases?" Researchers are working very hard to find the answer to this question. Many testing techniques attempt to provide answers to this question in their own ways. However, we do not have a standard yardstick for the selection of test cases.

We all know the importance of this area and expect some drastic solutions in the future. We also know that every project is a new project with new expectations, conditions and constraints. What is the bottom line for testing? At least, we may wish to touch this bottom line, which may incorporate the following:

(i) Execute every statement of the program at least once.
(ii) Execute all possible paths of the program at least once.
(iii) Execute every exit of the branch statement at least once.

This bottom line is also not easily achievable. Consider the following piece of source code:

1. if (x > 0)
2. {
3. a = a + b;
4. }
5. if (y>10)
6. {
7. c=c+d;
8. }

This code can be represented graphically as:

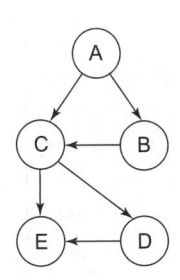

Line Numbers	Symbol for representation
1	A
2, 3, 4	B
5	C
6, 7, 8	D
End	E

18 Software Testing

The possible paths are: ACE, ABCE, ACDE and ABCDE. However, if we choose x = 9 and y = 15, all statements are covered. Hence only one test case is sufficient for 100% statement coverage by traversing only one path ABCDE. Therefore, 100% statement coverage may not be sufficient, even though that may be difficult to achieve in real life programs.

Myers [MYER04] has given an example in his book entitled "The art of software testing" which shows that the number of paths is too large to test. He considered a control flow graph (as given in Figure 1.5) of a 10 to 20 statement program with 'DO Loop' that iterates up to 20 times. Within 'DO Loop' there are many nested 'IF' statements. The assumption is that all decisions in the program are independent of each other. The number of unique paths is nothing but the number of unique ways to move from point X to point Y. Myers further stated that executing every statement of the program at least once may seem to be a reasonable goal. However many portions of the program may be missed with this type of criteria.

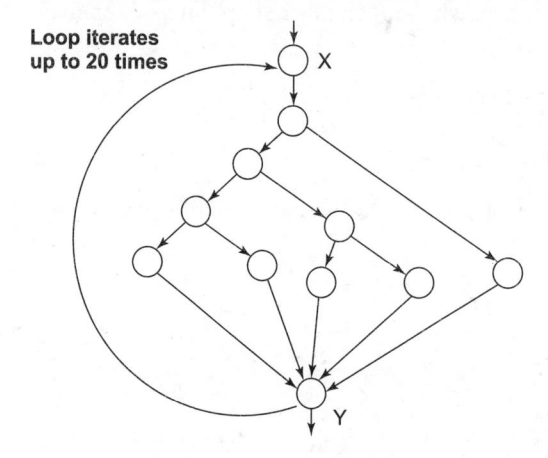

Figure 1.5. Control flow graph of a 10 to 20 statement program [MYER04]

"The total number of paths is approximately 10^{14} or 100 trillion. It is computed from $5^{20} + 5^{19} + \ldots\ldots 5^{1}$, where 5 is the number of independent paths of the control flow graph. If we write, execute and verify a test case every five minutes, it would take approximately one billion years to try every path. If we are 300 times faster, completing a test case one per second, we could complete the job in 3.2 million years." This is an extreme situation; however, in reality, all decisions are not independent. Hence, the total paths may be less than the calculated paths. But real programs are much more complex and larger in size. Hence, 'testing all paths' is very difficult if not impossible to achieve.

We may like to test a program for all possible valid and invalid inputs and furthermore, we may also like to execute all possible paths; but practically, it is quite difficult. Every exit condition of a branch statement is similarly difficult to test due to a large number of such conditions. We require effective planning, strategies and sufficient resources even to target the minimum possible bottom line. We should also check the program for very large numbers, very small numbers, numbers that are close to each other, negative numbers, some extreme cases, characters, special letters, symbols and some strange cases.

1.3 SOME TERMINOLOGIES

Some terminologies are discussed in this section, which are inter-related and confusing but commonly used in the area of software testing.

1.3.1 Program and Software

Both terms are used interchangeably, although they are quite different. The software is the superset of the program(s). It consists of one or many program(s), documentation manuals and operating procedure manuals. These components are shown in Figure 1.6.

```
                    ┌── Program(s)
                    │
        Software ───┼── Documentation manuals
                    │
                    └── Operating procedure manuals
```

Software = Program(s) + Documentation + Operations
                       manuals   procedure manuals

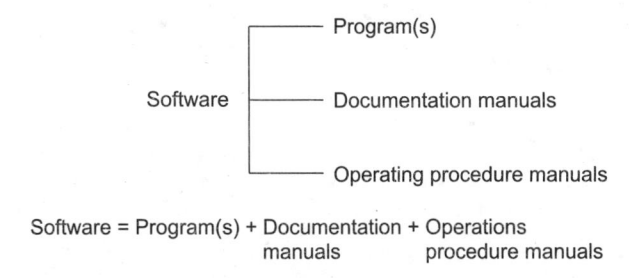

Figure 1.6. Components of the software

The program is a combination of source code and object code. Every phase of the software development life cycle requires preparation of a few documentation manuals which are shown in Figure 1.7. These are very helpful for development and maintenance activities.

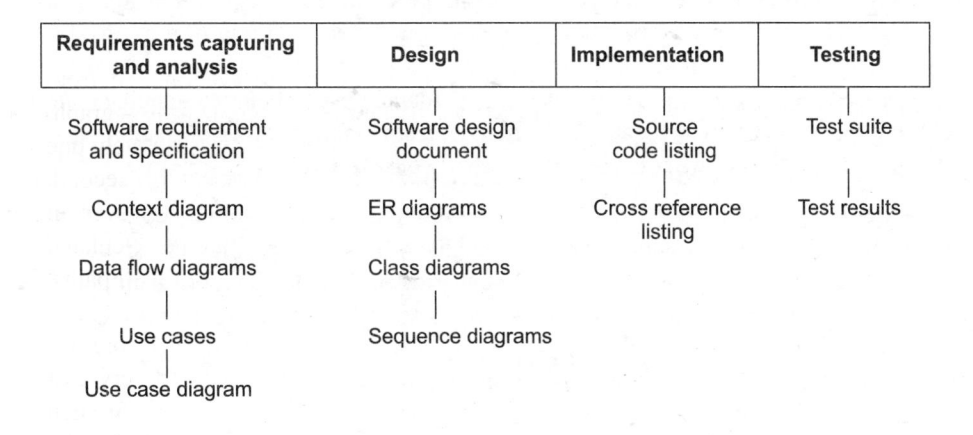

Requirements capturing and analysis	Design	Implementation	Testing
Software requirement and specification	Software design document	Source code listing	Test suite
Context diagram	ER diagrams	Cross reference listing	Test results
Data flow diagrams	Class diagrams		
Use cases	Sequence diagrams		
Use case diagram			

Figure 1.7. Documentation manuals

Operating procedure manuals consist of instructions to set up, install, use and to maintain the software. The list of operating procedure manuals / documents is given in Figure 1.8.

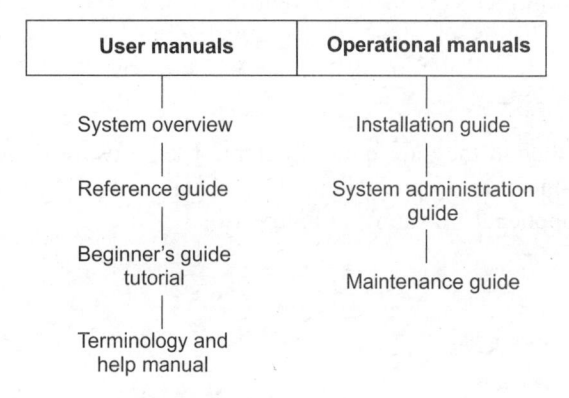

```
         User manuals           Operational manuals
              |                         |
       System overview            Installation guide
              |                         |
       Reference guide         System administration
              |                         guide
       Beginner's guide                 |
           tutorial               Maintenance guide
              |
       Terminology and
         help manual
```

Figure 1.8. Operating system manuals

1.3.2 Verification and Validation

These terms are used interchangeably and some of us may also feel that both are synonyms. The Institute of Electrical and Electronics Engineers (IEEE) has given definitions which are largely accepted by the software testing community. Verification is related to static testing which is performed manually. We only inspect and review the document. However, validation is dynamic in nature and requires the execution of the program.

Verification: As per IEEE [IEEE01], "It is the process of evaluating the system or component to determine whether the products of a given development phase satisfy the conditions imposed at the start of that phase." We apply verification activities from the early phases of the software development and check / review the documents generated after the completion of each phase. Hence, it is the process of reviewing the requirement document, design document, source code and other related documents of the project. This is manual testing and involves only looking at the documents in order to ensure what comes out is what we expected to get.

Validation: As per IEEE [IEEE01], "It is the process of evaluating a system or component during or at the end of development process to determine whether it satisfies the specified requirements." It requires the actual execution of the program. It is dynamic testing and requires a computer for execution of the program. Here, we experience failures and identify the causes of such failures.

Hence, testing includes both verification and validation. Thus

$$\text{Testing} = \text{Verification} + \text{Validation}$$

Both are essential and complementary activities of software testing. If effective verification is carried out, it may minimize the need of validation and more number of errors may be detected in the early phases of the software development. Unfortunately, testing is primarily validation oriented.

1.3.3 Fault, Error, Bug and Failure

All terms are used interchangeably although error, mistake and defect are synonyms in software testing terminology. When we make an error during coding, we call this a 'bug'. Hence, error / mistake / defect in coding is called a bug.

A fault is the representation of an error where representation is the mode of expression such as data flow diagrams, ER diagrams, source code, use cases, etc. If fault is in the source code, we call it a bug.

A failure is the result of execution of a fault and is dynamic in nature. When the expected output does not match with the observed output, we experience a failure. The program has to execute for a failure to occur. A fault may lead to many failures. A particular fault may cause different failures depending on the inputs to the program.

1.3.4 Test, Test Case and Test Suite

Test and test case terms are synonyms and may be used interchangeably. A test case consists of inputs given to the program and its expected outputs. Inputs may also contain pre-condition(s) (circumstances that hold prior to test case execution), if any, and actual inputs identified by some testing methods. Expected output may contain post-condition(s) (circumstances after the execution of a test case), if any, and outputs which may come as a result when selected inputs are given to the software. Every test case will have a unique identification number. When we do testing, we set desire pre-condition(s), if any, given selected inputs to the program and note the observed output(s). We compare the observed output(s) with the expected output(s) and if they are the same, the test case is successful. If they are different, that is the failure condition with selected input(s) and this should be recorded properly in order to find the cause of failure. A good test case has a high probability of showing a failure condition. Hence, test case designers should identify weak areas of the program and design test cases accordingly. The template for a typical test case is given in Table 1.7.

Table 1.7. Test case template

Test Case Identification Number:

Part I (Before Execution)

1. Purpose of test case:
2. Pre-condition(s): (optional)
3. Input(s) :
4. Expected Output(s) :
5. Post-condition(s) :
6. Written by :
7. Date of design :

Part II (After Execution)

1. Output(s) :
2. Post-condition(s) : (optional)

(Contd.)

(Contd.)

	Part II (After Execution)
3.	Pass / fail :
4.	If fails, any possible reason of failure (optional) :
5.	Suggestions (optional)
6.	Run by :
7.	Date of suggestion :

The set of test cases is called a test suite. We may have a test suite of all test cases, test suite of all successful test cases and test suite of all unsuccessful test cases. Any combination of test cases will generate a test suite. All test suites should be preserved as we preserve source code and other documents. They are equally valuable and useful for the purpose of maintenance of the software. Sometimes test suite of unsuccessful test cases gives very important information because these are the test cases which have made the program fail in the past.

1.3.5 Deliverables and Milestones

Different deliverables are generated during various phases of the software development. The examples are source code, Software Requirements and Specification document (SRS), Software Design Document (SDD), Installation guide, user reference manual, etc.

The milestones are the events that are used to ascertain the status of the project. For instance, finalization of SRS is a milestone; completion of SDD is another milestone. The milestones are essential for monitoring and planning the progress of the software development.

1.3.6 Alpha, Beta and Acceptance Testing

Customers may use the software in different and strange ways. Their involvement in testing may help to understand their minds and may force developers to make necessary changes in the software. These three terms are related to the customer's involvement in testing with different meanings.

Acceptance Testing: This term is used when the software is developed for a specific customer. The customer is involved during acceptance testing. He/she may design adhoc test cases or well-planned test cases and execute them to see the correctness of the software. This type of testing is called acceptance testing and may be carried out for a few weeks or months. The discovered errors are fixed and modified and then the software is delivered to the customer.

Alpha and Beta Testing: These terms are used when the software is developed as a product for anonymous customers. Therefore, acceptance testing is not possible. Some potential customers are identified to test the product. The alpha tests are conducted at the developer's site by the customer. These tests are conducted in a controlled environment and may start when the formal testing process is near completion. The beta tests are conducted by potential customers at their sites. Unlike alpha testing, the developer is not present here. It is carried out in an uncontrolled real life environment by many potential customers. Customers are expected to report failures, if any, to the company. These failure reports are studied by the developers and appropriate changes are made in the software. Beta tests have shown their advantages in the past and releasing a beta version of the software to the potential customer has become a common practice. The company gets the feedback of many potential customers without making any payment. The other good thing is that the reputation of the company is not at stake even if many failures are encountered.

1.3.7 Quality and Reliability

Software reliability is one of the important factors of software quality. Other factors are understandability, completeness, portability, consistency, maintainability, usability, efficiency, etc. These quality factors are known as non-functional requirements for a software system.

Software reliability is defined as "the probability of failure free operation for a specified time in a specified environment" [ANSI91]. Although software reliability is defined as a probabilistic function and comes with the notion of time, it is not a direct function of time. The software does not wear out like hardware during the software development life cycle. There is no aging concept in software and it will change only when we intentionally change or upgrade the software.

Software quality determines how well the software is designed (quality of design), and how well the software conforms to that design (quality of conformance).

Some software practitioners also feel that quality and reliability is the same thing. If we are testing a program till it is stable, reliable and dependable, we are assuring a high quality product. Unfortunately, that is not necessarily true. Reliability is just one part of quality. To produce a good quality product, a software tester must verify and validate throughout the software development process.

1.3.8 Testing, Quality Assurance and Quality Control

Most of us feel that these terms are similar and may be used interchangeably. This creates confusion about the purpose of the testing team and Quality Assurance (QA) team. As we have seen in the previous section (1.2.1), the purpose of testing is to find faults and find them in the early phases of software development. We remove faults and ensure the correctness of removal and also minimize the effect of change on other parts of the software.

The purpose of QA activity is to enforce standards and techniques to improve the development process and prevent the previous faults from ever occurring. A good QA activity enforces good software engineering practices which help to produce good quality software. The QA group monitors and guides throughout the software development life cycle. This is a defect prevention technique and concentrates on the process of the software development. Examples are reviews, audits, etc.

Quality control attempts to build a software system and test it thoroughly. If failures are experienced, it removes the cause of failures and ensures the correctness of removal. It concentrates on specific products rather than processes as in the case of QA. This is a defect detection and correction activity which is usually done after the completion of the software development. An example is software testing at various levels.

1.3.9 Static and Dynamic Testing

Static testing refers to testing activities without executing the source code. All verification activities like inspections, walkthroughs, reviews, etc. come under this category of testing.

This, if started in the early phases of the software development, gives good results at a very reasonable cost. Dynamic testing refers to executing the source code and seeing how it performs with specific inputs. All validation activities come in this category where execution of the program is essential.

1.3.10 Testing and Debugging

The purpose of testing is to find faults and find them as early as possible. When we find any such fault, the process used to determine the cause of this fault and to remove it is known as debugging. These are related activities and are carried out sequentially.

1.4 LIMITATIONS OF TESTING

We want to test everything before giving the software to the customers. This 'everything' is very illusive and has many meanings. What do we understand when we say 'everything'? We may expect one, two or all of the following when we refer to 'everything':

(i) Execute every statement of the program
(ii) Execute every true and false condition
(iii) Execute every condition of a decision node
(iv) Execute every possible path
(v) Execute the program with all valid inputs
(vi) Execute the program with all invalid inputs

These six objectives are impossible to achieve due to time and resource constraints as discussed in section 1.2.4. We may achieve a few of them. If we do any compromise, we may miss a bug. Input domain is too large to test and there are too many paths in any program. Hence 'Everything' is impossible and we have to settle for 'less than everything' in real life situations. Some of the other issues which further make the situation more complex and complicated are given in the subsequent sub-sections.

1.4.1 Errors in the Software Requirement and Specification Document

These issues are very difficult to identify. If 6+9=20 is written in the SRS document and our program prints output as 20 when 6 and 9 are inputs, is it a bug? If the program prints output as 15, when inputs are 6 and 9, how can we interpret? In this case, the actual output is so obvious that interpretation may not require time to take a correct decision. But in most of the situations, outputs are not so obvious. Some requirements may be misunderstood and some may be missed. Ambiguities of natural languages (like English) may give more than one meaning to a sentence and make life difficult for testers. Hence, problems in writing good SRS have also become one of the problems of software testing.

1.4.2 Logical Bugs

How do we handle logical bugs? An interesting example is given in Figure 1.9. In this function, statement "d = c++;" given in line number 4 is incorrect. As per requirements, it should have been "d = ++c"; but due to a typographical mistake and ignorance, "d = c++;" has been written. This is a logical error and cannot be detected by the compiler. Here, confusion is due to the use of prefix and postfix operators. A prefix operator first adds 1 to the operand and then the result is assigned to the variable on the left. On the other hand, a postfix operator first assigns the value to the variable on the left and then increment the operand [BALA07]. In this function the postfix operator is used instead of the prefix operator. The function returns the integer value of 'flag'. If this function is executed on a 16 bit computer, the valid integer range for input 'c' is −32768 to 32767. Hence, there are 65536 possible inputs to this program. We may not like to create 65536 test cases. After all, who will execute those cases, if at all created, one fine day? Which input values are to be selected for the detection of this bug? Ten test cases have been given in Table 1.8 and none of them could detect this bug. How many test cases out of possible 65536 test cases will find this bug? What are the chances that we will select all those test cases or any one of them in order to find this bug? Only two test cases out of 65536 can detect this bug and are given in Table 1.9. This example shows the impossibility of testing 'everything'. If a small function can create so many problems, we may appreciate the problems of real life large and complex programs. Logical bugs are extremely difficult to handle and become one of the serious concerns of testing.

Software testing has inherent difficulties which is making it impossible to completely test the software. It can only show that bugs are in the software but it cannot show that bugs are not in the software at all. With all the limitations, software testing still is mandatory and a very useful filter to detect errors, which may further be removed. However we all know that good testing cannot make the software better, only good coding with software engineering principles makes the software better. However, good testing techniques may detect a good number of errors and their removal may improve the quality of the software.

1. int funct1 (int c)
2. {
3. int d, flag;
4. d = c ++ ; // should be d = ++ c; as per requirements
5. if (d < 20000)
6.   flag = 1 ;
7. else
8.   flag = 0;
9. return (flag);
10. }

Figure 1.9. A typical example

Table 1.8. Test cases for function of Figure 1.9

Test case	Input c	Expected output	Actual output
1.	0	1	1
2.	1	1	1
3.	20000	0	0
4.	30000	0	0

(Contd.)

26 Software Testing

(Contd.)

Test case	Input c	Expected output	Actual output
5.	−10000	1	1
6.	−20000	1	1
7.	−1	1	1
8.	−16000	1	1
9.	27000	0	0
10.	32000	0	0

Table 1.9. Typical test cases where outputs are different

Input c	Expected output	Actual output
19999	0	1
32767	Integer out of specified range	0

1.4.3 Difficult to Measure the Progress of Testing

How to measure the progress of testing? Normally we count various things to measure and interpret these counts. Is experiencing more failures good news or bad news? The answer could be either. A higher number of failures may indicate that testing was thorough and very few faults remain in the software. Or, it may be treated as an indication of poor quality of the software with lots of faults; even though many have been exposed, lots of them still remain. These counts may be illusive and may not help us to measure the progress of testing.

This difficulty of measuring the progress of testing leads to another issue i.e. when to stop testing and release the software to the customer(s)? This is a sensitive decision and should be based on the status of testing. However, in the absence of testing standards, 'economics', 'time to market' and 'gut feeling' have become important issues over technical considerations for the release of any software. Many models are available with serious limitations and are not universally acceptable.

Software companies are facing serious challenges in testing their products and these challenges are growing bigger as the software grows more complex. Hence, we should recognize the complex nature of testing and take it seriously. The gap between standards and practices should be reduced in order to test the software effectively which may result in to good quality software.

1.5 THE V SHAPED SOFTWARE LIFE CYCLE MODEL

The V shaped model is the modified form of the waterfall model with a special focus on testing activities. The waterfall model allows us to start testing activities after the completion of the implementation phase. This was popular when testing was primarily validation oriented. Now, there is a shift in testing activities from validation to verification where we want to review / inspect every activity of the software development life cycle. We want to involve the testing persons from the requirement analysis and specification phase itself. They will review the SRS document and identify the weak areas, critical areas, ambiguous areas and misrepresented areas. This will improve the quality of the SRS document and may further minimize the errors.

These verification activities are treated as error preventive exercises and are applied at requirements analysis and specification phase, high level design phase, detailed design phase and implementation phase. We not only want to improve the quality of the end products at all phases by reviews, inspections and walkthroughs, but also want to design test cases and test plans during these phases. The designing of test cases after requirement analysis and specification phase, high level design phase, detailed design phase and implementation phase may help us to improve the quality of the final product and also reduce the cost and development time.

1.5.1 Graphical Representation

The shape of the model is like the English letter 'V' and it emphasizes testing activities in every phase. There are two parts of the software development life cycle in this model i.e. development and testing and are shown in Figure 1.10. We want to carry out development and testing activities in parallel and this model helps us to do the same in order to reduce time and cost.

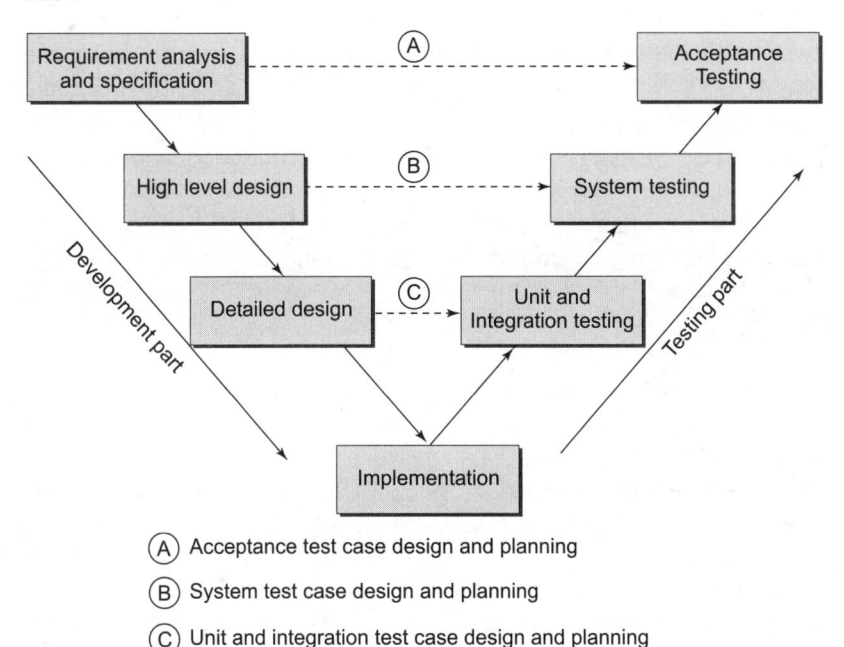

Figure 1.10. V shaped software development life cycle model

1.5.2 Relationship of Development and Testing Parts

The development part consists of the first four phases (i.e. requirements analysis and specification, high level design, detailed design and implementation) whereas the testing part has three phases (i.e. unit and integration testing, system testing and acceptance testing). The model establishes the relationship between the development and testing parts. The acceptance test case design and planning activities should be conducted along with the software requirements and specifications phase. Similarly the system test case design and planning activities should be carried out along with high level design phase. Unit and integration test case design and planning activities should be carried out along with the detailed design phase. The development work is to be done by the development team and testing is to be done by the testing team simultaneously. After the completion of implementation, we will have the required test cases for every phase of testing. The only remaining work is to execute these test cases and observe the responses of the outcome of the execution. This model brings the quality into the development of our products. The encouragement of writing test cases and test plans in the earlier phases of the software development life cycle is the real strength of this model. We require more resources to implement this model as compared to the waterfall model. This model also suffers from many disadvantages of the waterfall model like non-availability of a working version of the product until late in the life cycle, difficulty in accommodating any change, etc. This model has also limited applications in today's interactive software processes.

MULTIPLE CHOICE QUESTIONS

Note: *Select the most appropriate answer for the following questions.*

1.1 What is software testing?
   (a) It is the process of demonstrating that errors are not present.
   (b) It is the process of establishing confidence that a program does what it is supposed to do.
   (c) It is the process of executing a program with the intent of finding errors.
   (d) It is the process of showing the correctness of a program.

1.2 Why should testing be done?
   (a) To ensure the correctness of a program
   (b) To find errors in a program
   (c) To establish the reliability of a program
   (d) To certify the effectiveness of a program

1.3 Which phase consumes maximum effort to fix an error?
   (a) Requirements analysis and specifications
   (b) Design phase
   (c) Coding phase
   (d) Feasibility study phase

1.4 Which objective is most difficult to achieve?
   (a) Execute every statement of a program at least once
   (b) Execute every branch statement of a program at least once
   (c) Execute every path of a program at least once
   (d) Execute every condition of a branch statement of a program at least once

1.5 Software errors during coding are known as:
   (a) Bugs
   (b) Defects
   (c) Failures
   (d) Mistakes

1.6 The cost of fixing an error is:
   (a) More in requirements analysis and specification phase than coding phase
   (b) More in coding phase than requirements analysis and specification phase
   (c) Same in all phases of a software development life cycle
   (d) Negligible in all phases
1.7 Beta testing is done by:
   (a) Developers
   (b) Testers
   (c) Potential customers
   (d) Requirements writers
1.8 Alpha testing is carried out at the:
   (a) Developer's site in a controlled environment
   (b) Developer's site in a free environment
   (c) Customer's site in a controlled environment
   (d) Customer's site in a free environment
1.9 The purpose of acceptance testing is:
   (a) To perform testing from the business perspective
   (b) To find faults in the software
   (c) To test the software with associated hardware
   (d) To perform feasibility study
1.10 Acceptance testing is done by:
   (a) Developers
   (b) Customers
   (c) Testers
   (d) All of the above
1.11 Program is:
   (a) Subset of software
   (b) Superset of software
   (c) Set of software
   (d) Union of software
1.12 Which is not an infrastructure software?
   (a) Compiler
   (b) Operating system
   (c) Testing tools
   (d) Result Management Software
1.13 Software should have:
   (a) Program + operating system + compiler
   (b) Set of programs + operating system
   (c) Programs + documentation + operating procedures
   (d) None of the above
1.14 Concepts of software testing are applicable to:
   (a) Procedural programming languages
   (b) Object oriented programming languages
   (c) 'C', 'C++' and Java programming languages
   (d) All of the above

1.15 CASE Tool is:
   (a) Computer Aided Software Engineering Tool
   (b) Component Aided Software Engineering Tool
   (c) Constructive Aided Software Engineering Tool
   (d) Complete Analysis Software Enterprise Tool
1.16 One fault may lead to:
   (a) One failure
   (b) Many failures
   (c) No failure
   (d) All of the above
1.17 Test suite of a program is a:
   (a) Set of test cases
   (b) Set of inputs with pre-conditions
   (c) Set of outputs with post-conditions
   (d) Set of testing strategies
1.18 Alpha and Beta testing techniques are related to:
   (a) Unit testing
   (b) Integration testing
   (c) System testing
   (d) Testing by Customer
1.19 Testing a software is primarily focused on:
   (a) Verification activities only
   (b) Validation activities only
   (c) Verification and validation activities
   (d) None of the above
1.20 Testing a software with real data in real environment is known as:
   (a) Alpha testing
   (b) Beta testing
   (c) System testing
   (d) Integration testing
1.21 Verification activities are:
   (a) Performed manually
   (b) Related to reviewing the documents and source code
   (c) Known as static testing
   (d) All of the above
1.22 Validation activities are:
   (a) Dynamic activities and require program execution
   (b) Related to inspecting the source code
   (c) Related to static testing
   (d) Related to source code design and documentation
1.23 When the output of a program is different from the expected output, it is known as:
   (a) A fault
   (b) An error
   (c) A failure
   (d) A mistake

1.24 Software testing activities should be started:
   (a) After the completion of source code
   (b) After the completion of design phase
   (c) As early as possible in the software development life cycle
   (d) After the completion of software requirements and analysis phase
1.25 Software testing activities are important in:
   (a) Every phase of the software development life cycle
   (b) The last few phases of the software development life cycle
   (c) The software requirements and analysis phase
   (d) All of the above
1.26 The focus of acceptance testing is:
   (a) To find faults
   (b) To ensure correctness of software
   (c) To test integration related issues
   (d) To test from the user's perspective
1.27 A reliable software is one which is:
   (a) Liked by its users
   (b) Delivered on time and with budget
   (c) Unlikely to cause failures
   (d) Very easy to use
1.28 When to stop testing and release the software to customers should be decided on the basis of:
   (a) Market conditions
   (b) Budget and availability of resources
   (c) Test metrics
   (d) Capabilities of the testing persons
1.29 What are the good software testing practices?
   (a) Involve testing persons as early as possible in the software development life cycle
   (b) Apply effective verification techniques
   (c) Enforce inspections and reviews after every phase of the software development life cycle
   (d) All of the above
1.30 What is a test case?
   (a) Input(s), expected output(s), pre-condition(s) and post-condition(s)
   (b) Steps of execution
   (c) A list of activities which can be tested
   (d) None of the above
1.31 You cannot control what you cannot :
   (a) Define
   (b) Measure
   (c) Improve
   (d) Change
1.32 What is the major benefit of verifications in the early phases of the software development life cycle?

(a) It identifies changes in the SRS
(b) It reduces defect multiplication
(c) It allows involvement of testing persons
(d) It improves discipline in the various development activities

1.33 Behavioural specifications are required for:
(a) Modelling
(b) Verification
(c) Validation
(d) Testing

1.34 Which, in general, is the least expected skill of a testing person?
(a) Diplomatic
(b) Reliable
(c) Having good attention to detail
(d) Good developer

1.35 Debugging of a program is
(a) The process of executing the program
(b) The process of identifying a fault and removing it from the program
(c) The process of experiencing a failure
(d) The process of improving the quality of the program

1.36 All validation activities come under the category of:
(a) Dynamic testing
(b) Static testing
(c) Source code design
(d) None of the above

1.37 All verification activities come under the category of:
(a) Dynamic testing
(b) Static testing
(c) Source code design
(d) None of the above

1.38 Which is not a factor of software quality?
(a) Reliability
(b) Portability
(c) Efficiency
(d) Functionality

1.39 Which is the most important factor of software quality?
(a) Reliability
(b) Understandability
(c) Efficiency
(d) Consistency

1.40 Quality assurance activities concentrate on
(a) Software design
(b) Software performance
(c) Software products
(d) Software processes

1.41 Which is not the quality of a testing person?

(a) Cautious
(b) Curious
(c) Judgmental
(d) Critical

1.42 What should be the best possible objective for testing?
(a) Execute every statement at least once
(b) Execute every path at least once
(c) Execute every branch statement at least once
(d) Execute every condition of a branch statement at least once

1.43 Which is not a user manual?
(a) Reference guide
(b) Beginner's guide
(c) Sequence diagrams
(d) System overview

1.44 Which is not a documentation manual?
(a) SRS document
(b) SDD document
(c) Source code
(d) Installation guide

1.45 Which is not the limitation of testing?
(a) Difficult to measure the progress of testing
(b) Availability of testing tools
(c) Input domain is too large to test
(d) Too many paths in the program

1.46 How much percentage of cost is generally consumed in software testing with reference to software development cost?
(a) 10 – 20
(b) 40 – 50
(c) 80 – 90
(d) 70 – 80

1.47 How much testing is enough?
(a) Not easy to decide
(b) Depends on complexity and criticality
(c) Depends on abilities of testing persons
(d) Depends on maturity of developers

1.48 If an expected output is not specified then:
(a) We cannot execute the test case
(b) We may not be able to repeat the test
(c) We may not be able to decide if the test has passed or failed
(d) We may not be able to automate the testing activity

1.49 Which of the following is a reason for a software failure?
(a) Testing fault
(b) Software Fault
(c) Design Fault
(d) Requirement Fault

34 Software Testing

1.50 Why is it impossible to test a program completely?
 (a) Input domain is too large to test
 (b) Good testers are not available
 (c) Efficient testing tools are not available
 (d) None of the above

EXERCISES

1.1 What is software testing? Is it possible to do complete testing?
1.2 What are the limitations of testing? Discuss with the help of examples.
1.3 Describe some software failures. How can we minimize such failures?
1.4 Why should we test software? What are the associated risks, if we release it without testing?
1.5 Who should do the testing of the software? Is there any international standard?
1.6 What should we test? Discuss the areas which should be focused on during testing.
1.7 There are two limitations in software testing:
 (i) Input domain is too large to test
 (ii) Too many paths in the program
 Justify these limitations with the help of suitable examples.
1.8 What are logical bugs? How are they different from syntax bugs? How can we handle logical bugs effectively?
1.9 Write a program to add two digit integers. Can we test the program completely? If so, how many test cases are required? Assume that each test case can be executed and analyzed in one second; how long would it take to execute all test cases?
1.10 What is the testing process? How can it be implemented? What are its limitations?
1.11 Will exhaustive testing (even if possible for a very small program) guarantee that the program is 100% correct?
1.12 What are the objectives of testing? Why is the psychology of the testing person important?
1.13 Software does not break or wear out with time (unlike hardware). Why does software fail even after a good amount of testing?
1.14 What is the tester's role in software development?
1.15 When to stop testing is a very crucial decision. What factors should be considered for taking such a decision?
1.16 Differentiate between
 (i) Alpha and Beta testing
 (ii) Development and regression testing
 (iii) Fault, bug and failure
 (iv) Verification and validation
 (v) Static and dynamic testing
 (vi) Program and software
 (vii) Test, Test case and Test Suite
 (viii) Deliverable and milestones
 (ix) Quality and Reliability
 (x) Testing, Quality Assurance and Quality Control

1.17 Explain a typical test case template. What are the reasons for documenting test cases?
1.18 With the help of a suitable example, illustrate why exhaustive testing is not possible.
1.19 Define a test case. What are the objectives of test case design? Discuss the various steps involved.
1.20 What is the role of Quality Assurance in software development? How is it different from Quality Control?
1.21 What is software crisis? Was Y2K a software crisis?
1.22 What are the components of a software system? Discuss how a software differs from a program.
1.23 Differentiate between generic and customized software products. Which one has a large market share and why?
1.24 What is a software failure? Discuss the conditions of a failure. Mere presence of faults may not lead to failures. Explain with the help of an example.
1.25 Verification and validation are used interchangeably many times. Define these terms and establish their relationship with testing.
1.26 Testing is not a single phase in the software development life cycle. Explain and comment.
1.27 Discuss the advantages of testing with reference to the software product.
1.28 Discuss the significance of the V-shaped software life cycle model and also establish the relationship between its development and testing parts.
1.29 What is the relationship of the V-shaped software life cycle model with the waterfall model? How is acceptance testing related to requirement analysis and specification phase?
1.30 Differentiate between the V-shaped software life cycle model and the waterfall model.

FURTHER READING

The classic book on software testing which was the only book of note for years is:
    G.J. Myers, "The Art of Software Testing", John Wiley and Sons, Inc., 1977.
One of the first articles that describes the changes in growth of software testing is:
    D. Gelperin, B. Hetzel, "The Growth of Software Testing", Communications of the ACM, vol. 31, no. 6, June 1988.
Read the record report of Prof. J.L. Lions, Chairman Inquiry Board and Director General of ESA prepared on 19th July, 1996 for Identification of the Causes of Failure of Ariane 5:
    J.L. Lions, "Ariane 5 Flight 501 Failure", http://esamultimedia.esa.int/docs/esa-x-1819eng.pdf, July 19, Paris, 1996.
Many good books and articles have been written on the causes of software failure, including:
    S.A. Sherer, 'Software Failure Risk", Plenum, 1992.
    P. Neumann, "Computer Related Risks", Addison Wesley, 1995.
    S. Flowers, "Software Failure: Management Failure", John Wiley and Sons, 1996.

C. Jones, "Patterns of Software Systems Failure and Success", International Thomson Computer Press, 1996.

Ron Patton, "Software Testing", Techmedia, Delhi, India, 2002.

K. Ewusi-Mensah's, "Software Development Failures", MIT Press, 2003.

R.N. Charette, "Why Software Fails?", IEEE Spectrum, September 2005.

A very good article that shows why removing bugs is difficult and why testing is a constant challenge may be found in:

J A. Whittaker, "What Is Software Testing? And Why Is It So Hard?", IEEE Software, January/February, 2000.

An interesting article of Mann about bugs of Windows XP may be found at:

Charles C. Mann, "Why Software is so bad", Technology Review, www.technologyreview.com, 2002.

The report presented by RTI for the U.S. Department of Commerce's National Institute of Standards and Technology (NIST) is a very good study that quantifies the problem of software errors. The study states "Software errors cost U.S. economy $59.5 billion annually." The detailed report can be found at:

www.nist.gov/public_affairs/update/upd20020624.htm#Economics

M.P. Gallaher and B.M. Kropp, "Economic Impacts of Inadequate Infrastructure for Software Testing", NSIT Report, May 2002.

Some of the useful facts about software may be found in:

R. L. Glass, "Facts and Fallacies of Software Engineering", Pearson Education, 2003.

Further list of software failures may be read from:

http://www.sereferences.com/software-failure-list.php

A concise list of 28 best practices for software testing arranged in order of implementation is summarized in:

R. Chillarege, "Software Testing Best Practices", IBM Research Technical Report, 1999.

Bret Pettichord's Software testing hotlist can be checked from:

http://www.io.com/~wazmo/qa/

The online Forum on "Risks to the Public in Computers and Related Systems" is available at http://catless.ncl.ac.uk/risks.

2

Functional Testing

Software testing is very important but is an effort-consuming activity. A large number of test cases are possible and some of them may make the software fail. As we all know, if observed behaviour of the software is different from the expected behaviour, we treat this as a failure condition. Failure is a dynamic condition that always occurs after the execution of the software. Everyone is in search of such test cases which may make the software fail and every technique attempts to find ways to design those test cases which have a higher probability of showing a failure.

Functional testing techniques attempt to design those test cases which have a higher probability of making a software fail. These techniques also attempt to test every possible functionality of the software. Test cases are designed on the basis of functionality and the internal structure of the program is completely ignored. Observed output(s) is (are) compared with expected output(s) for selected input(s) with preconditions, if any. The software is treated as a black box and therefore, it is also known as black box testing as shown in Figure 2.1.

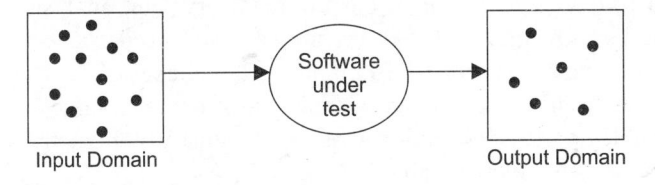

Figure 2.1. Functional (Black Box) testing

Every dot in the input domain represents a set of inputs and every dot in the output domain represents a set of outputs. Every set of input(s) will have a corresponding set of output(s). The test cases are designed on the basis of user requirements without considering the internal structure of the program. This black box knowledge is sufficient to design a good number of test cases. Many activities are performed in real life with only black box knowledge like driving a car, using a cell phone, operating a computer, etc. In functional testing techniques, execution of a program is essential and hence these testing techniques come under the category of 'validation'. Here, both valid and invalid inputs are chosen to see the observed behaviour of the program. These techniques can be used at all levels of software testing like unit, integration, system and acceptance testing. They also help the tester to design efficient and effective test cases to find faults in the software.

2.1 BOUNDARY VALUE ANALYSIS

This is a simple but popular functional testing technique. Here, we concentrate on input values and design test cases with input values that are on or close to boundary values. Experience has shown that such test cases have a higher probability of detecting a fault in the software. Suppose there is a program 'Square' which takes 'x' as an input and prints the square of 'x'as output. The range of 'x' is from 1 to 100. One possibility is to give all values from 1 to 100 one by one to the program and see the observed behaviour. We have to execute this program 100 times to check every input value. In boundary value analysis, we select values on or close to boundaries and all input values may have one of the following:

(i)   Minimum value
(ii) Just above minimum value
(iii) Maximum value
(iv) Just below maximum value
(v)   Nominal (Average) value

These values are shown in Figure 2.2 for the program 'Square'.

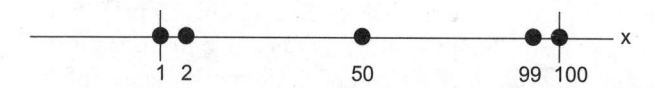

Figure 2.2. Five values for input 'x' of 'Square' program

These five values (1, 2, 50, 99 and 100) are selected on the basis of boundary value analysis and give reasonable confidence about the correctness of the program. There is no need to select all 100 inputs and execute the program one by one for all 100 inputs. The number of inputs selected by this technique is 4n + 1 where 'n' is the number of inputs. One nominal value is selected which may represent all values which are neither close to boundary nor on the boundary. Test cases for 'Square' program are given in Table 2.1.

Table 2.1. Test cases for the 'Square' program

Test Case	Input x	Expected output
1.	1	1
2.	2	4
3.	50	2500
4.	99	9801
5.	100	10000

Functional Testing 39

Consider a program 'Addition' with two input values x and y and it gives the addition of x and y as an output. The range of both input values are given as:

$$100 \leq x \leq 300$$

$$200 \leq y \leq 400$$

The selected values for *x* and *y* are given in Figure 2.3.

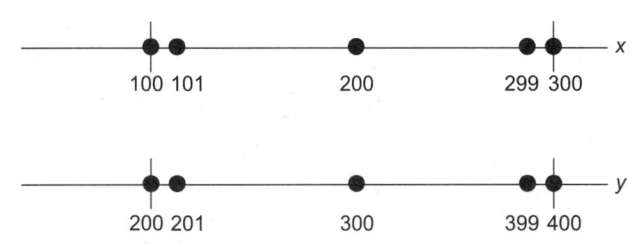

Figure 2.3. Selected values for input values x and y

The 'x' and 'y' inputs are required for the execution of the program. The input domain of this program 'Addition' is shown in Figure 2.4. Any point within the inner rectangle is a legitimate input to the program.

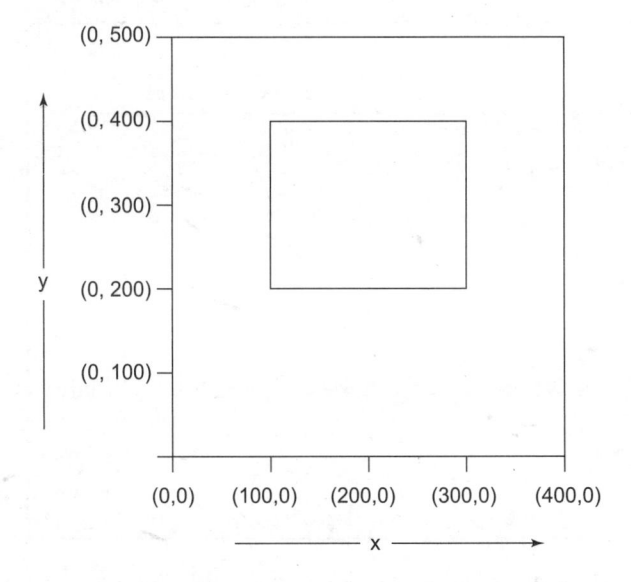

Figure 2.4. Valid input domain for the program 'Addition'

We also consider 'single fault' assumption theory of reliability which says that failures are rarely the result of the simultaneous occurrence of two (or more) faults. Normally, one fault is responsible for one failure. With this theory in mind, we select one input value on boundary (minimum), just above boundary (minimum $^+$), just below boundary (maximum $^-$), on boundary (maximum), nominal (average) and other n-1 input values as nominal values. The inputs are shown graphically in Figure 2.5 and the test cases for 'Addition' program are given in Table 2.2.

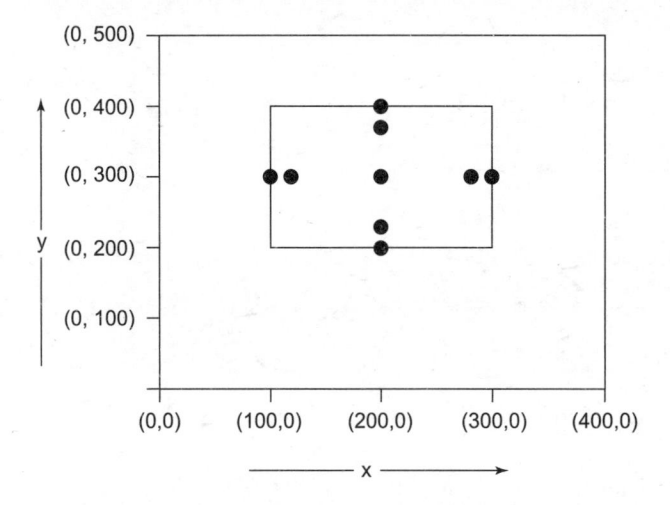

Figure 2.5. Graphical representation of inputs

Table 2.2. Test cases for the program 'Addition'

Test Case	x	y	Expected Output
1.	100	300	400
2.	101	300	401
3.	200	300	500
4.	299	300	599
5.	300	300	600
6.	200	200	400
7.	200	201	401
8.	200	300	500
9.	200	399	599
10.	200	400	600

In Table 2.2, two test cases are common (3 and 8), hence one must be selected. This technique generates 9 test cases where all inputs have valid values. Each dot of the Figure 2.5 represents a test case and inner rectangle is the domain of legitimate input values. Thus, for a program of 'n' variables, boundary value analysis yields 4n + 1 test cases.

Example 2.1: Consider a program for the determination of the largest amongst three numbers. Its input is a triple of positive integers (say x,y and z) and values are from interval [1, 300]. Design the boundary value test cases.

Solution: The boundary value test cases are given in Table 2.3.

Table 2.3. Boundary value test cases to find the largest among three numbers

Test Case	x	y	z	Expected output
1.	1	150	150	150
2.	2	150	150	150
3.	150	150	150	150
4.	299	150	150	299
5.	300	150	150	300
6.	150	1	150	150
7.	150	2	150	150
8.	150	299	150	299
9.	150	300	150	300
10.	150	150	1	150
11.	150	150	2	150
12.	150	150	299	299
13.	150	150	300	300

Example 2.2: Consider a program for the determination of division of a student based on the marks in three subjects. Its input is a triple of positive integers (say mark1, mark2, and mark3) and values are from interval [0, 100].
The division is calculated according to the following rules:

Marks Obtained (Average)	Division
75 – 100	First Division with distinction
60 – 74	First division
50 – 59	Second division
40 – 49	Third division
0 – 39	Fail

Total marks obtained are the average of marks obtained in the three subjects i.e.
$$\text{Average} = (\text{mark1} + \text{mark 2} + \text{mark3}) / 3$$

The program output may have one of the following words:
[Fail, Third Division, Second Division, First Division, First Division with Distinction]
Design the boundary value test cases.

Solution: The boundary value test cases are given in Table 2.4.

Table 2.4. Boundary value test cases for the program determining the division of a student

Test Case	mark1	mark2	mark3	Expected Output
1.	0	50	50	Fail
2.	1	50	50	Fail
3.	50	50	50	Second Division
4.	99	50	50	First Division
5.	100	50	50	First Division

(Contd.)

42 Software Testing

(Contd.)

Test Case	mark1	mark2	mark3	Expected Output
6.	50	0	50	Fail
7.	50	1	50	Fail
8.	50	99	50	First Division
9.	50	100	50	First Division
10.	50	50	0	Fail
11.	50	50	1	Fail
12.	50	50	99	First Division
13.	50	50	100	First Division

Example 2.3: Consider a program for classification of a triangle. Its input is a triple of positive integers (say a, b, c) and the input parameters are greater than zero and less than or equal to 100.

The triangle is classified according to the following rules:

Right angled triangle: $c^2 = a^2 + b^2$ or $a^2 = b^2 + c^2$ or $b^2 = c^2 + a^2$
Obtuse angled triangle: $c^2 > a^2 + b^2$ or $a^2 > b^2 + c^2$ or $b^2 > c^2 + a^2$
Acute angled triangle: $c^2 < a^2 + b^2$ and $a^2 < b^2 + c^2$ and $b^2 < c^2 + a^2$

The program output may have one of the following words:
[Acute angled triangle, Obtuse angled triangle, Right angled triangle, Invalid triangle]
Design the boundary value test cases.

Solution: The boundary value analysis test cases are given in Table 2.5.

Table 2.5. Boundary value test cases for triangle classification program

Test Case	a	b	c	Expected Output
1.	1	50	50	Acute angled triangle
2.	2	50	50	Acute angled triangle
3.	50	50	50	Acute angled triangle
4.	99	50	50	Obtuse angled triangle
5.	100	50	50	Invalid triangle
6.	50	1	50	Acute angled triangle
7.	50	2	50	Acute angled triangle
8.	50	99	50	Obtuse angled triangle
9.	50	100	50	Invalid triangle
10.	50	50	1	Acute angled triangle
11.	50	50	2	Acute angled triangle
12.	50	50	99	Obtuse angled triangle
13.	50	50	100	Invalid triangle

Example 2.4: Consider a program for determining the day of the week. Its input is a triple of day, month and year with the values in the range

$1 \leq$ month ≤ 12

$1 \leq$ day ≤ 31

$1900 \leq$ year ≤ 2058

The possible outputs would be the day of the week or invalid date. Design the boundary value test cases.

Solution: The boundary value test cases are given in Table 2.6.

Table 2.6. Boundary value test cases for the program determining the day of the week

Test Case	month	day	year	Expected Output
1.	1	15	1979	Monday
2.	2	15	1979	Thursday
3.	6	15	1979	Friday
4.	11	15	1979	Thursday
5.	12	15	1979	Saturday
6.	6	1	1979	Friday
7.	6	2	1979	Saturday
8.	6	30	1979	Saturday
9.	6	31	1979	Invalid Date
10.	6	15	1900	Friday
11.	6	15	1901	Saturday
12.	6	15	2057	Friday
13.	6	15	2058	Saturday

2.1.1 Robustness Testing

This is the extension of boundary value analysis. Here, we also select invalid values and see the responses of the program. Invalid values are also important to check the behaviour of the program. Hence, two additional states are added i.e. just below minimum value (minimum value $^-$) and just above maximum value (maximum value $^+$). We want to go beyond the legitimate domain of input values. This extended form of boundary value analysis is known as robustness testing. The inputs are shown graphically in Figure 2.6 and the test cases for the program 'Addition' are given in Table 2.7. There are four additional test cases which are outside the legitimate input domain. Thus, the total test cases in robustness testing are 6n + 1, where 'n' is the number of input values. All input values may have one of the following values:

(i) Minimum value
(ii) Just above minimum value
(iii) Just below minimum value
(iv) Just above maximum value
(v) Just below maximum value
(vi) Maximum value
(vii) Nominal (Average) value

44 Software Testing

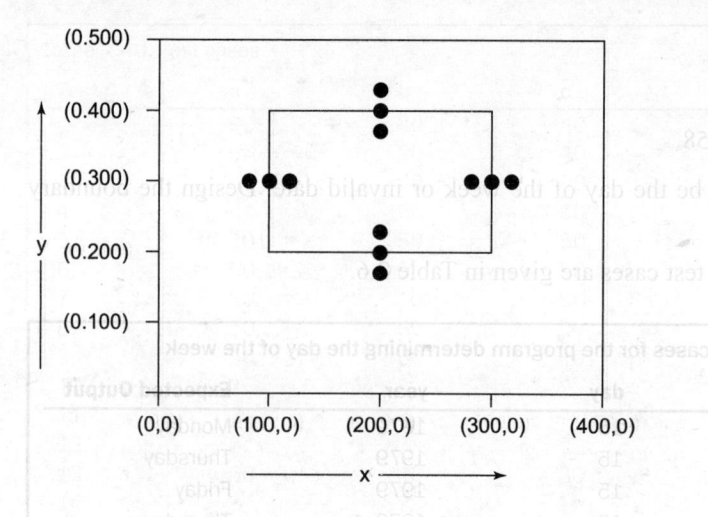

```
       (0.500)
          |
       (0.400)           •
          |              •
       (0.300)    • • •  • • •
          |              •
     y (0.200)           •
          |              •
       (0.100)
          |____|____|____|____|____
        (0,0) (100,0) (200,0) (300,0) (400,0)
                      ——— x ———>
```

Figure 2.6. Graphical representation of inputs

Table 2.7. Robustness test cases for two input values x and y

Test Case	x	y	Expected Output
1.	99	300	Invalid Input
2.	100	300	400
3.	101	300	401
4.	200	300	500
5.	299	300	599
6.	300	300	600
7.	301	300	Invalid Input
8.	200	199	Invalid Input
9.	200	200	400
10.	200	201	401
11.	200	399	599
12.	200	400	600
13.	200	401	Invalid Input

2.1.2 Worst-Case Testing

This is a special form of boundary value analysis where we don't consider the 'single fault' assumption theory of reliability. Now, failures are also due to occurrence of more than one fault simultaneously. The implication of this concept in boundary value analysis is that all input values may have one of the following:

(i) Minimum value
(ii) Just above minimum value

(iii) Just below maximum value
(iv) Maximum value
(v) Nominal (Average) value

The restriction of one input value at any of the above mentioned values and other input values must be at nominal is not valid in worst-case testing. This will increase the number of test cases from 4n + 1 test cases to 5^n test cases, where 'n' is the number of input values. The inputs for 'Addition' program are shown graphically in Figure 2.7. The program 'Addition' will have $5^2 = 25$ test cases and these test cases are given in Table 2.8.

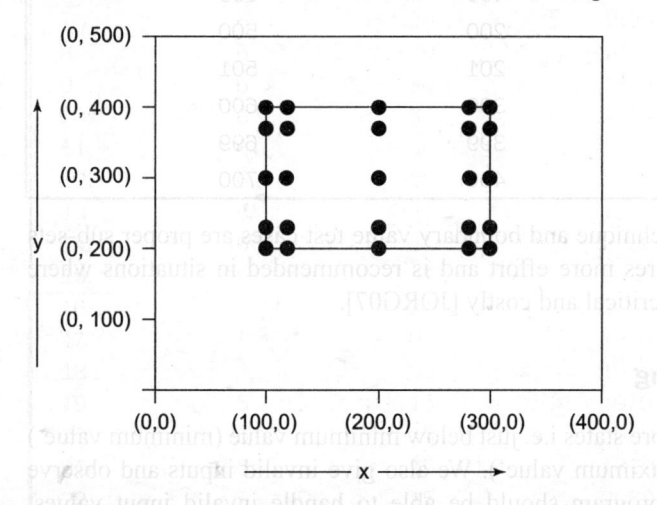

Figure 2.7. Graphical representation of inputs

Table 2.8. Worst test cases for the program 'Addition'

Test Case	x	y	Expected Output
1.	100	200	300
2.	100	201	301
3.	100	300	400
4.	100	399	499
5.	100	400	500
6.	101	200	301
7.	101	201	302
8.	101	300	401
9.	101	399	500
10.	101	400	501
11.	200	200	400
12.	200	201	401
13.	200	300	500
14.	200	399	599

(Contd.)

(Contd.)

Test Case	x	y	Expected Output
15.	200	400	600
16.	299	200	499
17.	299	201	500
18.	299	300	599
19.	299	399	698
20.	299	400	699
21.	300	200	500
22.	300	201	501
23.	300	300	600
24.	300	399	699
25.	300	400	700

This is a more comprehensive technique and boundary value test cases are proper sub-sets of worst case test cases. This requires more effort and is recommended in situations where failure of the program is extremely critical and costly [JORG07].

2.1.3 Robust Worst-Case Testing

In robustness testing, we add two more states i.e. just below minimum value (minimum value⁻) and just above maximum value (maximum value⁺). We also give invalid inputs and observe the behaviour of the program. A program should be able to handle invalid input values, otherwise it may fail and give unexpected output values. There are seven states (minimum ⁻, minimum, minimum ⁺, nominal, maximum ⁻, maximum, maximum ⁺) and a total of 7^n test cases will be generated. This will be the largest set of test cases and requires the maximum effort to generate such test cases. The inputs for the program 'Addition' are graphically shown in Figure 2.8. The program 'Addition' will have $7^2 = 49$ test cases and these test cases are shown in Table 2.9.

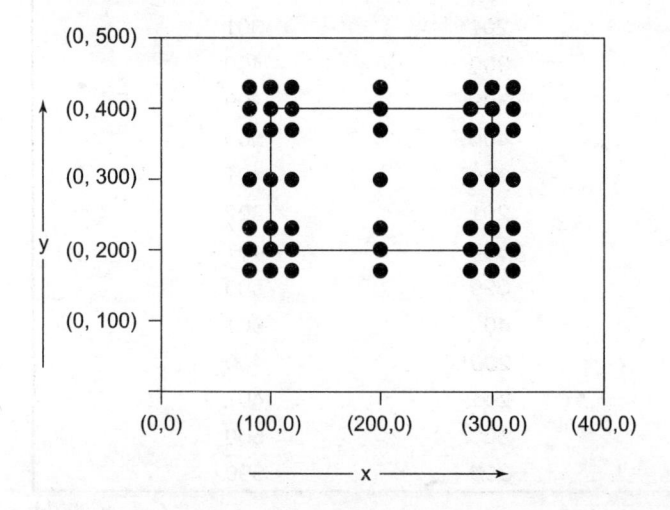

Figure 2.8. Graphical representation of inputs

Table 2.9. Robust worst test cases for the program 'Addition'

Test Case	x	y	Expected Output
1.	99	199	Invalid input
2.	99	200	Invalid input
3.	99	201	Invalid input
4.	99	300	Invalid input
5.	99	399	Invalid input
6.	99	400	Invalid input
7.	99	401	Invalid input
8.	100	199	Invalid input
9.	100	200	300
10.	100	201	301
11.	100	300	400
12.	100	399	499
13.	100	400	500
14.	100	401	Invalid input
15.	101	199	Invalid input
16.	101	200	301
17.	101	201	302
18.	101	300	401
19.	101	399	500
20.	101	400	501
21.	101	401	Invalid input
22.	200	199	Invalid input
23.	200	200	400
24.	200	201	401
25.	200	300	500
26.	200	399	599
27.	200	400	600
28.	200	401	Invalid input
29.	299	199	Invalid input
30.	299	200	499
31.	299	201	500
32.	299	300	599
33.	299	399	698
34.	299	400	699
35.	299	401	Invalid input
36.	300	199	Invalid input
37.	300	200	500
38.	300	201	501
39.	300	300	600
40.	300	399	699
41.	300	400	700
42.	300	401	Invalid input
43.	301	199	Invalid input
44.	301	200	Invalid input
45.	301	201	Invalid input
46.	301	300	Invalid input
47.	301	399	Invalid input
48.	301	400	Invalid input
49.	301	401	Invalid input

2.1.4 Applicability

Boundary value analysis is a simple technique and may prove to be effective when used correctly. Here, input values should be independent which restricts its applicability in many programs. This technique does not make sense for Boolean variables where input values are TRUE and FALSE only, and no choice is available for nominal values, just above boundary values, just below boundary values, etc. This technique can significantly reduce the number of test cases and is suited to programs in which input values are within ranges or within sets. This is equally applicable at the unit, integration, system and acceptance test levels. All we want is input values where boundaries can be identified from the requirements.

Example 2.5: Consider the program for the determination of the largest amongst three numbers as explained in example 2.1. Design the robust test cases and worst case test cases for this program.

Solution: The robust test cases and worst test cases are given in Table 2.10 and Table 2.11 respectively.

Table 2.10. Robust test cases for the program to find the largest among three numbers

Test Case	x	y	z	Expected output
1.	0	150	150	Invalid input
2.	1	150	150	150
3.	2	150	150	150
4.	150	150	150	150
5.	299	150	150	299
6.	300	150	150	300
7.	301	150	150	Invalid input
8.	150	0	150	Invalid input
9.	150	1	150	150
10.	150	2	150	150
11.	150	299	150	299
12.	150	300	150	300
13.	150	301	150	Invalid input
14.	150	150	0	Invalid input
15.	150	150	1	150
16.	150	150	2	150
17.	150	150	299	299
18.	150	150	300	300
19.	150	150	301	Invalid input

Table 2.11. Worst case test cases for the program to find the largest among three numbers

Test Case	x	y	z	Expected output
1.	1	1	1	1
2.	1	1	2	2
3.	1	1	150	150

(Contd.)

(Contd.)

Test Case	x	y	z	Expected output
4.	1	1	299	299
5.	1	1	300	300
6.	1	2	1	2
7.	1	2	2	2
8.	1	2	150	150
9.	1	2	299	299
10.	1	2	300	300
11.	1	150	1	150
12.	1	150	2	150
13.	1	150	150	150
14.	1	150	299	299
15.	1	150	300	300
16.	1	299	1	299
17.	1	299	2	299
18.	1	299	150	299
19.	1	299	299	299
20.	1	299	300	300
21.	1	300	1	300
22.	1	300	2	300
23.	1	300	150	300
24.	1	300	299	300
25.	1	300	300	300
26.	2	1	1	2
27.	2	1	2	2
28.	2	1	150	150
29.	2	1	299	299
30.	2	1	300	300
31.	2	2	1	2
32.	2	2	2	2
33.	2	2	150	150
34.	2	2	299	299
35.	2	2	300	300
36.	2	150	1	150
37.	2	150	2	150
38.	2	150	150	150
39.	2	150	299	299
40.	2	150	300	300
41.	2	299	1	299
42.	2	299	2	299
43.	2	299	150	299
44.	2	299	299	299
45.	2	299	300	300
46.	2	300	1	300
47.	2	300	2	300
48.	2	300	150	300
49.	2	300	299	300

(Contd.)

(Contd.)

Test Case	x	y	z	Expected output
50.	2	300	300	300
51.	150	1	1	150
52.	150	1	2	150
53.	150	1	150	150
54.	150	1	299	299
55.	150	1	300	300
56.	150	2	1	150
57.	150	2	2	150
58.	150	2	150	150
59.	150	2	299	299
60.	150	2	300	300
61.	150	150	1	150
62.	150	150	2	150
63.	150	150	150	150
64.	150	150	299	299
65.	150	150	300	300
66.	150	299	1	299
67.	150	299	2	299
68.	150	299	150	299
69.	150	299	299	299
70.	150	299	300	300
71.	150	300	1	300
72.	150	300	2	300
73.	150	300	150	300
74.	150	300	299	300
75.	150	300	300	300
76.	299	1	1	299
77.	299	1	2	299
78.	299	1	150	299
79.	299	1	299	299
80.	299	1	300	300
81.	299	2	1	299
82.	299	2	2	299
83.	299	2	150	299
84.	299	2	299	299
85.	299	2	300	300
86.	299	150	1	299
87.	299	150	2	299
88.	299	150	150	299
89.	299	150	299	299
90.	299	150	300	300
91.	299	299	1	299
92.	299	299	2	299
93.	299	299	150	299
94.	299	299	299	299
95.	299	299	300	300

(Contd.)

(Contd.)

Test Case	x	y	z	Expected output
96.	299	300	1	300
97.	299	300	2	300
98.	299	300	150	300
99.	299	300	299	300
100.	299	300	300	300
101.	300	1	1	300
102.	300	1	2	300
103.	300	1	150	300
104.	300	1	299	300
105.	300	1	300	300
106.	300	2	1	300
107.	300	2	2	300
108.	300	2	150	300
109.	300	2	299	300
110.	300	2	300	300
111.	300	150	1	300
112.	300	150	2	300
113.	300	150	150	300
114.	300	150	299	300
115.	300	150	300	300
116.	300	299	1	300
117.	300	299	2	300
118.	300	299	150	300
119.	300	299	299	300
120.	300	299	300	300
121.	300	300	1	300
122.	300	300	2	300
123.	300	300	150	300
124.	300	300	299	300
125.	300	300	300	300

Example 2.6: Consider the program for the determination of division of a student based on marks obtained in three subjects as explained in example 2.2. Design the robust test cases and worst case test cases for this program.

Solution: The robust test cases and worst test cases are given in Table 2.12 and Table 2.13 respectively.

Table 2.12. Robust test cases for the program determining the division of a student

Test Case	mark1	mark2	mark3	Expected Output
1.	−1	50	50	Invalid marks
2.	0	50	50	Fail
3.	1	50	50	Fail
4.	50	50	50	Second Division
5.	99	50	50	First Division
6.	100	50	50	First Division

(Contd.)

(Contd.)

Test Case	mark1	mark2	mark3	Expected Output
7.	101	50	50	Invalid marks
8.	50	−1	50	Invalid marks
9.	50	0	50	Fail
10.	50	1	50	Fail
11.	50	99	50	First Division
12.	50	100	50	First Division
13.	50	101	50	Invalid marks
14.	50	50	−1	Invalid marks
15.	50	50	0	Fail
16.	50	50	1	Fail
17.	50	50	99	First Division
18.	50	50	100	First Division
19.	50	50	101	Invalid Marks

Table 2.13. Worst case test cases for the program for determining the division of a student

Test Case	mark1	mark2	mark3	Expected Output
1	0	0	0	Fail
2.	0	0	1	Fail
3.	0	0	50	Fail
4.	0	0	99	Fail
5.	0	0	100	Fail
6.	0	1	0	Fail
7.	0	1	1	Fail
8.	0	1	50	Fail
9.	0	1	99	Fail
10.	0	1	100	Fail
11.	0	50	0	Fail
12.	0	50	1	Fail
13.	0	50	50	Fail
14.	0	50	99	Third division
15.	0	50	100	Second division
16.	0	99	0	Fail
17.	0	99	1	Fail
18.	0	99	50	Third division
19.	0	99	99	First division
20.	0	99	100	First division
21.	0	100	0	Fail
22.	0	100	1	Fail
23.	0	100	50	Second division
24.	0	100	99	First division
25.	0	100	100	First division
26.	1	0	0	Fail
27.	1	0	1	Fail
28.	1	0	50	Fail
29.	1	0	99	Fail
30.	1	0	100	Fail
31.	1	1	0	Fail
32.	1	1	1	Fail

(Contd.)

(Contd.)

Test Case	mark1	mark2	mark3	Expected Output
33.	1	1	50	Fail
34.	1	1	99	Fail
35.	1	1	100	Fail
36.	1	50	0	Fail
37.	1	50	1	Fail
38.	1	50	50	Fail
39.	1	50	99	Second division
40.	1	50	100	Second division
41.	1	99	0	Fail
42.	1	99	1	Fail
43.	1	99	50	Second division
44.	1	99	99	First division
45.	1	99	100	First division
46.	1	100	0	Fail
47.	1	100	1	Fail
48.	1	100	50	Second division
49.	1	100	99	First division
50.	1	100	100	First division
51.	50	0	0	Fail
52.	50	0	1	Fail
53.	50	0	50	Fail
54.	50	0	99	Third division
55.	50	0	100	Second division
56.	50	1	0	Fail
57.	50	1	1	Fail
58.	50	1	50	Fail
59.	50	1	99	Second division
60.	50	1	100	Second division
61.	50	50	0	Fail
62.	50	50	1	Fail
63.	50	50	50	Second division
64.	50	50	99	First division
65.	50	50	100	First division
66.	50	99	0	Third division
67.	50	99	1	Second division
68.	50	99	50	First division
69.	50	99	99	First division with distinction
70.	50	99	100	First division with distinction
71.	50	100	0	Second division
72.	50	100	1	Second division
73.	50	100	50	First division
74.	50	100	99	First division
75.	50	100	100	First division with distinction
76.	99	0	0	Fail
77.	99	0	1	Fail
78.	99	0	50	Third division
79.	99	0	99	First division
80.	99	0	100	First division
81.	99	1	0	Fail
82.	99	1	1	Fail

(Contd.)

(Contd.)

Test Case	mark1	mark2	mark3	Expected Output
83.	99	1	50	Second division
84.	99	1	99	First division
85.	99	1	100	First division
86.	99	50	0	Third division
87.	99	50	1	Second division
88.	99	50	50	First division
89.	99	50	99	First division with distinction
90.	99	50	100	First division with distinction
91.	99	99	0	First division
92.	99	99	1	First division
93.	99	99	50	First division with distinction
94.	99	99	99	First division with distinction
95.	99	99	100	First division with distinction
96.	99	100	0	First division
97.	99	100	1	First division
98.	99	100	50	First division with distinction
99.	99	100	99	First division with distinction
100.	99	100	100	First division with distinction
101.	100	0	0	Fail
102.	100	0	1	Fail
103.	100	0	50	Second division
104.	100	0	99	First division
105.	100	0	100	First division
106.	100	1	0	Fail
107.	100	1	1	Fail
108.	100	1	50	Second division
109.	100	1	99	First division
110.	100	1	100	First division
111.	100	50	0	Second division
112.	100	50	1	Second division
113.	100	50	50	First division
114.	100	50	99	First division with distinction
115.	100	50	100	First division with distinction
116.	100	99	0	First division
117.	100	99	1	First division
118.	100	99	50	First division with distinction
119.	100	99	99	First division wit distinction
120.	100	99	100	First division with distinction
121.	100	100	0	First division
122.	100	100	1	First division
123.	100	100	50	First division with distinction
124.	100	100	99	First division with distinction
125.	100	100	100	First division with distinction

Example 2.7: Consider the program for classification of a triangle in example 2.3. Generate robust and worst test cases for this program.

Solution: Robust test cases and worst test cases are given in Table 2.14 and Table 2.15 respectively.

Functional Testing 55

Table 2.14. Robust test cases for the triangle classification program

Test Case	a	b	c	Expected Output
1.	0	50	50	Input values out of range
2.	1	50	50	Acute angled triangle
3.	2	50	50	Acute angled triangle
4.	50	50	50	Acute angled triangle
5.	99	50	50	Obtuse angled triangle
6.	100	50	50	Invalid triangle
7.	101	50	50	Input values out of range
8.	50	0	50	Input values out of range
9.	50	1	50	Acute angled triangle
10.	50	2	50	Acute angled triangle
11.	50	99	50	Obtuse angled triangle
12.	50	100	50	Invalid triangle
13.	50	101	50	Input values out of range
14.	50	50	0	Input values out of range
15.	50	50	1	Acute angled triangle
16.	50	50	2	Acute angled triangle
17.	50	50	99	Obtuse angled triangle
18.	50	50	100	Invalid triangle
19.	50	50	101	Input values out of range

Table 2.15. Worst case test cases for the triangle classification program

Test Case	a	b	c	Expected Output
1.	1	1	1	Acute angled triangle
2.	1	1	2	Invalid triangle
3.	1	1	50	Invalid triangle
4.	1	1	99	Invalid triangle
5.	1	1	100	Invalid triangle
6.	1	2	1	Invalid triangle
7.	1	2	2	Acute angled triangle
8.	1	2	50	Invalid triangle
9.	1	2	99	Invalid triangle
10.	1	2	100	Invalid triangle
11.	1	50	1	Invalid triangle
12.	1	50	2	Invalid triangle
13.	1	50	50	Acute angled triangle
14.	1	50	99	Invalid triangle
15.	1	50	100	Invalid triangle
16.	1	99	1	Invalid triangle
17.	1	99	2	Invalid triangle

(Contd.)

(Contd.)

Test Case	a	b	c	Expected Output
18.	1	99	50	Invalid triangle
19.	1	99	99	Acute angled triangle
20.	1	99	100	Invalid triangle
21.	1	100	1	Invalid triangle
22.	1	100	2	Invalid triangle
23.	1	100	50	Invalid triangle
24.	1	100	99	Invalid triangle
25.	1	100	100	Acute angled triangle
26.	2	1	1	Invalid triangle
27.	2	1	2	Acute angled triangle
28.	2	1	50	Invalid triangle
29.	2	1	99	Invalid triangle
30.	2	1	100	Invalid triangle
31.	2	2	1	Acute angled triangle
32.	2	2	2	Acute angled triangle
33.	2	2	50	Invalid triangle
34.	2	2	99	Invalid triangle
35.	2	2	100	Invalid triangle
36.	2	50	1	Invalid triangle
37.	2	50	2	Invalid triangle
38.	2	50	50	Acute angled triangle
39.	2	50	99	Invalid triangle
40.	2	50	100	Invalid triangle
41.	2	99	1	Invalid triangle
42.	2	99	2	Invalid triangle
43.	2	99	50	Invalid triangle
44.	2	99	99	Acute angled
45.	2	99	100	Obtuse angled triangle
46.	2	100	1	Invalid triangle
47.	2	100	2	Invalid triangle
48.	2	100	50	Invalid triangle
49.	2	100	99	Obtuse angled triangle
50.	2	100	100	Acute angled triangle
51.	50	1	1	Invalid triangle
52.	50	1	2	Invalid triangle
53.	50	1	50	Acute angled triangle
54.	50	1	99	Invalid triangle
55.	50	1	100	Invalid triangle
56.	50	2	1	Invalid triangle

(Contd.)

(Contd.)

Test Case	a	b	c	Expected Output
57.	50	2	2	Invalid triangle
58.	50	2	50	Acute angled triangle
59.	50	2	99	Invalid triangle
60.	50	2	100	Invalid triangle
61.	50	50	1	Acute angled triangle
62.	50	50	2	Acute angled triangle
63.	50	50	50	Acute angled triangle
64.	50	50	99	Obtuse angled triangle
65.	50	50	100	Invalid triangle
66.	50	99	1	Invalid triangle
67.	50	99	2	Invalid triangle
68.	50	99	50	Obtuse angled triangle
69.	50	99	99	Acute angled triangle
70.	50	99	100	Acute angled triangle
71.	50	100	1	Invalid triangle
72.	50	100	2	Invalid triangle
73.	50	100	50	Invalid triangle
74.	50	100	99	Acute angled triangle
75.	50	100	100	Acute angled triangle
76.	99	1	1	Invalid triangle
77.	99	1	2	Invalid triangle
78.	99	1	50	Invalid triangle
79.	99	1	99	Acute angled triangle
80.	99	1	100	Invalid triangle
81.	99	2	1	Invalid triangle
82.	99	2	2	Invalid triangle
83.	99	2	50	Invalid triangle
84.	99	2	99	Acute angled triangle
85.	99	2	100	Obtuse angled triangle
86.	99	50	1	Invalid triangle
87.	99	50	2	Invalid triangle
88.	99	50	50	Obtuse angled triangle
89.	99	50	99	Acute angled triangle
90.	99	50	100	Acute angled triangle
91.	99	99	1	Acute angled triangle
92.	99	99	2	Acute angled triangle
93.	99	99	50	Acute angled triangle
94.	99	99	99	Acute angled triangle
95.	99	99	100	Acute angled triangle

(Contd.)

(Contd.)

Test Case	a	b	c	Expected Output
96.	99	100	1	Invalid triangle
97.	99	100	2	Obtuse angled triangle
98.	99	100	50	Acute angled triangle
99.	99	100	99	Acute angled triangle
100.	99	100	100	Acute angled triangle
101.	100	1	1	Invalid triangle
102.	100	1	2	Invalid triangle
103.	100	1	50	Invalid triangle
104.	100	1	99	Invalid triangle
105.	100	1	100	Acute angled triangle
106.	100	2	1	Invalid triangle
107.	100	2	2	Invalid triangle
108.	100	2	50	Invalid triangle
109.	100	2	99	Obtuse angled triangle
110.	100	2	100	Acute angled triangle
111.	100	50	1	Invalid triangle
112.	100	50	2	Invalid triangle
113.	100	50	50	Invalid triangle
114.	100	50	99	Acute angled triangle
115.	100	50	100	Acute angled triangle
116.	100	99	1	Invalid triangle
117.	100	99	2	Obtuse angled triangle
118.	100	99	50	Acute angled triangle
119.	100	99	99	Acute angled triangle
120.	100	99	100	Acute angled triangle
121.	100	100	1	Acute angled triangle
122.	100	100	2	Acute angled triangle
123.	100	100	50	Acute angled triangle
124.	100	100	99	Acute angled triangle
125.	100	100	100	Acute angled triangle

Example 2.8: Consider the program for the determination of day of the week as explained in example 2.4. Design the robust and worst test cases for this program.

Solution: Robust test cases and worst test cases are given in Table 2.16 and Table 2.17 respectively.

Table 2.16. Robust test cases for program for determining the day of the week

Test Case	month	day	year	Expected Output
1.	0	15	1979	Invalid date
2.	1	15	1979	Monday
3.	2	15	1979	Thursday
4.	6	15	1979	Friday
5.	11	15	1979	Thursday
6.	12	15	1979	Saturday
7.	13	15	1979	Invalid date
8.	6	0	1979	Invalid date
9.	6	1	1979	Friday
10.	6	2	1979	Saturday
11.	6	30	1979	Saturday
12.	6	31	1979	Invalid date
13.	6	32	1979	Invalid date
14.	6	15	1899	Invalid date (out of range)
15.	6	15	1900	Friday
16.	6	15	1901	Saturday
17.	6	15	2057	Friday
18.	6	15	2058	Saturday
19.	6	15	2059	Invalid date (out of range)

Table 2.17. Worst case test cases for the program determining day of the week

Test Case	month	day	year	Expected Output
1.	1	1	1900	Monday
2.	1	1	1901	Tuesday
3.	1	1	1979	Monday
4.	1	1	2057	Monday
5.	1	1	2058	Tuesday
6.	1	2	1900	Tuesday
7.	1	2	1901	Wednesday
8.	1	2	1979	Tuesday
9.	1	2	2057	Tuesday
10.	1	2	2058	Wednesday
11.	1	15	1900	Monday
12.	1	15	1901	Tuesday
13.	1	15	1979	Monday
14.	1	15	2057	Monday
15.	1	15	2058	Tuesday

(Contd.)

(Contd.)

Test Case	month	day	year	Expected Output
16.	1	30	1900	Tuesday
17.	1	30	1901	Wednesday
18.	1	30	1979	Tuesday
19.	1	30	2057	Tuesday
20.	1	30	2058	Wednesday
21.	1	31	1900	Wednesday
22.	1	31	1901	Thursday
23.	1	31	1979	Wednesday
24.	1	31	2057	Wednesday
25.	1	31	2058	Thursday
26.	2	1	1900	Thursday
27.	2	1	1901	Friday
28.	2	1	1979	Thursday
29.	2	1	2057	Thursday
30.	2	1	2058	Friday
31.	2	2	1900	Friday
32.	2	2	1901	Saturday
33.	2	2	1979	Friday
34.	2	2	2057	Friday
35.	2	2	2058	Saturday
36.	2	15	1900	Thursday
37.	2	15	1901	Friday
38.	2	15	1979	Thursday
39.	2	15	2057	Thursday
40.	2	15	2058	Friday
41.	2	30	1900	Invalid date
42.	2	30	1901	Invalid date
43.	2	30	1979	Invalid date
44.	2	30	2057	Invalid date
45.	2	30	2058	Invalid date
46.	2	31	1900	Invalid date
47.	2	31	1901	Invalid date
48.	2	31	1979	Invalid date
49.	2	31	2057	Invalid date
50.	2	31	2058	Invalid date
51.	6	1	1900	Friday
52.	6	1	1901	Saturday

(Contd.)

(Contd.)

Test Case	month	day	year	Expected Output
53.	6	1	1979	Friday
54.	6	1	2057	Friday
55.	6	1	2058	Saturday
56.	6	2	1900	Saturday
57.	6	2	1901	Sunday
58.	6	2	1979	Saturday
59.	6	2	2057	Saturday
60.	6	2	2058	Sunday
61.	6	15	1900	Friday
62.	6	15	1901	Saturday
63.	6	15	1979	Friday
64.	6	15	2057	Friday
65.	6	15	2058	Saturday
66.	6	30	1900	Saturday
67.	6	30	1901	Sunday
68.	6	30	1979	Saturday
69.	6	30	2057	Saturday
70.	6	30	2058	Sunday
71.	6	31	1900	Invalid date
72.	6	31	1901	Invalid date
73.	6	31	1979	Invalid date
74.	6	31	2057	Invalid date
75.	6	31	2058	Invalid date
76.	11	1	1900	Thursday
77.	11	1	1901	Friday
78.	11	1	1979	Thursday
79.	11	1	2057	Thursday
80.	11	1	2058	Friday
81.	11	2	1900	Friday
82.	11	2	1901	Saturday
83.	11	2	1979	Friday
84.	11	2	2057	Friday
85.	11	2	2058	Saturday
86.	11	15	1900	Thursday
87.	11	15	1901	Friday
88.	11	15	1979	Thursday
89.	11	15	2057	Thursday

(Contd.)

(Contd.)

Test Case	month	day	year	Expected Output
90.	11	15	2058	Friday
91.	11	30	1900	Friday
92.	11	30	1901	Saturday
93.	11	30	1979	Friday
94.	11	30	2057	Friday
95.	11	30	2058	Saturday
96.	11	31	1900	Invalid date
97.	11	31	1901	Invalid date
98.	11	31	1979	Invalid date
99.	11	31	2057	Invalid date
100.	11	31	2058	Invalid date
101.	12	1	1900	Saturday
102.	12	1	1901	Sunday
103.	12	1	1979	Saturday
104.	12	1	2057	Saturday
105.	12	1	2058	Sunday
106.	12	2	1900	Sunday
107.	12	2	1901	Monday
108.	12	2	1979	Sunday
109.	12	2	2057	Sunday
110.	12	2	2058	Monday
111.	12	15	1900	Saturday
112.	12	15	1901	Sunday
113.	12	15	1979	Saturday
114.	12	15	2057	Saturday
115.	12	15	2058	Sunday
116.	12	30	1900	Sunday
117.	12	30	1901	Monday
118.	12	30	1979	Sunday
119.	12	30	2057	Sunday
120.	12	30	2058	Monday
121.	12	31	1900	Monday
122.	12	31	1901	Tuesday
123.	12	31	1979	Monday
124.	12	31	2057	Monday
125.	12	31	2058	Tuesday

2.2 EQUIVALENCE CLASS TESTING

As we have discussed earlier, a large number of test cases are generated for any program. It is neither feasible nor desirable to execute all such test cases. We want to select a few test cases and still wish to achieve a reasonable level of coverage. Many test cases do not test any new thing and they just execute the same lines of source code again and again. We may divide input domain into various categories with some relationship and expect that every test case from a category exhibits the same behaviour. If categories are well selected, we may assume that if one representative test case works correctly, others may also give the same results. This assumption allows us to select exactly one test case from each category and if there are four categories, four test cases may be selected. Each category is called an equivalence class and this type of testing is known as equivalence class testing.

2.2.1 Creation of Equivalence Classes

The entire input domain can be divided into at least two equivalence classes: one containing all valid inputs and the other containing all invalid inputs. Each equivalence class can further be sub-divided into equivalence classes on which the program is required to behave differently. The input domain equivalence classes for the program 'Square' which takes 'x' as an input (range 1-100) and prints the square of 'x' (seen in Figure 2.2) are given as:

(i) $I_1 = \{ 1 \leq x \leq 100 \}$ (Valid input range from 1 to 100)
(ii) $I_2 = \{ x < 1 \}$ (Any invalid input where x is less than 1)
(iii) $I_3 = \{ x > 100 \}$ (Any invalid input where x is greater than 100)

Three test cases are generated covering every equivalence class and are given in Table 2.18.

Table 2.18. Test cases for program 'Square' based on input domain

Test Case	Input x	Expected Output
I_1	0	Invalid Input
I_2	50	2500
I_3	101	Invalid Input

The following equivalence classes can be generated for program 'Addition' for input domain:

(i) $I_1 = \{ 100 \leq x \leq 300$ and $200 \leq y \leq 400 \}$ (Both x and y are valid values)
(ii) $I_2 = \{ 100 \leq x \leq 300$ and $y < 200 \}$ (x is valid and y is invalid)
(iii) $I_3 = \{ 100 \leq x \leq 300$ and $y > 400 \}$ (x is valid and y is invalid)
(iv) $I_4 = \{ x < 100$ and $200 \leq y \leq 400 \}$ (x is invalid and y is valid)
(v) $I_5 = \{ x > 300$ and $200 \leq y \leq 400 \}$ (x is invalid and y is valid)
(vi) $I_6 = \{ x < 100$ and $y < 200 \}$ (Both inputs are invalid)
(vii) $I_7 = \{ x < 100$ and $y > 400 \}$ (Both inputs are invalid)
(viii) $I_8 = \{ x > 300$ and $y < 200 \}$ (Both inputs are invalid)
(ix) $I_9 = \{ x > 300$ and $y > 400 \}$ (Both inputs are invalid)

The graphical representation of inputs is shown in Figure 2.9 and the test cases are given in Table 2.19.

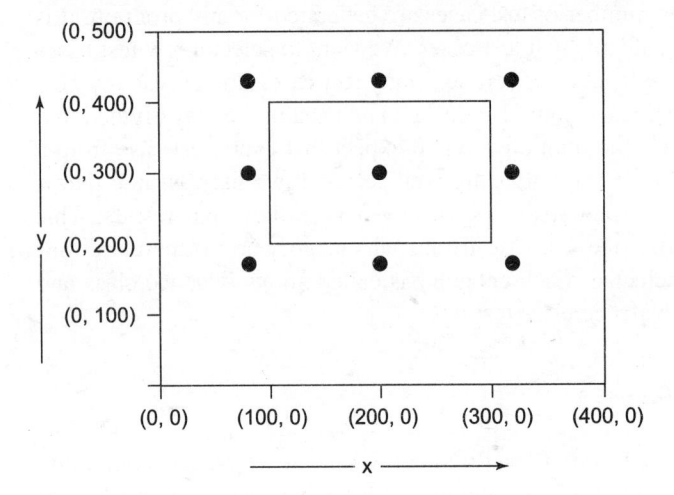

Figure 2.9. Graphical representation of inputs

Table 2.19. Test cases for the program 'Addition'

Test Case	x	y	Expected Output
I_1	200	300	500
I_2	200	199	Invalid input
I_3	200	401	Invalid input
I_4	99	300	Invalid input
I_5	301	300	Invalid input
I_6	99	199	Invalid input
I_7	99	401	Invalid input
I_8	301	199	Invalid input
I_9	301	401	Invalid input

The equivalence classes of input domain may be mutually exclusive (as shown in Figure 2.10 (a)) and they may have overlapping regions (as shown in Figure 2.10 (b)).

We may also partition output domain for the design of equivalence classes. Every output will lead to an equivalence class. Thus, for 'Square' program, the output domain equivalence classes are given as:

O_1 = {square of the input number 'x'}

O_2 = {Invalid input}

The test cases for output domain are shown in Table 2.20. Some of input and output domain test cases may be the same.

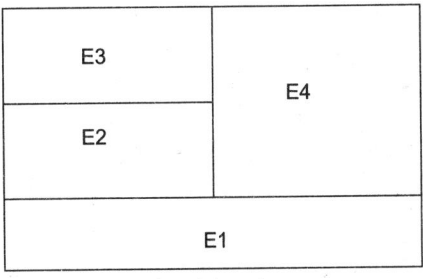

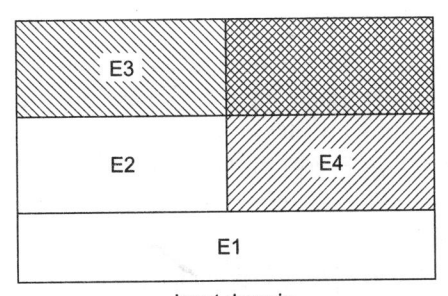

(a) Four mutually exclusive equivalence classes

(b) E3 and E4 have an overlapping region

Figure 2.10. Equivalence classes of input domain

Table 2.20. Test cases for program 'Square' based on output domain

Test Case	Input x	Expected Output
O_1	50	2500
O_2	0	Invalid Input

We may also design output domain equivalence classes for the program 'Addition' as given below:

O_1 = { Addition of two input numbers x and y }

O_2 = {Invalid Input}

The test cases are given in Table 2.21.

Table 2.21. Test cases for program 'Addition' based on output domain

Test Case	x	y	Expected Output
O_1	200	300	500
O_2	99	300	Invalid Input

In the above two examples, valid input domain has only one equivalence class. We may design more numbers of equivalence classes based on the type of problem and nature of inputs and outputs. Here, the most important task is the creation of equivalence classes which require domain knowledge and experience of testing. This technique reduces the number of test cases that should be designed and executed.

2.2.2 Applicability

It is applicable at unit, integration, system and acceptance test levels. The basic requirement is that inputs or outputs must be partitioned based on the requirements and every partition will give a test case. The selected test case may test the same thing, as would have been tested by another test case of the same equivalence class, and if one test case catches a bug, the other probably will too. If one test case does not find a bug, the other test cases of the same equivalence class may also not find any bug. We do not consider dependencies among different variables while designing equivalence classes.

The design of equivalence classes is subjective and two testing persons may design two different sets of partitions of input and output domains. This is understandable and correct as long as the partitions are reviewed and all agree that they acceptably cover the program under test.

Example 2.9: Consider the program for determination of the largest amongst three numbers specified in example 2.1. Identify the equivalence class test cases for output and input domain.

Solution: Output domain equivalence classes are:

$O_1 = \{<x, y, z> : $ Largest amongst three numbers x, y, z $\}$

$O_2 = \{<x, y, z> : $ Input values(s) is /are out of range with sides x, y, z $\}$

The test cases are given in Table 2.22.

Table 2.22. Output domain test cases to find the largest among three numbers

Test Case	x	y	z	Expected Output
O_1	150	140	110	150
O_2	301	50	50	Input values are out of range

Input domain based equivalence classes are:

$I_1 = \{ 1 \leq x \leq 300 $ and $ 1 \leq y \leq 300 $ and $ 1 \leq z \leq 300 \}$ (All inputs are valid)

$I_2 = \{ x < 1 $ and $ 1 \leq y \leq 300 $ and $ 1 \leq z \leq 300 \}$ (x is invalid , y is valid and z is valid)

$I_3 = \{ 1 \leq x \leq 300 $ and $ y < 1 $ and $ 1 \leq z \leq 300 \}$ (x is valid, y is invalid and z is valid)

$I_4 = \{ 1 \leq x \leq 300 $ and $ 1 \leq y \leq 300 $ and $ z < 1 \}$ (x is valid, y is valid and z is invalid)

$I_5 = \{ x > 300 $ and $ 1 \leq y \leq 300 $ and $ 1 \leq z \leq 300 \}$ (x is invalid, y is valid and z is valid)

$I_6 = \{ 1 \leq x \leq 300 $ and $ y > 300 $ and $ 1 \leq z \leq 300 \}$ (x is valid, y is invalid and z is valid)

$I_7 = \{ 1 \leq x \leq 300 $ and $ 1 \leq y \leq 300 $ and $ z > 300 \}$ (x is valid, y is valid and z is invalid)

$I_8 = \{ x < 1 $ and $ y < 1 $ and $ 1 \leq z \leq 300 \}$ (x is invalid, y is invalid and z is valid)

$I_9 = \{ 1 \leq x \leq 300 $ and $ y < 1 $ and $ z < 1 \}$ (x is valid, y is invalid and z is invalid)

$I_{10} = \{ x < 1 $ and $ 1 \leq y \leq 300 $ and $ z < 1 \}$ (x is invalid, y is valid and z is invalid)

$I_{11} = \{ x > 300 $ and $ y > 300 $ and $ 1 \leq z \leq 300 \}$ (x is invalid, y is invalid and z is valid)

$I_{12} = \{ 1 \leq x \leq 300 $ and $ y > 300 $ and $ z > 300 \}$ (x is valid, y is invalid and z is invalid)

$I_{13} = \{ x > 300 $ and $ 1 \leq y \leq 300 $ and $ z > 300 \}$ (x is invalid, y is valid and z is invalid)

$I_{14} = \{ x < 1 $ and $ y > 300 $ and $ 1 \leq z \leq 300 \}$ (x is invalid, y is invalid and z is valid)

$I_{15} = \{ x > 300 $ and $ y < 1 $ and $ 1 \leq z \leq 300 \}$ (x is invalid, y is invalid and z is valid)

$I_{16} = \{ 1 \leq x \leq 300 $ and $ y < 1 $ and $ z > 300 \}$ (x is valid, y is invalid and z is invalid)

I_{17} = { $1 \leq x \leq 300$ and $y > 300$ and $z < 1$ } (x is valid, y is invalid and z is invalid)
I_{18} = { $x < 1$ and $1 \leq y \leq 300$ and $z > 300$ } (x is invalid, y is valid and z is invalid)
I_{19} = { $x > 300$ and $1 \leq y \leq 300$ and $z < 1$ } (x is invalid, y is valid and z is invalid)
I_{20} = { $x < 1$ and $y < 1$ and $z < 1$ } (All inputs are invalid)
I_{21} = { $x > 300$. and $y > 300$ and $z > 300$ } (All inputs are invalid)
I_{22} = { $x < 1$ and $y < 1$ and $z > 300$ } (All inputs are invalid)
I_{23} = { $x < 1$ and $y > 300$ and $z < 1$ } (All inputs are invalid)
I_{24} = { $x > 300$ and $y < 1$ and $z < 1$ } (All inputs are invalid)
I_{25} = { $x > 300$ and $y > 300$ and $z < 1$ } (All inputs are invalid)
I_{26} = { $x > 300$ and $y < 1$ and $z > 300$ } (All inputs are invalid)
I_{27} = { $x < 1$ and $y > 300$ and $z > 300$ } (All inputs are invalid)

The input domain test cases are given in Table 2.23.

Table 2.23. Input domain test case

Test Case	x	y	z	Expected Output
I_1	150	40	50	150
I_2	0	50	50	Input values are out of range
I_3	50	0	50	Input values are out of range
I_4	50	50	0	Input values are out of range
I_5	101	50	50	Input values are out of range
I_6	50	101	50	Input values are out of range
I_7	50	50	101	Input values are out of range
I_8	0	0	50	Input values are out of range
I_9	50	0	0	Input values are out of range
I_{10}	0	50	0	Input values are out of range
I_{11}	301	301	50	Input values are out of range
I_{12}	50	301	301	Input values are out of range
I_{13}	301	50	301	Input values are out of range
I_{14}	0	301	50	Input values are out of range
I_{15}	301	0	50	Input values are out of range
I_{16}	50	0	301	Input values are out of range
I_{17}	50	301	0	Input values are out of range
I_{18}	0	50	301	Input values are out of range
I_{19}	301	50	0	Input values are out of range

(Contd.)

(Contd.)

Test Case	x	y	z	Expected Output
I_{20}	0	0	0	Input values are out of range
I_{21}	301	301	301	Input values are out of range
I_{22}	0	0	301	Input values are out of range
I_{23}	0	301	0	Input values are out of range
I_{24}	301	0	0	Input values are out of range
I_{25}	301	301	0	Input values are out of range
I_{26}	301	0	301	Input values are out of range
I_{27}	0	301	301	Input values are out of range

Example 2.10: Consider the program for the determination of division of a student as explained in example 2.2. Identify the equivalence class test cases for output and input domains.

Solution: Output domain equivalence class test cases can be identified as follows:

O_1 = { <mark1, mark2, mark3> : First Division with distinction if average >= 75 }
O_2 = { <mark1, mark2, mark3> : First Division if $60 \leq$ average ≤ 74}
O_3 = { <mark1, mark2, mark3> : Second Division if $50 \leq$ average ≤ 59 }
O_4 = { <mark1, mark2, mark3> : Third Division if $40 \leq$ average ≤ 49 }
O_5 = { <mark1, mark2, mark3> : Fail if average <40 }
O_6 = { <mark1, mark2, mark3> : Invalid marks if marks are not between 0 to 100 }

The test cases generated by output domain are given in Table 2.24.

Table 2.24. Output domain test cases

Test Case	mark1	mark2	mark3	Expected Output
O_1	75	80	85	First division with distinction
O_2	68	68	68	First division
O_3	55	55	55	Second division
O_4	45	45	45	Third division
O_5	25	25	25	Fail
O_6	-1	50	50	Invalid marks

We may have another set of test cases based on input domain.

I_1 = { $0 \leq$ mark1 ≤ 100 and $0 \leq$ mark2 ≤ 100 and $0 \leq$ mark3 ≤ 100 } (All inputs are valid)

I_2 = { mark1 < 0 and $0 \leq$ mark2 ≤ 100 and $0 \leq$ mark3 ≤ 100 } (mark1 is invalid, mark2 is valid and mark3 is valid)

I_3 = { $0 \leq mark1 \leq 100$ and $mark2 < 0$ and $0 \leq mark3 \leq 100$ } (mark1 is valid, mark2 is invalid and mark3 is valid)

I_4 = { $0 \leq mark1 \leq 100$ and $0 \leq mark2 \leq 100$ and $mark3 < 0$ } (mark1 is valid, mark2 is valid and mark3 is invalid)

I_5 = { $mark1 > 100$ and $0 \leq mark2 \leq 100$ and $0 \leq mark3 \leq 100$ } (mark1 is invalid, mark2 is valid and mark3 is valid)

I_6 = ($0 \leq mark1 \leq 100$ and $mark2 > 100$ and $0 \leq mark3 \leq 100$ } (mark1 is valid, mark2 is invalid and mark3 is valid)

I_7 = { $0 \leq mark1 \leq 100$ and $0 \leq mark2 \leq 100$ and $mark3 > 100$ } (mark 1 is valid, mark2 is valid and mark3 is invalid)

I_8 = { $mark1 < 0$ and $mark2 < 0$ and $0 \leq mark3 \leq 100$ } (mark1 is invalid, mark2 is invalid and mark3 is valid)

I_9 = { $0 \leq mark1 \leq 100$ and $mark2 < 0$ and $mark3 < 0$ } (mark1 is valid, mark2 is invalid and mark3 is invalid)

I_{10} = { $mark1 < 0$ and $0 \leq mark2 \leq 100$ and $mark3 < 0$ } (mark1 is invalid, mark2 is valid and mark3 is invalid)

I_{11} = { $mark1 > 100$ and $mark2 > 100$ and $0 \leq mark3 \leq 100$ } (mark1 is invalid, mark2 is invalid and mark3 is valid)

I_{12} = { $0 \leq mark1 \leq 100$ and $mark2 > 100$ and $mark3 > 100$ } (mark1 is valid, mark2 is invalid and mark3 is invalid)

I_{13} = { $mark1 > 100$ and $0 \leq mark2 \leq 100$ and $mark3 > 100$ } (mark1 is invalid, mark2 is valid and mark3 is invalid)

I_{14} = { $mark1 < 0$ and $mark2 > 100$ and $0 \leq mark3 \leq 100$ } (mark1 is invalid, mark2 is invalid and mark 3 is valid)

I_{15} = { $mark1 > 100$ and $mark2 < 0$ and $0 \leq mark3 \leq 100$ }{ (mark1 is invalid, mark2 is invalid and mark3 is valid)

I_{16} = { $0 \leq mark1 \leq 100$ and $mark2 < 0$ and $mark3 > 100$ } (mark1 is valid, mark2 is invalid and mark3 is invalid)

I_{17} = { $0 \leq mark1 \leq 100$ and $mark2 > 100$ and $mark3 < 0$ } (mark1 is valid, mark2 is invalid and mark3 is invalid)

I_{18} = { $mark1 < 0$ and $0 \leq mark2 \leq 100$ and $mark3 > 100$ } (mark1 is invalid, mark2 is valid and mark3 is invalid)

I_{19} = { $mark1 > 100$ and $0 \leq mark2 \leq 100$ and $mark3 < 0$ } (mark1 is invalid, mark2 is valid and mark3 is invalid)

I_{20} = { $mark1 < 0$ and $mark2 < 0$ and $mark3 < 0$ } (All inputs are invalid)

I_{21} = { $mark1 > 100$ and $mark2 > 100$ and $mark3 > 100$ } (All inputs are invalid)

I_{22} = { $mark1 < 0$ and $mark2 < 0$ and $mark3 > 100$ } (All inputs are invalid)

I_{23} = { $mark1 < 0$ and $mark2 > 100$ and $mark3 < 0$ } (All inputs are invalid)

I_{24} = { $mark1 > 100$ and $mark2 < 0$ and $mark3 < 0$ } (All inputs are invalid)

I_{25} = {$mark1 > 100$ and $mark2 > 100$ and $mark3 < 0$ } (All inputs are invalid)

I_{26} = { mark1 > 100 and mark2 < 0 and mark3 > 100 } (All inputs are invalid)
I_{27} = { mark1 < 0 and mark2 > 100 and mark3 > 100 } (All inputs are invalid)

Thus, 27 test cases are generated on the basis of input domain and are given in Table 3.25.

Table 2.25. Input domain test cases

Test Case	mark1	mark2	mark3	Expected Output
I_1	50	50	50	Second division
I_2	-1	50	50	Invalid marks
I_3	50	-1	50	Invalid marks
I_4	50	50	-1	Invalid marks
I_5	101	50	50	Invalid marks
I_6	50	101	50	Invalid marks
I_7	50	50	101	Invalid marks
I_8	-1	-1	50	Invalid marks
I_9	50	-1	-1	Invalid marks
I_{10}	-1	50	-1	Invalid marks
I_{11}	101	101	50	Invalid marks
I_{12}	50	101	101	Invalid marks
I_{13}	101	50	101	Invalid marks
I_{14}	-1	101	50	Invalid marks
I_{15}	101	-1	50	Invalid marks
I_{16}	50	-1	101	Invalid marks
I_{17}	50	101	-1	Invalid marks
I_{18}	-1	50	101	Invalid marks
I_{19}	101	50	-1	Invalid marks
I_{20}	-1	-1	-1	Invalid marks
I_{21}	101	101	101	Invalid marks
I_{22}	-1	-1	101	Invalid marks
I_{23}	-1	101	-1	Invalid marks
I_{24}	101	-1	-1	Invalid marks
I_{25}	101	101	-1	Invalid marks
I_{26}	101	-1	101	Invalid marks
I_{27}	-1	101	101	Invalid marks

Hence, the total number of equivalence class test cases are 27 (input domain) + 6 (output domain) which is equal to 33.

Example 2.11: Consider the program for classification of a triangle specified in example 2.3. Identify the equivalence class test cases for output and input domain.

Solution: Output domain equivalence classes are:

O_1 = { < a, b, c > : Right angled triangle with sides a, b, c }
O_2 = { < a, b, c > : Acute angled triangle with sides a, b, c }
O_3 = { < a, b, c > : Obtuse angled triangle with sides a, b, c}
O_4 = { < a, b, c > : Invalid triangle with sides a, b, c, }
O_5 = { < a, b, c > : Input values(s) is /are out of range with sides a, b, c }

The test cases are given in Table 2.26.

Table 2.26. Output domain test cases for triangle classification program

Test Case	a	b	c	Expected Output
O_1	50	40	30	Right angled triangle
O_2	50	49	49	Acute angled triangle
O_3	57	40	40	Obtuse angled triangle
O_4	50	50	100	Invalid triangle
O_5	101	50	50	Input values are out of range

Input domain based equivalence classes are:

I_1 = { $1 \le a \le 100$ and $1 \le b \le 100$ and $1 \le c \le 100$ } (All inputs are valid)

I_2 = { $a < 1$ and $1 \le b \le 100$ and $1 \le c \le 100$ } (a is invalid , b is valid and c is valid)

I_3 = { $1 \le a \le 100$ and $b < 1$ and $1 \le c \le 100$ } (a is valid, b is invalid and c is valid)

I_4 = { $1 \le a \le 100$ and $1 \le b \le 100$ and $c < 1$ } (a is valid, b is valid and c is invalid)

I_5 = { $a > 100$ and $1 \le b \le 100$ and $1 \le c \le 100$ } (a is invalid, b is valid and c is valid)

I_6 = { $1 \le a \le 100$ and $b > 100$ and $1 \le c \le 100$ } (a is valid, b is invalid and c is valid)

I_7 = { $1 \le a \le 100$ and $1 \le b \le 100$ and $c > 100$ } (a is valid, b is valid and c is invalid)

I_8 = { $a < 1$ and $b < 1$ and $1 \le c \le 100$ } (a is invalid, b is invalid and c is valid)

I_9 = { $1 \le a \le 100$ and $b < 1$ and $c < 1$ } (a is valid, b is invalid and c is invalid)

I_{10} = { $a < 1$ and $1 \le b \le 100$ and $c < 1$ } (a is invalid, b is valid and c is invalid)

I_{11} = { $a > 100$ and $b > 100$ and $1 \le c \le 100$ } (a is invalid, b is invalid and c is valid)

I_{12} = { $1 \le a \le 100$ and $b > 100$ and $c > 100$ }(a is valid, b is invalid and c is invalid)

I_{13} = { $a > 100$ and $1 \le b \le 100$ and $c > 100$ } (a is invalid, b is valid and c is invalid)

I_{14} = { a < 1 and b > 100 and 1 ≤ c ≤ 100 } (a is invalid, b is invalid and c is valid)

I_{15} = { a > 100 and b < 1 and 1 ≤ c ≤ 100 } (a is invalid, b is invalid and c is valid)

I_{16} = {1 ≤ a ≤ 100 and b < 1 and c > 100 } (a is valid, b is invalid and c is invalid)

I_{17} = { 1 ≤ a ≤ 100 and b > 100 and c < 1 } (a is valid, b is invalid and c is invalid)

I_{18} = { a < 1 and 1≤ b ≤ 100 and c > 100 } (a is invalid, b is valid and c is invalid)

I_{19} = { a > 100 and 1 ≤ b ≤ 100 and c < 1 } (a is invalid, b is valid and c is invalid)

I_{20} = { a < 1 and b < 1 and c < 1 } (All inputs are invalid)
I_{21} = { a > 100 and b > 100 and c > 100 } (All inputs are invalid)
I_{22} = { a < 1 and b < 1 and c > 100 } (All inputs are invalid)
I_{23} = { a < 1 and b > 100 and c < 1 } (All inputs are invalid)
I_{24} = { a > 100 and b < 1 and c < 1 } (All inputs are invalid)
I_{25} = { a > 100 and b > 100 and c < 1 } (All inputs are invalid)
I_{26} = { a > 100 and b < 1 and c > 100 } (All inputs are invalid)
I_{27} = { a < 1 and b > 100 and c > 100 } (All inputs are invalid)

Some input domain test cases can be obtained using the relationship amongst a, b and c.

I_{28} = { $a^2 = b^2 + c^2$ }
I_{29} = { $b^2 = c^2 + a^2$ }
I_{30} = { $c^2 = a^2 + b^2$ }
I_{31} = { $a^2 > b^2 + c^2$ }
I_{32} = { $b^2 > c^2 + a^2$ }
I_{33} = { $c^2 > a^2 + b^2$ }
I_{34} = { $a^2 < b^2 + c^2$ }
I_{35} = { $b^2 < c^2 + a^2$ }
I_{36} = { $c^2 < a^2 + b^2$ }
I_{37} = { a = b + c }
I_{38} = { a > b + c }
I_{39} = { b = c + a }
I_{40} = { b > c + a }
I_{41} = { c = a + b }
I_{42} = { c > a + b }
I_{43} = { $a^2 < b^2 + c^2$ && $b^2 < c^2 + a^2$ && $c^2 < a^2 + b^2$ }

The input domain test cases are given in Table 2.27.

Table 2.27. Input domain test cases

Test Case	a	b	c	Expected Output
I_1	50	50	50	Acute angled triangle
I_2	0	50	50	Input values are out of range
I_3	50	0	50	Input values are out of range
I_4	50	50	0	Input values are out of range
I_5	101	50	50	Input values are out of range
I_6	50	101	50	Input values are out of range
I_7	50	50	101	Input values are out of range
I_8	0	0	50	Input values are out of range
I_9	50	0	0	Input values are out of range
I_{10}	0	50	0	Input values are out of range
I_{11}	101	101	50	Input values are out of range
I_{12}	50	101	101	Input values are out of range
I_{13}	101	50	101	Input values are out of range
I_{14}	0	101	50	Input values are out of range
I_{15}	101	0	50	Input values are out of range
I_{16}	50	0	101	Input values are out of range
I_{17}	50	101	0	Input values are out of range
I_{18}	0	50	101	Input values are out of range
I_{19}	101	50	0	Input values are out of range
I_{20}	0	0	0	Input values are out of range
I_{21}	101	101	101	Input values are out of range
I_{22}	0	0	101	Input values are out of range
I_{23}	0	101	0	Input values are out of range
I_{24}	101	0	0	Input values are out of range
I_{25}	101	101	0	Input values are out of range
I_{26}	101	0	101	Input values are out of range
I_{27}	0	101	101	Input values are out of range
I_{28}	50	40	30	Right angled triangle
I_{29}	40	50	30	Right angled triangle
I_{30}	40	30	50	Right angled triangle
I_{31}	57	40	40	Obtuse angled triangle
I_{32}	40	57	50	Obtuse angled triangle
I_{33}	40	40	57	Obtuse angled triangle
I_{34}	50	49	49	Acute angled triangle
I_{35}	49	50	49	Acute angled triangle
I_{36}	49	49	50	Acute angled triangle
I_{37}	100	50	50	Invalid triangle
I_{38}	100	40	40	Invalid triangle
I_{39}	50	100	50	Invalid triangle
I_{40}	40	100	40	Invalid triangle
I_{41}	50	50	100	Invalid triangle
I_{42}	40	40	100	Invalid triangle
I_{43}	49	49	50	Acute angled triangle

74 Software Testing

Hence, total number of equivalence class test cases are 43 (input domain) and 5 (output domain) which is equal to 48.

Example 2.12: Consider the program for determining the day of the week as explained in example 2.4. Identify the equivalence class test cases for output and input domains.

Solution: Output domain equivalence classes are:

O_1 = { < Day, Month, Year > : Monday for all valid inputs }
O_2 = { < Day, Month, Year > : Tuesday for all valid inputs }
O_3 = { < Day, Month, Year > : Wednesday for all valid inputs}
O_4 = { < Day, Month, Year > : Thursday for all valid inputs}
O_5 = { < Day, Month, Year > : Friday for all valid inputs}
O_6 = { < Day, Month, Year > : Saturday for all valid inputs}
O_7 = { < Day, Month, Year > : Sunday for all valid inputs}
O_8 = { < Day, Month, Year > : Invalid Date if any of the input is invalid}
O_9 = { < Day, Month, Year > : Input out of range if any of the input is out of range}

The output domain test cases are given in Table 2.28.

Table 2.28. Output domain equivalence class test cases

Test Case	month	day	year	Expected Output
O_1	6	11	1979	Monday
O_2	6	12	1979	Tuesday
O_3	6	13	1979	Wednesday
O_4	6	14	1979	Thursday
O_5	6	15	1979	Friday
O_6	6	16	1979	Saturday
O_7	6	17	1979	Sunday
O_8	6	31	1979	Invalid date
O_9	6	32	1979	Inputs out of range

The input domain is partitioned as given below:

(i) Valid partitions
M1: Month has 30 Days
M2 : Month has 31 Days
M3 : Month is February
D1 : Days of a month from 1 to 28
D2 : Day = 29
D3 : Day = 30
D4 : Day = 31
Y1 : $1900 \leq year \leq 2058$ and is a common year
Y2 : $1900 \leq year \leq 2058$ and is a leap year.

(ii) Invalid partitions
M4 : Month < 1

M5 : Month > 12
D5 : Day < 1
D6 : Day > 31
Y3 : Year < 1900
Y4 : Year > 2058

We may have following equivalence classes which are based on input domain:

(a) Only for valid input domain

I_1 = { M1 and D1 and Y1 } (All inputs are valid)
I_2 = { M2 and D1 and Y1 } (All inputs are valid)
I_3 = { M3 and D1 and Y1 } (All inputs are valid)
I_4 = { M1 and D2 and Y1 } (All inputs are valid)
I_5 = { M2 and D2 and Y1 } (All inputs are valid)
I_6 = { M3 and D2 and Y1 } (All inputs are valid)
I_7 = { M1 and D3 and Y1 } (All inputs are valid)
I_8 = { M2 and D3 and Y1 } (All inputs are valid)
I_9 = { M3 and D3 and Y1 } (All inputs are valid)
I_{10} = { M1 and D4 and Y1 } (All inputs are valid)
I_{11} = { M2 and D4 and Y1 } (All inputs are valid)
I_{12} = { M3 and D4 and Y1 } (All inputs are valid)
I_{13} = { M1 and D1 and Y2 } (All Inputs are valid)
I_{14} = { M2 and D1 and Y2 } (All inputs are valid)
I_{15} = { M3 and D1 and Y2 } (All inputs are valid)
I_{16} = { M1 and D2 and Y2 } (All inputs are valid)
I_{17} = { M2 and D2 and Y2 } (All inputs are valid)
I_{18} = { M3 and D2 and Y2 } (All inputs are valid)
I_{19} = { M1 and D3 and Y2 } (All inputs are valid)
I_{20} = { M2 and D3 and Y2 } (All inputs are valid)
I_{21} = { M3 and D3 and Y2 } (All inputs are valid)
I_{22} = { M1 and D4 and Y2 } (All inputs are valid)
I_{23} = { M2 and D4 and Y2 } (All inputs are valid)
I_{24} = { M3 and D4 and Y2 } (All inputs are valid)

(b) Only for Invalid input domain

I_{25} = { M4 and D1 and Y1 } (Month is invalid, Day is valid and Year is valid)
I_{26} = { M5 and D1 and Y1 } (Month is invalid, Day is valid and Year is valid)
I_{27} = { M4 and D2 and Y1 } (Month is invalid, Day is valid and Year is valid)
I_{28} = { M5 and D2 and Y1 } (Month is invalid, Day is valid and Year is valid)
I_{29} = { M4 and D3 and Y1 } (Month is invalid, Day is valid and Year is valid)
I_{30} = { M5 and D3 and Y1 } (Month is invalid, Day is valid and Year is valid)

I_{31} = { M4 and D4 and Y1 } (Month is invalid, Day is valid and Year is valid)
I_{32} = { M5 and D4 and Y1 } (Month is invalid, Day is valid and year is valid)
I_{33} = { M4 and D1 and Y2 } (Month is invalid, Day is valid and Year is valid)
I_{34} = { M5 and D1 and Y2 } (Month is invalid, Day is valid and Year is valid)
I_{35} = { M4 and D2 and Y2 } (Month is invalid, Day is valid and Year is valid)
I_{36} = { M5 and D2 and Y2 } (Month is invalid, Day is valid and Year is valid)
I_{37} = { M4 and D3 and Y2 } (Month is invalid, Day is valid and Year is valid)
I_{38} = { M5 and D3 and Y2 } (Month is invalid, Day is valid and Year is valid)
I_{39} = { M4 and D4 and Y2 } (Month is invalid, Day is valid and Year is valid)
I_{40} = { M5 and D4 and Y2 } (Month is invalid, Day is valid and Year is valid)
I_{41} = { M1 and D5 and Y1 } (Month is valid, Day is invalid and Year is valid)
I_{42} = { M1 and D6 and Y1 } (Month is valid, Day is invalid and Year is valid)
I_{43} = { M2 and D5 and Y1 } (Month is valid, Day is invalid and Year is valid)
I_{44} = { M2 and D6 and Y1 } (Month is valid, Day is invalid and Year is valid)
I_{45} = { M3 and D5 and Y1 } (Month is valid, Day is invalid and Year is valid)
I_{46} = { M3 and D6 and Y1 } (Month is valid, Day is invalid and Year is valid)
I_{47} = { M1 and D5 and Y2 } (Month is valid, Day is invalid and Year is valid)
I_{48} = { M1 and D6 and Y2 } (Month is valid, Day is invalid and Year is valid)
I_{49} = { M2 and D5 and Y2 } (Month is valid, Day is invalid and Year is valid)
I_{50} = { M2 and D6 and Y2 } (Month is valid, Day is invalid and Year is valid)
I_{51} = { M3 and D5 and Y2 } (Month is valid, Day is invalid and Year is valid)
I_{52} = { M3 and D6 and Y2 } (Month is valid, Day is invalid and Year is valid)
I_{53} = { M1 and D1 and Y3 } (Month is valid, Day is valid and Year is invalid)
I_{54} = { M1 and D1 and Y4 } (Month is valid, Day is valid and Year is invalid)
I_{55} = { M2 and D1 and Y3 } (Month is valid, Day is valid and Year is invalid)
I_{56} = { M2 and D1 and Y4 } (Month is valid, Day is valid and Year is invalid)
I_{57} = { M3 and D1 and Y3 } (Month is valid, Day is valid and Year is invalid)
I_{58} = { M3 and D1 and Y4 } (Month is valid, Day is valid and Year is invalid)
I_{59} = { M1 and D2 and Y3 } (Month is valid, Day is valid and Year is invalid)
I_{60} = { M1 and D2 and Y4 } (Month is valid, Day is valid and Year is invalid)
I_{61} = { M2 and D2 and Y3 } (Month is valid, Day is valid and Year is invalid)
I_{62} = { M2 and D2 and Y4 } (Month is valid, Day is valid and Year is invalid)
I_{63} = { M3 and D2 and Y3 } (Month is valid, Day is valid and Year is invalid)
I_{64} = { M3 and D2 and Y4 } (Month is valid, Day is valid and Year is invalid)
I_{65} = { M1 and D3 and Y3 } (Month is valid, Day is valid and Year is invalid)
I_{66} = { M1 and D3 and Y3 } (Month is valid, Day is valid and Year is invalid)
I_{67} = { M2 and D3 and Y3 } (Month is valid, Day is valid and Year is invalid)

I_{68} = { M2 and D3 and Y4 } (Month is valid, Day is valid and Year is invalid)
I_{69} = { M3 and D3 and Y3 } (Month is valid, Day is valid and Year is invalid)
I_{70} = { M3 and D3 and Y4 } (Month is valid, Day is valid and Year is invalid)
I_{71} = { M1 and D4 and Y3 } (Month is valid, Day is valid and Year is invalid)
I_{72} = { M1 and D4 and Y4 } (Month is valid, Day is valid and Year is invalid)
I_{73} = { M2 and D4 and Y3 } (Month is valid, Day is valid and Year is invalid)
I_{74} = { M2 and D4 and Y4 } (Month is valid, Day is valid and Year is invalid)
I_{75} = { M3 and D4 and Y3 } (Month is valid, Day is valid and Year is invalid)
I_{76} = { M3 and D4 and Y4 } (Month is valid, Day is valid and Year is invalid)
I_{77} = { M4 and D5 and Y1 } (Month is invalid, Day is invalid and Year is valid)
1_{78} = { M4 and D5 and Y2 } (Month is invalid, Day is invalid and year is valid)
I_{79} = { M4 and D6 and Y1 } (Month is invalid, Day is invalid and Year is valid)
I_{80} = { M4 and D6 and Y2 } (Month is invalid, Day is invalid and Year is valid)
I_{81} = { M5 and D5 and Y1 } (Month is invalid, Day is invalid and Year is valid)
I_{82} = { M5 and D5 and Y2 } (Month is invalid, Day is invalid and Year is valid)
I_{83} = { M5 and D6 and Y1 } (Month is invalid, Day is invalid and Year is valid)
I_{84} = { M5 and D6 and Y2 } (Month is invalid, Day is invalid and Year is valid)
I_{85} = { M4 and D1 and Y3 } (Month is invalid, Day is valid and Year is invalid)
I_{86} = { M4 and D1 and Y4 } (Month is invalid, Day is valid and Year is invalid)
I_{87} = { M4 and D2 and Y3 } (Month is invalid, Day is valid and Year is invalid)
I_{88} = { M4 and D2 and Y4 } (Month is invalid, Day is valid and Year is invalid)
I_{89} = { M4 and D3 and Y3 } (Month is invalid, Day is valid and Year is invalid)
I_{90} = { M4 and D3 and Y4 } (Month is invalid, day is valid and Year is invalid)
I_{91} = { M4 and D4 and Y3 } (Month is invalid, Day is valid and Year is invalid)
I_{92} = { M4 and D4 and Y4 } (Month is invalid, Day is valid and Year is invalid)
I_{93} = { M5 and D1 and Y3 } (Month is invalid, Day is valid and Year is invalid)
I_{94} = { M5 and D1 and Y4 } (Month is invalid, Day is valid and Year is invalid)
I_{95} = { M5 and D2 and Y3 } (Month is invalid, Day is valid and year is invalid)
I_{96} = { M5 and D2 and Y4 } (Month is invalid, Day is valid and Year is invalid)
I_{97} = { M5 and D3 and Y3 } (Month is invalid, Day is valid and Year is invalid)
I_{98} = { M5 and D3 and Y4 } (Month is invalid, Day is valid and Year is invalid)
I_{99} = { M5 and D4 and Y3 } (Month is invalid, Day is valid and Year is invalid)
I_{100} = { M5 and D4 and Y4 } (Month is invalid, Day is valid and Year is invalid)
I_{101} = { M1 and D5 and Y3 } (Month is valid, Day is invalid and Year is invalid)
I_{102} = { M1 and D5 and Y4 } (Month is valid, Day is invalid and Year is invalid)
I_{103} = { M2 and D5 and Y3 } (Month is valid, Day is invalid and Year is invalid)
I_{104} = { M2 and D5 and Y4 } (Month is valid, Day is invalid and Year is invalid)

I_{105} = { M3 and D5 and Y3 } (Month is valid, Day is invalid and Year is invalid)
I_{106} = { M3 and D5 and Y4 } (Month is valid, Day is invalid and Year is invalid)
I_{107} = { M1 and D6 and Y3 } (Month is valid, Day is invalid and Year is invalid)
I_{108} = { M1 and D6 and Y4 } (Month is valid, Day is invalid and Year is invalid)
I_{109} = { M2 and D6 and Y3 } (Month is valid, Day is invalid and Year is invalid)
I_{110} = { M2 and D6 and Y4 } (Month is valid, Day is invalid and Year is invalid)
I_{111} = { M3 and D6 and Y3 } (Month is valid, Day is invalid and Year is invalid)
I_{112} = { M3 and D6 and Y4 } (Month is valid, Day is invalid and Year is invalid)
I_{113} = (M4 and D5 and Y3 } (All inputs are invalid)
I_{114} = { M4 and D5 and Y4 } (All inputs are invalid)
I_{115} = { M4 and D6 and Y3 } (All inputs are invalid)
I_{116} = { M4 and D6 and Y4 } (All inputs are invalid)
I_{117} = { M5 and D5 and Y3 } (All inputs are invalid)
I_{118} = { M5 and D5 and Y4 } (All inputs are invalid)
I_{119} = { M5 and D6 and Y3 } (All inputs are invalid)
I_{120} = { M5 and D6 and Y4 } (All inputs are invalid)

The test cases generated on the basis of input domain are given in Table 2.29.

Table 2.29. Input domain equivalence class test cases

Test Case	month	day	year	Expected Output
I_1	6	15	1979	Friday
I_2	5	15	1979	Tuesday
I_3	2	15	1979	Thursday
I_4	6	29	1979	Friday
I_5	5	29	1979	Tuesday
I_6	2	29	1979	Invalid Date
I_7	6	30	1979	Saturday
I_8	5	30	1979	Wednesday
I_9	2	30	1979	Invalid Date
I_{10}	6	31	1979	Invalid Date
I_{11}	5	31	1979	Thursday
I_{12}	2	31	1979	Invalid Date
I_{13}	6	15	2000	Thursday
I_{14}	5	15	2000	Monday
I_{15}	2	15	2000	Tuesday
I_{16}	6	29	2000	Thursday
I_{17}	5	29	2000	Monday
I_{18}	2	29	2000	Tuesday
I_{19}	6	30	2000	Friday
I_{20}	5	30	2000	Tuesday
I_{21}	2	30	2000	Invalid date
I_{22}	6	31	2000	Invalid date

(Contd.)

(Contd.)

Test Case	month	day	year	Expected Output
I_{23}	5	31	2000	Wednesday
I_{24}	2	31	2000	Invalid date
I_{25}	0	15	1979	Input(s) out of range
I_{26}	13	15	1979	Input(s) out of range
I_{27}	0	29	1979	Inputs(s) out of range
I_{28}	13	29	1979	Input(s) out of range
I_{29}	0	30	1979	Input(s) out of range
I_{30}	13	30	1979	Input(s) out of range
I_{31}	0	31	1979	Input(s) out of range
I_{32}	13	31	1979	Input(s) out of range
I_{33}	0	15	2000	Input(s) out of range
I_{34}	13	15	2000	Input(s) out of range
I_{35}	0	29	2000	Input(s) out of range
I_{36}	13	29	2000	Input(s) out of range
I_{37}	0	30	2000	Input(s) out of range
I_{38}	13	30	2000	Input(s) out of range
I_{39}	0	31	2000	Input(s) out of range
I_{40}	13	31	2000	Input(s) out of range
I_{41}	6	0	1979	Input(s) out of range
I_{42}	6	32	1979	Input(s) out of range
I_{43}	5	0	1979	Input(s) out of range
I_{44}	5	32	1979	Input(s) out of range
I_{45}	2	0	1979	Input(s) out of range
I_{46}	2	32	1979	Input(s) out of range
I_{47}	6	0	2000	Input(s) out of range
I_{48}	6	32	2000	Input(s) out of range
I_{49}	5	0	2000	Input(s) out of range
I_{50}	5	32	2000	Input(s) out of range
I_{51}	2	0	2000	Input(s) out of range
I_{52}	2	32	2000	Input(s) out of range
I_{53}	6	15	1899	Input(s) out of range
I_{54}	6	15	2059	Input(s) out of range
I_{55}	5	15	1899	Input(s) out of range
I_{56}	5	15	2059	Input(s) out of range
I_{57}	2	15	1899	Input(s) out of range
I_{58}	2	15	2059	Input(s) out of range
I_{59}	6	29	1899	Input(s) out of range
I_{60}	6	29	2059	Input(s) out of range
I_{61}	5	29	1899	Input(s) out of range
I_{62}	5	29	2059	Input(s) out of range
I_{63}	2	29	1899	Input(s) out of range
I_{64}	2	29	2059	Input(s) out of range
I_{65}	6	30	1899	Input(s) out of range
I_{66}	6	30	2059	Input(s) out of range
I_{67}	5	30	1899	Input(s) out of range
I_{68}	5	30	2059	Input(s) out of range

(Contd.)

(Contd.)

Test Case	month	day	year	Expected Output
I_{69}	2	30	1899	Input(s) out of range
I_{70}	2	30	2059	Input(s) out of range
I_{71}	6	31	1899	Input(s) out of range
I_{72}	6	31	2059	Input(s) out of range
I_{73}	5	31	1899	Input(s) out of range
I_{74}	5	31	2059	Input(s) out of range
I_{75}	2	31	1899	Input(s) out of range
I_{76}	2	31	2059	Input(s) out of range
I_{77}	0	0	1979	Input(s) out of range
I_{78}	0	0	2000	Input(s) out of range
I_{79}	0	32	1979	Input(s) out of range
I_{80}	0	32	2000	Input(s) out of range
I_{81}	13	0	1979	Input(s) out of range
I_{82}	13	0	2000	Input(s) out of range
I_{83}	13	32	1979	Input(s) out of range
I_{84}	13	32	2000	Input(s) out of range
I_{85}	0	15	1899	Input(s) out of range
I_{86}	0	15	2059	Input(s) out of range
I_{87}	0	20	1899	Input(s) out of range
I_{88}	0	29	2059	Input(s) out of range
I_{89}	0	30	1899	Input(s) out of range
I_{90}	0	30	2059	Input(s) out of range
I_{91}	0	31	1899	Input(s) out of range
I_{92}	0	31	2059	Input(s) out of range
I_{93}	13	15	1899	Input(s) out of range
I_{94}	13	15	2059	Input(s) out of range
I_{95}	13	29	1899	Input(s) out of range
I_{96}	13	29	2059	Input(s) out of range
I_{97}	13	30	1899	Input(s) out of range
I_{98}	13	30	2059	Input(s) out of range
I_{99}	13	31	1899	Input(s) out of range
I_{100}	13	31	2059	Input(s) out of range
I_{101}	5	0	1899	Input(s) out of range
I_{102}	5	0	2059	Input(s) out of range
I_{103}	6	0	1899	Input(s) out of range
I_{104}	6	0	2059	Input(s) out of range
I_{105}	2	0	1899	Input(s) out of range
I_{106}	2	0	2059	Input(s) out of range
I_{107}	5	32	1899	Input(s) out of range
I_{108}	5	32	2059	Input(s) out of range
I_{109}	6	32	1899	Input(s) out of range
I_{110}	6	32	2059	Input(s) out of range
I_{111}	2	32	1899	Input(s) out of range
I_{112}	2	32	2059	Input(s) out of range
I_{113}	0	0	1899	Input(s) out of range
I_{114}	0	0	2059	Input(s) out of range

(Contd.)

(Contd.)

Test Case	month	day	year	Expected Output
I_{115}	0	32	1899	Input(s) out of range
I_{116}	0	32	2059	Input(s) out of range
I_{117}	13	0	1899	Input(s) out of range
I_{118}	13	0	2059	Input(s) out of range
I_{119}	13	32	1899	Input(s) out of range
I_{120}	13	32	2059	Input(s) out of range

Hence, the total number of equivalence class test cases are 120 (input domain) + 9 (output domain) which is equal to 129. However, most of the outputs are 'Input out of range' and may not offer any value addition. This situation occurs when we choose more numbers of invalid equivalence classes.

It is clear that if the number of valid partitions of input domain increases, then the number of test cases increases very significantly and is equal to the product of the number of partitions of each input variable. In this example, there are 5 partitions of input variable 'month', 6 partitions of input variable 'day' and 4 partitions of input variable 'year' and thus leading to 5x6x4 = 120 equivalence classes of input domain.

2.3 DECISION TABLE BASED TESTING

Decision tables are used in many engineering disciplines to represent complex logical relationships. An output may be dependent on many input conditions and decision tables give a pictorial view of various combinations of input conditions. There are four portions of the decision table and are shown in Table 2.30. The decision table provides a set of conditions and their corresponding actions.

Table 2.30. Decision table

	Stubs	Entries
Condition	c_1 c_2 c_3	
Action	a_1 a_2 a_3 a_4	

Four Portions
1. Condition Stubs
2. Condition Entries
3. Action Stubs
4. Action Entries

2.3.1 Parts of the Decision Table

The four parts of the decision table are given as:

Condition Stubs: All the conditions are represented in this upper left section of the decision table. These conditions are used to determine a particular action or set of actions.

Action Stubs: All possible actions are listed in this lower left portion of the decision table.

Condition Entries: In the condition entries portion of the decision table, we have a number of columns and each column represents a rule. Values entered in this upper right portion of the table are known as inputs.

Action Entries: Each entry in the action entries portion has some associated action or set of actions in this lower right portion of the table. These values are known as outputs and are dependent upon the functionality of the program.

2.3.2 Limited Entry and Extended Entry Decision Tables

Decision table testing technique is used to design a complete set of test cases without using the internal structure of the program. Every column is associated with a rule and generates a test case. A typical decision table is given in Table 2.31.

Table 2.31. Typical structure of a decision table

Stubs	R_1	R_2	R_3	R_4
c_1	F	T	T	T
c_2	-	F	T	T
c_3	-	-	F	T
a_1	X	X		X
a_2			X	
a_3	X			

In Table 2.31, input values are only True (T) or False (F), which are binary conditions. The decision tables which use only binary conditions are known as limited entry decision tables. The decision tables which use multiple conditions where a condition may have many possibilities instead of only 'true' and 'false' are known as extended entry decision tables [COPE04].

2.3.3 'Do Not Care' Conditions and Rule Count

We consider the program for the classification of the triangle as explained in example 2.3. The decision table of the program is given in Table 2.32, where inputs are depicted using binary values.

Table 2.32. Decision table for triangle problem

Condition	c_1: a < b + c?	F	T	T	T	T	T	T	T	T	T
	c_2: b < c + a?	-	F	T	T	T	T	T	T	T	T
	c_3: c < a + b?	-	-	F	T	T	T	T	T	T	T
	c_4: $a^2 = b^2 + c^2$?	-	-	-	T	T	T	T	F	F	F	F
	c_5: $a^2 > b^2 + c^2$?	-	-	-	T	T	F	F	T	T	F	F
	c_6: $a_2 < b_2 + c_2$?	-	-	-	T	F	T	F	T	F	T	F
	Rule Count	32	16	8	1	1	1	1	1	1	1	1
Action	a_1 : Invalid triangle	X	X	X								
	a_2 : Right angled triangle						X					
	a_3 : Obtuse angled triangle								X			
	a_4 : Acute angled triangle									X		
	a_5 : Impossible				X	X	X		X			X

The 'do not care' conditions are represented by the '-'sign. A 'do not care' condition has no effect on the output. If we refer to column 1 of the decision table, where condition c_1: a < b + c is false, then other entries become 'do not care' entries. If c_1 is false, the output will be 'Invalid triangle' irrespective of any state (true or false) of other conditions like c_2, c_3, c_4, c_5 and c_6. These conditions become do not care conditions and are represented by '-'sign. If we do not do so and represent all true and false entries of every condition, the number of columns in the decision table will unnecessarily increase. This is nothing but a representation facility in the decision table to reduce the number of columns and avoid redundancy. Ideally, each column has one rule and that leads to a test case. A column in the entry portion of the table is known as a rule. In the Table 2.32, a term is used as 'rule count' and 32 is mentioned in column 1. The term 'rule count' is used with 'do not care' entries in the decision table and has a value 1, if 'do not care' conditions are not there, but it doubles for every 'do not care' entry. Hence each 'do not care' condition counts for two rules. Rule count can be calculated as:

$$\text{Rule count} = 2^{\text{number of do not care conditions}}$$

However, this is applicable only for limited entry decision tables where only 'true' and 'false' conditions are considered. Hence, the actual number of columns in any decision table is the sum of the rule counts of every column shown in the decision table. The triangle classification decision table has 11 columns as shown in Table 2.32. However the actual columns are a sum of rule counts and are equal to 64. Hence, this way of representation has reduced the number of columns from 64 to 11 without compromising any information. If rule count value of the decision table does not equal to the number of rules computed by the program, then the decision table is incomplete and needs revision.

2.3.4 Impossible Conditions

Decision tables are very popular for the generation of test cases. Sometimes, we may have to make a few attempts to reach the final solution. Some impossible conditions are also generated due to combinations of various inputs and an 'impossible' action is incorporated in the 'action stub' to show such a condition. We may have to redesign the input classes to reduce the impossible actions. Redundancy and inconsistency may create problems but may be reduced by proper designing of input classes depending upon the functionality of a program.

2.3.5 Applicability

Decision tables are popular in circumstances where an output is dependent on many conditions and a large number of decisions are required to be taken. They may also incorporate complex business rules and use them to design test cases. Every column of the decision table generates a test case. As the size of the program increases, handling of decision tables becomes difficult and cumbersome. In practice, they can be applied easily at unit level only. System testing and integration testing may not find its effective applications.

Example 2.13: Consider the problem for determining of the largest amongst three numbers as given in example 2.1. Identify the test cases using the decision table based testing.

Solution: The decision table is given in Table 2.33.

Table 2.33. Decision table

c_1: x >= 1?	F	T	T	T	T	T	T	T	T	T	T	T	T	T
c_2: x <= 300?	-	F	T	T	T	T	T	T	T	T	T	T	T	T
c_3: y >= 1?	-	-	F	T	T	T	T	T	T	T	T	T	T	T
c_4: y <= 300?	-	-	-	F	T	T	T	T	T	T	T	T	T	T
c_5: z >= 1?	-	-	-	-	F	T	T	T	T	T	T	T	T	T
c_6: z <= 300?	-	-	-	-	-	F	T	T	T	T	T	T	T	T
c_7: x>y?	-	-	-	-	-	-	T	T	T	T	F	F	F	F
c_8: y>z?	-	-	-	-	-	-	T	T	F	F	T	T	F	F
c_9: z>x?	-	-	-	-	-	-	T	F	T	F	T	F	T	F
Rule Count	256	128	64	32	16	8	1	1	1	1	1	1	1	1
a_1 : Invalid input	X	X	X	X	X	X								
a_2 : x is largest								X		X				
a_3 : y is largest											X	X		
a_4 : z is largest									X				X	
a_5 : Impossible							X							X

Table 2.34. Test cases of the given problem

Test Case	x	y	z	Expected Output
1.	0	50	50	Invalid marks
2.	301	50	50	Invalid marks
3.	50	0	50	Invalid marks
4.	50	301	50	Invalid marks
5.	50	50	0	Invalid marks
6.	50	50	301	Invalid marks
7.	?	?	?	Impossible
8.	150	130	110	150
9.	150	130	170	170
10.	150	130	140	150
11.	110	150	140	150
12.	140	150	120	150
13.	120	140	150	150
14.	?	?	?	Impossible

Example 2.14: Consider the problem for determining the division of the student in example 2.2. Identify the test cases using the decision table based testing.

Solution: This problem can be solved using either limited entry decision table or extended entry decision table. The effectiveness of any solution is dependent upon the creation of various conditions. The limited entry decision table is given in Table 2.35 and its associated test cases are given in Table 2.36. The impossible inputs are shown by '?' as given in test cases 8, 9, 10, 12, 13, 14, 16, 17, 19 and 22. There are 11 impossible test cases out of 22 test cases which is a very large number and compel us to look for other solutions.

Table 2.35. Limited entry decision table

Conditions	1	2	3	4	5	6	7	8	9	10	11	12	13	14	15	16	17	18	19	20	21	22
c_1 : mark1 >= 0 ?	F	T	T	T	T	T	T	T	T	T	T	T	T	T	T	T	T	T	T	T	T	T
c_2 : mark1 <= 100 ?	-	F	T	T	T	T	T	T	T	T	T	T	T	T	T	T	T	T	T	T	T	T
c_3 : mark2 >= 0 ?	-	-	F	T	T	T	T	T	T	T	T	T	T	T	T	T	T	T	T	T	T	T
c_4 : mark2 <= 100 ?	-	-	-	F	T	T	T	T	T	T	T	T	T	T	T	T	T	T	T	T	T	T
c_5 : mark3 >= 0 ?	-	-	-	-	F	T	T	T	T	T	T	T	T	T	T	T	T	T	T	T	T	T
c_6 : mark3 <= 100?	-	-	-	-	-	F	T	T	T	T	T	T	T	T	T	T	T	T	T	T	T	T
c_7 : 0 ≤ avg ≤ 39 ?	-	-	-	-	-	-	T	T	T	T	T	F	F	F	F	F	F	F	F	F	F	F
c_8 : 40 ≤ avg ≤ 49 ?	-	-	-	-	-	-	-	T	F	F	F	T	T	T	T	F	F	F	F	F	F	F
c_9 : 50 ≤ avg ≤ 59 ?	-	-	-	-	-	-	-	-	T	F	F	T	F	F	F	T	T	T	F	F	F	F
c_{10} : 60 ≤ avg ≤ 74 ?	-	-	-	-	-	-	-	-	-	T	F	-	T	F	F	-	T	F	T	T	F	F
c_{11} : avg ≥ 75 ?	-	-	-	-	-	-	-	-	-	-	F	-	-	T	F	-	-	F	-	F	T	F
Rule Count	1024	512	256	128	64	32	8	4	2	1	1	4	2	1	1	2	1	1	1	1	1	1
a_1 : Invalid marks	X	X	X	X	X	X																
a_2 : First division with distinction																					X	
a_3 : First division																				X		
a_4 : Second division																		X				
a_5 : Third division															X							
a_6 : Fail											X											
a_7 : Impossible							X	X	X	X		X	X	X		X	X	X	X			X

86　Software Testing

There are 22 test cases corresponding to each column in the decision table. The test cases are given in Table 2.36.

Table 2.36. Test cases of the given problem

Test Case	mark1	mark2	mark3	Expected Output
1.	−1	50	50	Invalid marks
2.	101	50	50	Invalid marks
3.	50	−1	50	Invalid marks
4.	50	101	50	Invalid marks
5.	50	50	−1	Invalid marks
6.	50	50	101	Invalid marks
7.	?	?	?	Impossible
8.	?	?	?	Impossible
9.	?	?	?	Impossible
10.	?	?	?	Impossible
11.	25	25	25	Fail
12.	?	?	?	Impossible
13.	?	?	?	Impossible
14.	?	?	?	Impossible
15.	45	45	45	Third division
16.	?	?	?	Impossible
17.	?	?	?	Impossible
18.	55	55	55	Second division
19.	?	?	?	Impossible
20.	65	65	65	First division
21.	80	80	80	First division with distinction
22.	?	?	?	Impossible

The input domain may be partitioned into the following equivalence classes:

$I_1 = \{ A1 : 0 \leq mark1 \leq 100 \}$
$I_2 = \{ A2 : mark1 < 0 \}$
$I_3 = \{ A3 : mark1 > 100 \}$
$I_4 = \{ B1 : 0 \leq mark2 \leq 100 \}$

$I_5 = \{B2 : mark2 < 0\}$

$I_6 = \{B3 : mark2 > 100\}$

$I_7 = \{C1 : 0 \leq mark3 \leq 100\}$

$I_8 = \{C2 : mark3 < 0\}$

$I_9 = \{C3 : mark3 > 100\}$

$I_{10} = \{D1 : 0 \leq avg \leq 39\}$

$I_{11} = \{D2 : 40 \leq avg \leq 49\}$

$I_{12} = \{D3 : 50 \leq avg \leq 59\}$

$I_{13} = \{D4 : 60 \leq avg \leq 74\}$

$I_{14} = \{D5 : avg \geq 75\}$

The extended entry decision table is given in Table 2.37.

Table 2.37. Extended entry decision table

Conditions	1	2	3	4	5	6	7	8	9	10	11
c_1 : mark1 in	A1	A1	A1	A1	A1	A1	A1	A1	A1	A2	A3
c_2 : mark 2 in	B1	B1	B1	B1	B1	B1	B1	B2	B3	-	-
c_3 : mark3 in	C1	C1	C1	C1	C1	C2	C3	-	-	-	-
c_4 : avg in	D1	D2	D3	D4	D5	-	-	-	-	-	-
Rule Count	1	1	1	1	1	5	5	15	15	45	45
a_1: Invalid Marks						X	X	X	X	X	X
a_2: First Division with Distinction						X					
a_3: First Division					X						
a_4: Second Division				X							
a_5: Third Division			X								
a_6: Fail		X									

Here $2^{\text{numbers of do not care conditions}}$ formula cannot be applied because this is an extended entry decision table where multiple conditions are used. We have made equivalence classes for mark1, mark2, mark3 and average value. In column 6, rule count is 5 because "average value" is 'do not care' otherwise the following combinations should have been shown:

A1, B1, C2, D1
A1, B1, C2, D2
A1, B1, C2, D3

A1, B1, C2, D4
A1, B1, C2, D5

These five combinations have been replaced by a 'do not care' condition for average value (D) and the result is shown as A1, B1, C2, —. Hence, rule count for extended decision table is given as:

Rule count = Cartesian product of number of equivalence classes of entries having 'do not care' conditions.

The test cases are given in Table 2.38. There are 11 test cases as compared to 22 test cases given in Table 2.36.

Table 2.38. Test cases of the given problem

Test Case	mark1	mark2	mark3	Expected Output
1.	25	25	25	Fail
2.	45	45	45	Third Division
3.	55	55	55	Second Division
4.	65	65	65	First Division
5.	80	80	80	First Division with Distinction
6.	50	50	-	Invalid marks
7.	50	50	101	Invalid marks
8.	50	-	50	Invalid marks
9.	50	101	50	Invalid marks
10.	-	50	50	Invalid marks
11.	101	50	50	Invalid marks

Example 2.15: Consider the program for classification of a triangle in example 2.3. Design the test cases using decision table based testing.

Solution: We may also choose conditions which include an invalid range of input domain, but this will increase the size of the decision table as shown in Table 2.39. We add an action to show that the inputs are out of range.

The decision table is given in Table 2.39 and has the corresponding test cases that are given in Table 2.40. The number of test cases is equal to the number of columns in the decision table. Hence, 17 test cases can be generated.

In the decision table given in Table 2.39, we assumed that 'a' is the longest side. This time we do not make this assumption and take all the possible conditions into consideration i.e. any of the sides 'a', 'b' or 'c' can be longest. It has 31 rules as compared to the 17 given in Table 2.40. The full decision table is given in Table 2.41. The corresponding 55 test cases are given in Table 2.42.

Table 2.39. Decision table

Conditions	1	2	3	4	5	6	7	8	9	10	11	12	13	14	15	16	17
c_1: a<b+c?	F	T	T	T	T	T	T	T	T	T	T	T	T	T	T	T	T
c_2: b<c+a?	-	F	T	T	T	T	T	T	T	T	T	T	T	T	T	T	T
c_3: c<a+b?	-	-	F	T	T	T	T	T	T	T	T	T	T	T	T	T	T
c_4: a > 0?	-	-	-	F	T	T	T	T	T	T	T	T	T	T	T	T	T
c_5: a <= 100?	-	-	-	-	F	T	T	T	T	T	T	T	T	T	T	T	T
c_6: b > 0?	-	-	-	-	-	F	T	T	T	T	T	T	T	T	T	T	T
c_7: b <= 100?	-	-	-	-	-	-	F	T	T	T	T	T	T	T	T	T	T
c_8: c > 0?	-	-	-	-	-	-	-	F	T	T	T	T	T	T	T	T	T
c_9: c <= 100?	-	-	-	-	-	-	-	-	F	T	T	T	T	T	T	T	T
c_{10}: $a^2 = b^2+c^2$?	-	-	-	-	-	-	-	-	-	T	T	T	T	F	F	F	F
c_{11}: $a^2 > b^2+c^2$?	-	-	-	-	-	-	-	-	-	T	T	F	F	T	T	F	F
c_{12}: $a^2 < b^2+c^2$?	-	-	-	-	-	-	-	-	-	T	F	T	F	T	F	T	F
Rule Count	1048	1024	512	256	128	64	32	16	8	1	1	1	1	1	1	1	1
a_1: Invalid Triangle	X	X	X														
a_2: Input(s) out of range				X	X	X	X	X	X								
a_3: Right angled triangle													X				
a_4: Obtuse angled triangle														X	X		
a_5: Acute angled triangle										X	X	X				X	
a_6: Impossible														X			X

Table 2.40. Test cases

Test Case	a	b	c	Expected Output
1.	90	40	40	Invalid Triangle
2.	40	90	40	Invalid Triangle
3.	40	40	90	Invalid Triangle
4.	0	50	50	Input(s) out of Range
5.	101	50	50	Input(s) out of Range
6.	50	0	50	Input(s) out of Range
7.	50	101	50	Input(s) out of Range
8.	50	50	0	Input(s) out of Range
9.	50	50	101	Input(s) out of Range
10.	?	?	?	Impossible
11.	?	?	?	Impossible
12.	?	?	?	Impossible
13.	50	40	30	Right Angled Triangle
14.	?	?	?	Impossible
15.	57	40	40	Obtuse Angled Triangle
16.	50	49	49	Acute Angled Triangle
17.	?	?	?	Impossible

Table 2.41. Modified decision table

Conditions	1	2	3	4	5	6	7	8	9	10	11
c_1: a < b+c?	F	T	T	T	T	T	T	T	T	T	T
c_2: b < c+a?	-	F	T	T	T	T	T	T	T	T	T
c_3: c < a+b?	-	-	F	T	T	T	T	T	T	T	T
c_4: a > 0?	-	-	-	F	T	T	T	T	T	T	T
c_5: a <= 100?	-	-	-	-	F	T	T	T	T	T	T
c_6: b > 0?	-	-	-	-	-	F	T	T	T	T	T
c_7: b <= 100?	-	-	-	-	-	-	F	T	T	T	T
c_8: c > 0?	-	-	-	-	-	-	-	F	T	T	T
c_9: c <= 100?	-	-	-	-	-	-	-	-	F	T	T
c_{10}: $a^2 = b^2+c^2$?	-	-	-	-	-	-	-	-	-	T	T
c_{11}: $b^2 = c^2+a^2$?	-	-	-	-	-	-	-	-	-	T	F
c_{12}: $c^2 = a^2+b^2$?	-	-	-	-	-	-	-	-	-	-	T
c_{13}: $a^2 > b^2+c^2$?	-	-	-	-	-	-	-	-	-	-	-
c_{14}: $b^2 > c^2+a^2$?	-	-	-	-	-	-	-	-	-	-	-
c_{15}: $c^2 > a^2+b^2$?	-	-	-	-	-	-	-	-	-	-	-
Rule Count	16384	8192	4096	2048	1024	512	256	128	64	16	8
a_1: Invalid triangle	X	X	X								
a_2: Input(s) out of range				X	X	X	X	X	X		
a_3: Right angled triangle											
a_4: Obtuse angled triangle											
a_5: Acute angled triangle											
a_6: Impossible										X	X

(Contd.)

(Contd.)

Conditions	12	13	14	15	16	17	18	19	20	21	22	23	24
c_1: a < b+c?	T	T	T	T	T	T	T	T	T	T	T	T	T
c_2: b < c+a?	T	T	T	T	T	T	T	T	T	T	T	T	T
c_3: c < a+b?	T	T	T	T	T	T	T	T	T	T	T	T	T
c_4: a > 0?	T	T	T	T	T	T	T	T	T	T	T	T	T
c_5: a <= 100?	T	T	T	T	T	T	T	T	T	T	T	T	T
c_6: b > 0?	T	T	T	T	T	T	T	T	T	T	T	T	T
c_7: b <= 100?	T	T	T	T	T	T	T	T	T	T	T	T	T
c_8: c > 0?	T	T	T	T	T	T	T	T	T	T	T	T	T
c_9: c <= 100?	T	T	T	T	T	T	T	T	T	T	T	T	T
c_{10}: $a^2 = b^2+c^2$?	T	T	T	T	F	F	F	F	F	F	F	F	F
c_{11}: $b^2 = c^2+a^2$?	F	F	F	F	T	T	T	T	T	F	F	F	F
c_{12}: $c^2 = a^2+b^2$?	F	F	F	F	T	F	F	F	F	T	T	T	T
c_{13}: $a^2 > b^2+c^2$?	T	F	F	F	-	T	F	F	F	T	F	F	F
c_{14}: $b^2 > c^2+a^2$?	-	T	F	F	-	-	T	F	T	-	T	F	F
c_{15}: $c^2 > a^2+b^2$?	-	-	T	F	-	-	-	T	F	-	-	T	F
Rule Count	4	2	1	1	8	4	2	1	1	4	2	1	1
a_1: Invalid triangle													
a_2: Input(s) out of range													
a_3: Right angled triangle				X				X					X
a_4: Obtuse angled triangle													
a_5: Acute angled triangle													
a_6: Impossible	X	X	X		X	X	X	X		X	X	X	

Conditions	25	26	27	28	29	30	31
c_1: a < b+c?	T	T	T	T	T	T	T
c_2: b < c+a?	T	T	T	T	T	T	T
c_3: c < a+b?	T	T	T	T	T	T	T
c_4: a > 0?	T	T	T	T	T	T	T
c_5: a <= 100?	T	T	T	T	T	T	T
c_6: b > 0?	T	T	T	T	T	T	T
c_7: b <= 100?	T	T	T	T	T	T	T
c_8: c > 0?	T	T	T	T	T	T	T
c_9: c <= 100?	T	T	T	T	T	T	T
c_{10}: $a^2 = b^2+c^2$?	F	F	F	F	F	F	F
c_{11}: $b^2 = c^2+a^2$?	F	F	F	F	F	F	F
c_{12}: $c^2 = a^2+b^2$?	F	F	F	F	F	F	F

(Contd.)

(Contd.)

Conditions	25	26	27	28	29	30	31
$c_{13}: a^2 > b^2+c^2$?	T	T	T	F	F	F	F
$c_{14}: b^2 > c^2+a^2$?	T	F	F	T	T	F	F
$c_{15}: c^2 > a^2+b^2$?	-	T	F	T	F	T	F
Rule Count	2	1	1	1	1	1	1
a_1 : Invalid triangle							
a_2 : Input(s) out of range							
a_3 : Right angled triangle							
a_4 : Obtuse angled triangle			X		X	X	
a_5 : Acute angled triangle							X
a_6 : Impossible	X	X		X			

The table has 31 columns (total = 32768)

Table 2.42. Test cases of the decision table given in table 2.41

Test Case	a	b	c	Expected Output
1.	90	40	40	Invalid Triangle
2.	40	90	40	Invalid Triangle
3.	40	40	90	Invalid Triangle
4.	0	50	50	Input(s) out of Range
5.	101	50	50	Input(s) out of Range
6.	50	0	50	Input(s) out of Range
7.	50	101	50	Input(s) out of Range
8.	50	50	0	Input(s) out of Range
9.	50	50	101	Input(s) out of Range
10.	?	?	?	Impossible
11.	?	?	?	Impossible
12.	?	?	?	Impossible
13.	?	?	?	Impossible
14.	?	?	?	Impossible
15.	50	40	30	Right Angled Triangle
16.	?	?	?	Impossible
17.	?	?	?	Impossible
18.	?	?	?	Impossible
19.	?	?	?	Impossible
20.	40	50	30	Right Angled Triangle

(Contd.)

(Contd.)

Test Case	a	b	c	Expected Output
21.	?	?	?	Impossible
22.	?	?	?	Impossible
23.	?	?	?	Impossible
24.	40	30	50	Right Angled Triangle
25.	?	?	?	Impossible
26.	?	?	?	Impossible
27.	57	40	40	Obtuse Angled Triangle
28.	?	?	?	Impossible
29.	40	57	40	Obtuse Angled Triangle
30.	40	40	57	Obtuse Angled Triangle
31.	50	49	49	Acute Angled Triangle

Example 2.16: Consider a program for the determination of day of the week specified in example 2.4. Identify the test cases using decision table based testing.

Solution: The input domain can be divided into the following classes:

I_1 = { M1 : month has 30 days }

I_2 = { M2 : month has 31 days }

I_3 = { M3 : month is February }

I_4 = { M4 : month <1 }

I_5 = { M5 : month > 12 }

I_6 = { D1 : 1 ≤ Day ≤ 28 }

I_7 = { D2 : Day = 29 }

I_8 = { D3 : Day = 30 }

I_9 = { D4 : Day = 31 }

I_{10} = { D5 : Day < 1 }

I_{11} = { D6 : Day > 31 }

I_{12} = { Y1 : 1900 ≤ Year ≤ 2058 and is a common year }

I_{13} = { Y2 : 1900 ≤ Year ≤ 2058 and is a leap year }

I_{14} : { Y3 : Year < 1900 }

I_{15} : { Y4 : year > 2058 }

The decision table is given in Table 2.43 and the corresponding test cases are given in Table 2.44.

Table 2.43. Decision table

Test Case	1	2	3	4	5	6	7	8	9	10	11	12	13	14	15	16	17	18	19	20
c_1: Months in	M1	M1	M1	M1	M1	M1	M1	M1	M1	M1	M1	M1	M1	M1	M1	M1	M1	M1	M2	M2
c_2: Days in	D1	D1	D1	D1	D2	D2	D2	D2	D3	D3	D3	D3	D4	D4	D4	D4	D5	D6	D1	D1
c_3: Years in	Y1	Y2	Y3	Y4	Y1	Y2	Y3	Y4	Y1	Y2	Y3	Y4	Y1	Y2	Y3	Y4	–	–	Y1	Y2
Rule Count	1	1	1	1	1	1	1	1	1	1	1	1	1	1	1	1	4	4	1	1
a_1: Invalid Date																				
a_2: Day of the week	X	X			X	X			X				X	X					X	X
a_3: Input out of range			X	X			X	X		X	X	X			X	X	X	X		

Test Case	21	22	23	24	25	26	27	28	29	30	31	32	33	34	35	36	37
c_1: Months in	M2	M2	M2	M2	M2	M2	M2	M2	M2	M2	M2	M2	M2	M2	M2	M2	M3
c_2: Days in	D1	D1	D2	D2	D2	D2	D3	D3	D3	D3	D4	D4	D4	D4	D5	D6	D1
c_3: Years in	Y3	Y4	Y1	Y2	Y3	Y4	Y1	Y2	Y3	Y4	Y1	Y2	Y3	Y4	–	–	Y1
Rule Count	1	1	1	1	1	1	1	1	1	1	1	1	1	1	4	4	1
a_1: Invalid Date																	
a_2: Day of the week				X			X	X			X	X					
a_3: Input out of range	X	X			X	X			X	X			X	X	X	X	

Test Case	38	39	40	41	42	43	44	45	46	47	48	49	50	51	52	53	54	55	56
c_1: Months in	M3	M3	M3	M3	M3	M3	M3	M3	M3	M3	M3	M3	M3	M3	M3	M3	M3	M4	M5
c_2: Days in	D1	D1	D1	D2	D2	D2	D2	D3	D3	D3	D3	D4	D4	D4	D4	D5	D6	–	–
c_3: Years in	Y2	Y3	Y4	Y1	Y2	Y3	Y4	Y1	Y2	Y3	Y4	Y1	Y2	Y3	Y4	–	–	–	–
Rule Count	1	1	1	1	1	1	1	1	1	1	1	1	1	1	1	1	1	24	24
a_1: Invalid Date	X				X			X	X			X	X						
a_2: Day of the week																			
a_3: Input out of range		X	X			X	X			X	X			X	X	X	X	X	X

Table 2.44. Test cases of the program day of the week

Test Case	month	day	year	Expected Output
1.	6	15	1979	Friday
2.	6	15	2000	Thursday
3.	6	15	1899	Input out of range
4.	6	15	2059	Input out of range
5.	6	29	1979	Friday
6.	6	29	2000	Thursday
7.	6	29	1899	Input out of range
8.	6	29	2059	Input out of range
9.	6	30	1979	Saturday
10.	6	30	2000	Friday
11.	6	30	1899	Input out of range
12.	6	30	2059	Input out of range
13.	6	31	1979	Invalid date
14.	6	31	2000	Invalid date
15.	6	31	1899	Input out of range
16.	6	31	2059	Input out of range
17.	6	0	1979	Input out of range
18.	6	32	1979	Input out of range
19.	5	15	1979	Tuesday
20.	5	15	2000	Monday
21.	5	15	1899	Input out of range
22.	5	15	2059	Input out of range
23.	5	29	1979	Tuesday
24.	5	29	2000	Monday
25.	5	29	1899	Input out of range
26.	5	29	2059	Input out of range
27.	5	30	1979	Wednesday
28.	5	30	2000	Tuesday
29.	5	30	1899	Input out of range
30.	5	30	2059	Input out of range
31.	5	31	1979	Thursday
32.	5	31	2000	Wednesday
33.	5	31	1899	Input out of range
34.	5	31	2059	Input out of range
35.	5	0	1979	Input out of range
36.	5	32	1979	Input out of range
37.	2	15	1979	Thursday
38.	2	15	2000	Tuesday
39.	2	15	1899	Input out of range
40.	2	15	2059	Input out of range
41.	2	29	1979	Invalid date
42.	2	29	2000	Tuesday
43.	2	29	1899	Input out of range
44.	2	29	2059	Input out of range
45.	2	30	1979	Invalid date

(Contd.)

(Contd.)

Test Case	month	day	year	Expected Output
46.	2	30	2000	Invalid date
47.	2	30	1899	Input out of range
48.	2	30	2059	Input out of range
49.	2	31	1979	Invalid date
50.	2	31	2000	Invalid date
51.	2	31	1899	Input out of range
52.	2	31	2059	Input out of range
53.	2	0	1979	Input out of range
54.	2	32	1979	Input out of range
55.	0	0	1899	Input out of range
56.	13	32	1899	Input out of range

The product of number of partitions of each input variable (or equivalence classes) is 120. The decision table has 56 columns and 56 corresponding test cases are shown in Table 2.44.

2.4 CAUSE-EFFECT GRAPHING TECHNIQUE

This technique is a popular technique for small programs and considers the combinations of various inputs which were not available in earlier discussed techniques like boundary value analysis and equivalence class testing. Such techniques do not allow combinations of inputs and consider all inputs as independent inputs. Two new terms are used here and these are causes and effects, which are nothing but inputs and outputs respectively. The steps for the generation of test cases are given in Figure 2.11.

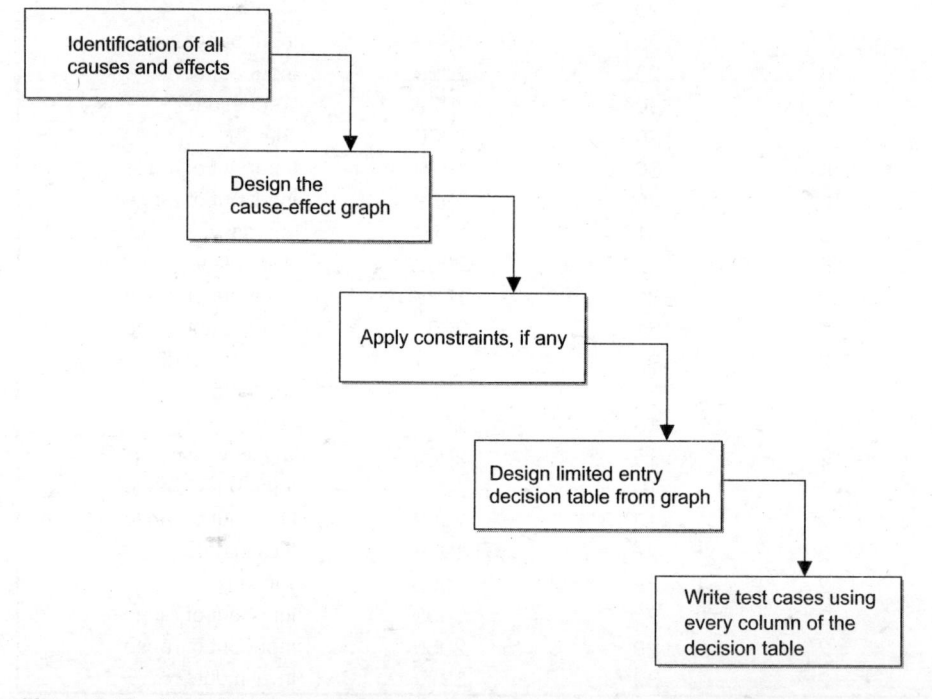

Figure 2.11. Steps for the generation of test cases

2.4.1 Identification of Causes and Effects

The SRS document is used for the identification of causes and effects. Causes which are inputs to the program and effects which are outputs of the program can easily be identified after reading the SRS document. A list is prepared for all causes and effects.

2.4.2 Design of Cause-Effect Graph

The relationship amongst causes and effects are established using cause-effect graph. The basic notations of the graph are shown in Figure 2.12.

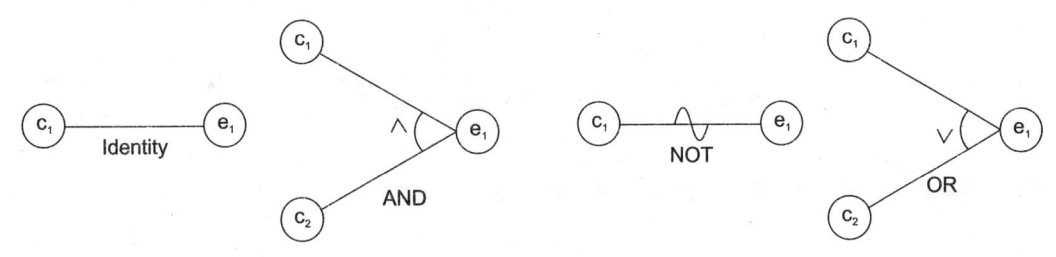

Figure 2.12. Basic notations used in cause-effect graph

In Figure 2.12, each node represents either true (present) or false (absent) state and may be assigned 1 and 0 value respectively. The purpose of four functions is given as:

(a) Identity: This function states that if c_1 is 1, then e_1 is 1; else e_1 is 0.
(b) NOT: This function states that if c_1 is 1, then e_1 is 0; else e_1 is 1.
(c) AND: This function states that if both c_1 and c_2 are 1, then e_1 is 1; else e_1 is 0.
(d) OR: This function states that if either c_1 or c_2 is 1, then e_1 is 1; else e_1 is 0.

The AND and OR functions are allowed to have any number of inputs.

2.4.3 Use of Constraints in Cause-Effect Graph

There may be a number of causes (inputs) in any program. We may like to explore the relationships amongst the causes and this process may lead to some impossible combinations of causes. Such impossible combinations or situations are represented by constraint symbols which are given in Figure 2.13.

The purpose of all five constraint symbols is given as:

(a) **Exclusive**
   The Exclusive (E) constraint states that at most one of c_1 or c_2 can be 1 (c_1 or c_2 cannot be 1 simultaneously). However, both c_1 and c_2 can be 0 simultaneously.
(b) **Inclusive**
   The Inclusive (I) constraints states that at least one of c_1 or c_2 must always be 1. Hence, both cannot be 0 simultaneously. However, both can be 1.
(c) **One and Only One**
   The one and only one (O) constraint states that one and only one of c_1 and c_2 must be 1.

98 Software Testing

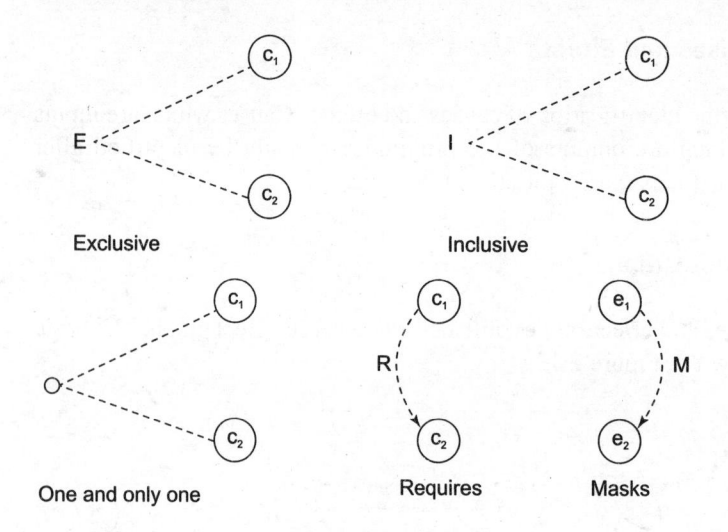

Figure 2.13. Constraint symbols for any cause-effect graph

    (d) Requires

        The requires (R) constraint states that for c_1 to be 1, c_2 must be 1; it is impossible for c_1 to be 1 if c_2 is 0.

    (e) Mask

        This constraint is applicable at the effect side of the cause-effect graph. This states that if effect e_1 is 1, effect e_2 is forced to be 0.

These five constraint symbols can be applied to a cause-effect graph depending upon the relationships amongst causes (a, b, c and d) and effects (e). They help us to represent real life situations in the cause-effect graph.

Consider the example of keeping the record of marital status and number of children of a citizen. The value of marital status must be 'U' or 'M'. The value of the number of children must be digit or null in case a citizen is unmarried. If the information entered by the user is correct then an update is made. If the value of marital status of the citizen is incorrect, then the error message 1 is issued. Similarly, if the value of number of children is incorrect, then the error message 2 is issued.

The causes are:

    c_1: marital status is 'U'
    c_2: marital status is 'M'
    c_3: number of children is a digit

and the effects are:

    e_1: updation made
    e_2: error message 1 is issued
    e_3: error message 2 is issued

The cause-effect graph is shown in Figure 2.14. There are two constraints exclusive (between c_1 and c_2) and requires (between c_3 and c_2), which are placed at appropriate places in the graph. Causes c_1 and c_2 cannot occur simultaneously and for cause c_3 to be true, cause c_2 has to be true. However, there is no mask constraint in this graph.

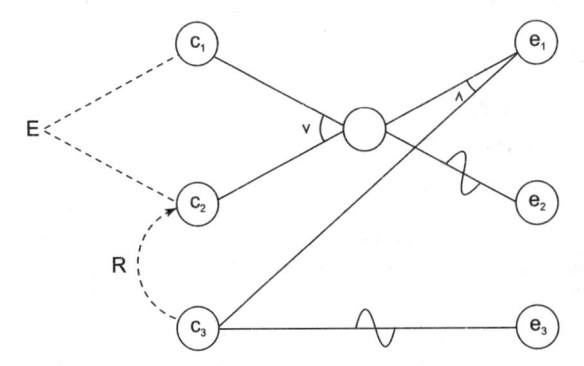

Figure 2.14. Example of cause-effect graph with exclusive (constraint) and requires constraint

2.4.4 Design of Limited Entry Decision Table

The cause-effect graph represents the relationships amongst the causes and effects. This graph may also help us to understand the various conditions/combinations amongst the causes and effects. These conditions/combinations are converted into the limited entry decision table. Each column of the table represents a test case.

2.4.5 Writing of Test Cases

Each column of the decision table represents a rule and gives us a test case. We may reduce the number of columns with the proper selection of various conditions and expected actions.

2.4.6 Applicability

Cause-effect graphing is a systematic method for generating test cases. It considers dependency of inputs using some constraints.

This technique is effective only for small programs because, as the size of the program increases, the number of causes and effects also increases and thus complexity of the cause-effect graph increases. For large-sized programs, a tool may help us to design the cause-effect graph with the minimum possible complexity.

It has very limited applications in unit testing and hardly any application in integration testing and system testing.

Example 2.17: A tourist of age greater than 21 years and having a clean driving record is supplied a rental car. A premium amount is also charged if the tourist is on business, otherwise it is not charged.

If the tourist is less than 21 year old, or does not have a clean driving record, the system will display the following message:
"Car cannot be supplied"
Draw the cause-effect graph and generate test cases.

Solution: The causes are

c_1: Age is over 21
c_2: Driving record is clean
c_3: Tourist is on business

and effects are

e_1: Supply a rental car without premium charge.
e_2: Supply a rental car with premium charge
e_3: Car cannot be supplied

The cause-effect graph is shown in Figure 2.15 and decision table is shown in Table 2.45. The test cases for the problem are given in Table 2.46.

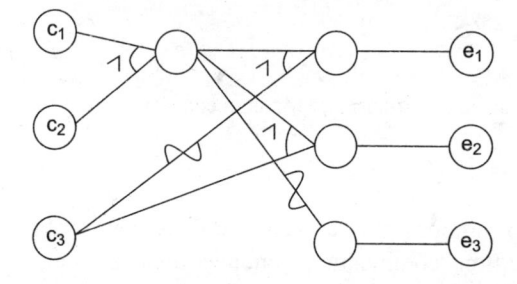

Figure 2.15. Cause-effect graph of rental car problem

Table 2.45. Decision table of rental car problem

Conditions	1	2	3	4
c_1: Over 21 ?	F	T	T	T
c_2: Driving record clean ?	-	F	T	T
c_3: On Business ?	-	-	F	T
e_1: Supply a rental car without premium charge			X	
e_2: Supply a rental car with premium charge				X
e_3: Car cannot be supplied	X	X		

Table 2.46. Test cases of the given decision table

Test Case	Age	Driving_record_clean	On_business	Expected Output
1.	20	Yes	Yes	Car cannot be supplied
2.	26	No	Yes	Car cannot be supplied
3.	62	Yes	No	Supply a rental car without premium charge
4.	62	Yes	Yes	Supply a rental car with premium charge.

Example 2.18: Consider the triangle classification problem ('a' is the largest side) specified in example 2.3. Draw the cause-effect graph and design decision table from it.

Solution:

The causes are:

- c_1 : side 'a' is less than the sum of sides 'b' and 'c'.
- c_2 : side 'b' is less than the sum of sides 'a' and 'c'.
- c_3 : side 'c' is less than the sum of sides 'a' and 'b'.
- c_4 : square of side 'a' is equal to the sum of squares of sides 'b' and 'c'.
- c_5 : square of side 'a' is greater than the sum of squares of sides 'b' and 'c'.
- c_6 : square of side 'a' is less than the sum of squares of sides 'b' and 'c'.

and effects are

- e_1 : Invalid Triangle
- e_2 : Right angle triangle
- e_3 : Obtuse angled triangle
- e_4 : Acute angled triangle
- e_5 : Impossible stage

The cause-effect graph is shown in Figure 2.16 and the decision table is shown in Table 2.47.

Table 2.47. Decision table

Conditions											
$c_1 : a<b+c$	0	1	1	1	1	1	1	1	1	1	1
$c_2 : b<a+c$	X	0	1	1	1	1	1	1	1	1	1
$c_3 : c<a+b$	X	X	0	1	1	1	1	1	1	1	1
$c_4 : a^2=b^2+c^2$	X	X	X	1	1	1	1	0	0	0	0
$c_5 : a^2>b^2+c^2$	X	X	X	1	1	0	0	1	1	0	0
$c_6 : a^2<b^2+c^2$	X	X	X	1	0	1	0	1	0	1	0
e_1 : Invalid Triangle	1	1	1								
e_2 : Right angled Triangle							1				
e_3 : Obtuse angled triangle									1		
e_4 : Acute angled triangle										1	
e_5 : Impossible					1	1	1		1		1

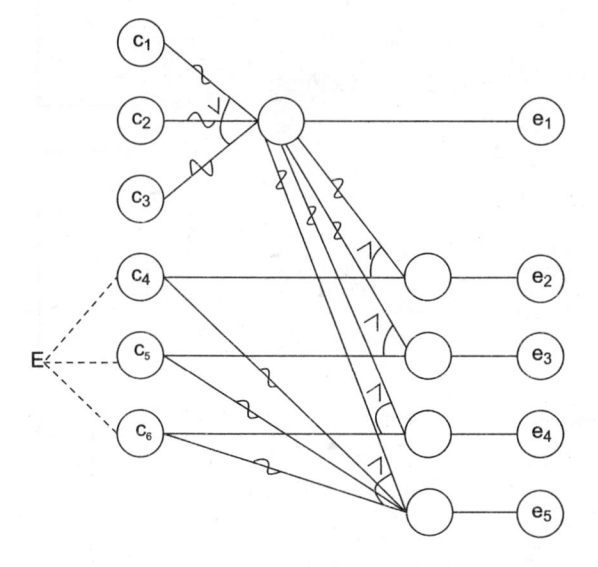

Figure 2.16. Cause-effect graph of triangle classification problem

MULTIPLE CHOICE QUESTIONS

Note: *Select the most appropriate answer for the following questions.*

2.1 What is functional testing?
 (f) Test cases are designed on the basis of internal structure of the source code.
 (g) Test cases are designed on the basis of functionality, and internal structure of the source code is completely ignored.
 (h) Test cases are designed on the basis of functionality and internal structure of the source code.
 (i) Test cases are designed on the basis of pre-conditions and post-conditions.

2.2 Which of the following statement is correct?
 (a) Functional testing is useful in every phase of the software development life cycle.
 (b) Functional testing is more useful than static testing because execution of a program gives more confidence.
 (c) Reviews are one form of functional testing.
 (d) Structural testing is more useful than functional testing.

2.3 Which of the following is not a form of functional testing?
 (a) Boundary value analysis
 (b) Equivalence class testing
 (c) Data flow testing
 (d) Decision table based testing

2.4 Functional testing is known as:
 (a) Regression Testing
 (b) Load Testing
 (c) Behaviour Testing
 (d) Structural Testing

2.5 For a function of 'n' variables, boundary value analysis generates:
 (a) $8n + 1$ test cases
 (b) $6n + 1$ test cases
 (c) $2n + 1$ test cases
 (d) $4n + 1$ test cases

2.6 For a function of 4 variables, boundary value analysis generates:
 (a) 9 test cases
 (b) 17 test cases
 (c) 33 test cases
 (d) 25 test cases

2.7 For a function of 'n' variables, robustness testing yields:
 (a) $6n + 1$ test cases
 (b) $8n + 1$ test cases
 (c) $2n + 1$ test cases
 (d) $4n + 1$ test cases

2.8 For a function of 'n' variables, worst case testing generates:
 (a) 6^n test cases
 (b) $4^n + 1$ test cases

(c) 5^n test cases
   (d) $6^n + 1$ test cases
2.9 For a function of 'n' variables, robust worst case testing generates:
   (a) 4^n test cases
   (b) 6^n test cases
   (c) 5^n test cases
   (d) 7^n test cases
2.10 A software is designed to calculate taxes to be paid as per details given below:
   (i)   Up to Rs. 40,000   :   Tax free
   (ii) Next Rs. 15,000   :   10% tax
   (iii) Next Rs. 65,000   :   15% tax
   (iv) Above this amount   :   20% tax
   Input to the software is the salary of an employee. Which of the following is a valid boundary analysis test case?
   (a) Rs. 40,000
   (b) Rs. 65,000
   (c) Rs. 1, 20,000
   (d) Rs. 80,000
2.11 'x' is an input to a program to calculate the square of the given number. The range for 'x' is from 1 to 100. In boundary value analysis, which are valid inputs?
   (a) 1,2,50,100,101
   (b) 1,2,99,100,101
   (c) 1,2,50,99,100
   (d) 0,1,2,99,100
2.12 'x' is an input to a program to calculate the square of the given number. The range for 'x' is from 1 to 100. In robustness testing, which are valid inputs?
   (a) 0, 1, 2, 50, 99, 100, 101
   (b) 0, 1, 2, 3, 99, 100, 101
   (c) 1, 2, 3, 50, 98, 99, 100
   (d) 1, 2, 50, 99, 100
2.13 Functionality of a software is tested by:
   (a) White box testing
   (b) Black box testing
   (c) Regression testing
   (d) None of the above
2.14 One weakness of boundary value analysis is:
   (a) It is not effective
   (b) It does not explore combinations of inputs
   (c) It explores combinations of inputs
   (d) None of the above
2.15 Boundary value analysis technique is effective when inputs are:
   (a) Dependent
   (b) Independent
   (c) Boolean
   (d) None of the above

2.16 Equivalence class testing is related to:
  (a) Mutation testing
  (b) Data flow testing
  (c) Functional testing
  (d) Structural testing
2.17 In a room air-conditioner, when the temperature reaches 28°C, the cooling is switched on. When the temperature falls to below 20°C, the cooling is switched off. What is the minimum set of test input values (in degree centigrade) to cover all equivalence classes?
  (a) 20, 22, 26
  (b) 19, 22, 24
  (c) 19, 24, 26
  (d) 19, 24, 29
2.18 If an input range is from 1 to 100, identify values from invalid equivalence classes.
  (a) 0, 101
  (b) 10, 101
  (c) 0, 10
  (d) None of the above
2.19 In an examination, the minimum passing marks is 50 out of 100 for each subject. Identify valid equivalence class values, if a student clears the examination of all three subjects.
  (a) 40, 60, 70
  (b) 38, 65, 75
  (c) 60, 65, 100
  (d) 49, 50, 65
2.20 How many minimum test cases should be selected from an equivalence class?
  (a) 2
  (b) 3
  (c) 1
  (d) 4
2.21 Decision tables are used in situations where:
  (a) An action is initiated on the basis of a varying set of conditions
  (b) No action is required under a varying set of conditions
  (c) A number of actions are taken under a varying set of conditions
  (d) None of the above
2.22 How many portions are available in a decision table?
  (a) 8
  (b) 2
  (c) 4
  (d) 1
2.23 How many minimum test cases are generated by a column of a decision table?
  (a) 0
  (b) 1
  (c) 2
  (d) 3

2.24 The decision table which uses only binary conditions is known as:
  (a) Limited entry decision table
  (b) Extended entry decision table
  (c) Advance decision table
  (d) None of the above
2.25 In cause-effect graphing technique, causes and effects are related to:
  (a) Outputs and inputs
  (b) Inputs and outputs
  (c) Sources and destinations
  (d) Destinations and sources
2.26 Cause-effect graphing is one form of:
  (a) Structural testing
  (b) Maintenance testing
  (c) Regression testing
  (d) Functional testing
2.27 Which is not a constraint applicable at the 'causes' side in the cause-effect graphing technique?
  (a) Exclusive
  (b) Inclusive
  (c) Masks
  (d) Requires
2.28 Which is not a basic notation used in a cause-effect graph?
  (a) NOT
  (b) OR
  (c) AND
  (d) NAND
2.29 Which is the term used for functional testing?
  (a) Black box testing
  (b) Behavioural testing
  (c) Functionality testing
  (d) All of the above
2.30 Functional testing does not involve:
  (a) Source code analysis
  (b) Black box testing techniques
  (c) Boundary value analysis
  (d) Robustness testing

EXERCISES

2.1 What is functional testing? How do we perform it in limited time and with limited resources?
2.2 What are the various types of functional testing techniques? Discuss any one with the help of an example.
2.3 Explain the boundary value analysis technique with a suitable example.

2.4 Why do we undertake robustness testing? What are the additional benefits? Show additional test cases with the help of an example and justify the significance of these test cases.

2.5 What is worst-case testing? How is it different from boundary value analysis? List the advantages of using this technique.

2.6 Explain the usefulness of robust worst-case testing. Should we really opt for this technique and select a large number of test cases? Discuss its applicability and limitations.

2.7 Consider a program that determines the previous date. Its inputs are a triple of day, month and year with its values in the range:
$1 \leq$ month ≤ 12
$1 \leq$ day ≤ 31
$1850 \leq$ year ≤ 2050
The possible outputs are 'previous date' or 'invalid input'. Design boundary value analysis test cases, robust test cases, worst-case test cases and robust worst-case test cases.

2.8 Consider the program to find the median of three numbers. Its input is a triple of positive integers (say x, y and z) and values are from interval [100,500]. Generate boundary, robust and worst-case test cases.

2.9 Consider a program that takes three numbers as input and print the values of these numbers in descending order. Its input is a triple of positive integers (say x, y and z) and values are from interval [300,700]. Generate boundary value, robust and worst case test cases.

2.10 Consider a three-input program to handle personal loans of a customer. Its input is a triple of positive integers (say principal, rate and term).
$1000 \leq$ principal ≤ 40000
$1 \leq$ rate ≤ 18
$1 \leq$ term ≤ 6
The program should calculate the interest for the whole term of the loan and the total amount of the personal loan. The output is:
interest = principal * (rate/100) * term
total_amount = principal + interest
Generate boundary value, robust and worst-case test cases

2.11 The BSE Electrical company charges its domestic consumers using the following slab:

Consumption units	Energy charges
0–150	2.00 per unit
151–300	Rs 200 + Rs. 3.00 per unit in excess of 150 units
301–400	Rs. 300 + Rs 3.90 per unit in excess of 300 units
>400	Rs. 350 + Rs 4.40 per unit in excess of 400 units

Identify the equivalence class test cases for output and input domain.

2.12 An telephone company charges its customer using the following calling rates:

Call	Rates
0-75	Rs. 500
76-200	Rs. 500 + Rs. 0.80 per call in excess of 75 calls
201-500	Rs. 500 + Rs. 1.00 per call in excess of 200 calls
>500	Rs. 500 + Rs 1.20 per unit in excess of 500 calls

Identify the equivalence class test cases for the output and input domain.

2.13 Consider an example of grading a student in a university. The grading is done as given below:

Average marks	Grade
90 – 100	Exemplary Performance
75 – 89	Distinction
60 – 74	First Division
50 – 59	Second Division
0 – 49	Fail

The marks of any three subjects are considered for the calculation of average marks. Generate boundary value analysis test cases and robust test cases. Also create equivalence classes and generate test cases.

2.14 Consider a program for the classification of a triangle. Its input is a triple of positive integers (say, a, b and c) from the interval [1, 100]. The output may be one of the following words [scalene, Isosceles, Equilateral, Not a triangle]. Design the boundary value test cases and robust worst-case test cases. Create equivalence classes and design test cases accordingly.

2.15 Consider a program that determines the next date. Given a month, day and year as input, it determines the date of the next day. The month, day and year have integer values subject to the following conditions:

C_1: $1 \leq month \leq 12$
C_2: $1 \leq day \leq 31$
C_3: $1800 \leq year \leq 2025$

We are allowed to add new conditions as per our requirements.
  (a) Generate boundary value analysis test cases, robust test cases, worst-case test cases and robust worst-case test cases
  (b) Create equivalence classes and generate test cases
  (c) Develop a decision table and generate test cases

2.16 Consider a program for the determination of the nature of roots of a quadratic equation. Its input is a triple of positive integers (say a, b and c) and values may be from interval [0, 100]. The output may have one of the following words:
[Not a quadratic equation, Real roots, Imaginary roots, Equal roots]
  (a) Design boundary value analysis test cases, robust test cases, worst-case test cases and robust worst-case test cases
  (b) Create equivalence classes and generate test cases
  (c) Develop a decision table and generate test cases

2.17 Explain the equivalence class testing technique. How is it different from boundary value analysis technique?

2.18 Discuss the significance of decision tables in testing. What is the purpose of a rule count? Explain the concept with the help of an example.
2.19 What is the cause-effect graphing technique? What are basic notations used in a cause-effect graph? Why and how are constraints used in such a graph?
2.20 Consider a program to multiply and divide two numbers. The inputs may be two valid integers (say a and b) in the range of [0, 100].
    (a) Generate boundary value analysis test cases and robust test cases
    (b) Create equivalence class and generate test cases
    (c) Develop a decision table and generate test cases
    (d) Design a cause-effect graph and write test cases accordingly
2.21 Consider the following points based on faculty appraisal and development system of a university:

Points Earned	University view
1 – 6	Work hard to improve
6 – 8	Satisfactory
8 – 10	Good
10 – 12	Very Good
12 – 15	Outstanding

Generate the test cases using equivalence class testing.
2.22 Consider a program to perform binary search and generate the test cases using equivalence class testing and decision table based testing.
2.23 Write a program to count the number of digits in a number. Its input is any number from interval [0, 9999]. Design the boundary value analysis test cases and robustness test cases.
2.24 Why is functional testing also known as black box testing? Discuss with the help of examples.
2.25 What are the limitations of boundary value analysis technique? Discuss the situations in which it is not effective.

FURTHER READING

A resource for pre-1981 literature which contains a huge bibliography up to 1981:
> E.F. Miller and W.E. Howden, "Tutorial: Software Testing and Validation Techniques", IEEE Computer Society, New York, 1981.

A hands-on guide to the black-box testing techniques:
> B. Beizer, "Black-Box Testing: Techniques for Functional Testing of Software and Systems", John Wiley and Sons, 1995.

An introductory book on software testing with a special focus on functional testing is:
> P. C. Jorgensen, "Software Testing: A Craftsman Approach", 3rd ed., Auerbach Publications, New York, 2007.

Other useful texts are:
> W.R. Elmendorf, "Cause Effect Graphs in Functional Testing", TR-00.2487, IBM System Development Division, Poughkeepsie, New York, 1973.

W.R. Elmendorf, "Functional analysis using cause-effect graphs", Proceedings of SHARE XLIII, SHARE, New York, pp. 567–577, 1974.

W.E. Howden, "Functional Program Testing", IEEE Transactions on Software Engineering, vol. 6, no. 2, March 1980.

W.E. Howden, "Validation of Scientific Programs", ACM Computing Surveys (CSUR), vol.14, no.2, pp.193–227, June 1982.

R.B. Hurley, "Decision Tables in Software Engineering", Van Nostrand Reinhod, New York, 1983.

V. Chvalovsky, "Decision tables", Software Practice and. Experience, vol. 13, pp. 423–429, 1983.

B. Korel and J. Laski, "A Tool for Data Flow Oriented Program Testing", Second Conference on Software Development Tools, Techniques, and Alternatives, San Francisco, CA, December 25, 1985.

V.R. Basili and R.W. Selby, "Comparing the Effectiveness of Software Testing Strategies", vol. 13, pp. 1278–1296, 1987.

3

Essentials of Graph Theory

Graph theory has been used extensively in computer science, electrical engineering, communication systems, operational research, economics, physics and many other areas. Any physical situation involving discrete objects may be represented by a graph along with their relationships amongst them. In practice, there are numerous applications of graphs in modern science and technology. Graph theory has recently been used for representing the connectivity of the World Wide Web. Global internet connectivity issues are studied using graphs like the number of links required to move from one web page to another and the links which are used to establish this connectivity. It has also provided many ways to test a program. Some testing techniques are available which are based on the concepts of graph theory.

3.1 WHAT IS A GRAPH?

A graph has a set of nodes and a set of edges that connect these nodes. A graph $G = (V, E)$ consists of a non-empty finite set V of nodes and a set E of edges containing ordered or unordered pairs of nodes.

$$V = (n_1, n_2, n_3........n_m) \text{ and } E = (e_1, e_2, e_3.........e_k)$$

If an edge $e_i \in E$ is associated with an ordered pair $<n_i, n_j>$ or an unordered pair (n_i, n_j), where $n_i, n_j \in V$, then the e_i is said to connect the nodes n_i and n_j. The edge e_i that connects the node n_i and n_j is called incident on each of the nodes. The pair of nodes that are connected by an edge are called adjacent nodes. A node, which is not connected to any other node, is called an isolated node. A graph with only isolated nodes is known as null graph.

If in graph $G = (V, E)$, each edge $e_i \in E$ is associated with an ordered pair of nodes, then graph G is called a directed graph or digraph. If each edge is associated with an unordered pair of nodes, then a graph G is called an undirected graph.

In diagrammatical representation of a graph, nodes are represented by circles and edges are represented by lines joining the two nodes incident on it and the same is shown in Figure 3.1.

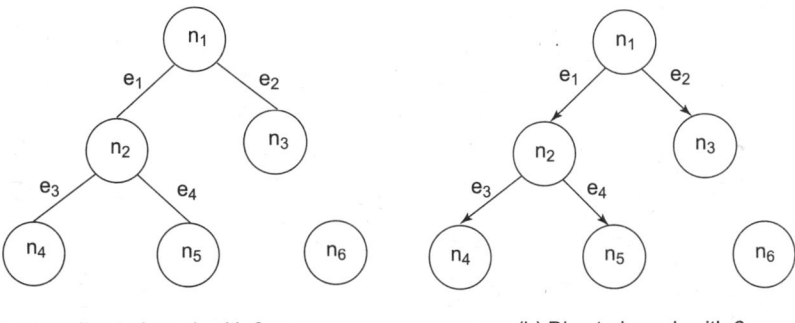

(a) Undirected graph with 6 nodes and 4 edges

(b) Directed graph with 6 nodes and 4 edges

Figure 3.1. Undirected and directed graphs

In the Figure 3.1(a), the node and edge sets are given as:

$$V = (n_1, n_2, n_3, n_4, n_5, n_6)$$
$$E = (e_1, e_2, e_3, e_4) = ((n_1, n_2), (n_1, n_3), (n_2, n_4), (n_2, n_5))$$

Similarly in Figure 3.1(b), the node and edge sets are

$$V = (n_1, n_2, n_3, n_4, n_5, n_6)$$
$$E = (e_1, e_2, e_3, e_4) = (<n_1, n_2>, <n_1, n_3>, <n_2, n_4>, <n_2, n_5>)$$

The only difference is that edges are the ordered pairs of nodes represented by $<n_1, n_2>$ rather than unordered pairs (n_1, n_2). For any graph (directed or undirected), a set of nodes and a set of edges between pairs of nodes are required for the construction of the graph.

An edge of a graph having the same node at its end points is called a loop. The direction of the edge is not important because the initial and final nodes are one and the same. In Figure 3.2(a), edge e_1 is a loop with node n_1 and may be represented as $e_1 = (n_1, n_1)$.

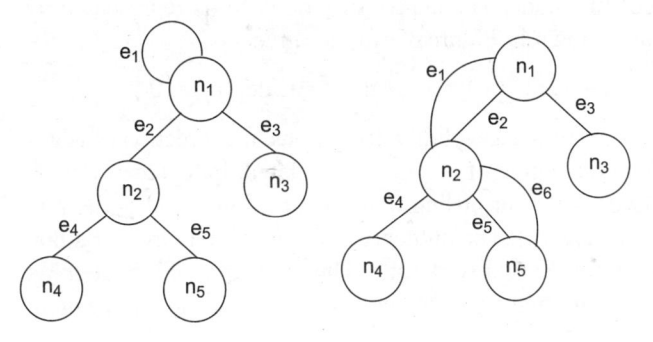

(a) Graph with loop e_1

(b) Graph with parallel edges e_1, e_2 and e_5, e_6

Figure 3.2. Undirected graphs with loop and parallel edges

If certain pairs of nodes are connected by more than one edge in a directed or undirected graph, then these edges are known as parallel edges. In Figure 3.2(b), e_1 and e_2 are parallel edges connecting nodes n_1 and n_2. Similarly e_5 and e_6 are also parallel edges connecting nodes n_2 and n_5. If a graph is a directed graph and parallel edges are in opposite directions, such edges are considered as distinct edges. A graph that has neither loops nor parallel edges is called a simple graph. A graph with one or more parallel edges is called a multigraph. These graphs are shown in Figure 3.3.

(a) Simple graph

(b) Undirected multigraph

(c) Directed multigraph with distinct edges

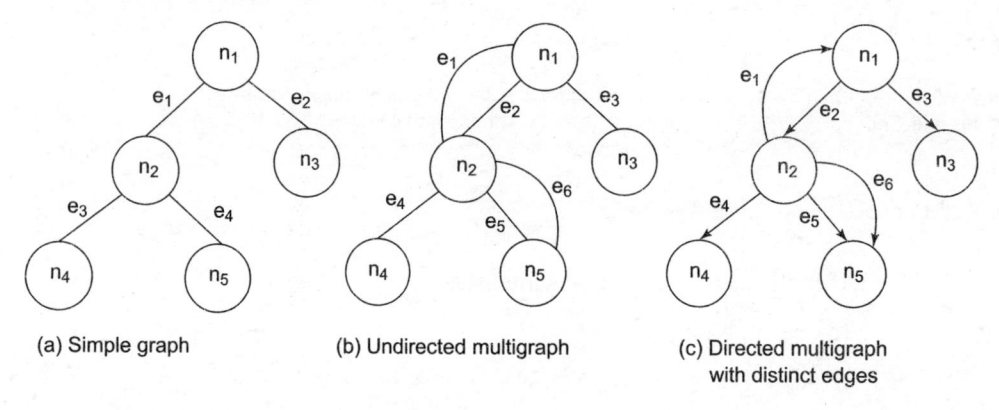

Figure 3.3. Types of graphs

A directed multigraph (see Figure 3.3 (c)) may have *distinct parallel* edges (like e_1 and e_2) and *parallel edges* (like e_5 and e_6). If numbers or weights are assigned to each edge of a graph, then such a graph is called a weighted graph.

3.1.1 Degree of a Node

The degree of a node in an undirected graph is the number of edges incident on it. However, a loop contributes twice to the degree of that node. The degree of a node 'n' is represented by deg(n). The degrees of nodes in a graph shown in Figure 3.1 (a) are given as:

$\deg(n_1) = 2$, $\deg(n_2) = 3$, $\deg(n_3) = 1$, $\deg(n_4) = 1$, $\deg(n_5) = 1$, $\deg(n_6) = 0$

The degree of an isolated node is always 0. In case of directed graphs, the direction of edges play an important role and indegree and outdegree of a node is calculated. Indegree of a node in a directed graph is the number of edges that are using that node as a terminal node. The indegree of a node 'n' is represented by indeg(n). The outdegree of a node in a directed graph is the number of edges that are using that node as a start node. The outdegree of a node 'n' is represented by outdeg(n). The indegrees and outdegrees of nodes in a graph shown in Figure 3.1(b) are given as:

$\text{indeg}(n_1) = 0$ $\text{outdeg}(n_1) = 2$

$\text{indeg}(n_2) = 1$ $\text{outdeg}(n_2) = 2$

$\text{indeg}(n_3) = 1$ $\text{outdeg}(n_3) = 0$

indeg(n_4) = 1   outdeg(n_4) = 0

indeg(n_5) = 1   outdeg(n_5) = 0

indeg(n_6) = 0   outdeg(n_6) = 0

The degree of a node in a directed graph is the sum of indegree and outdegree of that node. Hence, for node 'n' in a directed graph, the degree is given as:

deg(n) = indeg(n) + outdeg(n)

Few important characteristics of nodes are identified on the basis of indegree and outdegree and are given as:

(i) Source node: A node with indegree = 0 and outdegree ≥ 1
(ii) Destination node: A node with outdegree = 0 and in degree ≥ 1
(iii) Sequential node: A node with indegree = 1 and outdegree = 1
(iv) Predicate/decision node: A node with outdegree ≥ 2
(v) Junction node: indegree ≥ 2

In Figure 3.1(b), source nodes: n_1

Destination nodes: n_3, n_4, n_5

Sequential nodes: nil

Predicate nodes: n_1, n_2

There is no junction node in this graph and n_6 is an isolated node.

3.1.2 Regular Graph

If every node of a simple graph has the same degree, then the graph is called a regular graph. If the degree of a node is 'n', then it is called n-regular graph. Some of such graphs are shown in Figure 3.4.

2-regular graphs

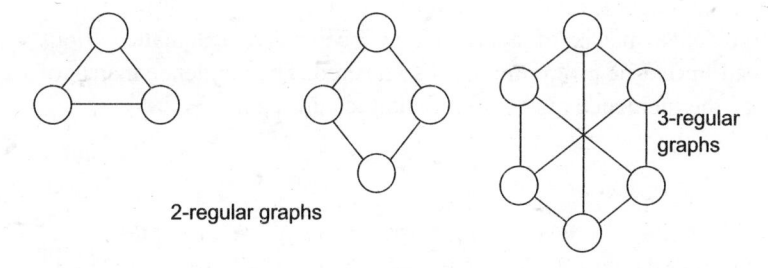

3-regular graphs

Figure 3.4. Regular graphs

3.2 MATRIX REPRESENTATION OF GRAPHS

In computer science, matrix representation of graphs is very popular due to its direct applications in programming. Each piece of information of a graph, which is shown diagrammatically, can be converted into matrix form. Some useful matrix representations are given in the following subsections which are used commonly in testing.

3.2.1 Incidence Matrix

Consider a graph G = (V, E) where

$$V = (n_1, n_2, n_3, \ldots n_m)$$
$$E = (e_1, e_2, e_3, \ldots e_k)$$

In this graph, there are 'm' nodes and 'k' edges. An incidence matrix is a matrix with 'm' rows and 'k' columns whose elements are defined such that:

$$a(i, j) = \begin{cases} 1 \text{ if } j^{th} \text{ edge } e_j \text{ is incident on } i^{th} \text{ node } n_i \\ 0 \text{ otherwise} \end{cases}$$

The incidence matrix of a graph shown in Figure 3.1(a) is given as:

$$\begin{array}{c} \\ n_1 \\ n_2 \\ n_3 \\ n_4 \\ n_5 \\ n_6 \end{array} \begin{array}{cccc} e_1 & e_2 & e_3 & e_4 \\ \begin{bmatrix} 1 & 1 & 0 & 0 \\ 1 & 0 & 1 & 1 \\ 0 & 1 & 0 & 0 \\ 0 & 0 & 1 & 0 \\ 0 & 0 & 0 & 1 \\ 0 & 0 & 0 & 0 \end{bmatrix} \end{array}$$

The sum of entries of any column of incidence matrix is always 2. This is because a column represents an edge which has only two endpoints. If, any time, the sum is not two, then there is some mistake in the transfer of information. If we add entries of a row, which is corresponding to a node, we get the degree of that node. If all entries of a row are 0's, then the corresponding node is an isolated node. Incidence matrix of a graph may be used to calculate various properties of a graph which can further be programmed, if so desired. The incidence matrix of a directed graph is the same as the incidence matrix of an undirected graph.

3.2.2 Adjacency Matrix

It is also known as connection matrix because it represents connections in a graph. The adjacency matrix of a graph G = (V, E) with 'm' nodes is a square matrix of size m×m whose elements are defined such that:

$$a(i, j) = \begin{cases} 1 \text{ if there is an edge from nodes } n_i \text{ and } n_j \\ 0 \text{ otherwise} \end{cases}$$

The adjacency matrix of a graph shown in Figure 3.1(a) is given as:

$$\begin{array}{c} \quad\; n_1\; n_2\; n_3\; n_4\; n_5\; n_6 \\ \begin{array}{c} n_1 \\ n_2 \\ n_3 \\ n_4 \\ n_5 \\ n_6 \end{array} \begin{bmatrix} 0 & 1 & 1 & 0 & 0 & 0 \\ 1 & 0 & 0 & 1 & 1 & 0 \\ 1 & 0 & 0 & 0 & 0 & 0 \\ 0 & 1 & 0 & 0 & 0 & 0 \\ 0 & 1 & 0 & 0 & 0 & 0 \\ 0 & 0 & 0 & 0 & 0 & 0 \end{bmatrix} \end{array}$$

If we add entries of any row, we get the degree of the node corresponding to that row. This is similar to incidence matrix. The adjacency matrix of an undirected graph is symmetric where $a(i, j) = a(j, i)$.

If we represent connections with the name of edges, then the matrix is called graph matrix. The size is the same as adjacent matrix i.e. number of nodes in a graph. The graph matrix of a graph shown in Figure 3.1(a) is given as:

$$\begin{array}{c} \quad\; n_1\; n_2\; n_3\; n_4\; n_5\; n_6 \\ \begin{array}{c} n_1 \\ n_2 \\ n_3 \\ n_4 \\ n_5 \\ n_6 \end{array} \begin{bmatrix} 0 & e_1 & e_2 & 0 & 0 & 0 \\ e_1 & 0 & 0 & e_3 & e_4 & 0 \\ e_2 & 0 & 0 & 0 & 0 & 0 \\ 0 & e_3 & 0 & 0 & 0 & 0 \\ 0 & e_4 & 0 & 0 & 0 & 0 \\ 0 & 0 & 0 & 0 & 0 & 0 \end{bmatrix} \end{array}$$

If connections are represented by 1, then it becomes the connection matrix.

The adjacency matrix of a directed graph $G = (V, E)$ with 'm' nodes is a square matrix of size m×m whose elements are such that:

$$a(i, j) = \begin{cases} 1 & \text{if there is an edge from nodes } n_i \text{ and } n_j \\ 0 & \text{otherwise} \end{cases}$$

The adjacency matrix of a directed graph may not be symmetric. If we add entries of a row, it becomes outdegree of the node and if we add entries of a column, it becomes indegree of the node. The adjacency matrix of a directed graph given in Figure 3.1(b) is given as:

$$\begin{array}{c} \quad\; n_1\; n_2\; n_3\; n_4\; n_5\; n_6 \\ \begin{array}{c} n_1 \\ n_2 \\ n_3 \\ n_4 \\ n_5 \\ n_6 \end{array} \begin{bmatrix} 0 & 1 & 1 & 0 & 0 & 0 \\ 0 & 0 & 0 & 1 & 1 & 0 \\ 0 & 0 & 0 & 0 & 0 & 0 \\ 0 & 0 & 0 & 0 & 0 & 0 \\ 0 & 0 & 0 & 0 & 0 & 0 \\ 0 & 0 & 0 & 0 & 0 & 0 \end{bmatrix} \end{array}$$

116 Software Testing

In directed graph, direction of an edge is considered, hence adjacency matrix of a directed graph is different from the undirected graph.

3.3 PATHS AND INDEPENDENT PATHS

A path in a graph is a sequence of adjacent nodes where nodes in sequence share a common edge or sequence of adjacent pair of edges where edges in sequence share a common node. The paths in a graph shown in Figure 3.1(a) are given in Table 3.1.

Table 3.1. Paths of undirected graph in Figure 3.1(a)

S.No.	Paths from initial node to final node	Sequence of nodes	Sequence of edges
1.	n_1 to n_4	n_1, n_2, n_4	e_1, e_3
2.	n_1 to n_5	n_1, n_2, n_5	e_1, e_4
3.	n_1 to n_2	n_1, n_2	e_1
4.	n_1 to n_3	n_1, n_3	e_2
5.	n_2 to n_4	n_2, n_4	e_3
6.	n_2 to n_5	n_2, n_5	e_4
7.	n_2 to n_1	n_2, n_1	e_1
8.	n_3 to n_1	n_3, n_1	e_2
9.	n_4 to n_2	n_4, n_2	e_3
10.	n_4 to n_1	n_4, n_2, n_1	e_3, e_1
11.	n_5 to n_2	n_5, n_2	e_4
12.	n_5 to n_1	n_5, n_2, n_1	e_4, e_1
13.	n_2 to n_3	n_2, n_1, n_3	e_1, e_2
14.	n_3 to n_2	n_3, n_1, n_2	e_2, e_1
15.	n_4 to n_3	n_4, n_2, n_1, n_3	e_3, e_1, e_2
16.	n_3 to n_4	n_3, n_1, n_2, n_4	e_2, e_1, e_3
17.	n_4 to n_5	n_4, n_2, n_5	e_3, e_4
18.	n_5 to n_4	n_5, n_2, n_4	e_4, e_3
19.	n_5 to n_3	n_5, n_2, n_1, n_3	e_4, e_1, e_2
20.	n_3 to n_5	n_3, n_1, n_2, n_5	e_2, e_1, e_4

A path represented by sequence of nodes is a more popular representation technique than sequence of edges.

An independent path in a graph is a path that has at least one new node or edge in its sequence from the initial node to its final node.

If there is no repetition of an edge in a path from the initial node to the final node, then the path is called a simple path. The number of edges in a path is called the length of the path.

The direction of an edge provides more meaning to a path. Hence, paths of a directed graph seem to be more practical and useful. They are also called chains. The paths in a directed graph shown in Figure 3.1(b) are given in Table 3.2.

Table 3.2. Paths of directed graph in Figure 3.1(b)

S.No.	Paths from initial node to final node	Sequence of nodes	Sequence of edges
1.	n_1 to n_4	n_1, n_2, n_4	e_1, e_3
2.	n_1 to n_5	n_1, n_2, n_5	e_1, e_4
3.	n_1 to n_2	n_1, n_2	e_1
4.	n_1 to n_3	n_1, n_3	e_2
5.	n_2 to n_4	n_2, n_4	e_3
6.	n_2 to n_5	n_2, n_5	e_4

3.3.1 Cycles

When the initial and final nodes of a path are the same and if length ≠ 0, the path is called a cycle. Consider the graph given in Figure 3.5 having 6 nodes and 6 edges with a cycle constituted by a path n_1, n_2, n_5, n_3, n_1 of length 4.

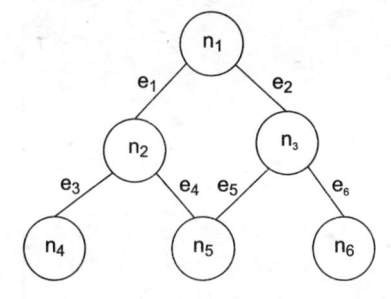

Figure 3.5. Cyclic graph

3.3.2 Connectedness of a Graph

An undirected graph is said to be connected if there is a path between every pair of nodes of the graph, otherwise it is said to be a disconnected graph. Two nodes are also said to be connected if there is a path between them.

A graph shown in Figure 3.3 (a) is a connected graph and a graph shown in Figure 3.1 (a) is a disconnected graph. The graph shown in Figure 3.6 is a disconnected graph with two portions of the graph.

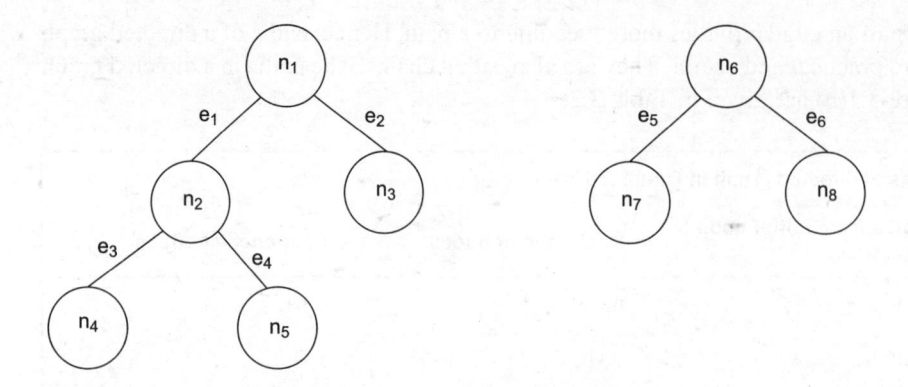

Figure 3.6. Disconnected graphs

A disconnected graph is the union of two or more disjoint portions of the graph. These disjoint portions are called the connected components of the graph.

A directed graph is said to be strongly connected if there is a path from node n_i to node n_j; where node n_i and n_j are any pair of nodes of the graph.

Every node of the graph should have a path to every other node of the graph in the strongly connected graphs. The directed graph shown in Figure 3.7 is a strongly connected graph.

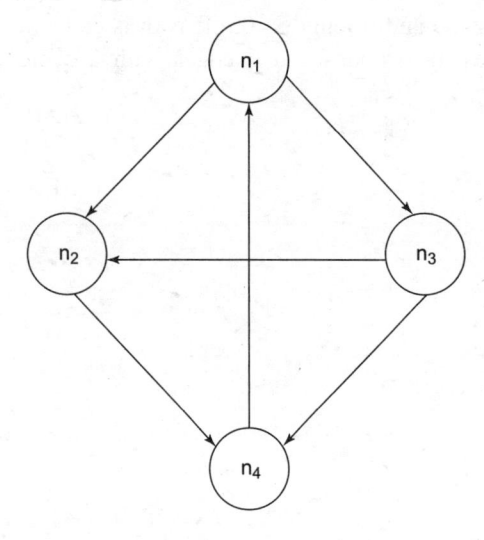

Figure 3.7. Strongly connected graph

The graph shown in Figure 3.7 has the following pair of nodes:
<n_1, n_2>, <n_1, n_3>, <n_4, n_1>, <n_3, n_2>, <n_2, n_4>, <n_3, n_4>. We identify paths for every pair of nodes.

    (a)   Pair <n_1, n_2>: Path = n_1, n_2
           Pair <n_2, n_1>: Path = n_2, n_4, n_1

(b) Pair $<n_1, n_3>$: Path = n_1, n_3
Pair $<n_3, n_1>$: Path = n_3, n_4, n_1
(c) Pair $<n_1, n_4>$: Path = n_1, n_2, n_4
Pair $<n_4, n_1>$: Path = n_4, n_1
(d) Pair $<n_2, n_3>$: Path = n_2, n_4, n_1, n_3
Pair $<n_3, n_2>$: Path = n_3, n_2
(e) Pair $<n_2, n_4>$: Path = n_2, n_4
Pair $<n_4, n_2>$: Path = n_4, n_1, n_2
(f) Pair $<n_3, n_4>$: Path = n_3, n_4
Pair $<n_4, n_3>$: Path = n_4, n_1, n_3
Hence this graph is strongly connected.

A directed graph is said to be weakly connected, if there is a path between every two nodes when the directions of the edges are not considered. A strongly connected directed graph will also be weakly connected when we do not consider the directions of edges. Consider the graph shown in Figure 3.8 which is weakly connected.

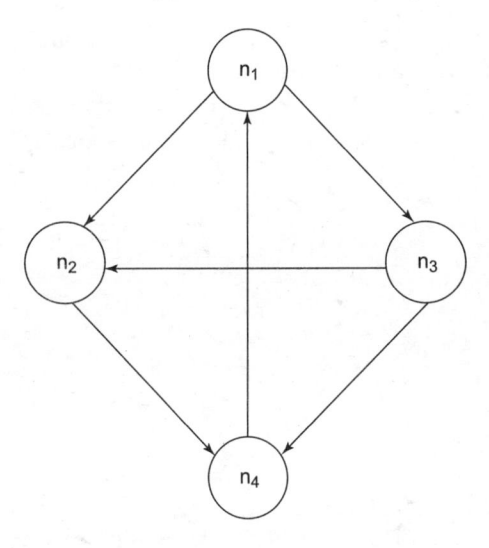

Figure 3.8. Weakly connected graph

When we do not consider the directions, it becomes an undirected graph where there is a path between every two nodes of the graph. Hence, this graph is weakly connected but not strongly connected.

Example 3.1: Consider the following undirected graph and find:

(a) The degree of all nodes
(b) The incidence matrix
(c) Adjacency matrix
(d) Paths

120 Software Testing

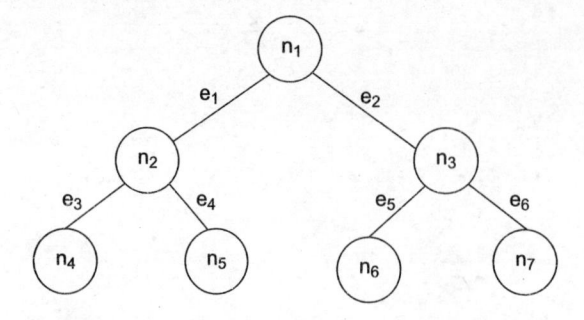

Solution:
This graph is an undirected graph with seven nodes and six edges

(a) The degrees of nodes are given as:
$deg(n_1) = 2$ $deg(n_5) = 1$
$deg(n_2) = 3$ $deg(n_6) = 1$
$deg(n_3) = 3$ $deg(n_7) = 1$
$deg(n_4) = 1$

(b) Incidence matrix of this graph has 7 × 6 size which is given as:

$$\begin{array}{c} \\ n_1 \\ n_2 \\ n_3 \\ n_4 \\ n_5 \\ n_6 \\ n_7 \end{array} \begin{array}{cccccc} e_1 & e_2 & e_3 & e_4 & e_5 & e_6 \\ \left[\begin{matrix} 1 & 1 & 0 & 0 & 0 & 0 \\ 1 & 0 & 1 & 1 & 0 & 0 \\ 0 & 1 & 0 & 0 & 1 & 1 \\ 0 & 0 & 1 & 0 & 0 & 0 \\ 0 & 0 & 0 & 1 & 0 & 0 \\ 0 & 0 & 0 & 0 & 1 & 0 \\ 0 & 0 & 0 & 0 & 0 & 1 \end{matrix}\right] \end{array}$$

(c) Adjacency matrix with size 7 × 7 is given as:

$$\begin{array}{c} \\ n_1 \\ n_2 \\ n_3 \\ n_4 \\ n_5 \\ n_6 \\ n_7 \end{array} \begin{array}{ccccccc} n_1 & n_2 & n_3 & n_4 & n_5 & n_6 & n_7 \\ \left[\begin{matrix} 0 & 1 & 1 & 0 & 0 & 0 & 0 \\ 1 & 0 & 0 & 1 & 1 & 0 & 0 \\ 1 & 0 & 0 & 0 & 0 & 1 & 1 \\ 0 & 1 & 0 & 0 & 0 & 0 & 0 \\ 0 & 1 & 0 & 0 & 0 & 0 & 0 \\ 0 & 0 & 1 & 0 & 0 & 0 & 0 \\ 0 & 0 & 1 & 0 & 0 & 0 & 0 \end{matrix}\right] \end{array}$$

(d) Paths of the graph are given as:

Essentials of Graph Theory   121

S. No.	Paths from initial node to final node	Sequence of nodes	Sequence of edges
1.	n_1 to n_2	n_1, n_2	e_1
2.	n_1 to n_4	n_1, n_2, n_4	e_1, e_3
3.	n_1 to n_5	n_1, n_2, n_5	e_1, e_4
4.	n_1 to n_3	n_1, n_3	e_2
5.	n_1 to n_6	n_1, n_3, n_6	e_2, e_5
6.	n_1 to n_7	n_1, n_3, n_7	e_2, e_6
7.	n_2 to n_1	n_2, n_1	e_1
8.	n_2 to n_4	n_2, n_4	e_3
9.	n_2 to n_5	n_2, n_5	e_4
10.	n_3 to n_1	n_3, n_1	e_2
11.	n_3 to n_6	n_3, n_6	e_5
12.	n_3 to n_7	n_3, n_7	e_6
13.	n_4 to n_2	n_4, n_2	e_3
14.	n_4 to n_1	n_4, n_2, n_1	e_3, e_1
15.	n_5 to n_2	n_5, n_2	e_4
16.	n_5 to n_1	n_5, n_2, n_1	e_4, e_1
17.	n_6 to n_3	n_6, n_2	e_5
18.	n_6 to n_1	n_6, n_3, n_1	e_5, e_2
19.	n_7 to n_3	n_7, n_3	e_6
20.	n_7 to n_1	n_7, n_3, n_1	e_6, e_2
21.	n_2 to n_3	n_2, n_1, n_3	e_1, e_2
22.	n_2 to n_6	n_2, n_1, n_3, n_6	e_1, e_2, e_5
23.	n_2 to n_7	n_2, n_1, n_3, n_7	e_1, e_2, e_6
24.	n_3 to n_2	n_3, n_1, n_2	e_2, e_1
25.	n_3 to n_4	n_3, n_1, n_2, n_4	e_2, e_1, e_3
26.	n_3 to n_5	n_3, n_1, n_2, n_5	e_1, e_2, e_4
27.	n_4 to n_3	n_4, n_2, n_1, n_3	e_3, e_1, e_2
28.	n_4 to n_5	n_4, n_2, n_5	e_3, e_4
29.	n_4 to n_6	n_4, n_2, n_1, n_3, n_6	e_3, e_1, e_2, e_5
30.	n_4 to n_7	n_4, n_2, n_1, n_3, n_7	e_3, e_1, e_2, e_6
31.	n_5 to n_3	n_5, n_2, n_1, n_3	e_4, e_1, e_2
32.	n_5 to n_4	n_5, n_2, n_4	e_4, e_3
33.	n_5 to n_6	n_5, n_2, n_1, n_3, n_6	e_4, e_1, e_2, e_5
34.	n_5 to n_7	n_5, n_2, n_1, n_3, n_7	e_4, e_1, e_2, e_6
35.	n_6 to n_2	n_6, n_3, n_1, n_2	e_5, e_2, e_1
36.	n_6 to n_4	n_6, n_3, n_1, n_2, n_4	e_5, e_2, e_1, e_3
37.	n_6 to n_5	n_6, n_3, n_1, n_2, n_5	e_5, e_2, e_1, e_4
38.	n_6 to n_7	n_6, n_3, n_7	e_5, e_6
39.	n_7 to n_2	n_7, n_3, n_1, n_2	e_6, e_2, e_1
40.	n_7 to n_4	n_7, n_3, n_1, n_2, n_4	e_6, e_2, e_1, e_3
41.	n_7 to n_5	n_7, n_3, n_1, n_2, n_5	e_6, e_2, e_1, e_4
42.	n_7 to n_6	n_7, n_3, n_6	e_6, e_5

Example 3.2: Consider the following directed graph and find:
(a) The degree of all nodes
(b) The incidence matrix
(c) Adjacency matrix
(d) Paths
(e) Connectedness

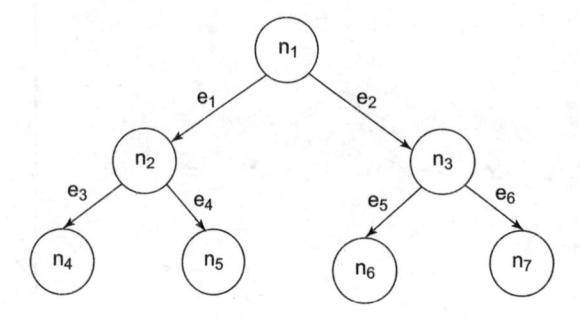

Solution:

This graph is a directed graph with seven nodes and six edges

(a) The degrees of all nodes are given as:

indeg(n_1) = 0	outdeg(n_1) = 2	deg(n_1) = 2
indeg(n_2) = 1	outdeg(n_2) = 2	deg(n_2) = 3
indeg(n_3) = 1	outdeg(n_3) = 2	deg(n_3) = 3
indeg(n_4) = 1	outdeg(n_4) = 0	deg(n_4) = 1
indeg(n_5) = 1	outdeg(n_5) = 0	deg(n_5) = 1
indeg(n_6) = 1	outdeg(n_6) = 0	deg(n_6) = 1
indeg(n_7) = 1	outdeg(n_7) = 0	deg(n_7) = 1

(b) Incidence matrix of this graph has 7 × 6 is given as:

$$\begin{array}{c} \\ n_1 \\ n_2 \\ n_3 \\ n_4 \\ n_5 \\ n_6 \\ n_7 \end{array} \begin{array}{c} e_1\ e_2\ e_3\ e_4\ e_5\ e_6 \\ \begin{bmatrix} 1 & 1 & 0 & 0 & 0 & 0 \\ 1 & 0 & 1 & 1 & 0 & 0 \\ 0 & 1 & 0 & 0 & 1 & 1 \\ 0 & 0 & 1 & 0 & 0 & 0 \\ 0 & 0 & 0 & 1 & 0 & 0 \\ 0 & 0 & 0 & 0 & 1 & 0 \\ 0 & 0 & 0 & 0 & 0 & 1 \end{bmatrix} \end{array}$$

(c) Adjacency matrix with size 7 × 7 is given as:

$$\begin{array}{c} \quad\;\; n_1\; n_2\; n_3\; n_4\; n_5\; n_6\; n_7 \\ \begin{array}{c} n_1 \\ n_2 \\ n_3 \\ n_4 \\ n_5 \\ n_6 \\ n_7 \end{array} \begin{bmatrix} 0 & 1 & 1 & 0 & 0 & 0 & 0 \\ 1 & 0 & 0 & 1 & 1 & 0 & 0 \\ 0 & 0 & 0 & 0 & 0 & 1 & 1 \\ 0 & 0 & 0 & 0 & 0 & 0 & 0 \\ 0 & 0 & 0 & 0 & 0 & 0 & 0 \\ 0 & 0 & 0 & 0 & 0 & 0 & 0 \\ 0 & 0 & 0 & 0 & 0 & 0 & 0 \end{bmatrix} \end{array}$$

(d) Paths of the graph are given as:

S. No.	Paths from initial node to final node	Sequence of nodes	Sequence of edges
1.	n_1 to n_2	n_1, n_2	e_1
2.	n_1 to n_4	n_1, n_2, n_4	e_1, e_3
3.	n_1 to n_5	n_1, n_2, n_5	e_1, e_4
4.	n_1 to n_3	n_1, n_3	e_2
5.	n_1 to n_6	n_1, n_3, n_6	e_2, e_5
6.	n_1 to n_7	n_1, n_3, n_7	e_2, e_6
7.	n_2 to n_4	n_2, n_4	e_3
.8.	n_2 to n_5	n_2, n_5	e_4
9.	n_3 to n_6	n_3, n_6	e_5
10.	n_3 to n_7	n_3, n_7	e_6

(e) This graph is weakly connected because there is no path between several nodes; for example, from node n_4 to n_2, n_6 to n_3, n_3 to n_1, n_2 to n_1, etc. however, if we do not consider directions, there is a path from every node to every other node which is the definition of a weakly connected graph.

3.4 GENERATION OF A GRAPH FROM PROGRAM

Graphs are extensively used in testing of computer programs. We may represent the flow of data and flow of control of any program in terms of directed graphs. A graph representing the flow of control of a program is called a program graph. The program graph may further be transformed into the DD path graph. Both of these graphs may provide foundations to many testing techniques.

3.4.1 Program Graphs

Program graph is a graphical representation of the source code of a program. The statements of a program are represented by nodes and flow of control by edges in the program graph. The definition of a program graph is [JORG07]:

> "A program graph is a directed graph in which nodes are either statements or fragments of a statement and edges represent flow of control."

The program graph helps us to understand the internal structure of the program which may provide the basis for designing the testing techniques. The basic constructs of the program graph are given in Figure 3.9.

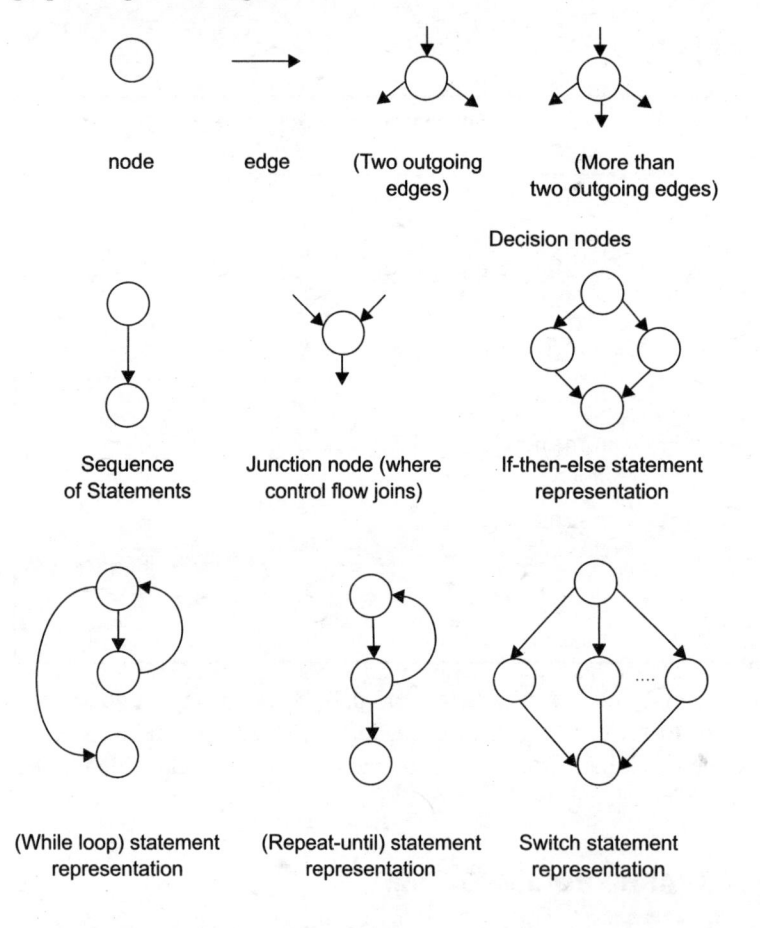

Figure 3.9. Basic constructs of a program graph

The basic constructs are used to convert a program in its program graph. We consider the program 'Square' which takes a number as an input and generates the square of the number. This program has 8 sequential statements which are represented by 8 nodes. All nodes are arranged sequentially which may lead to only one path in this program graph. Every program graph has one source node and one destination node.

We also consider a program given in Figure 3.11 that takes three numbers as input and prints the largest amongst these three numbers as output. The program graph of the program is given in Figure 3.12. There are 28 statements in the program which are represented by 28 nodes. All nodes are not in a sequence which may lead to many paths in the program graph.

```
  #include<stdio.h>
1  void main()
2  {
3  int num, result;
4  printf("Enter the number:");
5  scanf("%d", &num);
6  result=num*num;
7  printf("The result is: %d", result);
8  }
```

(a) Program to find 'square' of a number

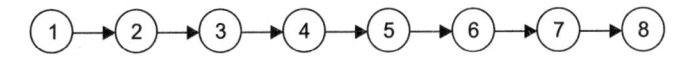

(1) → (2) → (3) → (4) → (5) → (6) → (7) → (8)

(b) Program graph for 'Square' program

Figure 3.10. Program 'Square' and its program graph

```
       #include<stdio.h>
       #include<conio.h>
1.     void main()
2.     {
3.     float A,B,C;
4.     clrscr();
5.     printf("Enter number 1:\n");
6.     scanf("%f", &A);
7.     printf("Enter number 2:\n");
8.     scanf("%f", &B);
9.     printf("Enter number 3:\n");
10.    scanf("%f", &C);
       /*Check for greatest of three numbers*/
11.    if(A>B) {
12.    if(A>C) {
13.        printf("The largest number is: %f\n",A);
14.    }
15.    else {
16.        printf("The largest number is: %f\n",C);
17.    }
18.    }
19.    else {
20.    if(C>B) {
21.        printf("The largest number is: %f\n",C);
22.    }
```

(Contd.)

(Contd.)

```
23.             else {
24.                     printf("The largest number is: %f\n",B);
25.                     }
26.             }
27.             getch();
28.     }
```

Figure 3.11. Program to find the largest among three numbers

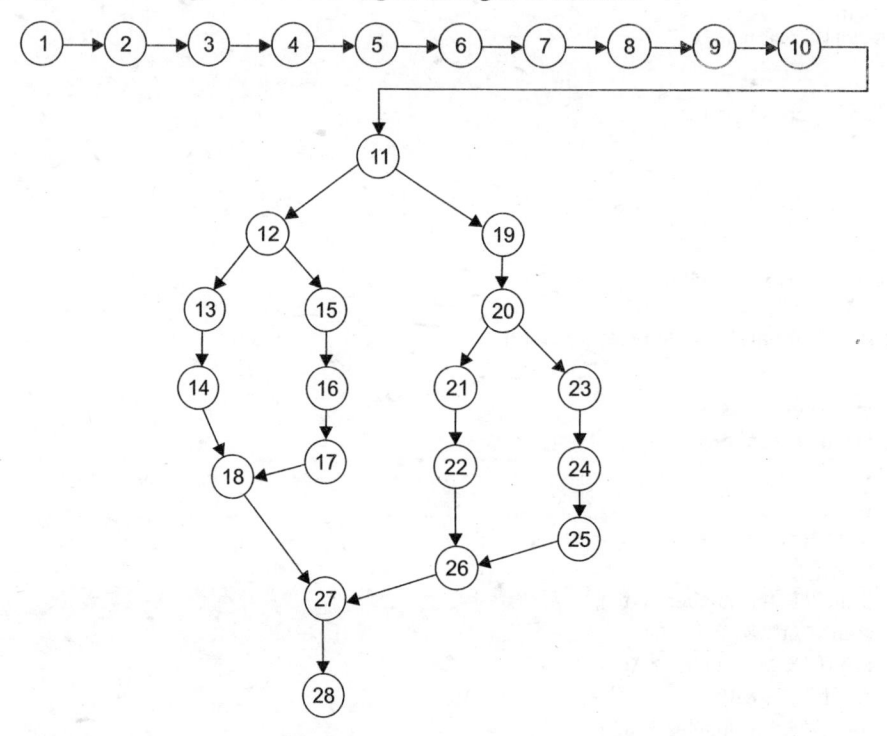

Figure 3.12. Program graph to find the largest number amongst three numbers as given in Figure 3.11.

Our example is simple, so it is easy to find all paths starting from the source node (node 1) and ending at the destination node (node 28). There are four possible paths. Every program graph may provide some interesting observations about the structure of the program. In our program graph given in Figure 3.12, nodes 2 to 10 are in sequence and nodes 11, 12, and 20 have two outgoing edges (predicate nodes) and nodes 18, 26, 27 have two incoming edges are (junction nodes).

We may also come to know whether the program is structured or not. A large program may be a structured program whereas a small program may be unstructured due to a loop in a program. If we have a loop in a program, large number of paths may be generated as shown in figure 1.5 of chapter 1. Myers [MYER04] has shown 10^{14} paths in a very small program graph due to a loop that iterates up to 20 times. This shows how an unstructured program may lead to difficulties in even finding every possible path in a program graph. Hence, testing a structured program is much easier as compared to any unstructured program.

3.4.2 DD Path Graphs

The Decision to Decision (DD) path graph is an extension of a program graph. It is widely known as DD path graph. There may be many nodes in a program graph which are in a sequence. When we enter into the first node of the sequence, we can exit only from the last node of that sequence. In DD path graph, such nodes which are in a sequence are combined into a block and are represented by a single node. Hence, the DD path graph is a directed graph in which nodes are sequences of statements and edges are control flow amongst the nodes. All programs have an entry and an exit and the corresponding program graph has a source node and a destination node. Similarly, the DD path graph also has a source node and a destination node.

We prepare a mapping table for the program graph and the DD path graph nodes. A mapping table maps nodes of the program graph to the corresponding nodes of the DD path graph. This may combine sequential nodes of the program graph into a block and that is represented by a single node in the DD path graph. This process may reduce the size of the program graph and convert it into a more meaningful DD path graph. We consider program 'Square' and its program graph given in Figure 3.10. We prepare a mapping table and a DD path graph as shown in Figure 3.13. All nodes are sequential nodes except node 1 and node 8 which are source node and destination node respectively.

Program graph nodes	DD path graph corresponding nodes	Remarks
1	S	Source node
2 – 7	N1	Sequential flow
8	D	Destination node

Mapping of program graph nodes and DD path graph nodes

DD Path graph

Figure 3.13. DD path graph and mapping table of program graph in Figure 3.10

We consider a program to find the 'largest amongst three numbers' as given in Figure 3.11. The program graph is also given in Figure 3.12. There are many sequential nodes, decision nodes, junction nodes available in its program graph. Its mapping table and the DD path graph are given in Table 3.3 and Figure 3.14 respectively.

Table 3.3. Mapping of program graph nodes and DD graph nodes

Program graph nodes	DD path graph corresponding node	Remarks
1	S	Source node
2 to 10	N1	Sequential nodes, there is a sequential flow from node 2 to 10
11	N2	Decision node, if true goto 12, else goto 19
12	N3	Decision node, if true goto 13 else goto 15
13, 14	N4	Sequential nodes
15, 16, 17	N5	Sequential nodes

(Contd.)

128 Software Testing

(Contd.)

Program graph nodes	DD path graph corresponding node	Remarks
18	N6	Junction node, two edges 14 and 17 are terminated here
19	N7	Intermediate node terminated at node 20
20	N8	Decision node, if true goto 21 else goto 23
21, 22	N9	Sequential nodes
23, 24, 25	N10	Sequential nodes
26	N11	Junction node, two edges 22 and 25 are terminated here
27	N12	Junction node, two edges 18 and 26 are terminated here
28	D	Destination node

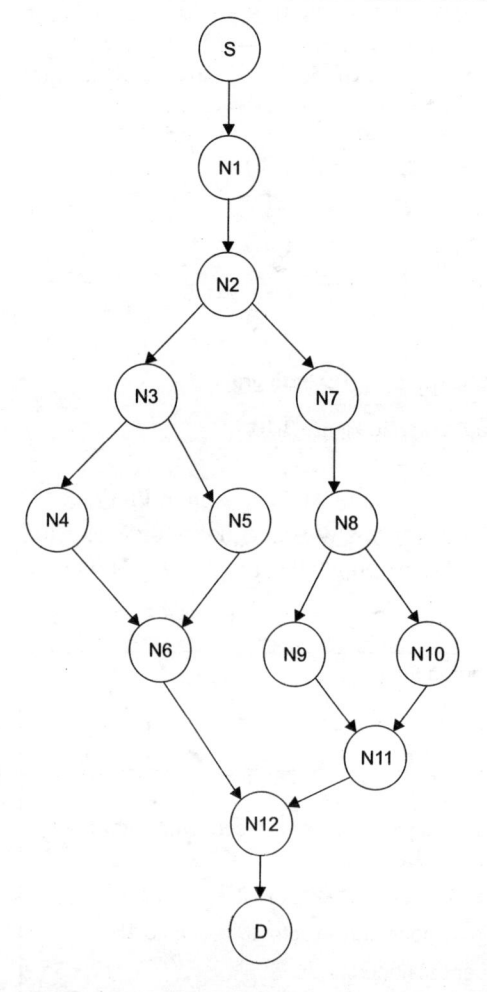

Figure 3.14. DD path graph of the program to find the largest among three numbers.

Essentials of Graph Theory   129

The DD path graphs are used to find paths of a program. We may like to test every identified path during testing which may give us some level of confidence about the correctness of the program.

Example 3.3: Consider the program for the determination of division of a student. Its input is a triple of positive integers (mark1, mark2, mark3) and values are from interval [0, 100].

The program is given in Figure 3.15. The output may be one of the following words:

[First division with distinction, First division, Second division, Third division, Fail, Invalid marks]. Draw the program graph and the DD path graph.

Solution:
The program graph is given in Figure 3.16. The mapping table of the DD path graph is given in Table 3.4 and DD path graph is given in Figure 3.17.

```
        /*Program to output division of a student based on the marks in three subjects*/
        #include<stdio.h>
        #include<conio.h>
1.      void main()
2.      {
3.      int mark1, mark2,mark3,avg;
4.      clrscr();
5.      printf("Enter marks of 3 subjects (between 0-100)\n");
6.      printf("Enter marks of first subject:");
7.      scanf("%d", &mark1);
8.      printf("Enter marks of second subject:");
9.      scanf("%d", &mark2);
10.     printf("Enter marks of third subject:");
11.     scanf("%d",&mark3);
12.     if(mark1>100||mark1<0||mark2>100||mark2<0||mark3>100||mark3<0) {
13.             printf("Invalid Marks! Please try again");
14.             }
15.     else {
16.     avg=(mark1+mark2+mark3)/3;
17.     if(avg<40) {
18.             printf("Fail");
19.             }
20.     else if(avg>=40&&avg<50) {
21.             printf("Third Division");
22.             }
23.     else if(avg>=50&&avg<60) {
24.             printf("Second Division");
25.             }
```

(Contd.)

130 Software Testing

(Contd.)

```
26.        else if(avg>=60&&avg<75) {
27.            printf("First Division");
28.        }
29.        else    {
30.            printf("First Division with Distinction");
31.        }
32.    }
33.    getch();
34. }
```

Figure 3.15. Source code of determination of division of a student problem

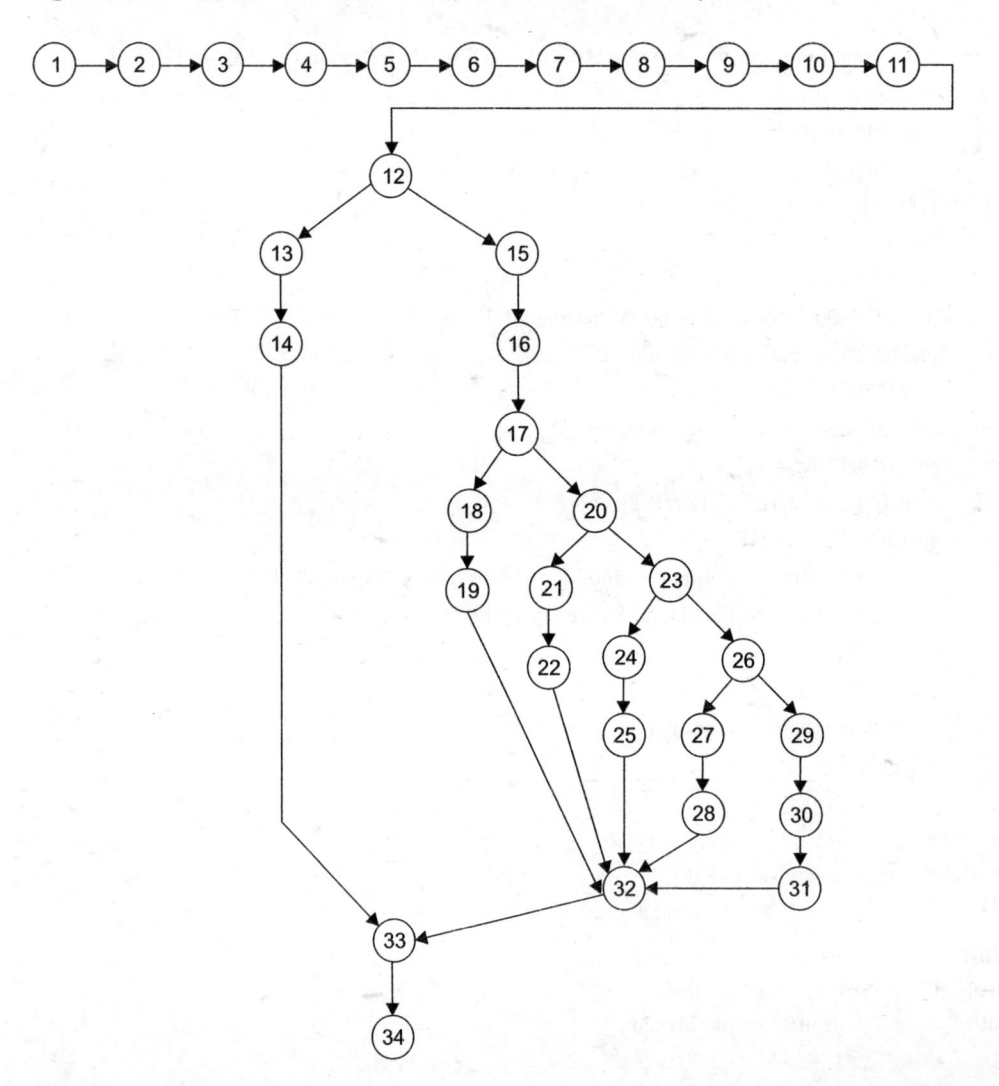

Figure 3.16. Program graph

Table 3.4. Mapping of program graph nodes and DD graph nodes

Program graph nodes	DD path graph corresponding node	Remarks
1	S	Source node
2 to 11	N1	Sequential nodes, there is a sequential flow from node 2 to 11
12	N2	Decision node, if true goto 13 else goto 15
13, 14	N3	Sequential nodes
15, 16	N4	Sequential nodes
17	N5	Decision node, if true goto 18 else goto 20
18, 19	N6	Sequential nodes
20	N7	Decision node, if true goto 21 else goto 23
21, 22	N8	Sequential nodes
23	N9	Decision node, if true goto 24 else goto 26
24, 25	N10	Sequential nodes
26	N11	Decision node, if true goto 27 else goto 29
27, 28	N12	Sequential nodes
29, 31	N13	Sequential nodes
32	N14	Junction node, five edges 19, 22, 25, 28 and 31 are terminated here
33	N15	Junction node, two edges 14 and 32 are terminated here
34	D	Destination node

Example 3.4: Consider the program for classification of a triangle. Its input is a triple of positive integers (say a, b and c) and values from the interval [1, 100]. The output may be [Right angled triangle, Acute angled triangle, Obtuse angled triangle, Invalid triangle, Input values are out of Range]. The program is given in Figure 3.18. Draw the program graph and the DD path graph.

Solution:
The program graph is shown in Figure 3.19. The mapping table is given in Table 3.5 and the DD path graph is given in Figure 3.20.

132 Software Testing

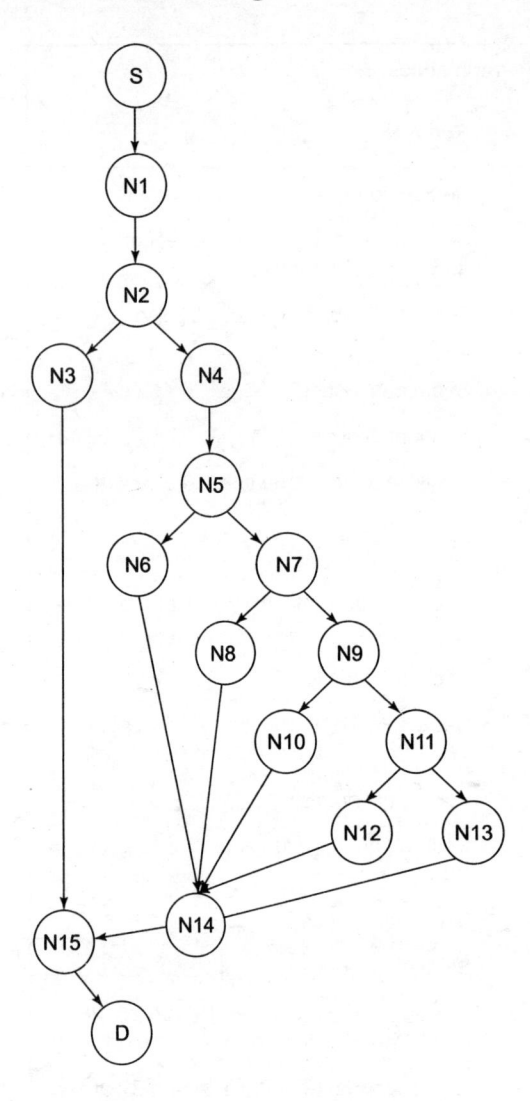

Figure 3.17. DD path graph of program to find division of a student

/*Program to classify whether a triangle is acute, obtuse or right angled given the sides of the triangle*/
//Header Files
#include<stdio.h>
#include<conio.h>
#include<math.h>
1. void main() //Main Begins
2. {

(Contd.)

(Contd.)

```
3.      double a,b,c;
4.      double a1,a2,a3;
5.      int valid=0;
6.      clrscr();
7.      printf("Enter first side of the triangle:"); /*Enter the sides of Triangle*/
8.      scanf("%lf",&a);
9.      printf("Enter second side of the triangle:");
10.     scanf("%lf",&b);
11.     printf("Enter third side of the triangle:");
12.     scanf("%lf",&c);
        /*Checks whether a triangle is valid or not*/
13.     if(a>0&&a<=100&&b>0&&b<=100&&c>0&&c<=100) {
14.         if((a+b)>c&&(b+c)>a&&(c+a)>b) {
15.             valid=1;
16.         }
17.         else {
18.             valid=-1;
19.         }
20.     }
21.     if(valid==1) {
22.         a1=(a*a+b*b)/(c*c);
23.         a2=(b*b+c*c)/(a*a);
24.         a3=(c*c+a*a)/(b*b);
25.         if(a1<1||a2<1||a3<1) {
26.             printf("Obtuse angled triangle");
27.         }
28.         else if(a1==1||a2==1||a3==1) {
29.             printf("Right angled triangle");
30.         }
31.         else {
32.             printf("Acute angled triangle");
33.         }
34.     }
35.     else if(valid==-1) {
36.         printf("\nInvalid Triangle");
37.     }
38.     else {
39.         printf("\nInput Values are Out of Range");
```

(Contd.)

134 Software Testing

(Contd.)

40.   }
41.   getch();
42.   } //Main Ends

Figure: 3.18. Source code for classification of triangle problem

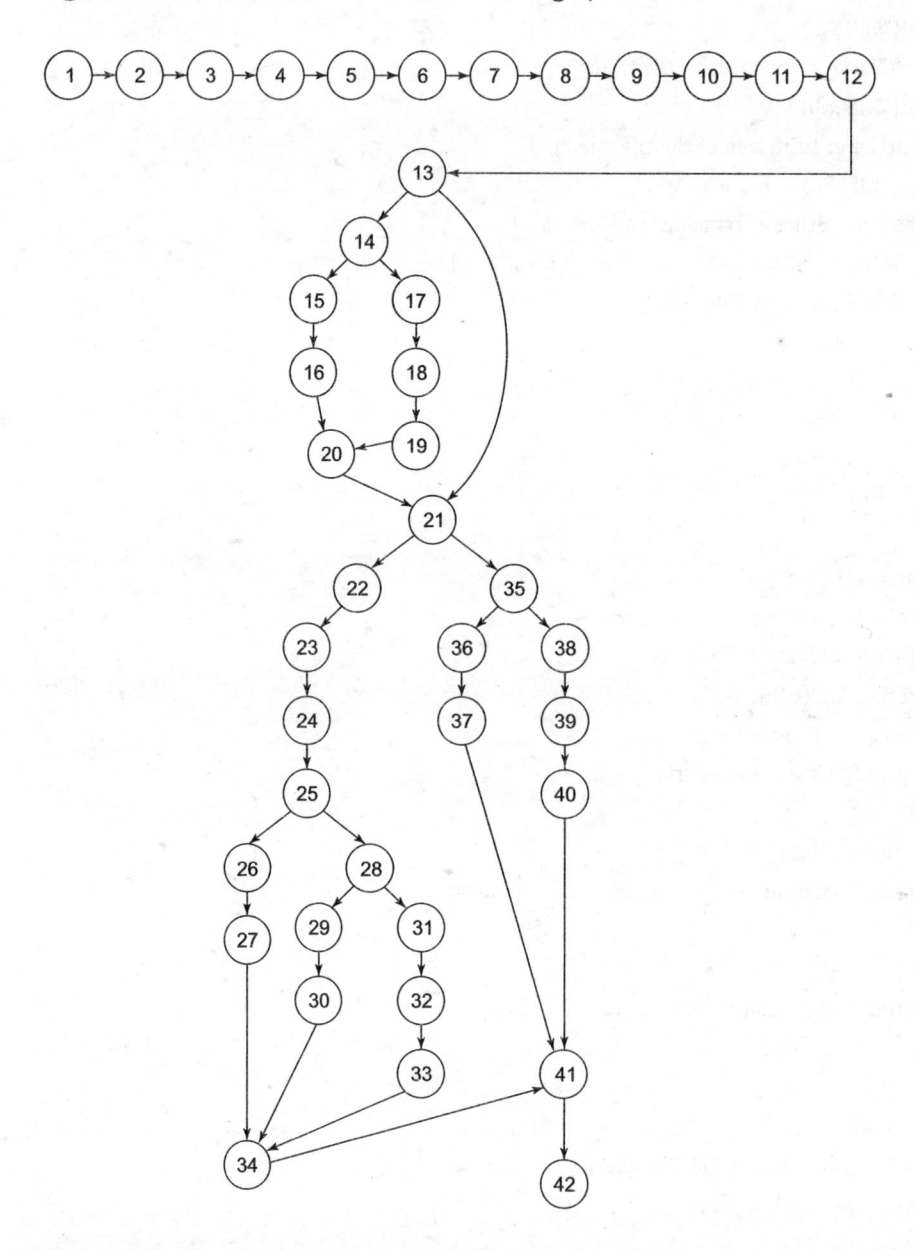

Figure 3.19. Program graph of classification of triangle problem

Table 3.5. Mapping of program graph nodes and DD graph nodes

Program graph nodes	DD path graph corresponding node	Remarks
1	S	Source node
2 to 12	N1	Sequential nodes, there is a sequential flow from node 2 to 12
13	N2	Decision node, if true goto 14 else goto 21
14	N3	Decision node, if true goto 15 else goto 17
15, 16	N4	Sequential nodes
17, 18, 19	N5	Sequential nodes
20	N6	Junction node, two edges 16 and 19 are terminated here
21	N7	Junction node, two edges 13 and 20 are terminated here. Also a decision node, if true goto 22, else goto 35
22, 23, 24	N8	Sequential nodes
25	N9	Decision node, if true goto 26 else goto 28
26, 27	N10	Sequential nodes
28	N11	Decision node, if true goto 29 else goto 31
29, 30	N12	Sequential nodes
31, 32, 33	N13	Sequential nodes
34	N14	Junction node, three edges 27, 30 and 33 are terminated here
35	N15	Decision node, if true goto 36 else goto 38
36, 37	N16	Sequential nodes
38, 39, 40	N17	Sequential nodes
41	N18	Three edges 34, 37 and 40 are terminated here.
42	D	Destination node.

136 Software Testing

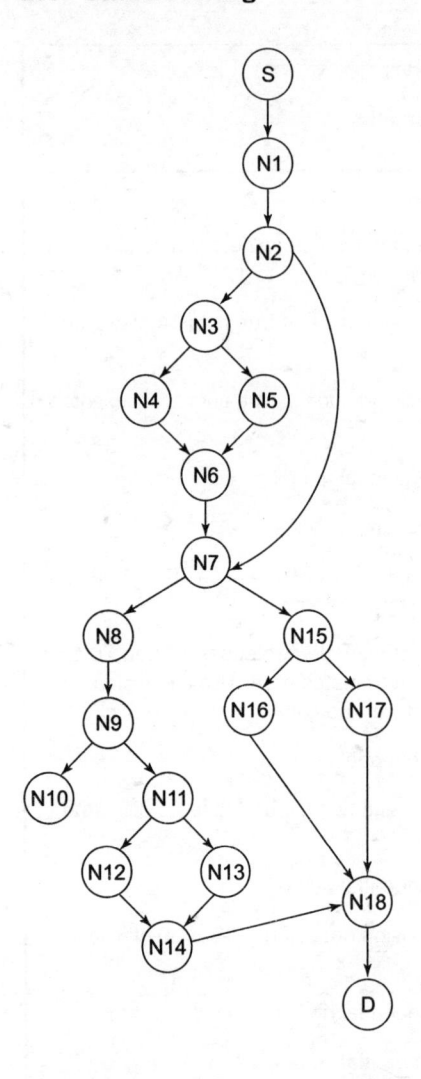

Figure 3.20. DD path graph of the program to classify a triangle

Example 3.5: Consider the program for determining the day of the week. Its input is a triple of day, month and year with the values in the range

$$1 \leq month \leq 12$$
$$1 \leq day \leq 31$$
$$1900 \leq year \leq 2058$$

The possible values of the output may be [Sunday, Monday, Tuesday, Wednesday, Thursday, Friday, Saturday, Invalid date]. The program is given in Figure 3.21.

Draw the program graph and the DD path graph.

```
                /*Program to compute day of the week*/
                /*Header Files*/
                #include<stdio.h>
                #include<conio.h>
1.              void main()
2.              {
3.              int day,month,year,century,Y,y1,M,date,validDate=0,leap=0;
4.              clrscr();
5.              printf("Enter day:");
6.              scanf("%d",&day);
7.              printf("Enter month:");
8.              scanf("%d",&month);
9.              printf("Enter year (between 1900 and 2058):");
10.             scanf("%d",&year);
                /*Check whether the date is valid or not*/
11.             if(year>=1900&&year<=2058) {
12.             if(year%4==0) { /*Check for leap year*/
13.                     leap=1;
14.                     if((year%100)==0&&(year%400)!=0) {
15.                             leap=0;
16.                     }
17.             }
18.             if(month==4||month==6||month==9||month==11){
19.             if(day>=1&&day<=30) {
20.                     validDate=1;
21.                     }
22.             else {
23.                     validDate=0;
24.                     }
25.             }
26.             else if(month==2){
27.             if(leap==1&&(day>=1&&day<=29)) {
28.                     validDate=1;
29.                     }
30.             else if(day>=1&&day<=28) {
31.                     validDate=1;
32.                     }
33.             else {
34.                     validDate=0;
35.                     }
36.             }
37.             else if((month>=1&&month<=12)&&(day>=1&&day<=31)){
```

(Contd.)

(Contd.)

```
38.                 validDate=1;
39.             }
40.         else {
41.                 validDate=0;
42.             }
43.         }
44.         if(validDate) { /*Calculation of Day in the week*/
45.             if(year>=1900&&year<2000){
46.             century=0;
47.             y1=year-1900;
48.             }
49.         else {
50.             century=6;
51.             y1=year-2000;
52.             }
53.         Y=y1+(y1/4);
54.         if(month==1) {
55.             if(leap==0) {
56.                 M=0; /*for non-leap year*/
57.                 }
58.         else {
59.                 M=6; /*for leap year*/
60.                 }
61.             }
62.         else if(month==2){
63.             if(leap==0) {
64.                 M=3; /*for non-leap year*/
65.                 }
66.         else {
67.                 M=2; //for leap year
68.                 }
69.             }
70.         else if((month==3)||(month==11)) {
71.                 M=3;
72.                 }
73.         else if((month==4)||(month==7)) {
74.                 M=6;
75.                 }
76.         else if(month==5) {
77.                 M=1;
78.                 }
79.         else if(month==6) {
80.                 M=4;
```

(Contd.)

(Contd.)

```
81.                    }
82.            else if(month==8) {
83.                    M=2;
84.                    }
85.            else if((month==9)||(month==12)) {
86.                    M=5;
87.                    }
88.            else {
89.                    M=0;
90.                    }
91.            date=(century+Y+M+day)%7;
92.            if(date==0) { /*Determine the day of the week*/
93.                    printf("Day of the week for [%d:%d:%d] is Sunday",day,month,year);
94.                    }
95.            else if(date==1) {
96.                    printf("Day of the week for [%d:%d:%d] is Monday",day,month,year);
97.                    }
98.            else if(date==2) {
99.                    printf("Day of the week for [%d:%d:%d] is Tuesday",day,month,year);
100.                   }
101.           else if(date==3) {
102.                   printf("Day of the week for [%d:%d:%d] is Wednesday",day,month,year);
103.                   }
104.           else if(date==4) {
105.                   printf("Day of the week for [%d:%d:%d] is Thursday",day,month,year);
106.                   }
107.           else if(date==5) {
108.                   printf("Day of the week for [%d:%d:%d] is Friday",day,month,year);
109.                   }
110.           else {
111.                   printf("Day of the week for [%d:%d:%d] is Saturday",day,month,year);
112.                   }
113.           }
114.           else {
115.                   printf("The date entered [%d:%d:%d] is invalid",day,month,year);
116.                   }
117.           getch();
118.           }
```

Figure 3.21. Source code for determination of day of the week

Solution:
The program graph is shown in Figure 3.22. The mapping table is given in Table 3.6 and the DD path graph is given in Figure 3.23.

140 Software Testing

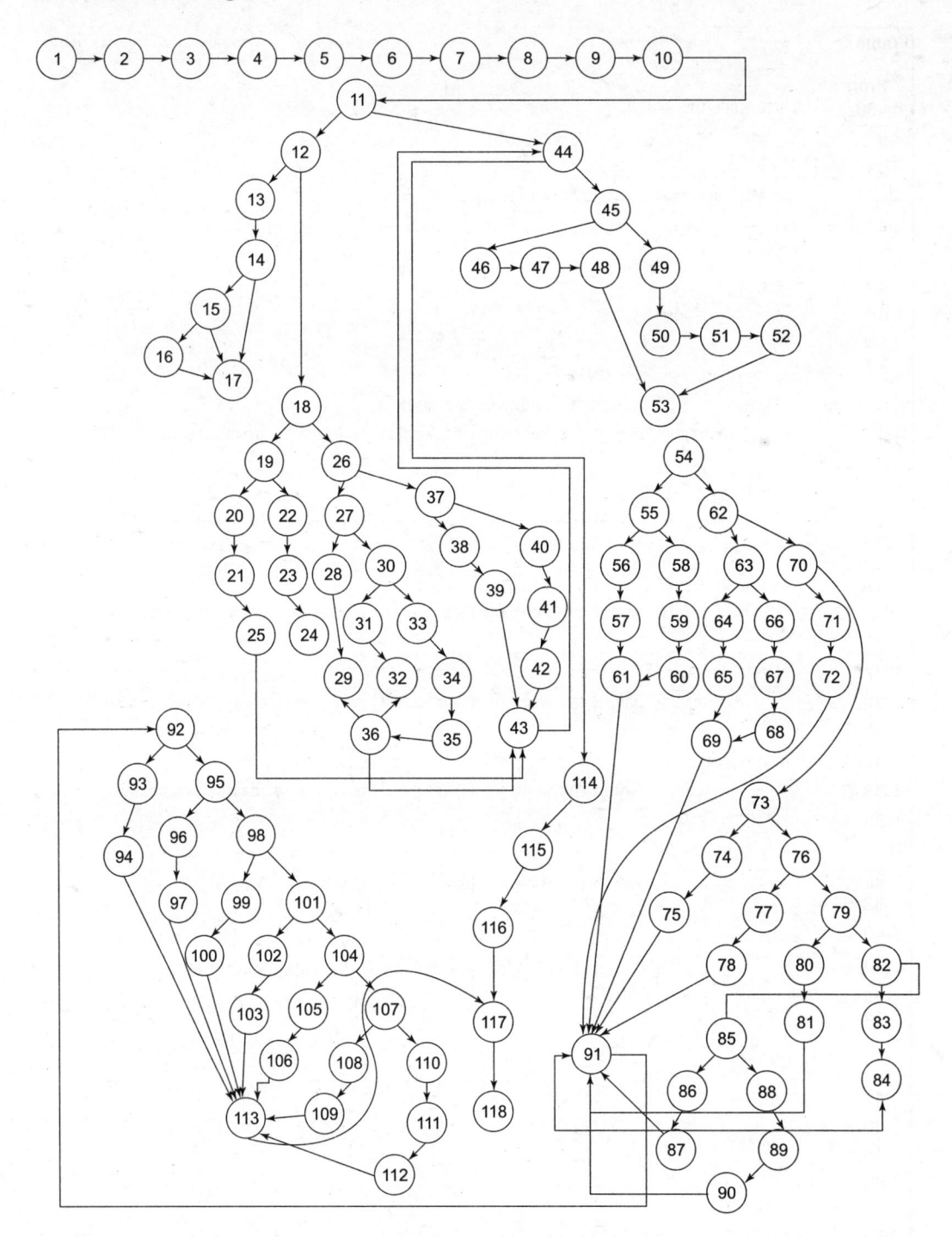

Figure 3.22. Program graph for determination of day of the week

Table 3.6. Mapping of program graph nodes to DD graph nodes

Program graph nodes	DD path graph corresponding node	Remarks
1	S	Source node
2 to 10	N1	Sequential nodes, there is a sequential flow from node 2 to 10
11	N2	Decision node, if true goto 12, else goto 44
12	N3	Decision node, if true goto 13, else goto 18
13	N4	Intermediate node terminated at node 14
14	N5	Decision node, if true goto 15, else goto 17
15, 16	N6	Sequential nodes
17	N7	Junction node, two edges 14 and 16 are terminated here
18	N8	Junction node, two edges 12 and 17 are terminated here. Also a decision node, if true goto 19, else goto 26
19	N9	Decision node, if true goto 20, else goto 22
20, 21	N10	Sequential nodes
22, 23, 24	N11	Sequential nodes
25	N12	Junction node, two edges 21 and 24 are terminated here
26	N13	Decision node, if true goto 27, else goto 37
27	N14	Decision node, if true goto 28, else goto 30
28, 29	N15	Sequential nodes
30	N16	Decision node, if true goto 31, else goto 33
31, 32	N17	Sequential nodes
33, 34, 35	N18	Sequential nodes
36	N19	Junction node, three edges 29, 32, and 35 are terminated here
37	N20	Decision node, if true goto 38, else goto 40
38, 39	N21	Sequential nodes
40, 41, 42	N22	Sequential nodes
43	N23	Four edges 25, 36, 39, and 42 are terminated here
44	N24	Junction node, two edges 11 and 43 are terminated here and also a decision node. If true goto 45, else goto 114
45	N25	Decision node, if true goto 46, else goto 49
46, 47, 48	N26	Sequential nodes
49, 50, 51, 52	N27	Sequential nodes
53	N28	Junction node, two edges 48 and 52 are terminated here
54	N29	Decision node, if true goto 55, else goto 62
55	N30	Decision node, if true goto 56, else goto 58
56, 57	N31	Sequential nodes
58, 59, 60	N32	Sequential nodes

(Contd.)

(*Contd.*)

Program graph nodes	DD path graph corresponding node	Remarks
61	N33	Junction node, two edges 57 and 60 are terminated here
62	N34	Decision node, if true goto 63, else goto 70
63	N35	Decision node, if true goto 64, else goto 66
64, 65	N36	Sequential nodes
66, 67, 68	N37	Sequential nodes
69	N38	Junction node, two edges 65 and 68 are terminated here
70	N39	Decision node, if true goto 71 else goto 73
71, 72	N40	Sequential nodes
73	N41	Decision node, if true goto 74 else goto 76
74, 75	N42	Sequential nodes
76	N43	Decision node, if true goto 77 else goto 79
77, 78	N44	Sequential nodes
79	N45	Decision node, if true goto 80 else goto 82
80, 81	N46	Sequential nodes
82	N47	Decision node, if true goto 83, else goto 85
83, 84	N48	Sequential nodes
85	N49	Decision node, if true goto 86, else goto 88
86, 87	N50	Sequential nodes
88, 89, 90	N51	Sequential nodes
91	N52	Junction node, nine edges 61, 69, 72, 75, 78, 81, 84, 87 and 90 are terminated here
92	N53	Decision node, if true goto 93, else goto 95
93, 94	N54	Sequential nodes
95	N55	Decision node, if true goto 96, else goto 98
96, 97	N56	Sequential nodes
98	N57	Decision node, if true goto 99, else goto 101
99, 100	N58	Sequential nodes
101	N59	Decision node, if true goto 102, else goto 104
102, 103	N60	Sequential nodes
104	N61	Decision node, if true goto 105, else goto 107
105, 106	N62	Sequential nodes
107	N63	Decision node, if true goto 108, else goto 110
108, 109	N64	Sequential nodes
110, 111, 112	N65	Sequential nodes
113	N66	Seven edges 94, 97, 100, 103, 106, 109 and 112 are terminated here
114, 115, 116	N67	Sequential nodes
117	N68	Junction node, two edges 116 and 113 are terminated here
118	D	Destination node

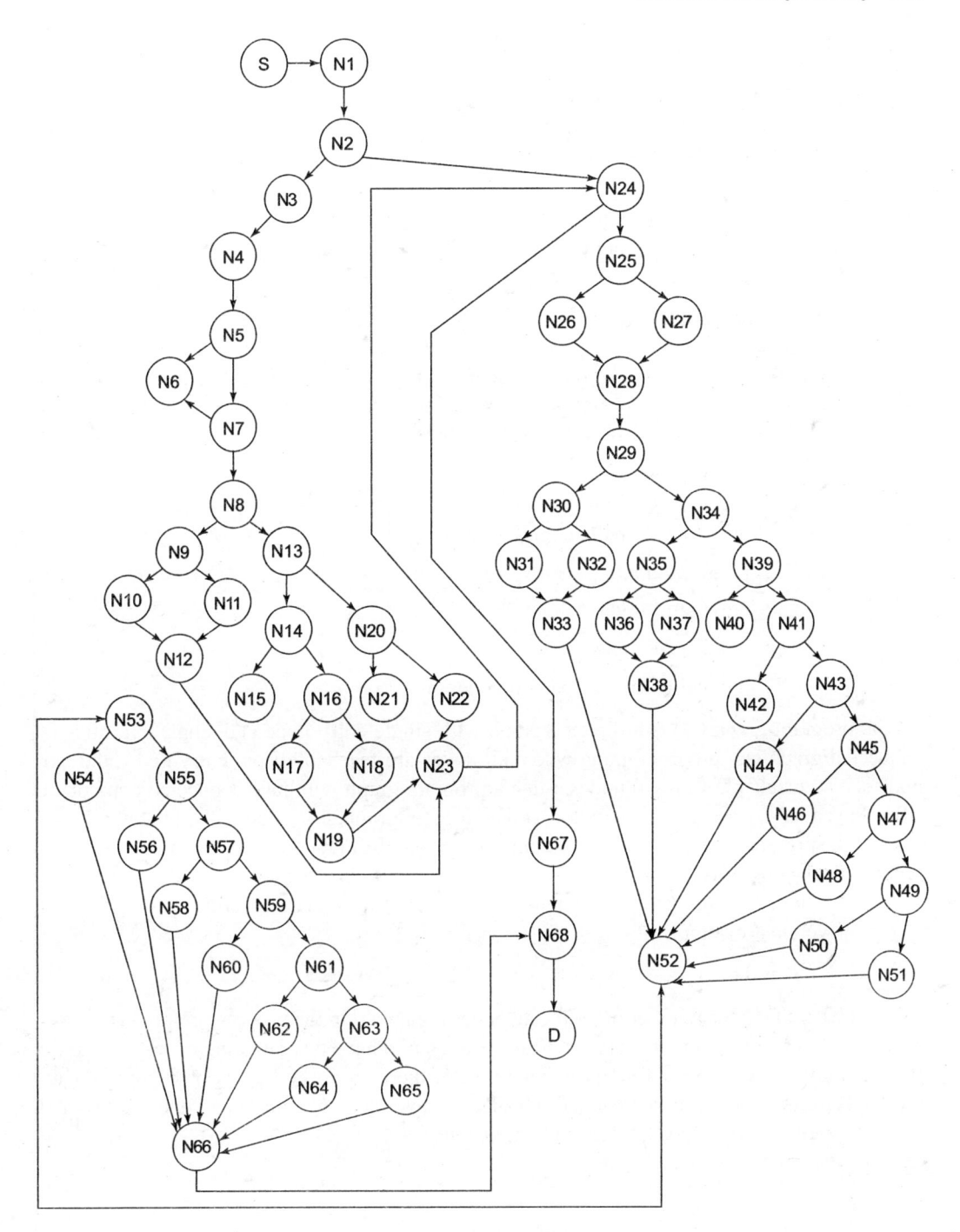

Figure 3.23. DD path graph for determination of day of the week

3.5 IDENTIFICATION OF INDEPENDENT PATHS

There are many paths in any program. If there are loops in a program, the number of paths increases drastically. In such situations, we may be traversing the same nodes and edges again and again. However, as defined earlier, an independent path should have at least one new node or edge which is to be traversed. We should identify every independent path of a program and pay special attention to these paths during testing. A few concepts of graph theory are used in testing techniques which may help us to identify independent paths.

3.5.1 Cyclomatic Complexity

This concept involves using cyclomatic number of graph theory which has been redefined as cyclomatic complexity. This is nothing but the number of independent paths through a program. McCabe [MCCA76] introduced this concept and gave three methods to calculate cyclomatic complexity.

(i) $V(G) = e - n + 2P$
where $V(G)$ = Cyclomatic complexity

   G : program graph

   n : number of nodes

   e : number of edges

   P : number of connected components

The program graph (G) is a directed graph with single entry node and single exit node. A connected graph is a program graph where all nodes are reachable from entry node, and exit node is also reachable from all nodes. Such a program graph will have connected component (P) value equal to one. If there are parts of the program graph, the value will be the number of parts of the program graph where one part may represent the main program and other parts may represent sub-programs.

(ii)   Cyclomatic complexity is equal to the number of regions of the program graph.
(iii) Cyclomatic complexity

   $V(G) = \Pi + 1$

where Π is the number of predicate nodes contained in the program graph (G).

The only restriction is that every predicate node should have two outgoing edges i.e. one for 'true' condition and another for 'false' condition. If there are more than two outgoing edges, the structure is required to be changed in order to have only two outgoing edges. If it is not possible, then this method ($\Pi + 1$) is not applicable.

Properties of cyclomatic complexity:

1. $V(G) \geq 1$
2. $V(G)$ is the maximum number of independent paths in program graph G.
3. Addition or deletion of functional statements to program graph G does not affect $V(G)$.
4. G has only one path if $V(G)=1$
5. $V(G)$ depends only on the decision structure of G.

We consider the program graph given in Figure 3.24.

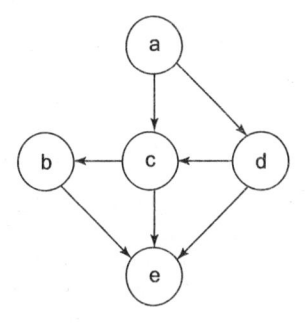

Figure 3.24. Program graph

The value of cyclomatic complexity can be calculated as:
(i) $V(G) = e - n + 2P$
    $= 7 - 5 + 2$
    $= 4$
(ii) $V(G)$ = No. of regions of the graph

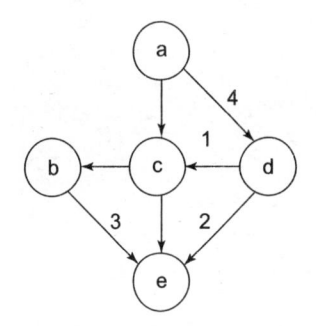

Hence, $V(G) = 4$
Three regions (1, 2 and 3) are inside and 4th is the outside region of the graph
(iii) $V(G) = \Pi + 1$
    $= 3 + 1 = 4$

There are three predicate nodes namely node a, node c and node d.
These four independent paths are given as:

        Path 1 :   ace
        Path 2 :   ade
        Path 3 :   adce
        Path 4 :   acbe

We consider another program graph given in Figure 3.25 with three parts of the program graph.

Part I (Main Program)

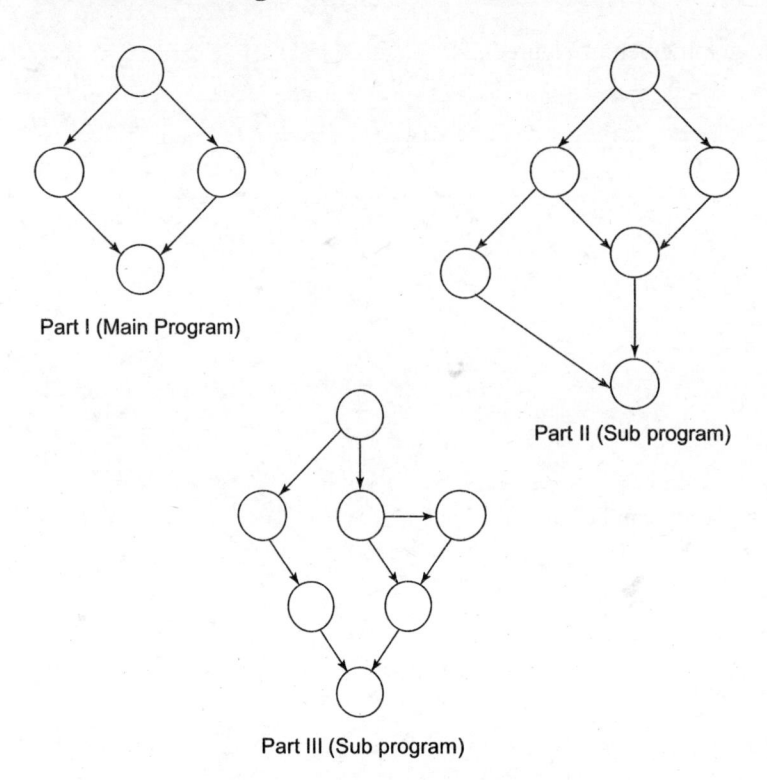

Part II (Sub program)

Part III (Sub program)

Figure 3.25. Program graph with 3 connected components

$$V(G) = e - n + 2P$$
$$= (4+7+8) - (4+6+7) + 2 \times 3$$
$$= 19 - 17 + 6$$
$$= 8$$

We calculate the cyclomatic complexity of each part of the graph independently.

$$V(G - \text{Part I}) = 4 - 4 + 2 = 2$$
$$V(G - \text{Part II}) = 7 - 6 + 2 = 3$$
$$V(G - \text{Part III}) = 8 - 7 + 2 = 3$$

Hence, V (G – Part I U G – Part II U G – Part III)

$$= V (G - \text{Part I}) + V (G - \text{Part II}) + V (G - \text{Part III})$$

In general, the cyclomatic complexity of a program graph with P connected components is equal to the summation of their individual cyclomatic complexities. To understand this, consider graph G_i where $1 \leq i \leq P$ denote the P connected components of a graph, and e_i and n_i are the number of edges and nodes in the ith connected component of the graph. Then, we may have the following equation:

$$V(G) = e - n + 2P = \sum_{i=1}^{P} e_i - \sum_{i=1}^{P} n_i + 2P$$

$$= \sum_{i=1}^{P}(e_i - n_i + 2) = \sum_{i=1}^{P} V(G_i)$$

The cyclomatic complexity is a popular measure to know the complexity of any program. It is easy to calculate and immediately provides an insight to the implementation of the program. McCabe suggested an upper limit for this cyclomatic complexity i.e. 10 [MACC76]. If this exceeds, developers have to redesign the program to reduce the cyclomatic complexity. The purpose is to keep the size of the program manageable and compel the testers to execute all independent paths. This technique is more popular at module level and forces everyone to minimize its value for the overall success of the program. There may be situations where this limit seems unreasonable; e.g. when a large number of independent cases follow a selection function like switch or case statement.

Example 3.6: Consider the following DD path graph (as given in Figure 3.14) and calculate the cyclomatic complexity. Also find independent paths.

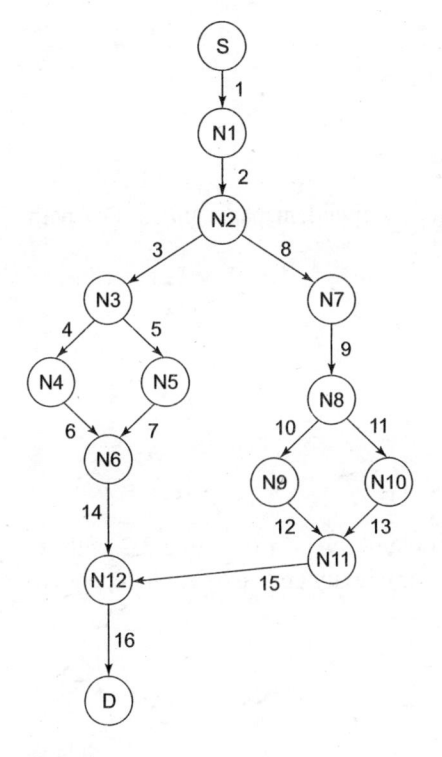

Solution:

(i) $V(G) = e - n + 2P$

           $= 16 - 14 + 2$

           $= 4$

(ii) V (G) = Number of Regions

$$= 4$$

(iii) V (G) = Π + 1

$$= 3 (N2, N3, N8) + 1$$

$$= 4$$

There are 4 independent paths as given below:

(i) S, N1, N2, N3, N4, N6, N12, D
(ii) S, N1, N2, N3, N5, N6, N12, D
(iii) S, N1, N2, N7, N8, N9, N11, N12, D
(iv) S, N1, N2, N8, N10, N11, N12, D

Example 3.7: Consider the problem for determination of division of a student with the DD path graph given in Figure 3.17. Find cyclomatic complexity and also find independent paths.

Solution:
Number of edges (e) = 21
Number of nodes (n) = 17

(i) V(G) = e − n + 2P = 21 − 17 + 2 = 6
(ii) V(G) = Π + 1 = 5 + 1 = 6
(iii) V(G) = Number of regions = 6

Hence cyclomatic complexity is 6 meaning there are six independent paths in the DD path graph.

The independent paths are:

(i) S, N1, N2, N3, N15, D
(ii) S, N1, N2, N4, N5, N6, N14, N15, D
(iii) S, N1, N2, N4, N5, N7, N8, N14, N15, D
(iv) S, N1, N2, N4, N5, N7, N9, N10, N14, N15, D
(v) S, N1, N2, N4, N5, N7, N9, N11, N12, N14, N15, D
(vi) S, N1, N2, N4, N5, N7, N9, N11, N13, N14, N15, D

Example 3.8: Consider the classification of triangle problem given in Example 3.2 with its DD path graph given in Figure 3.20. Find the cyclomatic complexity and also find independent paths.

Solution:
Number of edges (e) = 25
Number of nodes (n) = 20

(i) V(G) = e − n + 2P = 25 − 20 + 2 = 7
(ii) V(G) = Π + 1 = 6 + 1 = 7
(iii) V(G) = Number of regions = 7

Hence cyclomatic complexity is 7. There are seven independent paths as given below:

(i) S, N1, N2, N7, N15, N17, N18, D
(ii) S, N1, N2, N7, N15, N16, N18, D
(iii) S, N1, N2, N7, N8, N9, N11, N13, N14, N18, D
(iv) S, N1, N2, N7, N8, N9, N11, N12, N14, N18, D
(v) S, N1, N2, N7, N8, N9, N10, N14, N18, D
(vi) S, N1, N2, N3, N5, N6, N7, N8, N9, N10, N14, N18, D
(vii) S, N2, N3, N4, N6, N7, N8, N9, N10, N14, N18, D

Example 3.9: Consider the DD path graph given in Figure 3.23 for determination of the day problem. Calculate the cyclomatic complexity and also find independent paths.

Solution:
Number of edges (e) = 96
Number of nodes (n) = 70

(i) $V(G) = e - n + 2P$

$= 96 - 70 + 2 = 28$

(ii) $V(G)$ = Number of regions = 28
(iii) $V(G) = \Pi + 1$

$= 27 + 1 = 28$

Hence, there are 28 independent paths.
The independent paths are:

(i) S, N1, N2, N24, N25, N27, N28, N29, N34, N39, N41, N43, N45, N47, N49, N51, N52, N53, N54, N66, N68, D
(ii) S, N1, N2, N24, N25, N27, N28, N29, N34, N39, N41, N43, N45, N47, N49, N50, N52, N53, N54, N66, N68, D
(iii) S, N1, N2, N24, N25, N27, N28, N29, N34, N39, N41, N43, N45, N47, N48, N52, N53, N54, N66, N68, D
(iv) S, N1, N2, N24, N25, N27, N28, N29, N34, N39, N41, N43, N45, N46, N52, N53, N54, N66, N68, D
(v) S, N1, N2, N24, N25, N27, N28, N29, N34, N39, N41, N43, N44, N52, N53, N54, N66, N68, D
(vi) S, N1, N2, N24, N25, N27, N28, N29, N34, N39, N41, N42, N52, N53, N54, N66, N68, D
(vii) S, N1, N2, N24, N25, N27, N28, N29, N34, N39, N40, N52, N53, N54, N66, N68, D
(viii) S, N1, N2, N24, N25, N27, N28, N29, N34, N35, N37, N38, N52, N53, N54, N66, N68, D
(ix) S, N1, N2, N24, N25, N27, N28, N29, N34, N35, N36, N38, N52, N53, N54, N66, N68, D
(x) S, N1, N2, N24, N25, N27, N28, N29, N30, N32, N33, N52, N53, N54, N66, N68, D
(xi) S, N1, N2, N24, N25, N27, N28, N29, N30, N31, N33, N52, N53, N54, N66, N68, D
(xii) S, N1, N2, N24, N25, N26, N28, N29, N30, N31, N33, N52, N53, N54, N66, N68, D
(xiii) S, N1, N2, N24, N67, N68, D

150 Software Testing

(xiv) S, N1, N2, N3, N8, N13, N20, N22, N23, N24, N67, N68, D
(xv) S, N1, N2, N3, N8, N13, N20, N21, N23, N24, N67, N68, D
(xvi) S, N1, N2, N3, N8, N13, N14, N16, N18, N19, N23, N24, N67, N68, D
(xvii) S, N1, N2, N3, N8, N13, N14, N16, N17, N19, N23, N24, N67, N68, D
(xviii) S, N1, N2, N3, N8, N13, N14, N15, N19, N23, N24, N67, N68, D
(xix) S, N1, N2, N3, N8, N9, N11, N12, N23, N24, N67, N68, D
(xx) S, N1, N2, N3, N8, N9, N10, N12, N23, N24, N67, N68, D
(xxi) S, N1, N2, N3, N8, N9, N10, N12, N23, N24, N67, N68, D
(xxii) S, N1, N2, N3, N4, N5, N6, N7, N8, N9, N10, N12, N23, N24, N67, N68, D
(xxiii) S, N1, N2, N24, N25, N26, N28, N29, N30, N31, N52, N53, N55, N57, N59, N61, N63, N65, N66, N68, D
(xxiv) S, N1, N2, N24, N25, N26, N28, N29, N30N N31, N52, N53, N55, N57, N59, N61, N63, N64, N66, N68, D
(xxv) S, N1, N2, N24, N25, N26, N28, N29, N30, N31, N52, N53, N55, N57, N59, N61, N62, N66, N68, D
(xxvi) S, N1, N2, N24, N25, N26, N28, N29, N30, N31, N52, N53, N55, N57, N59, N60, N66, N68, D
(xxvii) S, N1, N2, N24, N25, N26, N28, N29, N30, N31, N52, N53, N55, N57, N58, N66, N68, D
(xxviii) S, N1, N2, N24, N25, N26, N28, N29, N30, N31, N52, N53, N55, N56, N66, N68, D

3.5.2 Graph Matrices

The graphs are commonly used in testing to find independent paths. Cyclomatic complexity also gives us the number of independent paths in any graph. When the size of the graph increases, it becomes difficult to identify those paths manually. We may do so with the help of a software tool and graph matrices may become the basis for designing such a tool.

A graph matrix is a square matrix with one row and one column for every node of the graph. The size of the matrix (number of rows and number of columns) is the number of nodes of the graph. Some examples of program graphs and their graph matrices are given in Figure 3.26.

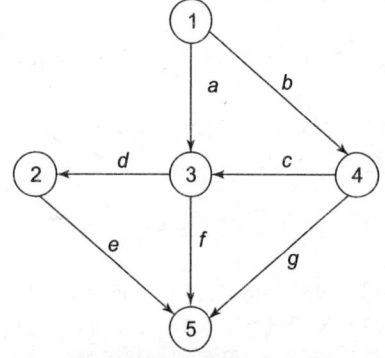

Cyclomatic Complexity = 4

	1	2	3	4	5
1			a	b	
2					e
3		d			f
4				c	g
5					

(a)

Essentials of Graph Theory

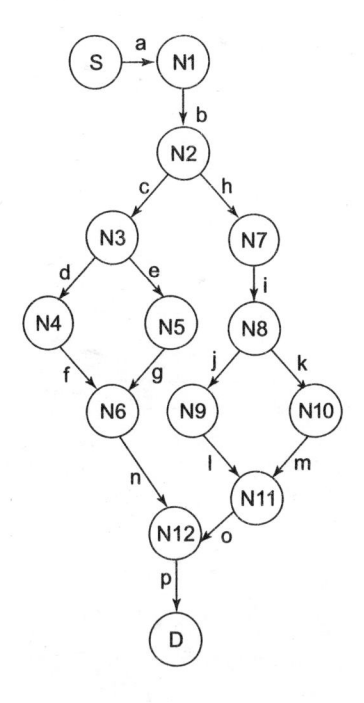

	S	N1	N2	N3	N4	N5	N6	N7	N8	N9	N10	N11	N12	D
S		a												
N1			b											
N2				c				h						
N3					d	e								
N4							f							
N5							g							
N6													n	
N7									i					
N8										j	k			
N9												l		
N10												m		
N11													o	
N12														p
D														

(b)

Figure 3.26. Program graphs and graph matrices

Graph matrix is the tabular representation of a program graph. If we assign weight for every entry in the table, then this may be used for the identification of independent paths. The simplest weight is 1, if there is a connection and 0 if there is no connection. A matrix with such weights is known as connection matrix. A connection matrix for Figure 3.26 (b) is obtained by replacing each entry with 1, if there is a link and 0 if there is no link.

152　Software Testing

We do not show 0 entries for simplicity and blank space is treated as 0 entry as shown in Figure 3.27.

	S	N1	N2	N3	N4	N5	N6	N7	N8	N9	N10	N11	N12	D	
S		1													1-1=0
N1			1												1-1=0
N2				1				1							2-1=1
N3					1	1									2-1=1
N4							1								1-1=0
N5							1								1-1=0
N6													1		1-1=0
N7									1						1-1=0
N8										1	1				2-1=1
N9												1			1-1=0
N10												1			1-1=0
N11													1		1-1=0
N12														1	1-1=0
D															3+1=4

Figure 3.27. Connection matrix for program graph shown in Figure 3.26(b)

The connection matrix can also be used to find cyclomatic complexity as shown in Figure 3.27. Each row with more than one entry represents a predicate node and cyclomatic complexity is predicate nodes plus one ($\Pi+1$).

As we know, each graph matrix expresses a direct link between nodes. If we take the square of the matrix, it shows 2-links relationships via one intermediate node. Hence, square matrix represents all paths of two links long. The Kth power of matrix represents all paths of K links long. We consider the graph matrix of the program graph given in Figure 3.26 (a) and find its square as shown below:

	1	2	3	4	5
1			a	b	
2					e
3		d			f
4			c		g
5					

[A]

	1	2	3	4	5
1		ad	bc		af+bg
2					
3					de
4		cd			cf
5					

$[A]^2$

There are two paths af and bg of two links between node 1 and node 5. There is no one link path from node 1 to node 5. We will get three links paths after taking the cube of this matrix as given below:

	1	2	3	4	5
1		bcd			ade+bcf
2					
3					
4					cde
5					

$[A]^3$

There are two 3-links paths from node 1 to node 5 which are ade and bcf. If we want to find four links paths, we extend this and find $[A]^4$ as given below:

	1	2	3	4	5
1					bcde
2					
3					
4					
5					

$$[A]^4$$

There is only one four links path – bcde, which is from node 1 to node 5. Our main objective is to use the graph matrix to find all paths between all nodes. This can be obtained by summing A, A^2, A^3....A^{n-1}. Hence, for the above examples, many paths are found and are given in Figure 3.28.

One link paths	:	a, b, c, d, e, f, g
Two links paths	:	ad, bc, af, bg, de, cd, cf
Three links paths	:	bcd, ade, bcf, cde
Four links paths	:	bcde

node 1 to node 2	:	ad, bcd
node 1 to node 3	:	a, bc
node 1 to node 4	:	b
node 1 to node 5	:	af, bg, ade, bcf, bcde
node 2 to node 1	:	-
node 2 to node 3	:	-
node 2 to node 4	:	-
node 2 to node 5	:	e
node 3 to node 1	:	-
node 3 to node 2	:	d
node 3 to node 4	:	-
node 3 to node 5	:	f, de
node 4 to node 1	:	-
node 4 to node 2	:	cd
node 4 to node 3	:	c
node 4 to node 5	:	g, cf, cde
node 5 to all other nodes	:	-

Figure 3.28. Various paths of program graph given in Figure 3.26(a)

As the cyclomatic complexity of this graph is 4, there should be 4 independent paths from node 1 (source node) to node 5 (destination node) given as:

Path 1 : af
Path 2 : bg
Path 3 : ade
Path 4 : bcf

Although 5 paths are shown, bcde does not contain any new edge or node. Thus, it cannot be treated as an independent path in this set of paths. This technique is easy to program and can be used easily for designing a testing tool for the calculation of cyclomatic complexity and generation of independent paths.

154 Software Testing

Example 3.10: Consider the program graph shown in Figure 3.29 and draw the graph and connection matrices. Find out the cyclomatic complexity and two/three link paths from a node to any other node.

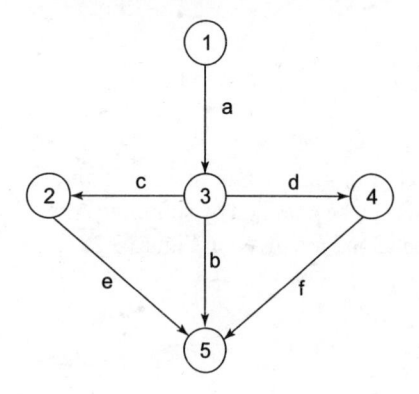

Figure 3.29. Program graph

Solution:

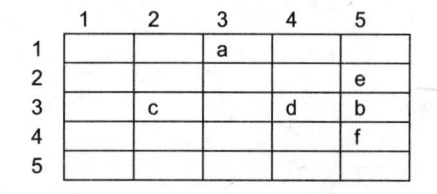

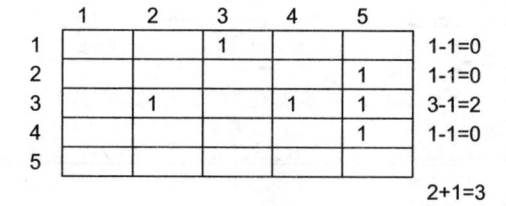

Graph Matrix (A)

	1	2	3	4	5
1			a		
2					e
3		c		d	b
4					f
5					

Connection Matrix

	1	2	3	4	5	
1			1			1-1=0
2					1	1-1=0
3		1		1	1	3-1=2
4					1	1-1=0
5						
						2+1=3

The graph and connection matrices are given below:

Cyclomatic complexity = e-n+2P = 6-5+2= 3

There are 3 regions in the program graph. The formula predicate node+1 (Π+1) is not applicable because predicate node 3 has three outgoing edges.

We generate square and cube matrices for [A]

	1	2	3	4	5
1		ac		ad	ab
2					
3		C		d	ce+df
4					
5					

[A²]

	1	2	3	4	5
1					ace+adf
2					
3					
4					
5					

[A³]

This indicates that there are the following two and three link paths:

Two links paths	ac, ad, ab, ce, df
Three links paths	ace, adf

The independent paths are:

1. ab
2. adf
3. ace

Example 3.11: Consider the DD path graph for determination of division problem shown in Figure 3.30 and draw the graph and connection matrices.

Solution: The graph and connection matrices are given in Figure 3.31 and Figure 3.32 respectively.

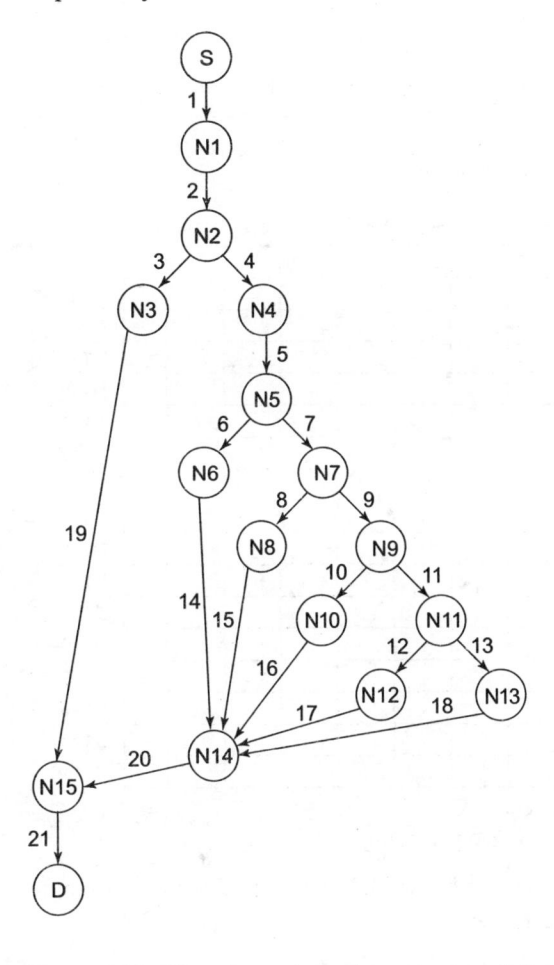

Figure 3.30. DD path graph for determination of division problem

156 Software Testing

	S	N1	N2	N3	N4	N5	N6	N7	N8	N9	N10	N11	N12	N13	N14	N15	D
S	1																
N1		2															
N2			3	4													
N3															19		
N4					5												
N5						6	7										
N6														14			
N7								8	9								
N8														15			
N9										10	11						
N10														16			
N11												12	13				
N12														17			
N13														18			
N14															20		
N15																	21
D																	

Figure 3.31. Graph matrix for determination of division problem

	S	N1	N2	N3	N4	N5	N6	N7	N8	N9	N10	N11	N12	N13	N14	N15	D	
S	1																	1-1=0
N1		1																1-1=0
N2			1	1														2-1=1
N3															1			1-1=0
N4					1													1-1=0
N5						1	1											2-1=1
N6														1				1-1=0
N7								1	1									2-1=1
N8														1				1-1=0
N9										1	1							2-1=1
N10														1				1-1=0
N11												1	1					2-1=1
N12														1				1-1=0
N13														1				1-1=0
N14															1			1-1=0
N15																1		1-1=0
D																		5+1=6

Figure 3.32. Connection matrix for determination of division problem

Example 3.12: Consider the DD path graph shown in Figure 3.33 for classification of triangle problem and draw the graph and connection matrices.

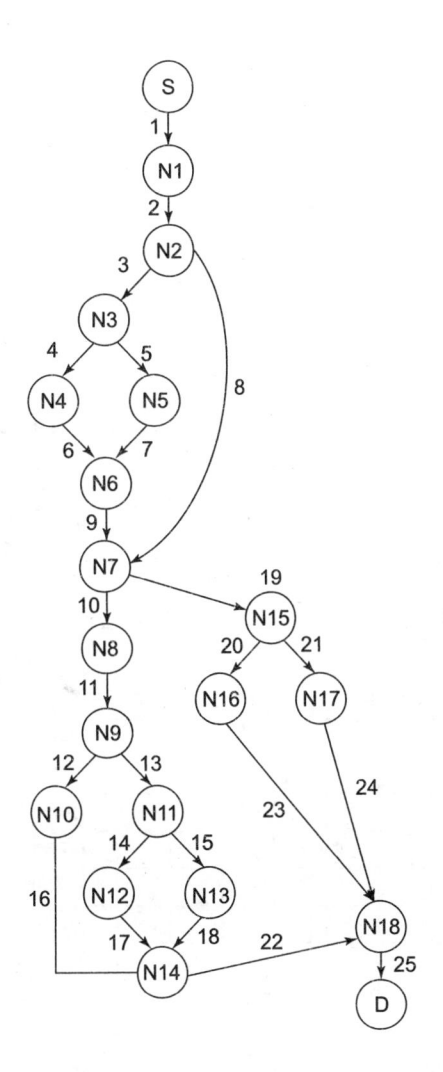

Figure 3.33. DD path graph for classification of triangle problem

Solution:
The graph and connection matrices are shown in Figure 3.34 and Figure 3.35 respectively.

	S	N1	N2	N3	N4	N5	N6	N7	N8	N9	N10	N11	N12	N13	N14	N15	N16	N17	N18	D
S	1																			
N1		2																		
N2			3				8													
N3				4	5															
N4						6														
N5						7														
N6							9													
N7								10							19					

(Contd.)

158 Software Testing

(Contd.)

	S	N1	N2	N3	N4	N5	N6	N7	N8	N9	N10	N11	N12	N13	N14	N15	N16	N17	N18	D
N8										11										
N9											12	13								
N10															16					
N11													14	15						
N12														17						
N13														18						
N14																	22			
N15																20	21			
N16																		23		
N17																		24		
N18																			25	
D																				

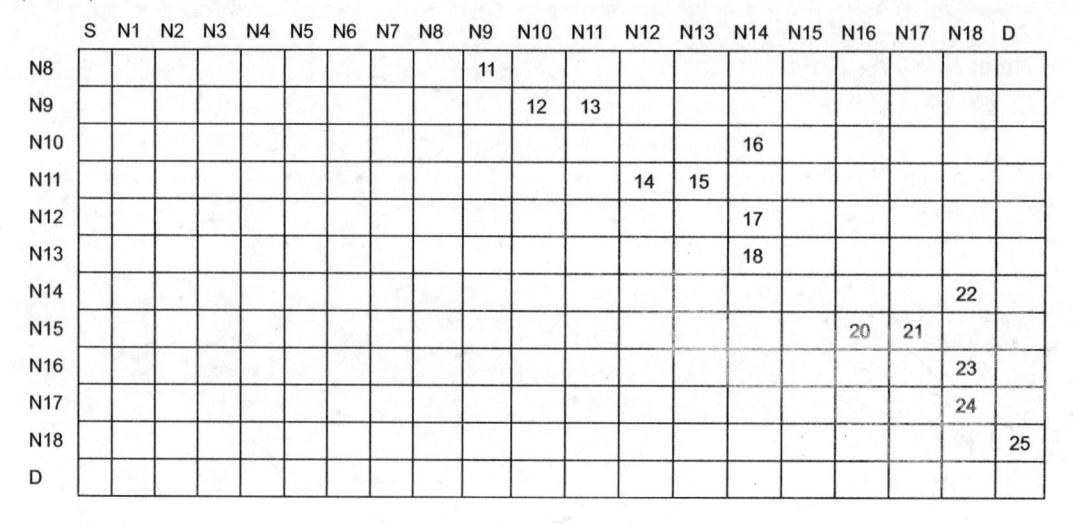

Figure 3.34. Graph matrix for classification of triangle problem

	S	N1	N2	N3	N4	N5	N6	N7	N8	N9	N10	N11	N12	N13	N14	N15	N16	N17	N18	D	
S	1																				1-1=0
N1		1																			1-1=0
N2			1			1															2-1=1
N3				1	1																2-1=1
N4					1																1-1=0
N5					1																1-1=0
N6							1														1-1=0
N7								1							1						2-1=1
N8									1												1-1=0
N9										1	1										2-1=1
N10															1						1-1=0
N11												1	1								2-1=1
N12														1							1-1=0
N13														1							1-1=0
N14																		1			1-1=0
N15																1	1				2-1=1
N16																		1			1-1=0
N17																		1			1-1=0
N18																				1	1-1=0
D																					

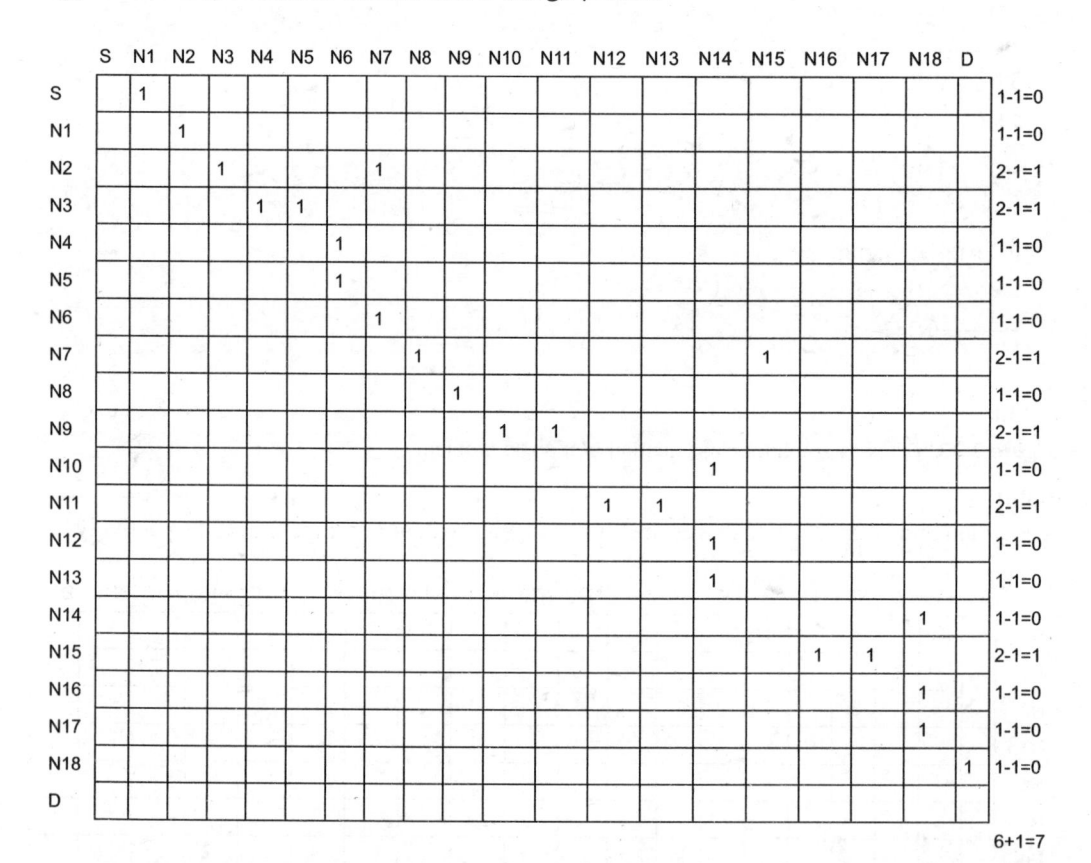

6+1=7

Figure 3.35 Connection matrix for classification of triangle problem

MULTIPLE CHOICE QUESTIONS

Note: *Select the most appropriate answer for the following questions.*

3.1 Cyclomatic complexity is designed by:
   (a) T.J. McCabe
   (b) B.W. Boehm
   (c) Victor Basili
   (d) Bev. Littlewood

3.2 Cyclomatic complexity can be calculated by:
   (a) V(G)= e-n+2P
   (b) V(G)= Π+1
   (c) V(G)= number of regions of the graph
   (d) All of the above

3.3 The cyclomatic complexity equation V(G)= Π+1 is applicable only if every predicate node has:
   (a) Two outgoing edges
   (b) Three or more outgoing edges
   (c) No outgoing edge
   (d) One outgoing edge

3.4 Cyclomatic complexity is equal to:
   (a) Number of paths in a graph
   (b) Number of independent paths in a graph
   (c) Number of edges in a graph
   (d) Number of nodes in a graph

3.5 A node with indegree ≠0 and outdegree =0 is called:
   (a) Source node
   (b) Destination node
   (c) Predicate node
   (d) None of the above

3.6 A node with indegree =0 and outdegree ≠0 is called:
   (a) Source node
   (b) Destination node
   (c) Predicate node
   (d) Transfer node

3.7 An independent path is:
   (a) Any path that has at least one new set of processing statements or new condition
   (b) Any path that has at most one new set of processing statements or new condition
   (c) Any path that has a few set of processing statements and few conditions
   (d) Any path that has feedback connection

3.8 DD path graph is called:
   (a) Defect to defect path graph
   (b) Design to defect path graph
   (c) Decision to decision path graph
   (d) Destination to decision path graph

3.9 Every node in the graph matrix is represented by:
   (a) One row and one column
   (b) Two rows and two columns
   (c) One row and two columns
   (d) Two rows and one column

3.10 The size of graph matrix is:
   (a) Number of edges in the flow graph
   (b) Number of nodes in the flow graph
   (c) Number of paths in the flow graph
   (d) Number of independent paths in the flow graph

3.11 A program with high cyclomatic complexity is:
   (a) Large in size
   (b) Small in size
   (c) Difficult to test
   (d) Easy to test

3.12 Developers may have to take some tough decisions when the cyclomatic complexity is:
   (a) 1
   (b) 5
   (c) 15
   (d) 75

3.13 Every node of a regular graph has:
   (a) Different degrees
   (b) Same degree
   (c) No degree
   (d) None of the above

3.14 The sum of entries of any column of incidence matrix is:
   (a) 2
   (b) 3
   (c) 1
   (d) 4

3.15 The sum of entries of any row of adjacency matrix gives:
   (a) Degree of a node
   (b) Paths in a graph
   (c) Connections in a graph
   (d) None of the above

3.16 The adjacency matrix of a directed graph:
   (a) May have diagonal entries equal to 1
   (b) May be symmetric
   (c) May not be symmetric
   (d) May be difficult to understand

3.17 Length of a path is equal to:
   (a) The number of edges in a graph
   (b) The number of nodes in a graph
   (c) The number of nodes in a path
   (d) The number of edges in a path

3.18 Strongly connected graph will always be:
  (a) Weakly connected
  (b) Large in size
  (c) Small in size
  (d) Loosely connected
3.19 A simple graph has:
  (a) Loops and parallel edges
  (b) No loop and a parallel edge
  (c) At least one loop
  (d) At most one loop
3.20 In a directed graph:
  (a) Edges are the un-ordered pairs of nodes
  (b) Edges are the ordered pairs of nodes
  (c) Edges and nodes are always equal
  (d) Edges and nodes are always same

EXERCISES

3.1 What is a graph? Define a simple graph, multigraph and regular graph with examples.
3.2 How do we calculate degree of a node? What is the degree of an isolated node?
3.3 What is the degree of a node in a directed graph? Explain the significance of indegree and outdegree of a node.
3.4 Consider the following graph and find the degree of every node. Is it a regular graph? Identify source nodes, destination nodes, sequential nodes, predicate nodes and junction nodes in this graph.

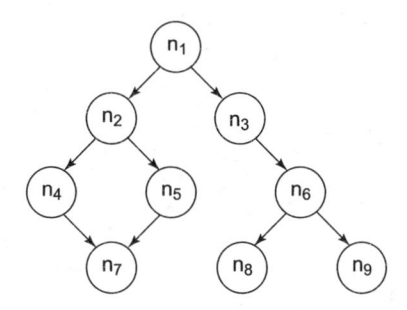

3.5 Consider the graph given in exercise 3.4 and find the following:
  (i) Incidence matrix
  (ii) Adjacency matrix
  (iii) Paths
  (iv) Connectedness
  (v) Cycles
3.6 Define incidence matrix and explain why the sum of entries of any column is always 2. What are various applications of incidence matrix in testing?

3.7 What is the relationship of an adjacency matrix with connection matrix?
3.8 What is a graph matrix? How is it related to a connection matrix?
3.9 Why is adjacency matrix not symmetric in a directed graph? How can we calculate indegree and outdegree of all nodes from the adjacency matrix?
3.10 What is a path? How is it different from an independent path?
3.11 Define the following in a graph:
   (i) Cycles
   (ii) Connectedness
3.12 Consider the following graph:

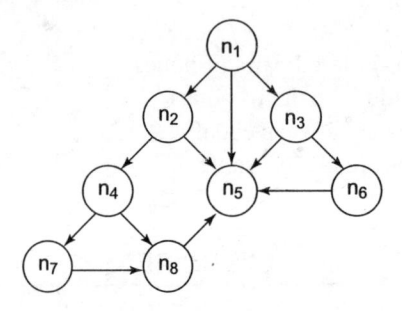

(i) Calculate the degree of every node and identify the cycles.
(ii) Is this graph strongly connected?
(iii) Draw the incidence matrix and adjacency matrix.
(iv) Find all paths.

3.13 What is cyclomatic complexity? Discuss different ways to compute it with examples.
3.14 Explain program graph notations. Use these notations to represent a program graph from a given program.
3.15 Consider the following program segment:
   /* sort takes an integer array and sorts it in ascending order*/

```
1.   void sort (int a [ ], int n) {
2.      int i, j;
3.      for(i=0;i<n-1;i++)
4.         for(i=i+1;j<n;j++)
5.            if(a[i]>a[j])
6.            {
7.               temp=a[i];
8.               a[i]=a[j];
9.               a[j]=temp;
10.           }
11.  }
```

(a) Draw the program graph for this program segment.
(b) Determine the cyclomatic complexity for this program (show the intermediate steps of your computation).
(c) How is the cyclomatic complexity metric useful?

3.16 Consider the following program segment:

```
1.  int find-maximum (int i, int j, int k)
2.  {
3.     int max;
4.     if(i>j) then
5.        if (i<k) then max=i;
6.           else max=k;
7.        else if (j>k) max=j
8.           else max=k
9.     return (max);
10. }
```

(a) Draw the control flow graph for this program segment.
(b) Determine the cyclomatic complexity for this program (show the intermediate steps of your computation).
(c) How is the cyclomatic complexity metric useful?

3.17 Write a program to determine whether a number is even or odd. Draw the program graph and DD path graph. Find the independent paths.

3.18 Consider the following program and draw the program path graph and DD path graph. Also find out cyclomatic complexity and independent paths.

```
void main ( )
{
    int x, y;
    scanf ("%d \n", &x);
    scanf ("%d \n", &y);
    while (x ! = y)
    {
      if (x > y)
         x = x - y;
      else y = y - x;
    }
    printf ("x = %d", x);
}
```

3.19 What are differences between a directed graph and un-directed graph? Which one is more relevant in software testing and why?

3.20 How do we define the connectedness of a graph? Why every strongly connected graph is also called weakly connected graph?

FURTHER READING

An early work on graph models of programs can be found in:
    C.V. Ramamoorthy, "Analysis of Graphs by Connectivity Considerations", Journal of the ACM, vol. 13, pp. 211–222, 1966.

The book by Veerarajan is an excellent text with an exhaustive number of examples:
    T. Veerarajan, "Discrete Mathematics with Graph Theory and Combinatorics", McGraw Hill, 2007.

Other similar books include:

- F. Harary, "Graph Theory", Addison-Wesley, 1969.
- W. Mayeda, "Graph Theory", John Wiley and Sons, New York, 1972.
- F. Harary, P. Frank; M. Edgar, "Graphical Enumeration", Academic Press, New York, 1973.
- M. Golumbic, "Algorithmic Graph Theory and Perfect Graphs", Academic Press, 1980.
- G. Chartrand, "Introductory Graph Theory", Dover, 1985.
- A. Gibbons, "Algorithmic Graph Theory", Cambridge University Press, 1985.
- N. Biggs, E. Lloyd, R. Wilson, "Graph Theory", Oxford University Press, 1986.
- Jonathan L Gross, and Jay Yellen, "Graph Theory and Its Applications", CRC Press, 1999.
- Jonathan L Gross, and Jay Yellen, "Handbook of Graph Theory", CRC Press, 2003.
- J.A. Bondy, U.S.R Murty,."Graph Theory", Springer, 2008.

The following paper gives a method for constructing a flow graph of a given function and determining the set of basis paths:

- Joseph Poole, "A Method to Determine a Basis Set of Paths to Perform Program Testing", NIST, 1991.

A classic paper that describes a graph-based complexity measure and illustrates how this measure can be used to compute program complexity is:

- T. McCabe, "A Complexity Measure", IEEE Transactions on Software Engineering, vol. 2, no. 4, pp. 308–320, December 1976.

Myers discussed several anomalies of the complexity measure where a program with low complexity gives high values of complexity measure:

- G. Myers, "An Extension to the Cyclomatic Measure of Program Complexity", SIGPLAN Notices, October 1977.

This excellent NIST report describes basis path testing using McCabe's cyclomatic complexity measure:

- Arthur H. Watson and Thomas J. McCabe, "Structured Testing: A Testing Methodology using the Cyclomatic Complexity Metric", NIST, September 1996.

For an introduction on graph matrix one may consult:

- B. Beizer, "Software Testing Techniques", The Coriolis Group, Inc, 1990.

4

Structural Testing

Structural testing is considered more technical than functional testing. It attempts to design test cases from the source code and not from the specifications. The source code becomes the base document which is examined thoroughly in order to understand the internal structure and other implementation details. It also gives insight in to the source code which may be used as an essential knowledge for the design of test cases. Structural testing techniques are also known as white box testing techniques due to consideration of internal structure and other implementation details of the program. Many structural testing techniques are available and some of them are given in this chapter like control flow testing, data flow testing, slice based testing and mutation testing.

4.1 CONTROL FLOW TESTING

This technique is very popular due to its simplicity and effectiveness. We identify paths of the program and write test cases to execute those paths. As we all know, path is a sequence of statements that begins at an entry and ends at an exit. As shown in chapter 1, there may be too many paths in a program and it may not be feasible to execute all of them. As the number of decisions increase in the program, the number of paths also increase accordingly.

Every path covers a portion of the program. We define 'coverage' as a 'percentage of source code that has been tested with respect to the total source code available for testing'. We may like to achieve a reasonable level of coverage using control flow testing. The most reasonable level may be to test every statement of a program at least once before the completion of testing. Hence, we may write test cases that ensure the execution of every statement. If we do so, we have some satisfaction about reasonable level of coverage. If we stop testing without achieving this level (every statement execution), we do unacceptable and intolerable activity which may lead to dangerous results in future. Testing techniques based on program coverage criterion may provide an insight about the effectiveness of test cases. Some of such techniques are discussed which are part of control flow testing.

4.1.1 Statement Coverage

We want to execute every statement of the program in order to achieve 100% statement coverage. Consider the following portion of a source code along with its program graph given in Figure 4.1.

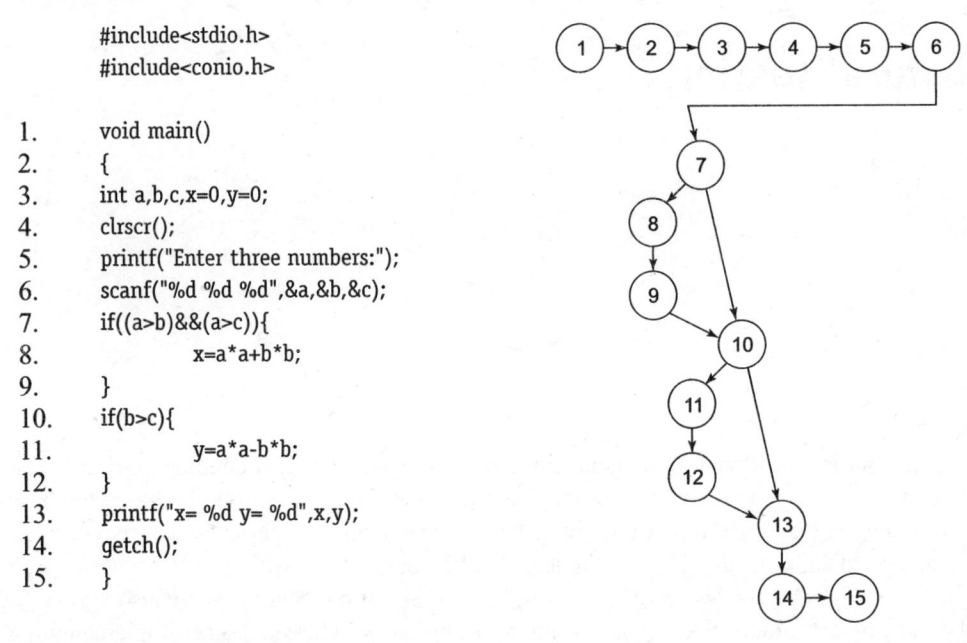

```
#include<stdio.h>
#include<conio.h>

1.   void main()
2.   {
3.      int a,b,c,x=0,y=0;
4.      clrscr();
5.      printf("Enter three numbers:");
6.      scanf("%d %d %d",&a,&b,&c);
7.      if((a>b)&&(a>c)){
8.         x=a*a+b*b;
9.      }
10.     if(b>c){
11.        y=a*a-b*b;
12.     }
13.     printf("x= %d y= %d",x,y);
14.     getch();
15.  }
```

Figure 4.1. Source code with program graph

If, we select inputs like:

a=9, b=8, c=7, all statements are executed and we have achieved 100% statement coverage by only one test case. The total paths of this program graph are given as:

(i) 1–7, 10, 13–15
(ii) 1–7, 10–15
(iii) 1–10, 13–15
(iv) 1–15

The cyclomatic complexity of this graph is:

$V(G) = e - n + 2P = 16 - 15 + 2 = 3$

$V(G) = $ no. of regions $= 3$

$V(G) = \Pi + 1 = 2 + 1 = 3$

Hence, independent paths are three and are given as:

(i) 1–7, 10, 13–15
(ii) 1–7, 10–15
(iii) 1–10, 13–15

Only one test case may cover all statements but will not execute all possible four paths and not even cover all independent paths (three in this case).

The objective of achieving 100% statement coverage is difficult in practice. A portion of the program may execute in exceptional circumstances and some conditions are rarely possible, and the affected portion of the program due to such conditions may not execute at all.

4.1.2 Branch Coverage

We want to test every branch of the program. Hence, we wish to test every 'True' and 'False' condition of the program. We consider the program given in Figure 4.1. If we select a = 9, b = 8, c = 7, we achieve 100% statement coverage and the path followed is given as (all true conditions):

Path = 1–15

We also want to select all false conditions with the following inputs:

a = 7, b = 8, c = 9, the path followed is
Path = 1–7, 10, 13–15

These two test cases out of four are sufficient to guarantee 100% branch coverage. The branch coverage does not guarantee 100% path coverage but it does guarantee 100% statement coverage.

4.1.3 Condition Coverage

Condition coverage is better than branch coverage because we want to test every condition at least once. However, branch coverage can be achieved without testing every condition.

Consider the seventh statement of the program given in Figure 4.1. The statement number 7 has two conditions (a>b) and (a>c). There are four possibilities namely:

(i) Both are true
(ii) First is true, second is false
(iii) First is false, second is true
(iv) Both are false

If a > b and a > c, then the statement number 7 will be true (first possibility). However, if a < b, then second condition (a > c) would not be tested and statement number 7 will be false (third and fourth possibilities). If a > b and a < c, statement number 7 will be false (second possibility). Hence, we should write test cases for every true and false condition. Selected inputs may be given as:

(i) a = 9, b = 8, c = 7 (first possibility when both are true)
(ii) a = 9, b = 8, c = 10 (second possibility – first is true, second is false)
(iii) a = 7, b = 8, c = 9 (third and fourth possibilities- first is false, statement number 7 is false)

Hence, these three test cases out of four are sufficient to ensure the execution of every condition of the program.

4.1.4 Path Coverage

In this coverage criteria, we want to test every path of the program. There are too many paths in any program due to loops and feedback connections. It may not be possible to achieve this goal of executing all paths in many programs. If we do so, we may be confident about the correctness of the program. If it is unachievable, at least all independent paths should be executed. The program given in Figure 4.1 has four paths as given as:

(i) 1–7, 10, 13–15
(ii) 1–7, 10–15
(iii) 1–10, 13–15
(iv) 1–15

Execution of all these paths increases confidence about the correctness of the program. Inputs for test cases are given as:

S. No.	Paths Id.	Paths	Inputs a	Inputs b	Inputs c	Expected Output
1.	Path-1	1–7,10, 13–15	7	8	9	x=0 y=0
2.	Path-2	1–7, 10–15	7	8	6	x=0 y=–15
3.	Path-3	1–10, 13–15	9	7	8	x=130 y=0
4.	Path-4	1–15	9	8	7	x=145 y=17

Some paths are possible from the program graph, but become impossible when we give inputs as per logic of the program. Hence, some combinations may be found to be impossible to create.

Path testing guarantee statement coverage, branch coverage and condition coverage. However, there are many paths in any program and it may not be possible to execute all the paths. We should do enough testing to achieve a reasonable level of coverage. We should execute at least (minimum level) all independent paths which are also referred to as basis paths to achieve reasonable coverage. These paths can be found using any method of cyclomatic complexity.

We have to decide our own coverage level before starting control flow testing. As we go up (statement coverage to path coverage) in the ladder, more resources and time may be required.

Example 4.1: Consider the program for the determination of the division of a student. The program and its program graph are given in Figure 3.15 and 3.16 of chapter 3 respectively. Derive test cases so that 100% path coverage is achieved.

Solution:
The test cases are given in Table 4.1.

Table 4.1. Test cases

S. No.	mark1	mark2	mark3	Expected output	Paths
1.	30	–1	20	Invalid marks	1–14, 33, 34
2.	40	20	45	Fail	1–12, 15–19, 32, 33,34
3.	45	47	50	Third division	1–13, 15–17, 20–22, 32–34
4.	55	60	57	Second division	1–12, 15–17, 20, 23, 26–28, 32–34
5.	65	70	75	First division	1–12, 15–17, 20, 23, 26–28,32–34
6.	80	85	90	First division with distinction	1–12, 15–17, 20, 23, 26, 29–34

Example 4.2: Consider the program and program graph given below. Derive test cases so that 100% statement coverage and path coverage is achieved.

```
     /*Program to validate input data*/
     #include<stdio.h>
     #include<string.h>
     #include<conio.h>
1.   void main()
2.   {
3.       char fname[30],address[100],Email[100];
4.       int valid=1,flag=1;
5.       clrscr();
6.       printf("Enter first name:");
7.       scanf("%s",fname);
8.       printf("\nEnter address:");
9.       scanf("%s",address);
10.      printf("\nEnter Email:");
11.      scanf("%s",Email);
12.      if(strlen(fname)<4||strlen(fname)>30){
13.          printf("\nInvalid first name");
14.          valid=0;
15.      }
16.      if(strlen(address)<4||strlen(address)>100){
17.          printf("\nInvalid address length");
18.          valid=0;
19.      }
20.      if(strlen(Email)<8||strlen(Email)>100){
21.          printf("\nInvalid Email length");
22.          flag=0;
23.          valid=0;
24.      }
25.      if(flag==1){
26.          if(strchr(Email,'.')==0||strchr(Email,'@')==0){
27.              printf("\nEmail must contain . and @ characters");
28.              valid=0;
29.          }
30.      }
31.      if(valid) {
32.          printf("\nFirst name: %s \t Address: %s \t Email: %s",fname,address,Email);
33.      }
34.      getch();
35.  }
```

170 Software Testing

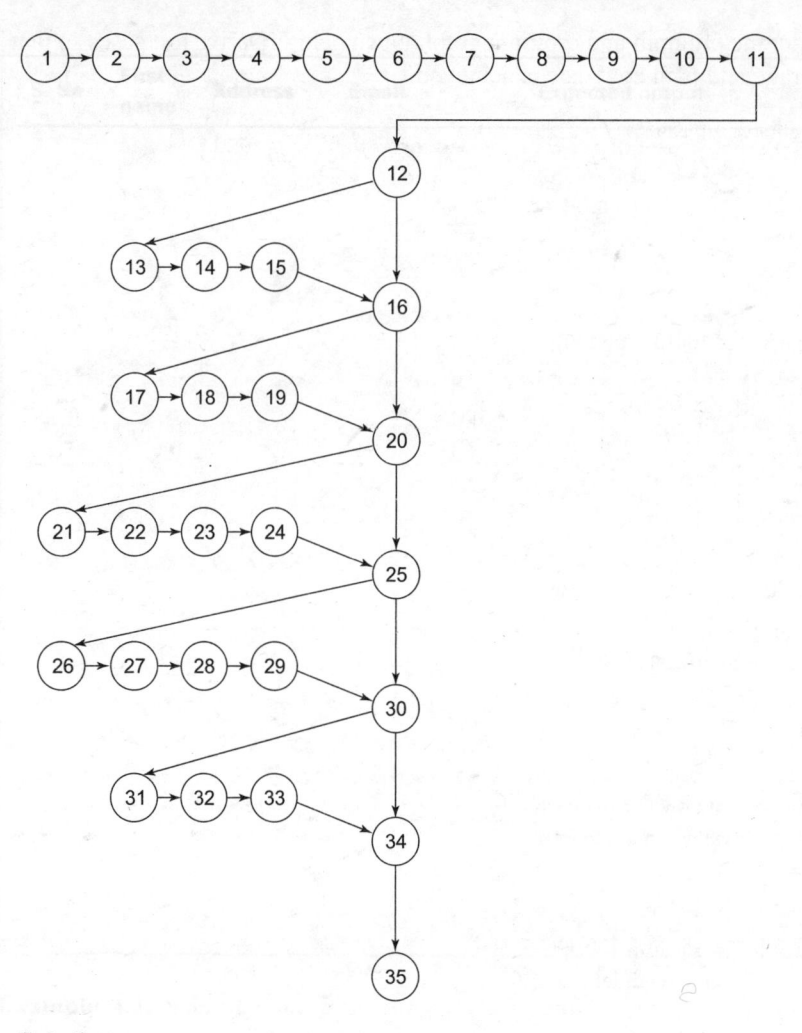

```
1 → 2 → 3 → 4 → 5 → 6 → 7 → 8 → 9 → 10 → 11
                        ↓
                       12
         13 → 14 → 15  ↓
                       16
         17 → 18 → 19  ↓
                       20
    21 → 22 → 23 → 24  ↓
                       25
26 → 27 → 28 → 29      ↓
                       30
    31 → 32 → 33       ↓
                       34
                       ↓
                       35
```

Solution:
The test cases to guarantee 100% statement and branch coverage are given in Table 4.2.

Table 4.2. Test cases for statement coverage

S. No.	First name	Address	Email	Expected output	Paths
1.	ashok	E-29, east-ofkailash	abc@yahoo.com	First name: ashok Address: E-29, east-ofkailash Email: abc@yahoo.com	1–12, 16, 20, 25, 31–35
2.	ruc	E29	abc	Invalid first name Invalid address length Invalid email length	1–25, 30, 31, 34, 35
3.	ruc	E-29	abc@yahoocom	Invalid first name Invalid address length Email must contain . and @ character	1–20, 25–31, 34, 35

(Contd.)

Total paths of the program graph are given in Table 4.3.

Table 4.3. Test cases for path coverage

S. No.	First name	Address	Email	Expected output	Paths
1.	-	-	-	-	1–35
2.	-	-	-	-	1–30, 34,35
3.	-	-	-	-	1–25, 30–35
4.	ruc	E29	abc	Invalid first name Invalid address length Invalid email length	1–25, 30, 31, 34, 35
5.	-	-	-	-	1–20, 25–35
6.	ruc	E-29	abc@yahoocom	Invalid first name Invalid address length Email must contain . and @ character	1–20, 25–31, 34, 35
7.	-	-	-	-	1–20, 25, 30–35
8.	ruc	E-29	Abs@yahoo.com	Invalid first name Invalid address length	1–20, 25, 30, 31, 34, 35
9.	-	-	-	-	1–16, 20–35
10.	-	-	-	-	1–16, 20–31, 34, 35
11.	-	-	-	-	1–16, 20–25, 30–35
12.	ruc	E-29, east-ofkailash	Abs	Invalid first name Invalid email length	1–16, 20–25, 30, 31, 34, 35
13.	-	-	-	-	1–16, 20, 25–35
14.	ruc	E-29, east-ofkailash	abc@yahoocom	Invalid first name Email must contain . and @ character	1–16, 20, 25–31, 34, 35
15.	-	-	-	-	1–16, 20, 25, 31–35
16.	ruc	E-29, east-ofkailash	abc@yahoo.com	Invalid first name	1–16, 20, 25, 30, 31, 34, 35
17.	-	-	-	-	1–12, 16–35
18.	-	-	-	-	1–12, 16–31, 34,35
19.	-	-	-	-	1–12, 16–25, 30–35
20.	ashok	E29	Abc	Invalid address length Invalid email length	1–12, 16–25, 30, 31, 34, 35
21.	-	-	-	-	1–12, 16–20, 25–35

(Contd.)

(Contd.)

S. No.	First name	Address	Email	Expected output	Paths
22.	ashok	E29	abc@yahoocom	Invalid address length Email must contain . and @ character	1-12, 16-20, 25-31, 34, 35
23.	-	-	-	-	1-12, 16-20, 25, 30-35
24.	ashok	E29	abc@yahoo.com	Invalid address length	1-12, 16-20, 25, 30, 31, 34, 35
25.	-	-	-	-	1-12, 16, 20-35
26.	-	-	-	-	1-12, 16, 20-31, 34, 35
27.	-	-	-	-	1-12, 16, 20-25, 30-35
28.	ashok	E-29, east-ofkailash	Abs	Invalid email length	1-12, 16, 20-25, 30, 31, 34, 35
29.	-	-	-	-	1-12, 16, 20, 25-35
30.	ashok	E-29, east-ofkailash	Abcyahoo.com	Email must contain . and @ character	1-12, 16, 20, 25-31, 34, 35
31.	ashok	E-29, east-ofkailash	abc@yahoo.com	First name: ashok Address: E-29, east-ofkailash Email: abc@yahoo.com	1-12, 16, 20, 25, 31-35
32.	-	-	-	-	1-12, 16, 20, 25, 30, 31, 34, 35

Example 4.3: Consider the program for classification of a triangle given in Figure 3.10. Derive test cases so that 100% statement coverage and path coverage is achieved.

Solution:

The test cases to guarantee 100% statement and branch coverage are given in Table 4.4.

Table 4.4. Test cases for statement coverage

S. No.	a	b	c	Expected output	Paths
1.	30	20	40	Obtuse angled triangle	1-16,20-27,34,41,42
2.	30	40	50	Right angled triangle	1-16,20-25,28-30,34,41,42
3.	40	50	60	Acute angled triangle	1-6,20-25,28,31-34,41,42
4.	30	10	15	Invalid triangle	1-14,17-21,35-37,41,42
5.	102	50	60	Input values out of range	1-13,21,35,38,39,40-42

Total paths of the program graph are given in Table 4.5.

Table 4.5. Test cases for path coverage

S. No.	a	b	c	Expected output	Paths
1.	102	−1	6	Input values out of range	1−13,21,35,38,39,40−42
2.	-	-	-	-	1−14,17−19,20,21,35,38,39,40−42
3.	-	-	-	-	1−16,20,21,35,38,39,40−42
4.	-	-	-	-	1−13,21,35,36,37,41,42
5.	30	10	15	Invalid triangle	1−14,17−21,35−37,41,42
6.	-	-	-	-	1−16,20,21,35−37,41,42
7.	-	-	-	-	1−13,21−25,28,31−34,41,42
8.	-	-	-	-	1−14,17−25,28,31−34,41,42
9.	40	50	60	Acute angled triangle	1−16,20−25,28,31−34,41,42
10.	-	-	-	-	1−13,21−25,28−30,34,41,42
11.	-	-	-	-	1−14,17−25,28−30,34,41,42
12.	30	40	50	Right angled triangle	1−16,20−25,28−30,34,41,42
13.	-	-	-	-	1−13,21−27,34,41,42
14.	-	-	-	-	1−14,17−27,34,41,42
15.	30	20	40	Obtuse angled triangle	1−16,20−27,34,41,42

Thus, there are 15 paths, out of which 10 paths are not possible to be executed as per the logic of the program.

4.2 DATA FLOW TESTING

In control flow testing, we find various paths of a program and design test cases to execute those paths. We may like to execute every statement of the program at least once before the completion of testing. Consider the following program:

```
1. # include < stdio.h>
2. void main ()
3. {
4.   int a, b, c;
5.   a = b + c;
6.   printf ("%d", a);
7. }
```

What will be the output? The value of 'a' may be the previous value stored in the memory location assigned to variable 'a' or a garbage value. If we execute the program, we may get an unexpected value (garbage value). The mistake is in the usage (reference) of this variable without first assigning a value to it. We may assume that all variables are automatically assigned to zero initially. This does not happen always. If we define at line number 4, 'static int a, b, c', then all variables are given zero value initially. However, this is a language and compiler dependent feature and may not be generalized.

Data flow testing may help us to minimize such mistakes. It has nothing to do with data-flow diagrams. It is based on variables, their usage and their definition(s) (assignment) in the program. The main points of concern are:

(i) Statements where variables receive values (definition).
(ii) Statements where these values are used (referenced).

Data flow testing focuses on variable definition and variable usage. In line number 5 of the above program, variable 'a' is defined and variables 'b' and 'c' are used. The variables are defined and used (referenced) throughout the program. Hence, this technique concentrates on how a variable is defined and used at different places of the program.

4.2.1 Define/Reference Anomalies

Some of the define / reference anomalies are given as:

(i) A variable is defined but never used / referenced.
(ii) A variable is used but never defined.
(iii) A variable is defined twice before it is used.
(iv) A variable is used before even first-definition.

We may define a variable, use a variable and redefine a variable. So, a variable must be first defined before any type of its usage. Define / reference anomalies may be identified by static analysis of the program i.e. analyzing program without executing it. This technique uses the program graphs to understand the 'define / use' conditions of all variables. Some terms are used frequently in data flow testing and such terms are discussed in the next sub-section.

4.2.2 Definitions

A program is first converted into a program graph. As we all know, every statement of a program is replaced by a node and flow of control by an edge to prepare a program graph. There may be many paths in the program graph.

(i) **Defining node**
A node of a program graph is a defining node for a variable v, if and only if, the value of the variable v is defined in the statement corresponding to that node. It is represented as DEF (v, n) where v is the variable and n is the node corresponding to the statement in which v is defined.

(ii) **Usage node**
A node of a program graph is a usage node for a variable v, if and only if, the value of the variable v is used in the statement corresponding to that node. It is represented as USE (v, n), where 'v' is the variable and 'n' in the node corresponding to the statement in which 'v' is used.
A usage node USE (v, n) is a predicate use node (denoted as P-use), if and only if, the statement corresponding to node 'n' is a predicate statement otherwise USE (v, n) is a computation use node (denoted as C-use).

(iii) **Definition use Path**
A definition use path (denoted as du-path) for a variable 'v' is a path between two nodes 'm' and 'n' where 'm' is the initial node in the path but the defining node for variable 'v' (denoted as DEF (v, m)) and 'n' is the final node in the path but usage node for variable 'v' (denoted as USE (v, n)).

(iv) **Definition clear path**
A definition clear path (denoted as dc-path) for a variable 'v' is a definition use path with initial and final nodes DEF (v, m) and USE (v, n) such that no other node in the path is a defining node of variable 'v'.

The du-paths and dc-paths describe the flow of data across program statements from statements where values are defined to statements where the values are used. A du-path for a variable 'v' may have many redefinitions of variable 'v' between initial node (DEF (v, m)) and final node (USE (v, n)). A dc-path for a variable 'v' will not have any definition of variable 'v' between initial node (DEF (v, m)) and final node (USE (v, n)). The du-paths that are not definition clear paths are potential troublesome paths. They should be identified and tested on topmost priority.

4.2.3 Identification of du and dc Paths

The various steps for the identification of du and dc paths are given as:

(i) Draw the program graph of the program.
(ii) Find all variables of the program and prepare a table for define / use status of all variables using the following format:

S. No.	Variable(s)	Defined at node	Used at node

(iii) Generate all du-paths from define/use variable table of step (iii) using the following format:

S. No.	Variable	du-path(begin, end)

(iv) Identify those du-paths which are not dc-paths.

4.2.4 Testing Strategies Using du-Paths

We want to generate test cases which trace every definition to each of its use and every use is traced to each of its definition. Some of the testing strategies are given as:

(i) **Test all du-paths**
All du-paths generated for all variables are tested. This is the strongest data flow testing strategy covering all possible du-paths.

(ii) Test all uses

Find at least one path from every definition of every variable to every use of that variable which can be reached by that definition.

For every use of a variable, there is a path from the definition of that variable to the use of that variable.

(iii) Test all definitions

Find paths from every definition of every variable to at least one use of that variable; we may choose any strategy for testing. As we go from 'test all du-paths' (no. (i)) to 'test all definitions' (no.(iii)), the number of paths are reduced. However, it is best to test all du-paths (no. (i)) and give priority to those du-paths which are not definition clear paths. The first requires that each definition reaches all possible uses through all possible du-paths, the second requires that each definition reaches all possible uses, and the third requires that each definition reaches at least one use.

4.2.5 Generation of Test Cases

After finding paths, test cases are generated by giving values to the input parameter. We get different test suites for each variable.

Consider the program given in Figure 3.11 to find the largest number amongst three numbers. Its program graph is given in Figure 3.12. There are three variables in the program namely A, B and C. Define /use nodes for all these variables are given below:

S. No.	Variable	Defined at node	Used at node
1.	A	6	11, 12, 13
2.	B	8	11, 20, 24
3.	C	10	12, 16, 20, 21

The du-paths with beginning node and end node are given as:

Variable	du-path (Begin, end)
A	6, 11 6, 12 6, 13
B	8, 11 8, 20 8, 24
C	10, 12 10, 16 10, 20 10, 21

The first strategy (best) is to test all du-paths, the second is to test all uses and the third is to test all definitions. The du-paths as per these three strategies are given as:

Structural Testing

	Paths	Definition clear?
All	6-11	Yes
du paths	6-12	Yes
and	6-13	Yes
all uses	8-11	Yes
(Both are same in this	8-11, 19, 20	Yes
example)	8-11, 19, 20, 23, 24	Yes
	10-12	Yes
	10-12, 15, 16	Yes
	10, 11, 19, 20	Yes
	10, 11, 19-21	Yes
All definitions	6-11	Yes
	8-11	Yes
	10-12	Yes

Here all du-paths and all-uses paths are the same (10 du-paths). But in the 3rd case, for all definitions, there are three paths.

Test cases are given below:

Test all du-paths

S. No.	Inputs A	Inputs B	Inputs C	Expected Output	Remarks
1.	9	8	7	9	6-11
2.	9	8	7	9	6-12
3.	9	8	7	9	6-13
4.	7	9	8	9	8-11
5.	7	9	8	9	8-11, 19, 20
6.	7	9	8	9	8-11, 19, 20, 23, 24
7.	8	7	9	9	10-12
8.	8	7	9	9	10-12, ,15, 16
9.	7	8	9	9	10, 11, 19, 20
10.	7	8	9	9	10, 11, 19-21

Test All definitions

S. No.	Inputs A	Inputs B	Inputs C	Expected Output	Remarks
1.	9	8	7	9	6-11
2.	7	9	8	9	8-11
3.	8	7	9	9	10-12

In this example all du-paths and all uses yield the same number of paths. This may not always be true. If we consider the following graph and find du paths with all three strategies, we will get a different number of all-du paths and all-uses paths.

178　Software Testing

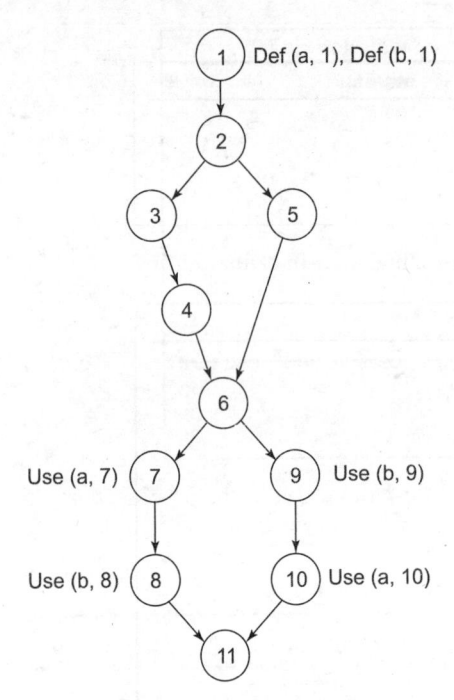

```
        (1) Def (a, 1), Def (b, 1)
         |
        (2)
        / \
      (3) (5)
       |   |
      (4)  |
        \ /
        (6)
        / \
Use(a,7)(7) (9) Use (b, 9)
        |   |
Use(b,8)(8)(10) Use (a, 10)
        \ /
        (11)
```

Def/Use nodes table

S. No.	Variables	Defined at node	Used at node
1.	a	1	7, 10
2.	b	1	8, 9

The du paths are identified as:

S. No.	Variables	du-paths (Begin, end)
1.	a	1, 7
		1, 10
2.	b	1, 8
		1, 9

The du-paths are identified as per three testing strategies:

	Paths	Definition clear?
All du paths	1–4, 6, 7	Yes
(8 paths)	1, 2, 5–7	Yes
	1–4, 6, 9, 10	Yes
	1, 2, 5, 6, 9, 10	Yes
	1–4, 6, 7, 8	Yes
	1, 2, 5–8	Yes
	1–4, 6, 9	Yes
	1, 2, 5, 6, 9	Yes

(Contd.)

(Contd.)

	Paths	Definition clear?
All uses (4 paths)	1-4, 6, 7	Yes
	1-4, 6, 9, 10	Yes
	1-4, 6-8	Yes
	1-4, 6, 9	Yes
All definitions (2 paths)	1-4, 6, 7	Yes
	1-4, 6-8	Yes

Hence the number of paths is different in all testing strategies. When we find all du-paths, some paths may become impossible paths. We show them in order to show all combinations.

Example 4.4: Consider the program for the determination of the division problem. Its input is a triple of positive integers (mark1, mark2, mark3) and values for each of these may be from interval [0, 100]. The program is given in Figure 3.15. The output may have one of the options given below:

(i) Fail
(ii) Third division
(iii) Second division
(iv) First division
(v) First division with distinction
(vi) Invalid marks

Find all du-paths and identify those du-paths that are definition clear. Also find all du-paths, all-uses and all-definitions and generate test cases for these paths.

Solution:

(i) The program graph is given in Figure 3.16. The variables used in the program are mark1, mark2, mark3, avg.
(ii) The define/ use nodes for all variables are given below:

S. No.	Variable	Defined at node	Used at node
1.	mark1	7	12, 16
2.	mark2	9	12, 16
3.	mark3	11	12, 16
4.	avg	16	17, 20, 23, 26

(iii) The du-paths with beginning and ending nodes are given as:

S. No.	Variable	Du-path (begin, end)
1.	mark1	7, 12
		7, 16
2.	mark2	9, 12
		9, 16
3.	mark3	11, 12
		11, 16

(Contd.)

(Contd.)

S. No.	Variable	Du-path (begin, end)
4.	Avg	16, 17
		16, 20
		16, 23
		16, 26

(iv) All du-paths, all-uses and all-definitions are given below:

	Paths	Definition clear?
All du-paths and all-uses	7–12	Yes
	7–12, 15, 16	Yes
	9–12	Yes
	9–12, 15, 16	Yes
	11, 12	Yes
	11, 12, 15, 16	Yes
	16, 17	Yes
	16, 17, 20	Yes
	16, 17, 20, 23	Yes
	16, 17, 20, 23, 26	Yes
All definitions	7–12	Yes
	9–12	Yes
	11, 12	Yes
	16, 17	Yes

Test cases for all du-paths and all-uses are given in Table 4.6 and test cases for all definitions are given in Table 4.7.

Table 4.6. Test cases for all du-paths and all-uses

S. No.	mark1	mark2	mark3	Expected Output	Remarks
1.	101	50	50	Invalid marks	7–12
2.	60	50	40	Second division	7–12, 15, 16
3.	50	101	50	Invalid marks	9–12
4.	60	70	80	First division	9–12, 15, 16
5.	50	50	101	Invalid marks	11, 12
6.	60	75	80	First division	11, 12, 15, 16
7.	30	40	30	Fail	16, 17
8.	45	50	50	Third division	16, 17, 20
9.	55	60	50	Second division	16, 17, 20, 23
10.	65	70	70	First division	16, 17, 20, 23, 26

Table 4.7. Test cases for all definitions

S. No.	mark1	mark2	mark3	Expected Output	Remarks
1.	101	50	50	Invalid marks	7–12
2.	50	101	50	Invalid marks	9–12
3.	50	50	101	Invalid marks	11, 12
4.	30	40	30	Fail	16, 17

Example 4.5: Consider the program of classification of a triangle. Its input is a triple of positive integers (a, b and c) and values for each of these may be from interval [0, 100]. The program is given in Figure 3.18. The output may have one of the options given below:

(i) Obtuse angled triangle
(ii) Acute angled triangle
(iii) Right angled triangle
(iv) Invalid triangle
(v) Input values out of range

Find all du-paths and identify those du-paths that are definition clear. Also find all du-paths, all-uses and all definitions and generate test cases from them.

Solution:

(i) The program graph is given in Figure 3.19. The variables used are a, b, c, a1, a2, a3, valid.

(ii) Define / use nodes for all variables are given below:

S. No.	Variable	Defined at node	Used at node
1.	a	8	13, 14, 22, 23, 24
2.	b	10	13, 14, 22, 23, 24
3.	c	12	13, 14, 22-24
4.	a1	22	25. 28
5.	a2	23	25, 28
6.	a3	24	25, 28
7.	valid	5, 15, 18	21, 35

(iii) The du-paths with beginning and ending nodes are given as:

S. No.	Variable	du-path (Begin, end)
1.	a	8, 13
		8, 14
		8, 22
		8, 23
		8, 24
2.	b	10, 13
		10, 14
		10, 22
		10, 23
		10, 24
3.	c	12, 13
		12, 14
		12, 22
		12, 23
		12, 24
4.	a1	22. 25
		22, 28

(Contd.)

(Contd.)

S. No.	Variable	du-path (Begin, end)
5.	a2	23, 25
		23, 28
6.	a3	24, 25
		24, 28
7.	Valid	5, 21
		5, 35
		15, 21
		15, 35
		18, 21
		18, 35

All du-paths are given in Table 4.8 and the test cases for all du-paths are given in Table 4.9.

Table 4.8. All du-paths

All du-paths	Definition clear?	All du paths	Definition clear?
8–13	Yes	12–14, 17–22	Yes
8–14	Yes	12, 13, 21, 22	Yes
8–16, 20–22	Yes	12–16, 20–23	Yes
8–14, 17–22	Yes	12–14, 17–23	Yes
8–13, 21,22	Yes	12, 13, 21–23	Yes
8–16, 20–23	Yes	12–16, 20–24	Yes
8–14, 17–23	Yes	12–14, 17–24	Yes
8–13, 21–23	Yes	12, 13, 21–24	Yes
8–16, 20–24	Yes	22–25	Yes
8–14, 17–24	Yes	22–25, 28	Yes
8–13, 21–24	Yes	23–25	Yes
10–13	Yes	23–25, 28	Yes
10–14	Yes	24, 25	Yes
10–16, 20–22	Yes	24, 25, 28	Yes
10–14, 17–22	Yes	5–16, 20, 21	No
10–13, 21,22	Yes	5–14, 17–21	No
10–16, 20–23	Yes	5–13, 21	Yes
10–14, 17–23	Yes	5–16, 20, 21, 35	No
10–13, 21–23	Yes	5–14, 17–21, 35	No
10–16, 20–24	Yes	5–13, 21, 35	Yes
10–14, 17–24	Yes	15, 16, 20, 21	Yes
10–13, 21–24	Yes	15, 16, 20, 21, 35	Yes
12, 13	Yes	18–21	Yes
12–14	Yes	18–21, 35	Yes
12–16, 20–22	Yes		

We consider all combinations for the design of du-paths. In this process, test cases corresponding to some paths are not possible, but these paths are shown in the list of 'all du-paths'. They may be considered only for completion purpose.

Table 4.9. Test cases for all du-paths

S. No.	A	b	c	Expected output	Remarks
1.	30	20	40	Obtuse angled triangle	8–13
2.	30	20	40	Obtuse angled triangle	8–14
3.	30	20	40	Obtuse angled triangle	8–16, 20–22
4.	–	–	–	–	8–14, 17–22
5.	–	–	–	–	8–13, 21,22
6.	30	20	40	Obtuse angled triangle	8–16, 20–23
7.	–	–	–	–	8–14, 17–23
8.	–	–	–	–	8–13, 21–23
9.	30	20	40	Obtuse angled triangle	8–16, 20–24
10.	–	–	–	–	8–14, 17–24
11.	–	–	–	–	8–13, 21–24
12.	30	20	40	Obtuse angled triangle	10–13
13.	30	20	40	Obtuse angled triangle	10–14
14.	30	20	40	Obtuse angled triangle	10–16, 20–22
15.	–	–	–	–	10–14, 17–22
16.	–	–	–	–	10–13, 21,22
17.	30	20	40	Obtuse angled triangle	10–16, 20–23
18.	–	–	–	–	10–14, 17–23
19.	–	–	–	–	10–13, 21–23
20.	30	20	40	Obtuse angled triangle	10–16, 20–24
21.	–	–	–	–	10–14, 17–24
22.	–	–	–	–	10–13, 21–24
23.	30	20	40	Obtuse angled triangle	12, 13
24.	30	20	40	Obtuse angled triangle	12–14
25.	30	20	40	Obtuse angled triangle	12–16, 20–22
26.	–	–	–	–	12–14, 17–22
27.	–	–	–	–	12, 13, 21, 22
28.	30	20	40	Obtuse angled triangle	12–16, 20–23
29.	–	–	–	–	12–14, 17–23
30.	–	–	–	–	12, 13, 21–23
31.	30	20	40	Obtuse angled triangle	12–16, 20–24
32.	–	–	–	–	12–14, 17–24
33.	–	–	–	–	12, 13, 21–24
34.	30	20	40	Obtuse angled triangle	22–25

(Contd.)

(Contd.)

S. No.	A	b	c	Expected output	Remarks
35.	30	40	50	Right angled triangle	22–25, 28
36.	30	20	40	Obtuse angled triangle	23–25
37.	30	40	50	Right angled triangle	23–25, 28
38.	30	20	40	Obtuse angled triangle	24, 25
39.	30	40	50	Right angled triangle	24, 25, 28
40.	30	20	40	Obtuse angled triangle	5–16, 20, 21
41.	30	10	15	Invalid triangle	5–14, 17–21
42.	102	–1	6	Input values out of range	5–13, 21
43.	-	-	-	-	5–16, 20, 21, 35
44.	30	10	15	Invalid triangle	5–14, 17–21, 35
45.	102	–1	6	Input values out of range	5–13, 21, 35
46.	30	20	40	Obtuse angled triangle	15, 16, 20, 21
47.	-	-	-	-	15, 16, 20, 21, 35
48.	30	10	15	Invalid triangle	18–21
49.	30	10	15	Invalid triangle	18–21, 35

The 'all-uses' paths are given in Table 4.10 and the test cases for all du-paths are given in Table 4.11. The 'all-definitions' paths and the test cases are given in Tables 4.12 and 4.13 respectively.

Table 4.10. All uses paths for triangle classification problem

All uses	Definition clear?	All uses	Definition clear?
8–13	Yes	12–16, 20–24	Yes
8–14	Yes	22–25	Yes
8–16, 20–22	Yes	22–25, 28	Yes
8–16, 20–23	Yes	23–25	Yes
8–16, 20–24	Yes	23–25, 28	Yes
10–13	Yes	24, 25	Yes
10–14	Yes	24, 25, 28	Yes
10–16, 20–22	Yes	5–16, 20, 21	No
10–13, 21–23	Yes	5–14, 17–21, 35	No
10–16, 20–24	Yes	15, 16, 20, 21	Yes
12,13	Yes	15, 16, 20, 21, 35	Yes
12–14	Yes	18–21	Yes
12–16, 20, 21, 22	Yes	18–21, 35	Yes
12–16, 20–23	Yes		

Table 4.11. Test cases for all uses paths

S. No.	a	b	c	Expected output	Remarks
1.	30	20	40	Obtuse angled triangle	8–13
2.	30	20	40	Obtuse angled triangle	8–14
3.	30	20	40	Obtuse angled triangle	8–16, 20–22
4.	30	20	40	Obtuse angled triangle	8–16, 20–23
5.	30	20	40	Obtuse angled triangle	8–16, 20–24
6.	30	20	40	Obtuse angled triangle	10–13
7.	30	20	40	Obtuse angled triangle	10–14
8.	30	20	40	Obtuse angled triangle	10–16, 20–22
9.	30	20	40	Obtuse angled triangle	10–13, 21–23
10.	30	20	40	Obtuse angled triangle	10–16, 20–24
11.	30	20	40	Obtuse angled triangle	12,13
12.	30	20	40	Obtuse angled triangle	12–14
13.	30	20	40	Obtuse angled triangle	12–16, 20, 21, 22
14.	30	20	40	Obtuse angled triangle	12–16, 20–23
15.	30	20	40	Obtuse angled triangle	12–16, 20–24
16.	30	20	40	Obtuse angled triangle	22–25
17.	30	40	50	Right angled triangle	22–25, 28
18.	30	20	40	Obtuse angled triangle	23–25
19.	30	40	50	Right angled triangle	23–25, 28
20.	30	20	40	Obtuse angled triangle	24, 25
21.	30	40	50	Right angled triangle	24, 25, 28
22.	30	20	40	Obtuse angled triangle	5–16, 20, 21
23.	30	10	15	Invalid triangle	5–14, 17–21, 35
24.	30	20	40	Obtuse angled triangle	15, 16, 20, 21
25.	-	-	-	-	15, 16, 20, 21, 35
26.	30	10	15	Invalid triangle	18–21
27.	30	10	15	Invalid triangle	18–21, 35

Table 4.12. All definitions paths for triangle classification problem

All definitions	Definition clear?
8–13	Yes
10–13	Yes
12, 13	Yes
22–25	Yes
23–25	Yes
24,25	Yes
5–16, 20, 21	No
15, 16, 20, 21	Yes
18–21	Yes

Table 4.13. Test cases for all definitions paths

S. No.	a	b	c	Expected output	Remarks
1.	30	20	40	Obtuse angled triangle	8–13
2.	30	20	40	Obtuse angled triangle	10–13
3.	30	20	40	Obtuse angled triangle	12, 13
4.	30	20	40	Obtuse angled triangle	22–25
5.	30	20	40	Obtuse angled triangle	23–25
6.	30	20	40	Obtuse angled triangle	24, 25
7.	30	20	40	Obtuse angled triangle	5–16, 20, 21
8.	30	20	40	Obtuse angled triangle	15, 16, 20, 21
9.	30	10	15	Invalid triangle	18–21

Example 4.6: Consider the program given in Figure 3.21 for the determination of day of the week. Its input is at triple of positive integers (day, month, year) from the interval

$1 \leq day \leq 31$

$1 \leq month \leq 12$

$1900 \leq year \leq 2058$

The output may be:

[Sunday, Monday, Tuesday, Wednesday, Thursday, Friday, Saturday]

Find all du-paths and identify those du-paths that are definition clear. Also find all du-paths, all-uses and all-definitions and generate test cases for these paths.

Solution:

(i) The program graph is given in Figure 3.22. The variables used in the program are day, month, year, century, Y, Y1, M, date, validDate, leap.

(ii) Define / use nodes for all variables are given below:

S. No.	Variable	Defined at node	Used at node
1.	Day	6	19, 27, 30, 37, 91 93, 96, 99, 102 105, 108, 111, 115
2.	Month	8	18, 26, 37, 54 62, 70, 73, 76, 79 82, 85, 93, 96, 99 102, 105, 108, 111, 115
3.	Year	10	11, 12, 14, 45, 47 51, 93, 96, 99, 102 105, 108, 111, 115
4.	Century	46, 50	91
5.	Y	53	91
6.	Y1	47, 51	53

(Contd.)

(Contd.)

S. No.	Variable	Defined at node	Used at node
7.	M	56, 59, 64 67, 71, 74 77, 80, 83 86, 89	91
8.	Date	91	92, 95, 98, 101, 104, 107
9.	ValidDate	3, 20, 23 28, 31, 34, 38, 41	44
10.	Leap	3, 13, 15	27, 55, 63

(iii) The du-paths with beginning and ending nodes are given as:

S. No.	Variable	du-path (begin, end)
1.	Day	6, 19
		6, 27
		6, 30
		6, 37
		6, 91
		6, 93
		6, 96
		6, 99
		6, 102
		6, 105
		6, 108
		6, 111
		6, 115
2.	Month	8, 18
		8, 26
		8, 37
		8, 54
		8, 62
		8, 70
		8, 73
		8, 76
		8, 79
		8, 82
		8, 85
		8, 93
		8, 96
		8, 99
		8, 102
		8, 105
		8, 108
		8, 111
		8, 115

(Contd.)

(Contd.)

S. No.	Variable	du-path (begin, end)
3.	Year	10, 11
		10, 12
		10, 14
		10, 45
		10, 47
		10, 51
		10, 93
		10, 96
		10, 99
		10, 102
		10, 105
		10, 108
		10, 111
		10, 115
4.	Century	46, 91
		50, 91
5.	Y	53, 91
6.	Y1	47, 53
		51, 53
7.	M	56, 91
		59, 91
		64, 91
		67, 91
		71, 91
		74, 91
		77, 91
		80, 91
		83, 91
		86, 91
		89, 91
8.	Date	91, 92
		91, 95
		91, 98
		91, 101
		91, 104
		91, 107
9.	ValidDate	3, 44
		20, 44
		23, 44
		28, 44
		31, 44
		34, 44
		38, 44
		41, 44

(Contd.)

(Contd.)

S. No.	Variable	du-path (begin, end)
10.	Leap	3, 27
		3, 55
		3, 63
		13, 27
		13, 55
		13, 63
		15, 27
		15, 55
		15, 63

There are more than 10,000 du-paths and it is neither possible nor desirable to show all of them. The all uses paths and their respective test cases are shown in Table 4.14 and Table 4.15 respectively. The 'all definitions' paths are shown in Table 4.16 and their corresponding test cases are given in Table 4.17.

Table 4.14. All uses paths for determination of the day of week problem

All uses	Definition clear?
6–19	Yes
6–18, 26, 27	Yes
6–18, 26, 27, 30	Yes
6–18, 26, 37	Yes
6–21, 25, 43–48, 53, 54, 62, 70, 73, 76, 79–81, 91	Yes
6–21, 25, 43–48, 53, 54, 62, 70, 73, 76, 79–81, 91-93	Yes
6–21, 25, 43–48, 53, 54, 62, 70, 73, 76, 79–81, 91, 92, 95, 96	Yes
6–21, 25, 43–48, 53, 54, 62, 70, 73, 76, 79–81, 91, 92, 95, 98, 99	Yes
6–21, 25, 43–48, 53, 54, 62, 70, 73, 76, 79–81, 91, 92, 95, 98, 101, 102	Yes
6–21, 43–48, 53, 54, 62, 70, 73, 76, 79–81, 91, 92, 95, 98, 101, 104, 105	Yes
6–21, 25, 43–48, 53, 54, 62, 70, 73, 76, 79–81, 91, 92, 95, 98, 101,104, 107, 108	Yes
6–21, 25, 43–48, 53, 54, 62, 70, 73, 76, 79–81, 91, 92, 95, 98, 101, 104, 107, 110, 111	Yes
6–11, 44, 114, 115	Yes
8–18	Yes
8–18, 26	Yes
8–18, 26, 37	Yes
8–21, 25, 43–48, 53, 54	Yes
8–21, 25, 43–48, 53, 54, 62	Yes
8–25, 43–48, 53, 54, 62, 70	Yes
8–21, 25, 43–48, 53, 54, 62, 70, 73	**Yes**
8–21, 25, 43–48, 53, 54, 62, 70, 73, 76	**Yes**

(Contd.)

(*Contd.*)

All uses	Definition clear?
8–21, 25, 43–48, 53, 54, 62, 70, 73, 76, 79	Yes
8–21, 25, 43–48, 53, 54, 62, 70, 73, 76, 79, 82	Yes
8–21, 25, 43–48, 53, 54, 62, 70, 73, 76, 79, 82, 85	Yes
8–21, 25, 43–48, 53, 54, 62, 70, 73, 76, 79–81, 91, 92, 93	Yes
8–21, 25, 43–48, 53, 54, 62, 70, 73, 76, 79–81, 91, 92, 95, 96	Yes
8–21, 25, 43–48, 53, 54, 62, 70, 73, 76, 79–81, 91, 92, 95, 98, 99	Yes
8–21, 25, 43–48, 53, 54, 62, 70, 73, 76, 79–81, 91, 92, 95, 98, 101, 102	Yes
8–21, 25, 43–48, 53, 54, 62, 70, 73, 76, 79–81, 91, 92, 95, 98, 101, 104, 105	Yes
8–21, 25, 43–48, 53, 54, 62, 70, 73, 76, 79–81, 91, 92, 95, 98, 101, 104, 107, 108	Yes
8–21, 25, 43–48, 53, 54, 62, 70, 73, 76, 79–81, 91, 92, 95, 98, 101, 104, 107, 110, 111	Yes
8–11, 44, 114, 115	Yes
10, 11	Yes
10–12	Yes
10–14	Yes
10–21, 25, 43–45	Yes
10–21, 25, 43–47	Yes
10–21, 25, 43–45, 49–51	Yes
10–21, 25, 43–48, 53, 54, 62, 70, 73, 76, 79–81, 91–93	Yes
10–21, 25, 43–48, 53, 54, 62, 70, 73, 76, 79–81, 91, 92, 95, 96	Yes
10–21, 25, 43–48, 53, 54, 62, 70, 73, 76, 79–81, 91, 92, 95, 98, 99	Yes
10–21, 25, 43–48, 53, 54, 62, 70, 73, 76, 79–81, 91, 92, 95, 98, 101, 102	Yes
10–21, 25, 43–48, 53, 54, 62, 70, 73, 76, 79–81, 91, 92, 95, 98, 101, 104, 105	Yes
10–21, 25, 43–48, 53, 54, 62, 70, 73, 76, 79–81, 91, 92, 95, 98, 101, 104, 107, 108	Yes
10–21, 25, 43–48, 53, 54, 62, 70, 73, 76, 79–81, 91, 92, 95, 98, 101, 104, 107, 110, 111	Yes
10, 11, 44, 114, 115	Yes
46–48, 53–57, 61, 91	Yes
50–57, 61, 91	Yes
53–61, 91	Yes
47, 48, 53	Yes
51–53	Yes
56, 57, 61, 91	Yes
59–61, 91	Yes

(*Contd.*)

(Contd.)

All uses	Definition clear?
64, 65, 69, 91	Yes
67–69, 91	Yes
71, 72, 91	Yes
74, 75, 91	Yes
77, 78, 91	Yes
80, 81, 91	Yes
83, 84, 91	Yes
86, 87, 91	Yes
89, 90, 91	Yes
91, 92	Yes
91, 92, 95	Yes
91, 92, 95, 98	Yes
91, 92, 95, 98, 101	Yes
91, 92, 95, 98, 101, 104	Yes
91, 92, 95, 98, 101, 104, 107	Yes
3–11, 44	No
20, 21, 25, 43, 44	Yes
23–25, 43, 44	Yes
28, 29, 36, 43, 44	Yes
31, 32, 36, 43, 44	Yes
34–36, 43, 44	Yes
38, 39, 43, 44	Yes
41–44	Yes
3–18, 26, 27	No
3–18, 26, 37–39, 43–48, 53–55	No
3–18, 26, 27, 30–32, 36, 43–48, 53, 54, 62, 63	No
13–18, 26, 27	No
13–18, 26, 37–39, 43–48, 53–55	No
13–18, 26, 27, 30–32, 36, 43–48, 53, 54, 62, 63	No
15–18, 26, 27	Yes
15–18, 26, 37–39, 43–48, 53–55	Yes
15–18, 26, 27, 30–32, 36, 43–48, 53, 54, 62, 63	Yes

Table 4.15. Test cases for all uses

S. No.	Month	Day	Year	Expected output	Remarks
1.	6	15	1900	Friday	6–19
2.	2	15	1900	Thursday	6–18, 26, 27
3.	2	15	1900	Thursday	6–18, 26, 27, 30
4.	7	15	1900	Sunday	6–18, 26, 37
5.	6	15	1900	Friday	6–21, 25, 43–48, 53, 54, 62, 70, 73, 76, 79–81, 91
6.	6	10	1900	Sunday	6–21, 25, 43–48, 53, 54, 62, 70, 73, 76, 79–81, 91–93
7.	6	11	1900	Monday	6–21, 25, 43–48, 53, 54, 62, 70, 73, 76, 79–81, 91, 92, 95, 96
8.	6	12	1900	Tuesday	6–21, 25, 43–48, 53, 54, 62, 70, 73, 76, 79–81, 91, 92, 95, 98, 99
9.	6	13	1900	Wednesday	6–21, 25, 43–48, 53, 54, 62, 70, 73, 76, 79–81, 91, 92, 95, 98, 101, 102
10.	6	14	1900	Thursday	6–21, 43–48, 53, 54, 62, 70, 73, 76, 79–81, 91, 92, 95, 98, 101, 104, 105
11.	6	15	1900	Friday	6–21, 25, 43–48, 53, 54, 62, 70, 73, 76, 79–81, 91, 92, 95, 98, 101, 104, 107, 108
12.	6	16	1900	Saturday	6–21, 25, 43–48, 53, 54, 62, 70, 73, 76, 79–81, 91, 92, 95, 98, 101, 104, 107, 110, 111
13.	6	15	2059	Invalid Date	6–11, 44, 114, 115
14.	6	15	1900	Friday	8–18
15.	2	15	1900	Thursday	8–18, 26
16.	1	15	1900	Monday	8–18, 26, 37
17.	6	15	1900	Friday	8–21, 25, 43–48, 53, 54
18.	6	15	1900	Friday	8–21, 25, 43–48, 53, 54, 62
19.	6	15	1900	Friday	8–25, 43–48, 53, 54, 62, 70
20.	4	15	1900	Sunday	8–21, 25, 43–48, 53, 54, 62, 70, 73
21.	6	15	1900	Friday	8–21, 25, 43–48, 53, 54, 62, 70, 73, 76
22.	6	15	1900	Friday	8–21, 25, 43–48, 53, 54, 62, 70, 73, 76, 79
23.	9	15	1900	Saturday	8–21, 25, 43–48, 53, 54, 62, 70, 73, 76, 79, 82

(Contd.)

(Contd.)

S. No.	Month	Day	Year	Expected output	Remarks
24.	9	15	1900	Saturday	8–21, 25, 43–48, 53, 54, 62, 70, 73, 76, 79, 82, 85
25.	6	10	1900	Sunday	8–21, 25, 43–48, 53, 54, 62, 70, 73, 76, 79–81, 91, 92, 93
26.	6	11	1900	Monday	8–21, 25, 43–48, 53, 54, 62, 70, 73, 76, 79–81, 91, 92, 95, 96
27.	6	12	1900	Tuesday	8–21, 25, 43–48, 53, 54, 62, 70, 73, 76, 79–81, 91, 92, 95, 98, 99
28.	6	13	1900	Wednesday	8–21, 25, 43–48, 53, 54, 62, 70, 73, 76, 79, 80, 81, 91, 92, 95, 98, 101, 102
29.	6	14	1900	Thursday	8–21, 25, 43–48, 53, 54, 62, 70, 73, 76, 79, 80, 81, 91, 92, 95, 98, 101, 104, 105
30.	6	15	1900	Friday	8–21, 25, 43–48, 53, 54, 62, 70, 73, 76, 79, 80, 81, 91, 92, 95, 98, 101, 104, 107, 108
31.	6	16	1900	Saturday	8–21, 25, 43–48, 53, 54, 62, 70, 73, 76, 79, 80, 81, 91, 92, 95, 98, 101, 104, 107, 110, 111
32.	6	15	2059	Invalid Date	8–11, 44, 114, 115
33.	6	15	1900	Friday	10, 11
34.	6	15	1900	Friday	10–12
35.	6	15	1900	Friday	10–14
36.	6	15	1900	Friday	10–21, 25, 43–45
37.	6	15	1900	Friday	10–21, 25, 43–47
38.	6	15	2009	Monday	10–21, 25, 43–45, 49–51
39.	6	10	1900	Sunday	10–21, 25, 43–48, 53, 54, 62, 70, 73, 76, 79–81, 91–93
40.	6	11	1900	Monday	10–21, 25, 43–48, 53, 54, 62, 70, 73, 76, 79–81, 91, 92, 95, 96
41.	6	12	1900	Tuesday	10–21, 25, 43–48, 53, 54, 62, 70, 73, 76, 79–81, 91, 92, 95, 98, 99
42.	6	13	1900	Wednesday	10–21, 25, 43–48, 53, 54, 62, 70, 73, 76, 79–81, 91, 92, 95, 98, 101, 102
43.	6	14	1900	Thursday	10–21, 25, 43–48, 53, 54, 62, 70, 73, 76, 79–81, 91, 92, 95, 98, 101, 104, 105
44.	6	15	1900	Friday	10–21, 25, 43–48, 53, 54, 62, 70, 73, 76, 79–81, 91, 92, 95, 98, 101, 104, 107, 108

(Contd.)

194 Software Testing

(Contd.)

S. No.	Month	Day	Year	Expected output	Remarks
45.	6	16	1900	Saturday	10–21, 25, 43–48, 53, 54, 62, 70, 73, 76, 79–81, 91, 92, 95, 98, 101, 104, 107, 110, 111
46.	6	15	2059	Invalid Date	10, 11, 44, 114, 115
47.	1	15	1900	Monday	46–48, 53–57, 61, 91
48.	1	15	2009	Thursday	50–57, 61, 91
49.	1	15	2009	Thursday	53–61, 91
50.	6	15	1900	Friday	47, 48, 53
51.	6	15	2009	Monday	51–53
52.	1	15	2009	Thursday	56, 57, 61, 91
53.	1	15	2000	Saturday	59–61, 91
54.	1	15	2009	Thursday	64, 65, 69, 91
55.	2	15	2000	Tuesday	67–69, 91
56.	3	15	2009	Sunday	71, 72, 91
57.	4	15	2009	Wednesday	74, 75, 91
58.	5	15	2009	Friday	77, 78, 91
59.	6	15	2009	Monday	80, 81, 91
60.	8	15	2009	Saturday	83, 84, 91
61.	9	15	2009	Tuesday	86, 87, 91
62.	7	15	2009	Wednesday	89, 90, 91
63.	5	7	2009	Sunday	91, 92
64.	6	7	2009	Monday	91, 92, 95
65.	7	7	2009	Tuesday	91, 92, 95, 98
66.	8	7	2009	Wednesday	91, 92, 95, 98, 101
67.	9	7	2009	Thursday	91, 92, 95, 98, 101, 104
68.	10	7	2009	Friday	91, 92, 95, 98, 101, 104, 107
69.	6	15	1900	Friday	3–11, 44
70.	6	15	1900	Friday	20, 21, 25, 43, 44
71.	6	31	2009	Invalid Date	23–25, 43, 44

(Contd.)

(Contd.)

S. No.	Month	Day	Year	Expected output	Remarks
72.	2	15	2000	Tuesday	28, 29, 36, 43, 44
73.	2	15	2009	Sunday	31, 32, 36, 43, 44
74.	2	30	2009	Invalid Date	34–36, 43, 44
75.	8	15	2009	Saturday	38, 39, 43, 44
76.	13	1	2009	Invalid Date	41–44
77.	2	15	1900	Thursday	3–18, 26, 27
78.	1	15	1900	Monday	3–18, 26, 37–39, 43–48, 53–55
79.	2	15	1900	Thursday	3–18, 26, 27, 30–32, 36, 43–48, 53, 54, 62, 63
80.	2	15	1900	Thursday	13–18, 26, 27
81.	1	15	1900	Monday	13–18, 26, 37–39, 43–48, 53–55
82.	2	15	1900	Thursday	13–18, 26, 27, 30–32, 36, 43–48, 53, 54, 62, 63
83.	2	15	1900	Thursday	15–18, 26, 27
84.	1	15	1900	Monday	15–18, 26, 37–39, 43–48, 53–55
85.	2	15	1900	Thursday	15–18, 26, 27, 30–32, 36, 43–48, 53, 54, 62, 63

Table 4.16. All definitions paths for determination of the day of week problem

All definitions	Definition clear?
6–19	Yes
8–18	Yes
10, 11	Yes
46–48, 53–57, 61, 91	Yes
50–57, 61, 91	Yes
53–57, 61, 91	Yes
47, 48, 53	Yes
51–53	Yes
56, 57, 61, 91	Yes
59, 60, 61, 91	Yes
64, 65, 69, 91	Yes
67–69, 91	Yes
71, 72, 91	Yes
74, 75, 91	Yes

(Contd.)

(*Contd.*)

All definitions	Definition clear?
77, 78, 91	Yes
80, 81, 91	Yes
83, 84, 91	Yes
86, 87, 91	Yes
89–91	Yes
91, 92	Yes
3–11, 44	No
20, 21, 25, 43, 44	Yes
23–25, 43, 44	Yes
28, 29, 36, 43, 44	Yes
31, 32, 36, 43, 44	Yes
34–36, 43, 44	Yes
38, 39, 43, 44	Yes
41–44	Yes
3–18, 26, 27	No
13–18, 26, 27	No
15–18, 26, 27	Yes

Table 4.17. Test cases for all definitions

S. No.	Month	Day	Year	Expected output	Remarks
1.	6	15	1900	Friday	6–19
2.	6	15	1900	Friday	8–18
3.	6	15	1900	Friday	10, 11
4.	1	15	1900	Monday	46–48, 53–57, 61, 91
5.	1	15	2009	Thursday	50–57, 61, 91
6.	1	15	2009	Thursday	53–57, 61, 91
7.	6	15	1900	Friday	47, 48, 53
8.	6	15	2009	Monday	51–53
9.	1	15	2009	Thursday	56, 57, 61, 91
10.	1	15	2000	Saturday	59, 60, 61, 91
11.	1	15	2009	Thursday	64, 65, 69, 91
12.	2	15	2000	Tuesday	67–69, 91
13.	3	15	2009	Sunday	71, 72, 91
14.	4	15	2009	Wednesday	74, 75, 91
15.	5	15	2009	Friday	77, 78, 91
16.	6	15	2009	Monday	80, 81, 91
17.	8	15	2009	Saturday	83, 84, 91

(*Contd.*)

(Contd.)

S. No.	Month	Day	Year	Expected output	Remarks
18.	9	15	2009	Tuesday	86, 87, 91
19.	7	15	2009	Wednesday	89–91
20.	6	15	2009	Monday	91, 92
21.	6	15	2059	Invalid Date	3–11, 44
22.	6	15	1900	Friday	20, 21, 25, 43, 44
23.	6	31	2009	Invalid Date	23–25, 43, 44
24.	2	15	2000	Tuesday	28, 29, 36, 43, 44
25.	2	15	2009	Sunday	31, 32, 36, 43, 44
26.	2	30	2009	Invalid Date	34–36, 43, 44
27.	8	15	2009	Saturday	38, 39, 43, 44
28.	13	1	2009	Invalid Date	41–44
29.	2	15	1900	Thursday	3–18, 26, 27
30.	2	15	1900	Thursday	13–18, 26, 27
31.	2	15	1900	Thursday	15–18, 26, 27

4.3 SLICE BASED TESTING

Program slicing was introduced by Mark Weiser [WEIS84] where we prepare various subsets (called slices) of a program with respect to its variables and their selected locations in the program. Each variable with one of its location will give us a program slice. A large program may have many smaller programs (its slices), each constructed for different variable subsets. The slices are typically simpler than the original program, thereby simplifying the process of testing of the program. Keith and James [KEIT91] have explained this concept as:

"Program slicing is a technique for restricting the behaviour of a program to some specified subset of interest. A slice $S(v, n)$ of program P on variable v, or set of variables, at statement n yields the portions of the program that contributed to the value of v just before statement n is executed. $S(v, n)$ is called a slicing criteria. Slices can be computed automatically on source programs by analyzing data flow. A program slice has the added advantage of being an executable program."

Hence, slices are smaller than the original program and may be executed independently. Only two things are important here, variable and its selected location in the program.

4.3.1 Guidelines for Slicing

There are many variables in the program but their usage may be different in different statements. The following guidelines may be used for the creation of program slices.

1. All statements where variables are defined and redefined should be considered. Consider the program for classification of a triangle (given in Figure 3.18) where variable 'valid' is defined at line number 5 and redefined at line number 15 and line number 18.

5   int valid = 0
15 valid = 1
18 valid = −1

Hence, we may create S(valid, 5), S(valid, 15) and S(valid, 18) slices for variable 'valid' of the program.

2. All statements where variables receive values externally should be considered. Consider the triangle problem (given in Figure 3.18) where variables 'a', 'b' and 'c' receive values externally at line number 8, line number 10 and line number 12 respectively as shown below:

8   scanf ("%lf", &a);
10 scanf ("%lf", &b);
12 scanf ("%lf", &c);

Hence, we may create S(a, 8), S(b, 10) and S(c, 12) slices for these variables.

3. All statements where output of a variable is printed should be considered. Consider the program to find the largest amongst three numbers (given in Figure 3.11) where variable 'C' is printed at line number 16 and 21 as given below:

16 printf ("The largest number is: % f \n", C);
21 printf ("The largest number is: % f \n", C)

Hence, we may create S(C, 16) and S(C, 21) as slices for 'C' variable

4. All statements where some relevant output is printed should be considered. Consider the triangle classification program where line number 26, 29, 32, 36 and 39 are used for printing the classification of the triangle (given in Figure 3.18) which is very relevant as per logic of the program. The statements are given as:

26 printf ("Obtuse angled triangle");
29 printf ("Right angled triangle");
32 printf ("Acute angled triangle");
36 printf ("\nInvalid triangle");
39 printf ("\nInput Values out of Range");

We may create S(a1, 26), S(a1, 29), S(a1, 32), S(valid, 36) and S(valid, 39) as slices. These are important slices for the purpose of testing.

5. The status of all variables may be considered at the last statement of the program. We consider the triangle classification program (given in figure 3.18) where line number 42 is the last statement of the program. We may create S(a1, 42), S(a2, 42), S(a3, 42), S(valid, 42), S(a, 42), S(b,42) and S(c, 42) as slices.

4.3.2 Creation of Program Slices

Consider the portion of a program given in Figure 4.2 for the identification of its slices.

1. a = 3;
2. b = 6;
3. c = b^2;
4. d = $a^2 + b^2$;
5. c = a + b;

Figure 4.2. Portion of a program

We identify two slices for variable 'c' at statement number 3 and statement number 5 as given in Figure 4.3.

1.	a	=	3;
2.	b	=	6;
5.	c	=	a + b;

S(c, 5)

Variable 'c' at statement 5

2.	b	=	6;
3.	c	=	b^2;

S(c, 3)

Variable 'c' at statement 5

Figure 4.3. Two slices for variable 'c'

Consider the program given in Figure 4.4.

1. void main ( )
2. {
3. int a, b, c, d, e;
4. printf ("Enter the values of a, b and c \ n");
5. scanf ("%d %d %d", & a, &b, &c);
6. d = a+b;
7. e = b+c:
8. printf ("%d", d);
9. printf ("%d", e);
10. }

Figure 4.4. Example program

Many slices may be created as per criterion (mentioned in section 4.3.1) of the program given in the Figure 4.4. Some of these slices are shown below:

```
1.  main ( )
2.  {
3.  int a, b, c, d, e;
4.  printf ("Enter the values of a, b and c \ n");
5.  scanf ("%d %d %d", &a, &b, &c);
7.  e = b + c;
9.  printf ("%d", e);
10. }
```

Slice on criterion S (e, 10) = (1, 2, 3, 4, 5, 7, 9, 10)

```
1. main ( )
2. {
3.   int a, b, c, d, e;
4.   printf ("Enter the values of a, b and c \ n");
5.   scanf ("%d %d %d", &a, &b, &c);
6.   d = a + b;
8.   printf ("%d", d);
10. }
```

Slice on criterion S (d,10) = (1, 2, 3, 4, 5, 6, 8, 10)

```
1. main ( )
2. {
3.   int a, b, c, d, e;
4.   printf ("Enter the values of a, b and c \ n");
5.   scanf ("%d %d %d", &a, &b, &c);
7.   e = b + c;
10. }
```

Slice on criterion S (e,7) = (1, 2, 3, 4, 5, 7, 10)

```
1. main ( )
2. {
3.   int a, b, c, d, e;
4.   printf ("Enter the values of a, b and c \ n");
5.   scanf ("%d %d %d", &a, &b, &c);
6.   d = a + b;
10. }
```

Slice on criterion S (d,6) = (1, 2, 3, 4, 5, 6, 10)

```
1. main ( )
2. {
3.   int a, b, c, d, e;
4.   printf ("Enter the values of a, b and c \ n");
5.   scanf ("%d %d %d", &a, &b, &c);
10. }
```

Slice on criterion S (a, 5) = (1, 2, 3, 4, 5, 10)

We also consider the program to find the largest number amongst three numbers as given in Figure 3.11. There are three variables A, B and C in the program. We may create many slices like S (A, 28), S (B, 28), S (C, 28) which are given in Figure 4.8.

Some other slices and the portions of the program covered by these slices are given as:

S (A, 6) = {1– 6, 28}
S (A, 13) = {1–14, 18, 27, 28}
S (B, 8) = {1– 4, 7, 8, 28}
S (B, 24) = {1–11, 18–20, 22–28}
S (C, 10) = {1– 4, 9, 10, 28}
S (C, 16) = {1–12, 14–18, 27, 28}
S (C, 21) = {1–11, 18–22, 26–28}

It is a good programming practice to create a block even for a single statement. If we consider C++/C/Java programming languages, every single statement should be covered with curly braces { }. However, if we do not do so, the compiler will not show any warning / error message. In the process of generating slices we delete many statements (which are not required in the slice). It is essential to keep the starting and ending brackets of the block of the deleted statements. It is also advisable to give a comment 'do nothing' in order to improve the readability of the source code.

```
    #include<stdio.h>
    #include<conio.h>
1.  void main()
2.  {
3.  float A,B,C;
4.  clrscr();
5.  printf("Enter number 1:\n");
6.  scanf("%f", &A);
7.  printf("Enter number 2:\n");
8.  scanf("%f", &B);
9.  printf("Enter number 3:\n");
10. scanf("%f", &C);
11. if(A>B) {
12. if(A>C) {
13. printf("The largest number is: %f\n",A);
14.     }
18. }
27. getch();
28. }
```

```
    #include<stdio.h>
    #include<conio.h>
1.  void main()
2.  {
3.  float A,B,C;
4.  clrscr();
5.  printf("Enter number 1:\n");
6.  scanf("%f", &A);
7.  printf("Enter number 2:\n");
8.  scanf("%f", &B);
9.  printf("Enter number 3:\n");
10. scanf("%f", &C);
11. if(A>B) { /*do nothing*/
18. }
19. else {
20. if(C>B) { /*do nothing*/
22.     }
23. else {
24. printf("The largest number is: %f\n",B);
25.     }
26. }
27. getch();
28. }
```

(a) S(A, 28) ={1–14, 18, 27, 28}   (b) S(B, 28) ={1–11, 18–20, 22–28}

(Contd.)

(Contd.)

```
         #include<stdio.h>
         #include<conio.h>
1.   void main()
2.   {
3.      float A,B,C;
4.      clrscr();
5.      printf("Enter number 1:\n");
6.      scanf("%f", &A);
7.      printf("Enter number 2:\n");
8.      scanf("%f", &B);
9.      printf("Enter number 3:\n");
10.     scanf("%f", &C);
11.     if(A>B) { /*do nothing*/
18.     }
19.     else {
20.     if(C>B) {
21.             printf("The largest number is: %f\n",C);
22.             }
26.     }
27.     getch();
28.  }
```
(c) S(C, 28)={1-11, 18-22, 26-28}

Figure 4.5. Some slices of program in Figure 3.11

A statement may have many variables. However, only one variable should be used to generate a slice at a time. Different variables in the same statement will generate a different program slice. Hence, there may be a number of slices of a program depending upon the slicing criteria. Every slice is smaller than the original program and can be executed independently. Each slice may have one or more test cases and may help us to focus on the definition, redefinition, last statement of the program, and printing/reading of a variable in the slice. Program slicing has many applications in testing, debugging, program comprehension and software measurement. A statement may have many variables. We should use only one variable of a statement for generating a slice.

4.3.3 Generation of Test Cases

Every slice should be independently executable and may cover some lines of source code of the program as shown in previous examples. The test cases for the slices of the program given in Figure 3.3 (to find the largest number amongst three numbers) are shown in Table 4.18. The generated slices are S(A, 6), S(A, 13), S(A, 28), S(B, 8), S(B, 24), S(B, 28), S(C, 10), S(C, 16), S(C, 21), S(C, 28) as discussed in previous section 4.3.1.

Table 4.18. Test cases using program slices of program to find the largest among three numbers

S. No.	Slice	Lines covered	A	B	C	Expected output
1.	S(A, 6)	1–6, 28	9			No output
2.	S(A, 13)	1–14, 18, 27, 28	9	8	7	9
3.	S(A, 28)	1–14, 18, 27, 28	8	8	7	9
4.	S(B, 8)	1–4, 7, 8, 28		9		No output
5.	S(B, 24)	1–11, 18–20, 22–28	7	9	8	9
6.	S(B, 28)	1–11, 19, 20, 23–28	7	9	8	9
7.	S(C, 10)	1–4, 9, 10, 28			9	No output
8.	S(C, 16)	1–12, 14–18, 27, 28	8	7	9	9
9.	S(C, 21)	1–11, 18–22, 26–28	7	8	9	9
10.	S(C, 28)	1–11, 18–22, 26–28	7	8	9	9

Slice based testing is a popular structural testing technique and focuses on a portion of the program with respect to a variable location in any statement of the program. Hence slicing simplifies the way of testing a program's behaviour with respect to a particular subset of its variables. But slicing cannot test a behaviour which is not represented by a set of variables or a variable of the program.

Example 4.7: Consider the program for determination of division of a student. Consider all variables and generate possible program slices. Design at least one test case from every slice.

Solution:
There are four variables – mark1, mark2, mark3 and avg in the program. We may create many slices as given below:

$$S\,(mark1, 7) = \{1\text{–}7, 34\}$$
$$S\,(mark1, 13) = \{1\text{–}14, 33, 34\}$$
$$S\,(mark2, 9) = \{1\text{–}5, 8, 9, 34\}$$
$$S\,(mark2, 13) = \{1\text{–}14, 33, 34\}$$
$$S\,(mark3, 11) = \{1\text{–}5, 10, 11, 34\}$$
$$S\,(mark3, 13) = \{1\text{–}14, 33, 34\}$$
$$S\,(avg, 16) = \{1\text{–}12, 14\text{–}16, 32, 34\}$$
$$S\,(avg, 18) = \{1\text{–}12, 14\text{–}19, 32\text{–}34\}$$
$$S\,(avg, 21) = \{1\text{–}12, 14\text{–}17, 19\text{–}22, 29, 31\text{–}34\}$$
$$S\,(avg, 24) = \{1\text{–}12, 14\text{–}17, 19, 20, 22\text{–}25, 29, 31\text{–}34\}$$
$$S\,(avg, 27) = \{1\text{–}12, 14\text{–}17, 19, 20, 22, 23, 25\text{–}29, 31\text{–}34\}$$
$$S\,(avg, 30) = \{1\text{–}12, 14\text{–}17, 19, 20, 22, 23, 25, 26, 28\text{–}34\}$$

The program slices are given in Figure 4.6 and their corresponding test cases are given in Table 4.19.

```
    #include<stdio.h>
    #include<conio.h>
1.  void main()
2.  {
3.  int mark1, mark2,mark3,avg;
4.  clrscr();
5.  printf("Enter marks of 3 subjects
    (between 0-100)\n");
6.  printf("Enter marks of first
    subject:");
7.  scanf("%d", &mark1);
34. }
```
(a) S(mark1,7)/S(mark1,34)

```
    #include<stdio.h>
    #include<conio.h>
1.  void main()
2.  {
3.  int mark1, mark2,mark3,avg;
4.  clrscr();
5.  printf("Enter marks of 3 subjects (between
    0-100)\n");
8.  printf("Enter marks of second subject:");
9.  scanf("%d", &mark2);
34. }
```
(b) S(mark2,9)/S(mark2,34)

```
    #include<stdio.h>
    #include<conio.h>
1.  void main()
2.  {
3.  int mark1, mark2,mark3,avg;
4.  clrscr();
5.  printf("Enter marks of 3 subjects
    (between 0-100)\n");
10. printf("Enter marks of third subject:");
11. scanf("%d",&mark3);
34. }
```
(c) S(mark3,11)/S(mark3,34)

```
    #include<stdio.h>
    #include<conio.h>
1.  void main()
2.  {
3.  int mark1, mark2,mark3,avg;
4.  clrscr();
5.  printf("Enter marks of 3 subjects (between
    0-100)\n");
6.  printf("Enter marks of first subject:");
7.  scanf("%d", &mark1);
8.  printf("Enter marks of second subject:");
9.  scanf("%d", &mark2);
10. printf("Enter marks of third subject:");
11. scanf("%d",&mark3);
12. if(mark1>100||mark1<0||mark2>100||mark2<0||
    mark3>100||mark3<0){
13. printf("Invalid Marks! Please try again");
14. }
33. getch();
34. }
```
(d) S(mark1,13)/S(mark2,13)/S(mark3,13)

(Contd.)

(Contd.)

```
          #include<stdio.h>                              #include<conio.h>
          #include<conio.h>                              #include<conio.h>
1.   void main()                              1.   void main()
2.   {                                        2.   {
3.   int mark1, mark2,mark3,avg;              3.   int mark1, mark2,mark3,avg;
4.   clrscr();                                4.   clrscr();
5.   printf("Enter marks of 3 subjects (between   5.   printf("Enter marks of 3 subjects
     0-100)\n");                                    (between 0-100)\n");
6.   printf("Enter marks of first subject:");  6.   printf("Enter marks of first subject:");
7.   scanf("%d", &mark1);                     7.   scanf("%d", &mark1);
8.   printf("Enter marks of second subject:"); 8.   printf("Enter marks of second subject:");
9.   scanf("%d", &mark2);                     9.   scanf("%d", &mark2);
10.  printf("Enter marks of third subject:"); 10.  printf("Enter marks of third subject:");
11.  scanf("%d",&mark3);                      11.  scanf("%d",&mark3);
12.  if(mark1>100||mark1<0||mark2>100||mark2  12.  if(mark1>100||mark1<0||mark2>100||mark2
     <0||mark3>100||mark3<0){ /* do nothing*/      <0||mark3>100||mark3<0){
14.       }                                   14.  } /* do nothing*/
15.  else {                                   15.  else {
16.  avg=(mark1+mark2+mark3)/3;               16.  avg=(mark1+mark2+mark3)/3;
17.  if(avg<40){                              17.  if(avg<40){ /* do nothing*/
18.       printf("Fail");                     19.       }
19.       }                                   20.  else if(avg>=40&&avg<50) {
32.  }                                        21.       printf("Third Division");
33.  getch();                                 22.  }
34.  }                                        29.  else { /* do nothing*/
                                              31.       }
                                              32.  }
                                              33.  getch();
                                              34.  }
          (e) S(avg,18)                                 (f) S(avg,21)

          #include<stdio.h>                              #include<stdio.h>
          #include<conio.h>                              #include<conio.h>
1.   void main()                              1.   void main()
2.   {                                        2.   {
3.   int mark1, mark2,mark3,avg;              3.   int mark1, mark2,mark3,avg;
4.   clrscr();                                4.   clrscr();
5.   printf("Enter marks of 3 subjects (between   5.   printf("Enter marks of 3 subjects
     0-100)\n");                                    (between 0-100)\n");
```

(Contd.)

(Contd.)

6.	printf("Enter marks of first subject:");	6.	printf("Enter marks of first subject:");
7.	scanf("%d", &mark1);	7.	scanf("%d", &mark1);
8.	printf("Enter marks of second subject:");	8.	printf("Enter marks of second subject:");
9.	scanf("%d", &mark2);	9.	scanf("%d", &mark2);
10.	printf("Enter marks of third subject:");	10.	printf("Enter marks of third subject:");
11.	scanf("%d",&mark3);	11.	scanf("%d",&mark3);
12.	if(mark1>100||mark1<0||mark2>100||mark2<0||mark3>100||mark3<0) { /* do nothing*/	12.	if(mark1>100||mark1<0||mark2>100||mark2<0||mark3>100||mark3<0) { /* do nothing*/
14.	}	14.	}
15.	else {	15.	else {
16.	avg=(mark1+mark2+mark3)/3;	16.	avg=(mark1+mark2+mark3)/3;
17.	if(avg<40) { /* do nothing*/	17.	if(avg<40) { /* do nothing*/
19.	}	19.	}
20.	else if(avg>=40&&avg<50) { /* do nothing*/	20.	else if(avg>=40&&avg<50) { /* do nothing*/
22.	}	22.	}
23.	else if(avg>=50&&avg<60) {	23.	else if(avg>=50&&avg<60) {
24.	printf("Second Division");	25.	}
25.	}	26.	else if(avg>=60&&avg<75) {
29.	else { /* do nothing*/	27.	printf("First Division");
31.	}	28.	}
32.	}	29.	else { /* do nothing*/
33.	getch();	31.	}
34.	}	32.	}
		33.	getch();
		34.	}
	(g) S(avg,24)		(h) S(avg,27)

#include<stdio.h>

#include<conio.h>

1. void main()
2. {
3. int mark1, mark2,mark3,avg;
4. clrscr();
5. printf("Enter marks of 3 subjects (between 0-100)\n");
6. printf("Enter marks of first subject:");
7. scanf("%d", &mark1);
8. printf("Enter marks of second subject:");

(Contd.)

(Contd.)

9.   scanf("%d", &mark2);
10.   printf("Enter marks of third subject:");
11.   scanf("%d",&mark3);
12.   if(mark1>100||mark1<0||mark2>100||mark2<0||mark3>100||mark3<0) { /* do nothing*/
14.   }
15.   else {
16.   avg=(mark1+mark2+mark3)/3;
17.   if(avg<40) { /* do nothing*/
19.   }
20.   else if(avg>=40&&avg<50) {/* do nothing*/
22.   }
23.   else if(avg>=50&&avg<60) {/* do nothing*/
25.   }
26.   else if(avg>=60&&avg<75) {/* do nothing*/
28.   }
29.   else   {
30.   printf("First Division with Distinction");
31.   }
32.   }
33.   getch();
34. }

(i) S(avg,30)/S(avg,34)

Figure 4.6. Slices of program for determination of division of a student

Table 4.19. Test cases using program slices

S. No.	Slice	Line covered	mark1	mark2	mark3	Expected output
1.	S(mark1, 7)	1–7, 34	65			No output
2.	S(mark1, 13)	1–14, 33, 34	101	40	50	Invalid marks
3.	S(mark1, 34)	1–7, 34	65			No output
4.	S(mark2, 9)	1–5, 8, 9, 34		65		No output
5.	S(mark2, 13)	1–14, 33, 34	40	101	50	Invalid marks
6.	S(mark2, 34)	1–5, 8, 9, 34		65		No output
7.	S(mark3, 11)	1–5, 10, 11, 34			65	No output
8.	S(mark3, 13)	1–14, 33, 34	40	50	101	Invalid marks

(Contd.)

(Contd.)

S. No.	Slice	Line covered	mark1	mark2	mark3	Expected output
9.	S(mark3, 34)	1–5, 10, 11, 34			65	No output
10.	S(avg, 16)	1–12, 14–16, 32, 34	45	50	45	No output
11.	S(avg, 18)	1–12, 14–19, 32–34	40	30	20	Fail
12.	S(avg, 21)	1–12, 14–17, 19–22, 29, 32–34	45	50	45	Third division
13.	S(avg, 24)	1–12, 14–17, 19, 20, 22–25, 29, 31–34	55	60	57	Second division
14.	S(avg, 27)	1–12, 14–17, 19, 20, 22, 23, 25–29, 31–34	65	67	65	First division
15.	S(avg, 30)	1–12, 14–17, 19, 20, 22, 23, 25, 26, 28–34	79	80	85	First division with distinction
16.	S(avg, 34)	1–12, 14–17, 19, 20, 22, 23, 25, 26, 28–34	79	80	85	First division with distinction
17.	S(avg, 16)	1–12, 14–16, 32, 34	45	50	45	No output

Example 4.8: Consider the program for classification of a triangle. Consider all variables and generate possible program slices. Design at least one test case from every slice.

Solution:

There are seven variables 'a', 'b', 'c', 'a1', 'a2', 'a3' and 'valid' in the program. We may create many slices as given below:

    i.   S (a, 8)   = {1–8, 42}
    ii.   S (b, 10)   = {1–6, 9, 10, 42}
    iii.   S (c, 12)   = {1–6, 11, 12, 42}
    iv.   S (a1, 22)   = {1–16, 20–22, 34, 42}
    v.   S (a1, 26)   = {1–16, 20–22, 25–27, 34, 41, 42}
    vi.   S (a1, 29)   = {1–16, 20–22, 25, 27–31, 33, 34, 41, 42}
    vii.   S (a1, 32)   = {1–16, 20–22, 25, 27, 28, 30–34, 41, 42}
    viii.   S (a2, 23)   = {1–16, 20, 21,23, 34, 42}
    ix.   S (a2, 26)   = {1–16, 20, 21, 23, 25–27, 34, 41, 42)
    x.   S (a2, 29)   = {1–16, 20, 21, 23, 25, 27–31, 33, 34, 41, 42}
    xi.   S (a2, 32)   = {1–16, 20, 21, 23, 25, 27, 28, 30–34, 41, 42}
    xii.   S (a3, 26)   = {1–16, 20, 21, 24–27, 34, 41, 42}
    xiii.   S (a3, 29)   = {1–16, 20, 21, 24, 25, 27–31, 33, 34, 41,42}
    xiv.   S (a3, 32)   = {1–16, 20, 21, 24, 25, 27, 28, 30–34, 41, 42}
    xv.   S (valid, 5)   = {1–5, 42}
    xvi.   S (valid, 15) = {1–16, 20, 42}
    xvii.   S (valid, 18) = {1–14, 16–20, 42}
    xviii.   S (valid, 36) = {1–14, 16–20, 21, 34–38, 40–42}
    xix.   S (valid, 39) = {1–13, 20, 21, 34, 35, 37–42}

The test cases of the above slices are given in Table 4.20.

Table 4.20. Test cases using program slices

S. No.	Slice	Path	a	b	c	Expected output
1.	S(a, 8)/S(a,42)	1-8, 42	20			No output
2.	S(b, 10)/S(b,42)	1-6, 9, 10, 42		20		No output
3.	S(c, 12)/S(c,42)	1-6, 11, 12, 42			20	No output
4.	S(a1, 22)	1-16, 20-22, 34, 42	30	20	40	No output
5.	S(a1, 26)	1-16, 20-22, 25-27, 34, 41, 42	30	20	40	Obtuse angled triangle
6.	S(a1, 29)	1-16, 20-22, 25, 27-31, 33, 34, 41, 42	30	40	50	Right angled triangle
7.	S(a1, 32)	1-16, 20-22, 25, 27, 28, 30-34, 41, 42	50	60	40	Acute angled triangle
8.	S(a1, 42)	1-16, 20-22, 34, 42	30	20	40	No output
9.	S(a2, 23)	1-16, 20, 21, 23, 34, 42	30	20	40	No output
10.	S(a2, 26)	1-16, 20, 21, 23, 25-27, 34, 41, 42	40	30	20	Obtuse angled triangle
11.	S(a2, 29)	1-16, 20, 21, 23, 25, 27-31, 33, 34, 41, 42	50	40	30	Right angled triangle
12.	S(a2, 32)	1-16, 20, 21, 23, 25, 27, 28, 30-34, 41, 42	40	50	60	Acute angled triangle
13.	S(a2, 42)	1-16, 20, 21, 23, 34, 42	30	20	40	No output
14.	S(a3, 24)	1-16, 20, 21, 24, 34, 42	30	20	40	No output
15.	S(a3, 26)	1-16, 20, 21, 24-27, 34, 41, 42	20	40	30	Obtuse angled triangle
16.	S(a3, 29)	1-16, 20, 21, 24, 25, 27-31, 33, 34, 41, 42	40	50	30	Right angled triangle
17.	S(a3, 32)	1-16, 20, 21, 24, 25, 27, 28, 30-34, 41, 42	50	40	60	Acute angled triangle
18.	S(a3, 42)	1-16, 20, 21, 24, 34, 42	30	20	40	No output
19.	S(valid,5)	1-2, 5, 42				No output
20.	S(valid,15)	1-16, 20, 42	20	40	30	No output
21.	S(valid,18)	1-14, 16-20, 42	30	10	15	No output
22.	S(valid,36)	1-14, 16-20, 21, 34-38, 40-42	30	10	15	Invalid triangle
23.	S(valid,39)	1-13, 20, 21, 34, 35, 37-42	102	-1	6	Input values out of range
24.	S(valid,42)	1-14, 16-20, 42	30	10	15	No output

Example 4.9. Consider the program for determination of day of the week given in Figure 3.13. Consider variables day, validDate, leap and generate possible program slices. Design at least one test case from each slice.

Solution:
There are ten variables – day, month, year, century Y, Y1, M, date, valid date, and leap. We may create many slices for variables day, validDate and leap as given below:

1. S(day, 6)   = {1-6, 118}
2. S(day, 93)   = {1-11, 18-21, 25, 43-48, 53, 54, 61, 62, 69, 70, 72, 73, 75, 76, 78-81, 88, 90-94, 113, 117, 118}
3. S(day, 96)   = {1-11, 18-21, 25, 43-48, 53, 54, 61, 62, 69, 70, 72, 73, 75, 76, 78-81, 88, 90-92, 94-97, 110, 112, 113, 117, 118}
4. S(day, 99)   = {1-11, 18-21, 25, 43-48, 53, 54, 61, 62, 69, 70, 72, 73, 75, 76, 78-81, 88, 90-92, 94, 95, 97-100, 110, 112, 113, 117, 118}
5. S(day, 102)   = {1-11, 18-21, 25, 43-48, 53, 54, 61, 62, 69, 70, 72, 73, 75, 76, 78-81, 88, 90-92, 94, 95, 97, 98, 100-103, 110, 112, 113, 117, 118}
6. S(day, 105)   = {1-11, 18-21, 25, 43-48, 53, 54, 61, 62, 69, 70, 72, 73, 75, 76, 78-81, 88, 90-92, 94, 95, 97, 98, 100, 101, 103-106, 110, 112, 113, 117, 118}
7. S(day, 108)   = {1-11, 18-21, 25, 43-48, 53, 54, 61, 62, 69, 70, 72, 73, 75, 76, 78-81, 88, 90-92, 94, 95, 97, 98, 100, 101, 103, 104, 106-110, 112, 113, 117, 118}
8. S(day, 111)   = {1-11, 18-21, 25, 43-48, 53, 54, 61, 62, 69, 70, 72, 73, 75, 76, 78-81, 88, 90-92, 94, 95, 97, 98, 100, 101, 103, 104, 106, 107, 109-113, 117, 118}
9. S(day, 115)   = {1-11, 43, 44, 113-118}
10. S(day, 118)   = {1-6, 118}
11. S(validDate,3) = {1-3, 118}
12. S(validDate,20) = {1-11, 18-21, 25, 43, 118}
13. S(validDate,23) = {1-11, 18, 19, 21-25, 43, 118}
14. S(validDate,28) = {1-13, 17, 18, 25, 26-29, 36, 40, 42, 43, 118}
15. S(validDate,31) = {1-11, 18, 25, 26, 27, 29-33, 35, 36, 40, 42, 43, 118}
16. S(validDate,34) = {1-11, 18, 25, 26, 27, 29, 30, 32-36, 40, 42, 43, 118}
17.. S(validDate,38) = {1-11, 18, 25, 26, 36-40, 42, 43, 118}
18. S(validDate,41) = {1-11, 18, 25, 26, 36, 37, 39-43, 118}
19. S(validDate,118)= {1-11, 18, 25, 26, 36, 37, 39-43, 118}
20. S(leap,3)   = {1-3, 118}
21. S(leap,13)   = {1-13, 17, 43, 118}
22. S(leap,15)   = {1-17, 43, 118}
23. S(leap,118)   = {1-17, 43, 118}

The test cases for the above slices are given in Table 4.21.

Table 4.21. Test cases using program slices

S. No.	Slice	Lines covered	Month	Day	Year	Expected output
1.	S(day, 6)	1–6, 118	6	–	–	No output
2.	S(day, 93)	1–11, 18–21, 25, 43–48, 53, 54, 61, 62, 69, 70, 72, 73, 75, 76, 78–81, 88, 90–94, 113, 117, 118	6	13	1999	Sunday
3.	S(day, 96)	1–11, 18–21, 25, 43–48, 53, 54, 61, 62, 69, 70, 72, 73, 75, 76, 78–81, 88, 90–92, 94–97, 110, 112, 113, 117, 118	6	14	1999	Monday
4.	S(day, 99)	1–11, 18–21, 25, 43–48, 53, 54, 61, 62, 69, 70, 72, 73, 75, 76, 78–81, 88, 90–92, 94, 95, 97–100, 110, 112, 113, 117, 118	6	15	1999	Tuesday
5.	S(day, 102)	1–11, 18–21, 25, 43–48, 53, 54, 61, 62, 69, 70, 72, 73, 75, 76, 78–81, 88, 90–92, 94, 95, 97, 98, 100–103, 110, 112, 113, 117, 118	6	16	1999	Wednesday
6.	S(day, 105)	1–11, 18–21, 25, 43–48, 53, 54, 61, 62, 69, 70, 72, 73, 75, 76, 78–81, 88, 90–92, 94, 95, 97, 98, 100, 101, 103–106, 110, 112, 113, 117, 118	6	17	1999	Thursday
7.	S(day, 108)	1–11, 18–21, 25, 43–48, 53, 54, 61, 62, 69, 70, 72, 73, 75, 76, 78–81, 88, 90–92, 94, 95, 97, 98, 100, 101, 103, 104, 106–110, 112, 113, 117, 118	6	18	1999	Friday
8.	S(day, 111)	1–11, 18–21, 25, 43–48, 53, 54, 61, 62, 69, 70, 72, 73, 75, 76, 78–81, 88, 90–92, 94, 95, 97, 98, 100, 101, 103, 104, 106, 107, 109–113, 117, 118	6	19	1999	Saturday
9.	S(day, 115)	1–11, 43, 44, 113–118	6	31	2059	Invalid Date
10.	S(day, 118)	1–6, 118	6	19	1999	Saturday
11.	S(validDate,3)	1–3, 118	–	–	–	No output
12.	S(validDate,20)	1–11, 18–21, 25, 43, 118	6	15	2009	No output
13.	S(validDate,23)	1–11, 18, 19, 21–25, 43, 118	6	31	2009	No output
14.	S(validDate,28)	1–13, 17, 18, 25, 26–29, 36, 40, 42, 43, 118	2	15	2000	No output

(Contd.)

(Contd.)

S. No.	Slice	Lines covered	Month	Day	Year	Expected output
15.	S(validDate,31)	1-11, 18, 25, 26, 27, 29-33, 35, 36, 40, 42, 43, 118	2	15	2009	No output
16.	S(validDate,34)	1-11, 18, 25, 26, 27, 29, 30, 32-36, 40, 42, 43, 118	2	29	2009	No output
17.	S(validDate,38)	1-11, 18, 25, 26, 36-40, 42, 43, 118	8	15	2009	No output
18.	S(validDate,41)	1-11, 18, 25, 26, 36, 37, 39-43, 118	13	15	2009	No output
19.	S(validDate,118)	1-11, 18, 25, 26, 36, 37, 39-43, 118	13	15	2009	No output
20.	S(leap,3)	1-3, 118	-	-	-	No output
21.	S(leap,13)	1-13, 17, 43, 118	8	15	2000	No output
22.	S(leap,15)	1-17, 43, 118	8	15	1900	No output
23.	S(leap,118)	1-17, 43, 118	8	15	1900	No output

4.4 MUTATION TESTING

It is a popular technique to assess the effectiveness of a test suite. We may have a large number of test cases for any program. We neither have time nor resources to execute all of them. We may select a few test cases using any testing technique and prepare a test suite. How do we assess the effectiveness of a selected test suite? Is this test suite adequate for the program? If the test suite is not able to make the program fail, there may be one of the following reasons:

(i) The test suite is effective but hardly any errors are there in the program. How will a test suite detect errors when they are not there?

(ii) The test suite is not effective and could not find any errors. Although there may be errors, they could not be detected due to poor selection of test suite. How will errors be detected when the test suite is not effective?

In both the cases, we are not able to find errors, but the reasons are different. In the first case, the program quality is good and the test suite is effective and in the second case, the program quality is not that good and the test suite is also not that effective. When the test suite is not able to detect errors, how do we know whether the test suite is not effective or the program quality is good? Hence, assessing the effectiveness and quality of a test suite is very important. Mutation testing may help us to assess the effectiveness of a test suite and may also enhance the test suite, if it is not adequate for a program.

4.4.1 Mutation and Mutants

The process of changing a program is known as mutation. This change may be limited to one, two or very few changes in the program. We prepare a copy of the program under test and make a change in a statement of the program. This changed version of the program is known as a mutant of the original program. The behaviour of the mutant may be different from the original program due to the introduction of a change. However, the original program and mutant are syntactically correct and should compile correctly. To mutate a program means to change a program. We generally make only one or two changes in order to assess the effectiveness of the selected test suite. We may make many mutants of a program by making small changes in the program. Every mutant will have a different change in a program. Consider a program to find the largest amongst three numbers as given in Figure 3.11 and its two mutants are given in Figure 4.7 and Figure 4.8. Every change of a program may give a different output as compared to the original program.

Many changes can be made in the program given in Figure 3.11 till it is syntactically correct. Mutant M_1 is obtained by replacing the operator '>' of line number 11 by the operator '='. Mutant M_2 is obtained by changing the operator '>' of line number 20 to operator '<'. These changes are simple changes. Only one change has been made in the original program to obtain mutant M_1 and mutant M_2.

```
            #include<stdio.h>
            #include<conio.h>
1.          void main()
2.          {
3.              float A,B,C;
4.              clrscr();
5.              printf("Enter number 1:\n");
6.              scanf("%f", &A);
7.              printf("Enter number 2:\n");
8.              scanf("%f", &B);
9.              printf("Enter number 3:\n");
10.             scanf("%f", &C);
                /*Check for greatest of three numbers*/
11.             if(A>B){      ← if(A=B) {  mutated statement ('>' is replaced by '=')
12.                if(A>C) {
13.                    printf("The largest number is: %f\n",A);
14.                }
15.                else {
16.                    printf("The largest number is: %f\n",C);
17.                }
18.             }
19.             else {
20.                if(C>B) {
21.                    printf("The largest number is: %f\n",C);
22.                }
23.                else {
24.                    printf("The largest number is: %f\n",B);
25.                }
26.             }
```

(Contd.)

(Contd.)
27.   getch();
28.   }

M₁ : First order mutant

Figure 4.7. Mutant₁ (M₁) of program to find the largest among three numbers

```
       #include<stdio.h>
       #include<conio.h>
1.     void main()
2.     {
3.     float A,B,C;
4.     clrscr();
5.     printf("Enter number 1:\n");
6.     scanf("%f", &A);
7.     printf("Enter number 2:\n");
8.     scanf("%f", &B);
9.     printf("Enter number 3:\n");
10.    scanf("%f", &C);
       /*Check for greatest of three numbers*/
11.    if(A>B) {
12.    if(A>C) {
13.         printf("The largest number is: %f\n",A);
14.    }
15.    else {
16.         printf("The largest number is: %f\n",C);
17.    }
18.    }
19.    else {
20.    if(C>B) {      ← if(C<B) { mutated statement ('>' is replaced by '<')
21.         printf("The largest number is: %f\n",C);
22.    }
23.    else {
24.         printf("The largest number is: %f\n",B);
25.    }
26.    }
27.    getch();
28.    }
```

M₂ : First order mutant

Figure 4.8. Mutant₂ (M₂) of program to find the largest among three numbers

Structural Testing

The mutants generated by making only one change are known as first order mutants. We may obtain second order mutants by making two simple changes in the program and third order mutants by making three simple changes, and so on. The second order mutant (M_3) of the program given in Figure 3.11 is obtained by making two changes in the program and thus changing operator '>' of line number 11 to operator '<' and operator '>' of line number 20 to '≥' as given in Figure 4.9. The second order mutants and above are called higher order mutants. Generally, in practice, we prefer to use only first order mutants in order to simplify the process of mutation.

```
        #include<stdio.h>
        #include<conio.h>
1.      void main()
2.      {
3.         float A,B,C;
4.         clrscr();
5.         printf("Enter number 1:\n");
6.         scanf("%f", &A);
7.         printf("Enter number 2:\n");
8.         scanf("%f", &B);
9.         printf("Enter number 3:\n");
10.        scanf("%f", &C);
           /*Check for greatest of three numbers*/
11.        if(A>B) {      ← if(A<B) { mutated statement (replacing '>' by '<')
12.           if(A>C) {
13.              printf("The largest number is: %f\n",A);
14.           }
15.           else {
16.              printf("The largest number is: %f\n",C);
17.           }
18.        }
19.        else {
20.           if(C>B) {    ← if(C≥B) { mutated statement (replacing '>' by '≥')
21.              printf("The largest number is: %f\n",C);
22.           }
23.           else {
24.              printf("The largest number is: %f\n",B);
25.           }
26.        }
27.        getch();
28.     }
        M₃ : Second order mutant
```

Figure 4.9. Mutant₃ (M_3) of program to find the largest among three numbers

4.4.2 Mutation Operators

Mutants are produced by applying mutant operators. An operator is essentially a grammatical rule that changes a single expression to another expression. The changed expression should be grammatically correct as per the used language. If one or more mutant operators are applied to all expressions of a program, we may be able to generate a large set of mutants. We should measure the degree to which the program is changed. If the original expression is x + 1, and the mutant for that expression is x + 2, that is considered as a lesser change as compared to a mutant where the changed expression is (y * 2) by changing both operands and the operator. We may have a ranking scheme, where a first order mutant is a single change to an expression, a second order mutant is a mutation to a first order mutant, and so on. Higher order mutants become difficult to manage, control and trace. They are not popular in practice and first order mutants are recommended to be used. To kill a mutant, we should be able to execute the changed statement of the program. If we are not able to do so, the fault will not be detected. If x − y is changed to x − 5 to make a mutant, then we should not use the value of y to be equal to 5. If we do so, the fault will not be revealed. Some of the mutant operators for object oriented languages like Java, C++ are given as:

(i) Changing the access modifier, like public to private.
(ii) Static modifier change
(iii) Argument order change
(iv) Super Keyword change
(v) Operator change
(vi) Any operand change by a numeric value.

4.4.3 Mutation Score

When we execute a mutant using a test suite, we may have any of the following outcomes:

(i) The results of the program are affected by the change and any test case of the test suite detects it. If this happens, then the mutant is called a killed mutant.
(ii) The results of the program are not affected by the change and any test case of the test suite does not detect the mutation. The mutant is called a live mutant.

The mutation score associated with a test suite and its mutants is calculated as:

$$\text{Mutation Score} = \frac{\text{Number of mutants killed}}{\text{Total number of mutants}}$$

The total number of mutants is equal to the number of killed mutants plus the number of live mutants. The mutation score measures how sensitive the program is to the changes and how accurate the test suite is. A mutation score is always between 0 and 1. A higher value of mutation score indicates the effectiveness of the test suite although effectiveness also depends on the types of faults that the mutation operators are designed to represent.

The live mutants are important for us and should be analyzed thoroughly. Why is it that any test case of the test suite not able to detect the changed behaviour of the program? One of the reasons may be that the changed statement was not executed by these test cases. If executed, then also it has no effect on the behaviour of the program. We should write new test cases for live mutants and kill all these mutants. The test cases that identify the changed behaviour should be preserved and transferred to the original test suite in order to enhance the capability of the test suite. Hence, the purpose of mutation testing is not only to assess the capability of a test suite but also to enhance the test suite. Some mutation testing tools are also available in the market like Insure++, Jester for Java (open source) and Nester for C++ (open source).

Example 4.10: Consider the program to find the largest of three numbers as given in figure 3.11. The test suite selected by a testing technique is given as:

S. No.	A	B	C	Expected Output
1.	6	10	2	10
2.	10	6	2	10
3.	6	2	10	10
4.	6	10	20	20

Generate five mutants (M_1 to M_5) and calculate the mutation score of this test suite.

Solution:
The mutated line numbers and changed lines are shown in Table 4.22.

Table 4.22. Mutated statements

Mutant No.	Line no.	Original line	Modified Line
M_1	11	if(A>B)	if (A<B)
M_2	11	if(A>B)	if(A>(B+C))
M_3	12	if(A>C)	if(A<C)
M_4	20	if(C>B)	if(C=B)
M_5	16	printf("The Largest number is:%f\n",C);	printf("The Largest number is:%f\n",B);

The actual output obtained by executing the mutants M_1-M_5 is shown in Tables 4.23-4.27.

Table 4.23. Actual output of mutant M_1

Test case	A	B	C	Expected output	Actual output
1.	6	10	2	10	6
2.	10	6	2	10	6
3.	6	2	10	10	10
4.	6	10	20	20	20

Table 4.24. Actual output of mutant M_2

Test case	A	B	C	Expected output	Actual output
1.	6	10	2	10	10
2.	10	6	2	10	10
3.	6	2	10	10	10
4.	6	10	20	20	20

Table 4.25. Actual output of mutant M_3

Test case	A	B	C	Expected output	Actual output
1.	6	10	2	10	10
2.	10	6	2	10	2
3.	6	2	10	10	6
4.	6	10	20	20	20

Table 4.26. Actual output of mutant M_4

Test case	A	B	C	Expected output	Actual output
1.	6	10	2	10	10
2.	10	6	2	10	10
3.	6	2	10	10	10
4.	6	10	20	20	10

Table 4.27. Actual output of mutant M_5

Test case	A	B	C	Expected output	Actual output
1.	6	10	2	10	10
2.	10	6	2	10	10
3.	6	2	10	10	2
4.	6	10	20	20	20

$$\text{Mutation Score} = \frac{\text{Number of mutants killed}}{\text{Total number of mutants}}$$
$$= \frac{4}{5}$$
$$= 0.8$$

Higher the mutant score, better is the effectiveness of the test suite. The mutant M_2 is live in the example. We may have to write a specific test case to kill this mutant. The additional test case is given in Table 4.28.

Table 4.28. Additional test case

Test case	A	B	C	Expected output
5.	10	5	6	10

Now when we execute the test case 5, the actual output will be different from the expected output (see Table 4.29), hence the mutant will be killed.

Table 4.29. Output of added test case

Test case	A	B	C	Expected output	Actual output
5.	10	5	6	10	6

Structural Testing

This test case is very important and should be added to the given test suite. Therefore, the revised test suite is given in Table 4.30.

Table 4.30. Revised test suite

Test case	A	B	C	Expected output
1.	6	10	2	10
2.	10	6	2	10
3.	6	2	10	10
4.	6	10	20	20
5.	10	5	6	10

Example 4.11: Consider the program for classification of triangle given in Figure 3.18. The test suite A and B are selected by two different testing techniques and are given in Table 4.31 and Table 4.32, respectively. The five first order mutants and the modified lines are given in Table 4.33. Calculate the mutation score of each test suite and compare their effectiveness. Also, add any additional test case, if required.

Table 4.31. Test suite A

Test case	a	b	c	Expected output
1.	30	40	90	Invalid triangle
2.	30	20	40	Obtuse angled triangle
3.	50	40	60	Acute angled triangle
4.	30	40	50	Right angled triangle
5.	-1	50	40	Input values are out of range
6.	50	150	90	Input values are out of range
7.	50	40	-1	Input values are out of range

Table 4.32. Test suite B

Test case	a	b	c	Expected output
1.	40	90	20	Invalid triangle
2.	40	30	60	Obtuse angled triangle
3.	40	50	60	Acute angled triangle
4.	30	40	50	Right angled triangle
5.	-1	50	40	Input values are out of range
6.	30	101	90	Input values are out of range
7.	30	90	0	Input values are out of range

Table 4.33. Mutated lines

Mutant No.	Line no.	Original line	Modified Line
M_1	13	if(a>0&&a<=100&&b>0&&b<=100&&c>0&&c<=100) {	if(a>0||a<=100&&b>0&&b<=100&&c>0&&c<=100) {
M_2	14	if((a+b)>c&&(b+c)>a&&(c+a)>b) {	if((a+b)>c&&(b+c)>a&&(b+a)>b) {
M_3	21	if(valid==1) {	if(valid>1) {
M_4	23	a2=(b*b+c*c)/(a*a);	a2=(b*b+c*c)*(a*a);
M_5	25	if(a1<1||a2<1||a3<1) {	if(a1>1||a2<1||a3<1) {

Solution:

(a) Test cases for Test Suite A

The actual outputs of mutants M_1-M_5 on test suite A are shown in Tables 4.34-4.38.

Table 4.34. Actual output of $M_1(A)$

Test case	a	b	c	Expected output	Actual output
1.	30	40	90	Invalid triangle	Invalid triangle
2.	30	20	40	Obtuse angled triangle	Obtuse angled triangle
3.	50	40	60	Acute angled triangle	Acute angled triangle
4.	30	40	50	Right angled triangle	Right angled triangle
5.	-1	50	40	Input values are out of range	Invalid triangle
6.	50	150	90	Input values are out of range	Invalid triangle
7.	50	40	-1	Input values are out of range	Invalid triangle

Table 4.35. Actual output of $M_2(A)$

Test case	a	b	c	Expected output	Actual output
1.	30	40	90	Invalid triangle	Invalid triangle
2.	30	20	40	Obtuse angled triangle	Obtuse angled triangle
3.	50	40	60	Acute angled triangle	Acute angled triangle
4.	30	40	50	Right angled triangle	Right angled triangle
5.	-1	50	40	Input values are out of range	Input values are out of range
6.	50	150	90	Input values are out of range	Input values are out of range
7.	50	40	-1	Input values are out of range	Input values are out of range

Table 4.36. Actual output of $M_3(A)$

Test case	a	b	c	Expected output	Actual output
1.	30	40	90	Invalid triangle	Invalid triangle
2.	30	20	40	Obtuse angled triangle	Input values are out of range
3.	50	40	60	Acute angled triangle	Input values are out of range
4.	30	40	50	Right angled triangle	Input values are out of range
5.	-1	50	40	Input values are out of range	Input values are out of range
6.	50	150	90	Input values are out of range	Input values are out of range
7.	50	40	-1	Input values are out of range	Input values are out of range

Table 4.37. Actual output of $M_4(A)$

Test case	a	b	c	Expected output	Actual output
1.	30	40	90	Invalid triangle	Invalid triangle
2.	30	20	40	Obtuse angled triangle	Obtuse angled triangle
3.	50	40	60	Acute angled triangle	Acute angled triangle
4.	30	40	50	Right angled triangle	Right angled triangle
5.	-1	50	40	Input values are out of range	Input values are out of range
6.	50	150	90	Input values are out of range	Input values are out of range
7.	50	40	-1	Input values are out of range	Input values are out of range

Table 4.38. Actual output of $M_5(A)$

Test case	a	b	c	Expected output	Actual output
1.	30	40	90	Invalid triangle	Invalid triangle
2.	30	20	40	Obtuse angled triangle	Acute angled triangle
3.	50	40	60	Acute angled triangle	Obtuse angled triangle
4.	30	40	50	Right angled triangle	Right angled triangle
5.	-1	50	40	Input values are out of range	Input values are out of range
6.	50	150	90	Input values are out of range	Input values are out of range
7.	50	40	-1	Input values are out of range	Input values are out of range

Two mutants are M_2 and M_4 are live. Thus, the mutation score using test suite A is 0.6.

$$\text{Mutation Score} = \frac{\text{Number of mutants killed}}{\text{Total number of mutants}}$$
$$= \frac{3}{5}$$
$$= 0.6$$

(b) Test cases for Test Suite B

The actual outputs of mutants M_1-M_5 on test suite B are shown in Tables 4.39-4.43.

Table 4.39. Actual output of $M_1(B)$

Test case	a	b	c	Expected output	Actual output
1.	40	90	20	Invalid triangle	Invalid triangle
2.	40	30	60	Obtuse angled triangle	Obtuse angled triangle
3.	40	50	60	Acute angled triangle	Acute angled triangle
4.	30	40	50	Right angled triangle	Right angled triangle
5.	-1	50	40	Input values are out of range	Invalid triangle
6.	30	101	90	Input values are out of range	Obtuse angled triangle
7.	30	90	0	Input values are out of range	Invalid triangle

Table 4.40. Actual output of $M_2(B)$

Test case	a	b	c	Expected output	Actual output
1.	40	90	20	Invalid triangle	Obtuse angled triangle
2.	40	30	60	Obtuse angled triangle	Obtuse angled triangle
3.	40	50	60	Acute angled triangle	Acute angled triangle
4.	30	40	50	Right angled triangle	Right angled triangle
5.	-1	50	40	Input values are out of range	Input values are out of range
6.	30	101	90	Input values are out of range	Input values are out of range
7.	30	90	0	Input values are out of range	Input values are out of range

Table 4.41. Actual output of $M_3(B)$

Test case	a	b	c	Expected output	Actual output
1.	40	90	20	Invalid triangle	Invalid triangle
2.	40	30	60	Obtuse angled triangle	Input values are out of range
3.	40	50	60	Acute angled triangle	Input values are out of range
4.	30	40	50	Right angled triangle	Input values are out of range
5.	-1	50	40	Input values are out of range	Input values are out of range
6.	30	101	90	Input values are out of range	Input values are out of range
7.	30	90	0	Input values are out of range	Input values are out of range

Table 4.42. Actual output of $M_4(B)$

Test case	a	b	c	Expected output	Actual output
1.	40	90	20	Invalid triangle	Invalid triangle
2.	40	30	60	Obtuse angled triangle	Obtuse angled triangle
3.	40	50	60	Acute angled triangle	Acute angled triangle
4.	30	40	50	Right angled triangle	Right angled triangle
5.	-1	50	40	Input values are out of range	Input values are out of range
6.	30	101	90	Input values are out of range	Input values are out of range
7.	30	90	0	Input values are out of range	Input values are out of range

Table 4.43. Actual output of $M_5(B)$

Test case	a	b	c	Expected output	Actual output
1.	40	90	20	Invalid triangle	Invalid triangle
2.	40	30	60	Obtuse angled triangle	Acute angled triangle
3.	40	50	60	Acute angled triangle	Obtuse angled triangle
4.	30	40	50	Right angled triangle	Right angled triangle
5.	-1	50	40	Input values are out of range	Input values are out of range
6.	30	101	90	Input values are out of range	Input values are out of range
7.	30	90	0	Input values are out of range	Input values are out of range

$$\text{Mutation Score} = \frac{\text{Number of mutants killed}}{\text{Total number of mutants}}$$
$$= \frac{4}{5}$$
$$= 0.8$$

The mutation score of Test suite B is higher as compared to the mutation score of test suite A, hence test suite B is more effective in comparison to test suite A. In order to kill the live mutant (M_4), an additional test case should be added to test suite B as shown in Table 4.44.

Table 4.44. Additional test case

Test case	a	b	c	Expected output
8.	40	30	20	Obtuse angled triangle

The revised test suite B is given in Table 4.45.

Table 4.45. Revised test suite B

Test case	a	b	c	Expected output
1.	40	90	20	Invalid triangle
2.	40	30	60	Obtuse angled triangle
3.	40	50	60	Acute angled triangle
4.	30	40	50	Right angled triangle
5.	−1	50	40	Input values are out of range
6.	30	101	90	Input values are out of range
7.	30	90	0	Input values are out of range
8.	40	30	20	Obtuse angled triangle

MULTIPLE CHOICE QUESTIONS

Note: *Select the most appropriate answer for the following questions.*

4.1 Which is not a structural testing technique?
 (a) Mutation testing
 (b) Data flow testing
 (c) Slice based testing
 (d) Decision table based testing

4.2 Which is a structural testing technique?
 (a) Data flow testing
 (b) Control flow testing
 (c) Mutation testing
 (d) All of the above

4.3 Data flow testing is related to:
 (a) ER diagrams
 (b) Data flow diagrams
 (c) Data dictionaries
 (d) None of the above

4.4 Mutation testing is related to:
 (a) Fault seeding
 (b) Fault severity
 (c) Fault impact analysis
 (d) None of the above

4.5 Mutation score does not indicate anything about:
 (a) Size of a test suite
 (b) Effectiveness of a test suite
 (c) Performance of a test suite
 (d) Usefulness of a test suite

4.6 100% statement coverage and branch coverage means:
(a) Every statement has been tested
(b) Every outcome of a branch statement has been tested
(c) Every statement and every branch has been tested
(d) Every condition has been tested

4.7 How many test cases are required for 100% statement and branch coverage of the following source code?

```
void main ( )
{
    int a, b;
    scanf ("%d", &a);
    scanf ("%d", &b);
    if (a>b) {
        printf ("a is large");
    }
    else {
        printf ("b is large");
    }
}
```

(a) 1 test case for statement coverage, 2 for branch coverage.
(b) 2 test case for statement coverage, 1 for branch coverage.
(c) 2 test case for statement coverage, 2 for branch coverage.
(d) 1 test case for statement coverage, 3 for branch coverage.

4.8 Which of the following statements about the relationship of statement coverage and decision coverage is correct?
(a) 100% statement coverage means 100% decision coverage.
(b) 100% decision coverage means 100% statement coverage.
(c) 90% statement coverage means 90% decision coverage.
(d) 90% decision coverage means 90% statement coverage.

4.9 In data flow testing, which criterion generates the maximum number of test cases?
(a) Test all du-paths
(b) Test all uses
(c) Test all definitions
(d) All of the above generates the same number of test cases

4.10 Statements coverage will not check for :
(a) Missing statements
(b) Extra statements
(c) Dead statements
(d) Unused statements

4.11 Statement coverage is commonly used to measure:
(a) Test effectiveness
(b) Number of faults
(c) Testing time
(d) Complexity of code

4.12 Structural testing techniques may help us to:
- (a) Understand the source code
- (b) Generate test cases using various paths
- (c) Comprehend the program
- (d) All of the above

4.13 A program slice is:
- (a) More complex than the original program
- (b) Larger than the original program
- (c) Smaller than the original program
- (d) More critical than the original program

4.14 Which mutants are more popular in practice?
- (a) First order mutant
- (b) Second order mutant
- (c) Third order mutant
- (d) Zero order mutant

4.15 Source code coverage measurement is :
- (a) A partial measure of test effectiveness
- (b) Not related to testing
- (c) Easily achievable in practice
- (d) None of the above

4.16 Which of the following is not related?
- (a) White box
- (b) Black box
- (c) Glass box
- (d) Structural

4.17 Mutation score is related to:
- (a) Effectiveness of a test suite
- (b) Size of a test suite
- (c) Complexity of a test suite
- (d) Criticality of a test suite

4.18 Which is a mutation testing tool?
- (a) Insure++
- (b) Jester for Java
- (c) Nester for c++
- (d) All of the above

4.19 Which is difficult to achieve?
- (a) 100% statement coverage
- (b) 100% branch coverage
- (c) 100% condition coverage
- (d) 100% path coverage

4.20 Program slicing was introduced by:
- (a) Mark Weiser
- (b) Victor Basili
- (c) L. Briand
- (d) Mc Cabe

EXERCISES

4.1 What is structural testing? How is it different from functional testing?
4.2 What are different types of structural testing techniques? Discuss any two techniques with the help of examples.
4.3 Discuss the significance of path testing. How can we make it more effective?
4.4 Show with the help of an example that a very high level of statement coverage does not mean that the program is defect-free.
4.5 Write a program to find roots of a quadratic equation.
   (a) Draw program graph, DD path graph. Also find independent paths and generate test cases.
   (b) Find all du-paths and identify those du-paths that are not dc paths. Write test cases for every du-path.
4.6 Explain define/use testing. Consider the NextDate function and write a program in 'C' language. Find all du paths and dc paths. Design test cases for every definition to every usage.
4.7 Consider a program for classification of a triangle. Its input is a triple of positive integers (say a, b and c) from interval [1, 100]. The output may be one of the following:
   [Scalene, Isosceles, Equilateral, Not a triangle, invalid inputs]
   (a) Draw a program graph, DD path graph and write test cases for every independent path.
   (b) Find all du-paths and identify those du-paths that are not dc paths. Write test cases for every du-path.
4.8 What is slice based testing? How can it improve testing? Explain the concept with the help of an example and write test cases accordingly.
4.9 What is mutation testing? What is the purpose of mutation score? Why are higher order mutants not preferred?
4.10 Differentiate between black box and white box testing. Consider a program to find the largest number amongst three numbers. Generate test cases using one black box testing and one white box testing technique.
4.11 How is data flow testing performed? Is it possible to design data flow test cases manually? Justify your answer.
4.12 What do you mean by a program graph? What is its use? How can we use it in the design of du-paths?
4.13 Write a program to print the grade of a student according to the following criteria:
   (i)   marks > 80   A+ Grade
   (ii) 70 < marks ≤ 80   A Grade
   (iii) 60 < marks ≤ 70   B Grade
   (iv) 50 < marks ≤ 60   C Grade
   (v)   40 < marks ≤ 50   D Grade
   Generate all du-paths and write test cases for all du-paths.
4.14 Consider the program given below. Find all du-paths and identify those du-paths that are definition clear. Also find all du-paths, all-uses and all-definitions and generate test cases for these paths.

/* Program to calculate total telephone bill amount to be paid by an customer*/

```
       #include<stdio.h>
       #include<conio.h>
1.     void main()
2.     {
3.     int custnum,numcalls,valid=0;
4.     float netamount;
5.     clrscr();
6.     printf("Enter customer number & number of calls:");
7.     scanf("%d %d",&custnum,&numcalls);
8.     if(custnum>10&&custnum<20000){
9.             valid=1;
10.    if(numcalls<0){
11.            valid=-1;
12.    }
13.    }
14.    if(valid==1){
15.    if(numcalls<76){
16.            netamount=500;
17.    }
18.    else if(numcalls>75&&numcalls<201){
19.            netamount=500+0.80*(numcalls-75);
20.    }
21.    else if(numcalls>200&&numcalls<501){
22.            netamount=500+1.00*(numcalls-200);
23.    }
24.    else{
25.            netamount=500+1.20*(numcalls-500);
26.    }
27.    printf("\nCustomer number: %d\t Total Charges:%.3f",custnum,netamount);
28.    }
29.    else if(valid==0){
30.            printf("Invalid customer number");
31.    }
32.    else{
33.            printf("Invalid number of calls");
34.    }
35.    getch();
36.    }
```

4.15 Consider the program for determination of the total telephone bill amount to be paid by a customer given in exercise 4.14. Consider all variables and generate possible program slices. Design at least one test case from every slice.

4.16 Consider the program for determination of the total telephone bill amount to be paid by a customer given in exercise 4.14. Generate two first order mutants and one second order mutant. Design a test suite of five test cases and calculate the mutation score of the test suite.

4.17 Consider a program to input two numbers and print them in ascending order given below. Find all du-paths and identify those du-paths that are definition clear. Also find all du-paths, all-uses and all-definitions and generate test cases for these paths.

```
#include<stdio.h>
#include<conio.h>
```

```
1.   void main()
2.   {
3.   int a,b,t;
4.   clrscr();
5.   printf("Enter first number:");
6.   scanf("%d",&a);
7.   printf("Enter second number:");
8.   scanf("%d",&b);
9.   if(a<b){
10.  t=a;
11.  a=b;
12.  b=t;
13.  }
14.  printf("%d %d",a,b);
15.  getch();
16.  }
```

4.18 Consider a program to input two numbers and print them in ascending order given in exercise 4.17. Consider all variables and generate possible program slices. Design at least one test case from every slice.

4.19 Establish the relationship between data flow testing and slice based testing.

4.20 What is the importance of mutation testing? Why is it becoming popular?

FURTHER READING

Copeland's book provides introduction to levels of converge:
    Lee Copeland, "A Practitioner's Guide to Software Test Design", Artech House, 2004.

Key concepts and definitions for structural data flow testing are given by Weyuker:
    Weyuker, Elaine J. "Data Flow Testing", In MARC94, pp. 247–249.

The research paper explains the basic concepts of data flow testing with an example:
    J. Badlaney R. Ghatol R. Jadhwani, "An Introduction to Data-Flow Testing", TR-2006-22, 2006.

An edited tutorial on testing and collection of important publications may be found in:

> T.J. McCabe, "Structured Testing", Silver Spring, M.D, IEEE Computer Society Press, 1982.

Path covering changes and issues are found in:

> S.C. Ntafos, "A Graph Theoretic Approach to Program Testing", Ph.D Dissertation, Northwestern University, 1978.

Some important issues of complexity of data flow testing are discussed in:

> E.J. Weyuker, "An Empirical Study of the Complexity of Data Flow Testing", Second Workshop on Software Testing, Verification and Analysis, Banff, Canada, pp. 19–21, July 1988.

A comparison of du-paths and branch coverage metrics can be found in:

> M.D. Weiser, J.D. Gannon and P.R. McMullin, "Comparison of Structural Test Coverage Metrics," IEEE Software, vol. 2, pp. 80–85, March 1985.

Weiser was probably the first one to introduce program slicing:

> M. Weiser, "Program Slicing", Proceedings of the Fifth International Conference on Software Engineering pp. 439–449, March 1981.

M. Weiser, "Programmers use Slices when Debugging", Communications of ACM, vol. 25, no. 7, pp. 446–452, 1982.

> M. Weiser, "Program Slicing", IEEE Transactions on Software Engineering, SE-10, pp. 352–357, 1984.

Dasso provides an introduction to mutation testing in Chapter 7 of the book:

> Aristides Dasso, Ana Funes, "Verification, Validation and Testing in Software Engineering", Idea Group Inc, 2007.

The following research paper provides a comprehensive analysis and survey on mutation testing:

> Yue Jia, Mark Harman, "An Analysis and Survey of the Development of Mutation Testing", CREST Centre, King's College London, Technical Report TR-09-06. http://www.dcs.kcl.ac.uk/pg/jiayue/repository/TR-09-06.pdf, September 2009.

A publicly available repository that provides complete literature on mutation testing can accessed from:

> http://www.dcs.kcl.ac.uk/pg/jiayue/repository/

Other useful research papers may be:

> S. Rapps and E.J. Weyuker, "Selecting Software Test Data Using Data Flow Information", IEEE Transactions on Software Engineering, vol. 11, no. 4, pp. 367–375, 1985.
>
> K.C. Tai, "What to do beyond Branch Testing," ACM SIGSOFT Software Engineering Notes, vol. 14, no. 2, pp. 58–61, April 1989.
>
> A. J. Offutt and D. Lee Stephen, "An Empirical Evaluation of Weak Mutation", IEEE Transactions on Software Engineering, vol. 20, no. 5, pp. 337–344, May 1994.
>
> A. Watson, T.J. McCabe, "Structured Testing: A Testing Methodology Using the Cyclomatic Complexity Metric", NIST, 1996.
>
> A. J. Offutt and J. Pan, "Detecting Equivalent Mutants and the Feasible Path Problem", Software Testing, Verification, and Reliability, vol. 7, no. 3, pp. 165–192, September 1997.

5

Software Verification

Software verification has proved its effectiveness in the software world and its usage is increasing day by day. The most important aspect of software verification is its implementation in the early phases of the software development life cycle. There was a time when people used to say that "testing is a post-mortem activity where testers are only finding the damages already been done and making changes in the program to get rid of these damages." Testing primarily used to be validation oriented where the program was required for execution and was available only in the later phases of software development. Any testing activity which requires program execution comes under the 'validation' category. In short, whenever we execute the program with its input(s) and get output(s), that type of testing is known as software validation.

What is software verification? How can we apply this in the early phases of software development? If we review any document for the purpose of finding faults, it is called verification. Reviewing a document is possible from the first phase of software development i.e. software requirement and analysis phase where the end product is the SRS document.

Verification is the process of manually examining / reviewing a document. The document may be SRS, SDD, the program itself or any document prepared during any phase of software development. We may call this as static testing because the execution of the program is not required. We evaluate, review and inspect documents which are generated after the completion of every phase of software development. As per IEEE, "verification is the process of evaluating the system or component to determine whether the products of a given development phase satisfy the conditions imposed at the start of that phase" [IEEE01]. Testing includes both verification and validation activities and they are complementary to each other. If effective verification is carried out, we may detect a number of faults in the early phases of the software development life cycle and ultimately may be able to produce a quality product within time and budget.

5.1 VERIFICATION METHODS

The objective of any verification method is to review the documents with the purpose of finding faults. Many methods are commonly used in practice like peer reviews, walkthroughs, inspections, etc. Verification helps in prevention of potential faults, which may lead to failure of software.

After the completion of the implementation phase, we start testing the program by executing it. We may carry out verification also by reviewing the program manually and examining the critical areas carefully. Verification and validation activities may be performed after the implementation phase. However, only verification is possible in the phases prior to implementation like the requirement phase, the design phase and even most of the implementation phase.

5.1.1 Peer Reviews

Any type of testing (verification or validation), even adhoc and undisciplined, is better than no testing if it is carried out by person(s) other than the developers / writers of the document with the purpose of finding faults. This is the simplest way of reviewing the documents / programs to find out faults during verification. We give the document(s) / program(s) to someone else and ask to review the document(s) / program(s). We expect views about the quality of the document(s) and also expect to find faults. This type of informal activity may give very good results without spending any significant resources. Many studies have shown the importance of peer review due to its efficiency and significance. Our thrust should be to find faults in the document(s) / program(s) and not in the persons who have developed them. The activities involved may be SRS document verification, SDD verification and program verification. The reviewer may prepare a report of observations and findings or may inform verbally during discussions. This is an informal activity to be carried out by peers and may be very effective if reviewers have domain knowledge, good programming skills and proper involvement.

5.1.2 Walkthroughs

Walkthroughs are more formal and systematic than peer reviews. In a walkthrough, the author of the document presents the document to a small group of two to seven persons. Participants are not expected to prepare anything. Only the presenter, who is the author, prepares for the meeting. The document(s) is / are distributed to all participants. During the meeting, the author introduces the material in order to make them familiar with it. All participants are free to ask questions. All participants may write their observations on any display mechanism like boards, sheets, projection systems, etc. so that every one may see and give views. After the review, the author writes a report about findings and any faults pointed out in the meeting.

The disadvantages of this system are the non-preparation of participants and incompleteness of the document(s) presented by the author(s). The author may hide some critical areas and unnecessarily emphasize on some specific areas of his / her interest. The participants may not be able to ask many penetrating questions. Walkthroughs may help us to find potential faults and may also be used for sharing the documents with others.

5.1.3 Inspections

Many names are used for this verification method like formal reviews, technical reviews, inspections, formal technical reviews, etc. This is the most structured and most formal type of verification method and is commonly known as inspections. These are different from peer reviews and walkthroughs. The presenter is not the author but some other person who prepares and understands the document being presented. This forces that person to learn and review that document prior to the meeting. The document(s) is / are distributed to all participants in advance in order to give them sufficient time for preparation. Rules for such meetings are fixed and communicated to all participants. A team of three to six participants are constituted which is led by an impartial moderator. A presenter and a recorder are also added to this team to assure that the rules are followed and views are documented properly.

Every person in the group participates openly, actively and follows the rules about how such a review is to be conducted. Everyone may get time to express their views, potential faults and critical areas. Important points are displayed by some display mechanism so that everyone can see them. The moderator, preferably a senior person, conducts such meetings and respects everyone's views. The idea is not to criticize anyone but to understand their views in order to improve the quality of the document being presented. Sometimes a checklist is also used to review the document.

After the meeting, a report is prepared by the moderator and circulated to all participants. They may give their views again, if any, or discuss with the moderator. A final report is prepared after incorporating necessary suggestions by the moderator. Inspections are very effective to find potential faults and problems in the document like SRS, SDD, source code, etc. Critical inspections always help find many faults and improve these documents, and prevent the propagation of a fault from one phase to another phase of the software development life cycle.

5.1.4 Applications

All three verification methods are popular and have their own strengths and weaknesses. These methods are compared on specific issues and this comparison is given in Table 5.1.

Table 5.1. Comparison of verification methods

S. No.	Method	Presenter	Number of Participants	Prior preparation	Report	Strengths	Weaknesses
1.	Peer reviews	No one	1 or 2	Not required	Optional	Inexpensive but find some faults	Output is dependent on the ability of the reviewer
2.	Walkthrough	Author	2 to 7 participants	Only presenter is required to be prepared	Prepared by presenter	Knowledge sharing	Find few faults and not very expensive
3.	Inspections	Someone other than author	3 to 6 participants	All participants are required to be prepared	Prepared by moderator	Effective and find many faults	Expensive and requires very skilled participants

The SRS verification offers the biggest potential saving to the software development effort. Inspections must be carried out at this level. For any reasonably sized project, the SRS document becomes critical and the source of many faults. Inspections shall improve this document and faults are removed at this stage itself without much impact and cost. For small sized projects, peer reviews may be useful but results are heavily dependent on the ability and involvement of the reviewer. Walkthroughs are normally used to sensitize participants about the new initiative of the organization. Their views may add new functionality or may identify weak areas of the project.

Verification is always more effective than validation. It may find faults that are nearly impossible to detect during validation. Most importantly, it allows us to find faults at the earliest possible time and in the early phases of software development. However, in most organizations the distribution of verification / validation is 20/80, or even less for verification.

5.2 SOFTWARE REQUIREMENTS SPECIFICATION (SRS) DOCUMENT VERIFICATION

The outcome of the first phase of the software development life cycle is the SRS document. This describes 'What do we expect from the system?' However, it does not carry any details about 'How do we achieve these expectations?' After the finalization of the SRS, the developer knows what to develop and the customer knows what to expect. The SRS also becomes a legal document to resolve any conflict between the customer and the developer.

The SRS document should cover both functional requirements and non-functional requirements. Functional requirements are the expectations from the proposed software. They explain what the software has to do. They are also known as product features. Non-functional requirements are quality requirements that stipulate how well the software does what it has to do. Some of the non-functional requirements are reliability, usability, portability, maintainability and testability.

5.2.1 Nature of the SRS Document

The SRS should include the following:

(i) Expectations from the software: The SRS document should clearly specify 'what do we expect from the software?' and broadly describe functions of the software.
(ii) Interfaces of the software: The software will interact with many persons, hardware, other devices and external software. These interfaces should be written and 'forms' for interaction may also be provided.
(iii) Non-functional requirements: These requirements are very important for the success of the software. They may help us to design a performance criterion in terms of the requirements – response time, speed, availability, recovery time of various software functions, etc. Some non-functional requirements become attributes of the software like portability, correctness, maintainability, reliability, security, etc. These non-functional requirements should also be properly placed in the SRS document.
(iv) Implementation difficulties and limitations: There may be some limitations of the programming language, database integration, etc. All constraints of project implementation including resource limitations and operating environment should also be specified.

The SRS writer(s) should not include design and implementation details. It should be written in simple, clear and unambiguous language which may be understandable to all developers and customers.

5.2.2 Characteristics and Organization of the SRS Document

The SRS document acts as a contract between the developer and customer. This document should have the following characteristics as given in IEEE recommended practice for software requirements specifications (IEEE std. 830 – 1998) [IEEE98a]: "Correct, unambiguous, complete, consistent and ranked for importance and / or stability, verifiable, modifiable, traceable." These characteristics should be checked and a good SRS document should address these issues.

The IEEE has published guidelines and standards to organize an SRS document (IEEE93, IEEE98a). It provides different ways to organize the SRS document depending upon the nature of the project. The first two sections of the SRS document are the same for all projects. The specific tailoring occurs in section 3 entitled 'specific requirements'. The general organization of the SRS document is given in Table 5.2.

Table 5.2. Organization of the SRS [IEEE98a]

1. Introduction
    - 1.1 Purpose0
    - 1.2 Scope
    - 1.3 Definitions, Acronyms and Abbreviations
    - 1.4 References
    - 1.5 Overview
2. The Overall Description
    - 2.1 Product Perspective
        - 2.1.1 System Interfaces
        - 2.1.2 Interfaces
        - 2.1.3 Hardware Interfaces
        - 2.1.4 Software Interfaces
        - 2.1.5 Communications interfaces
        - 2.1.6 Memory Constraints
        - 2.1.7 Operations
        - 2.1.8 Site Adaptation Requirements
    - 2.2 Product Functions
    - 2.3 User Characteristics
    - 2.4 Constraints
    - 2.5 Assumptions and Dependencies
    - 2.6 Apportioning of Requirements
3. Specific Requirements
    - 3.1 External interfaces
    - 3.2 Functions
    - 3.3 Performance Requirements
    - 3.4 Logical Database Requirements
    - 3.5 Design Constraints
        - 3.5.1 Standards Compliance
    - 3.6 Software System Attributes
        - 3.6.1 Reliability
        - 3.6.2 Availability
        - 3.6.3 Security
        - 3.6.4 Maintainability
        - 3.6.5 Portability
    - 3.7 Organizing the Specific Requirements
        - 3.7.1 System Mode
        - 3.7.2 User Class
        - 3.7.3 Objects
        - 3.7.4 Feature
        - 3.7.5 Stimulus
        - 3.7.6 Response
        - 3.7.7 Functional Hierarchy
    - 3.8 Additional Comments
4. Change Management Process
5. Document Approvals
6. Supporting Information

IEEE Std 830–1998 Recommended Practice for Software Requirements Specifications – reprinted with permission from IEEE, 3 Park Avenue, New York, NY 10016 – 5997 USA, Copyright 1998, by IEEE.

5.2.3 SRS Document Checklist

The SRS document is reviewed by the testing person(s) by using any verification method (like peer reviews, walkthroughs, inspections, etc.). We may use inspections due to their effectiveness and capability to produce good results. We may conduct reviews twice or even more often. Every review will improve the quality of the document but may consume resources and increase the cost of the software development.

A checklist is a popular verification tool which consists of a list of critical information content that a deliverable should contain. A checklist may also look for duplicate information, missing information, unclear information, wrong information, etc. Checklists are used during reviewing and may make reviews more structured and effective. An SRS document checklist should address the following issues:

(i) **Correctness**

Every requirement stated in the SRS should correctly represent an expectation from the proposed software. We do not have standards, guidelines or tools to ensure the correctness of the software. If the expectation is that the software should respond to all button presses within 2 seconds, but the SRS states that 'the software shall respond to all buttons presses within 20 seconds', then that requirement is incorrectly documented.

(ii) **Ambiguity**

There may be an ambiguity in a stated requirement. If a requirement conveys more than one meaning, it is a serious problem. Every requirement must have a single interpretation only. We give a portion of the SRS document (having one or two requirements) to 10 persons and ask their interpretations. If we get more than one interpretation, then there may be an ambiguity in the requirement(s). Hence, requirement statement should be short, explicit, precise and clear. However, it is difficult to achieve this due to the usage of natural languages (like English), which are inherently ambiguous. A checklist should focus on ambiguous words and should have potential ambiguity indicators.

(iii) **Completeness**

The SRS document should contain all significant functional requirements and non-functional requirements. It should also have forms (external interfaces) with validity checks, constraints, attributes and full labels and references of all figures, tables, diagrams, etc. The completeness of the SRS document must be checked thoroughly by a checklist.

(iv) **Consistency**

Consistency of the document may be maintained if the stated requirements do not differ with other stated requirements within the SRS document. For example, in the overall description of the SRS document, it may be stated that the passing percentage is 50 in 'result management software' and elsewhere, the passing percentage is mentioned as 40. In one section, it is written that the semester mark sheet will be issued to colleges and elsewhere it is mentioned that the semester mark sheet will be issued directly to students. These are examples of inconsistencies and should be avoided. The checklist should highlight such issues and should be designed to find inconsistencies.

(v) **Verifiability**

The SRS document is said to be verifiable, if and only if, every requirement stated therein is verifiable. Non-verifiable requirements include statements like 'good interfaces', 'excellent response time', 'usually', 'well', etc. These statements should not be used.

An example of a verifiable statement is 'semester mark sheet shall be displayed on the screen within 10 seconds'. We should use measurable terms and avoid vague terms. The checklist should check the non-verifiable requirements.

(vi) Modifiability

The SRS document should incorporate modifications without disturbing its structure and style. Thus, changes may be made easily, completely and consistently while retaining the framework. Modifiability is a very important characteristic due to frequent changes in the requirements. What is constant in life? It is change and if we can handle it properly, then it may have a very positive impact on the quality of the SRS document.

(vii) Traceability

The SRS document is traceable if the origin of each requirement is clear and may also help for future development. Traceability may help to structure the document and should find place in the design of the checklist.

(viii) Feasibility

Some of the requirements may not be feasible to implement due to technical reasons or lack of resources. Such requirements should be identified and accordingly removed from the SRS document. A checklist may also help to find non-feasible requirements.

The SRS document is the source of all future problems. It must be reviewed effectively to improve its quality. Every review process will add to the improvement of its quality which is dependent on the characteristics discussed above. A checklist should be designed to address the above-mentioned issues. A well-designed and meaningful checklist may help the objective of producing good quality maintainable software, delivered on time and within budget. There may be many ways to design a checklist. A good checklist must address the above-mentioned characteristics. A generic checklist is given in Table 5.3, which may be tailored as per the need of a project.

Section - I

Name of reviewer	
Organization	
Group Number	
Date of review	
Project Title	

Section – II

Table 5.3. Checklist for the SRS document

S. No.	Description	Yes/No/NA	Remarks
	Introduction		
1.	Is the purpose of the project clearly defined?		
2.	Is the scope clearly defined?		
3.	Is document format as per standard / guidelines (e.g. IEEE 830-1998)		
4.	Is the project formally approved by the customer?		
5.	Are all requirements, interfaces, constraints, definitions, etc. listed in the appropriate sections?		

(Contd.)

(Contd.)

S. No.	Description	Yes/No/NA	Remarks
6.	Is the expected response time from the user's point of view, specified for all operations?		
7.	Do all stated requirements express the expectations of the customer?		
8.	Are there areas not addressed in the SRS document that need to be?		
9.	Are non-functional requirements stated?		
10.	Are validity checks properly defined for every input condition?		
	Ambiguity		
11	Are functional requirements separated from non-functional requirements?		
12.	Is any requirement conveying more than one interpretation?		
13.	Are all requirements clearly understandable?		
14.	Does any requirement conflict with or duplicate with other requirements?		
15.	Are there ambiguous or implied requirements?		
	Completeness		
16.	Are all functional and non-functional requirements stated?		
17.	Are forms available with validity checks?		
18.	Are all reports available in the specified format?		
19.	Are all references, constraints, assumptions, terms and unit of measures clearly stated?		
20.	Has analysis been performed to identify missing requirements?		
	Consistency		
21.	Are the requirements specified at a consistent level of detail?		
22.	Should any requirement be specified in more detail?		
23.	Should any requirement be specified in less detail?		
24.	Are the requirements consistent with other documents of the project?		
25.	Is there any difference in the stated requirement at two places?		
	Verifiability		
26.	Are all stated requirements verifiable?		
27.	Are requirements written in a language and vocabulary that the stakeholders can understand?		
28.	Are there any non-verifiable words?		
29.	Are all paths of a use case verifiable?		
30.	Is each requirement testable?		
	Modifiability		
31.	Are all stated requirements modifiable?		
32.	Have redundant requirements been consolidated?		
33.	Has the document been designed to incorporate changes?		

(Contd.)

(Contd.)

S. No.	Description	Yes/No/NA	Remarks
34.	Is the format structure and style of the document standard?		
35.	Is there any procedure to document a change?		
	Traceability		
36.	Can any requirement be traced back to its origin or source?		
37.	Is every requirement uniquely identifiable?		
38.	Are all requirements clearly understandable for implementation?		
39.	Has each requirement been cross referenced to requirements in previous project documents that are relevant?		
40.	Is each requirement identified such that it facilitates referencing of each requirement in future development and enhancement efforts?		
	Feasibility		
41.	Is every stated requirement feasible?		
42.	Is any requirement non-feasible due to technical reasons?		
43.	Is any requirement non-feasible due to lack of resources?		
44.	Is any requirement feasible but very difficult to implement?		
45.	Is any requirement very complex?		
	General		
46.	Is the document concise and easy to follow?		
47.	Are requirements stated clearly and consistently without contradicting themselves or other requirements?		
48.	Are all forms, figures and tables uniquely numbered?		
49.	Are hardware and other communication requirements stated clearly?		
50.	Are all stated requirements necessary?		

5.3 SOFTWARE DESIGN DESCRIPTION (SDD) DOCUMENT VERIFICATION

We prepare the SDD document from the SRS document. Every requirement stated therein is translated into design information required for planning and implementation of a software system. It represents the system as a combination of design entities and also describes the important properties and relationship among those entities. A design entity is an element (unit) of a design that is structurally and functionally distinct from other elements and that is separately named and referenced. Our objective is to partition the system into separate units that can be considered, implemented and changed independently.

The design entities may have different nature, but may also have common characteristics. Each entity shall have a purpose, function and a name. There is a common relationship among entities such as interfaces or shared data. The common characteristics are described by attributes of entities. Attributes are the questions about entities. The answer to these questions is the values of the attributes. The collection of answers provides a complete description of an entity. The SDD should address all design entities along with their attributes.

5.3.1 Organization of the SDD Document

We may have different views about the essential aspects of software design. However, we have the IEEE recommended practice for software design description (IEEE STD 1016-1998), which is a popular way to organize an SDD document [IEEE98b]. The organization of SDD is given in as per IEEE STD 1016-1998. The entity / attribute information may be organized in several ways to reveal all the essential aspects of a design. Hence, there may be a number of ways to view the design. Each design view gives a separate concern about the system. These views provide a comprehensive description of the design in a concise and usable form that simplifies information access and assimilation. Two popular design techniques are function oriented design and object oriented design. We may use any approach depending on the nature and complexity of the project. Our purpose is to prepare a quality document that translates all requirements into design entities along with its attributes. The verification process may be carried out many times in order to improve the quality of the SDD. The SDD provides a bridge between software requirements and implementation. Hence, strength of the bridge is the strength of the final software system.

5.3.2 The SDD Document Checklist

The SDD document verification checklist may provide opportunities to reviewers for focusing on important areas of the design. The software design starts as a process for translating requirements stated in the SRS document in a user-oriented functional design. The system developers, customers and project team may finalise this design and use it as a basis for a more technical system design. A checklist may help to structure the design review process. There are many ways to design a checklist which may vary with the nature, scope, size and complexity of the project. One form of checklist is given in Table 5.4. However, organizations may modify this checklist depending on software engineering practices and type of the project.

Section – I

Name of reviewer	
Organization	
Group Number	
Date of review	
Project title	

Section – II

Table 5.4. Checklist for the SDD Document

S. No.	Description	Yes/No/NA	Remarks
	General Issues		
1.	Is the document easy to read?		
2.	Is the document easy to understand?		

(Contd.)

(Contd.)

S. No.	Description	Yes/No/NA	Remarks
3.	Is the document format as per IEEE std. 1016-1998?		
4.	Does the document look professional?		
5.	Is system architecture (including hardware, software, database and data communication structures) specified?		
	System Architecture		
6.	Is the architecture understandable?		
7.	Are figures used to show the architecture of the system?		
8.	Are all essentials described clearly and consistently? (Essentials may be software component(s), networks, hardware, databases, operating system, etc).		
9.	Is the software architecture consistent with existing policies, guidelines and standards?		
10.	Is the architecture complete with essential details?		
	Software Design		
11.	Is the design as per standards?		
12.	Are all design entities described?		
13.	Are all attributes defined clearly?		
14.	Are all interfaces shown amongst the design entities?		
15.	Are all stated objectives addressed?		
16.	Is the data dictionary specified in tabular form?		
	Data Design		
17.	Are all definitions of data elements included in the data dictionary?		
18.	Are all appropriate attributes that describe each data element included in the data dictionary?		
19.	Is interface data design described?		
20.	Is data design consistent with existing policies, procedures, guidelines, standards and technological directives?		
	Interface Design		
21.	Is the user interface for every application described?		
22.	Are all fields available on every screen?		
23.	Is the quality of screen acceptable?		
24.	Are all major functions supporting each interface addressed?		
25.	Are all validity checks for every field specified?		
	Traceability		
26.	Is every requirement stated in the SRS addressed in design?		
27.	Does every design entity address at least one requirement?		
28.	Is there any missing requirement?		
29.	Is the Requirement Traceability Matrix (RTM) prepared?		
30.	Does the RTM indicate that every requirement has been addressed clearly?		

5.4 SOURCE CODE REVIEWS

A source code review involves one or more reviewers examining the source code and providing feedback to the developers, both positive and negative. Reviewers should not be from the development team. Robert Bogue [BOGU09] has given his views about source code reviews as:

> "Code reviews in most organizations are a painful experience for everyone involved. The developer often feels like it's a bashing session designed to beat out their will. The development leads are often confused as to what is important to point out and what is not. And other developers that may be involved often use this as a chance to show how much better they can be by pointing out possible issues in someone else's code."

We may review the source code for syntax, standards defined, readability and maintainability. Typically, reviews will have a standard checklist as a guide for finding common mistakes and to validate the source code against established coding standards. The source code reviews always improve the quality and find all types of faults. The faults may be due to poor structure, violation of business rules, simple omissions, etc. Reviewing the source code has proved to be an effective way to find faults and is considered as a good practice for software development.

5.4.1 Issues Related to Source Code Reviews

We should follow good software engineering practices to produce good quality maintainable software within time at a reasonable cost. Source code reviews help us to achieve this objective. Some of the recommended software engineering practices are given as:

1. Always use meaningful variables.
2. Avoid confusing words in names. Do not abbreviate 'Number' to 'No'; 'Num' is a better choice.
3. Declare local variables and avoid global variables to the extent possible. Thus, minimize the scope of variables.
4. Minimize the visibility of variables.
5. Do not overload variables with multiple meanings.
6. Define all variables with meaningful, consistent and clear names.
7. Do not unnecessarily declare variables.
8. Use comments to increase the readability of the source code.
9. Generally, comments should describe what the source code does and not how the source code works.
10. Always update comments while changing the source code.
11. Use spaces and not TABS.
12. All divisors should be tested for zero or garbage value.
13. Always remove unused lines of the source code.
14. Minimize the module coupling and maximize the module strength.
15. File names should only contain A-Z, a-z, 0-9, '_' and '.'.
16. The source code file names should be all lower case.
17. All loops, branches and logic constructs should be complete, correct and properly nested and also avoid deep nesting.

18. Complex algorithms should be thoroughly explained.
19. The reasons for declaring static variables should be given.
20. Always ensure that loops iterate the correct number of times.
21. When memory is not required, it is essential to make it free.
22. Release all allocated memory and resources after the usage.
23. Stack space should be available for running a recursive function. Generally, it is better to write iterative functions.
24. Do not reinvent the wheel. Use existing source code as much as possible. However, do not over-rely on this source code during testing. This portion should also be tested thoroughly.

We may add many such issues which are to be addressed during reviewing. A good checklist may help the reviewers to organize and structure the review process of the source code.

5.4.2 Checklist of Source Code Reviews

A checklist should at least address the above-mentioned issues. However, other issues may also be added depending on the nature and complexity of the project. A generic checklist is given in Table 5.5. We may also prepare a programming language specific checklist which may also consider the specific language issues.

Section – I

Name of reviewer	
Organization	
Group Number	
Date of review	
Project title	

Section – II

Table 5.5. Source code reviews checklist

S. No.	Description	Yes/No/NA	Remarks
	Structure		
1.	Does the source code correctly and completely implement the design?		
2.	Is there any coding standard being followed?		
3.	Has the developer tested the source code?		
4.	Does the source code execute as expected?		
5.	Is the source code clear and easy to understand?		
6.	Are all functions in the design coded?		
7.	Is the source code properly structured?		
8.	Are there any blocks of repeated source code that can be combined to form a single module?		
9.	Is any module very complex and should be decomposed into two or more modules?		
10.	Is the source code fault tolerant?		

(Contd.)

(Contd.)

Variables

11. Are all variables clearly defined with appropriate names?
12. Are there any redundant and unused variables?
13. Is there unnecessary usage of global variables?
14. Are variable declarations properly commented?
15. Are all variables properly initialized?
16. Is the scope of every variable minimized?
17. Is any variable name ambiguous?
18. Are all variable names spelt correctly and consistently?

Comments

19. Is readability of the source code acceptable?
20. Is the source code well commented and documented properly?
21. Are all given comments necessary?
22. Is there any requirement of additional comments?
23. Are all comments consistent with the source code?

Loop and Branches

24. Are all loops, logic constructs and branches correct, complete and appropriately nested?
25. Does the source code make use of an infinite loop?
26. Does the loop execute the number of times specified?
27. Are loop exit conditions accurate?
28. Does every case statement have a default?

General

29. Is every allocated memory de-allocated?
30. Does the source code make use of exception handling?
31. Does the source code appear to pose a security concern?
32. Does the source code avoid deadlocks?
33. Does the implementation match the documentation?
34. Is there any identifier that conflicts with the keyword?
35. Is the source code maintainable?

5.5 USER DOCUMENTATION VERIFICATION

We prepare many documents during the software development life cycle. Some are for the users like installation guide, beginner's guide / tutorial, system administration guide, etc. and these are known as user manuals. Some are prepared for internal purposes like SRS, SDD, program listing, cross-reference listing, test suite, etc., and are known as documentation manuals. Verification of the internal documents is essential for the success of implementation and quality of the final product and the same has been discussed in sections 5.2, 5.3 and 5.4. The documents which are given to the customer are also important for the overall success of the project. These are part of the software supplied along with other deliverables. User documentation may be provided as a user manual in electronic form, as a printed booklet, or in the form of online help.

5.5.1 Review Process Issues

These documents should be reviewed thoroughly and proper consistency should be maintained in all documents. The documents should be written in simple, clear and short sentences. Installation procedure of the software must be explained step by step with proper justifications. All tables, figures and graphs should be numbered properly. Explanations, if possible, should be supported by suitable examples. A checklist may help to structure the review process and must highlight these issues.

5.5.2 User Documentation Checklist

A checklist always helps the review process. A generic checklist for user documentation is given in Table 5.6. However, this may be modified depending on the nature, complexity and applicability of the project.

Section – I

Name of reviewer	
Organization	
Group Number	
Date of review	
Project title	

Section – II

Table 5.6. User documentation checklist

S. No.	Description	Yes/No/NA	Remarks
	General Issues		
1.	Is the document easy to read?		
2.	Is the document easy to understand?		
3.	Is the document well organized? Are things easy to find?		
4.	Does the document look professional?		
5.	Are spellings and grammar correct?		
6.	Are all references properly placed in text?		
7.	Is consistency maintained?		
8.	Are all abbreviations and assumptions properly written at proper places?		
	Installation Issues		
9.	Is everything operated as stated in the document?		
10.	Is there any step omitted?		

(Contd.)

(Contd.)

S. No.	Description	Yes/No/NA	Remarks
11.	Does it specify a minimum system configuration requirement?		
12.	Does it specify reasons for failure of a particular activity?		
	Operational Issues		
13.	Does it clearly describe all toolbars, menus, commands and options?		
14.	Do toolbars, menus and commands options operate as stated?		
15.	Are examples documented correctly?		
16.	Are all steps explained?		
17.	Does the document specify all steps as accepted to operate a Graphical User Interface (GUI)?		
18.	Does it include sample screenshots identical to GUI?		
	Issues of tables, graphs and figures		
19.	Are all tables, graphs and figures properly numbered?		
20.	Are they identical to actual GUI?		
21.	Are they properly referenced in the text?		
22.	Are they properly placed?		
23.	Are they consistent with previous tables, graphs and figures?		
24.	Are all given tables, graphs and figures necessary?		
25.	Are there any requirements of new figures, graphs or tables?		

5.6 SOFTWARE PROJECT AUDIT

Audit of a software project is a very important activity and may be carried out at any time during the software development life cycle. Generally, auditors are appointed by the top management to review the progress of the project. The auditors are different from the developers and testers and may not have any involvement in the project. They may examine the progress of the project and quality of the processes with respect to many attributes like project planning, management, quality management, resourcing, users, development approaches, testing, application architecture, data architecture and technical architecture. The auditing process is a continuous activity and may be carried out many times during the software development life cycle. We may audit the SRS, SDD and other relevant documents including the source code. The audit process is a verification activity and the auditor prepares an audited report after examining the relevant records and documents. This report may help the management to initiate timely action, if required. The management may get to know about delays, if any, in the development, involvement of users, implementation of software engineering practices and standards, status of risk assessment activities, etc. A project audit and review checklist has been developed by Hetty Baiz and Nancy Costa at Princeton University [HETT01] which is an excellent work for auditing any software project. The same checklist is given in section 5.6.3 and it is recommended to use the same for auditing a software project.

5.6.1 Relevance Scale

A relevance scale has been given in project audit and review checklist to measure the relevance of any attribute at the time of auditing the project. Many attributes have been identified in the checklist. We have to find their relevance to the project at the state when the audit is being conducted. The relevance scale is given as:

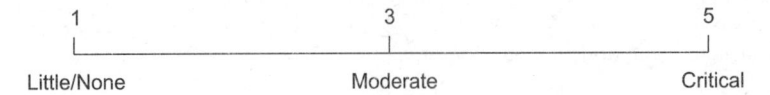

```
1                         3                         5
|-------------------------|-------------------------|
Little/None            Moderate                  Critical
```

Relevance (at the point) scale when the audit is conducted

5.6.2 Theory and Practice Scale

We may have to further indicate the strengths and weaknesses of the attributes given in project audit and review checklist, in theory and practice on the scale as given below:

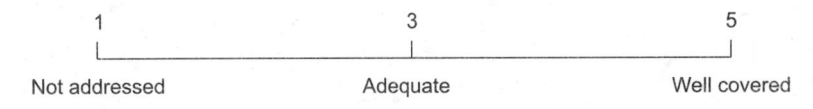

```
1                         3                         5
|-------------------------|-------------------------|
Not addressed          Adequate                Well covered
```

Theory and Practice Scale

An attribute may be relevant moderately at one point of time and may not be relevant at another point of time. The theory and practice scale is very useful and indicates the implementation status of any attribute. The checklist also provides a column for assessment where auditors may give their views, if required, about the attribute in addition to relevance and practice columns.

This type of quantification is very useful to monitor the progress of the software project. Auditors should always be non-judgmental and should have good communication skills. They also need to behave in a positive way in order to get the clear and correct picture of the project. Project audits must be carried out many times during development. They will definitely improve the performance, quality and progress of the project.

5.6.3 Project Audit and Review Checklist

This checklist has been designed by Hetty Baiz and Nancy Costa at Princeton University, New Jersey, USA [HETT01] which has been used by many organizations. All activities are reviewed on the basis of its relevance and strength/weakness at any point of time. Relevance scale and theory and practice scale may help us to understand the status of various attributes. This may also indicate the health of the project during its design implementation. An audit checklist is given below which is to be filled using relevance scale and theory and practice scale.

Project Audit and Review Checklist (Reproduced with permission of authors and special thanks to Princeton University, NJ, USA.)

Item	Attribute	Relevance	Practice	Assessment
1	**Project Planning**			
1.1	Does the project have a formal Project Plan?			
1.2	Are the following key elements of a Project Plan present? a. Project Definition and Scope b. Project Objectives c. Cost / Benefit Analysis d. Staffing Requirements e. Time Line f. Risk Analysis g. Critical Success Criteria (if we meet these, we've met our goals)			
1.3	Have all stakeholders been identified?			
1.4	Is a Stakeholder Management plan in place? Have project accountabilities and responsibilities been clearly defined?			
1.5	Have the scope, objectives, costs, benefits and impacts been communicated to all involved and/or impacted stakeholders and work groups?			
1.6	a) Have all involved stakeholders and work groups committed to the project? b) Have all necessary approvals been obtained?			
1.7	Has a project Communications Plan been developed?			
1.8	Are funding and staffing resource estimates sufficiently detailed and documented for use in planning and tracking the project?			
1.9	Does a documented project organizational policy and plan (i.e. governance model) exist?			
1.10	Have adequate resources been provided by the management to ensure project success?			
1.11	Is the current scope of the project substantially different from that originally defined in the approved project plan?			
1.12	Has the approach and development strategy of the project been defined, documented and accepted by the appropriate stakeholders?			
1.13	Have project management standards and procedures been established and documented?			
1.14	Is there a Steering Committee in place?			
1.15	Is the Steering Committee active in project oversight?			

(Contd.)

(Contd.)

Item	Attribute	Relevance	Practice	Assessment
1.16	Are there procedures in place to effectively manage interdependencies with other projects / systems?			
2	**Project Management**			
2.1	Have the key elements of a coherent project management strategy been established? a. Project tracking plan and methodology b. Project status reporting structure and process c. Change Management plan and tracking d. Issues Management process and tracking plan e. Risk Management Plan f. Software Quality Assurance g. Software Configuration Management			
2.2	**Project Scheduling and Tracking**			
2.2.1	Has a structured approach been used to break work effort into manageable components?			
2.2.2	Are team members involved in the development of activity and task decomposition?			
2.2.3	Are individual tasks of reasonable duration (8–40 hours)?			
2.2.4	Are milestone deliverables effectively tracked and compared to the project plan?			
2.2.5	Does the detailed project plan identify individual responsibilities for the next 4–6 weeks?			
2.2.6	Have activity relationships and interdependencies within tasks been adequately identified?			
2.2.7	Are target dates established for each milestone deliverable?			
2.2.8	Are corrective actions taken when actual results are substantially different from the detailed project plan? Describe.			
2.2.9	Are changes in deliverable commitments agreed to by all affected groups and individuals?			
2.2.10	Is the organization structure for both tracking and controlling project activities work, products and costs (effort, schedule and budget) well defined and assigned to a specific individual?			
2.2.11	Are measurements and feedback mechanisms incorporated in tracking work effort and refining work estimating techniques?			
2.2.12	Have procedures for identifying variances from estimates and adjusting the detailed work program been established?			
2.2.13	Is project work proceeding in accordance with the original project schedule?			

(Contd.)

(Contd.)

Item	Attribute	Relevance	Practice	Assessment
2.2.14	If not, have all project delays been adequately accounted for, communicated to all stakeholders and adjustments made in overall project schedule?			
2.2.15	Is there general agreement and acceptance of the current status and progress of the project?			
2.2.16	Is PERT / Critical Path or equivalent methodology being used? Can you see the critical path on the plan?			
2.2.17	Is an industry recognized mechanized support tool(s) being used for project scheduling and tracking?			
2.2.18	Is it possible to track all classes of project work (e.g. scheduled, un-scheduled, defect repair, etc.)? Can you compare work done to the baseline?			
2.3	**Project Status Reporting**			
2.3.1	Is the project status reviewed with senior management at appropriate intervals? What are they? a. Overall status b. Project performance (achievements and milestones) c. Open issues d. Risks e. Action items f. Cost and time performance against plan g. Quality metrics h. Client involvement			
2.3.2	Are internal project status meetings held at reasonable intervals?			
2.3.3	Are sub-project reviews held at reasonable intervals?			
2.3.4	Have adequate procedures been put in place for project co-ordination and status reporting across project boundaries (i.e. interdependent software development among interfacing systems)?			
2.3.5	Do project teams and team members report on status / activities / progress?			
2.4	**Project Estimating**			
2.4.1	Are multiple estimation methods being employed?			
2.4.2	Are current project time and resource estimates reasonable based on the current project stage?			
2.4.3	Are actuals compared against estimates to analyze and correct variances?			
2.4.4	Are software metrics formally captured, analyzed and used as a basis for other project estimates?			

(Contd.)

(Contd.)

Item	Attribute	Relevance	Practice	Assessment
2.4.5	Is the PPO estimating methodology being used and followed?			
2.4.6	Do the estimating techniques include any of the following features? a. Ranged estimates b. Sensitivity analysis c. Risk rating d. Quality Assurance overheads e. Contingency			
2.4.7	Are project team members involved in detailed estimating and scheduling?			
2.4.8	Are stakeholders aware and supportive of the principles and practices of modern software estimation?			
2.5	**Risk Management**			
2.5.1	Was an original risk assessment completed?			
2.5.2	Is there a process in place to monitor project risks?			
2.5.3	Has provision been made to reassess project risks at various project stages?			
2.5.4	Have all unresolved risks been documented? Have all unimplemented risk strategies been escalated to an issues log?			
3	**Quality Management**			
3.1	Does the project have a 'Quality Culture'?			
3.2	Is there a Quality Plan covering all Policies, Guidelines and Procedures?			
3.3	Quality Assurance			
3.3.1	Has an overall Quality Assurance Plan been developed for the project?			
3.3.2	Does the plan address key project elements? a. Project Planning b. Project Management c. Software Quality Assurance (SQA)			
3.3.3	Does the SQA process provide objective verification of adherence to applicable standards, procedures and requirements?			
3.3.4	Are all key components of an SQA plan present? a. SQA Plan b. Software Configuration Management (SCM) c. Software development standards and methods d. Methodology e. Testing Standards and Methodology f. Data Architecture Standards g. Data Naming Conventions h. Technology Architecture i. Software Metrics			

(Contd.)

(Contd.)

Item	Attribute	Relevance	Practice	Assessment
3.3.5	Are the results of SQA reviews provided to affected groups and individuals?			
3.3.6	Are adequate resources provided for the SQA function? Are SQA resources experienced?			
3.3.7	Are the SQA processes in place and being effectively used?			
3.4	Is there a set of procedures defining the scope, procedures and deliverables defining Quality Control?			
3.5	Are quality metrics defined?			
3.6	Is there a set of procedures to capture, analyze and act on quality metrics?			
3.7	**Software Configuration Management (SCM)**			
3.7.1	Has SCM been implemented for this project?			
3.7.2	Has an industry recognized SCM software version management and control tool been implemented?			
3.7.3	Is SCM version management and control effectively linked with the testing function to ensure that integration and regression testing have been performed?			
3.7.4	Has an automated Change Management tool been implemented?			
3.7.5	Is the SCM function adequately staffed?			
3.7.6	Is the Testing Co-ordination function separate from the development staff?			
4.0	**Management Procedures**			
4.1	**Vendor Management**			
4.1.1	Is there a formal set of procedures (for status reporting, contract negotiation and review, time/invoice reconciliation, etc.) supporting Vendor Management?			
4.2	**Issues Management**			
4.2.1	Is there a formal set of procedures supporting Issues Management?			
4.2.2	Is there any form of automated support for Issues Management?			
4.2.3	Are issues raised, assessed, actioned and resolved in a timely and efficient manner?			
4.3	**Stakeholder Management**			
4.3.1	Is there a formal set of procedures supporting Stakeholder Management?			
4.3.2	Is it standard practice to formally commit stakeholders to the project via agreements?			
4.3.3	Does a comprehensive set of Stakeholder Agreements exist? Do we have statements delineating what each stakeholder has agreed to do?			
5.0	**Resourcing**			

(Contd.)

(Contd.)

Item	Attribute	Relevance	Practice	Assessment
5.1	Are all resource assumptions documented?			
5.2	Does the project team have the skills necessary to successfully complete current project(s) and support the application?			
5.3	Have arrangements been made to obtain special expertise or competence by consulting or referencing: a. Similar projects? b. Published materials? c. Personnel with expertise? d. Outside experts?			
5.4	Have the personnel with the necessary skills and competence been identified and has an agreement for their participation in the project been reached with the appropriate management?			
5.5	Is there a project organization chart showing the reporting relationships and responsibilities for each position?			
5.6	Has a proper project work location been established that will allow the team to work together with user personnel?			
5.7	Does the detailed work plan match the complexity of tasks with the capabilities of personnel?			
5.8	Has allowance been made for vacations, holidays, training (learning time for each team member), staff promotions and staff turnovers?			
5.9	Has adequate time for orientation and training of project staff been provided for in relation to the technical nature of the Application and the experience levels of the project personnel?			
5.10	Has appropriate allowance been made for the effect of the learning curve on all personnel joining the project who do not have the required prior industry, functional and technical expertise?			
5.11	Are the appropriate IT resources adequate to meet planned commitments?			
5.12	Are enough systems and user personnel assigned to the project?			
5.13	Are the people assigned to the project sufficiently qualified?			
5.14	Do project managers participating in the project adequately know its true status first-hand? a. Is a qualified person sufficiently involved in each critical area? b. Are communication lines working?			
5.15	Is a senior systems department representative allocated to each user department to provide liaison and support? Does the project have both a business team leader and a technical team leader?			

(Contd.)

(Contd.)

Item	Attribute	Relevance	Practice	Assessment
5.16	Does the project team have a good understanding of the existing and/or proposed hardware / software environments?			
5.17	Are project leaders committed to this project full time?			
5.18	Are project team members committed full-time?			
5.19	Is the Production Support function adequately resourced? Is the Production Support function resourced full-time?			
5.20	Is there a production support plan with a plan for transition from development to production?			
6.0	**Users**			
6.1	Is user involvement adequate?			
6.2	Are the people assigned to the project sufficiently qualified?			
6.3	Is there a formal Service Level Agreement (SLA) with the appropriate client departments?			
6.4	Does the SLA define: a. The Project/Application Scope? b. The objectives of the Agreement? c. The business areas to be supported? d. The systems / applications to be supported? e. The basis for costs and charges? f. The extent of user participation? g. The frequency of progress reporting – i.e. weekly, bi-weekly, monthly, etc.? h. The form of the final report? i. The work plan(s)?			
6.5	Are the project team members located locally to the users?			
6.6	Has provision been made for training the staff, including: a. Formal training related to the project? b. On the job training? c. Formal training not related to the project? d. Vendor training?			
6.7	Are users adequately trained and are all training requirements fulfilled?			
7.0	**Development Approach**			
7.1	**Methodologies**			
7.1.1	Is a recognized development method(s) been followed?			
7.1.2	If more than one method has been implemented, does a documented process exist for effective integration between / among methods?			
7.1.3	Is the selected method appropriate for the Application, Technical and Data Architectures?			
7.2	**CASE**			
7.2.1	Are CASE tools being used?			

(Contd.)

(Contd.)

Item	Attribute	Relevance	Practice	Assessment
7.2.2	Does the CASE 'integration strategy' include a process for reverse integration (i.e. updating the analysis tool if a change is made at the design level)?			
7.3	Are structured requirements and design reviews and/or walkthroughs in use?			
7.4	Are detailed design and code inspections in use?			
7.5	**Analysis and Design**			
7.5.1	Are requirements and design standards in place?			
7.5.2	Are specifications clearly traceable from physical design to logical requirements?			
7.5.3	Are the requirements and design methods suitable for the type of application and environment?			
7.5.4	Do the design specification documents reference: a. Purpose / scope? b. Glossary of terms? c. Requirements specifications? d. Modular decomposition diagrams? e. Technical environment specification? f. Constraints? g. Testing and Data Conversion strategy?			
7.6	**Development/Construction**			
7.6.1	Are coding standards in place?			
7.6.2	Is there a clearly documented relationship between logical (conceptual) design and technical design?			
7.6.3	Is design and code re-use supported?			
7.6.4	Are program control procedures in place?			
7.6.5	Are there procedures to govern unit test cases, conditions, expected results, logs and sign-offs?			
7.6.6	Do adequate development and test environments exist?			
7.7	**Testing**			
7.7.1	Which of the following test phases are covered by the methodology: a. Unit Testing? b. System Testing? c. Integration Testing? d. User Acceptance Testing?			
7.7.2	Is a test strategy in place?			
7.7.3	Do detailed test plans/cases exist?			
7.7.4	Are all necessary Quality Control procedures in place?			
7.7.5	Is there an audit trail of all tests and results?			
7.7.6	Are effective testing tools incorporated?			

(Contd.)

(Contd.)

Item	Attribute	Relevance	Practice	Assessment
7.7.7	Is adequate allowance made for regression testing?			
7.7.8	Is adequate allowance made for defect repair both before and after implementation?			
7.7.9	Will the following components of systems testing be carried out? a. Communications b. Volume c. Stress d. Recovery e. Usability f. Operations g. Environment h. Security i. Efficiency/performance			
8.0	**Application Architecture**			
8.1	Are object-based designs and layered architecture principles being employed?			
8.2	Does the application conform to recognized industry architecture standards?			
8.3	Is the application being implemented using client / server architecture?			
8.4	Is business process re-engineering being undertaken in parallel with and/or as part of this project?			
8.5	Are there limitations to business operation flexibility due to the chosen Application Architecture?			
8.6	Are application interfaces designed in such a way as to facilitate maintenance and change?			
8.7	Does the Application Architecture support information needs at all levels of user operations (Strategic/Tactical/Operational)?			
8.8	**Client/Server**			
8.8.1	Are there design limitations which are impacting service delivery and/or performance?			
8.8.2	Is the current architecture scalable?			
9.0	**Data Architecture and Standards**			
9.1	Is the project operating under a formal set of data architecture standards?			
9.2	Does a formal data architecture and model exist for the application?			
9.3	Has a fully attributed data model been developed for the application?			
9.4	Has the data model been integrated with the other users and system views of the data?			
9.5	Is an industry recognized mechanized tool being used to support the data modelling area?			
9.6	Has a set of data naming conventions and/or standards been established?			
9.7	Is an active data dictionary in place?			

(Contd.)

(Contd.)

Item	Attribute	Relevance	Practice	Assessment
9.8	Is the data dictionary fully integrated with the development method?			
9.9	Has the DBMS been optimized to support any of the following: a. OLTP? b. Decision Support/EIS? c. Data Warehousing?			
9.10	Is the DBMS cost effective against expectations as defined in the Business Case?			
9.11	Is the DBMS portable across target platforms?			
9.12	Does DBMS vendor support meet formal agreements and/or expectations?			
9.13	Is there (or has there been) significant interruptions to development or support activities due to DBMS behaviour?			
9.14	Does or will the DBMS support extensibility appropriate for current and future business needs?			
9.15	Is there a clear upgrade path to future Phases of the DBMS?			
9.16	If an alternative DBMS is being considered, is there a proven conversion path?			
9.17	Is the DBMS consistent with SOE?			
9.18	Is the DBMS regarded as 'State-of-the-Art'?			
10.0	**Technical Architecture**			
10.1	Is the choice of hardware platform consistent with the Standard Operating Environment (SOE)?			
10.2	Is the software environment consistent with SOE?			
10.3	Is the development language platform-independent?			
10.4	Is the mixture of technologies proven, stable and easily supportable?			
10.5	Is TCP/IP or other industry recognized application interface standard being employed?			
10.6	Does the user interface employ GUI representation?			
10.7	Is the application software cost effective against expectations as defined in the Business Case?			
10.8	Is the application software portable across target platforms?			
10.9	Does the application software vendor(s) support meet formal agreements and/or expectations?			
10.10	Is there (or has there been) significant interruptions to development or support activities due to application software behaviour?			
10.11	Does or will the application software support extensibility appropriate for current and future business needs?			
10.12	Is there a clear upgrade path to future phases of the application software?			
10.13	Is the software regarded as 'State-of-the-Art'?			

5.7 CASE STUDY

Consider the problem statement of a university registration system. Prepare the software requirement checklist with the details of faults in the given SRS.

Problem Statement

A university is organized in different teaching schools and each school conducts a variety of programmes. Admissions to the various programmes offered by each school are done through counselling. Admission slips are issued to the admitted students giving their Roll Numbers, Name of the School and Name of the Programme. Students are registered in various schools manually based on the admission slips. Students are assigned papers (compulsory, elective and practical) depending upon the scheme of the selected programme. Every school is responsible for its registration process and the following records are prepared and maintained manually:

1. List of students registered in a programme.
2. List of students registered for a particular paper.
3. List of papers offered in a particular semester.
4. List of faculty in a school.
5. Personal details of the students.
6. Registration card for every registered student.

The university decides to automate the manual registration process in order to improve the existing system. The proposed system should perform the following functions:

(i)   Issue of login Id and password to the members i.e. student and faculty.
(ii) Maintain the personal details of the students.
(iii) Maintain the details of the faculty.
(iv) Maintain the details of the various papers - Theory (compulsory and elective) and practical as per the scheme of the programme.
(v)   Issue of registration card to the student in every semester.
(vi) List of registered students
   - Roll number wise
   - Programme wise
   - Semester wise
   - Paper wise
(vii) List of programmes offered by the university.
(viii) List of papers offered in a particular semester for a particular programme.
(ix)   List of faculty in a school.

Contents

1. Introduction
   1.1. Purpose
   1.2. Scope

1.3. Definitions, Acronyms, and Abbreviations
1.4 References
1.5 Overview
2. Overall Description
    2.1 Product Perspective
        2.1.1 System Interfaces
        2.1.2 User Interfaces
        2.1.3 Hardware Interfaces
        2.1.4 Software Interfaces
        2.1.5 Communication Interfaces
        2.1.6 Memory Constraints
        2.1.7 Operations
        2.1.8 Site Adaptation Requirements
    2.2 Product Functions
    2.3 User Characteristics
    2.4 Constraints
    2.5 Assumptions and Dependencies
    2.6 Apportioning of Requirements
3. Specific Requirements
    3.1 External Interface Requirements
        3.1.1 User Interfaces
        3.1.2 Hardware Interfaces
        3.1.3 Software Interfaces
        3.1.4 Communication Interfaces
    3.2 Functional Requirements
        3.2.1 Login
        3.2.2 Maintain School Details
        3.2.3 Maintain Programme Details
        3.2.4 Maintain Scheme Details
        3.2.5 Maintain Paper Details
        3.2.6 Maintain Student Details
        3.2.7 Maintain Faculty Details
        3.2.8 Maintain Student Registration Form
        3.2.9 Generate Reports
        3.2.10 Generate Registration Card
    3.3 Performance Requirements
    3.4 Design Constraints
    3.5 Software System Attributes
    3.6 Logical Database Requirements
    3.7 Other Requirements

Software Requirements Specification (SRS) Document for University Registration System

1. Introduction

A university is organized in different teaching schools and each school conducts a variety of programmes. Admissions to the various programmes offered by each school are done through counselling. Admission slips are issued to the admitted students giving their Roll Numbers, Name of the School and the Name of the Programme.

After admission, every student has to register in the University Registration System (URS) which is open for a specific period at the beginning of the academic session. Every student has to obtain a login Id and password from the 'System Administrator'. After successfully logging on to the system, a student needs to enter his/her personal details in the system. The student also needs to select elective papers of his/her choice as per the programme scheme. Compulsory papers (theory and practical) offered in that semester are then assigned automatically. On submitting the requisite details, a Registration Card giving the personal information and list of the papers to be studied during the semester is issued to the student.

Faculty members can also access the URS by obtaining login Id and password from the system administrator. They can view the details of the students who have been registered for various programmes in a school.

1.1 Purpose

The University Registration System (URS) maintains the information regarding various papers to be studied by a student in a particular programme. A paper may be a theory paper. A theory paper may be of two types: compulsory paper and elective paper. Compulsory papers are assigned automatically whereas a student has to select the elective papers of his/her choice in a particular semester.

1.2 Scope

The proposed 'University Registration System' shall perform the following functions:

(i) Issue of login Id and password to the members i.e. student and faculty.
(ii) Maintain the personal details of the students.
(iii) Maintain the details of the various papers - Theory (compulsory and elective) and practical as per the scheme of the programme.
(iv) Issue of registration card to the student in every semester.
(v) List of registered students
  - Roll number wise
  - Programme wise
  - Semester wise
  - Paper wise
» List of programmes offered by the university.

- » List of papers offered in a particular semester for a particular programme.
- » List of faculty in a school.

1.3 Definitions, Acronyms, and Abbreviations

URS: University Registration System

User: Any user (Student, Faculty or Administrator)

RAM: Random Access Memory

Student: Any candidate admitted in a programme (UG or PG) offered by a school.

Status: Status of the Student – Registered or Unregistered in URS.

System Administrator/Administrator: User having all the privileges to operate the URS.

Faculty: Teaching Staff of the University – Professor, Reader, Lecturer

School: Academic Unit that offers various Programmes

Programme: Degree Programme (UG or PG) as offered by a School

Semester: Duration for which a student has to study (normally 20 weeks) before appearing in the university examinations. There are two semesters in a year.

Scheme: Details of compulsory and elective papers (including practicals) offered in a semester for a programme.

1.4 References

(a) 'A Practitioner's Guide to Software Test Design' by Lee Copeland, Artech House, 2004.
(b) 'Software Engineering' by K.K. Aggarwal and Yogesh Singh, New Age Publishing House, 2nd Ed.
(c) IEEE Recommended Practice for Software Requirements Specifications – IEEE Std 830-1998.
(d) IEEE Standard for Software Test Documentation – IEEE Std. 829-1998.

1.5 Overview

The rest of the SRS document describes various system requirements, interfaces, features and functionalities in detail.

2. Overall Description

The URS registers a student for a semester to a programme offered by a school of a university. It is assumed that the student has already been admitted in the university, for a specific programme. The system administrator will receive lists of the admitted students (school-wise and programme-wise) from the academic section responsible for counselling. The establishment section will provide the list of the faculty members appointed in the school. Based on this information, the system administrator will generate the login Id and password for the faculty and the students.

The user can access URS on the University's LAN. Students are permitted to Add, Modify and View their information only after successfully logging on to the system. After registration, students can print their registration card. Faculty members can make the query about the registered students and view/print the information of the registered students, papers offered in the various programmes, etc. The system administrator is the master user of the URS and will maintain the records of the students, faculty and generate their login Id and password.

The user will have to maintain the following information:

(i)   Login details
(ii) School details
(iii) Programme details
(iv) Scheme details
(v)   Paper details
(vi) Student details
(vii) Faculty details

The user requires the following reports from the proposed system:

(i) Registration card
(ii) List of registered students
   - Roll number wise
   - Programme wise
   - Semester wise
   - Paper wise
» List of programmes offered by the university.
(iii) List of papers offered in a particular semester of a particular programme.
(iv) List of faculty in a school.

2.1.1 Product Perspective

The proposed system shall be developed using client/server architecture and be compatible with Microsoft Windows Operating System. The front end of the system will be developed using Visual Basic 6.0 and the backend will be developed using MS SQL Server 2000.

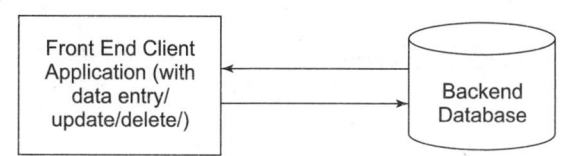

2.1.2 System Interfaces

None

2.1.3 User Interfaces

The URS will have the following user-friendly and menu driven interfaces:

(i) **Login:** to allow the entry of only authorized users through valid login Id and password.
(ii) **School Details:** to maintain school details.
(iii) **Programme Details:** to maintain programme details.
(iv) **Scheme Details:** to maintain scheme details of a programme.
(v) **Paper Details:** to maintain paper details of a scheme for a particular programme.
(vi) **Student Details:** to maintain student's details that will include personal information and papers to be studied in the current semester.
(vii) **Faculty Details:** to maintain the faculty details.

The software should generate the following viewable and printable reports:

(i) **Registration Card:** It will contain the roll number, name of the student, school, programme, semester and the papers in which the student is registered. The registration card will be generated after filling the necessary information in the student registration form.
(ii) **List of Students:** It will be generated roll number wise, programme wise, semester wise and paper wise.
(iii) **List of Programmes:** It will give the details of programmes offered by various schools of the university.
(iv) **List of Papers:** It will give the list of papers offered in a particular semester for a particular programme.

2.1.4 Hardware Interfaces

(i) Screen resolution of at least 640 × 480 or above.
(ii) Support for printer (dot matrix, DeskJet, LaserJet)
(iii) Computer systems will be in the networked environment as it is a multi-user system.

2.1.5 Software Interfaces

(i) MS-Windows Operating System
(ii) Microsoft Visual Basic 6.0 for designing front-end
(iii) MS SQL Server 2000 for backend

2.1.6 Communication Interfaces

None

2.1.7 Memory Constraints

At least 512 MB RAM and 500 MB space of hard disk will be required to run the software.

2.1.8 Operations

None

2.1.9 Site Adaptation Requirements

The terminal at the client site will have to support the hardware and software interfaces specified in the section 2.1.3 and 2.1.4 respectively.

2.2 Product Functions

The URS will allow access only to authorized users with specific roles (System administrator, Faculty and Student). Depending upon the user's role, he/she will be able to access only specific modules of the system.

A summary of major functions that the URS will perform include:

(i) A login facility for enabling only authorized access to the system.
(ii) The system administrator will be able to add, modify or delete programmes, schools, schemes, papers and login information.
(iii) Students will be able to add/modify his/her details and register for papers to be studied in the current semester.
(iv) The system administrator/student will be able to generate the student registration card of a particular semester for a particular programme.
(v) The system administrator/faculty will be able to generate reports.

2.3 User Characteristics

(i) Qualification: At least matriculation and comfortable with English.
(ii) Experience: Should be well versed/informed about the registration process of the university.
(iii) Technical Experience: Elementary knowledge of computers.

2.4 Constraints

(i) There will be only one administrator.
(ii) The delete operation is available only to the administrator. To reduce the complexity of the system, there is no check on the delete operation. Hence, the administrator should be very careful before deletion of any record and he/she will be responsible for data consistency.

2.5 Assumptions and Dependencies

(i) The login Id and password must be created by the system administrator and communicated to the concerned user confidentially to avoid unauthorized access to the system.

(ii) It is assumed that a student registering for the subsequent semester has been promoted to that semester by the university as per rules and has paid the requisite university fee.

2.6 Apportioning of Requirements

Not Required

Specific Requirements

This section contains the software requirements in detail along with the various screens to be developed.

3.1 External Interface Requirements

3.1.1 User Interfaces

The following user interfaces (or screens) will be provided by the system.

(i) Login Form
This will be the first form, which will be displayed. It will allow the user to access the different forms based on his/her role.

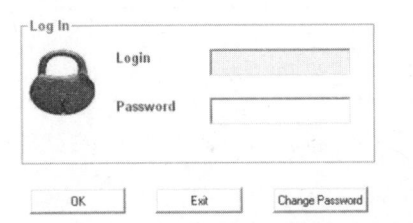

Various fields available on this form will be:

- *Login Id:* Alphanumeric of 11 characters in length and digits from 0 to 9 only are allowed. Alphabets, special characters and blank spaces are not allowed.
- *Password:* Alphanumeric in the range of 4 to 15 characters in length. Blank spaces are not allowed. However, special characters are allowed.

(ii) Change Password

The 'change password' form facilitates the user to change the password. Various fields available on this form will be:

- *Login Id:* Alphanumeric of 11 characters in length and digits from 0 to 9 only are allowed. Special characters and blank spaces are not allowed.
- *Old Password:* Alphanumeric in the range of 4 to 15 characters in length. Blank spaces are not allowed. However, special characters are allowed.
- *New Password:* Alphanumeric in the range of 4 to 15 characters in length. Blank spaces are not allowed. However, special characters are allowed.
- *Confirm Password*: Alphanumeric in the range of 4 to 15 characters in length. Blank spaces are not allowed. However, special characters are allowed. The contents of this field must match with the contents of the new password field.

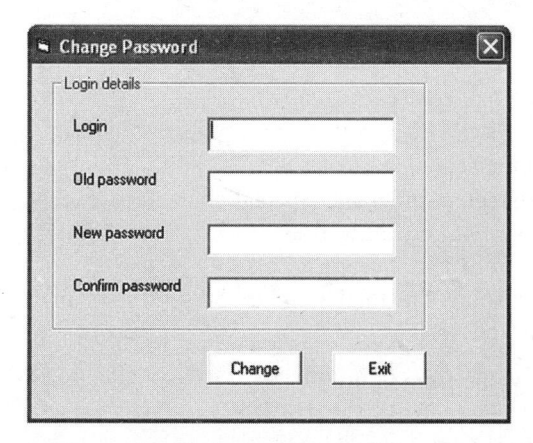

(iii) School Details

This form will allow the user to add/edit/delete/view information about new/existing school(s).

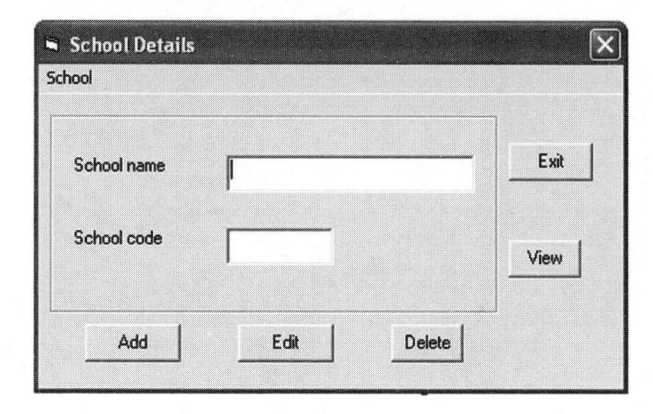

Various fields available on this form will be:

- *School Name:* Alphanumeric of 10 to 50 characters in length. Digits and special characters are not allowed. Blank spaces between characters are allowed.
- *School Code:* Numeric and will have a value from 101 to 199.

(iv) **Programme Details**

This form will allow the user to add/edit/delete/view information about new/existing programme(s) of the school that was selected in the 'Programme Details' form.

[Programme Details form image]

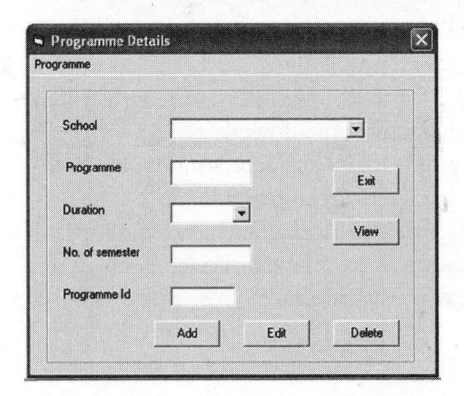

Various fields available on this form will be:

- *School*: This will display the name of all the schools.
- *Programme:* Alphanumeric of 3 to 50 characters in length. Special characters (except brackets) are not allowed. Numeric data will not be allowed.
- *Duration:* Numeric and can have a value from 1 to 7 years.
- *Number of Semesters:* This field will display the total number of semesters in a programme. Numeric can have a value from 2 to 14.
- *Programme Id:* Numeric and can have a value from 01 to 99.

(v) **Scheme Details**

This form will allow the user to add/edit/delete/view information about new/existing scheme(s) for the schools and programmes that were selected in the 'Scheme Details' form. The list of schools and programmes available in that particular school will be displayed. The list of semesters available in that particular programme will also be displayed.

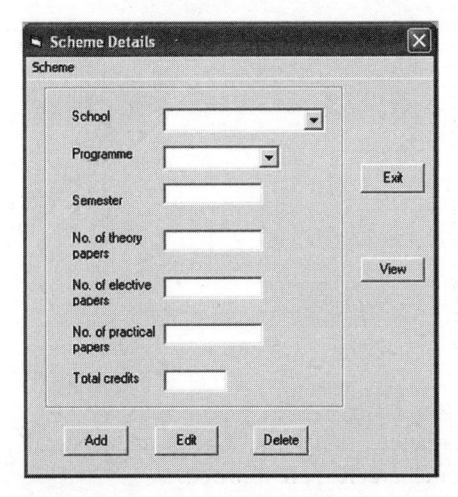

[Scheme Details form image]

Various fields available on this form will be:

- *School*: This will display the name of all the schools.
- *Programme:* This will display the name of all the programmes of the selected school.
- *Semester:* This will display the current semester of the selected programme. Numeric and can have a value from 1 to 14.
- *Number of Theory (Core) Papers:* Numeric and will have a value from 0 to 10. Core papers in the semester may be 'zero' depending upon the scheme of the programme.
- *Number of Elective Papers:* Numeric and will have a value from 0 to 10. Elective papers in the semester may be 'zero' depending upon the scheme of the programme.
- *Number of Practical Papers:* Numeric and will have a value from 0 to 10. Practical papers in the semester may be 'zero' depending upon the scheme of the programme.
- *Total Credits:* This will display total credits of the current semester. Numeric and will have a value from 5 to 99.

(vi) Paper Details

This form will allow the user to add/edit/delete/view information about new/existing paper(s) for the school, the programme and the semester that were selected in the 'Paper Details' form.

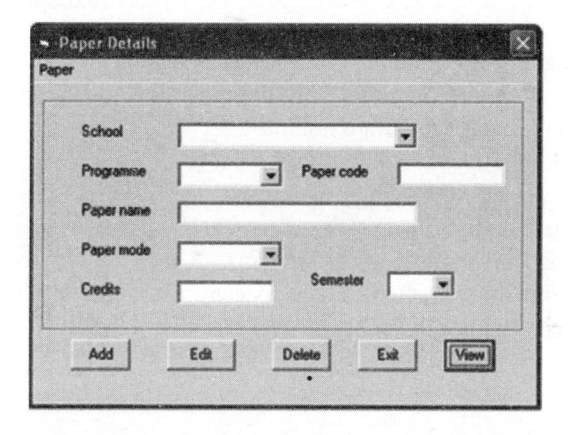

Various fields available on this form will be:

- *School:* This will display all the schools.
- *Programme:* This will display all the programmes available in the selected school.
- *Semester:* This will display the number of all the semesters available in the selected programme.
- *Paper Code:* Alphanumeric with length of 5 to 7 characters. Special characters and blank spaces are not allowed.
- *Paper Name:* Alphanumeric with length of 3 to 30 characters. This field can have only alphabetic letters. Special characters are allowed. However blank spaces are not allowed.
- *Paper Type:* Compulsory/Elective/Practical.
- *Credits:* Numeric and will have a value from 1 to 30.

(vii) Student Details

This form will allow the user to add/edit/delete/view information about new/existing student(s) for a particular year.

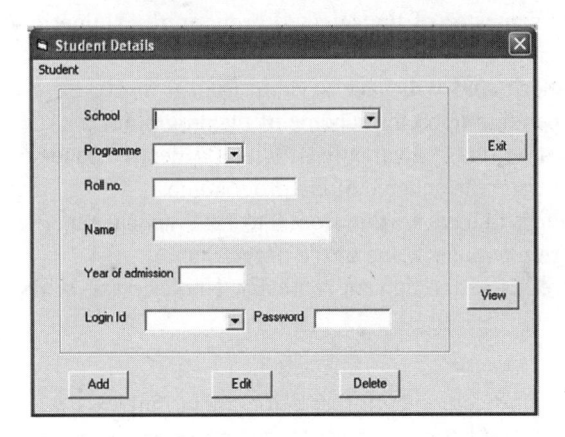

Various fields available on this form will be:

- *School:* This will display all the schools.
- *Programme:* This will display all the programmes available in the selected school.
- *Roll number:* Alphanumeric of 11 characters in length and only digits from 0 to 9 are allowed. Alphabets, special characters and blank spaces are not allowed.
- *Name:* Alphanumeric with length of 3 to 50 characters. Blank spaces are allowed. Special characters are not allowed.
- *Year of admission:* Numeric of length up to 4 digits.
- *Login Id:* This will be displayed (same as Roll number of the student).
- *Password:* Alphanumeric with length of 4 to 15 characters. Blank spaces are not allowed. However, special characters are allowed. It initially contains 8 digits of a randomly generated number.

(viii) Faculty Details

This form will allow the user to add/edit/delete/view information about new/existing faculty(ies) in a particular school.

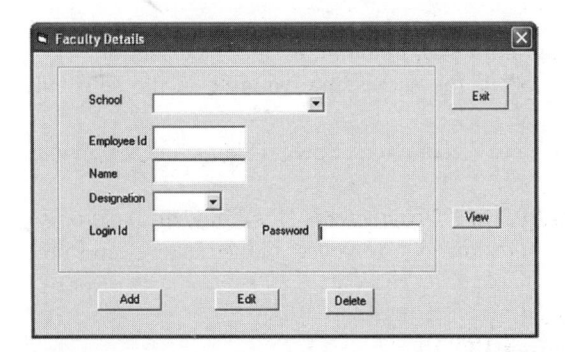

Various fields available on this form will be:

- *School*: This will display the name of all the schools.
- *Employee Id:* Alphanumeric of 11 characters in length and only digits from 0 to 9 are allowed. Alphabets, special characters and blank spaces are not allowed.
- *Name:* This will have only alphabetic letters and length of 3 to 50 characters. Blank spaces are allowed.
- *Designation:* This will have values: Professor, Reader or Lecturer.
- *Login Id:* Same as employee Id.
- *Password:* Alphanumeric with length of 4 to 15 characters. Blank spaces are not allowed. However, special characters are allowed. Initially it contains 8 digits of a randomly generated number.

(ix) **Student Registration Details**

This form will be available to the user only when registration for a semester is open. It will be filled by the student in order to register himself/herself for the current semester. Every student will be permitted to fill only his/her form.

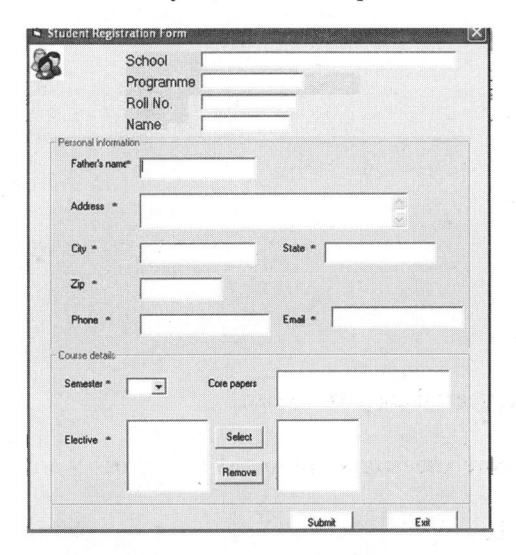

Various fields available on this form will be:

- *Father's Name:* Alphanumeric with length of 3 to 50 characters. Alphabetic letters and blank spaces are allowed. Special characters are not allowed (except'.'Character).
- *Address:* Alphanumeric with length of 10 to 200 characters. Blank spaces are allowed.
- *City:* Alphanumeric with length of 3 to 20 characters. Alphabetic letters and blank spaces are allowed. Special characters are not allowed.
- *State:* Alphanumeric with length of 3 to 20 characters. Alphabetic letters and blank spaces are allowed. Special characters are not allowed.
- *Zip:* Numeric and can have length of 6 digits.
- *Phone:* Numeric and can have length up to 11 digits.
- *Email:* Alphanumeric and can have length up to 50 characters. The email must have one '@' and '.' symbol.

- *Semester:* This will display the number of all the semesters available in the selected programme.
- *Core:* This will display all the core papers in the semester selected by the user.
- *Elective:* This will display all the elective papers available in the semester selected by the user.

3.1.2 Hardware Interfaces

As stated in Section 2.1.3

3.1.3 Software Interfaces

As stated in Section 2.1.4

3.1.4 Communication Interfaces

None

3.2 Functional Requirements

3.2.1 Login

A. Validity Checks

- (i) Every user will have a unique login Id.
- (ii) The Login Id cannot be blank.
- (iii) The Login Id will not accept alphabetic, special and blank spaces.
- (iv) The Password cannot be blank.
- (v) Alphabets, digits, hyphen and underscore characters are allowed in the password field.
- (vi) The Password will not accept blank spaces.

B. Sequencing information

None

C. Error Handling/Response to Abnormal Situations

If the flow of any of the validations does not hold true, an appropriate error message will be prompted to the user for doing the needful.

3.2.2 School Details

A. Validity Checks

- (i) Every school will have a unique school name.
- (ii) The school code cannot be blank.

(iii) The school code will have only 3 digits.
(iv) The school name cannot be blank.
(v) The school name will only accept alphabetic characters and blank spaces.
(vi) The school name cannot accept special characters and numeric digits.

B. Sequencing information

None

D. Error Handling/Response to Abnormal Situations

If the flow of any of the validations does not hold true, an appropriate error message will be prompted to the user for doing the needful.

3.2.3 Programme Details

A. Validity Checks

(i) Every programme will have a unique programme code and name.
(ii) The programme name cannot be blank.
(iii) The programme name can be of length of 3 to 50 characters.
(iv) The programme name can only have alphabets and brackets.
(v) The programme name cannot have special characters, digits and blank spaces.
(vi) The duration cannot be blank.
(vii) The duration can have a value from 1 to 7.
(viii) The number of semesters cannot be blank.
(ix) The number of semesters can have a value from 2 to 14.
(x) The programme code cannot be blank.
(xi) The programme code cannot have special characters, digits and blank spaces.
(xii) The programme code can have only 2 digits.

B. Sequencing information

The school details will have to be entered into the system before any programme details can be entered into the system.

C. Error Handling/Response to Abnormal Situations

If any of the validations/sequencing flow does not hold true, an appropriate error message will be prompted to the user for doing the needful.

3.2.4 Scheme Details

A. Validity Checks

(i) Every scheme will have a unique semester.
(ii) The school name cannot be blank.
(iii) The programme name cannot be blank.
(iv) The number of theory papers cannot be blank.

(v) The number of theory papers can have a value between 0 and 10.
(vi) The number of elective papers cannot be blank.
(vii) The number of elective papers can have a value between 0 and 10.
(viii) The number of practical papers cannot be blank.
(ix) The number of practical papers can have a value between 0 and 10.
(x) The semester cannot be blank.
(xi) The semester can have a value between 1 and 14.
(xii) The total credit cannot be blank.
(xiii) The total credit can have a value between 5 and 99.

B. Sequencing information

The school and programme details will have to be entered into the system before any scheme details can be entered into the system.

C. Error Handling/Response to Abnormal Situations

If the flow of any of the validations/sequencing does not hold true, an appropriate error message will be prompted to the user for doing the needful.

3.2.5 Paper Details

A. Validity Checks

(i) A scheme will have more than one paper.
(ii) No two semesters will have the same paper i.e. a paper will be offered only in a particular semester for a given programme.
(iii) The school name cannot be blank.
(iv) The programme name cannot be blank.
(v) The semester cannot be blank.
(vi) The semester can have a value only between 1 and 14.
(vii) The paper code cannot be blank.
(viii) The paper code cannot accept special characters.
(ix) The paper code can have both alphabetic and numeric characters.
(x) The paper code can include blank spaces.
(xi) The paper code can have length of 5 to 7 characters.
(xii) The paper name cannot be blank.
(xiii) The paper name can only have alphanumeric (alphabets and digits) or blank space characters.
(xiv) The paper name cannot have special characters.
(xv) The paper type may be compulsory, elective or practical.
(xvi) The credit cannot be blank.
(xvii) The credit can have a value only between 1 and 30.

B. Sequencing information

The school, programme and scheme details will have to be entered into the system before any paper details can be entered into the system.

C. Error Handling/Response to Abnormal Situations

If the flow of any of the validations/sequencing does not hold true, an appropriate error message will be prompted to the user for doing the needful.

3.2.6 Student Details

A. Validity Checks

(i) Every student will have a unique roll number.
(ii) The programme name cannot be blank.
(iii) The roll number cannot be blank.
(iv) The length of the roll number for any user can only be equal to 11 digits.
(v) The roll number cannot contain alphabets, special characters and blank spaces.
(vi) The student name cannot be blank.
(vii) The length of the student name can be of 3 to 50 characters.
(viii) The student name will only accept alphabetic characters and blank spaces.
(ix) The year of admission cannot be blank.
(x) The year of admission can have only 4 digits.
(xi) The password cannot be blank (this is initially auto-generated with 8 digits).
(xii) The password can have length from 4 to 15 characters.
(xiii) Alphabets, digits, hyphen and underscore characters are allowed in the password field.
(xiv) However blank spaces are not allowed.
(xv) The roll number and login Id are the same.

B. Sequencing information

The school and programme details will have to be entered into the system before any student details can be entered into the system.

C. Error Handling/Response to Abnormal Situations

If the flow of any of the validations/sequencing does not hold true, an appropriate error message will be prompted to the user for doing the needful.

3.2.7 Faculty Details

A. Validity Checks

(i) Every faculty will have a unique Employee Id.
(ii) The Employee Id cannot be blank.
(iii) The length of the Employee Id will be equal to 11 digits only.
(iv) The Employee Id cannot contain alphabets, special characters and blank spaces.
(v) The faculty name cannot be blank.
(vi) The faculty name will only accept alphabetic characters and blank spaces and will not accept special characters.
(vii) The designation cannot be blank.
(viii) The password cannot be blank (initially auto-generated with 8 digits).

- (ix) The password can have a length from 4 to 15 characters.
- (x) Alphabets, digits, hyphen and underscore characters are allowed in the password field. However blank spaces are not allowed.

B. Sequencing information

School details should be available in the system.

C. Error Handling/Response to Abnormal Situations

If the flow of any of the validations/sequencing does not hold true, an appropriate error message will be prompted to the user for doing the needful.

3.2.8 Registration Form

A. Validity Checks

- (i) The father's name cannot be blank.
- (ii) The address cannot be blank.
- (iii) The address can have a length from 10 to 200 characters.
- (iv) The city cannot be blank.
- (v) The city can have a length of up to 20 characters.
- (vi) The city cannot include special characters and numeric digits, but blank spaces are allowed.
- (vii) The state cannot be blank.
- (viii) The state can have a length of up to 20 characters.
- (ix) The state cannot include special characters and numeric digits, but blank spaces are allowed.
- (x) The zip code cannot be blank.
- (xi) The zip code cannot include alphabets, special characters and blank spaces.
- (xii) The zip code can have a length of 6 digits.
- (xiii) The phone number cannot be blank.
- (xiv) The phone number cannot include alphabets, special characters and blank spaces.
- (xv) The phone number can be of up to 11 digits.
- (xvi) The email address cannot be blank.
- (xvii) The email address can have a length of up to 50 characters (including @ and . character).
- (xviii) The semester should not be blank.
- (xix) A semester may or may not have an elective paper.
- (xx) The student cannot select more than the required number elective papers.
- (xxi) The student is required to register within the given registration time.

B. Sequencing information

Student details will have to be entered into the system before any student registration details can be entered into the system.

C. Error Handling/Response to Abnormal Situations

If the flow of any of the validations/sequencing does not hold true, an appropriate error message will be prompted to the user for doing the needful.

3.2.9 Generate Report

A. Validity Checks

(i) Only an authorized user will be allowed to access the 'Generate Reports' module.

B. Sequencing information

Reports can be generated only after the school, programme, scheme, paper and student registration details have been entered into the system.

C. Error Handling/Response to Abnormal Situations

If the flow of any of the validations/sequencing does not hold true, an appropriate error message will be prompted to the user for doing the needful.

3.2.10 Generate Registration Card

A. Validity Checks

(i) Only an authorized user will be allowed to access the 'Generate Registration Card' module.

B. Sequencing information

The registration card can be generated only after school, programme, scheme, paper and student registration details have been entered into the system for that student for the given semester.

3.3 Performance Requirements

(a) Should run on 500 MHz, 512 MB RAM machine.
(b) Responses should be within 2 seconds.

3.4 Design Constraints

None

3.5 Software System Attributes

Security

The application will be password protected. Users will have to enter the correct login Id and password to access the application.

Maintainability

The application will be designed in a maintainable manner. It will be easy to incorporate new requirements in the individual modules.

Portability

The application will be easily portable on any windows-based system that has SQL Server installed.

3.6 Logical Database Requirements

The following information will be placed in a database:

Table Name	Description
Login	Records the login details of the user.
School	Records the details of the various Schools in the University
Programme	Records programmes offered in a school.
Scheme	Stores the details of the Scheme of a Programme such as number of compulsory (core) papers, number of elective papers in a semester and the total number of theory and practical papers offered.
Paper	Stores details of Papers offered in a Programme.
Student	Records the student details.
Faculty	Records faculty details.
StudentPaperList	Records semester wise Papers selected by a student.
RegistrationOpen	A student can register only in a semester that is open for a specific duration. If the registration closes, he cannot register. The student may not be permitted to register more than one time in a semester.

Results after Verification

The SRS document is reviewed on the basis of the checklist and results are given below:

S. No.	Description	Yes/No/NA	Remarks
	Introduction		
1.	Is the purpose of the project clearly defined?	No	Refer A
2.	Is the scope clearly defined?	No	Refer B
3.	Is the document format as per standard/guidelines (Ex. IEEE 830-1993)?	Yes	-
4.	Is the project formally approved by the customer?	NA	-
5.	Are all requirements, interfaces, constraints, definitions etc. listed in the appropriate sections?	Yes	-
	Correctness		
6.	Is the expected response time from the user's point of view specified for all operations?	Yes	-
7.	Are all stated requirements expressing the functionality?	Yes	-
8.	Are there areas not addressed in the SRS document that need to be covered?	Yes	Refer C
9.	Are non-functional requirements stated?	No	Refer D
10.	Are validity checks properly defined for every input condition?	No	Refer E
	Ambiguity		
11.	Are functional requirements separated from non-functional requirements?	Yes	-

(Contd.)

(Contd.)

S. No.	Description	Yes/No/NA	Remarks
12.	Does any requirement convey more than one interpretation?	No	-
13.	Are all requirements clearly understandable?	Yes	-
14.	Does any requirement conflict with or duplicate with other requirements?	No	-
15.	Are there ambiguous or implied requirements?	No	-
Completeness			
16.	Are all functional and non-functional requirements stated?	No	Refer D
17.	Are forms available with validity checks?	Yes	-
18.	Are all reports available in the specified format?	No	Refer F
19.	Are all references, constraints, assumptions, terms and unit of measures clearly stated?	No	Refer G
20.	Has analysis been performed to identify missing requirements?	No	Refer H
Consistency			
21.	Are the requirements specified at a consistent level of detail?	No	Refer I
22.	Should any requirements be specified in more detail?	Yes	Refer I
23.	Should any requirements be specified in less detail?	No	-
24.	Are the requirements consistent with other documents of the project?	NA	-
25.	Is there any difference in the stated requirements at two places?	No	-
Verifiability			
26.	Are all stated requirements verifiable?	Yes	-
27.	Are requirements written in a language and vocabulary that the stakeholders understand?	No	Refer J
28.	Are there any non-verifiable words?	Yes	Refer K
29.	Are all paths of a use case verifiable?	NA	-
30.	Is each requirement testable?	Yes	-
Modifiability			
31.	Are all stated requirements modifiable?	Yes	-
32.	Have redundant requirements been consolidated?	Yes	-
33.	Has the document been designed to incorporate changes?	Yes	-
34.	Are the format structures and styles of the document standard?	Yes	-
35.	Is there any procedure to document a change?	No	-
Traceability			
36.	Can any requirement be traced to its origin or source?	Yes	-
37.	Is every requirement uniquely identifiable?	No	-
38.	Are all requirements clearly understandable for implementation?	Yes	-
39.	Has each requirement been cross-referenced to requirements in the documents of comparable previous projects?	NA	-
40.	Is each requirement identified such that it facilitates referencing of each requirement in future development and enhancement efforts?	Yes	-
41.	Is every stated requirement feasible?	Yes	-

(Contd.)

(Contd.)

S.No.	Description	Yes/No/NA	Remarks
42.	Is any requirement non-feasible due to technical reasons?	No	-
43.	Is any requirement non-feasible due to lack of resources?	No	-
44.	Is any requirement feasible but very difficult to implement?	No	-
45.	Is any requirement very complex?	No	-
	General		
46.	Is the document concise and easy to follow?	Yes	-
47.	Are requirements stated clearly and consistently without contradicting themselves or other requirements?	Yes	-
48.	Are all forms, figures and tables uniquely numbered?	No	-
49.	Are hardware and other communication requirements stated clearly?	No	Refer L
50.	Are all stated requirements necessary?	Yes	-

Remarks

A. Section 1.1: A paper can either be a theory paper or a practical paper.
B. In section 1.2, it is not stated that the faculty details will be maintained.
C. The layout of the student registration card and reports that the system will generate has not been given.
D. All functional requirements have not been stated. In section 3.5, the non-functional requirements – usability and reliability have not been mentioned.
E. (i) In section 3.2.1, the range of values of login id and password have not been defined.
   (ii) In section 3.2.2, it is not mentioned that a school code cannot contain alphanumeric, special characters and blank spaces.
   (iii) In section 3.2.2, the range of values of the school name has not been defined.
   (iv) In section 3.2.3, it is not mentioned that a school name cannot be blank.
   (v) In section 3.2.6, it is not mentioned that a school name cannot be blank.
   (vi) In section 3.2.7, it is not mentioned that a school name cannot be blank.
   (vii) In section 3.2.8, a range of values of the father's name is not mentioned. It is also not mentioned that a father's name cannot contain digits and special characters, but can contain blank spaces.
   (viii) In section 3.2.8, the minimum length of the city and state field has not mentioned.
   (ix) In section 3.2.8, the validity check that an email address cannot contain blank spaces has not been stated.
   (x) In section 3.2.8, there should be a separate validity check to verify that an email should contain '@' and '.' characters.
F. In section 3.1.1, neither is there any snapshot of the student registration card and output reports nor have the contents been mentioned.
G. (i) In section 1.3, the abbreviation of LAN has not been given.
   (ii) In section 2.5, the assumption that the registration process will be open only for a specific duration is not stated.
   (iii) In section 2.5, the dependencies that the list of students will be obtained from the academic section and the list of faculty will be obtained from the establishment section have not been stated.
H. (i) A data entry operator will be needed in order to add/modify/delete student and faculty details.

(ii) In section 2.2, product functions do not specify a major function that the URS would perform i.e. add/modify/delete faculty details.
I. In section 3.1.1, the details about format/layout of registration card and reports have not been provided.
J. An ambiguous word 'User' has been used throughout the SRS without specifying that the specified user under question is either an administrator, data entry operator, student or a faculty.
K. The word 'user' is non verifiable.
L. In section 3.1.4, the communication interfaces have not been stated.

The corrected SRS is provided in Appendix A.

MULTIPLE CHOICE QUESTIONS

Note: *Select the most appropriate answer for the following questions.*

5.1 Software verification includes:
 (a) Reviews
 (b) Inspections
 (c) Walkthroughs
 (d) All of the above.

5.2 Which of the following is not true?
 (a) Verification is the process of executing a program.
 (b) Verification is the process of examining a program.
 (c) Verification is the process of inspecting a program.
 (d) Verification is the process of understanding a program.

5.3 Which of the following is not a verification method?
 (a) Peer reviews
 (b) Cause effect graphing
 (c) Walkthroughs
 (d) Inspections

5.4 In walkthroughs, who presents the document to the members?
 (a) Author
 (b) Moderator
 (c) Customer
 (d) Developer

5.5 Which of the following is not a weakness of walkthroughs?
 (a) The presenter may hide critical areas.
 (b) Participants may not ask penetrating questions.
 (c) Documents are shown to all participants.
 (d) None of the above.

5.6 Which of the following is not used as a term for inspections?
 (a) Formal technical reviews
 (b) Peer reviews
 (c) Technical reviews
 (d) Reviews

5.7 In inspections, who presents the document to the members?
   (a) Author
   (b) Developer
   (c) Specialized person
   (d) Customer
5.8 Which verification method requires maximum participants?
   (a) Peer reviews
   (b) Walkthroughs
   (c) Inspections
   (d) None of the above.
5.9 What is the IEEE standard for SRS document?
   (a) IEEE std. 830 – 1998
   (b) IEEE std. 829 – 1993
   (c) IEEE std. 860 – 1998
   (d) IEEE std. 863 – 1998
5.10 What is the IEEE standard for SDD document?
   (a) IEEE std. 830 – 1998
   (b) IEEE std. 1016 – 1998
   (c) IEEE std. 829 – 1998
   (d) IEEE std. 831 – 1998
5.11 SRS stands for:
   (a) Software Requirements specifications
   (b) System Requirements Specifications
   (c) Systematic Requirements Specifications
   (d) Sequential Requirements Specifications
5.12 Verification of the SRS documents is carried out to:
   (a) Document the requirements
   (b) Improve the quality
   (c) Capture the requirements
   (d) Notify the requirements
5.13 Which is not a characteristic of a good SRS?
   (a) Correct
   (b) Complete
   (c) Consistent
   (d) Brief
5.14 Software verification activities are most useful at the level of:
   (a) SRS document
   (b) SDD document
   (c) Source code
   (d) Documentations
5.15 Source code should be examined to check:
   (a) Syntax errors
   (b) Semantics errors
   (c) Standards
   (d) All of the above

5.16 What is the advantage of source code inspections?
  (a) Examine the source code before the execution environment is ready.
  (b) It can be performed by inexperienced persons.
  (c) It is not expensive.
  (d) Source code writers can do it.
5.17 Peer reviews are also known as:
  (a) Inspections
  (b) Walkthroughs
  (c) Informal reviews
  (d) Formal reviews
5.18 What is not included in the cost of performing inspections?
  (a) Setting up forms and databases
  (b) Statistical analysis of various metrics
  (c) Time spent on documenting outside meeting
  (d) Writing the documents to be inspected
5.19 Reviews, inspections and dynamic testing have the same objective of:
  (a) Identifying faults
  (b) Fixing faults
  (c) Removing faults
  (d) All of the above
5.20 Quality assurance methods are usually considered as:
  (a) Defective
  (b) Preventive
  (c) Corrective
  (d) Perfective
5.21 What is the basic difference between a walkthrough and an inspection?
  (a) An inspection is led by the author, while a walkthrough is led by the moderator.
  (b) An inspection is led by the moderator, while a walkthrough is led by the author.
  (c) Authors are not present during inspections while they handle every aspect of the walkthrough.
  (d) None of the above.
5.22 Software quality is determined by:
  (a) The number of bugs only
  (b) The sales level of the software
  (c) How well the software meets the needs of the business
  (d) None of the above
5.23 Typical defects that are easier to find in reviews than in dynamic testing are:
  (a) Deviations from standards
  (b) Requirement defects
  (c) Design defects
  (d) All of the above
5.24 Which should not be included as a success factor for a review?
  (a) Management supports a good review process
  (b) Defects found are discussed openly
  (c) Each review does not have a predefined objective
  (d) None of the above

5.25 The later in the development life cycle a fault is discovered, the more expensive it is to fix. Why?
   (a) Due to poor documentation, it takes longer to find out what the software is doing.
   (b) Wages are rising.
   (c) The fault has already resulted in many faults in documentation, generated faulty source code, etc
   (d) None of the above

5.26 Inspections can find all of the following except:
   (a) Variables not defined in the source code
   (b) Omission of requirements
   (c) Errors in documents and the source code
   (d) How much of the source code has been covered

5.27 During software development, when should we start testing activities?
   (a) After the completion of code
   (b) After the completion of design
   (c) After the completion of requirements capturing
   (d) After the completion of feasibility study

5.28 In reviews, the moderator's job is to:
   (a) Prepare minutes of the meeting
   (b) Prepare documents for review
   (c) Mediate between participants
   (d) Guide the users about quality

5.29 What can static analysis not identify?
   (a) Memory leaks
   (b) Data of defined variables but which are not used
   (c) Data of variables used but not defined
   (d) Array bound violations

5.30 Which of the following statements are not true?
   (a) Inspections are very important for fault identifications.
   (b) Inspections should be led by a senior trained person.
   (c) Inspections are carried out using documents.
   (d) Inspections may often not require documents.

EXERCISES

5.1 Differentiate between verification and validation. Describe various verification methods.
5.2 Which verification method is most popular and why?
5.3 Describe the following verification methods:
   (a) Peer views
   (b) Walkthroughs
   (c) Inspections
5.4 Explain the issues which must be addressed by the SRS document checklist.
5.5 Discuss the areas which must be included in a good SDD design checklist. How is it useful to improve the quality of the document?

5.6 Discuss some of the issues related to source code reviews. How can we incorporate these issues in the source code review checklist?

5.7 Design a checklist for user documentation verification.

5.8 Why do we opt for software project audit? What are the requirements of a relevance scale and theory and practice scale? Discuss some of the issues which must be addressed in project audit and review checklist.

5.9 Establish a relationship between verification, validation and testing. Which is most important and why?

5.10 Discuss some characteristics which the SRS document must address. How can these be incorporated in a checklist?

5.11 What is the purpose of preparing a checklist? Discuss with the help of a checklist.

5.12 What types of reviews are conducted throughout the software development life cycle?

5.13 With the help of an example, explain how you will review an SRS document to ensure that the software development has been correctly carried out.

5.14 What are the differences between inspections and walkthroughs? Compare the relative merits of both.

5.15 Could review and inspections be considered as part of testing? If yes, why? Give suitable examples.

FURTHER READING

Horch presents reviews as one of the elements of software quality system. Chapter 3 of the book gives a full account on reviews:

John W. Horch, "Practical Guide to Software Quality Management", Artech House, 2003.

The books by Rakitin and Hollocker provide a full account on how to start a review.

Charles P. Hollocker, "Software Reviews and Audits Handbook", New York: John Wiley & Sons, 1990.

Steve Rakitin, "Software Verification and Validation for Practitioners and Managers", Second Edition, Norwood, MA: Artech House, 2001.

The book by Tom provides an excellent introduction on software inspection and is full of a large number of real-life case studies.

Gilb, Tom and D. Graham, "Software Inspections", MA: Addison-Wesley, 1993.

Fagan shows that by using inspection, cost of errors may be reduced significantly in the initial phases of software development.

Fagan, M. E., "Design and Code Inspections to Reduce Errors in Program Development", IBM Systems Journal, vol. 15, no. 3, 1976.

Strauss provides a comprehensive guide to software inspections method that may reduce program defects in the early phases of software design and development:

S.H Strauss, Susan H., and Robert G. Ebenau, "Software Inspection Process", New York: McGraw-Hill, 1994.

Wheeler provides a summary of a number of papers on software inspections. The book traces the software industry's experiences on software inspections and it can be seen from the best papers published on this topic:

> David A.Wheeler, "Software Inspection: An Industry Best Practice", Los Alamitos, CA: IEEE Computer Society Press, 1996.

Wiegers book is an important contribution in the area of peer reviews. The author provides a good description on how to create work culture within a software organization:

> Wiegers, Karl Eugene, "Peer Reviews in Software: A Practical Guide", MA: Addison-Wesley, 2001.

The following book may provide a useful guidance to practitioners and programmers on group walkthroughs:

> E. Yourdon, "Structured Walk-throughs", Englewood Cliffs, NJ: Prentice Hall, 1989.

The IEEE standard for Software Requirements Specifications presents content and qualities of a good requirement and provides an outline and description of a Software Requirements Specifications document:

> IEEE, "IEEE Recommended Practice for Software Requirements Specifications (IEEE Std 830–1998)", 1998.

The IEEE standard on software design provides recommendations on the organization of software design description document:

> IEEE, "IEEE Recommended Practice for Software Design Description (IEEE Std 1016–1998)", 1998.

Baiz and Costa have designed an excellent audit checklist which is based on relevance scale and theory and practice scale:

> Hatty Baiz and Nancy Costa, "Project Audit and Review Checklist", Princeton Project Office, Princeton University, New Jersey, USA, hetty@princeton.edu, ncosta@princeton.edu, 2001.

6

Creating Test Cases from Requirements and Use Cases

We prepare 'Software requirements and specifications' document to define and specify user requirements. In the initial years of software development, requirement writers used to write stories to explain the expected behaviour of the system and its interactions with the external world. Ivar Jacobson and his team [JACO99] gave a new dimension and direction to this area and developed a Unified Modeling Language (UML) for software development. They introduced use case approach for requirements elicitation and modeling. This is a more formal way to write requirements. The customer knows what to expect, the developer understands what to code, the technical writer comprehends what to document and the tester gets what to test. The use cases address primarily the functional requirements, meaning thereby, the perspective of the users sitting outside the system. Use cases capture the expectations in terms of achieving goals and interactions of the users with the system.

The IEEE Std 830-1998 requires us to follow a systematic approach which may include the design of use cases, various forms for interaction with the user, data validations, reports, error handling and response to unexpected situations. This is an important document designed in the initial phases of the software development. In this chapter, techniques have been discussed to design test cases from requirements. Database testing has also been introduced to design test cases using interface forms.

6.1 USE CASE DIAGRAM AND USE CASES

Use case diagram is also used along with use cases to explain the functionality of the system. This is a graphical representation and gives the top view of the system along with its users and use cases. Use case diagram may be decomposed into a further level of abstraction. Use cases and use case diagrams are normally used together to define the behaviour of a system.

A use case diagram visually explains what happens when an actor interacts with the system. Actor represents the role of a user that interacts with the system. They are outsiders to the system and can be human beings, other systems, devices, etc. We should not confuse the actors with the devices they use. Devices are mechanisms that actors use to communicate with the system, but they are not actors themselves. We use the computer keyboard for interaction; in such a case, we are the actors, and not the keyboard that helps us to interact with the computer. We use the printer to generate a report; in such case, the printer does not become an actor because it is only used to convey the information. However, if we want to take information from an external database, then, this database becomes an actor for our system.

A use case is started by a user for a specific purpose and completes when that purpose is satisfied. It describes a sequence of actions a system performs to produce an observable output for the interacting user (actor). The importance of a use case is effectively given by Greg Fournier [FOUR09] as:

> "The real value of a use case is the dynamic relationship between the actor and the system. A well written use case clarifies how a system is used by the actor for a given goal or reason. If there are any questions about what a system does to provide some specific value to someone or something outside the system, including conditional behaviour and handling conditions of when something goes wrong, the use case is the place to find the answers."

A use case describes who (any user) does what (interaction) with the system, for what goal, without considering the internal details of the system. A complete set of use cases explains the various ways to use the system. Hence, use cases define expected behaviours of the system and helps us to define the scope of the system.

6.1.1 Identification of Actors

An actor represents the role of a user that interacts with the system. An actor may be a human being or a system that may interact with a use case keeping in view a particular goal in mind. Some of the examples of the actors used in the case study of 'University registration system' (discussed in Section 5.7) are given as:

(i) Administrator
(ii) Student
(iii) Faculty
(iv) Data entry operator

The URS will allow the above actors to interact with the system with their specific roles. Depending upon the role, an actor will be able to access only the defined information from the system. We may define the role of every actor as:

(i) Administrator: Able to add, modify or delete a programme, school, scheme, paper, student, faculty and login information. Able to generate student registration card and other reports.
(ii) Student: Able to add and modify his/her details and register for papers to be studied in the current semester. Able to generate student registration card.

(iii) Faculty: Able to generate desired reports.
(iv) Data entry operator: Able to add, modify or delete student and faculty information.

The identification of actors with their specified roles may define the scope for every actor and its expected actions. Every actor may interact with one or more use cases designed for the specified purpose.

6.1.2 Identification of Use Cases

Whenever we design a system, we expect some functionalities from the system. To achieve such functionalities, many actors interact with the system with some specified expectations. The actor acts from the outside and may provide some inputs to the system and expect some outputs from the system. After the finalization of requirements, we expect to create use cases for the system. Some guidelines for the creation of use cases are given as:

(i) Every use case should have a specified functionality.
(ii) Every use case will have a name. Every name should be unique, meaningful and purposeful to avoid confusion in the system.
(iii) One or more actors will interact with a use case.
(iv) An actor will initiate a use case.
(v) The role of actors should always be clearly defined for every use case. Who will initiate the use case and under which conditions, should be clearly specified.

We should always remember that use cases describe who (actor) does what (interaction) with the system, for what goal, without considering the internal details of the system.

In the URS, we may identify the following use cases for each of the actors.

S. No.	Use Case	Actors	Description
1.	Login	Administrator, student, faculty, DEO	Login
			Change password
2.	Maintain School Details	Administrator	Add School
			Edit School
			Delete School
			View School
3.	Maintain Programme Details	Administrator	Add Programme
			Edit Programme
			Delete Programme
			View Programme
4.	Maintain Scheme Details	Administrator	Add Scheme
			Edit Scheme
			Delete Scheme
			View Scheme

(Contd.)

(Contd.)

S. No.	Use Case	Actors	Description
5.	Maintain Paper Details	Administrator	Add Paper
			Edit Paper
			Delete Paper
			View Paper
6.	Maintain Student Details	Administrator, DEO	Add Student
			Edit Student
			Delete Student
			View Student
7.	Maintain Faculty Details	Administrator, DEO	Add Faculty
			Edit Faculty
			Delete Faculty
			View Faculty
8.	Maintain Student Registration Details	Administrator, student	Add Student Information
			Select Papers offered by the programme
9.	Generate Report	Administrator, faculty	Roll number wise
			Programme wise
			Semester wise
			Paper wise
10.	Generate Registration Card	Administrator, student	Printing of Registration card

We should identify use cases very carefully, because it has serious implications on the overall design of the system. Use cases should not be too small or too big. The basic flow and all alternative flows should also be specified. Identifying and writing good use cases means providing better foundations for the intended system.

6.1.3 Drawing of Use Case Diagram

The use case diagram shows actors, use cases and the relationship between them. It gives the pictorial view of the system. In use case diagram, actors are represented as stick figures and use cases are represented as ovals. The relationship between an actor and a use case is represented by a solid arrow. The components of the use case diagram are given in Figure 6.1.

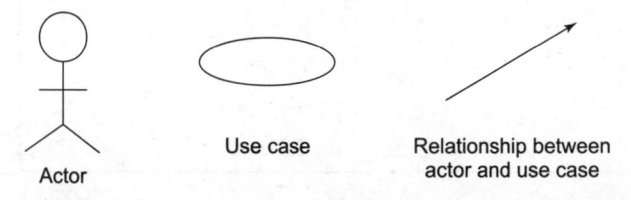

Figure 6.1. Components of use case diagram

Actors appear outside of a system. A relationship is shown by an arrow and is between the actor and a use case and vice versa. A relationship between a 'user' (actor) and 'login' use case is shown as:

If the system is small, one diagram may be sufficient to represent the whole system, but for large systems, we may require to represent the whole system in many diagrams. The use case diagram of the URS is given in Figure 6.2. There are ten use cases and four actors. The administrator interacts with all use cases, whereas a student may interact only with 'Login', 'Maintain student registration' details and 'Generate registration card' use cases.

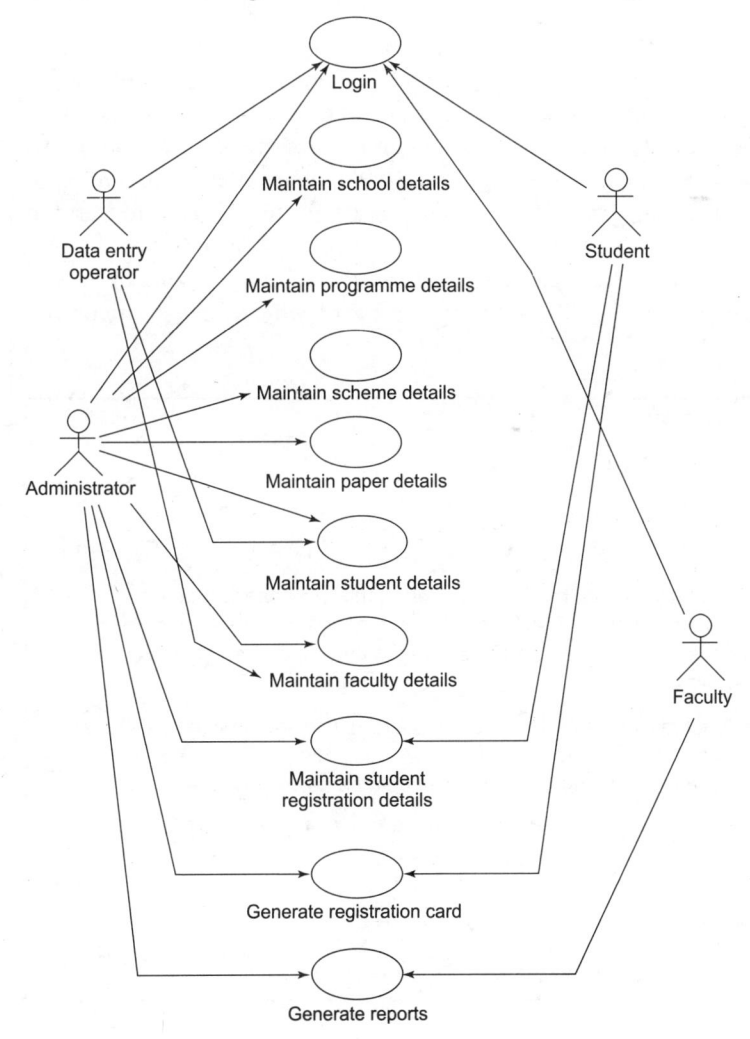

Figure 6.2. Use case diagram of the URS

6.1.4 Writing of Use Case Description

Actors interact with the use cases for predefined purposes. Hence, each actor does something with the system and the system responds accordingly. Each step is considered as a sequence of events and is called a flow. There are two types of flows:

(i) **Basic Flow:** It is the main flow and describes the sequence of events that takes place most of the time between the actor and the system to achieve the purpose of the use case.

(ii) **Alternative Flows:** If the basic flow is not successful due to any condition, the system takes an alternative flow. An alternative flow may occur due to failure of an expected service because of occurrence of exceptions/errors. There may be more than one alternative flow of a use case, but may not occur most of the time. Any alternative flow takes place under certain conditions in order to fulfil the purpose of a use case.

There is no standard method for writing use cases. Jacobson et al. [JACO99] has given a use case template which is given in Table 6.1. This captures the requirements effectively and has become a popular template. Another similar template is given in Table 6.2 which is also used by many companies [COCK01, QUAT03]. All pre-conditions that are required for the use case to perform should be identified. Post conditions, which will emerge after the execution of a use case, should also be defined. The pre-condition is necessary for the use case to start but is not sufficient to start the use case. The use case must be started by an actor when the pre-condition is true. A post-condition describes the state of the system after the ending of the use case. A post-condition for a use case should be true regardless of which flow (basic or any alternative flows) is executed.

Table 6.1. Jacobson's use case template

1. **Brief Description.** Describe a quick background of the use case.

2. **Actors.** List the actors that interact and participate in this use case.

3. **Flow of Events.**
   3.1. **Basic flow.** List the primary events that will occur when this use case is executed.
   3.2. **Alternative flows.** Any subsidiary events that can occur in the use case should be separately listed. List each such event as an alternative flow. A use case can have as many alternative flows as required.

4. **Special Requirements.** Business rules for the basic and alternative flow should be listed as special requirements in the use case narration. These business rules will also be used for writing test cases. Both success and failure scenarios should be described here.

5. **Pre-conditions.** Pre-conditions that need to be satisfied for the use case to perform should be listed.

6. **Post-conditions.** Define the different states in which we expect the system to be in, after the use case executes.

7. **Extension Points.** List of related use cases, if any.

> **Table 6.2.** Alternative use case template
>
> 1. **Introduction.** Describe the brief purpose of the use case.
> 2. **Actors.** List the actors that interact and participate in this use case.
> 3. **Pre-condition.** Define the condition that needs to be satisfied for the use case to execute.
> 4. **Post-condition.** After the execution of the use case, different states of the systems are defined here.
> 5. **Flow of Events.**
>   5.1. **Basic flow.** List the primary events that will occur when this use case is executed.
>   5.2. **Alternative flow.** Any other possible flow in this use case should be separately listed. A use case may have many alternative flows.
> 6. **Special Requirements.** Business rules for the basic and alternative flows should be listed as special requirements. Both success and failure scenarios should be described.
> 7. **Associated use cases.** List the related use cases, if any.

We may write a 'Login' use case description of the URS using the template given in Table 6.2 and the same is given below:

> **Use Case Description of login use case**
>
> **1 Introduction**
> This use case documents the steps that must be followed in order to log into the URS
>
> **2 Actors**
> - Administrator
> - Student
> - Faculty
> - Data Entry Operator
>
> **3 Pre-Condition**
> The user must have a valid login Id and password.
>
> **4 Post-Condition**
> If the use case is successful, the actor is logged into the system. If not, the system state remains unchanged.
>
> **5 Basic Flow**
> It starts when the actor wishes to login to the URS.
> (v) The system requests that the actor specify the function he/she would like to perform (either Login, Change Password).
> (vi) Once the actor provides the requested information, one of the flows is executed.
>   - If the actor selects 'Login', the Login flow is executed.
>   - If the actor selects 'Change Password', the Change Password flow is executed.
>
> **Basic Flow 1: Login**
> (i) The system requests that the actor enters his/her login Id and password information.
> (ii) The actor enters his/her login Id and password.
> (iii) The actor enters into the system.
>
> **Basic Flow 2: Change Password**
> (i) The system requests that the actor enter his/her login Id, old password, new password and confirm the new password information.
> (ii) The actor enters login Id, old password and new password, and confirms the new password information.
> (iii) The system validates the new password entered and the password change is confirmed.

(Contd.)

> **Use Case** Description of login use case
>
> **6 Alternative flows**
>   **Alternative Flow 1: Invalid login Id/password**
>   If in the Login basic flow, the actor enters an invalid login Id and/or password or leaves the login Id and /or password empty, the system displays an error message. The actor returns to the beginning of the basic flow.
>   **Alternative Flow 2: Invalid Entry**
>   If in the Change Password basic flow, the actor enters an invalid login Id, old password, new password or the new password does not match with the confirmed password, the system displays an error message. The actor returns to the beginning of the basic flow.
>   **Alternative Flow 3: User Exits**
>   This allows the user to exit during the use case. The use case ends.
>
> **7 Special Requirement**
>   None
>
> **8 Associated use cases**
>   None

The use cases describe the flow of events which include the basic flow and alternative flows and this description should be long enough to clearly explain its various steps. The basic flow and alternative flows are written in simple and clear sentences in order to satisfy all the stakeholders. A login use case, which allows entering the correct login Id and password, has two basic flows (the user is allowed to enter after giving the correct login Id and password and change password) and many alternative flows (incorrect login Id and/or password, invalid entry and user Exits). If an alternative flow has other alternative flows, the use case may have a longer description of the flows and may become a complex use case.

We should write the basic flow independently of the alternative flows and no knowledge of alternative flows is considered. The basic flow must be complete in itself without reference to the alternative flows. The alternative flow knows the details of when and where it is applicable which is opposite to the basic flow. It inserts into the basic flow when a particular condition is true [BITT03].

6.2 GENERATION OF TEST CASES FROM USE CASES

We may start writing the test cases as soon as use cases are available. This may happen well before any source code is written. It is always advisable to follow a systematic approach for the generation of test cases. These test cases may give us better coverage of the source code during testing. Any adhoc way may generate many duplicate test cases that may result in to poor coverage of the source code. A systematic approach may include the following steps:

  (i)   Generation of scenario diagrams
  (ii) Creation of use case scenario matrix
  (iii) Identification of variables in a use case
  (iv) Identification of different input states of available variables
  (v)   Design of test case matrix
  (vi) Assigning actual values to variables

If all steps are followed in the above mentioned sequence, we may have a good number of planned and systematic test cases which will result in an efficient and effective testing process.

6.2.1 Generation of Scenario Diagrams

A use case scenario is an instance of a use case or a complete path through the use case [HEUM01]. The basic flow is one scenario and every alternative path gives another scenario. Use case scenarios may also be generated due to various combinations of alternative flows. The basic and alternative flows for a use case are shown in Figure 6.3.

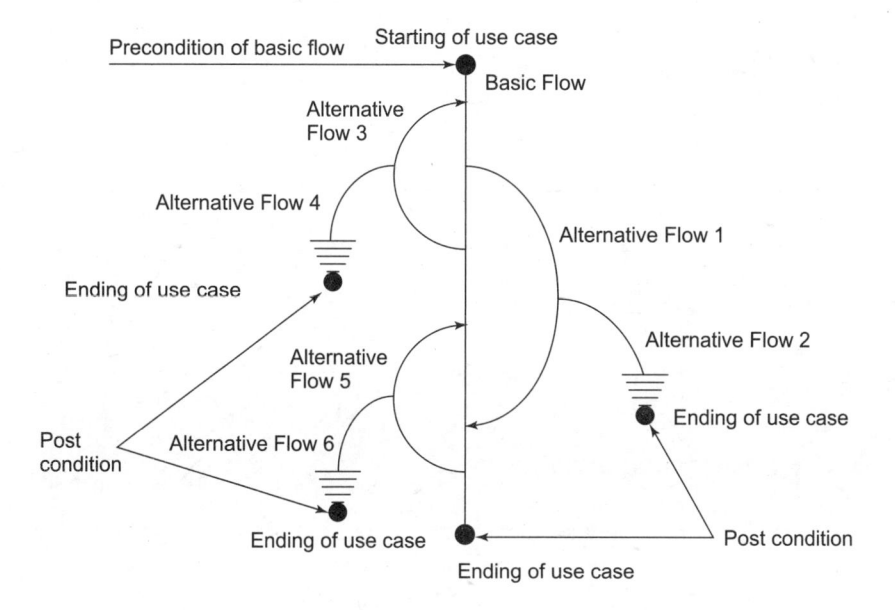

Figure 6.3. Basic and alternative flows with pre- and post-conditions

The basic flow is represented by a straight arrow and the alternative flows by the curves. Some alternative flows return to the basic flow, while others end the use case. At the end of the basic flow, a post-condition is generated while at the starting of the basic flow, a pre-condition is required to be set.

There are the following basic and alternative flows in login use case:

Basic flow:

(i) Login
(ii) Change password

Alternative flows:

(i) Invalid Login Id/password
(ii) Invalid entry
(iii) User exits

294 Software Testing

The basic and alternative flows for login use case are given in Figure 6.4. In Figure 6.4 (a), there is one basic flow which will be executed when the correct login Id and password are given. This basic flow is expected to be executed most of the time. If any input (Login Id or password) is invalid, then the alternative flow will be executed and the actor will return to the beginning of the basic flow. If at any time, the user decides to exit, then alternative flow 3 will be executed.

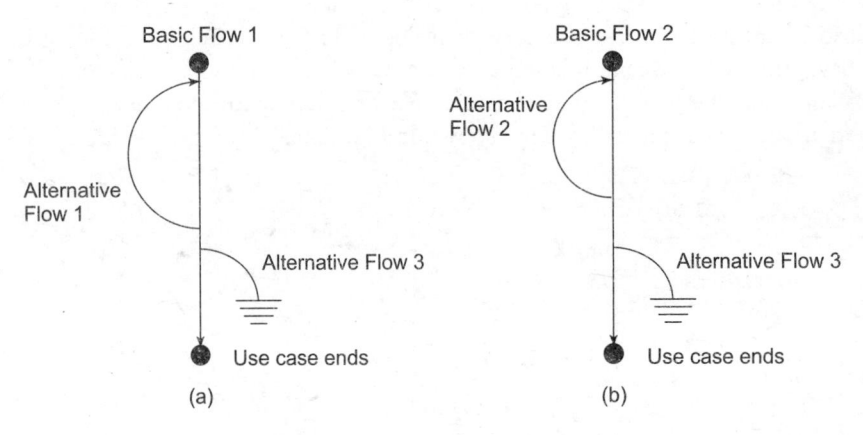

Figure 6.4. Basic and alternative flows for login use case (a) Login (b) Change password
Alternative Flow 1: Invalid login Id/password
Alternative Flow 2: Invalid Entry
Alternative Flow 3: User exits

6.2.2 Creation of Use Case Scenario Matrix

Use case scenario diagrams generate many scenarios due to the basic flow, every alternative flow along with the basic flow and various combinations of the basic and alternative flows. A scenario matrix gives all possible scenarios of the use case scenario diagram. The scenario matrix given in Table 6.3 gives all possible scenarios for the diagram given in Figure 6.3.

Table 6.3. Scenario matrix for the flow of events shown in Figure 6.3

Scenario 1	Basic Flow			
Scenario 2	Basic Flow	Alternative Flow 1		
Scenario 3	Basic Flow	Alternative Flow 1	Alternative Flow 2	
Scenario 4	Basic Flow	Alternative Flow 3		
Scenario 5	Basic Flow	Alternative Flow 3	Alternative Flow 4	
Scenario 6	Basic Flow	Alternative Flow 3	Alternative Flow1	
Scenario 7	Basic Flow	Alternative Flow 3	Alternative Flow 1	Alternative Flow 2
Scenario 8	Basic Flow	Alternative Flow 5		

(Contd.)

(Contd.)

Scenario 9	Basic Flow	Alternative Flow 5	Alternative Flow 6	
Scenario 10	Basic Flow	Alternative Flow 3	Alternative Flow 5	
Scenario 11	Basic Flow	Alternative Flow 3	Alternative Flow 5	Alternative Flow 6

In the basic and alternative flows scenario diagram of the login use case, there are six possible paths (see Figure 6.4). These six paths become six scenarios of login use case and are given in Table 6.4. Moreover, the path 'Basic Flow 1, Alternative Flow 1 and Alternative Flow 3' is impossible as per the use case description, because after giving incorrect login ID/password, the actor returns to the beginning of the basic flow 1. Similarly, both 'Basic Flow 2, Alternative Flow 2 and Alternative Flow 3' are also impossible. All valid combinations of the basic flow and the alternative flows may be generated as per given use case description.

Table 6.4. Scenario matrix for the login use case

Scenario 1- Login	Basic Flow 1	
Scenario 2- Login alternative flow: Invalid login Id/password	Basic Flow 1	Alternative Flow 1
Scenario 3- Login alternative flow: User Exits	Basic Flow 1	Alternative Flow 3
Scenario 4- Change Password	Basic Flow 2	
Scenario 5- Change password alternative flow: Invalid Entry	Basic Flow 2	Alternative Flow 2
Scenario 6- Change password alternative flow: User Exits	Basic Flow 2	Alternative Flow 3

6.2.3 Identification of Variables in a Use Case

We have to identify all input variables which have been used in every use case. For a login use case, we use 'login Id' and 'password' as inputs for entering into the use case. These are two input variables for the 'Login' use case. A variable may also be used as a selection variable where many options are available for a variable. A selection variable may be values of buttons available which provide input to the use case at some intermediate step of the use case. For example, 'Updation confirmed?' will provide two options to an actor 'Yes/No' and thus based on this selection input, the decision on whether updation is to be made or not, is made. We may select a semester from a drop down menu. The following variables are used in the login use case:

(i) Login Id
(ii) Password
(iii) Old password
(iv) New password
(v) Confirm password

These variables are inputs to the system and when an input or combination of specified inputs is given, a particular behaviour (output) is expected from the system. Hence, identification of these variables is important and helps in designing the test cases.

6.2.4 Identification of Different Input States of a Variable

An input variable may have different states and the behaviour of the system may change if the state of a variable is changed. Any variable may have at least two states i.e. valid state and invalid state. If we consider the 'Login Id' variable of the login use case, it is expected that the "Login Id should be alphanumeric of length 11 characters and only digits from 0 to 9 are allowed. Alphabets, special characters and blank spaces are not allowed." Hence, one state is the valid login Id as per the given directions and another state is the invalid login Id which is different from the given directions. There may be many different states of invalid variable. If a variable is in an invalid state, then a different process flow is executed (different alternative flow) or the system gives an unexpected output. The invalid variable should be given different inputs and appropriate values should be given at the time of designing the test cases.

6.2.5 Design of Test Case Matrix

We identify all variables and their different states for the purpose of designing test cases. One way to do so is to create a test case matrix where rows of the matrix contain test cases and the first column contains the scenario name and description and the remaining columns may contain the various input variables including the selection variables. The last column contains the expected output when these inputs are given to the system. A typical test case matrix is given in Table 6.5.

Table 6.5. A typical test case matrix

Test Case Id	Scenario Name and Description	Input 1	Input 2	Input 3 (selection variable)	Expected Output
TC1					
TC2					
TC3					
TC4					

The test case matrix for login use case is given in Table 6.6.

6.2.6 Assigning Actual Values to Variables

In test case matrix, we have written only 'valid input', 'invalid input' and 'not applicable (n/a)' in the input value columns of various variables. Now, we want to assign actual values in these columns in order to use them at the time of execution to get the actual output. We may also add two additional columns with titles 'Actual output' and 'Pass/fail' which will be used at the time of executing these test cases. There should be at least one test case for each scenario, but more test cases may be designed, depending upon availability, time and resources. These test cases may be very useful, effective and are also designed at an early stage of the software development life cycle. The test cases for the 'Login' use case are given in Table 6.7.

Table 6.6. Test case matrix for the login use case

Test case Id	Scenario Name and description	Input 1 Login Id	Input 2 Password	Input 3 Old password	Input 4 New password	Input 5 Confirm password	Expected output	Remarks (if any)
TC1	Scenario 1- Login	Valid input	Valid input	n/a	n/a	n/a	User is allowed to login	–
TC2	Scenario 2- Login alternative flow: Invalid Entry	Invalid input	Valid input	n/a	n/a	n/a	Login id invalid	Login Id is not in the specified format
TC3		Valid input	Valid input	n/a	n/a	n/a	Login id invalid	Login id does not exist in database
TC4		Valid input	Invalid input	n/a	n/a	n/a	Password invalid	Password is not in the specified format
TC5		Valid input	Valid input	n/a	n/a	n/a	Password invalid	Password does not exist in database
TC6		Invalid input	Invalid input	n/a	n/a	n/a	Login id and password invalid	Login id and Password are not in the specified format
TC7	Scenario 3- Login alternative flow: Exit	Valid /Invalid input	Valid /Invalid input	n/a	n/a	n/a	User comes out of the system	–
TC8	Scenario 4- Change password	Valid input	n/a	Valid input	Valid input	Valid input	User is allowed to change password	
TC9	Scenario 5- Change password alternative flow: Invalid entry	Invalid input	n/a	Valid /Invalid input	Valid /Invalid input	Valid /Invalid input	Old password invalid	Password is changed in the database
TC10		Valid input	n/a	Invalid input	Valid /Invalid input	Valid /Invalid input	Old password invalid	Login Id is not in the specified format
TC11		Valid input	n/a	Valid input	Invalid input	Valid /Invalid input	New password invalid	If old password is not valid, other entries become 'do not care' entries
TC12		Valid input	n/a	Valid input	Valid input	Valid input	Confirm password does not match new password	Password is not in the specified format
TC13	Scenario 6- Change password alternative flow: Exit	Valid /Invalid input	n/a	Valid /Invalid input	Valid /Invalid input	Valid /Invalid input	User is allowed to exit and returns to login screen	New and confirm password entries are different

Table 6.7. Test case matrix with actual data values for the login use case

Test case Id	Scenario Name and description	Login Id	Password	Old password	New password	Confirm password	Expected output	Remarks (if any)
TC1	Scenario 1- Login	01164521657	Abc123	n/a	n/a	n/a	User is allowed to login	–
TC2	Scenario 2- Login alternative flow: Invalid Entry	1234	Abc123	n/a	n/a	n/a	Login id invalid	Login id is not in specified format which is less than 11 characters
TC3		01164521658	Abc123	n/a	n/a	n/a	Login id invalid	Login id does not exist in database
TC4		01164521657	R34	n/a	n/a	n/a	Password invalid	Password is not in specified format which is less than 4 characters
TC5		01164521657	Abc124	n/a	n/a	n/a	Login id invalid	Password does not exist in database
TC6		1234	R34	n/a	n/a	n/a	Login id/password invalid	Login id and password are not in the specified format. Login id is less than 11 characters and password is less than 4 characters.
TC7	Scenario 3- Login alternative flow: Exit	*	*	n/a	n/a	n/a	User comes out of the system	–
TC8	Scenario 4- Change password	01164521657	n/a	Abc123	Abc124	Abc124	User is allowed to change password	–
TC9	Scenario 5- Change password alternative flow: Invalid entry	01165	n/a	*	*	*	Login Id invalid	Login Id is not in the specified format.
TC10		01164521657	n/a	Abc1	*	*	Old password invalid	Old password does not match the corresponding password in the database. Other entries (new password and confirm password) become 'do not care'.
TC11		01164521657	n/a	Abc123	R12	*	New password invalid	New password is not in the specified format which is less than 4 characters. Other entries (confirm password) become 'do not care'.
TC12		01164521657	n/a	Abc123	Abc124	Abc125	Confirm password does not match new password	–
TC13	Scenario 6- Change password alternative flow: Exit	*	n/a	*	*	*	User is allowed to exit and returns to login screen	–

*: 'do not care' conditions (valid/invalid inputs); n/a: option(s) not available for respective scenario

The use cases are available after finalizing the SRS document. If we start writing test cases in the beginning, we may be able to identify defects at the early phases of the software development. This will help to ensure complete test coverage as a complete test suite will be designed directly from the use cases. This technique is becoming popular due to its applicability in the early phases of software development. The technique is simple and directly applicable from the use cases that are part of the SRS which is designed as per IEEE standard 830-1998.

Example 6.1: Consider the problem statement of the URS as given in chapter 5. Write the use case description of use cases and generate test cases from these use cases.

Solution:

The use case description of 'maintain school details' use case is given below:

---

1 Introduction
Allow the administrator to maintain details of schools in the university. This includes adding, updating, deleting and viewing school information.

2 Actors
Administrator

3 Pre-Conditions
The administrator must be logged onto the system before this use case begins.

4 Post-Conditions
If the use case is successful, the school information is added/updated/deleted/viewed from the system. Otherwise, the system state is unchanged.

5 Basic Flow
This use case starts when the administrator wishes to add/edit/delete/view school information.
(i) The system requests that the administrator specify the function he/she would like to perform (either Add a school, Edit a school, Delete a school or View a school).
(ii) Once the administrator provides the requested information, one of the flows is executed.
- If the administrator selects 'Add a School', the **Add a School** flow is executed.
- If the administrator selects 'Edit a School', the **Edit a School** flow is executed.
- If the administrator selects 'Delete a School', the **Delete a School** flow is executed.
- If the administrator selects 'View a School', the **View a School** flow is executed.

Basic Flow 1: Add a School
The system requests that the administrator enter the school information. This includes:
(i) The system requests the administrator to enter the:
   1. School name
   2. School code
(ii) Once the administrator provides the requested information, the school is added to the system.

Basic Flow 2: Edit a School
(i) The system requests the administrator to enter the school code.
(ii) The administrator enters the code of the school. The system retrieves and displays the school name information.
(iii) The administrator makes the desired changes to the school information. This includes any of the information specified in the 'Add a School' flow.
(iv) The system prompts the administrator to confirm the updation of the school.
(v) After confirming the changes, the system updates the school record with the updated information.

(Contd.)

(Contd.)

Basic Flow 3: Delete a School
(i) The system requests the administrator to specify the code of the school.
(ii) The administrator enters the code of the school. The system retrieves and displays the school information.
(iii) The system prompts the administrator to confirm the deletion of the school.
(iv) The administrator confirms the deletion.
(v) The system deletes the school record.

Basic Flow 4: View a School
(i) The system requests that the administrator specify the school code.
(ii) The system retrieves and displays the school information.

6 Alternative Flows

Alternative Flow 1: Invalid Entry
If in the **Add a School or Edit a School** flows, the actor enters an invalid school name/code or the actor leaves the school name/code blank, the system displays an error message. The actor returns to the basic flow and may re-enter the invalid entry.

Alternative Flow 2: School Code Already Exists
If in the **Add a School** flow, a specified school code already exists, the system displays an error message. The administrator returns to the basic flow and may re-enter the school code.

Alternative Flow 3: School Not Found
If in the **Edit a School or Delete a School or View a School** flows, a school with the specified school code does not exist, the system displays an error message. The administrator returns to the basic flow and may re-enter the school code.

Alternative Flow 4: Edit Cancelled
If in the **Edit a School** flow, the administrator decides not to edit the school, the edit is cancelled and the **Basic Flow** is re-started at the beginning.

Alternative Flow 5: Delete Cancelled
If in the **Delete a School** flow, the administrator decides not to delete the school, the delete is cancelled and the **Basic Flow** is re-started at the beginning.

Alternative Flow 6: Deletion not allowed
If in the **Delete a School** flow, a programme detail of the school code exists then the system displays an error message. The administrator returns to the basic flow.

Alternative Flow 7: User Exits
This allows the user to exit during the use case. The use case ends.

7 Special Requirements
None.

8 Associated Use cases
Login

The Use Case Scenario diagram of 'Maintain school details' use case is given in Figure 6.5 and the scenario matrix is given in Table 6.8. The test case matrix is given in Table 6.9 and corresponding matrix with actual data values is given in Table 6.10.

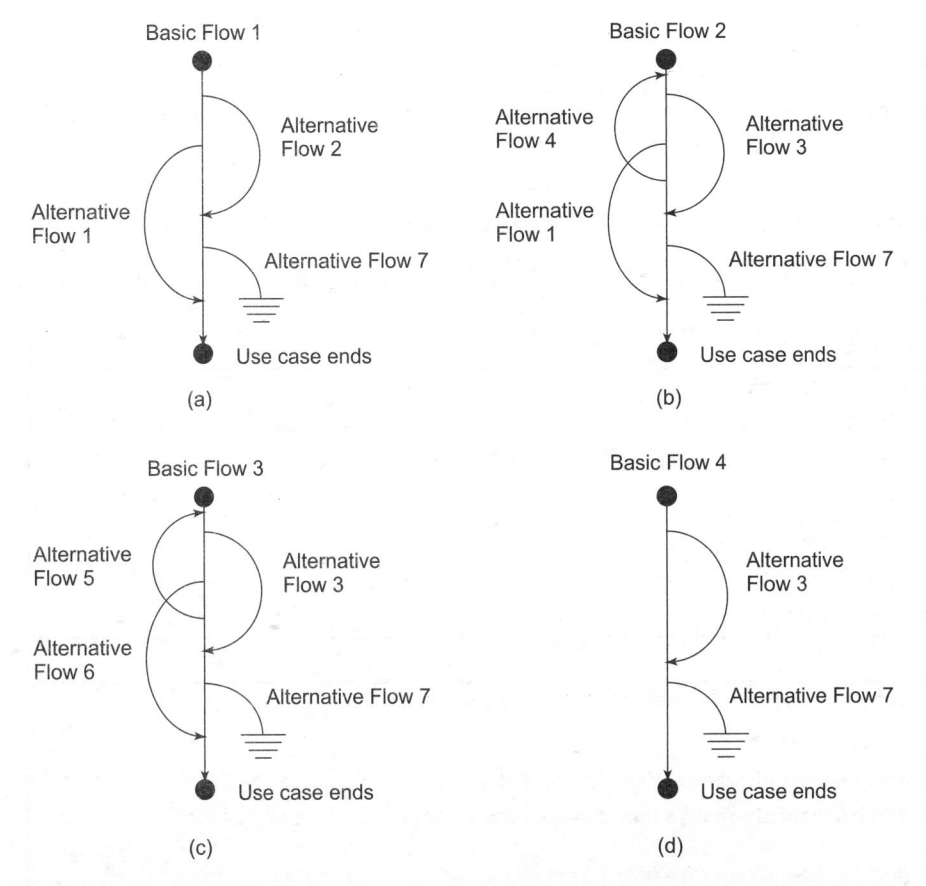

Creating Test Cases from Requirements and Use Cases 301

Figure 6.5. Basic and alternative flows for 'maintain school', 'programme', 'scheme', 'paper', or 'student details' use cases (a) Add details (b) Edit details (c) Delete details (d) View details

The scenario diagram is the same for Maintain Programme details, 'Maintain Scheme details', 'Maintain Paper details', and 'Maintain Student details'.

Maintain School Details	Maintain Programme Details
Alternative Flow 1: Invalid Entry	**Alternative Flow 1:** Invalid Entry
Alternative Flow 2: School already exists	**Alternative Flow 2:** Programme already exists
Alternative Flow 3: School not found	**Alternative Flow 3:** Programme not found
Alternative Flow 4: Edit cancelled	**Alternative Flow 4:** Edit cancelled
Alternative Flow 5: Delete cancelled	**Alternative Flow 5:** Delete cancelled
Alternative Flow 6: Deletion not allowed	**Alternative Flow 6:** Deletion not allowed
Alternative Flow 7: User exits	**Alternative Flow 7:** User exits
Maintain Scheme Details	**Maintain Paper Details**
Alternative Flow 1: Invalid Entry	**Alternative Flow 1:** Invalid Entry
Alternative Flow 2: Scheme already exists	**Alternative Flow 2:** Paper already exists

(Contd.)

(*Contd.*)

Maintain Scheme Details	Maintain Paper Details
Alternative Flow 3: Scheme not found	**Alternative Flow 3:** Paper not found
Alternative Flow 4: Edit cancelled	**Alternative Flow 4:** Edit cancelled
Alternative Flow 5: Delete cancelled	**Alternative Flow 5:** Delete cancelled
Alternative Flow 6: Deletion not allowed	**Alternative Flow 6:** Deletion not allowed
Alternative Flow 7: User exits	**Alternative Flow 7:** User exits

Maintain Student Details
Alternative Flow 1: Invalid Entry
Alternative Flow 2: Roll number already exists
Alternative Flow 3: Student not found
Alternative Flow 4: Edit cancelled
Alternative Flow 5: Delete cancelled
Alternative Flow 6: Deletion not allowed
Alternative Flow 7: User exits

Table 6.8. Scenario matrix for the 'maintain school details' use case

Scenario	Flows
Scenario 1- Add a school	Basic Flow 1
Scenario 2- Add a school alternative flow: Invalid Entry	Basic Flow 1 Alternative Flow 1
Scenario 3- Add a school alternative flow: School code already exists	Basic Flow 1 Alternative Flow 2
Scenario 4- Add a school alternative flow: User exits	Basic Flow 1 Alternative Flow 7
Scenario 5- Edit a school	Basic Flow 2
Scenario 6- Edit a school alternative flow: Invalid Entry	Basic Flow 2 Alternative Flow 1
Scenario 7- Edit a school alternative flow: School not found	Basic Flow 2 Alternative Flow 3
Scenario 8- Edit a school alternative flow: Edit cancelled	Basic Flow 2 Alternative Flow 4
Scenario 9- Edit a school alternative flow: User exits	Basic Flow 2 Alternative Flow 7
Scenario 10- Delete a school	Basic Flow 3
Scenario 11- Delete a school alternative flow: School not found	Basic Flow 3 Alternative Flow 3
Scenario 12- Delete a school alternative flow: Delete cancelled	Basic Flow 3 Alternative Flow 5
Scenario 13- Delete a school alternative flow: Delete not allowed	Basic Flow 3 Alternative Flow 6
Scenario 14- Delete a school alternative flow: User exits	Basic Flow 3 Alternative Flow 7
Scenario 15- View a school	Basic Flow 4
Scenario 16- View a school alternative flow: School not found	Basic Flow 4 Alternative Flow 3
Scenario 17- View a school alternative flow: User exits	Basic Flow 4 Alternative Flow 7

As shown in Table 6.8, there are 17 scenarios for 'Maintain School Details' use case. For 'Maintain School Details' use case, we identify four input variables for various basic flows in the use case. There are two input variables (school code, school name) and two selection variables (edit confirmed, delete confirmed) in this use case. These inputs will be available for the respective flows as specified in the use case.

Creating Test Cases from Requirements and Use Cases 303

Table 6.9. Test case matrix for the 'maintain school details' use case

Test case Id	Scenario and description	Input 1 School code	Input 2 School name	Edit confirmed	Deletion confirmed	Expected result	Remarks (if any)
TC1	Scenario 1- Add a school	Valid input	Valid input	n/a	n/a	School is added successfully	–
TC2	Scenario 2- Add a school alternative flow: Invalid entry	Invalid input	Valid/invalid input	n/a	n/a	Invalid school code	School code is not in the specified format. School name becomes do not care.
TC3	Scenario 2- Add a school alternative flow: Invalid entry	Valid input	Invalid input	n/a	n/a	Invalid school name	School name is not in the specified format
TC4	Scenario 3- Add a school alternative flow: School code already exists	Valid input	Valid input	n/a	n/a	School code already exist	The school with the same code is already present in the database
TC5	Scenario 4- Add a school alternative flow: User exits	Valid / Invalid input	Valid /Invalid input	n/a	n/a	User is allowed to exit and returns to Main menu	–
TC6	Scenario 5- Edit a school	Valid input	Valid input	Yes	n/a	School is updated successfully	–
TC7	Scenario 6- Edit a school alternative flow: Invalid entry	Invalid input	Valid/invalid input	n/a	n/a	Invalid school code	School code is not in the specified format
TC8	Scenario 7- Edit a school alternative flow: School not found	Valid input	n/a	n/a	n/a	School not found	School with the specified code does not exist in the database
TC9	Scenario 8- Edit cancelled	Valid input	Valid input	No	n/a	Main screen of school appears	–
TC10	Scenario 9- Edit a school alternative flow: User exits	Valid / Invalid input	Valid /Invalid input	n/a	n/a	User is allowed to exit and returns to Main menu	–

(Contd.)

(Contd.)

Test case Id	Scenario and description	Input 1 School code	Input 2 School name	Edit confirmed	Deletion confirmed	Expected result	Remarks (if any)
TC11	**Scenario 10- Delete a school**	Valid input	n/a	n/a	Yes	School is deleted successfully	–
TC12	**Scenario 11- Delete a school alternative flow: School not found**	Valid input	n/a	n/a	n/a	School not found	School with the specified code does not exist in the database
TC13	**Scenario 12- Delete a school alternative flow: Delete cancelled**	Valid input	n/a	n/a	No	Main screen of school appears	User does not confirm the delete operation
TC14	**Scenario 13- Delete a school alternative flow: Deletion not allowed**	Valid input	n/a	n/a	n/a	Deletion not allowed	Programme of the school exists
TC15	**Scenario 14- Delete a school alternative flow: User exits**	Valid / Invalid input	Valid /Invalid input	n/a	n/a	User is allowed to exit and returns to Main menu	–
TC16	**Scenario 15- View a school**	Valid input	n/a	n/a	n/a	School is displayed successfully	The school name with the specified code is displayed on the screen
TC17	**Scenario 16- View a school alternative flow: School not found**	Valid input	n/a	n/a	n/a	School not found	The school with the specified code does not exist in the database
TC18	**Scenario 17- View a school alternative flow: User exits**	Valid / Invalid input	Valid /Invalid input	n/a	n/a	User is allowed to exit and returns to Main menu	–

n/a: option(s) not available for respective scenario

There are 18 test cases created for the given 17 scenarios as shown in Table 6.9. Two test cases are designed for scenario 2. After constructing these test cases, actual input values are given to all the variables in order to generate actual output and verify whether the test case passes or fails (refer Table 6.10).

Table 6.10. Test case matrix with actual data values for the 'maintain school details' use case

Test case Id	Scenario and description	School ID	School Name	Edit confirmed	Deletion confirmed	Expected result	Remarks (if any)
TC1	Scenario 1- Add a school	101	University School of Information technology	n/a	n/a	School is added successfully	–
TC2	Scenario 2- Add a school alternative flow: Invalid entry	1001	*	n/a	n/a	Invalid school code	School code is not of specified length
TC3	Scenario 2- Add a school alternative flow : Invalid entry	101	12univ	n/a	n/a	Invalid school name	School name is not in the specified format i.e. it contains digits in the beginning
TC4	Scenario 3- Add a school alternative flow: School code already exists	102	University School of Management Studies	n/a	n/a	School code already exists	Entry with the same school code already exists in the database
TC5	Scenario 4- Add a school alternative flow: User exits	*	*	n/a	n/a	User is allowed to exit and returns to Main menu	–
TC6	Scenario 5- Edit a school	102	University School of Management Studies	Yes	n/a	School is updated successfully	–
TC7	Scenario 6- Edit a school alternative flow: Invalid entry	101	univ	n/a	n/a	Invalid school name	School name is not in the specified format which is less than 10 characters
TC8	Scenario 7- Edit a school alternative flow: School not found	103	n/a	n/a	n/a	School not found	School code does not exist in the database
TC9	Scenario 8- Edit cancelled	101	University School of Information technology	No	n/a	Main screen of school appears	User does not confirm the edit operation

(Contd.)

(Contd.)

Test case Id	Scenario and description	School ID	School Name	Edit confirmed	Deletion confirmed	Expected result	Remarks (if any)
TC10	Scenario 9- Edit a school alternative flow: User exits	*	*	n/a	n/a	User is allowed to exit and returns to Main menu	--
TC11	Scenario 10- Delete a school	101	n/a	n/a	Yes	School is deleted successfully	--
TC12	Scenario 11- Delete a school alternative flow: School not found	103	n/a	n/a	n/a	School not found	School code does not exist in the database
TC13	Scenario 12- Delete a school alternative flow: Delete cancelled	102	n/a	n/a	No	Main screen of school appears	--
TC14	Scenario 13- Delete a school alternative flow: Deletion not allowed	102	n/a	n/a	n/a	Deletion not allowed	Programme of the school exists
TC15	Scenario 14- Delete a school alternative flow: User exits	*	*	n/a	n/a	User is allowed to exit and returns to Main menu	--
TC16	Scenario 15- View a school	101	n/a	n/a	n/a	School is displayed successfully	--
TC17	Scenario 16- View a school alternative flow: School not found	103	n/a	n/a	n/a	School not found	School code does not exist in the database
TC18	Scenario 17- View a school alternative flow: User exits	*	*	n/a	n/a	User is allowed to exit and returns to Main menu	--

*: 'do not care' conditions (valid/invalid inputs)
n/a: option(s) that are not available for respective scenario

The use case description of 'Maintain programme details' use case is given below:

1. **Introduction**
   Allow the administrator to maintain details of the programme in the school. This includes adding, updating, deleting and viewing programme information.
2. **Actors**
   Administrator
3. **Pre-Conditions**
   The administrator must be logged onto the system and school details for which the programme details are to be added/updated/deleted/viewed must be available in the system before this use case begins.
4. **Post-Conditions**
   If the use case is successful, the programme information is added/updated/deleted/viewed from the system. Otherwise, the system state is unchanged.
5. **Basic Flow**
   This use case starts when the administrator wishes to add/edit/delete/view programme information
   (i) The system requests that the administrator specify the function he/she would like to perform (either 'Add a programme', 'Edit a programme', 'Delete a programme' or 'View a programme')
   (ii) Once the administrator provides the requested information, one of the flows is executed.
   - If the administrator selects 'Add a Programme', the **Add a Programme** flow is executed.
   - If the administrator selects 'Edit a Programme', the **Edit a Programme** flow is executed.
   - If the administrator selects 'Delete a Programme', the **Delete a Programme** flow is executed.
   - If the administrator selects 'View a Programme', the **View a Programme** flow is executed.

   Basic Flow 1: Add a Programme
   The system requests that the administrator enters the programme information. This includes:
   (i) The system requests the administrator to select an already existing school and also enter:
      1. Programme name
      2. Duration (select through drop down menu)
      3. Number of semesters
      4. Programme code
   (ii) Once the administrator provides the requested information, the programme is added to the system.

   Basic Flow 2: Edit a Programme
   (i) The system requests that the administrator enters the programme code.
   (ii) The administrator enters the programme code. The system retrieves and displays the programme information.
   (iii) The administrator makes the desired changes to the programme information. This includes any of the information specified in the **Add a Programme** flow.
   (iv) The system prompts the administrator to confirm the updation of the programme.
   (v) After confirming the changes, the system updates the programme record with the updated information.

   Basic Flow 3: Delete a Programme
   (i) The system requests that the administrator specify the programme code.
   (ii) The administrator enters the programme code. The system retrieves and displays the programme information.
   (iii) The system prompts the administrator to confirm the deletion of the programme.
   (iv) The administrator confirms the deletion.
   (v) The system deletes the programme record.

   Basic Flow 4: View a Programme
   (i) The system requests that the administrator specify the programme code.
   (ii) The system retrieves and displays the programme information.

(Contd.)

(*Contd.*)

> 6. **Alternative Flows**
>   **Alternative Flow 1: Invalid Entry**
>   If in the 'Add a Programme' or 'Edit a Programme' flows, the actor enters invalid programme/duration/number of semesters/programme code or the actor leaves the programme/duration/number of semesters/programme code empty, the system displays an error message. The actor returns to the basic flow and may re-enter the invalid entry.
>   **Alternative Flow 2: Programme code already exists**
>   If in the 'Add a Programme' flow, a programme with a specified programme code already exists, the system displays an error message. The administrator returns to the basic flow and may renter the programme code.
>   **Alternative Flow 3: Programme not found**
>   If in the 'Edit a Programme' or 'Delete a Programme' or 'View a Programme' flows, a programme with the specified programme code does not exist, the system displays an error message. The administrator returns to the basic flow and may re-enter the programme code.
>   **Alternative Flow 4: Edit cancelled**
>   If in the 'Edit a Programme' flow, the administrator decides not to edit the programme, the edit is cancelled and the Basic Flow is re-started at the beginning.
>   **Alternative Flow 5: Delete cancelled**
>   If in the 'Delete a Programme' flow, the administrator decides not to delete the programme, the delete is cancelled and the Basic Flow is re-started at the beginning.
>   **Alternative Flow 6: Deletion not allowed**
>   If in the 'Delete a Programme' flow, a scheme detail of the programme code exists then the system displays an error message. The administrator returns to the basic flow.
>   **Alternative Flow 7: User exits**
>   This allows the user to exit during the use case. The use case ends.
> 7. **Special Requirements**
>   None.
> 8. **Associated use cases**
>   Login, Maintain School Details, Maintain Scheme Details.

The Use Case Scenario of 'Maintain programme details' use case is given in Figure 6.5 and the scenario matrix is given in Table 6.11.

Table 6.11. Scenario matrix for the 'maintain programme details' use case

Scenario	Flows
Scenario 1- Add a programme	Basic Flow 1
Scenario 2- Add a programme alternative flow: Invalid entry	Basic Flow 1 Alternative Flow 1
Scenario 3- Add a programme alternative flow: Programme code already exists	Basic Flow 1 Alternative Flow 2
Scenario 4- Add a programme alternative flow: User exits	Basic Flow 1 Alternative Flow 7
Scenario 5- Edit a programme alternative flow: Edit a programme	Basic Flow 2
Scenario 6- Edit a programme alternative flow: Invalid entry	Basic Flow 2 Alternative Flow 1
Scenario 7- Edit a programme alternative flow: Programme not found	Basic Flow 2 Alternative Flow 3
Scenario 8- Edit a programme alternative flow: Edit cancelled	Basic Flow 2 Alternative Flow 4
Scenario 9- Edit a programme alternative flow: User exits	Basic Flow 2 Alternative Flow 7
Scenario 10- Delete a programme	Basic Flow 3
Scenario 11- Delete a programme alternative flow: Programme not found	Basic Flow 3 Alternative Flow 3
Scenario 12- Delete a programme alternative flow: Deletion cancelled	Basic Flow 3 Alternative Flow 5
Scenario 13- Delete a programme alternative flow: Deletion not allowed	Basic Flow 3 Alternative Flow 6
Scenario 14- Delete a programme alternative flow: User exits	Basic Flow 3 Alternative Flow 7
Scenario 15- View a programme	Basic Flow 4
Scenario 16- View a programme alternative flow: Programme not found	Basic Flow 4 Alternative Flow 3
Scenario 17- View a programme alternative flow: User exits	Basic Flow 4 Alternative Flow 7

From the use case, we identify seven input variables, out of which four are selection variables. The input variables are programme name, duration, number of semesters and programme code. The selection variables include school name, duration, edit confirmed and delete confirmed. The test case matrix is given in Table 6.12 and the corresponding matrix with actual data values is given in Table 6.13.

Table 6.12. Test case matrix for the 'maintain programme details' use case

Test case Id	Scenario Name and description	Input 1 School selected	Input 2 Programme name	Input 3 Duration	Input 4 Number of semesters	Input 5 Programme code	Edit confirmed	Deletion confirmed	Expected output	Remarks (if any)
TC1	Scenario 1- Add a programme	Yes	Valid input	Valid input	Valid input	Valid input	n/a	n/a	User is allowed to add a programme	–
TC2	Scenario 2- Add a programme alternative flow: Invalid entry	No	Valid/ Invalid input	Valid/ Invalid input	Valid/ Invalid input	Valid/ Invalid input	n/a	n/a	School not selected	User did not select a school
TC3	—do—	Yes	Invalid input	Valid/ Invalid input	Valid/ Invalid input	Valid/ Invalid input	n/a	n/a	Programme name invalid	Programme name is not in the specified format
TC4	—do—	Yes	Valid input	Invalid input	Valid/ Invalid input	Valid/ Invalid input	n/a	n/a	Duration invalid	Duration is not selected
TC5	—do—	Yes	Valid input	Valid input	Invalid input	Valid/ Invalid input	n/a	n/a	Number of semesters invalid	–
TC6	—do—	Yes	Valid input	Valid input	Valid input	Invalid input	n/a	n/a	Programme code invalid	Programme code is not in the specified format
TC7	Scenario 3- Add a programme alternative flow: Programme code already exist	Yes	Valid input	Valid input	Valid input	Valid input	n/a	n/a	Programme code already exists	Entry with the same programme code already exists in the database

(Contd.)

(Contd.)

Test case Id	Scenario Name and description	Input 1 School selected	Input 2 Programme name	Input 3 Duration	Input 4 Number of semesters	Input 5 Programme code	Edit confirmed	Deletion confirmed	Expected output	Remarks (if any)
TC8	Scenario 4- Add a programme alternative flow: User exits	Yes	Valid / Invalid input	Valid / Invalid input	Valid / Invalid input	Valid / Invalid input	n/a	n/a	User is allowed to exit and returns to Main menu	–
TC9	Scenario 5- Edit a programme alternative flow	n/a	Valid input	Valid input	Valid input	Valid input	Yes	n/a	Programme is successfully updated	–
TC10	Scenario 6-Edit a programme alternative flow: Invalid entry	n/a	Invalid input	Valid/ Invalid input	Valid/ Invalid input	Valid/ Invalid input	n/a	n/a	Programme name invalid	Programme name is not in the specified format
TC11	—do—	n/a	Valid input	Invalid input	Valid/ Invalid input	Valid/ Invalid input	n/a	n/a	Duration invalid	Duration is not selected
TC12	—do—	n/a	Valid input	Valid input	Invalid input	Valid/ Invalid input	n/a	n/a	Number of semesters invalid	–
TC13	Scenario 7- Edit a programme alternative flow: Programme not found	n/a	n/a	n/a	n/a	Valid input	n/a	n/a	Programme not found	Programme with the specified programme code does not exist in the database
TC14	Scenario 8- Edit a programme alternative flow: Edit cancelled	n/a	Valid input	Valid input	Valid input	Valid input	No	n/a	Sub menu of programme appears	User does not confirm the edit operation

(Contd.)

Creating Test Cases from Requirements and Use Cases   311

(Contd.)

Test case Id	Scenario Name and description	Input 1 School selected	Input 2 Programme name	Input 3 Duration	Input 4 Number of semesters	Input 5 Programme code	Edit confirmed	Deletion confirmed	Expected output	Remarks (if any)
TC15	Scenario 9- Edit a programme alternative flow: User exits	n/a	Valid / Invalid input	Valid / Invalid input	Valid / Invalid input	Valid / Invalid input	n/a	n/a	User is allowed to exit and returns to Main menu	--
TC16	Scenario 10- Delete a programme	n/a	n/a	n/a	n/a	Valid input	n/a	Yes	Programme is successfully deleted	--
TC17	Scenario 11- Delete a programme alternative flow: Programme not found	n/a	n/a	n/a	n/a	Valid input	n/a	n/a	Programme not found	Programme with the specified programme code does not exist in the database
TC18	Scenario 12- Delete a programme alternative flow: Deletion cancelled	n/a	n/a	n/a	n/a	Valid input	n/a	No	Deletion cancelled	User does not confirm the deletion operation
TC19	Scenario 13- Delete a programme alternative flow: Deletion not allowed	n/a	n/a	n/a	n/a	Valid input	n/a	n/a	Deletion not allowed	Scheme of the programme exists
TC20	Scenario 14- Delete a programme alternative flow: User exits	n/a	n/a	n/a	n/a	Valid / Invalid input	n/a	n/a	User is allowed to exit and returns to Main menu	--

(Contd.)

(Contd.)

Test case Id	Scenario Name and description	Input 1 School selected	Input 2 Programme name	Input 3 Duration	Input 4 Number of semesters	Input 5 Programme code	Edit confirmed	Deletion confirmed	Expected output	Remarks (if any)
TC21	Scenario 15- View a programme	n/a	n/a	n/a	n/a	Valid input	n/a	n/a	Programme details are displayed	–
TC22	Scenario 16- View a programme alternative flow: Programme not found	n/a	n/a	n/a	n/a	Valid input	n/a	n/a	Programme not found	Programme with the specified programme code does not exist in the database
TC23	Scenario 17- View a programme alternative flow: User exits	n/a	n/a	n/a	n/a	Valid / Invalid input	n/a	n/a	User is allowed to exit and returns to Main menu	–

n/a: option(s) not available for respective scenario

Creating Test Cases from Requirements and Use Cases 313

Table 6.13. Test case matrix with actual data values for the programme use case

Test case Id	Scenario name and description	School selected	Programme name	Duration	Number of semesters	Programme code	Edit confirmed	Deletion confirmed	Expected output	Remarks (if any)
TC1	Scenario 1- Add a programme	Yes	MCA	3	6	12	n/a	n/a	User is allowed to add a programme	—
TC2	Scenario 2- Add a programme alternative flow: Invalid entry	No	*	*	*	*	n/a	n/a	School not selected	User did not select a school
TC3	—do—	Yes	M12Ca	*	*	*	n/a	n/a	Programme name invalid	Programme name is not in the specified format i.e. it contains digits
TC4	—do—	Yes	MCA	*	*	*	n/a	n/a	Duration invalid	Duration not selected
TC5	—do—	Yes	MCA	3	12	*	n/a	n/a	Number of semesters invalid	Number of semesters should be 6 as duration of the programme is 3
TC6	—do—	Yes	MCA	3	6	12d	n/a	n/a	Programme code invalid	Programme code is a numeric field and cannot contain alphabets
TC7	Scenario 3- Add a programme alternative flow: Programme code already exists	Yes	BTech(IT)	4	8	13	n/a	n/a	Programme code already exists	Programme with the same programme code exists in the database
TC8	Scenario 4- Add a programme alternative flow: User exits	Yes	*	*	*	*	n/a	n/a	User is allowed to exit and returns to Main menu	—

(Contd.)

314 Software Testing

(Contd.)

Test case Id	Scenario name and description	School selected	Programme name	Duration	Number of semesters	Programme code	Edit confirmed	Deletion confirmed	Expected output	Remarks (if any)
TC9	Scenario 5- Edit a programme alternative flow	n/a	BTech(IT)	4	8	13	Yes	n/a	Programme is successfully edited	–
TC10	Scenario 6-Edit a programme alternative flow: Invalid entry	n/a	Mca123	*	*	*	n/a	n/a	Programme name invalid in 'Edit a programme' flow	Programme name is not in the specified format and contains digits
TC11	–do–	n/a	BTech(IT)	*	*	*	n/a	n/a	Duration invalid	Duration not selected
TC12	–do–	n/a	BTech(IT)	4	13	*	n/a	n/a	Number of semesters	Number of semesters should be 8 as duration is 4
TC13	Scenario 7 - Edit a programme alternative flow: Programme not found	n/a	n/a	n/a	n/a	14	n/a	n/a	Programme not found	Programme with the specified programme code does not exist in the database
TC14	Scenario 8- Edit a programme alternative flow: Edit cancelled	n/a	BTech(IT)	4	8	13	No	n/a	Blank form appears	User does not confirm the edit operation
TC15	Scenario 9- Edit a programme alternative flow: User exits	n/a	*	*	*	*	n/a	n/a	User is allowed to exit and returns to Main menu	–
TC16	Scenario 10- Delete a programme	n/a	n/a	n/a	n/a	12	n/a	Yes	Programme is successfully deleted	–
TC17	Scenario 11- Delete a programme alternative flow: Programme not found	n/a	n/a	n/a	n/a	16	n/a	n/a	Programme not found	Programme with the specified programme code does not exist in the database

(Contd.)

(Contd.)

Test case Id	Scenario name and description	School selected	Programme name	Duration	Number of semesters	Programme code	Edit confirmed	Deletion confirmed	Expected output	Remarks (if any)
TC18	Scenario 12- Delete a programme alternative flow: Deletion cancelled	n/a	n/a	n/a	n/a	13	n/a	No	Sub menu of programme appears	User does not confirm the delete operation
TC19	Scenario 13- Delete a programme alternative flow: Deletion not allowed	n/a	n/a	n/a	n/a	13	n/a	n/a	Deletion not allowed	Scheme of the record already exists, hence the programme with the specified code cannot be deleted
TC20	Scenario 14- Delete a programme alternative flow: User exits	n/a	n/a	n/a	n/a	*	n/a	n/a	User is allowed to exit and returns to Main menu	–
TC21	Scenario 15- View a programme	n/a	n/a	n/a	n/a	13	n/a	n/a	Programme details are displayed	–
TC22	Scenario 16- View a programme alternative flow: Programme not found	n/a	n/a	n/a	n/a	16	n/a	n/a	Programme not found	Programme with the specified programme code does not exist in the database
TC23	Scenario 17- View a programme alternative flow: User exits	n/a	n/a	n/a	n/a	*	n/a	n/a	User is allowed to exit and returns to Main menu	–

*: 'do not care' conditions (valid/invalid inputs)
n/a: option(s) not available for respective scenario

The test cases for other use cases of the URS case study are given in Appendix II.

6.3 GUIDELINES FOR GENERATING VALIDITY CHECKS

We want to have guidelines for generating validity checks for input data. We may have to give many inputs to a program via forms, data files and / or input statement(s). Ideally, we want to enter correct data and for this purpose we should test various conditions with invalid inputs to the program. Some of the guidelines are given in the following sub-sections.

6.3.1 Data Type

If input x is defined as an integer, then x should also be checked for float, char, double, etc. values. We should clearly state what can be accepted as an input. In the login form, (please refer to Figure 6.7), we should clearly state the type of both the inputs i.e. Login Id and password. For example, the Login Id input should be numeric and should not accept alphabets, special characters and blank spaces. Similarly, the password input will accept alphabets, digits, hyphen and underscore but will not accept blank spaces. We should generate validity checks for every 'do' and every 'do not' case.

6.3.2 Data Range

The range of inputs should also be clearly specified. If x is defined as an integer, its range, (say $1 \leq x \leq 100$) should also be defined. Validity checks may be written for conditions when $x \leq 1$ and $x > 100$. For example, in login form, length of the login-id is defined as 11 digits and the password as 4 to 15 digits. We should generate validity checks for both valid and invalid range of inputs.

6.3.3 Special Data Conditions

Some special conditions may need to be checked for specified inputs. For example, in the e-mail address, '@' and '.'symbols are essential and must be checked. We should write validity checks for such special symbols which are essential for any specific input.

6.3.4 Mandatory Data Inputs

Some inputs are compulsory for the execution of a program. These mandatory fields should be identified and validity checks be written accordingly. In the login form, both inputs (login Id and password) are mandatory. Some fields (data inputs) may not be mandatory like telephone number in a student registration form. We should provide validity checks to verify that mandatory fields are entered by the user.

6.3.5 Domain Specific Checks

Some validity checks should be written on the basis of the expected functionality. In the URS, no two semesters should have a common paper. The roll number should be used as a login Id. A student cannot select more than the required number of elective papers in a semester. These domain specific issues should be written as validity checks in order to verify their correctness.

6.4 STRATEGIES FOR DATA VALIDITY

What are data validity checks? Are they required to be tested? Why should data validation be given focus in testing? Why do we expect valid data? These questions are important and their answers may motivate us to generate test cases using data validity checks.

Valid data means correct data which is expected in every software. The software should provide checks for validating data entered into the system. Whenever and wherever we attempt to enter invalid data, an appropriate message should be displayed. Ideally, the software should only allow the entry of valid data into the system. If we are able to do so with a good design, we may be able to minimize many problems. In order to give proper focus on data validations, there is a provision of writing data validity checks for every form / screen in the SRS document. These data validity checks may become the basis for the generation of test cases.

Data validity strategies are often influenced by the design of the software. Three popular strategies for data validation are discussed which may be applied at the early phases of the software development life cycle.

6.4.1 Accept Only Known Valid Data

We all want to enter valid data into the system. If our software accepts only correct data, our design is a successful design. If it does not happen, we may enter invalid data into the system, which may further complicate many issues. Invalid data may force the software to behave unexpectedly and may lead to a failure. Hence, software should accept only input(s) that is / are known to be safe and expected.

Consider the SRS document of the URS (refer Appendix I). The login form is given in Figure 6.6 that allows users to enter into the system using a valid login Id and a valid password. Some data validity checks are also given in Table 6.14. Our login form should only accept valid login Id and valid password and allow the user to enter into the system. If we give valid entries for both login ID and password, we should enter into the system, otherwise proper error message(s) should be displayed. In order to ensure validity of data, we should generate test cases to check the validity of the data and to also check the conditions when we enter invalid data. Both valid and invalid data inputs will generate test cases that may check the entry of data into the software. We have identified 8 validity checks shown in Table 6.14 and may generate test cases as given in Table 6.15. If the first input is invalid, the second input automatically becomes 'do not care' and an appropriate error message is displayed. Every validity check condition at least generates a test case. In Table 6.15, two test cases (TC1, TC10) accept only valid data. We have identified three test cases for VC4 and two test cases for VC6.

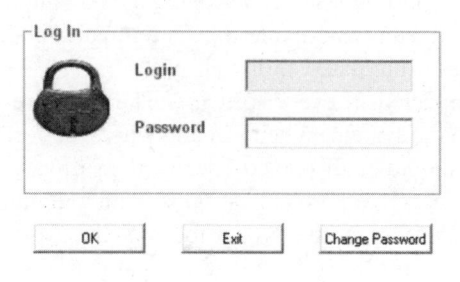

Figure 6.6. Login form

Table 6.14. Validity checks for login form

Validity check Number	Description
VC1	Every user will have a unique login Id.
VC2	Login Id cannot be blank.
VC3	Login Id can only have 11 digits.
VC4	Login Id will not accept alphabetic, special and blank spaces.
VC5	Password cannot be blank.
VC6	Length of password can only be 4 to 15 digits.
VC7	Alphabets, digits, hyphen and underscore characters are allowed in password field.
VC8	Password will not accept blank spaces.

Table 6.15. Test case with actual data values for the login form

Test case Id	Validity check Number	Login id	Password	Expected output	Remarks
TC1	VC1	10234567899	Rkhj7689	User successfully logs into the system	-
TC2	VC2		*	Please Enter Login Id	Login id cannot be blank
TC3	VC3	1234	*	Invalid login id	Login id should have 11 digits
TC4	VC4	Ae455678521	*	Invalid login id	Login id cannot have alphanumeric characters
TC5	VC4	123$4567867	*	Invalid login id	Login id cannot have special characters
TC6	VC4	123 45667897	*	Invalid login id	Login id cannot have blank spaces
TC7	VC5	10234567899		Please Enter Password	Password cannot be blank
TC8	VC6	10234567899	Ruc	Invalid password	Password cannot be less than 4 characters in length
TC9	VC6	10234567899	Rtyuiopki1123678	Invalid password	Password cannot be greater than 15 characters in length
TC10	VC7	10234567899	Rty_uyo	User successfully logs into the system	Password can have underscore character
TC11	VC8	10234567899	Rt yuii	Invalid password	Password cannot have blank spaces

*: 'do not care' conditions (valid/invalid inputs)

Additional validity checks are designed in order to validate various inputs in the 'Change password' form. The 'Change password' form is given in Figure 6.7 and the validity checks are given in Table 6.16. The corresponding test cases for each validity check are given in Table 6.17.

Figure 6.7. Change password form

Table 6.16. Validity checks for change password form

Validity check Number	Description
VC9	Login Id cannot be blank.
VC10	Login Id can only have 11 digits.
VC11	Login Id will not accept alphabetic, special and blank spaces.
VC12	Old password cannot be blank.
VC13	Length of old password can only be 4 to 15 digits.
VC14	Alphabets, digits, hyphen and underscore characters are allowed in old password field.
VC15	Old password will not accept blank spaces.
VC16	New password cannot be blank.
VC17	Length of new password can only be 4 to 15 digits.
VC18	Alphabets, digits, hyphen and underscore characters are allowed in new password field.
VC19	New password will not accept blank spaces.
VC20	'Confirm password' cannot be blank.
VC21	'Confirm password' should match with new password.

Table 6.17. Test case with actual data values for the 'Change Password' form

Test case Id	Validity check No.	Login id	Old password	New Password	Confirm Password	Expected output	Remarks
TC1	VC9		*	*	*	Please Enter Login Id	Login id cannot be blank
TC2	VC10	1234	*	*	*	Invalid login id	Login id should have 11 digits
TC3	VC11	Ae455678521	*	*	*	Invalid login id	Login id cannot have alphanumeric characters
TC4	VC11	123$4567867	*	*	*	Invalid login id	Login id cannot have special characters
TC5	VC11	123 45667897	*	*	*	Invalid login id	Login id cannot have blank spaces
TC6	VC12	10234567899		*	*	Please Enter Old Password	Password cannot be blank
TC7	VC13	10234567899	Ruc	*	*	Invalid old password	Password cannot be less than 4 characters long
TC8	VC14	10234567899	Rtyuiopki1123678	*	*	Invalid old password	Password cannot be greater than 15 characters in length
TC9	VC14	10234567899	Rty_uyo	*	*	–	Password can have underscore character
TC10	VC15	10234567899	Rt yuii	*	*	Invalid old password	Password cannot have blank spaces
TC11	VC16	10234567899	Ruc_ui		*	–	Password cannot be blank
TC12	VC17	10234567899	Ruc_ui	Rrk	*	Invalid new password	Password cannot be less than 4 characters long
TC13	VC17	10234567899	Ruc_ui	Rtyuiopki1123678	*	Invalid new password	Password cannot be greater than 15 characters in length
TC14	VC18	10234567899	Ruc_ui	Rty_uyo	*	Invalid new password	New password can have underscore character
TC15	VC19	10234567899	Ruc_ui	Rty uyo	*	Invalid new password	New password cannot have blank spaces
TC16	VC20	10234567899	Ruc_ui	Rty_uyo		–	'Confirm Password' cannot be blank
TC17	VC21	10234567899	Ruc_ui	Rty_uyo	Rty_uyo	Invalid 'Confirm Password'	'Confirm Password' should match with new password

*: 'do not care' conditions (valid/invalid inputs)

6.4.2 Reject Known Bad Data

We should be able to identify the correctness of the data. If the input data is not as expected, the software should reject it and an appropriate error message should be displayed. We should check the data type from the form itself. If the integer type x is the input and we enter x as a float, an error should immediately be displayed. The software should accept values in the specified range. If the input is beyond range, it should not be accepted at all. Many test cases of Table 6.15 check this concept and reject known bad data (refer TC3, TC4, TC5, TC6, TC8, TC9, and TC11) by giving appropriate error messages.

6.4.3 Sanitize All Data

Data sanitization is the process of purifying (filtering) undesirable data in order to make it harmless and safe for the system. We may sanitize data at the input stage where data is entered by the user. We may also sanitize the data at the output stage where data is displayed to the user in such a way that it becomes more useful and meaningful. For example, when an integer variable is used, its lower and upper permissible limits must be specified and provisions should be made in the program to prevent the entry of any value outside the permissible limit. These limits are hardware dependent and may change, if not earlier specified. In case of Boolean variable, provision should be made in the program to reject any value which is not from the following list:
List = (true, false, 0, 1, yes, no)

Hence, we should attempt to make undesired data harmless, especially when dealing with rejecting bad inputs. This may be easy to write but extremely difficult to do in practice. It is advisable to reject undesired data if we want to play safe and secure.

Example 6.2: Consider the 'Maintain School detail' form of the URS as given in Figure 6.8. The validity checks for the 'Maintain school details' form are given in Table 6.18. Generate test cases from these validity checks.

Figure 6.8. Maintain school details form

Table 6.18. Validity checks for school form

Validity check Number	Description
VC1	Only Administrator will be authorized to access the 'Maintain School Details' module. Test case of this validity check cannot be generated as access to the module is provided to the actor at the time of login.
VC2	Every school will have a unique school name.
VC3	School code cannot be blank.
VC4	School code cannot contain alphanumeric, special and blank characters.
VC5	School code will have only 3 digits.
VC6	School name cannot be blank.
VC7	School name will only accept alphabetic characters and blank spaces.
VC8	School name cannot accept special characters and numeric digits.
VC9	School name can have from 10 to 50 characters.

Solution:

Test cases based on validity checks for 'Maintain school details' form are given in Table 6.19.

Table 6.19. Test case with actual data values for the school form

Test case Id	Validity check No.	School ID	School Name	Expected result	Remarks (if any)
TC1	VC2	101	University School of Information Technology	User successfully adds the school record	--
TC2	VC3		*	Please enter school code	School code cannot be blank
TC3	VC4	1rr	*	Invalid school code	School code cannot contain alphanumeric characters
TC3	VC4	1_*	*	Invalid school code	School code cannot contain special characters
TC3	VC4	1 3	*	Invalid school code	School code cannot contain blank characters
TC4	VC5	1012	*	Invalid school code	School code can have length of 3 digits
TC5	VC6	102		Invalid school name	School name cannot be blank
TC6	VC7	102	University School of Management Studies	User successfully adds the school record	--
TC7	VC8	103	University 434	Invalid school name	School name cannot contain digits
TC8	VC8	104	University_school_of_ basic_applied_science	Invalid school name	School name cannot contain special characters
TC9	VC9	105	univer	Invalid school name	School name cannot contain less than 10 characters
TC10	VC9	106	>50	Invalid school name	School name cannot contain more than 50 characters

*: 'do not care' conditions (valid/invalid inputs)

324 Software Testing

Example 6.3: Consider the 'Maintain programme detail' form of the URS as given in Figure 6.9. This form will be accessible only to the system administrator. It will allow him/her to add/edit/delete/view information about new/existing programme(s) for the school that was selected in the 'Programme Details' form. Generate the test cases using validity checks given in Table 6.20.

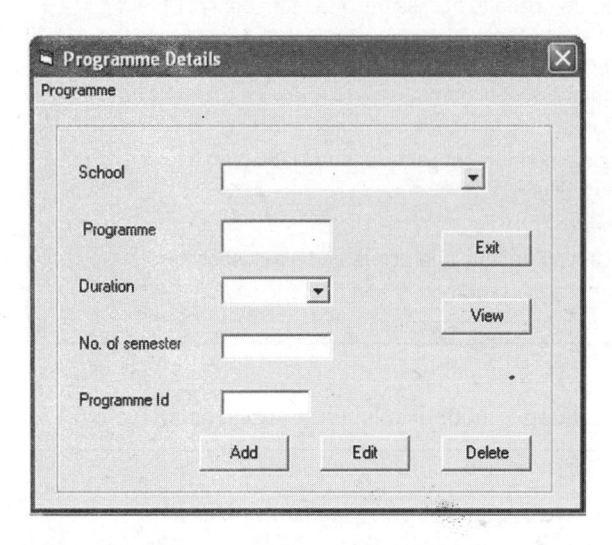

Figure 6.9. Maintain program details form

Table 6.20. Validity checks for program form	
Validity check No.	**Description**
VC1	Only Administrator will be authorized to access the 'Maintain Programme Details' module.
VC2	Every programme will have a unique programme code and name.
VC3	School name cannot be blank.
VC4	Programme name cannot be blank.
VC5	Programme name can be of length 3 to 50 characters.
VC6	Programme name can only have alphabets and brackets.
VC7	Programme name cannot have special characters, digits and blank spaces.
VC8	Duration cannot be blank.
VC9	Duration can have a value from 1 to 7.
VC10	Number of semesters cannot be blank.
VC11	Number of semesters can have a value from 2 to 14.
VC12	Programme code cannot be blank.
VC13	Programme code cannot have special characters, digits and blank spaces.
VC14	Programme code can have only 2 digits.

Solution:

The test cases based on validity checks of the 'Maintain Programme Detail' form are given in Table 6.21.

Creating Test Cases from Requirements and Use Cases 325

Table 6.21. Test case with actual data values for the program form

Test case Id	Validity check No.	School selected	Programme name	Duration	Number of semesters	Programme code	Expected output	Remarks (if any)
TC1	VC2	Yes	MCA	3	6	12	User is allowed to add a programme	–
TC2	VC3		*	*	*	*	Please select school	User should select a school
TC3	VC4	Yes	*	*	*	*	Please enter programme name	Programme name cannot be blank
TC4	VC5	Yes	MC	*	*	*	Invalid programme name	Programme cannot be less than 3 characters
TC5	VC5	Yes	>50	*	*	*	Invalid programme name	Programme cannot be greater than 50 characters
TC6	VC6	Yes	MCA(SE)	*	*	*	–	Valid programme name
TC7	VC7	Yes	MC_A(Se)	*	*	*	Invalid programme name	Programme cannot contain special characters
TC8	VC7	Yes	MC1234	*	*	*	Invalid programme name	Programme cannot contain digits
TC9	VC8	Yes	MCA	*	*	*	Please enter duration	Duration cannot be blank
TC10	VC9	Yes	MCA	8	*	*	Invalid duration	Duration can have value between 1 to 7
TC11	VC10	Yes	MCA	3	*	*	Please enter number of semesters	Number of semesters cannot be blank
TC12	VC11	Yes	MCA	3	15	*	Invalid number of semesters	Number of semesters can have value between 2 to 14
TC13	VC12	Yes	MCA	3	6	*	Please enter programme code	
TC14	VC13	Yes	MCA	3	6	12a	Invalid programme code	Programme code cannot contain alphanumeric characters
TC15	VC13	Yes	MCA	3	6	1_0	Invalid programme code	Programme code cannot contain special characters
TC16	VC13	Yes	MCA	3	6	1 2	Invalid programme code	Programme code cannot contain blank spaces
TC17	VC14	Yes	MCA	3	6	123	Invalid programme code	Programme code can only contain 2 digits

*: 'do not care' conditions (valid/invalid inputs)
The validity checks for other forms of the URS case study are given in Appendix III.

6.5 DATABASE TESTING

In many software applications, we create and maintain databases. Items are added, viewed, edited and deleted regularly as per requirements of the users. These operations are generally performed using the interface forms where special provisions are provided for such operations. These interface forms provide graphical interface to the users so that the user can add/edit/delete/view information to and from the database easily, efficiently and in a user-friendly manner. When a user wants to add an item, he/she is expected to be connected to the database. Similar types of actions are required for other operations like 'delete an item', 'edit an item' or 'view an item'. As a tester, we may like to verify the following:

(i) Is an item added in the database after the execution of 'Add' operation?
(ii) Is an operation deleted from the database after the execution of 'Delete' operation?
(iii) Is an item edited as desired in the database after the execution of 'Edit' operation?
(iv) Is an item viewed as expected after correctly retrieving from the database after the execution of 'View' operation?

We consider the 'School details' form of the URS for the purpose of verifying various available operations. This form allows the user to add/delete/edit/view information about new/existing school(s). The 'School detail' form is given in Figure 6.7 with the following fields:

(i) School Name: Alphanumeric of length of 10 to 50 characters. Digits and special characters are not allowed. Blank spaces between characters are allowed.
(ii) School Code: Numeric and will have a value from 101 to 199.

There are five buttons i.e. Add, Edit, Delete, View and Exit, for various operations. All operations except 'Exit' require the involvement of the database to get the desired output.

The test cases for all the four operations of the 'School details' form are given in Table 6.22 and testers are expected to verify every step very carefully.

Table 6.22. Operations of 'school details' form

'ADD' OPERATION

Test Case ID	Input	Expected Output	Actual Output	Status (Pass/Fail)	Comments
1.	Pre-requisites: The administrator should be logged into the system. Objective: To add the details of a new school to the system and confirm the operation from the database.				
	Open the 'School Details' form from the admin menu	The school details main window opens			
	Select 'Add' from the drop down menu	The current form changes into 'Add' mode			
	Enter a school name, press the 'Tab' button	Name of the school is displayed in the field and focus comes on the school code field			
	Enter the school code, press the 'Add' button	The school is added in the database			
	Click 'View' from the drop down menu option	The drop down menu appears with all existing school codes in the database			
	Select the code just added, Click the 'View' button	All details entered for the new school are displayed in the window			

(Contd.)

(Contd.)

'EDIT' OPERATION					
Test Case ID	Input	Expected Output	Actual Output	Status (Pass/Fail)	Comments
2.	**Pre-requisites: The administrator should be logged into the system and some school details should have been entered.**				
	Objective: To edit the details of a school and confirm the operation from the database.				
	Open the 'School Details' form from the admin menu	The school details main window opens			
	Select 'Edit' from the drop down menu	The current form comes into edit mode. List of all school codes appears in the drop down list			
	Select a school code from the drop down list in the corresponding field	Details for the school are displayed in the window			
	Change the school name, click the 'Edit' button	Confirmation message window appears			
	Click the 'Yes' button in the confirmation message window	Confirmation window closes and database status updated, focus returns to the school details window			
	Click the 'No' button in the confirmation message window	Edit operation is cancelled and database status does not change			
	Click 'View' from the menu	A drop down list appears			
	Choose the same school code that was edited	Check that all the details are changed			
3.	**Pre-requisites: The administrator should be logged into the system and some school details should have been entered.**				
	Objective: Cancel the 'edit' operation and confirm that the record is not deleted.				
	Open the 'School Details' form from the admin menu	The school details main window opens			

(Contd.)

(Contd.)

Test Case ID	Input	Expected Output	Actual Output	Status (Pass/Fail)	Comments
	Select 'Edit' from the drop down menu	The current form comes into edit mode. List of all school codes appears in the drop down list			
	Select a school code from the drop down list in the corresponding field	Details for the school are displayed in the window			
	Change the school name, click the 'Edit' button	Confirmation message window appears			
	Click the 'No' button in the confirmation message window	Edit operation is cancelled and database status does not change			
	Click 'View' from the menu	A drop down list appears			
	Choose the same school code that was edited	The information of the selected school code should not have been updated			

'DELETE' OPERATION

Test Case ID	Input	Expected Output	Actual Output	Status (Pass/Fail)	Comments
4.	**Pre-requisites: The administrator should be logged into the system and some school details should have been entered.** **Objective: To delete the details of a school from the system and confirm the operation from the database.**				
	Open the 'School Details' form from the admin menu	The 'School Details' main window opens			
	Select 'Delete' from the drop down menu	The current form comes into delete mode. List of all school codes appears in the drop down list			
	Select 'Delete' from the drop down menu				
	Select a 'School Code' from the drop down list in the corresponding field	All the details of the school are displayed			

(Contd.)

(Contd.)

Test Case ID	Input	Expected Output	Actual Output	Status (Pass/Fail)	Comments
	Click the 'Delete' button	Confirmation message window appears			
	Click the 'Yes' button	If no programme of the school exists then deletion is performed and a message window appears 'Record has been deleted successfully'			
	Click the 'Ok' button				
	Click 'View' from the menu	The current form changes into view mode			
	Click on the 'School Code' field	List of the existing school codes appears. It should not contain the code of the deleted school.			
5.	**Objective: To delete the details of a school when the scheme of the school already exists.**				
	Open the 'School Details' form from admin menu	The 'School Details' main window opens			
	Select 'Delete' from the drop down menu	The current form comes into delete mode. List of all school codes appear in the drop down list			
	Select a 'School Code' from the drop down list in the corresponding field	All the details of the school are displayed			
	Click the 'Delete' button	Confirmation message window appears			
	Click the 'Yes' button	If the programme of the school exists then deletion is not performed and a message window appears 'Deletion not allowed'			

(Contd.)

(Contd.)

Test Case ID	Input	Expected Output	Actual Output	Status (Pass/Fail)	Comments
	Click the 'Ok' button				
	Click 'View' from the menu	The current form changes into view mode			
	Click on the 'School Code' field	List of the existing 'School codes appear. It should contain the code of school which could not be deleted.			
6	**Objective: Cancel the 'Delete' operation and confirm that the record is not deleted.**				
	Open the 'School Details' screen	The 'School Details' main window opens			
	Select 'Delete' from menu	List of all school codes appear in the drop down list			
	Select a 'School Code' from the drop down list	All the details of the school are displayed			
	Click the 'Delete' button	Confirmation message window appears			
	Click the 'No' button	Deletion operation is cancelled and main window appears			
	Click 'View' from the drop down menu	The current form comes into view mode			
	Click on the 'School Code' field	List of the existing school codes appear. It should contain the code of the school which was not deleted.			

'VIEW' OPERATION

Test Case ID	Input	Expected Output	Actual Output	Status (Pass/Fail)	Comments
7	**Pre-requisites: The administrator should be logged into the system and some programme details should have been entered.**				

(Contd.)

(Contd.)

Test Case ID	Input	Expected Output	Actual Output	Status (Pass/Fail)	Comments
	Objective: To View the details of a school.				
	Open the school details form	The 'School Details' main window opens			
	Click 'View' from the menu	The current form changes into view mode			
	Select school code click 'View' button	All the details of the school are displayed			

Database testing is very popular in applications where huge databases are maintained and items are regularly searched, added, deleted, updated and viewed. Many queries are generated by various users simultaneously and the database should be able to handle them in a reasonable time frame, for example, web testing, inventory management and other large database applications. Testing of stress level for a database is a real challenge for the testers. Some commercially available tools make tall claims about stress testing; however their applicability is not universally acceptable.

MULTIPLE CHOICE QUESTIONS

Note: *Select the most appropriate answer for the following questions.*

6.1 Which is not a component of a use case diagram?
   (a) Actor
   (b) Use case
   (c) Relationship between actor and use case
   (d) Test case

6.2 Which is not included in a use case template?
   (a) Actors
   (b) Pre-conditions and post-conditions
   (c) Test cases
   (d) Flow of events

6.3 UML stands for any one of the following:
   (a) Unified Modeling Language
   (b) Unified Machine Language
   (c) United Modeling Language
   (d) United Machine Language

6.4 Which of the following is not correct
   (a) An actor initiates a use case.
   (b) Every use case has a specified functionality.
   (c) One or more actors may interact with a use case.
   (d) Two use cases may have the same name.

6.5 Use case scenario is:
   (a) An input of a use case
   (b) An instance of a use case
   (c) An output of a use case
   (d) An information of a use case
6.6 Which is not an accepted strategy for data validity?
   (a) Accept only known valid data
   (b) Reject known bad data
   (c) Sanitize all data
   (d) Reject non-effective data
6.7 Guidelines for generating validity checks should include the following:
   (a) Mandatory data inputs
   (b) Blank data inputs
   (c) Data range
   (d) All of the above
6.8 The most popular area of database testing is:
   (a) Websites
   (b) Networks
   (c) Scientific applications
   (d) Operating systems
6.9 Which is not an actor in use cases?
   (a) External data base
   (b) Administrator
   (c) Keyboard
   (d) Data entry operator
6.10 Every use case may have:
   (a) At least one actor
   (b) At most one actor
   (c) No actor
   (d) None of the above
6.11 A use case scenario may generate:
   (a) At most one test case
   (b) At least one test case
   (c) No test case
   (d) None of the above
6.12 Use cases and use case diagrams are used to define:
   (a) Complexity of a system
   (b) Criticality of a system
   (c) Stability of a system
   (d) Behaviour of a system
6.13 Special requirements in a use case template define:
   (a) Business rules
   (b) Reliability requirements
   (c) Expectations of the users
   (d) Associated use cases

6.14 Any variable in a use case has:
   (a) At least one valid value and one invalid value
   (b) At most one valid value
   (c) At most one invalid value
   (d) At most one valid value and one invalid value
6.15 A selection variable in a form:
   (a) Has one option
   (b) Has many options
   (c) Has no option
   (d) None of the above

EXERCISES

6.1 What is a use case? How is it different from a use case diagram? What are the components of a use case diagram?
6.2 How do we write use cases? Describe the basic and alternative flows in a use case. Discuss any popular template for writing a use case.
6.3 Explain the various steps for the generation of test cases from the use cases. Why do we identify variables in a use case?
6.4 Design a problem statement for library management system and generate the following:
   (i) Use cases
   (ii) Use case diagram
   (iii) Basic and alternative flows in use cases
   (iv) Test cases from use cases.
6.5 Consider the problem of railway reservation system and design the following:
   (i) Use cases
   (ii) Use case diagram
   (iii) Test cases from use cases
   What is the role of an actor in use case diagram? Discuss with the help of a suitable example.
6.6 Discuss the guidelines for the creation of use cases for designing of any system. Is there any limit for the number of use cases in any system?
6.7 Consider the problem statement of a university registration system as given in Chapter 5. Write the 'maintain scheme detail' use case description and also generate test cases accordingly.
6.8 What are various strategies for data validity? Discuss with the help of an example.
6.9 Consider the scheme detail form given in chapter 5 of a university registration system. Write the validity checks and generate test cases from the validity checks.
6.10 What are the guidelines for generating the validity checks? Explain with the help of an example.
6.11 Why should we do database testing? Write some advantages and applications of data base testing.

6.12 Write the problem statement for library management system. Design test cases for various operations using database testing.
6.13 Design the test cases for all operations of 'maintain scheme detail' form of university registration system using database testing.
6.14 Why do we consider domain specific checks very important for generating validity checks? How are they related with the functionality of the system?
6.15 Why should data validation be given focus in testing? Why do we expect valid data? How do we prevent the entry of invalid data in a system?

FURTHER READING

Jacobson provides a classic introduction to use case approach:
> I.V. Jacobson, "Object Oriented Software Engineering: A Use Case Driven Approach", Pearson Education, 1999.

Cockburn provides guidance for writing and managing use cases. This may help to reduce common problems associated with use cases:
> A. Cockburn, "Writing Effective Use Cases", Pearson Education, 2001.

Hurlbut's paper provides a survey on approaches for formalizing and writing use cases:
> R. Hurlbut, "A Survey of Approaches for Describing and Formalizing Use-Cases," Technical Report 97–03, Department of Computer Science, Illinois Institute of Technology, USA, 1997.

Fournier has discussed the relationship between actor and system in:
> G. Fournier, "Essential Software Testing-A Use Case Approach", CRC Press, 2009.

Other useful texts are available at:
> G. Booch, J. Rumbaugh and I.V. Jacobson, "The Unified Modeling Language User Guide", Addison-Wesley, Boston, 1999.
> Rational Requisite Pro, "User's Guide", Rational Software Corporation, 2003.
> "Rational Rose User's Guide", IBM Corporation, 2003.
> N.R. Tague, "The Quality Toolbox," ASQ Quality Press, 2004.

The most current information about UML can be found at:
> http://www.rational.com
> http://www.omg.org

7

Selection, Minimization and Prioritization of Test Cases for Regression Testing

Software maintenance is becoming important and expensive day by day. Development of software may take a few years (2 to 4 years), but the same may have to be maintained for several years (10 to 15 years). Software maintenance accounts for as much as two-thirds of the cost of software production [BEIZ90].

Software inevitably changes, whatever well-written and designed initially it may be. There are many reasons for such changes:

(i) Some errors may have been discovered during the actual use of the software.
(ii) The user may have requested for additional functionality.
(iii) Software may have to be modified due to change in some external policies and principles. When European countries had decided to go for a single European currency, this change affected all banking system software.
(iv) Some restructuring work may have to be done to improve the efficiency and performance of the software.
(v) Software may have to be modified due to change in existing technologies.
(vi) Some obsolete capabilities may have to be deleted.

This list is endless but the message is loud and clear i.e. 'change is inevitable'. Hence, software always changes in order to address the above mentioned issues. This changed software is required to be re-tested in order to ensure that changes work correctly and these changes have not adversely affected other parts of the software. This is necessary because small changes in one part of the software program may have subtle undesired effects in other seemingly unrelated parts of the software.

7.1 WHAT IS REGRESSION TESTING?

When we develop software, we use development testing to obtain confidence in the correctness of the software. Development testing involves constructing a test plan that describes how we should test the software and then, designing and running a suite of test cases that satisfy the requirements of the test plan. When we modify software, we typically re-test it. This process of re-testing is called regression testing.

Hence, regression testing is the process of re-testing the modified parts of the software and ensuring that no new errors have been introduced into previously tested source code due to these modifications. Therefore, regression testing tests both the modified source code and other parts of the source code that may be affected by the change. It serves several purposes like:

- Increases confidence in the correctness of the modified program.
- Locates errors in the modified program.
- Preserves the quality and reliability of the software.
- Ensures the software's continued operation.

We typically think of regression testing as a software maintenance activity; however, we also perform regression testing during the latter stage of software development. This latter stage starts after we have developed test plans and test suites and used them initially to test the software. During this stage of development, we fine-tune the source code and correct errors in it, hence these activities resemble maintenance activities. The comparison of development testing and regression testing is given in Table 7.1.

Table 7.1. Comparison of regression and development testing

S.No.	Development Testing	Regression Testing
1.	We write test cases.	We may use already available test cases.
2.	We want to test all portions of the source code.	We want to test only modified portion of the source code and the portion affected by the modifications.
3.	We do development testing just once in the lifetime of the software.	We may have to do regression testing many times in the lifetime of the software.
4.	We do development testing to obtain confidence about the correctness of the software.	We do regression testing to obtain confidence about the correctness of the modified portion of the software.
5.	Performed under the pressure of release date.	Performed in crisis situations, under greater time constraints.
6.	Separate allocation of budget and time.	Practically no time and generally no separate budget allocation.
7.	Focus is on the whole software with the objective of finding faults.	Focus is only on the modified portion and other affected portions with the objective of ensuring the correctness of the modifications.
8.	Time and effort consuming activity (40% to 70%).	Not much time and effort is consumed as compared to development testing.

7.1.1 Regression Testing Process

Regression testing is a very costly process and consumes a significant amount of resources. The question is "how to reduce this cost?" Whenever a failure is experienced, it is reported to the software team. The team may like to debug the source code to know the reason(s) for this failure. After identification of the reason(s), the source code is modified and we generally do not expect the same failure again. In order to ensure this correctness, we re-test the source code with a focus on modified portion(s) of the source code and also on affected portion(s) of the source code due to modifications. We need test cases that target the modified and affected portions of the source code. We may write new test cases, which may be a 'time and effort consuming' activity. We neither have enough time nor reasonable resources to write new test cases for every failure. Another option is to use the existing test cases which were designed for development testing and some of them might have been used during development testing. The existing test suite may be useful and may reduce the cost of regression testing. As we all know, the size of the existing test suite may be very large and it may not be possible to execute all tests. The greatest challenge is to reduce the size of the existing test suite for a particular failure. The various steps are shown in Figure 7.1. Hence, test case selection for a failure is the main key for regression testing.

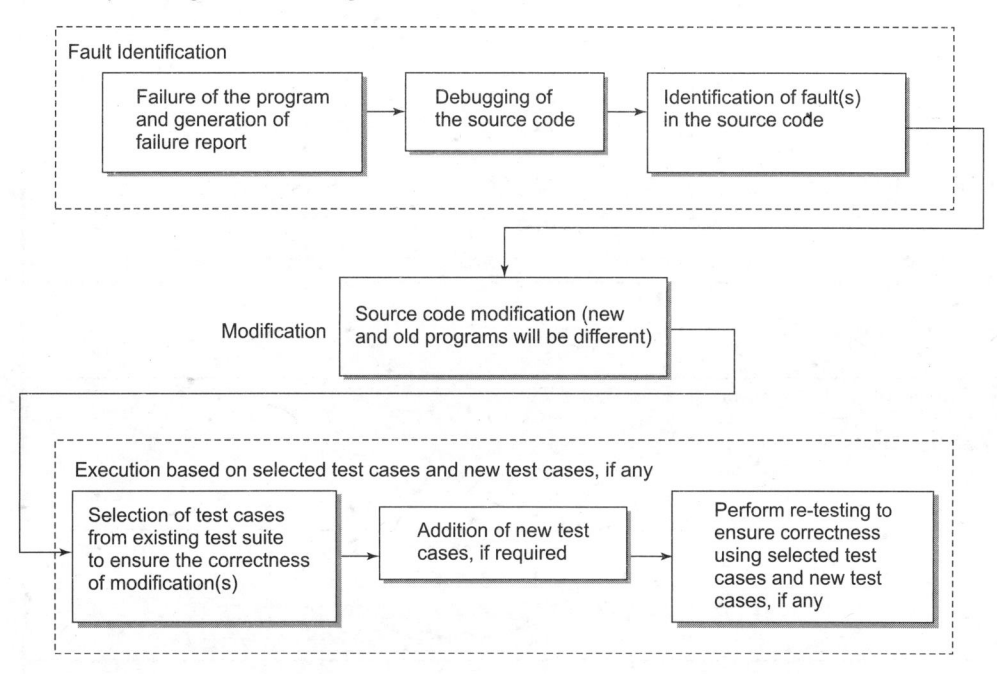

Figure 7.1. Steps of regression testing process

7.1.2 Selection of Test Cases

We want to use the existing test suite for regression testing. How should we select an appropriate number of test cases for a failure? The range is from "one test case" to "all test cases". A 'regression test cases' selection technique may help us to do this selection process. The effectiveness of the selection technique may decide the selection of the most appropriate test cases from the test suite. Many techniques have been developed for procedural and object oriented programming languages. Testing professionals are, however, reluctant to omit any test case from a test suite that might expose a fault in the modified program. We consider a program given in Figure 7.2 along with its modified version where the modification is in line 6 (replacing operator '*' by '-'). A test suite is also given in Table 7.2.

```
1.  main( )                              1.  main ( )
2.  {                                    2.  {
3.  int a, b, x, y, z;                   3.  int a, b, x, y, z;
4.  scanf ("%d, %d", &a, &b);            4.  scanf ("%d, %d", &a, &b);
5.  x = a + b ;                          5.  x = a + b;
6.  y = a* b;                            6.  y = a - b;
7.  if (x ≥ y) {                         7.  if (x ≥ y) {
8.  z = x / y ;                          8.  z = x / y ;
9.  }                                    9.  }
10. else {                               10. else {
11. z = x * y ;                          11. z = x * y ;
12. }                                    12. }
13. printf ("z = %d \ n", z );           13. printf ("z = %d \ n", z);
14. }                                    14. }
(a) Original program with fault in line 6.   (b) Modified program with modification in line 6.
```

Figure 7.2. Program for printing value of z

Table 7.2. Test suite for program given in Figure 7.2

Set of Test Cases

S. No.	Inputs a	b	Execution History
1	2	1	1, 2, 3, 4, 5, 6, 7, 8, 9, 13, 14
2	1	1	1, 2, 3, 4, 5, 6, 7, 8, 9, 13, 14
3	3	2	1, 2, 3, 4, 5, 6, 7, 10, 11, 12, 13, 14
4	3	3	1, 2, 3, 4, 5, 6, 7, 10, 11, 12, 13, 14

In this case, the modified line is line number 6 where 'a*b' is replaced by 'a-b'. All four test cases of the test suite execute this modified line 6. We may decide to execute all four tests for the modified program. If we do so, test case 2 with inputs a = 1 and b = 1 will experience a 'divide by zero' problem, whereas others will not. However, we may like to reduce the number of test cases for the modified program. We may select all test cases which are executing the modified line. Here, line number 6 is modified. All four test cases are executing the modified line (line number 6) and hence are selected. There is no reduction in terms of the number of test cases. If we see the execution history, we find that test case 1 and test case 2 have the same execution history. Similarly, test case 3 and test case 4 have the same execution history. We choose any one test case of the same execution history to avoid repetition. For execution history 1 (i.e. 1, 2, 3, 4, 5, 6, 7, 8, 10, 11), if we select test case 1, the program will execute well, but if we select test case 2, the program will experience 'divide by zero' problem. If several test cases execute a particular modified line, and all of these test cases reach a particular affected source code segment, minimization methods require selection of only one such test case, unless they select the others for coverage elsewhere. Therefore, either test case 1 or test case 2 may have to be selected. If we select test case 1, we miss the opportunity to detect the fault that test case 2 detects. Minimization techniques may omit some test cases that might expose fault(s) in the modified program. Hence, we should be very careful in the process of minimization of test cases and always try to use safe regression test selection technique (if at all it is possible). A safe regression test selection technique should select all test cases that can expose faults in the modified program.

7.2 REGRESSION TEST CASES SELECTION

Test suite design is an expensive process and its size can grow quite large. Most of the times, running an entire test suite is not possible as it requires a significant amount of time to run all test cases. Many techniques are available for the selection of test cases for the purpose of regression testing.

7.2.1 Select All Test Cases

This is the simplest technique where we do not want to take any risk. We want to run all test cases for any change in the program. This is the safest technique, without any risk. A program may fail many times and every time we will execute the entire test suite. This technique is practical only when the size of the test suite is small. For any reasonable or large sized test suite, it becomes impractical to execute all test cases.

7.2.2 Select Test Cases Randomly

We may select test cases randomly to reduce the size of the test suite. We decide how many test cases are required to be selected depending upon time and available resources. When we decide the number, the same number of test cases is selected randomly. If the number is large, we may get a good number of test cases for execution and testing may be of some use. But, if the number is small, testing may not be useful at all. In this technique, our assumption is that all test cases are equally good in their fault detection ability. However, in most of the situations, this assumption may not be true. We want to re-test the source code for the purpose of checking the correctness of the modified portion of the program. Many randomly selected test cases may not have any relationship with the modified portion of the program. However, random selection may be better than no regression testing at all.

7.2.3 Select Modification Traversing Test Cases

We select only those test cases that execute the modified portion of the program and the portion which is affected by the modification(s). Other test cases of the test suite are discarded.

Actually, we want to select all those test cases that reveal faults in the modified program. These test cases are known as fault revealing test cases. There is no effective technique by which we can find fault revealing test cases for the modified program. This is the best selection approach, which we want, but we do not have techniques for the same. Another lower objective may be to select those test cases that reveal the difference in the output of the original program and the modified program. These test cases are known as modification revealing test cases. These test cases target that portion of the source code which makes the output of the original program and the modified program differ. Unfortunately, we do not have any effective technique to do this. Therefore, it is difficult to find fault revealing test cases and modification revealing test cases.

The reasonable objective is to select all those test cases that traverse the modified source code and the source code affected by modification(s). These test cases are known as modification traversing test cases. It is easy to develop techniques for modification traversing test cases and some are available too. Out of all modification traversing test cases, some may be modification revealing test cases and out of some modification revealing test cases, some may be fault revealing test cases. Many modification traversing techniques are available but their applications are limited due to the varied nature of software projects. Aditya Mathur has rightly mentioned that [MATH08]:

> *"The sophistication of techniques to select modification traversing tests requires automation. It is impractical to apply these techniques to large commercial systems unless a tool is available that incorporates at least one safe test minimization technique. Further, while test selection appears attractive from the test effort point of view, it might not be a practical technique when tests are dependent on each other in complex ways and that this dependency cannot be incorporated in the test selection tool".*

We may effectively implement any test case selection technique with the help of a testing tool. The modified source code and source code affected by modification(s) may have to be identified systematically and this selected area of the source code becomes the concern of test case selection. As the size of the source code increases, the complexity also increases, and need for an efficient technique also increases accordingly.

7.3 REDUCING THE NUMBER OF TEST CASES

Test case reduction is an essential activity and we may select those test cases that execute the modification(s) and the portion of the program that is affected by the modification(s). We may minimize the test suite or prioritize the test suite in order to execute the selected number of test cases.

7.3.1 Minimization of Test Cases

We select all those test cases that traverse the modified portion of the program and the portion that is affected by the modification(s). If we find the selected number very large, we may still reduce this using any test case minimization technique. These test case minimization techniques attempt to find redundant test cases. A redundant test case is one which achieves an objective which has already been achieved by another test case. The objective may be source code coverage, requirement coverage, variables coverage, branch coverage, specific lines of source code coverage, etc. A minimization technique may further reduce the size of the selected test cases based on some criteria. We should always remember that any type of minimization is risky and may omit some fault revealing test cases.

7.3.2 Prioritization of Test Cases

We may indicate the order with which a test case may be addressed. This process is known as prioritization of test cases. A test case with the highest rank has the highest priority and the test case with the second highest rank has the second highest priority and as so on. Prioritization does not discard any test case. The efficiency of the regression testing is dependent upon the criteria of prioritization. There are two varieties of test case prioritization i.e. general test case prioritization and version specific test case prioritization. In general test case prioritization, for a given program with its test suite, we prioritize the test cases that will be useful over a succession of subsequent modified versions of the original program without any knowledge of modification(s). In the version specific test case prioritization, we prioritize the test cases, when the original program is changed to the modified program, with the knowledge of the changes that have been made in the original program.

Prioritization guidelines should address two fundamental issues like:

(i) What functions of the software must be tested?
(ii) What are the consequences if some functions are not tested?

Every reduction activity has an associated risk. All prioritization guidelines should be designed on the basis of risk analysis. All risky functions should be tested on higher priority. The risk analysis may be based on complexity, criticality, impact of failure, etc. The most important is the 'impact of failure' which may range from 'no impact' to 'loss of human life' and must be studied very carefully.

The simplest priority category scheme is to assign a priority code to every test case. The priority code may be based on the assumption that "test case of priority code 1 is more important than test case of priority code 2." We may have priority codes as follows:

Priority code 1 : Essential test case
Priority code 2 : Important test case
Priority code 3 : Execute, if time permits
Priority code 4 : Not important test case
Priority code 5 : Redundant test case

There may be other ways for assigning priorities based on customer requirements or market conditions like:

Priority code 1 : Important for the customer
Priority code 2 : Required to increase customer satisfaction
Priority code 3 : Help to increase market share of the product

We may design any priority category scheme, but a scheme based on technical considerations always improves the quality of the product and should always be encouraged.

7.4 RISK ANALYSIS

Unexpected behaviours of a software programme always carry huge information and most of the time they disturb every associate person. No one likes such unexpected behaviour and everyone prays that they never face these situations in their professional career. In practice, the situation is entirely different and developers do face such unexpected situations frequently and, moreover, work hard to find the solutions of the problems highlighted by these unexpected behaviours.

We may be able to minimize these situations, if we are able to minimize the risky areas of the software. Hence, risk analysis has become an important area and in most of the projects we are doing it to minimize the risk.

7.4.1 What is Risk?

Tomorrow's problems are today's risks. Therefore, a simple definition of risk is a problem that may cause some loss or threaten the success of the project, but, which has not happened yet. Risk is defined as the "probability of occurrence of an undesirable event and the impact of occurrence of that event." To understand whether an event is really risky needs an understanding of the potential consequences of the occurrences / non-occurrences of that event. Risks may delay and over-budget a project. Risky projects may also not meet specified quality levels. Hence, there are two things associated with risk as given below:

(i) Probability of occurrence of a problem (i.e. an event)
(ii) Impact of that problem

Risk analysis is a process of identifying the potential problems and then assigning a 'probability of occurrence of the problem' value and 'impact of that problem' value for each identified problem. Both of these values are assigned on a scale of 1 (low) to 10 (high). A factor 'risk exposure' is calculated for every problem which is the product of 'probability of occurrence of the problem' value and 'impact of that problem' value. The risks may be ranked on the basis of its risk exposure. A risk analysis table may be prepared as given in Table 7.3. These values may be calculated on the basis of historical data, past experience, intuition and criticality of the problem. We should not confuse with the mathematical scale of probability values which is from 0 to 1. Here, the scale of 1 to 10 is used for assigning values to both the components of the risk exposure.

Table 7.3. Risk analysis table

S. No.	Potential Problem	Probability of occurrence of problem	Impact of that Problem	Risk Exposure
1.				
2.				
3.				
4.				

The case study of 'University Registration System' given in chapter 5 is considered and its potential problems are identified. Risk exposure factor for every problem is calculated on the basis of 'probability of occurrence of the problem' and 'impact of that problem'. The risk analysis is given in Table 7.4.

Table 7.4. Risk analysis table of 'University Registration System'

S. No.	Potential Problems	Probability of occurrence of problem	Impact of that Problem	Risk Exposure
1.	Issued password not available	2	3	6
2.	Wrong entry in students detail form	6	2	12
3.	Wrong entry in scheme detail form	3	3	9
4.	Printing mistake in registration card	2	2	4
5.	Unauthorised access	1	10	10
6.	Database corrupted	2	9	18
7.	Ambiguous documentation	8	1	8
8.	Lists not in proper format	3	2	6
9.	Issued login-id is not in specified format	2	1	2
10.	School not available in the database	2	4	8

The potential problems ranked by risk exposure are 6, 2, 5, 3, 7, 10, 1, 8, 4 and 9.

7.4.2 Risk Matrix

Risk matrix is used to capture identified problems, estimate their probability of occurrence with impact and rank the risks based on this information. We may use the risk matrix to assign thresholds that group the potential problems into priority categories. The risk matrix is shown in Figure 7.3 with four quadrants. Each quadrant represents a priority category.

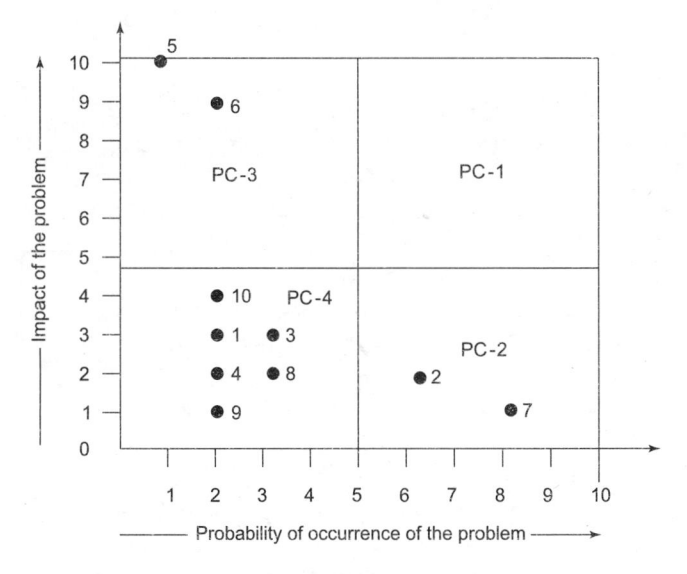

Figure 7.3. Threshold by quadrant

The priority category in defined as:

Priority category 1 (PC-1) = High probability value and high impact value
Priority category 2 (PC-2) = High probability value and low impact value
Priority category 3 (PC-3) = Low probability value and high impact value
Priority category 4 (PC-4) = Low probability value and low impact value

In this case, a risk with high probability value is given more importance than a problem with high impact value. We may change this and may decide to give more importance to high impact value over the high probability value and is shown in Figure 7.4. Hence, PC-2 and PC-3 will swap, but PC-1 and PC-4 will remain the same.

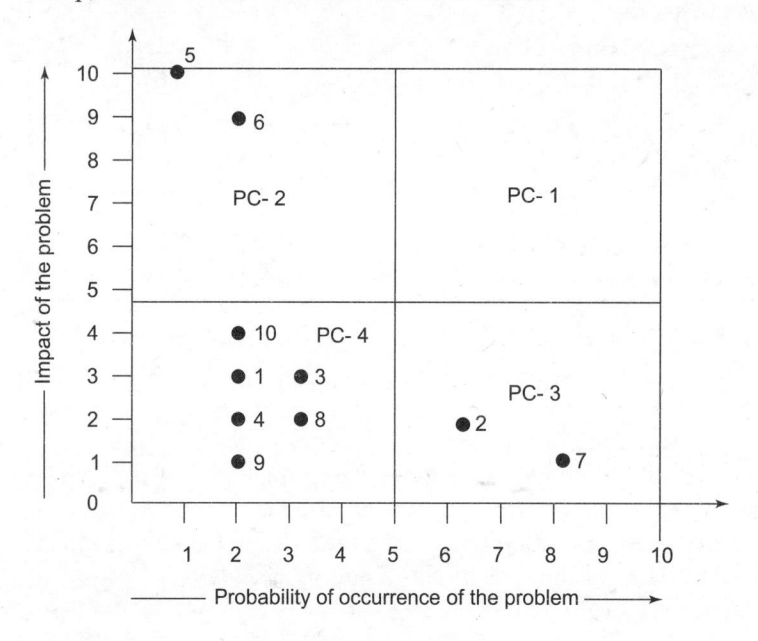

Figure 7.4. Alternative threshold by quadrant

There may be situations where we do not want to give importance to any value and assign equal importance. In this case, the diagonal band prioritization scheme may be more suitable as shown in Figure 7.5. This scheme is more appropriate in situations where we have difficulty in assigning importance to either 'probability of occurrence of the problem' value or 'impact of that problem' value.

We may also feel that high impact value must be given highest priority irrespective of the 'probability of occurrence' value. A high impact problem should be addressed first, irrespective of its probability of occurrence value. This prioritization scheme is given in Figure 7.6. Here, the highest priority (PC-1) is assigned to high impact value and for the other four quadrants; any prioritization scheme may be selected. We may also assign high priority to high 'probability of occurrence' values irrespective of the impact value as shown in Figure 7.7. This scheme may not be popular in practice. Generally, we are afraid of the impact of the problem. If the impact value is low, we are not much concerned. In the risk analysis table (see Table 7.4), ambiguous documentations (S. No. 7) have high 'probability of occurrence of problem' value (8), but impact value is very low (1). Hence, these faults are not considered risky faults as compared to 'unauthorized access' (S. No. 5) where 'probability of occurrence' value is very low (1) and impact value is very high (10).

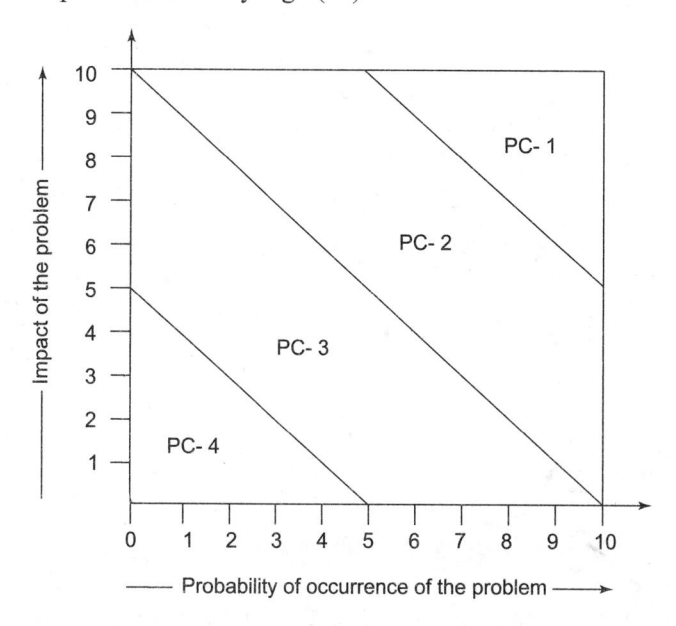

Figure 7.5. Threshold by diagonal quadrant

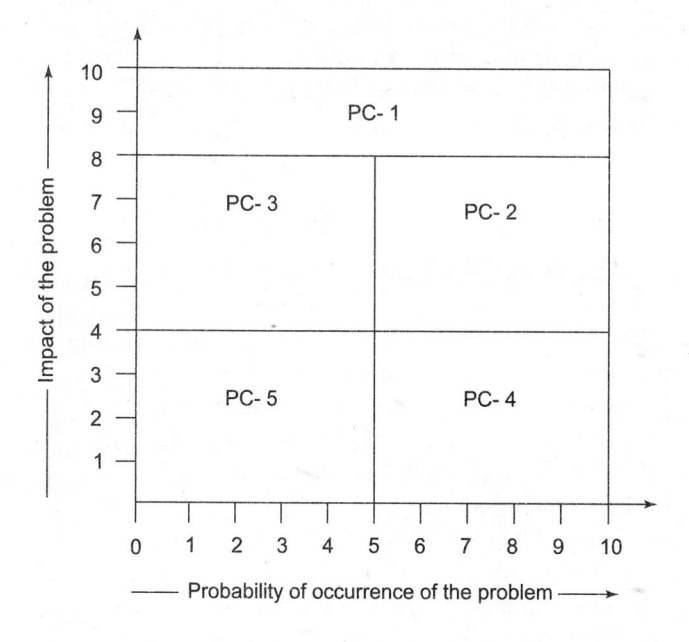

Figure 7.6. Threshold based on high 'Impact of Problem' value

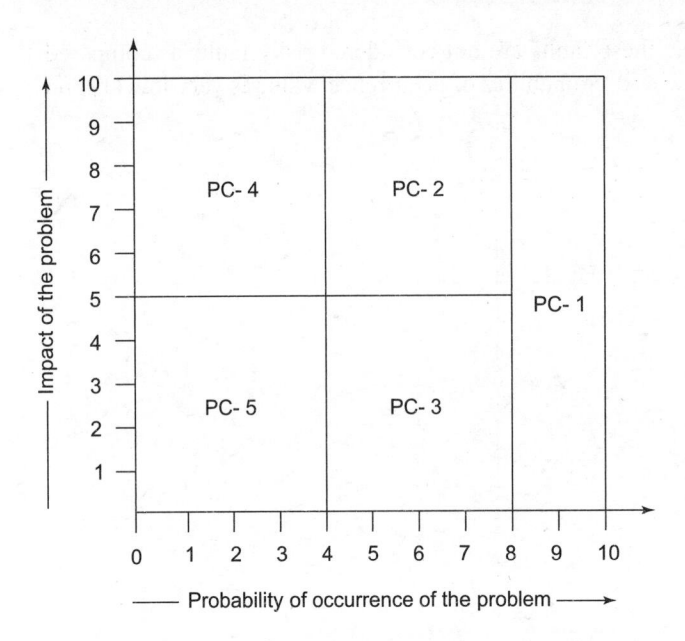

Figure 7.7. Threshold based on high 'probability of occurrence of problem' value

After the risks are ranked, the high priority risks are identified. These risks are required to be managed first and then other priority risks in descending order. These risks should be discussed in a team and proper action should be recommended to manage these risks. A risk matrix has become a powerful tool for designing prioritization schemes. Estimating the probability of occurrence of a problem may be difficult in practice. Fortunately, all that matters when using a risk matrix is the relative order of the probability estimates (which risks are more likely to occur) on the scale of 1 to 10. The impact of the problem may be critical, serious, moderate, minor or negligible. These two values are essential for risk exposure which is used to prioritize the risks.

7.5 CODE COVERAGE PRIORITIZATION TECHNIQUE

We consider a program P with its modified program P' and its test suite T created to test P. When we modify P to P', we would like to execute modified portion(s) of the source code and the portion(s) affected by the modification(s) to see the correctness of modification(s). We neither have time nor resources to execute all test cases of T. Our objective is to reduce the size of T to T' using some selection criteria, which may help us to execute the modified portion of the source code and the portion(s) affected by modification(s).

A code coverage based technique [KAUR06, AGGA04] has been developed which is based on version specific test case prioritization and selects T' from T which is a subset of T. The technique also prioritizes test cases of T' and recommends use of high priority test cases first and then low priority test cases in descending order till time and resources are available or a reasonable level of confidence is achieved.

7.5.1 Test Cases Selection Criteria

The technique is based on version specific test case prioritization where information about changes in the program is known. Hence, prioritization is focused around the changes in the modified program. We may like to execute all modified lines of source code with a minimum number of selected test cases. This technique identifies those test cases that:

(i) Execute the modified lines of source code at least once
(ii) Execute the lines of source code after deletion of deleted lines from the execution history of the test case and are not redundant.

The technique uses two algorithms – one for 'modification' and the other for 'deletion'. The following information is available with us and has been used to design the technique:

(i) Program P with its modified program P'.
(ii) Test suite T with test cases t1, t2, t3,.....tn.
(iii) Execution history (number of lines of source code covered by a test case) of each test case of test suite T.
(iv) Line numbers of lines of source code covered by each test case are stored in a two dimensional array (t_{11}, t_{12}, t_{13},......t_{ij}).

7.5.2 Modification Algorithm

The 'modification' portion of the technique is used to minimize and prioritize test cases based on the modified lines of source code. The 'modification' algorithm uses the following information given in Table 7.5.

Table 7.5. Variables used by 'modification' algorithm

S. No.	Variable name	Description
1.	T1	It is a two dimensional array and is used to store line numbers of lines of source code covered by each test case.
2.	modloc	It is used to store the total number of modified lines of source code.
3.	mod_locode	It is a one-dimensional array and is used to store line numbers of modified lines of source code.
4.	nfound	It is a one-dimensional array and is used to store the number of lines of source code matched with modified lines of each test case.
5.	pos	It is a one-dimensional array and is used to set the position of each test case when nfound is sorted.
6.	candidate	It is a one-dimensional array. It sets the bit to 1 corresponding to the position of the test case to be removed.
7.	priority	It is a one-dimensional array and is used to set the priority of the selected test case.

The following steps have been followed in order to select and prioritize test cases from test suite T based on the modification in the program P.

Step I: Initialization of variables

Consider a hypothetical program of 60 lines of code with a test suite of 10 test cases. The execution history is given in Table 7.6. We assume that lines 1, 2, 5, 15, 35, 45, 55 are modified.

Table 7.6. Test cases with execution history

Test case Id	Execution history
T1	1, 2, 20, 30, 40, 50
T2	1, 3, 4, 21, 31, 41, 51
T3	5, 6, 7, 8, 22, 32, 42, 52
T4	6, 9, 10, 23, 24, 33, 43, 54
T5	5, 9, 11, 12, 13, 14, 15, 20, 29, 37, 38, 39
T6	15, 16, 17, 18, 19, 23, 24, 25, 34, 35, 36
T7	26, 27, 28, 40, 41, 44, 45, 46
T8	46, 47, 48, 49, 50, 53, 55
T9	55, 56, 57, 58, 59
T10	3, 4, 60

The first portion of the 'modification' algorithm is used to initialize and read values of variables T1, modloc and mod_locode.

First portion of the 'modification' algorithm

1. Repeat for i=1 to number of test cases
   (a) Repeat for j=1 to number of test cases
       (i) Initialize array T1[i][j] to zero
2. Repeat for i=1 to number of test cases
   (a) Repeat for j=1 to number of test cases
       (i) Store line numbers of line of source code covered by each test case.
3. Repeat for i=1 to number of modified lines of source code
   (a) Store line numbers of modified lines of source code in array mod_locode.

Step II: Selection and prioritization of test cases

The second portion of the algorithm counts the number of modified lines of source code covered by each test case (nfound).

Second portion of the 'modification' algorithm

2. Repeat for all true cases
   (a) Repeat for i=1 to number of test cases
       (i) Initialize array nfound[i] to zeroes
       (ii) Set pos[i] =i
   (b) Repeat for i=1 to number of test cases
       (i) Initialize l to zero

Selection, Minimization and Prioritization of Test Cases for Regression Testing 349

> (ii) Repeat for j=1 to length of the test case
>   If candidate[i] ≠ 1 then
>   Repeat for k=1 to modified lines of source code
>   If t1[i][j]=mod_locode[k] then
>   Increment nfound[i] by one
>   Increment l by one

The status of test cases covering modified lines of source code is given in Table 7.7.

Table 7.7. Test cases with number of matches found

Test Cases	Numbers of lines matched	Number of Matches (nfound)
T1	1, 2	2
T2	1	1
T3	5	1
T4	-	0
T5	5, 15	2
T6	15, 35	2
T7	45	1
T8	55	1
T9	55	1
T10	-	0

    Consider the third portion of 'modification' algorithm. In this portion, we sort the nfound array and select the test case with the highest value of nfound as a candidate for selection. The test cases are arranged in increasing order of priority.

> **Third portion of the '"modification' algorithm**
>
> (c) Initialize l to zero
> (d) Repeat for i=0 to number of test cases
>   (i) Repeat for j=1 to number of test cases
>   If nfound[i]>0 then
>   t=nfound[i]
>   nfound[i]=nfound[j]
>   nfound[j]=t
>   t=pos[i]
>   pos[i]=pos[j]
>   pos[j]=t
> (e) Repeat for i=1 to number of test cases
>   (i) If nfound[i]=1 then
>   Increment count
> (f) If count = 0 then
>   (i) Goto end of the algorithm
> (g) Initialize candidate[pos[0]] = 1
> (h) Initialize priority[pos[0]]= m+1

    The test cases with less value have higher priority than the test cases with higher value. Hence, the test cases are sorted on the basis of number of modified lines covered as shown in Table 7.8.

Table 7.8. Test cases in decreasing order of number of modified lines covered

Test Cases	Numbers of lines matched	Number of Matches (nfound)	Candidate	Priority
T1	1, 2	2	1	1
T5	5, 15	2	0	0
T6	15, 35	2	0	0
T2	1	1	0	0
T3	5	1	0	0
T7	45	1	0	0
T8	55	1	0	0
T9	55	1	0	0
T4	-	0	0	0
T10	-	0	0	0

The test case with candidate=1 is selected in each iteration. In the fourth portion of the algorithm, the modified lines of source code included in the selected test case are removed from the mod_locode array. This process continues until there are no remaining modified lines of source code covered by any test case.

Fourth portion of the 'modification' algorithm

(a) Repeat for i=1 to length of selected test cases
   (i) Repeat for j=1 to modified lines of source code
      If t1[pos[0]][i] = mod[j] then
         mod[j] = 0

Since test case T1 is selected and it covers 1 and 2 lines of source code, these lines will be removed from the mod_locode array.

mod_locode = [1, 2, 5, 15, 35, 45, 55] - [1, 2] = [5, 15, 35, 45, 55]

The remaining iterations of the 'modification' algorithm are shown in tables 7.9-7.12.

Table 7.9. Test cases in descending order of number of matches found (iteration 2)

Test Cases	Number of matches (nfound)	Matches found	Candidate	Priority
T5	2	5, 15	1	2
T6	2	15, 35	0	0
T3	1	5	0	0
T7	1	45	0	0
T8	1	55	0	0
T9	1	55	0	0
T2	0	-	0	0
T4	0	-	0	0
T10	0	-	0	0

mod_locode = [5, 15, 35, 45, 55] – [5, 15] = [35, 45, 55]

Table 7.10. Test cases in descending order of number of matches found (iteration 3)

Test Cases	Number of matches (nfound)	Matches found	Candidate	Priority
T6	1	35	1	3
T7	1	45	0	0
T8	1	55	0	0
T9	1	55	0	0
T2	0	-	0	0
T3	0	-	0	0
T4	0	-	0	0
T10	0	-	0	0

mod_locode = [35, 45, 55] – [35] = [45, 55]

Table 7.11. Test cases in descending order of number of matches found (iteration 4)

Test Cases	Number of matches (nfound)	Matches found	Candidate	Priority
T7	1	45	1	4
T8	1	55	0	0
T9	1	55	0	0
T2	0	-	0	0
T3	0	-	0	0
T4	0	-	0	0
T10	0	-	0	0

mod_locode = [45, 55] – [45] = [55]

Table 7.12. Test cases in descending order of number of matches found (iteration 5)

Test Cases	Number of matches (nfound)	Matches found	Candidate	Priority
T8	1	55	1	5
T9	1	55	0	0
T2	0	-	0	0
T3	0	-	0	0
T4	0	-	0	0
T10	0	-	0	0

mod_locode = [55] – [55] = [Nil]

Hence test cases T1, T5, T6, T7 and T8 need to be executed on the basis of their corresponding priority. Out of ten test cases, we need to run only 5 test cases for 100% code coverage of modified lines of source code. This is 50% reduction of test cases.

7.5.3 Deletion Algorithm

The 'deletion' portion of the technique is used to (i) update the execution history of test cases by removing the deleted lines of source code (ii) identify and remove those test cases that cover only those lines which are covered by other test cases of the program. The information used in the algorithm is given in Table 7.13.

Table 7.13. Variables used by 'deletion' algorithm

S. No.	Variable	Description
1.	T1	It is a two-dimensional array. It keeps the number of lines of source code covered by each test case i.
2.	deloc	It is used to store the total number of lines of source code deleted.
3.	del_locode	It is a one-dimensional array and is used to store line numbers of deleted lines of source code.
4.	count	It is a two-dimensional array. It sets the position corresponding to every matched line of source code of each test case to 1.
5.	match	It is a one-dimensional array. It stores the total count of the number of 1's in the count array for each test case.
6.	deleted	It is a one-dimensional array. It keeps the record of redundant test cases. If the value corresponding to test case i is 1 in deleted array, then that test case is redundant and should be removed.

Step I: Initialization of variables

We consider a hypothetical program of 20 lines with a test suite of 5 test cases. The execution history is given in Table 7.14.

Table 7.14. Test cases with execution history

Test case Id	Execution history
T1	1, 5, 7, 15, 20
T2	2, 3, 4, 5, 8, 16, 20
T3	6, 8, 9, 10, 11, 12, 13, 14, 17, 18
T4	1, 2, 5, 8, 17, 19
T5	1, 2, 6, 8, 9, 13

We assume that line numbers 6, 13, 17 and 20 are modified, and line numbers 4, 7 and 15 are deleted from the source code. The information is stored as:

delloc = 3
del_locode = [4, 7, 15]
modloc = 4
mod_locode = [6, 13, 17, 20]

First portion of the "deletion" algorithm

1. Repeat for i=1 to number of test cases
   (a) Repeat for j=1 to length of test case i
       (i) Repeat for l to number of deleted lines of source code
           If T1[i][j]=del_locode then
               Repeat for k=j to length of test case i
                   T1[i][k]=T1[i][k+1]
                   Initialize T1[i][k] to zero
                   Decrement c[i] by one

After deleting line numbers 4, 7, and 15, the modified execution history is given in Table 7.15.

Table 7.15. Modified execution history after deleting line numbers 4, 7 and 15

Test case Id	Execution history
T1	1, 5, 20
T2	2, 3, 5, 8, 16, 20
T3	6, 8, 9, 10, 11, 12, 13, 14, 17, 18
T4	1, 2, 5, 8, 17, 19
T5	1, 2, 6, 8, 9, 13

Step II: Identification of redundant test cases

We want to find redundant test cases. A test case is a redundant test case, if it covers only those lines which are covered by other test cases of the program. This situation may arise due to deletion of a few lines of the program.

Consider the second portion of the 'deletion' algorithm. In this portion, the test case array is initialized with line numbers of lines of source code covered by each test case.

Second portion of the 'deletion' algorithm

2. Repeat for i=1 to number of test cases
   (a) Repeat for j=1 to number of test cases
       (i) Initialize array t1[i][j] to zero
       (ii) Initialize array count[i][j] to zero
3. Repeat for i=1 to number of test cases
   (a) Initialize deleted[i] and match [i] to zero
4. Repeat for i=1 to number of test cases
   (a) Initialize c[i] to number of line numbers in each test case i
   (b) Repeat for j=1 to c[i]
   (c) Initialize t1[i][j] to line numbers of line of source code covered by each test case

354   Software Testing

The third portion of the algorithm compares lines covered by each test case with lines covered by other test cases. A two-dimensional array count is used to keep the record of line number matched in each test case. If all the lines covered by a test case are being covered by some other test case, then that test case is redundant and should not be selected for execution.

Third portion of the 'deletion' algorithm

5. Repeat for i=1 to number of test cases
   (a) Repeat for j=1 to number of test cases
       (i) If i≠j and deleted[j]≠1 then
           Repeat for k=1 to until t1[i][k]≠0
           Repeat for l=1 until t1[j][l]≠0
           If t1[i][k]=t1[j][l] then
               Initialize count [i][k]=1
   (b) Repeat for m=1 to c[i]
       (i) If count[i][m]=1 then
           Increment match[i] with 1
   (c) If match[i]=c[i] then
       (i) Initialize deleted[i] to 1
6. Repeat for i=1 to number of test cases
   (a) If deleted[i] =1 then
       Remove test case i (as it is a redundant test case)

On comparing all values in each test case with all values of other test cases, we found that test case 1 and test case 5 are redundant test cases. These two test cases do not cover any line which is not covered by other test cases as shown in Table 7.16.

Table 7.16. Redundant test cases

Test Case	Line Number of LOC	Found In Test Case	Redundant Y/N
T1	1	T4	Y
	5	T2	Y
	20	T2	Y
T5	6	T3	Y
	8	T3	Y
	9	T3	Y
	1	T4	Y
	2	T2	Y
	13	T3	Y

The remaining test cases are = [T2, T3, T4] and are given in Table 7.17.

Table 7.17. Modified table after removing T1 and T5

Test case Id	Execution history
T2	2, 3, 5, 8, 16, 20
T3	6, 8, 9, 10, 11, 12, 13, 14, 17, 18
T4	1, 2, 5, 8, 17, 19

Now we will minimize and prioritize test cases using 'modification' algorithm given in section 7.5.2. The status of test cases covering the modified lines is given in Table 7.18.

Table 7.18. Test cases with modified lines

Test Cases	Number of lines matched (found)	Number of matches (nfound)
T2	20	1
T3	6, 13, 17	3
T4	17	1

Test cases are sorted on the basis of number of modified lines covered as shown in tables 7.19-7.20.

Table 7.19. Test cases in descending order of number of modified lines covered

Test Cases	Number of matches (nfound)	Numbers of lines matched	Candidate	Priority
T3	3	6, 13, 17	1	1
T2	1	20	0	0
T4	1	17	0	0

mod_locode = [6, 13, 17, 20] – [6, 13, 17] = [20]

Table 7.20. Test cases in descending order of number of modified lines covered (iteration 2)

Test Cases	Number of matches (nfound)	Numbers of lines matched	Candidate	Priority
T2	1	20	1	2
T4	0	-	0	0

Hence, test cases T2 and T3 are needed to be executed and redundant test cases are T1 and T5.

Out of the five test cases, we need to run only 2 test cases for 100% code coverage of modified code coverage. This is a 60% reduction. If we run only those test cases that cover any modified lines, then T2, T3 and T4 are selected. This technique not only selects test cases, but also prioritizes test cases.

356 Software Testing

Example 7.1: Consider the algorithm for deletion and modification of lines of source code in test cases. Write a program in C to implement, minimize and prioritize test cases using the above technique.

Solution:

```
#include<stdio.h>
#include<conio.h>
void main()
{
int t1[50][50]={0};
int count[50][50]={0};
int deleted[50],deloc,del_loc[50],k,c[50],l,num,m,n,match[50],i,j;
clrscr();
for(i=0;i<50;i++){
deleted[i]=0;
match[i]=0;
}

printf("Enter the number of test cases\n");
scanf("%d",&num);
for(i=0;i<num;i++){
    printf("Enter the length of test case %d\n",i+1);
    scanf("%d",&c[i]);
    printf("Enter the values of test case\n");
    for(j=0;j<c[i];j++){
        scanf("%d",&t1[i][j]);
        }
    }

printf("\nEnter the deleted lines of code:");
scanf("%d",&deloc);

for(i=0;i<deloc;i++)
    {
        scanf("%d",&del_loc[i]);
    }
for(i=0;i<num;i++){
    for(j=0;j<c[i];j++){
        for(l=0;l<deloc;l++){
        if(t1[i][j]==del_loc[l]){
            for(k=j;k<c[i];k++){
            t1[i][k]=t1[i][k+1];
            }
            t1[i][k]=0;
            c[i]--;
        }
    }
}
```

```c
        }
    }
    printf("Test case execution history after deletion:\n");
    for(i=0;i<num;i++){
        printf("T%d\t",i+1);
        for(j=0;j<c[i];j++){
            printf("%d ",t1[i][j]);
        }
    printf("\n");
    }
    for(i=0;i<num;i++){
        for(j=0;j<num;j++){
            if(i!=j&&deleted[j]!=1){
                for(k=0;t1[i][k]!=0;k++){
                    for(l=0;t1[j][l]!=0;l++){
                        if(t1[i][k]==t1[j][l])
                            count[i][k]=1;
                    }
                }
            }
        }
    for(m=0;m<c[i];m++)
        if(count[i][m]==1)
            match[i]++;
    if(match[i]==c[i])
        deleted[i]=1;
    }
    for(i=0;i<num;i++)
    if(deleted[i]==1)
    printf("Remove Test case %d\n",i+1);
    getch();
}
```

OUTPUT

Enter the number of test cases
5
Enter the length of test case 1
5
Enter the values of test case
1 5 7 15 20
Enter the length of test case 2
7
Enter the values of test case
2 3 4 5 8 16 20
Enter the length of test case 3
10

Enter the values of test case
6 8 9 10 11 12 13 14 17 18
Enter the length of test case 4
6
Enter the values of test case
1 2 5 8 17 19
Enter the length of test case 5
6
Enter the values of test case
1 2 6 8 9 13
Enter the deleted lines of code:3
4 7 15
Test case execution history after deletion:
T1   1 5 20
T2   2 3 5 8 16 20
T3   6 8 9 10 11 12 13 14 17 18
T4   1 2 5 8 17 19
T5   1 2 6 8 9 13
Remove Test case 1
Remove Test case 5

/*Program for test case selection for modified lines using regression test case selection algorithm*/

```c
#include<stdio.h>
#include<conio.h>

void main()
{
int t1[50][50];
int count=0;
int candidate[50]={0},priority[50]={0},m=0,pos[50],found[50][50],k,t,c[50],l,num,n,index[50],i,j,modnum,nfound[50],mod[50];
clrscr();
printf("Enter the number of test cases:");
scanf("%d",&num);
for(i=0;i<num;i++){
    printf("\nEnter the length of test case%d:",i+1);
    scanf("%d",&c[i]);
    }

for(i=0;i<50;i++)
    for(j=0;j<50;j++)
        found[i][j]=0;
for(i=0;i<num;i++)
    for(j=0;j<c[i];j++){
        t1[i][j]=0;
    }
for(i=0;i<num;i++){
    printf("Enter the values of test case %d\n",i+1);
    for(j=0;j<c[i];j++){
```

```
            scanf("%d",&t1[i][j]);
            }
            pos[i]=i;
    }
printf("\nEnter number of modified lines of code:");
scanf("%d",&modnum);
printf("Enter the lines of code modified:");
for(i=0;i<modnum;i++)
    scanf("%d",&mod[i]);
while(1)
{
count=0;
for(i=0;i<num;i++) {
    nfound[i]=0;
    pos[i]=i;
    }
for(i=0;i<num;i++){
l=0;
    for(j=0;j<c[i];j++){
    if(candidate[i]!=1){
    for(k=0;k<modnum;k++) {
        if(t1[i][j]==mod[k]){
            nfound[i]++;
            found[i][l]=mod[k];
            l++;
            }
    }
    }
}
}

l=0;
for(i=0;i<num;i++)
for(j=0;j<num-1;j++)
    if(nfound[i]>nfound[j]){
        t=nfound[i];
        nfound[i]=nfound[j];
        nfound[j]=t;
        t=pos[i];
        pos[i]=pos[j];
        pos[j]=t;
    }

for(i=0;i<num;i++)
    if(nfound[i]>0)
        count++;
if(count==0)
```

```c
            break;
candidate[pos[0]]=1;
priority[pos[0]]=++m;

printf("\nTestcase\tMatches");
for(i=0;i<num;i++) {
    printf("\n%d\t\t%d",pos[i]+1,nfound[i]);
    getch();
    }

for(i=0;i<c[pos[0]];i++)
    for(j=0;j<modnum;j++)
        if(t1[pos[0]][i]==mod[j]){
            mod[j]=0;
            }

printf("\nModified Array:");
for(i=0;i<modnum;i++){
    if(mod[i]==0){
        continue;
        }
    else {
        printf("%d\t",mod[i]);
        }
    }
}

count=0;
printf("\nTest case selected.....\n");
for(i=0;i<num;i++)
    if(candidate[i]==1){
        printf("\nT%d\t Priority%d\n ",i+1,priority[i]);
        count++;
        }
if(count==0){
    printf("\nNone");
    }
getch();
}
```

OUTPUT

Enter the number of test cases:10
Enter the length of test case1:6
Enter the length of test case2:7
Enter the length of test case3:8
Enter the length of test case4:8

Enter the length of test case5:12
Enter the length of test case6:11
Enter the length of test case7:8
Enter the length of test case8:7
Enter the length of test case9:5
Enter the length of test case10:3
Enter the values of test case 1
1 2 20 30 40 50
Enter the values of test case 2
1 3 4 21 31 41 51
Enter the values of test case 3
5 6 7 8 22 32 42 52
Enter the values of test case 4
6 9 10 23 24 33 43 54
Enter the values of test case 5
5 9 11 12 13 14 15 20 29 37 38 39
Enter the values of test case 6
15 16 17 18 19 23 24 25 34 35 36
Enter the values of test case 7
26 27 28 40 41 44 45 46
Enter the values of test case 8
46 47 48 49 50 53 55
Enter the values of test case 9
55 56 57 58 59
Enter the values of test case 10
3 4 60
Enter the number of modified lines of code:7
Enter the lines of code modified:1 2 5 15 35 45 55

Test case	Matches
1	2
5	2
6	2
3	1
2	1
7	1
8	1
9	1
4	0
10	0

Modified Array:5   15   35   45   55

Test case	Matches
5	2
6	2
3	1
7	1
8	1
9	1

```
4      0
2      0
1      0
10     0
```
Modified Array:35   45   55
Test case   Matches
```
6      1
7      1
8      1
9      1
5      0
1      0
2      0
3      0
4      0
10     0
```
Modified Array:45   55
Test case   Matches
```
7      1
8      1
9      1
4      0
5      0
6      0
1      0
2      0
3      0
10     0
```
Modified Array:55
Test case   Matches
```
8      1
9      1
3      0
4      0
5      0
6      0
7      0
1      0
2      0
10     0
```
Modified Array:
Test case selected.....
T1   Priority1
T5   Priority2
T6   Priority3
T7   Priority4
T8   Priority5

MULTIPLE CHOICE QUESTIONS

Note: *Select the most appropriate answer for the following questions.*

7.1 Regression testing should be performed:
   (a) After every month of release of software
   (b) After the changes in the software
   (c) After the release of the software
   (d) After the completion of development of software

7.2 Regression testing is primarily related to:
   (a) Functional testing
   (b) Data flow testing
   (c) Maintenance testing
   (d) Development testing

7.3 Which test cases are easy to identify?
   (a) Fault revealing
   (b) Modification revealing
   (c) Modification traversing
   (d) Bug revealing

7.4 Which of the following is not achieved by regression testing?
   (a) Locate errors in the modified program
   (b) Increase confidence in the correctness of the modified program
   (c) Ensure the continued operation of the program
   (d) Increase the functionality of the program

7.5 Which activity is performed in crisis situations and under greater time constraints?
   (a) Regression testing
   (b) Development testing
   (c) Verification
   (d) Validation

7.6 Regression testing process may include:
   (a) Fault Identification
   (b) Code modification
   (c) Test cases selection
   (d) All of the above

7.7 Which regression test cases selection technique is more useful?
   (a) Select all test cases
   (b) Select test cases randomly
   (c) Select modification traversing test cases
   (d) Select 50% of available test cases

7.8 Risk should include:
   (a) Probability of occurrence of a problem
   (b) Impact of that problem
   (c) Test cases
   (d) (a) and (b) both

7.9 Which is not the way to organize a risk matrix?
   (a) Threshold by quadrant
   (b) Threshold by diagonal quadrant
   (c) Threshold by available test cases
   (d) Threshold based on high impact of the problem

7.10 Which prioritization technique is used when we assign equal importance to 'probability of occurrence' and 'Impact of problem' in risk matrix?
   (a) Threshold by quadrant
   (b) Threshold by diagonal quadrant
   (c) Threshold based on high impact of the problem
   (d) Threshold based on high probability of occurrence of problem

7.11 In prioritizing what to test, the most important objective is to:
   (a) Find as many faults as possible
   (b) Test high risk areas
   (c) Obtain good test coverage
   (d) Test easy areas

7.12 Test cases are prioritized so that:
   (a) We shorten the time of testing
   (b) We do the best testing in the time available
   (c) We do more effective testing
   (d) We find more faults

7.13 A regression test:
   (a) Will always be automated
   (b) Will help to ensure that unchanged areas have not been affected
   (c) Will help to ensure that changed areas have not been affected
   (d) Will run during acceptance testing

7.14 Which of the following uses impact analysis most?
   (a) Acceptance testing
   (b) System testing
   (c) Regression testing
   (d) Unit testing

7.15 Which of the following is most benefited when a tool is used with test capture and replay facility?
   (a) Regression testing
   (b) Integration testing
   (c) System testing
   (d) Acceptance testing

EXERCISES

7.1 (a) What is regression testing? Discuss various categories of selective re-test problem.
   (b) Discuss an algorithm for the prioritization of test cases.

7.2 What are the factors responsible for requirement changes? How are the requirements traced?

7.3 Identify the reasons which are responsible for changes in the software. Comment on the statement "change is inevitable."

7.4 Compare regression testing with development testing. Do we perform regression testing before the release of the software?

7.5 Is it necessary to perform regression testing? Highlight some issues and difficulties of regression testing.

7.6 Explain the various steps of the regression testing process. Which step is the most important and why?

7.7 Discuss techniques for selection of test cases during regression testing. Why do we rely on the selection of test cases based on modification traversing?

7.8 What are selective re-test techniques? How are they different from the 'retest all' technique?

7.9 What are the categories to evaluate regression test selection technique? Why do we use such categorization?

7.10 (a) Discuss the priority category schemes for the prioritization of test cases.
(b) What is the role of risk matrix for the reduction of test cases?

7.11 How is risk analysis used in testing? How can we prioritize test cases using risk factor?

7.12 What is a risk matrix? How do we assign thresholds that group the potential problems into priority categories?

7.13 Explain the following:
(a) Modification traversing test cases
(b) Modification revealing test cases

7.14 What is the difference between general test case prioritization and version specific test case prioritization? Discuss any prioritization technique with the help of an example.

7.15 Explain the 'code coverage prioritization' technique. What are the test cases selection criteria? Write the modification algorithm which is used to minimize and prioritize test cases.

FURTHER READING

Many test cases may be generated using test design techniques. Applying risk analysis may help the software tester to select the most important test cases that address the most significant features. Tamres describes risk analysis in order to prioritize test cases:

L. Tamres, "Introduction to Software Testing", Pearson Education, 2005.

The following article provides a full account on design and maintenance of behavioural regression test suites that may help to change code with confidence:

Nada daVeiga, "Change Code without Fear: Utilize a Regression Safety Net", DDJ, February 2008.

Useful recommendations x on regression testing by Microsoft can be obtained from:

Microsoft regression testing recommendations, http://msdn.microsoft.com/en-us/library/aa292167(VS.71).aspx

Fischer proposed a minimisation based regression test selection technique. This technique uses linear equations in order to represent relationships between basic block and test cases. A safe regression test selection algorithm was proposed by Rothermal and Harrold. They use control flow graphs for a program or procedure and these graphs were used to select test cases that execute modified source code from the given test suite. Harrold and Soffa present a data flow coverage based regression test selection technique. An empirical study is conducted by Graves in order to examine the costs and benefits of various regression test selection techniques:

    K. Fischer, F. Raji, and A. Chruscicki, "A Methodology for Retesting Modified Software", Proceedings of the National Telecommunications Conference B-6-3, Nov: 1–6, 1981.

    G. Rothermel and M. Harrold, "A Safe, Efficient Algorithm for Regression Test Selection", Proceedings of International Conference on Software Maintenance pp. 358–367, 1993.

    T. Graves, M.J. Harrold, J.M. Kim, A. Porter, and G. Rothermel, "An Empirical Study of Regression Test Selection Techniques", Proceedings of 20th International Conference on Software Engineering, Kyoto, Japan. IEEE Computer Society Press: Los Alamitos, CA, pp.188–197, 1998.

    M.J Harrold, and M.L Soffa, "An Incremental Approach to Unit Testing during Maintenance", Proceedings of the Conference on Software Maintenance (Oct.). pp. 362–367, 1998.

Other similar studies include:

    Kim, J. M., and A. Porter, "A History-Based Test Prioritization Technique for Regression Testing in Resource Constrained Environments", Proceedings of the 24th International Conference on Software Engineering, pp. 119–129, 2002.

    J. Laski and W. Szermer, "Identification of Program Modifications and Its Applications in Software Maintenance", Proceedings of the 1992 Conference on Software Maintenance (Nov.), pp. 282–290, 1992.

    Z. Li, M. Harman, and R. M. Hierons "Search Algorithms for Regression Test Case Prioritization", IEEE Trans. on Software Engineering, vol. 33, no. 4, April 2007.

    W. E. Wong, J. R. Horgan, S. London and H. Aggarwal, "A Study of Effective Regression in Practice", Proceedings of the 8th International Symposium on software reliability Engineering, pp. 230–238, Nov. 1994.

A useful introduction to regression testing performed in a real-life environment is given by Onomo:

    A.K. Onomo, Wei-Tek Tsai, M. Poonawala, H. Suganuma, "Regression Testing in an Industrial Environment," Communications of the ACM, vol. 45, no. 5, pp. 81–86, May 1998.

Some other good survey papers on regression testing include:

    Emelie Engström, Per Runeson and Mats Skoglund, "A Systematic Review on Regression Test Selection Techniques", Information and Software Technology, vol. 52, no. 1, pp. 14–30, January 2010.

    S. Yoo and M. Harman, "Regression Testing Minimization, Selection and Prioritization: A Survey", March 2010, DOI: 10.1002/stvr.430.

The following research paper provides an excellent comparison in order to analyze the costs and benefits of several regression test selection algorithms:

    T.L. Graves, M.J. Harrold, J.M. Kim, A. Porter, G. Rothermel, "An Empirical Study: Regression Test Selection Techniques", ACM Transactions on Software Engineering and Methodology, vol. 10 , no. 2, pp. 180–208, April 2001.

Other similar study includes:

    Gregg Rothermel, Mary Jean Harrold, Jeffery von Ronne, Christie Hong, "Empirical Studies of Test-suite Reduction", Software Testing, Verification and Reliability, vol. 12, no. 4, pp. 219–249, 2002.

8

Software Testing Activities

We start testing activities from the first phase of the software development life cycle. We may generate test cases from the SRS and SDD documents and use them during system and acceptance testing. Hence, development and testing activities are carried out simultaneously in order to produce good quality maintainable software in time and within budget. We may carry out testing at many levels and may also take help of a software testing tool. Whenever we experience a failure, we debug the source code to find reasons for such a failure. Finding the reasons for a failure is a very significant testing activity and consumes a huge amount of resources and may also delay the release of the software.

8.1 LEVELS OF TESTING

Software testing is generally carried out at different levels. There are four such levels namely unit testing, integration testing, system testing and acceptance testing as shown in Figure 8.1. The first three levels of testing activities are done by the testers and the last level of testing (acceptance) is done by the customer(s)/user(s). Each level has specific testing objectives. For example, at the unit testing level, independent units are tested using functional and/or structural testing techniques. At the integration testing level, two or more units are combined and testing is carried out to test the integration related issues of various units. At the system testing level, the system is tested as a whole and primarily functional testing techniques are used to test the system. Non-functional requirements like performance, reliability, usability, testability, etc. are also tested at this level. Load/stress testing is also performed at this level. The last level i.e. acceptance testing, is done by the customer(s)/user(s) for the purpose of accepting the final product.

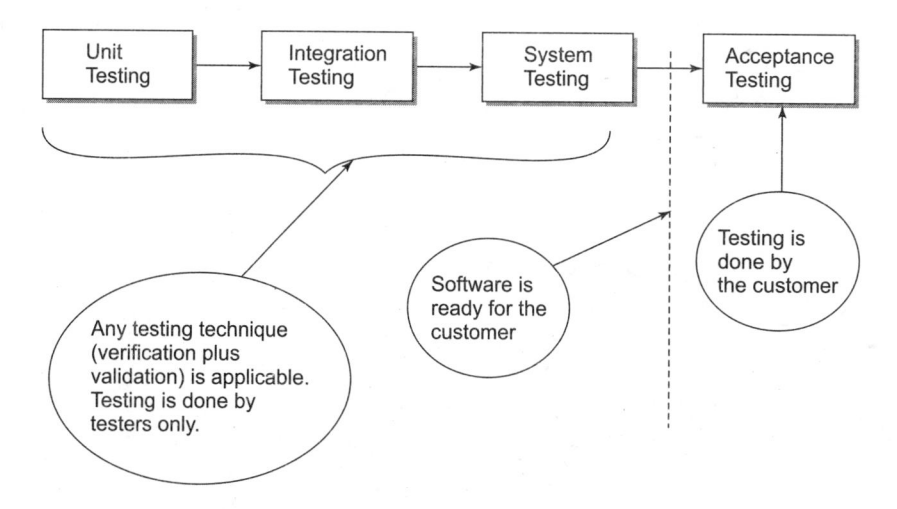

Figure 8.1. Levels of testing

8.1.1 Unit Testing

We develop software in parts / units and every unit is expected to have a defined functionality. We may call it a component, module, procedure, function, etc., which will have a purpose and may be developed independently and simultaneously. A. Bertolino and E. Marchetti have defined a unit as [BERT07]:

> "A unit is the smallest testable piece of software, which may consist of hundreds or even just few lines of source code, and generally represents the result of the work of one or few developers. The unit test cases' purpose is to ensure that the unit satisfies its functional specification and / or that its implemented structure matches the intended design structure. [BEIZ90, PFLE01]."

There are also problems with unit testing. How can we run a unit independently? A unit may not be completely independent. It may be calling a few units and also be called by one or more units. We may have to write additional source code to execute a unit. A unit X may call a unit Y and a unit Y may call a unit A and a unit B as shown in Figure 8.2(a). To execute a unit Y independently, we may have to write additional source code in a unit Y which may handle the activities of a unit X and the activities of a unit A and a unit B. The additional source code to handle the activities of a unit X is called 'driver' and the additional source code to handle the activities of a unit A and a unit B is called 'stub'. The complete additional source code which is written for the design of stub and driver is called scaffolding.

The scaffolding should be removed after the completion of unit testing. This may help us to locate an error easily due to small size of a unit. Many white box testing techniques may be effectively applicable at unit level. We should keep stubs and drivers simple and small in size to reduce the cost of testing. If we design units in such a way that they can be tested without writing stubs and drivers, we may be very efficient and lucky. Generally, in practice, it may be difficult and thus the requirement of stubs and drivers may not be eliminated. We may only minimize the requirement of scaffolding depending upon the functionality and its division in various units.

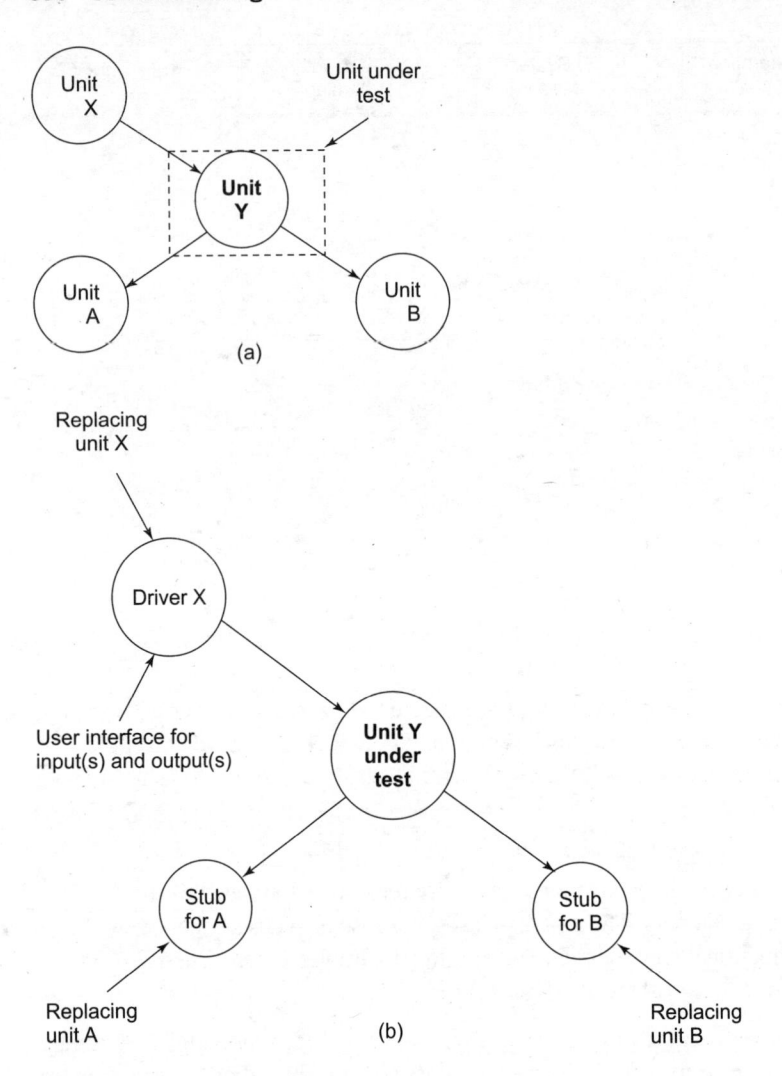

Figure 8.2. Unit under test with stubs and driver

8.1.2 Integration Testing

A software program may have many units. We test units independently during unit testing after writing the required stubs and drivers. When we combine two units, we may like to test the interfaces amongst these units. We combine two or more units because they share some relationship. This relationship is represented by an interface and is known as coupling. The coupling is the measure of the degree of interdependence between units. Two units with high coupling are strongly connected and thus, dependent on each other. Two units with low coupling are weakly connected and thus have low dependency on each other. Hence, highly coupled units are heavily dependent on other units and loosely **coupled** units are comparatively less dependent on other units as shown in Figure 8.3.

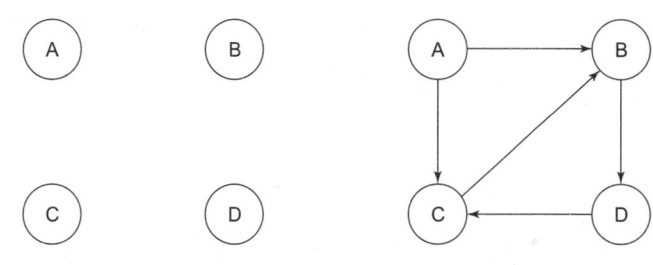

(a) Uncoupled: No dependencies
(b) Loosely coupled units: Few dependencies
(c) Highly coupled units: Many dependencies

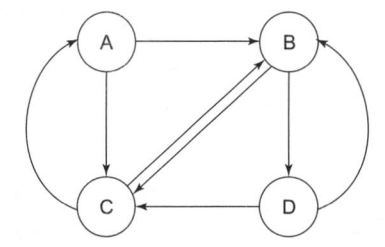

Figure 8.3. Coupling amongst units

Coupling increases as the number of calls amongst units increases or the amount of shared data increases. A design with high coupling may have more errors. Loose coupling minimizes the interdependence, and some of the steps to minimize coupling are given as:

(i) Pass only data, not the control information.
(ii) Avoid passing undesired data.
(iii) Minimize parent/child relationship between calling and called units.
(iv) Minimize the number of parameters to be passed between two units.
(v) Avoid passing complete data structure.
(vi) Do not declare global variables.
(vii) Minimize the scope of variables.

Different types of coupling are data (best), stamp, control, external, common and content (worst). When we design test cases for interfaces, we should be very clear about the coupling amongst units and if it is high, a large number of test cases should be designed to test that particular interface.

A good design should have low coupling and thus interfaces become very important. When interfaces are important, their testing will also be important. In integration testing, we focus on the issues related to interfaces amongst units. There are several integration strategies that really have little basis in a rational methodology and are given in Figure 8.4. Top down integration starts from the main unit and keeps on adding all called units of the next level. This portion should be tested thoroughly by focusing on interface issues. After completion of integration testing at this level, add the next level of units and so on till we reach the lowest level units (leaf units). There will not be any requirement of drivers and only stubs will be designed. In bottom-up integration, we start from the bottom, (i.e. from leaf units) and keep on adding upper level units till we reach the top (i.e. root node). There will not be any need of stubs. A sandwich

372 Software Testing

strategy runs from top and bottom concurrently, depending upon the availability of units and may meet somewhere in the middle.

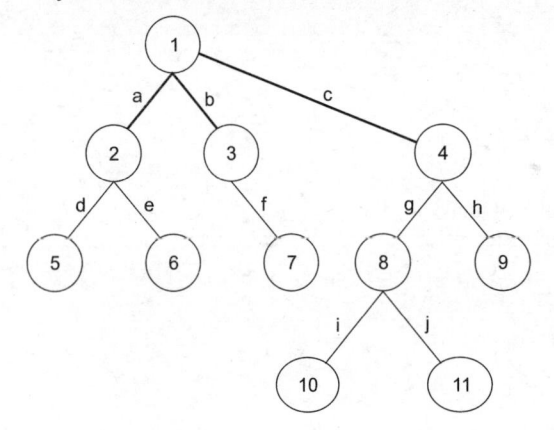

(a) Top down integration (focus starts from edges a, b, c and so on)

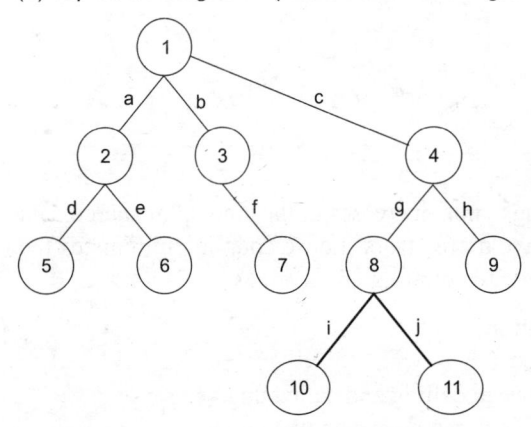

(b) Bottom up integration (focus starts from edges i, j and so on)

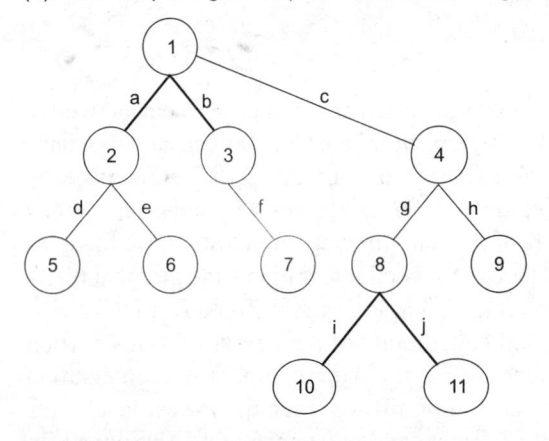

(c) Sandwich integration (focus starts from a, b, i, j and so on)

Figure 8.4. Integration approaches

Each approach has its own advantages and disadvantages. In practice, sandwich integration approach is more popular. This can be started as and when two related units are available. We may use any functional or structural testing techniques to design test cases.

Functional testing techniques are easy to implement with a particular focus on the interfaces and some structural testing techniques may also be used. When a new unit is added as a part of integration testing, then the software is considered as a changed software. New paths are designed and new input(s) and output(s) conditions may emerge and new control logic may be invoked. These changes may also cause problems with units that previously worked flawlessly.

8.1.3 System Testing

We perform system testing after the completion of unit and integration testing. We test complete software along with its expected environment. We generally use functional testing techniques, although a few structural testing techniques may also be used.

A system is defined as a combination of the software, hardware and other associated parts that together provide product features and solutions. System testing ensures that each system function works as expected and it also tests for non-functional requirements like performance, security, reliability, stress, load, etc. This is the only phase of testing which tests both functional and non-functional requirements of the system. A team of the testing persons does the system testing under the supervision of a test team leader. We also review all associated documents and manuals of the software. This verification activity is equally important and may improve the quality of the final product.

Utmost care should be taken for the defects found during the system testing phase. A proper impact analysis should be done before fixing the defect. Sometimes, if the system permits, instead of fixing the defects, they are just documented and mentioned as the known limitations. This may happen in a situation when fixing is very time consuming or technically it is not possible in the present design, etc. Progress of system testing also builds confidence in the development team as this is the first phase in which the complete product is tested with a specific focus on the customer's expectations. After the completion of this phase, customers are invited to test the software.

8.1.4 Acceptance Testing

This is the extension of system testing. When the testing team feels that the product is ready for the customer(s), they invite the customer(s) for demonstration. After demonstration of the product, customer(s) may like to use the product to assess their satisfaction and confidence. This may range from adhoc usage to systematic well-planned usage of the product. This type of usage is essential before accepting the final product. The testing done for the purpose of accepting a product is known as acceptance testing. This may be carried out by the customer(s) or persons authorized by the customer(s). The venue may be the developer's site or the customer's site depending on mutual agreement. Generally, acceptance testing is carried out at the customer's site. Acceptance testing is carried out only when the software is developed for a particular customer(s). If we develop 'standardised' software for anonymous users at large (like operating systems, compilers, case tools, etc.), then acceptance testing is not feasible. In such cases, potential customers are identified to test the software and this type of testing is called alpha / beta testing. Beta testing is done by many potential customers at their sites without any involvement of developers / testers. However, alpha testing is done by some potential customers at the developer's site under the direction and supervision of developers testers.

8.2 DEBUGGING

Whenever a software fails, we would like to understand the reason(s) for such a failure. After knowing the reason(s), we may attempt to find the solution and may make necessary changes in the source code accordingly. These changes will hopefully remove the reason(s) for that software failure. The process of identifying and correcting a software error is known as debugging. It starts after receiving a failure report and completes after ensuring that all corrections have been rightly placed and the software does not fail with the same set of input(s). The debugging is quite a difficult phase and may become one of the reasons for the software delays.

Every bug detection process is different and it is difficult to know how long it will take to detect and fix a bug. Sometimes, it may not be possible to detect a bug or if a bug is detected, it may not be feasible to correct it at all. These situations should be handled very carefully. In order to remove bugs, developers should understand that a problem prevails and then he/she should do the classification of the bug. The next step is to identify the location of the bug in the source code and finally take the corrective action to remove the bug.

8.2.1 Why Debugging is so Difficult?

Debugging is a difficult process. This is probably due to human involvement and their psychology. Developers become uncomfortable after receiving any request of debugging. It is taken against their professional pride. Shneiderman [SHNE80] has rightly commented on the human aspect of debugging as:

> "It is one of the most frustrating parts of programming. It has elements of problem solving or brain teasers, coupled with the annoying recognition that we have made a mistake. Heightened anxiety and the unwillingness to accept the possibility of errors, increase the task difficulty. Fortunately, there is a great sigh of relief and a lessening of tension when the bug is ultimately corrected."

These comments explain the difficulty of debugging. Pressman [PRES97] has given some clues about the characteristics of bugs as:

> "The debugging process attempts to match symptom with cause, thereby leading to error correction. The symptom and the cause may be geographically remote. That is, symptom may appear in one part of program, while the cause may actually be located in other part. Highly coupled program structures may further complicate this situation. Symptom may also disappear temporarily

when another error is corrected. In real time applications, it may be difficult to accurately reproduce the input conditions. In some cases, symptom may be due to causes that are distributed across a number of tasks running on different processors."

There may be many reasons which may make the debugging process difficult and time consuming. However, psychological reasons are more prevalent over technical reasons. Over the years, debugging techniques have substantially improved and they will continue to develop significantly in the near future. Some debugging tools are available and they minimize the human involvement in the debugging process. However, it is still a difficult area and consumes a significant amount of time and resources.

8.2.2 Debugging Process

Debugging means detecting and removing bugs from the programs. Whenever a program generates an unexpected behaviour, it is known as a failure of the program. This failure may be mild, annoying, disturbing, serious, extreme, catastrophic or infectious. Depending on the type of failure, actions are required to be taken. The debugging process starts after receiving a failure report either from the testing team or from users. The steps of the debugging process are replication of the bug, understanding the bug, locating the bug, fixing the bug and retesting the program. These steps are explained below:

(i) **Replication of the bug:** The first step in fixing a bug is to replicate it. This means to recreate the undesired behaviour under controlled conditions. The same set of input(s) should be given under similar conditions to the program and the program after execution, should produce a similar unexpected behaviour. If this happens, we are able to replicate a bug. In many cases, this is simple and straight forward. We execute the program on a particular input(s) or we press a particular button on a particular dialog, and the bug occurs. In other cases, replication may be very difficult. It may require many steps or in an interactive program such as a game, it may require precise timing. In worst cases, replication may be nearly impossible. If we do not replicate the bug, how will we verify the fix? Hence, failure to replicate a bug is a real problem. If we cannot do it, any action, which cannot be verified, has no meaning, howsoever important it may be. Some of the reasons for non-replication of a bug are:

- The user incorrectly reported the problem.
- The program has failed due to hardware problems like memory overflow, poor network connectivity, network congestion, non-availability of system buses, deadlock conditions, etc.
- The program has failed due to system software problems. The reason may be the usage of a different type of operating system, compilers, device drivers, etc. There may be any of the above-mentioned reasons for the failure of the program, although there is no inherent bug in the program for this particular failure.

Our effort should be to replicate the bug. If we cannot do so, it is advisable to keep the matter pending till we are able to replicate it. There is no point in playing with the source code for a situation which is not reproducible.

(ii) **Understanding the bug**

After replicating the bug, we may like to understand the bug. This means, we want to find the reason(s) for this failure. There may be one or more reasons and is generally the most time consuming activity. We should understand the program very clearly for understanding a bug. If we are the designers and source code writers, there may not be any problem for understanding the bug. If not, then we may have serious problems. If readability of the program is good and associated documents are available, we may be able to manage the problem. If readability is not that good, (which happens in many situations) and associated documents are not proper and complete, the situation becomes very difficult and complex. We may call the designers; if we are lucky, they may be available with the company and we may get them. In case of the designers not being available, the situation becomes challenging and in practice many times, we have to face this and struggle with the source code and documents written by the persons not available with the company. We may have to put effort in order to understand the program. We may start from the first statement of the source code to the last statement with a special focus on critical and complex areas of the source code. We should be able to know where to look in the source code for any particular activity. The source code should also tell us the general way in which the program acts.

The worst cases are large programs written by many persons over many years. These programs may not have consistency and may become poorly readable over time due to various maintenance activities. We should simply do the best and try to avoid making the mess worse. We may also take the help of source code analysis tools for examining large programs. A debugger may also be helpful for understanding the program. A debugger inspects a program statement-wise and may be able to show the dynamic behaviour of the program using a breakpoint. The breakpoints are used to pause the program at any time needed. At every breakpoint, we may look at values of variables, contents of relevant memory locations, registers, etc. The main point is that in order to understand a bug, program understanding is essential. We should put the desired effort before finding the reasons for the software failure. If we fail to do so, unnecessarily, we may waste our effort, which is neither required nor desired.

(iii) **Locate the bug**

There are two portions of the source code which need to be considered for locating a bug. The first portion of the source code is one which causes the visible incorrect behaviour and the second portion of the source code is one which is actually incorrect. In most of the situations, both portions may overlap and sometimes, both portions may be in different parts of the program. We should first find the source code which causes the incorrect behaviour. After knowing the incorrect behaviour and its related portion of the source code, we may find the portion of the source code which is at fault. Sometimes, it may be very easy to identify the problematic source code (the second portion of the source code) with manual inspection. Otherwise, we may have to take the help of a debugger. If we have 'core dumps', a debugger can immediately identify the line which fails. A 'core dumps' is the printout of all registers and relevant memory locations. We should document them and also retain them for possible future use. We may provide breakpoints while replicating the bug and this process may also help us to locate the bug.

Sometimes simple print statements may help us to locate the sources of the bad behaviour. This simple way provides us the status of various variables at different locations of the program with a specific set of inputs. A sequence of print statements may also portray the dynamics of variable changes. However, it is cumbersome to use in large programs. They may also generate superfluous data which may be difficult to analyze and manage.

We may add check routines in the source code to verify the correctness of the data structures. This may help us to know the problematic areas of the source code. If execution of these check routines is not very time consuming, then we may always add them. If it is time consuming, we may design a mechanism to make them operational, whenever required.

The most useful and powerful way is to inspect the source code. This may help us to understand the program, understand the bug and finally locate the bug. A clear understanding of the program is an absolute requirement of any debugging activity. Sometimes, the bug may not be in the program at all. It may be in a library routine or in the operating system, or in the compiler. These cases are very rare, but there are chances and if everything fails, we may have to look for such options.

(iv) **Fix the bug and re-test the program**

After locating the bug, we may like to fix the bug. The fixing of a bug is a programming exercise rather than a debugging activity. After making necessary changes in the source code, we may have to re-test the source code in order to ensure that the corrections have been rightly done at right place. Every change may affect other portions of the source code too. Hence an impact analysis is required to identify the affected portion and that portion should also be re-tested thoroughly. This re-testing activity is called regression testing which is a very important activity of any debugging process.

8.2.3 Debugging Approaches

There are many popular debugging approaches, but success of any approach is dependent upon the understanding of the program. If the persons involved in debugging understand the program correctly, they may be able to detect and remove the bugs.

(i) **Trial and Error Method**

This approach is dependent on the ability and experience of the debugging persons. After getting a failure report, it is analyzed and the program is inspected. Based on experience and intelligence, and also using the 'hit and trial' technique, the bug is located and a solution is found. This is a slow approach and becomes impractical in large programs.

(ii) **Backtracking**

This can be used successfully in small programs. We start at the point where the program gives an incorrect result such as an unexpected output is printed. After analyzing the output, we trace backward the source code manually until a cause of the failure is found. The source code, from the statement where symptoms of the failure is found, to the statement where the cause of failure is found, is analyzed properly. This technique brackets the locations of the bug in the program. Subsequent careful study of the bracketed location may help us to rectify the bug. Another obvious variation of backtracking is forward tracking, where we use print statements or other means to examine a succession of intermediate results to determine at what point the result first became wrong. These approaches (backtracking and forward tracking) may be useful only when the size of the program is small. As the program size increases, it becomes difficult to manage these approaches.

(iii) **Brute Force**

This is probably the most common and efficient approach to identify the cause of a software failure. In this approach, memory dumps are taken, run time traces are invoked and the program is loaded with print statements. When this is done, we may find a clue by the information produced which leads to identification of cause of a bug. Memory traces are similar to memory dumps, except that the printout contains only certain memory and register contents and printing is conditional on some event occurring. Typically conditional events are entry, exit or use of one of the following:

- A particular subroutine, statement or database
- Communication with I/O devices
- Value of a variable
- Timed actions (periodic or random) in certain real time system.

A special problem with trace programs is that the conditions are entered in the source code and any changes require a recompilation. A huge amount of data is generated, which, although may help to identify the cause, but may be difficult to manage and analyze.

(iv) **Cause Elimination**

Cause elimination is manifested by induction or deduction and also introduces the concept of binary partitioning. Data related to error occurrence are organized to isolate potential causes. Alternatively, a list of all possible causes is developed and tests are conducted to eliminate each. Therefore, we may rule out causes one by one until a single one remains for validation. The cause is identified, properly fixed and re-tested accordingly.

8.2.4 Debugging Tools

Many debugging tools are available to support the debugging process. Some of the manual activities can also be automated using a tool. We may need a tool that may execute every statement of a program at a time and print values of any variable after executing every statement of the program. We will be free from inserting print statements in the program manually. Thus, run time debuggers are designed. Fundamentally, a run time debugger is similar to an automatic print statement generator. It helps us to trace the program path and the defined variables without having to put print statements in the source code. Every compiler available in the market comes with run time debugger. It allows us to compile and run the program with a single compilation, rather than modifying the source code and recompiling as we try to narrow down the bug.

Run time debuggers may detect bugs in the program, but may fail to find the causes of failures. We may need a special tool to find causes of failures and correct the bug. Some errors like memory corruption and memory leaks may be detected automatically. The automation was the modification in the debugging process because it automated the process of finding the bug. A tool may detect an error and our job is to simply fix it. These tools are known as 'automatic debugger' and are available in different varieties. One variety may be a library of functions that may be connected into the program. During execution of the program, these functions are called and the debugger looks for memory corruption and other similar issues. If anything is found, it is reported accordingly.

Compilers are also used for finding bugs. Of course, they check only syntax errors and particular types of run time errors. Compilers should give proper and detailed messages of errors that will be of great help to the debugging process. Compilers may give all such information in the attribute table, which is printed along with the listing. The attribute table contains various levels of warnings which have been picked up by the compiler scan and which are noted. Hence, compilers come with an error detection feature and there is no excuse to design compilers without meaningful error messages.

We may apply a wide variety of tools like run time debugger, automatic debugger, automatic test case generators, memory dumps, cross reference maps, compilers, etc. during the debugging process. However, tools are not the substitute for careful examination of the source code after thorough understanding.

8.3 SOFTWARE TESTING TOOLS

The most important effort-consuming task in software testing is to design the test cases. The execution of these test cases may not require much time and resources. Hence, the designing part is more significant than the execution part. Both parts are normally handled manually. Do we really need a tool? If yes, where and when can we use it – in the first part (designing of test cases) or second part (execution of test cases) or both? Software testing tools may be used to reduce the time of testing and to make testing as easy and pleasant as possible. Automated testing may be carried out without human involvement. This may help us in the areas where a similar dataset is to be given as input to the program again and again. A tool may undertake repeated testing, unattended (and without human intervention), during nights or on weekends.

Many non-functional requirements may be tested with the help of a tool. We want to test the performance of a software under load, which may require many computers, manpower and other resources. A tool may simulate multiple users on one computer and also a situation when many users are accessing a database simultaneously.

There are three broad categories of software testing tools i.e. static, dynamic and process management. Most of the tools fall clearly into one of these categories but there are a few exceptions like mutation analysis system which falls in more than one category. A wide variety of tools are available with different scope and quality and they assist us in many ways.

8.3.1 Static Software Testing Tools

Static software testing tools are those that perform analysis of the programs without executing them at all. They may also find the source code which will be hard to test and maintain. As we all know, static testing is about prevention and dynamic testing is about cure. We should use both the tools but prevention is always better than cure. These tools will find more bugs as compared to dynamic testing tools (where we execute the program). There are many areas for which effective static testing tools are available, and they have shown their results for the improvement of the quality of the software.

(i) **Complexity analysis tools**

Complexity of a program plays a very important role while determining its quality. A popular measure of complexity is the cyclomatic complexity as discussed in chapter 4. This gives us the idea about the number of independent paths in the program and is dependent upon the number of decisions in the program. A higher value of cyclomatic complexity may indicate poor design and risky implementation. This may also be applied at the module level, and higher cyclomatic complexity value modules may either be redesigned or may be tested very thoroughly. There are other complexity measures also which are used in practice like Halstead software size measures, knot complexity measure, etc. Tools are available which are based on any of the complexity measures. These tools may take the program as an input, process it and produce a complexity value as output. This value may be an indicator of the quality of design and implementation.

(ii) **Syntax and semantic analysis tools**

These tools find syntax and semantic errors. Although the compiler may detect all syntax errors during compilation, early detection of such errors may help to minimize other associated errors. Semantic errors are very significant and compilers are helpless in finding such errors. There are tools in the market that may analyze the program and find errors. Non-declaration of a variable, double declaration of a variable, 'divide by zero' issue, unspecified inputs and non-initialization of a variable are some of the issues which may be detected by semantic analysis tools. These tools are language dependent and may parse the source code, maintain a list of errors and provide implementation information. The parser may find semantic errors as well as make an inference as to what is syntactically correct.

(iii) **Flow graph generator tools**

These tools are language dependent and take the program as an input and convert it to its flow graph. The flow graph may be used for many purposes like complexity calculation, paths identification, generation of definition use paths, program slicing, etc. These tools assist us to understand the risky and poorly designed areas of the source code.

(iv) **Code comprehension tools**

These tools may help us to understand unfamiliar source code. They may also identify dead source code, duplicate source code and areas that may require special attention and should be reviewed seriously.

(v) **Code inspectors**

Source code inspectors do the simple job of enforcing standards in a uniform way for many programs. They inspect the programs and force us to implement the guidelines of good programming practices. Although they are language dependent, most of the guidelines of good programming practices are similar in many languages. These tools are simple and may find many critical and weak areas of the program. They may also suggest possible changes in the source code for improvement.

8.3.2 Dynamic Software Testing Tools

Dynamic software testing tools select test cases and execute the program to get the results. They also analyze the results and find reasons for failures (if any) of the program. They will be used after the implementation of the program and may also test non-functional requirements like efficiency, performance, reliability, etc.

(i) **Coverage analysis tools**

These tools are used to find the level of coverage of the program after executing the selected test cases. They give us an idea about the effectiveness of the selected test cases. They highlight the unexecuted portion of the source code and force us to design special test cases for that portion of the source code. There are many levels of coverage like statement coverage, branch coverage, condition coverage, multiple condition coverage, path coverage, etc. We may like to ensure that at least every statement must be executed once and every outcome of the branch statement must be executed once. This minimum level of coverage may be shown by a tool after executing an appropriate set of test cases. There are tools available for checking statement coverage, branch coverage, condition coverage, multiple conditions coverage and path coverage. The profiler displays the number of times each statement is executed. We may study the output to know which portion of the source code is not executed. We may design test cases for those portions of the source code in order to achieve the desired level of coverage. Some tools are also available to check whether the source code is as per standards or not and also generate a number of commented lines, non-commented lines, local variables, global variables, duplicate declaration of variables, etc. Some tools check the portability of the source code. A source code is not portable if some operating system dependent features are used. Some tools are Automated QA's time, Parasoft's Insure++ and Telelogic's Logicscope.

(vi) **Performance testing tools**

We may like to test the performance of the software under stress / load. For example, if we are testing a result management software, we may observe the performance when 10 users are entering the data and also when 100 users are entering the data simultaneously. Similarly, we may like to test a website with 10 users, 100 users, 1000 users, etc. working simultaneously. This may require huge resources and sometimes, it may not be possible to create such real life environment for testing in the company. A tool may help us to simulate such situations and test these situations in various stress conditions. This is the most popular area for the usage of any tool and many popular tools are available in the market. These tools simulate multiple users on a single computer. We may also see the response time for a database when 10 users access the database, when 100 users access the database and when 1000 users access the data base simultaneously. Will the response time be 10 seconds or 100 seconds or even 1000 seconds? No user may like to tolerate the response time in minutes. Performance testing includes load and stress testing. Some of the popular tools are Mercury Interactive's Load Runner, Apache's J Meter, Segue Software's Silk Performer, IBM Rational's Performance Tester, Comuware's QALOAD and AutoTester's AutoController.

(vii) **Functional / Regression Testing Tools**
These tools are used to test the software on the basis of its functionality without considering the implementation details. They may also generate test cases automatically and execute them without human intervention. Many combinations of inputs may be considered for generating test cases automatically and these test cases may be executed, thus, relieving us from repeated testing activities. Some of the popular available tools are IBM Rational's Robot, Mercury Interactive's Win Runner, Comuware's QA Centre and Segue Software's Silktest.

8.3.3 Process Management Tools

These tools help us to manage and improve the software testing process. We may create a test plan, allocate resources and prepare a schedule for unattended testing for tracking the status of a bug using such tools. They improve many aspects of testing and make it a disciplined process. Some of the tools are IBM Rational Test Manager, Mercury Interactive's Test Director, Segue Software's Silk Plan Pro and Compuware's QA Director. Some configuration management tools are also available which may help bug tracking, its management and correctness like IBM Rational Software's Clear DDTs, Bugzilla and Samba's Jitterbug.

Selection of any tool is dependent upon the application, expectations, quality requirements and available trained manpower in the organization. Tools assist us to make testing effective, efficient and performance oriented.

8.4 SOFTWARE TEST PLAN

It is a document to specify the systematic approach to plan the testing activities of the software. If we carry out testing as per a well-designed systematic test plan document, the effectiveness of testing will improve and that may further help to produce a good quality product. The test plan document may force us to maintain a certain level of standards and disciplined approach to testing. Many software test plan documents are available, but the most popular document is the IEEE standard for Software Test Documentation (Std 829 – 1998). This document addresses the scope, schedule, milestones and purpose of various testing activities. It also specifies the items and features to be tested and features which are not to be tested. Pass/fail criteria, roles and responsibilities of persons involved, associated risks and constraints are also described in this document. The structure of the IEEE Std 829 – 1998 test plan document is given in [IEEE98c]. All ten sections have a specific purpose. Some changes may be made as per requirement of the project. A test plan document is prepared after the completion of the SRS document and may be modified along with the progress of the project. We should clearly specify the test coverage criteria and testing techniques to achieve the criteria. We should also describe who will perform testing, at what level and when. Roles and responsibilities of testers must be clearly documented.

MULTIPLE CHOICE QUESTIONS

Note: *Select the most appropriate answer for the following questions.*

8.1 The purpose of acceptance testing is:
   (a) To find faults in the system
   (b) To ensure the correctness of the system
   (c) To test the system from the business perspective
   (d) To demonstrate the effectiveness of the system

8.2 Which of the following is not part of system testing?
   (a) Performance, load and stress testing
   (b) Bottom up integration testing
   (c) Usability testing
   (d) Business perspective testing

8.3 Which of the following is not the integration testing strategy?
   (a) Top down
   (b) Bottom up
   (c) Sandwich
   (d) Design based

8.4 Which is not covered under the category of static testing tools?
   (a) Complexity analysis tools
   (b) Coverage analysis tools
   (c) Syntax and semantic analysis tools
   (d) Code Inspectors

8.5 Which is not covered under the category of dynamic testing tools?
   (a) Flow graph generator tools
   (b) Performance testing tools
   (c) Regression testing tools
   (d) Coverage analysis tools

8.6 Which is not a performance testing tool?
   (a) Mercury Interactive's Load Runner
   (b) Apache's J Meter,
   (c) IBM Rational's Performance tester
   (d) Parasoft's Insure ++

8.7 Select a functional / regression testing tool out of the following:
   (a) IBM Rational's Robot
   (b) Comuware's QALOAD
   (c) Automated QA's time
   (d) Telelogic's Logic scope

8.8 Find a process management tool out of the following:
   (a) IBM Rational Test Manager
   (b) Mercury Interactive's Test Director

(c) Segue Software's Silk Plan Pro
(d) All of the above

8.9 Which is not a coverage analysis tool?
(a) Automated QA's time
(b) Parasoft's Insure ++
(c) Telelogic's Logic Scope
(d) Apache's J Meter

8.10 Which is not a functional / regression testing tool?
(a) Mercury Interactive Win Runner
(b) IBM Rational's Robot
(c) Bugzilla
(d) Segue Software's Silk test

8.11 Which is not the specified testing level?
(a) Integration testing
(b) Acceptance testing
(c) Regression testing
(d) System testing

8.12 Which type of testing is done by the customers?
(a) Unit testing
(b) Integration testing
(c) System testing
(d) Acceptance testing

8.13 Which one is not a step to minimize the coupling?
(a) Pass only control information, not data
(b) Avoid passing undesired data
(c) Do not declare global variables
(d) Minimize the scope of variables

8.14 Choose the most desirable type of coupling:
(a) Data coupling
(b) Stamp coupling
(c) Control coupling
(d) Common coupling

8.15 Choose the worst type of coupling
(a) Stamp coupling
(b) Content coupling
(c) Common coupling
(d) Control coupling

8.16 Which is the most popular integration testing approach?
(a) Bottom up integration
(b) Top down integration
(c) Sandwich integration
(d) None of the above

8.17 Which is not covered in the debugging process?
  (a) Replication of the bug
  (b) Understanding of the bug
  (c) Selection of the bug tracking tool
  (d) Fix the bug and re-test the program

8.18 Which is not a debugging approach?
  (a) Brute force
  (b) Backtracking
  (c) Cause elimination
  (d) Bug multiplication

8.19 Binary partitioning is related to:
  (a) Cause elimination
  (b) Brute force
  (c) Backtracking
  (d) Trial and Error method

8.20 Which is not a popular debugging tool?
  (a) Run time debugger
  (b) Compiler
  (c) Memory dumps
  (d) Samba's Jitterbug

8.21 Finding reasons for a failure is known as:
  (a) Debugging
  (b) Testing
  (c) Verification
  (d) Validation

8.22 Which of the following terms is not used for a unit?
  (a) Component
  (b) Module
  (c) Function
  (d) Documentation

8.23 Non-functional requirements testing is performed at the level of:
  (a) System testing
  (b) Acceptance testing
  (c) Unit testing
  (d) (a) and (b) both

8.24 The debugging process attempts to match:
  (a) Symptom with cause
  (b) Cause with inputs
  (c) Symptoms with outputs
  (d) Inputs with outputs

8.25 Static testing tools perform the analysis of programs:
  (a) After their execution
  (b) Without their execution
  (c) During their execution
  (d) None of the above

EXERCISES

8.1 What are the various levels of testing? Explain the objectives of every level. Who should do testing at every level and why?

8.2 Is unit testing possible or even desirable in all circumstances? Justify your answer with examples.

8.3 What is scaffolding? Why do we use stubs and drivers during unit testing?

8.4 What are the various steps to minimize the coupling amongst various units? Discuss different types of coupling from the best coupling to the worst coupling.

8.5 Compare the top down and bottom up integration testing approaches to test a program.

8.6 What is debugging? Discuss two debugging techniques. Write features of these techniques and compare the important features.

8.7 Why is debugging so difficult? What are the various steps of a debugging process?

8.8 What are the popular debugging approaches? Which one is more popular and why?

8.9 Explain the significance of debugging tools. List some commercially available debugging tools.

8.10 (a) Discuss the static and dynamic testing tools with the help of examples.
  (b) Discuss some of the areas where testing cannot be performed effectively without the help of a testing tool.

8.11 Write short notes on:
  (i) Coverage analysis tools
  (ii) Performance testing tools
  (iii) Functional / Regression testing tools

8.12 What are non-functional requirements? How can we use software tools to test these requirements? Discuss some popular tools along with their areas of applications.

8.13 Explain stress, load and performance testing.

8.14 Differentiate between the following:
  (a) Integration testing and system testing
  (b) System testing and acceptance testing
  (c) Unit testing and integration testing
  (d) Testing and debugging

8.15 What are the objectives of process management tools? Describe the process of selection of such a tool. List some commercially available process management tools.

8.16 What is the use of a software test plan document in testing? Is there any standard available?
8.17 Discuss the outline of a test plan document as per IEEE Std 829-1998.
8.18 Consider the problem of the URS given in chapter 5, and design a software test plan document.
8.19 Which is the most popular level of testing a software in practice and why?
8.20 Which is the most popular integration testing approach? Discuss with suitable examples.

FURTHER READING

The IEEE standard on software unit testing presents a standard approach to unit testing that can be used as sound software engineering practice. It also provides guidelines for a software practitioner for implementation and usage of software unit testing:

IEEE Standards Board, "IEEE Standard for Software Unit Testing: An American National Standard", ANSI/IEEE Std 1008–1987.

For a comprehensive set of 27 guidelines on unit testing refer to:

"Unit Testing Guidelines", Geotechnical Software Services, http://geosoft.no/development/unittesting.html, 2007.

An excellent book on "The Art of Unit Testing" was written by Osherove:

R. Osherove, "The Art of Unit Testing", Manning Publications.

The following survey paper defines a number of practices that may be followed during unit testing:

Per Runeson, "A Survey of Unit Testing Practices", IEEE Software, vol. 23, no. 4, pp. 22–29, July/Aug. 2006, doi:10.1109/MS.2006.91.

Agans provides nine main debugging rules and several sub-debugging rules. These sub-rules are derived from common sense and several years of experience:

David J. Agans, "Debugging: The Nine Indispensable Rules for Finding Even the Most Elusive Software and Hardware Problems", AMACOM, 2002.

An introduction to debugging approaches may be found in Chapter 7 in Myers' book:

G.J Myers, "The Art of Software Testing," John Wiley & Sons, 2004.

A software practitioner spends lots of time in identifying and fixing bugs. The essay written by Taylor provides a good discussion on debugging:

Ian Lance Taylor, "Debugging", http://www.airs.com/ian/, 2003.

Other similar books include:

John Robbins, "Debugging Applications", Microsoft Press, 2000.

Matthew A. Telles, Yuan Hsieh, "The Science of Debugging", The Coriolis Group, 2001.

Dmitry Vostokov, "Memory Dump Analysis Anthology", vol. 1, OpenTask, 2008.

A comprehensive list of software testing tools can be obtained from:
   http://www.dmoz.org/Computers/Programming/Software_Testing/Products_and_Tools/
   http://www.aptest.com/resources.html#app-func

The IEEE standard for test documentation (IEEE, 1998) provides a comprehensive set of documents for test planning:
   IEEE, "IEEE Standard for Test Documentation (IEEE Std 829 –1998)", 1998.

A good survey on dynamic analysis may be found in:
   W.E. Howden, "A Survey of Dynamic Analysis Methods", In tutorial: Program Testing and Validation Techniques, IEEE Computer Society Press, 1981.

9

Object Oriented Testing

What is object orientation? Why is it becoming important and relevant in software development? How is it improving the life of software developers? Is it a buzzword? Many such questions come into our mind whenever we think about object orientation of software engineering. Companies are releasing the object oriented versions of existing software products. Customers are also expecting object oriented software solutions. Many developers are of the view that structural programming, modular design concepts and conventional development approaches are old fashioned activities and may not be able to handle today's challenges. They may also feel that real world situations are effectively handled by object oriented concepts using modeling in order to understand them clearly. Object oriented modeling may improve the quality of the SRS document, the SDD document and may help us to produce good quality maintainable software. The software developed using object orientation may require a different set of testing techniques, although few existing concepts may also be applicable with some modifications.

9.1 WHAT IS OBJECT ORIENTATION?

We may model real world situations using object oriented concepts. Suppose we want to send a book to our teacher who does not stay in the same city, we cannot go to his house for delivery of the book because he stays in a city which is 500 km away from our city. As we all know, sending a book is not a difficult task. We may go to a nearby courier agent (say Fast Track Courier) and ask to deliver the book to our teacher on his address. After this, we are sure that the book will be delivered automatically and also within the specified time (say two days). The agents of Fast Track Courier will perform the job without disturbing us at all.

Our objective is that we want to send a book to our teacher who does not stay in our city. This objective may be simply achieved, when we identify a proper 'agent' (say Fast Track Courier) and give a 'message' to send the book on an address of the teacher. It is the 'responsibility' of the identified agent (Fast Track Agent) to send the book. There are many 'methods' or ways to perform this task. We are not required to know the details of the operations to be performed to complete this task. Our interest is very limited and focused. If we investigate further, we may come to know that there are many ways to send a book like using train network, bus network, air network or combinations of two or more available networks. The selection of any method is the prerogative of our agent (say, agent of Fast Track Company). The agent may transfer the book to another agent with the delivery address and a message to transfer to the next agent and so on. Our task may be done by a sequence of requests from one agent to another.

In object orientation, an action is initiated by sending a message (request) to an agent who is responsible for that action. An agent acts as a receiver and if it accepts a message (request), it becomes its responsibility to initiate the desired action using some method to complete the task.

In real world situations, we do not need to know all operations of our agents to complete the assigned task. This concept of 'information hiding' with respect to message passing has become very popular in object oriented modeling. Another dimension is the interpretation of the message by the receiver. All actions are dependent upon the interpretation of the received message. Different receivers may interpret the same message differently. They may decide to use different methods for the same message. Fast Track Agency may use air network while another agency may use train network and so on. If we request our tailor to send the book, he may not have any solution for our problem. The tailor will only deny such requests. Hence, a message should be issued to a proper agent (receiver) in order to complete the task. Object orientation is centered around a few basic concepts like objects, classes, messages, interfaces, inheritance and polymorphism. These concepts help us to model a real world situation which provides the foundation for object oriented software engineering.

9.1.1 Classes and Objects

We consider the same example of sending a book to a teacher. The selection of the courier company is based on its reputation and proximity to our house. A courier management system is required in order to send a book to a teacher. All courier types (such as book, pen, etc.) may be combined to form a group and this group is known as a class. All objects are instances of a class. The class describes the structure of the instances which include behaviour and information. In our example, courier (containing courier details) is a class and all courier types are its objects as shown in Figure 9.1.

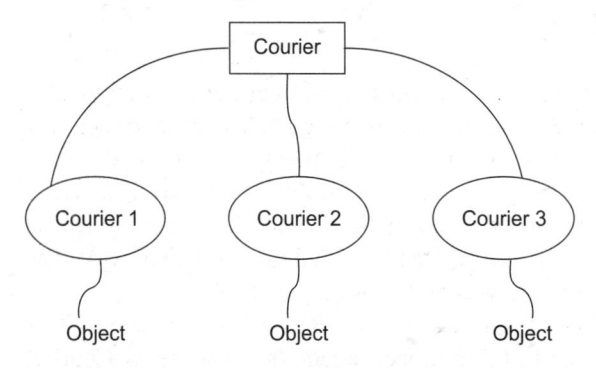

Figure 9.1. Class and its objects

All objects have unique identification and are distinguishable. There may be four horses having same attributes colour, breed and size but all are distinguishable due to their colour. The term identity means that objects are distinguished by their inherent existence and not by descriptive properties [JOSH03].

What types of things become objects? Anything and everything may become an object. In our example, customer, courier and tracking are nothing but objects. The class of an object provides the structure for the object i.e. its state and operations. A courier class is shown in Figure 9.2 with eight attributes and four operations.

Courier
Description
Weight
Length
Width
Height
Cost
DeliveryStatus
Address
addcourierdetail()
deletecourier()
updatecourier()
viewstatus()

Name

Attributes / State / Information

Operations / Behaviour

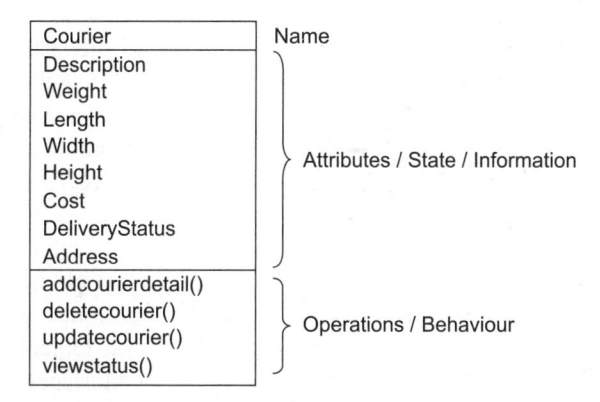

Figure 9.2. Class courier

An attribute (or information / state) is a data value held by the object of a class. The courier may have different height, weight, width, length, description and it may be delivered or not. The attributes are shown as the second part of the class courier as given in Figure 9.2. Operations (or behaviour) are the functions which may be applied on a class. All objects of a class have the same operations. A class courier shown in Figure 9.2 has four operations namely 'addcourierdetail', 'deletecourier', 'updatecourier' and 'viewstatus'. These four operations are defined for a Class Courier in the Figure 9.2. In short, every object has a list of functions (operation part) and data values required to store information (Attribute part).

I. Jacobson has defined a class as [JACO98]:

"A class represents a template for several objects and describes how these objects are structured internally. Objects of the same class have the same definition both for their operations and for their information structures."

In an object oriented system, every object has a class and the object is called an instance of that class. We use object and instance as synonyms and an object is defined as [JACO98]:

"An instance is an object created from a class. The class describes the (behaviour and information) structure of the instance, while the current state of the instance is defined by the operations performed on the instance."

9.1.2 Inheritance

We may have more information about Fast Track Courier Company not necessarily because it is a courier company but because it is a company. As a company, it will have employees, balance sheet, profit / loss account and a chief executive officer. It will also charge for its services and products from the customers. These things are also true for transport companies, automobile companies, aircraft companies, etc. Since the category 'courier company' is a more specialized form of the category 'company' and any knowledge of a company is also true for a courier company and subsequently also true for Fast Track Courier Company.

We may organize our knowledge in terms of hierarchy of categories as shown in Figure 9.3.

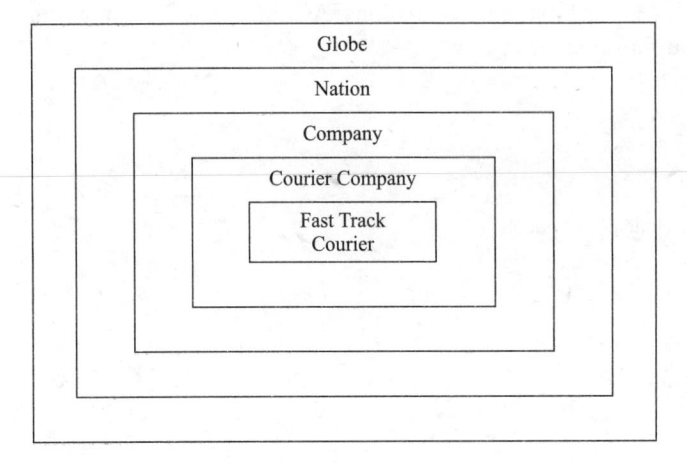

Figure 9.3. The categories around fast track courier

Fast Track Courier is a specialized category of a courier company; however, 'courier company' is a specialized category of a company. Moreover, a nation may have many companies and around the globe, we have many nations; all knowledge gathered so far, may not be directly applicable to Fast Track Company. Knowledge of a more general category, which is also applicable to a specialized category, is called inheritance. We may say that Fast Track Courier will inherit attributes of the category 'courier company' and 'courier company' will inherit the attributes of the category 'company'. This category is nothing but the class in the object oriented system. There is another tree-like structure used to represent a hierarchy of classes and is shown in Figure 9.4.

Information of a courier company is available to Fast Track Company because it is a sub-class of the class 'courier company'. The same information of a courier company is also applicable to Air World Courier and Express Courier because they are also sub-classes of the class 'courier company'. All classes inherit information from the upper classes. Hence information from a base class is common to all the derived classes; however, each derived class also has some additional information of its own. Each derived class inherits the attributes of its base class and this process is known as inheritance. In general, low level classes (known as sub-classes or derived classes) inherit state and behaviour from their high level class (known as a super class or base class).

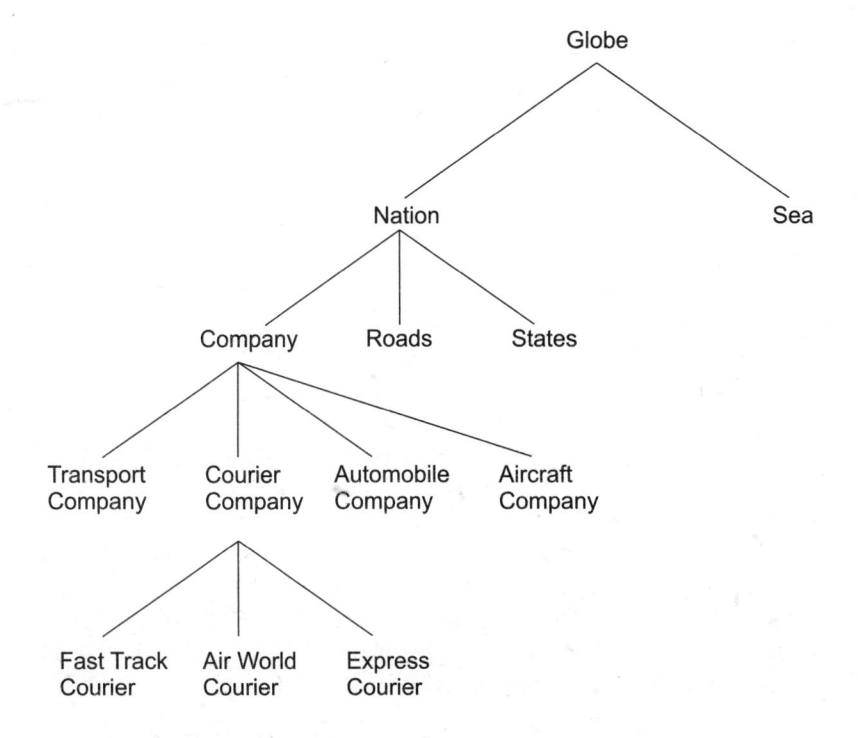

```
                      Globe
                    /      \
                Nation       Sea
               / |  \
        Company Roads States
        /  |   \    \
Transport Courier Automobile Aircraft
Company   Company  Company   Company
         / |  \
Fast Track Air World Express
Courier    Courier   Courier
```

Figure 9.4. A class hierarchy

9.1.3 Messages, Methods, Responsibility, Abstraction

Objects communicate through passing messages. A message is a request for performing an operation by some object in the system. A message may consist of the identification of the target object, name of the requested operation and other relevant information for processing the request. An object which originates a message is called the sender and the object which receives a message is called the receiver. An object may send a message to another object or even to itself to perform designed functions. A 'method' is the sequence of steps (or set of operations) to be performed to fulfil the assigned task. There may be many methods available for any task. It is the responsibility of the receiver of the message to choose an appropriate method to complete a task effectively and efficiently. In Figure 9.2, four methods, 'addcourierdetail', 'deletecourier', 'updatecourier' and 'viewstatus' are available for courier class. In order to retrieve the delivery status of the courier, the 'viewstatus' method must be invoked.

Responsibility is an important concept of an object oriented system. Behaviour of an object is described in terms of responsibilities. Fast Track Courier is free to use any method to send the book without our involvement and interference. This type of independence increases the level of abstraction. This improves the independence amongst the objects which is very important for solving any complex problem. The complexity of a problem is managed using the right level of abstraction which is the elimination of the irrelevant and the amplification of the essentials. We learn driving a car by knowing driving essentials like steering wheel, ignition, clutch, break, gear system without knowing any details of the type of engine, batteries, control system, etc. These details may not be required for a learner and may create unnecessary confusion. Hence, abstraction concept provides independence and improves the clarity of the system.

9.1.4 Polymorphism

The dictionary meaning of polymorphism is 'many forms'. In the real world, the same operations may have different meanings in different situations. For example, 'Human' is a sub-class of 'Mammal'. Similarly 'Dog', 'Bird', 'Horse' are also sub-classes of 'Mammal'. If a message 'come fast' is issued to all mammals, all may not behave in the same way. The horse and dog may run, the bird may fly and the human may take an aircraft. The behaviour of mammals is different on the same message. This concept is known as polymorphism, where the same message is sent to different objects irrespective of their class, but the responses of objects may be different. When we abstract the interface of an operation and leave the implementation details to sub-classes, this activity is called polymorphism. This operation is called polymorphic operation. We may create a super class by pulling out important states, behaviours and interfaces of the classes. This may further simplify the complexity of a problem. An object may not need to know the class of another object to whom it wishes to send a message, when we have polymorphism. This may be defined as [JACO98]:

> "Polymorphism means that the sender of a stimulus (message) does not need to know the receiving instance's class. The receiving instance can belong to an arbitrary class."

Polymorphism is considered to be an important concept of any object oriented programming language. As we all know, arithmetic operators such as +, =, - are used to operate on primary data types such as int, float, etc. We may overload these operators so that they may operate in the same way on objects (user defined data types) as they operate on primary data types. Thus, the same operators will have multiple forms.

9.1.5 Encapsulation

Encapsulation is also known as information hiding concept. It is a way in which both data and functions (or operations) that operate on data are combined into a single unit. The only way to access the data is through functions, which operate on the data. The data is hidden from the external world. Hence, it is safe from outside (external) and accidental modifications. For example, any object will have attributes (data) and operations which operate on the specified data only.

If data of any object needs to be modified, it may be done through the specified functions only. The process of encapsulating the data and functions into a single unit simplifies the activities of writing, modifying, debugging and maintaining the program.

In a university, every school may access and maintain its data on its own. One school is not allowed to access the data of another school directly. This is possible only by sending a request to the other school for the data. Hence, the data and functions that operate on the data are specific to each school and are encapsulated into a single unit that is the school of a university.

9.2 WHAT IS OBJECT ORIENTED TESTING?

Object oriented programming concepts are different from conventional programming and have become the preferred choice for a large scale system design. The fundamental entity is the class that provides an excellent structuring mechanism. It allows us to divide a system into well-defined units which may then be implemented separately. We still do unit testing although the meaning of unit has changed. We also do integration and system testing to test the correctness of implementation. We also do regression testing in order to ensure that changes have been implemented correctly. However, many concepts and techniques are different from conventional testing.

9.2.1 What is a Unit?

In conventional programming, a unit is the smallest portion of the program that can be compiled and executed. We may call it a module, component, function or procedure. In object oriented system, we have two options for a unit. We may treat each class as a unit or may treat each method within a class as a unit. If a class is tested thoroughly, it can be reused without being unit tested again. Unit testing of a class with a super class may be impossible to do without the super classes' methods/variables. One of the solutions is to merge the super class and the class under test so that all methods and variables are available. This may solve the immediate testing problem and is called flattening of classes. But classes would not be flattened in the final product, so potential issues may still prevail. We may have to redo flattening after completion when dealing with multiple inheritance. If we decide to choose method as a unit, then these issues will be more complicated and difficult to implement. Generally, classes are selected as a unit for the purpose of unit testing.

9.2.2 Levels of Testing

We may have 3 or 4 levels of testing depending on our approach. The various testing levels are:

(i) Method testing (Unit testing)
(ii) Class testing (Unit testing)
(iii) Inter-class testing (Integration testing)
(iv) System testing

In order to test a class, we may create an instance of the class i.e. object, and pass the appropriate parameters to the constructor. We may further call the methods of the object passing parameters and receive the results. We should also examine the internal data of the object. The encapsulation plays an important role in class testing because data and function (operations) are combined in a class. We concentrate on each encapsulated class during unit testing but each function may be difficult to test independently. Inter-class testing considers the parameter passing issues between two classes and is similar to integration testing. System testing considers the whole system and test cases are generated using functional testing techniques.

Integration testing in object oriented system is also called inter-class testing. We do not have hierarchical control structure in object orientation and thus conventional integration testing techniques like top down, bottom up and sandwich integration cannot be applied. There are three popular techniques for inter-class testing in object oriented systems. The first is the thread based testing where we integrate classes that are needed to respond to an input given to the system. Whenever we give input to a system, one or more classes are required to be executed that respond to that input to get the result. We combine such classes which execute together for a particular input or set of inputs and this is treated as a thread. We may have many threads in a system, depending on various inputs. Thread based testing is easy to implement and has proved as an effective testing technique. The second is the use case based testing where we combine classes that are required by one use case.

The third is the cluster testing where we combine classes that are required to demonstrate one collaboration. In all three approaches, we combine classes on the basis of a concept and execute them to see the outcome. Thread based testing is more popular due to its simplicity and easy implementability.

The advantage of object oriented system is that the test cases can be generated earlier in the process, even when the SRS document is being designed. Early generation of test cases may help the designers to better understand and express requirements and to ensure that specified requirements are testable. Use cases are used to generate a good number of test cases. This process is very effective and also saves time and effort. Developers and testers understand requirements clearly and may design an effective and stable system. We may also generate test cases from the SDD document. Both the teams (testers and developers) may review the SRS and the SDD documents thoroughly in order to detect many errors before coding. However, testing of source code is still a very important part of testing and all generated test cases will be used to show their usefulness and effectiveness. We may also generate test cases on the basis of the availability of the source code.

Path testing, state based testing and class testing are popular object oriented testing techniques and are discussed in subsequent sections.

9.3 PATH TESTING

As discussed earlier, path testing is a structural testing technique where the source code is required for the generation of test cases. In object oriented testing, we also identify paths from the source code and write test cases for the execution of such paths. Most of the concepts of conventional testing such as generating test cases from independent paths are also applicable in object oriented testing.

9.3.1 Activity Diagram

The first step of path testing is to convert source code into its activity diagram. In Unified Modeling Language (UML), activity diagram is used to represent sequences in which all activities are performed. This is similar to a flow graph which is the basis of conventional path testing. Activity diagram may be generated from a use case or from a class. It may represent basic flow and also possible alternative flows. As shown in Figure 9.5, the start state is represented by a solid circle and the end state is represented by a solid circle inside a circle. The activities are represented by rectangles with rounded corners along with their descriptions. Activities are nothing but the set of operations. After execution of these set of activities, a transition takes place to another activity. Transitions are represented by an arrow. When multiple activities are performed simultaneously, the situation is represented by a symbol 'fork'. The parallel activities are combined after the completion of such activities by a symbol 'join'. The number of fork and join in an activity diagram are the same. The branches are used to describe what activities are performed after evaluating a set of conditions. Branches may also be represented as diamonds with multiple labelled exit arrows. A guard condition is a boolean expression and is also written along with branches. An activity diagram consisting of seven activities is shown in Figure 9.5.

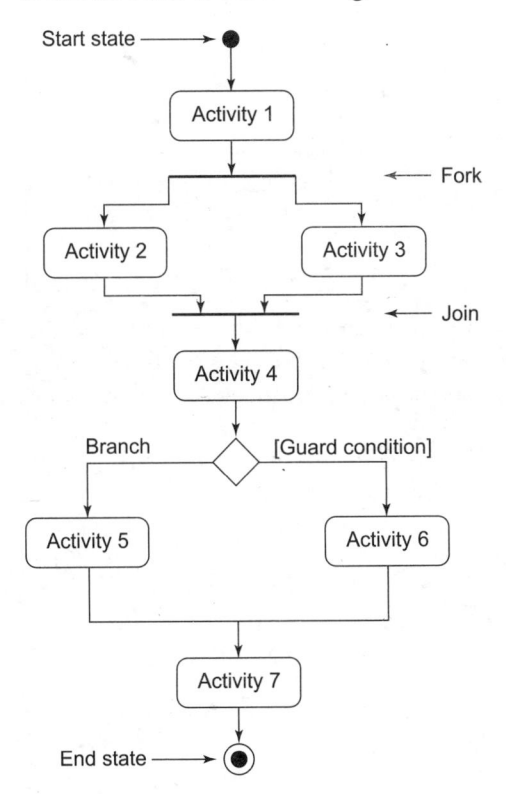

Figure 9.5. An example of an activity diagram

In the activity diagram given in Figure 9.5, Activity 2 and Activity 3 are performed simultaneously and combined by a join symbol. After Activity 4, a decision is represented by a diamond symbol and if the guard condition is true, Activity 5 is performed, otherwise Activity 6 is performed. The fork has one incoming transition (Activity 1 is split into sub-activities) and two outgoing transitions. Similarly join has two incoming transitions and one outgoing transition. The symbols of an activity diagram are given in Table 9.1.

Table 9.1. Symbols of an activity diagram

S. No.	Symbol	Notation	Remarks
1.	Fork		To represent multiple parallel activities i.e. an activity is split into two or more activities.
2.	Join		To represent the combination of two or more parallel activities after completion of respective activities.
3.	Transition	⟶	To represent transfer of flow of control from one activity to another.
4.	Activity	▭	To represent a set of operations known as an activity.
5.	Start	●	To represent start state of an activity diagram.
6.	End	◉	To represent end state of an activity diagram.
7.	Branch	[Guard condition]	To represent the transfer of flow on the basis of evaluation of boolean expression known as guard condition.

An activity diagram represents the flow of activities through the class. We may read the diagram from top to bottom i.e. from start symbol to end symbol. It provides the basis for the path testing where we may like to execute each independent path of the activity diagram at least once.

We consider the program given in Figure 9.6 for determination of division of a student. We give marks in three subjects as input to calculate the division of a student. There are three methods in this program – getdata, validate and calculate. The activity diagram for validate and calculate functions is given in Figure 9.7 and Figure 9.8.

```
#include<iostream.h>
#include<conio.h>

class student
{
int mark1;
int mark2;
int mark3;
public:
void getdata()
{
cout<<"Enter marks of 3 subjects (between 0-100)\n";
cout<<"Enter marks of first subject:";
cin>>mark1;
```

(Contd.)

(*Contd.*)
```
cout<<"Enter marks of second subject:";
cin>>mark2;
cout<<"Enter marks of third subject:";
cin>>mark3;
}
void validate()
{
if(mark1>100||mark1<0||mark2>100||mark2<0||mark3>100||mark3<0){
    cout<<"Invalid Marks! Please try again";
    }
else{
    calculate();
}
}
void calculate();
};

void student::calculate()
{
int avg;
avg=(mark1+mark2+mark3)/3;
if(avg<40) {
    cout<<"Fail";
}
else if(avg>=40&&avg<50){
    cout<<"Third Division";
}
else if(avg>=50&&avg<60){
    cout<<"Second Division";
}
else if(avg>=60&&avg<75){
    cout<<"First Division";
}
else{
    cout<<"First Division with Distinction";
}
}
void main()
{
clrscr();
student s1;
s1.getdata();
s1.validate();
getch();
}
```

Figure 9.6. Program to determine division of a student

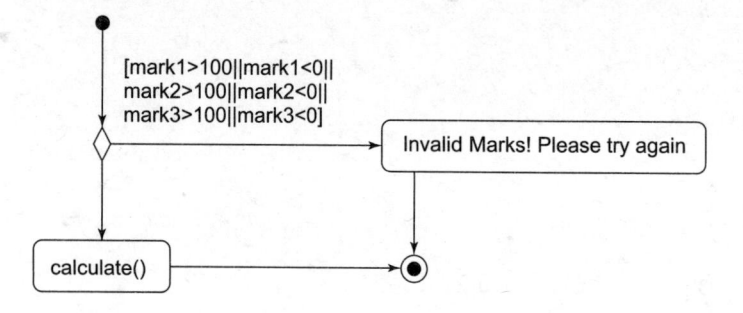

Figure 9.7. Activity diagram of function validate()

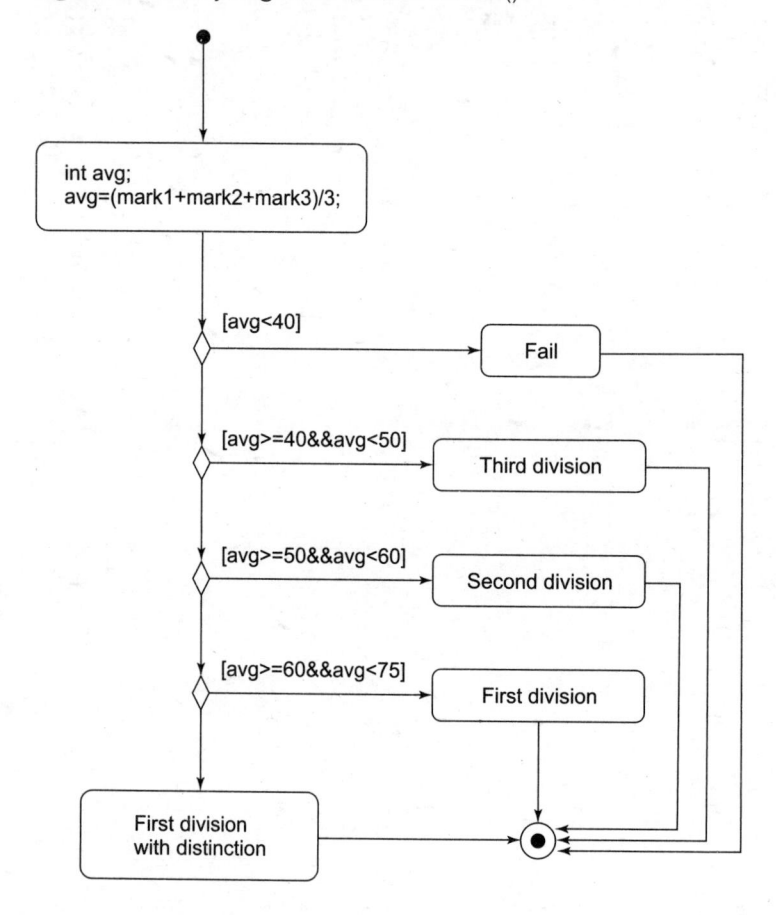

Figure 9.8. Activity diagram of function calculate()

9.3.2 Calculation of Cyclomatic Complexity

As defined earlier in chapter 4, cyclomatic complexity of a graph is given as:

V(G)=e-n+2P

Where e: number of edges of a graph G

n: number of nodes of a graph G

P: number of connected components

The same concepts of a flow graph are applicable to an activity diagram, for the calculation of cyclomatic complexity. Nodes of a flow graph are represented as branches, activities, initial state and end state in an activity diagram. The edges of a flow graph are represented as transitions in the activity diagram. We may calculate the cyclomatic complexity in the same way and cyclomatic complexity of an activity diagram given in Figure 9.5 is 2. Hence, there are two independent paths in the activity diagram.

We consider the activity diagram given in Figure 9.7 for validate function and cyclomatic complexity is calculated as

Cyclomatic complexity = e-n+2P = transitions − activities/branches +2P

$$= 5 - 5 + 2$$
$$= 2$$

Similarly, for activity diagram for calculate function given in Figure 9.8, cyclomatic complexity is:

Cyclomatic complexity = e-n+2P

$$= 15 - 12 + 2$$
$$= 5$$

Hence, there are two and five independent paths of validate and calculate functions, respectively.

9.3.3 Generation of Test Cases

After the identification of independent paths, we may generate test cases that traverse all independent paths at the time of executing the program. This process will ensure that each transition of the activity diagram is traversed at least once.

In general, path testing may detect only errors that result from executing a path in the program. It may not be able to detect the errors due to omissions of some important characteristics of the program. It is heavily dependent on the control structure of the program and if we execute all paths (if possible), an effective coverage is achieved. This effective coverage may contribute to the delivery of good quality maintainable software.

Test cases from activity diagrams of validate and calculate functions (refer to figures 9.7 and 9.8) are shown in Table 9.2 and Table 9.3.

Path testing is very useful in object oriented systems. An activity diagram provides a pictorial view of a class which helps us to identify various independent paths. However, as the size of a class increases, design of an activity diagram becomes complex and difficult. This technique is applicable to the classes of reasonable size.

Table 9.2. Test cases for validate function

Test case	mark1	mark2	mark3	Path
1.	101	40	50	Invalid marks
2.	90	75	75	calculate()

Table 9.3. Test cases for calculate function

Test case	mark1	mark2	mark3	Path
1.	40	30	40	Fail
2.	45	47	48	Third division
3.	55	57	60	Second division
4.	70	65	60	First division
5.	80	85	78	First division with distinction

Example 9.1: Consider the program given in Figure 9.9 for determination of the largest amongst three numbers. There are three methods in this program – getdata, validate and maximum. Design test cases for validate and maximum methods of the class using path testing.

```
#include<iostream.h>
#include<conio.h>
class greatest
{
float A;
float B;
float C;
public:
void getdata()
{
cout<<"Enter number 1:\n";
cin>>A;
cout<<"Enter number 2:\n";
cin>>B;
cout<<"Enter number 3:\n";
cin>>C;
}
void validate()
{
if(A<0||A>400||B<0||B>400||C<0||C>400){
    cout<<"Input out of range";
}
else{
maximum();
}
}
void maximum();
};
void greatest::maximum()
{
/*Check for greatest of three numbers*/
if(A>B) {
if(A>C) {
    cout<<A;
```

```
        }
    else {
        cout<<C;
        }
    }
else {
if(C>B) {
    cout<<C;
    }
else {
    cout<<B;
    }
}
}
void main()
{
clrscr();
greatest g1;
g1.getdata();
g1.validate();
getch();
}
```

Figure 9.9. Program to determine largest among three numbers

Solution:

The activity diagram for validate and calculate functions is given in Figure 9.10 and Figure 9.11 and their test cases are shown in Table 9.4 and Table 9.5.

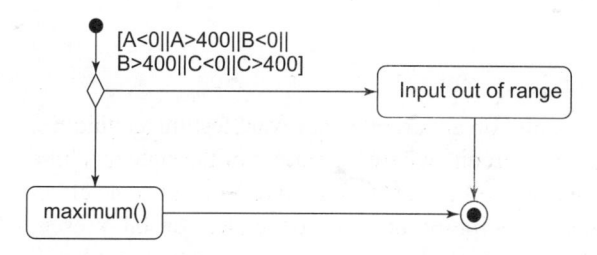

Figure 9.10. Activity diagram for function validate()

Table 9.4. Test cases of activity diagram in Figure 9.10

Test case	A	B	C	Path
1.	500	40	50	Input out of range
2.	90	75	75	maximum()

Cyclomatic complexity = e-n+2P = transitions − activities/branches +2P

$$= 5 - 5 + 2$$
$$= 2$$

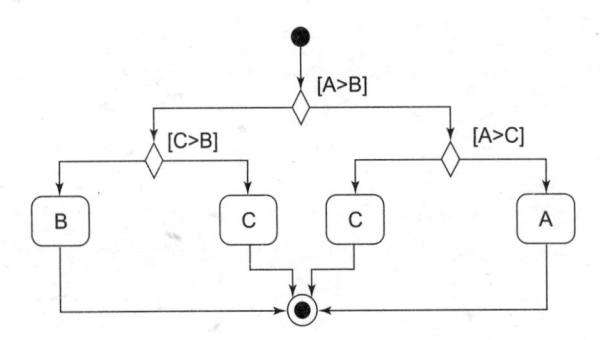

Figure 9.11. Activity diagram for function maximum()

Cyclomatic complexity = e − n + 2P = transitions − activities/branches +2P

11 − 9 + 2 = 4

Table 9.5. Test cases of activity diagram in Figure 9.11

Test case	A	B	C	Expected output
1.	100	87	56	100
2.	87	56	100	100
3.	56	87	100	100
4.	87	100	56	100

9.4 STATE BASED TESTING

State based testing is used as one of the most useful object oriented software testing techniques. It uses the concept of state machine of electronic circuits where the output of the state machine is dependent not only on the present state but also on the past state. A state represents the effect of previous inputs. Hence, in state machine, the output is not only dependent on the present inputs but also on the previous inputs. In electronic circuits, such circuits are called sequential circuits. If the output of a state is only dependent on present inputs, such circuits are called combinational circuits. In state based testing, the resulting state is compared with the expected state.

9.4.1 What is a State Machine?

State machines are used to model the behaviour of objects. A state machine represents various states which an object is expected to visit during its lifetime in response to events or methods along with its responses to these events or methods. A state is represented by rectangles with rounded corners and transitions are represented by edges (arrows). Events and actions are represented by annotations on the directed edges. A typical state machine is shown in Figure 9.12 and descriptions of its associated terms are given in Table 9.6.

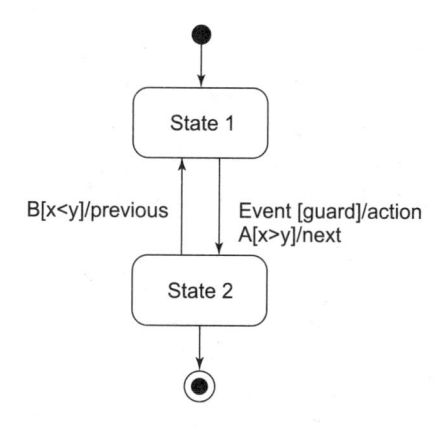

Figure 9.12. A typical state machine diagram

Table 9.6. Terminologies used in state chart diagram

S. No.	Terminologies used in statechart diagram	Description	Remarks
1.	State	Abstract situation in the life cycle of an entity that occurs in response to occurrence of some event.	State1, state2
2.	Event	An input (a message or method call).	A, B
3.	Action	An output or the result of an activity.	Next, previous
4.	Transition	Change of state after occurrence of an event.	When x>y and A is the input, state is changed from state1 to state2
5.	Guard condition	Predicate expression with an event, stating a Boolean restriction for a transition to fire.	Two predicate expressions x>y and x<y

In the Figure 9.12, there are two states – state1 and state2. If at state1, input A is given and (x>y), then state1 is changed to state2 with an output 'next'. At state2, if the input is B and (x<y), then state2 is changed to state1 with an output 'previous'. Hence, a transition transfers a system from one state to another state. The first state is called the accepting state and another is called the resultant state. Both states (accepting and resultant) may also be the same in case of self-loop conditions. The state in question is the current state or present state. Transition occurs from the current state to the resultant state.

We consider an example of a process i.e. program under execution that may have the following states:

» **New:** The process is created
» **Ready:** The process is waiting for the processor to be allocated.
» **Running:** The process is allocated to the processor and is being executed.
» **Time expired:** The time allocated to the process in execution expires.
» **Waiting:** The process is waiting for some I/O or event to occur.
» **Terminated:** The process under execution has completed.

The state machine for life cycle of a process is shown in Figure 9.13. There are six states in the state machine – new, ready, running, time expired, waiting and terminated. The waiting state is decomposed into three concurrent sub-states – I/O operation, child process and interrupt process. The three processes are separated by dashed lines. After the completion of these sub-states the flow of control joins to the ready state.

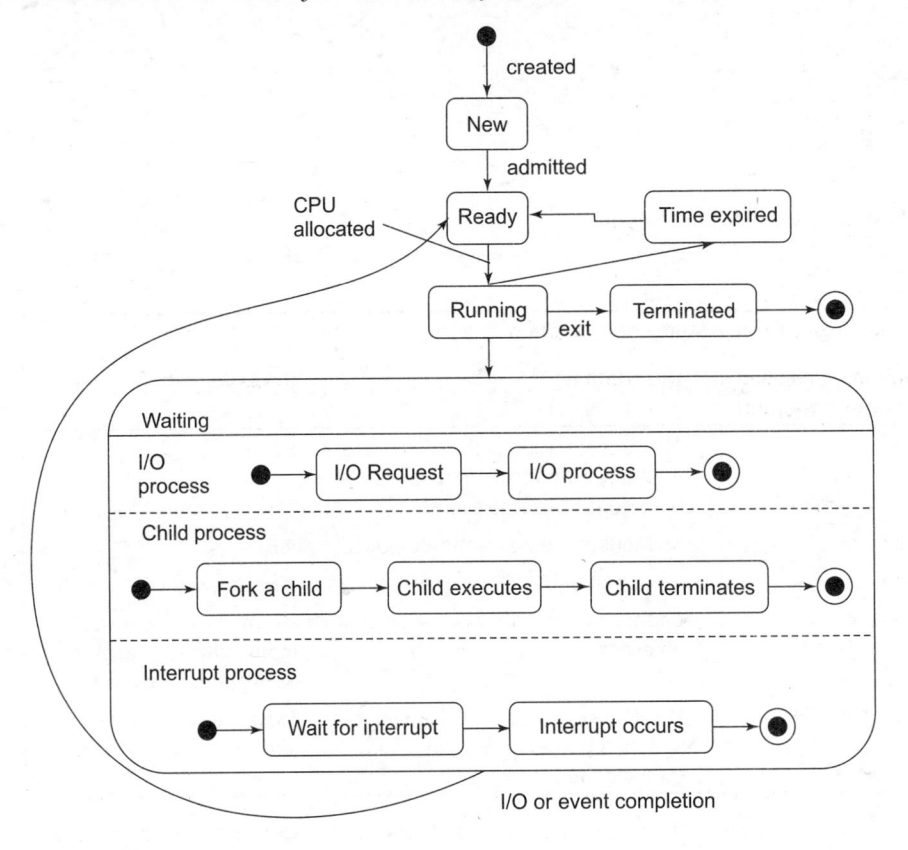

Figure 9.13. Typical life cycle of a process

9.4.2 State Chart Diagram

In Unified Modeling Language (UML), a state machine is graphically represented by a state chart diagram. It shows the flow of control from one state to another state. Here too, states are represented by rectangles with rounded corners and transitions are represented by edges (arrows).

Two special states are used i.e. α (alpha) and ω (omega) state for representing the constructor and destructor of a class. These states may simplify testing of multiple constructors, exception handling and destructors. Binder [BIND99] has explained this concept very effectively as:

> "The α state is a null state representing the declaration of an object before its construction. It may accept only a constructor, new, or a similar initialization message. The ω state is reached after an object has been destructed or deleted, or has gone out of scope. It allows for explicit modeling and systematic testing of destructors, garbage collection, and other termination actions."

Alpha and omega states are different from start state and end state of a state chart diagram. These are additional states to make things more explicit and meaningful.

We consider an example of a class 'stack' where two operations – push and pop, are allowed. The functionality of a stack suggests three states – empty, holding and full. There are four events – new, push, pop and destroy, with the following purposes:

(i) **New:** Creates an empty stack.
(ii) **Push:** Push an element in the stack, if space is available.
(iii) **Pop:** Pop out an element from the stack, if it is available.
(iv) **Destroy:** Destroy the stack after the completion of its requirement i.e. instance of the stack class is destroyed.

The state chart diagram for class stack is given in the Figure 9.14.

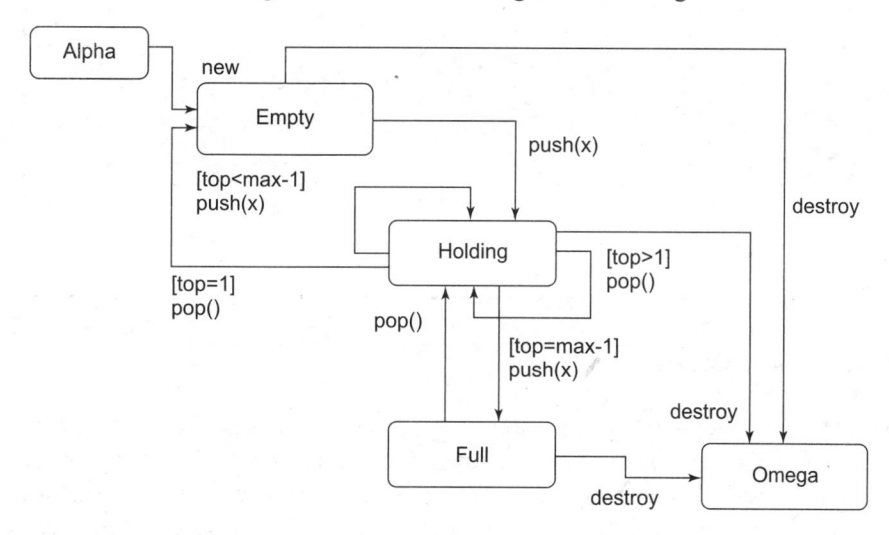

Figure 9.14. State chart diagram for class stack

9.4.3 State Transition Tables

State chart diagrams provide a graphical view of the system and help us to understand the behaviour of the system. Test cases may be designed on the basis of understanding the behaviour. However, drawing a large state chart diagram is difficult, risky and error prone. If states are more than 10 or 15, it is difficult to keep track of various transitions. In practice, we may have to handle systems with 100 states or more. State transition tables are used when the number of states is more these tables and provide information in a compact tabular form. In state transition tables, rows represent the present acceptable state and columns represent the resultant state. The state transition table of a class stack is given in Table 9.7.

State transition tables represent every transition, event and action and may help us to design the test cases.

Table 9.7. State transition table for stack class

State	Event/method	Resultant state				
		Alpha	Empty	Holding	Full	Omega
Alpha	new		√			
	push(x)					
	pop()					
	destroy					
Empty	new					
	push(x)			√		
	pop()					
	destroy					√
Holding	new					
	push(x)			√	√	
	pop()		√	√		
	destroy					√
Full	new					
	push(x)					
	pop()			√		
	destroy					√

9.4.4 Generation of Test Cases

There are many possible testing strategies for the generation of test cases. We may identify paths from the state chart diagram and execute all of them. This seems to be difficult in practice due to a large number of paths. Another option is to exercise all transitions at least once; this may mean all events' coverage, all states' coverage and all actions' coverage. A state chart diagram and state transition tables may help us to do so and we may be able to generate a good number of systematic and planned test cases. The test cases for stack class are given in Table 9.8. Here we generate test cases for each independent path in the state transition diagram given in Figure 9.12. Some illegal transitions are also shown in Table 9.9 in order to give an idea about undesired actions. What will happen if an illegal event is given to a state? These test cases are also important and may help to find faults in the state chart diagram.

Table 9.8. Test cases for class stack

Test case id	Test case input		Expected result	
	Event (method)	Test condition	Action	State
1.1	New			Empty
1.2	Push(x)			Holding
1.3	Pop()	Top=1	Return x	Empty
1.4	destroy			Omega
2.1	New			Empty
2.2	Push(x)			Holding
2.3	Pop()	Top>1	Return x	holding
2.4	destroy			Omega
3.1	New			Empty
3.2	Push(x)	Top<max-1		Holding
3.3	Push(x)			holding
3.4	destroy			Omega
4.1	New			Empty
4.2	Push(x)			Holding
4.3	Push(x)	Top=max-1		Full
4.4	Pop()			Holding
4.5	destroy			Omega
5.1	New			Empty
5.2	Push(x)			Holding
5.3	Push(x)	Top=max-1		Full
5.4	destroy			omega
6.1	New			empty
6.2	destroy			Omega

Table 9.9. Illegal test case for class stack

Test case id	Test condition		Expected result
	Test state	Test event	Action
7.0	Empty	New	Illegal exception
8.0	Empty	Pop()	Illegal exception
9.0	Holding	New	Illegal exception
10.0	Holding	Push (top=max)	Illegal exception
11.0	Holding	Pop (top=0)	Illegal exception
12.0	Full	New	Illegal exception
13.0	Full	Push	Illegal exception
14.0	Omega	any	Illegal exception

Example 9.2: Consider the example of withdrawing cash from an ATM machine. The process consists of the following steps:

(i) The customer will be asked to insert the ATM card and enter the PIN number.
(ii) If the PIN number is valid, the withdrawal transaction will be performed:
   (a) The customer selects amount.
   (b) The system verifies that it has sufficient money to satisfy the request; then the appropriate amount of cash is dispensed by the machine and a receipt is issued.
   (c) If sufficient amount is not available in the account, a message "Balance not sufficient" is issued.
(iii) If the bank reports that the customer's PIN is invalid, then the customer will have to re-enter the PIN.

Draw a Statechart diagram and generate test cases using state based testing.

Solution:

State chart diagram for withdrawal of cash from an ATM machine is shown in Figure 9.15 and test cases are given in Table 9.10.

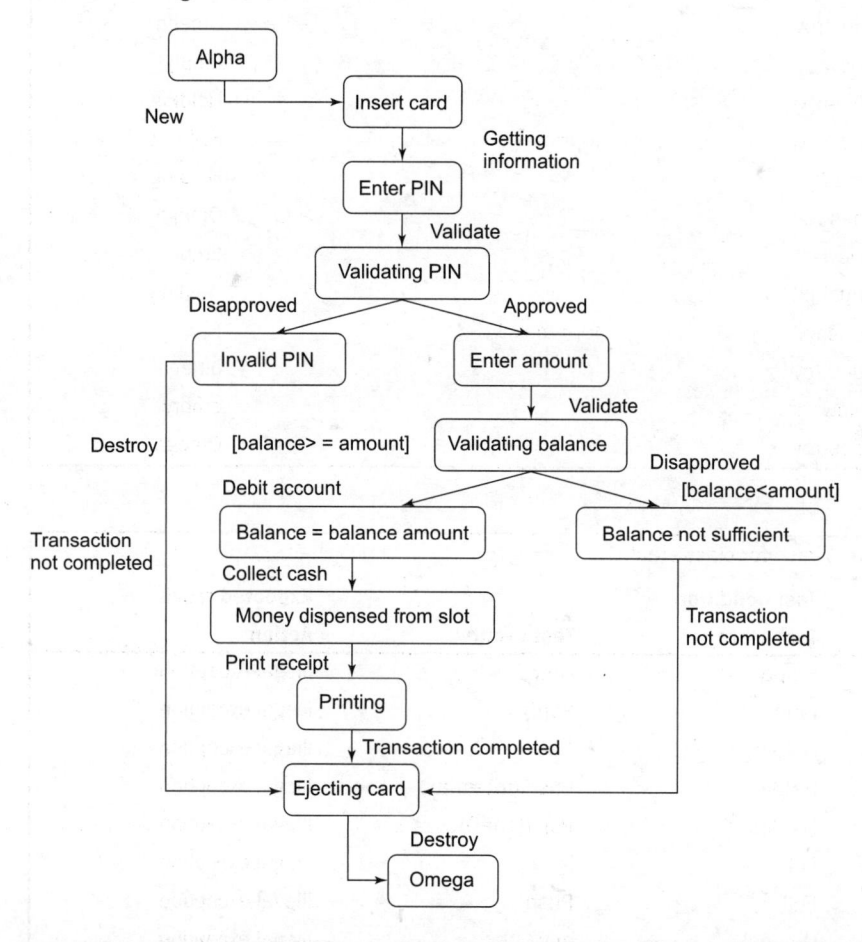

Figure 9.15. State chart diagram of withdrawal from ATM

Table 9.10. Test cases of withdrawal from ATM

Test case ID	Test case input		Expected output	
	Event	Test condition	Action	State
1.1	New			Insert card
1.2	Getting information			Enter pin
1.3	Validate			Validating PIN
1.4	Disapproved			Invalid pin
1.5	Transaction not completed		Collect card	Ejecting card
1.6	Destroy			Omega
2.1	New			Insert card
2.2	Getting information			Enter pin
2.3	Validate			Validating
2.4	Approved			Enter amount
2.5	Validate			Validating balance
2.6	Disapproved	Balance<amount		Balance not sufficient
2.7	Transaction not completed		Collect card	Ejecting card
2.8	Destroy			Omega
3.1	New			Insert card
3.2	Getting information			Enter pin
3.3	Validate			Validating
3.4	Approved			Enter amount
3.5	Validate			Validating balance
3.6	Debit amount	Balance>=amount		Balance=balance-amount
3.7	Collect cash			Money dispensed from slot
3.8	Print receipt		Collect receipt	Printing
3.9	Transaction completed		Collect card	Ejecting card
3.10	Destroy			Omega

9.5 CLASS TESTING

A class is very important in object oriented programming. Every instance of a class is known as an object. Testing of a class is very significant and critical in object oriented testing where we want to verify the implementation of a class with respect to its specifications. If the implementation is as per specifications, then it is expected that every instance of the class may behave in the specified way. Class testing is similar to the unit testing of a conventional system. We require stubs and drivers for testing a 'unit' and sometimes, it may require significant effort. Similarly, classes also cannot be tested in isolation. They may also require additional source code (similar to stubs and drivers) for testing independently.

9.5.1 How Should We Test a Class?

We want to test the source code of a class. Validation and verification techniques are equally applicable to test a class. We may review the source code during verification and may be able to detect a good number of errors. Reviews are very common in practice, but their effectiveness is heavily dependent on the ability of the reviewer(s).

Another type of testing is validation where we may execute a class using a set of test cases. This is also common in practice but significant effort may be required to write test drivers and sometime this effort may be more than the effort of developing the 'unit' under test. After writing test cases for a class, we must design a test driver to execute each of the test cases and record the output of every test case. The test driver creates one or more instances of a class to execute a test case. We should always remember that classes are tested by creating instances and testing the behaviour of those instances [MCGR01].

9.5.2 Issues Related to Class Testing

How should we test a class? We may test it independently, as a unit or as a group of a system. The decision is dependent on the amount of effort required to develop a test driver, severity of class in the system and associated risk with it and so on. If a class has been developed to be a part of a class library, thorough testing is essential even if the cost of developing a test driver is very high.

Classes should be tested by its developers after developing a test driver. Developers are familiar with the internal design, complexities and other critical issues of a class under test and this knowledge may help to design test cases and develop test driver(s). Class should be tested with respect to its specifications. If some unspecified behaviours have been implemented, we may not be able to test them. We should always be very careful for additional functionalities which are not specified. Generally, we should discourage this practice and if it has been implemented in the SRS document, it should immediately be specified. A test plan with a test suite may discipline the testers to follow a predefined path. This is particularly essential when developers are also the testers.

9.5.3 Generating Test Cases

One of the methods of generating test cases is from pre and post conditions specified in the use cases. As discussed in chapter 6, use cases help us to generate very effective test cases. The pre and post conditions of every method may be used to generate test cases for class testing. Every method of a class has a pre-condition that needs to be satisfied before the execution. Similarly, every method of a class has a post-condition that is the resultant state after the execution of the method. Consider a class 'stack' given in Figure 9.16 with two attributes (x and top) and three methods (stack(), push(x), pop()).

```
        Stack
    ─────────────
     x: integer
     top: integer
    ─────────────
     Stack()
     push(x)
     pop()
```

Figure 9.16. Specification for the class stack

We should first specify the pre and post conditions for every operation/method of a class. We may identify requirements for all possible combinations of situations in which a pre-condition can hold and post-conditions can be achieved. We may generate test cases to address what happens when a pre-condition is violated [MCGR01]. We consider the stack class given in Figure 9.16 and identify the following pre and post conditions of all the methods in the class:

(i) Stack::Stack()
    (a) Pre=true
    (b) Post: top=0
(ii) Stack::push(x)
    (a) Pre: top<MAX
    (b) Post: top=top+1
(iii) Stack::pop()
    (a) Pre: top>0
    (b) Post: top=top-1

After the identification of pre and post conditions, we may establish logical relationships between pre and post conditions. Every logical relationship may generate a test case. We consider the push() operation and establish the following logical relationships:

1. (pre condition: top<MAX; post condition: top=top+1)
2. (pre condition: not (top<MAX) ; post condition: exception)

Similarly for pop() operation, the following logical relationships are established:

3. (pre condition: top>0; post condition: top=top-1)
4. (pre condition: not (top>0) ; post condition: exception)

We may identify test cases for every operation/method using pre and post conditions. We should generate test cases when a pre-condition is true and false. Both are equally important to verify the behaviour of a class. We may generate test cases for push(x) and pop() operations (refer Table 9.11 and Table 9.12).

Table 9.11. Test cases of function push()

Test input	Condition	Expected output
23	top<MAX	Element '23' inserted successfully
34	top=MAX	Stack overflow

414 Software Testing

Table 9.12. Test cases of function pop()

Test input	Condition	Expected output
-	top>0	23
-	top=0	Stack underflow

Example 9.3. Consider the example of withdrawing cash from an ATM machine given in example 9.2. Generate test cases using class testing.

Solution:

The class ATMWithdrawal is given in Figure 9.17.

ATMWithdrawal
accountID: integer amount: integer
ATMWithdrawal (accid, amt) Withdraw()

Figure 9.17. Class ATM withdrawal

The pre and post conditions of function Withdraw() are given as:

ATMWirthdrawal::Withdraw()
Pre: true
Post: if(PIN is valid) then
    if (balance>=amount) then
        balance=balance-amount
    else
        Display "Insufficient balance"
  else
    Display "Invalid PIN"
(true, PIN is valid and balance>=amount)
(true, PIN is valid and balance<amount)
(true, PIN is invalid)

Test cases are given in Table 9.13.

Table 9.13. Test cases for function withdraw()

S. No.	AccountID	Amount	Expected output
1.	4321	1000	Balance update/Debit account
2.	4321	2000	Insufficient balance
3.	4322	-	Invalid PIN

MULTIPLE CHOICE QUESTIONS

Note: *Select the most appropriate answer for the following questions.*

9.1 A class has:
  (e) Attributes and operations
  (f) Attributes and states
  (g) Operations and Behaviour
  (h) State and information

9.2 An object is:
  (a) An information of a class
  (b) An instance of a class
  (c) An attribute of a class
  (d) An operation of a class

9.3 The objects of the same class have:
  (a) Different definition for operations and information
  (b) Same definition for operations and information
  (c) Different operations
  (d) Different formats

9.4 All classes inherit information from:
  (a) The lower classes
  (b) The same classes
  (c) The upper classes
  (d) The lower and upper classes

9.5 Encapsulation is known as:
  (a) Information sharing concept
  (b) Information retrieval concept
  (c) Information hiding concept
  (d) Information transfer concept

9.6 A method is:
  (a) The sequence of steps to be performed to fulfil the assigned task
  (b) The set of operations for a particular task
  (c) Both (a) and (b)
  (d) None of the above

9.7 Which is not a defined testing level?
  (a) Method testing
  (b) Class testing
  (c) Interclass testing
  (d) Regression testing

9.8 Which is not a symbol of an activity diagram?
  (a) Join
  (b) Fork
  (c) Operation
  (d) Transition

9.9 An activity diagram represents the flow of activities through the:
   (a) Classes
   (b) Methods
   (c) Objects
   (d) Programs
9.10 Path testing may not be able to detect errors due to:
   (a) Omissions of some characteristics of the program
   (b) Implementation
   (c) Complexity of the code
   (d) None of the above
9.11 In state chart diagrams, transitions are represented by:
   (a) Edges
   (b) States
   (c) Variables
   (d) Circles
9.12 In state chart diagrams, states are represented by:
   (a) Edges
   (b) Rounded rectangles
   (c) Circles
   (d) Arrows
9.13 Guard condition in state chart diagram is:
   (a) Predicate expression with an event
   (b) Regular expression
   (c) Sequential expression
   (d) Last expression
9.14 What is α state?
   (a) Intermediate state
   (b) Null state
   (c) End state
   (d) Initial state
9.15 What is ω state?
   (a) Last state
   (b) Intermediate state
   (c) Start state
   (d) Initial state
9.16 Which is not an object oriented testing technique?
   (a) State based testing
   (b) Class testing
   (c) Equivalence class testing
   (d) Path testing
9.17 Classes are tested by creating:
   (a) Other classes
   (b) Polymorphism
   (c) Class hierarchy
   (d) Instances

9.18 What types of things become objects?
  (a) Real World entities
  (b) Humans
  (c) Humans and animals
  (d) Any living thing
9.19 Classes should be tested by their:
  (a) Customers
  (b) Developers
  (c) Testers
  (d) Managers
9.20 Object orientation is centered around concepts like:
  (a) Objects and classes
  (b) Messages and inheritance
  (c) Polymorphism and encapsulation
  (d) All of the above

EXERCISES

9.1 (a) What is object orientation? How is it close to real life situations? Explain basic concepts which help us to model a real life situation.
   (b) Describe the following terms:
   Messages, Methods, Responsibility, Abstraction
9.2 (a) How is object oriented testing different from procedural testing?
   (b) Discuss the following terms:
      (i) Object
      (ii) Class
      (iii) Message
      (iv) Inheritance
      (v) Polymorphism
9.3 (a) Explain the issues in object oriented testing.
   (b) What are various levels of testing? Which testing level is easy to test and why?
9.4 Explain the testing process for object oriented programs.
9.5 Write the limitations of the basic state model. How are they overcome in state charts?
9.6 What is state based testing? Draw the state machine model for a 'traffic light controller'. What are the limitations of a basic state model? How are they overcome in a state chart?
9.7 What is an activity diagram? What are the basic symbols used in the construction of such diagram? Explain with the help of an example.
9.8 How can we calculate cyclomatic complexity from an activity diagram? What does it signify? What is the relationship of cyclomatic complexity with number of test cases?
9.9 Write a program for finding the roots of a quadratic equation. Draw the activity diagram and calculate the cyclomatic complexity. Generate the test cases on the basis of cyclomatic complexity.

9.10 What is path testing? How can we perform it in object oriented software? Explain the various steps of path testing.

9.11 What is a state chart diagram? Discuss the components of a state chart diagram. Explain with the help of an example.

9.12 Draw the state chart diagram of a 'queue'. Identify the operations of a 'queue' and generate the state transition table. Write test cases from the state transition table.

9.13 What is class testing? What are various issues related to class testing?

9.14 Define a class 'queue'. Identify pre and post conditions of various operations and generate the test cases.

9.15 Write short notes on:
   (a) Class hierarchy
   (b) Inheritance and Polymorphism
   (c) Encapsulation

FURTHER READING

The basic concepts of object-oriented programming in a language independent manner are presented in:

    T. Budd, "An Introduction to Object-Oriented Programming", Pearson Education, India, 1997.

The definitions of object, class, inheritance and aggregation may be read from:

    Edward V. Berard, "Basic Object-Oriented Concepts", http://www.ipipan.gda.pl/~marek/objects/TOA/oobasics/oobasics.html

Booch and his colleagues provide an excellent tutorial on nine diagrams of Unified Modeling Language:

    G. Booch, J. Rumbaugh and I.V. Jacobson., "The Unified Modeling Language User Guide", Addison-Wesley, Boston, 1999.

A useful guide to designing test cases for object-oriented applications. This book provides comprehensive and detailed coverage of techniques to develop testable models from unified Modeling Language and state machines:

    R.V. Binder, "Testing Object Oriented Systems: Models, Patterns and Tools", Addison-Wesley, 1999.

Binder has significantly contributed in the area on object-oriented testing:

    R. Binder, "State-based Testing", Object Magazine, vol. 5, no.4, pp. 75–78, July-Aug, 1995.

    R. Binder, "State-based testing: Sneak paths and Conditional Transitions", Object magazine, vol. 5, no. 6, pp. 87–89, Nov-Dec 1995.

    R. Binder, "Testing Object-Oriented Systems: A Status Report," Released online by RBSC Corporation, 1995. Available at http://stsc.hill.af.mil/crosstalk/1995/April/testinoo.asp.

McGregor and Sykes provide good differences of testing traditional and object-oriented software. They also describe methods for testing of classes:

    J.D. McGregor and David A. Sykes, "A Practical Guide to Testing Object Oriented Software", Addison Wesley, 2001.

A complete bibliographical list on object-oriented testing can be obtained from: http://oo-testing.com/bib/

A study on mutation analysis on object oriented programs can be found in:

Y.S. Ma and Y.R. Kwon, "A Study on Method and Tool of Mutation Analysis for Object Oriented Programs", Software Engineering Review, vol. 15, no. 2, pp. 41–52, 2002.

10

Metrics and Models in Software Testing

How do we measure the progress of testing? When do we release the software? Why do we devote more time and resources for testing a particular module? What is the reliability of software at the time of release? Who is responsible for the selection of a poor test suite? How many faults do we expect during testing? How much time and resources are required for software testing? How do we know the effectiveness of a test suite? We may keep on framing such questions without much effort. However, finding answers to such questions is not easy and may require a significant amount of effort. Software testing metrics may help us to measure and quantify many things which may help us find some answers to such important questions.

10.1 SOFTWARE METRICS

"What cannot be measured cannot be controlled" is a reality in this world. If we want to control something, we should first be able to measure it. Therefore, everything should be measurable. If a thing is not measurable, we should make an effort to make it measurable. The area of measurement is very important in every field and we have mature and establish metrics to quantify various things. However, in software engineering this 'area of measurement' is still in its developing stage and it may require a significant effort to make it mature, scientific and effective.

10.1.1 Measure, Measurement and Metrics

These terms are often used interchangeably. However, we should understand the difference between these terms. Pressman explained this clearly as [PRES05]:

"A measure provides a quantitative indication of the extent, amount, dimension, capacity or size of some attributes of a product or process. Measurement is the act of determining a measure. The metric is a quantitative measure of the degree to which a product or process possesses a given attribute." For example, a measure is the number of failures experienced during testing. Measurement is the way of recording such failures. A software metric may be an average number of failures experienced per hour during testing.

Fenton [FENT04] has defined measurement as:

> "It is the process by which numbers or symbols are assigned to attributes of entities in the real world in such a way as to describe them according to clearly defined rules."

The basic issue is that we want to measure every attribute of an entity. We should have established metrics to do so. However, we are in the process of developing metrics for many attributes of various entities used in software engineering.

Software metrics can be defined as [GOOD93]: "The continuous application of measurement based techniques to the software development process and its products to supply meaningful and timely management information, together with the use of those techniques to improve that process and its products."

Many things are covered in this definition. Software metrics are related to measures which, in turn, involve numbers for quantification. These numbers are used to produce a better product and improve its related process. We may like to measure quality attributes such as testability, complexity, reliability, maintainability, efficiency, portability, enhanceability, usability, etc. for a software. Similarly, we may also like to measure size, effort, development time and resources for a software.

10.1.2 Applications

Software metrics are applicable in all phases of the software development life cycle. In the software requirements and analysis phase, where output is the SRS document, we may have to estimate the cost, manpower requirement and development time for the software. The customer may like to know the cost of the software and development time before signing the contract. As we all know, the SRS document acts as a contract between customer and developer. The readability and effectiveness of the SRS document may help to increase the confidence level of the customer and may provide better foundations for designing the product. Some metrics are available for cost and size estimation like COCOMO, Putnam resource allocation model, function point estimation model, etc. Some metrics are also available for the SRS document like the number of mistakes found during verification, change request frequency, readability, etc. In the design phase, we may like to measure stability of a design, coupling amongst modules, cohesion of a module, etc. We may also like to measure the amount of data input to a software, processed by the software and also produced by the software. A count of the amount of data input to, processed in, and output from the software is called a data structure metric. Many such metrics are available like number of variables, number of operators, number of operands, number of live variables, variable spans, module weakness, etc. Some information flow metrics are also popular like FAN IN, FAN OUT, etc.

Use cases may also be used to design metrics like counting actors, counting use cases, counting the number of links, etc. Some metrics may also be designed for various applications of websites like number of static web pages, number of dynamic web pages, number of internal page links, word count, number of static and dynamic content objects, time taken to search a web page and retrieve the desired information, similarity of web pages, etc. Software metrics have a number of applications during the implementation phase and after the completion of such a phase. Halstead software size measures are applicable after coding like token count, program length, program volume, program level, difficulty, estimation of time and effort, language level, etc. Some complexity measures are also popular like cyclomatic complexity, knot count, feature count, etc. Software metrics have found a good number of applications during testing. One area is the reliability estimation where popular models are Musa's basic execution time model and Logarithmic Poisson execution time model. Jelinski Moranda model [JELI72] is also used for the calculation of reliability. Source code coverage metrics are available that calculate the percentage of source code covered during testing. Test suite effectiveness may also be measured. The number of failures experienced per unit of time, number of paths, number of independent paths, number of du paths, percentage of statement coverage and percentage of branch condition covered are also useful software metrics. The maintenance phase may have many metrics like number of faults reported per year, number of requests for changes per year, percentage of source code modified per year, percentage of obsolete source code per year, etc.

We may find a number of applications of software metrics in every phase of the software development life cycle. They provide meaningful and timely information which may help us to take corrective actions as and when required. Effective implementation of metrics may improve the quality of software and may help us to deliver the software in time and within budget.

10.2 CATEGORIES OF METRICS

There are two broad categories of software metrics, namely, product metrics and process metrics. Product metrics describe the characteristics of the product such as size, complexity, design features, performance, efficiency, reliability, portability, etc. Process metrics describe the effectiveness and quality of the processes that produce the software product. Examples are effort required in the process, time to produce the product, effectiveness of defect removal during development, number of defects found during testing, maturity of the process, etc. [AGGA08].

10.2.1 Product Metrics for Testing

These metrics provide information about the testing status of a software product. The data for such metrics are also generated during testing and may help us to know the quality of the product. Some of the basic metrics are given as:

(i) Number of failures experienced in a time interval
(ii) Time interval between failures
(iii) Cumulative failures experienced up to a specified time
(iv) Time of failure
(v) Estimated time for testing
(vi) Actual testing time

With these basic metrics, we may find some additional metrics as given below:

(i) $\quad \%$ of time spent $= \dfrac{\text{Actual time spent}}{\text{Estimated testing time}} \times 100$

(ii) Average time interval between failures
(iii) Maximum and minimum failures experienced in any time interval
(iv) Average number of failures experienced in time intervals
(v) Time remaining to complete the testing

We may design similar metrics to find the indications about the quality of the product.

10.2.2 Process Metrics for Testing

These metrics are developed to monitor the progress of testing, status of design and development of test cases, and outcome of test cases after execution.
Some of the basic process metrics are given below:

(i) Number of test cases designed
(ii) Number of test cases executed
(iii) Number of test cases passed
(iv) Number of test cases failed
(v) Test case execution time
(vi) Total execution time
(vii) Time spent for the development of a test case
(viii) Total time spent for the development of all test cases

On the basis of the above direct measures, we may design the following additional metrics which may convert the base metric data into more useful information.

(i) % of test cases executed
(ii) % of test cases passed
(iii) % of test cases failed
(iv) Total actual execution time / total estimated execution time
(v) Average execution time of a test case

These metrics, although simple, may help us to know the progress of testing and may provide meaningful information to the testers and the project manager.

An effective test plan may force us to capture data and convert it into useful metrics for both, process and product. This document also guides the organization for future projects and may also suggest changes in the existing processes in order to produce a good quality maintainable software product.

10.3 OBJECT ORIENTED METRICS USED IN TESTING

Object oriented metrics capture many attributes of a software product and some of them are relevant in testing. Measuring structural design attributes of a software system, such as coupling, cohesion or complexity, is a promising approach towards early quality assessments.

There are several metrics available in the literature to capture the quality of design and source code.

10.3.1 Coupling Metrics

Coupling relations increase complexity, reduce encapsulation, potential reuse, and limit understanding and maintainability. Coupling metrics require information about attribute usage and method invocations of other classes. These metrics are given in Table 10.1. Higher values of coupling metrics indicate that a class under test will require a higher number of stubs during testing. In addition, each interface will require to be tested thoroughly.

Table 10.1. Coupling metrics

Metric	Definition	Source
Coupling between Objects (CBO)	CBO for a class is a count of the number of other classes to which it is coupled.	[CHID94]
Data Abstraction Coupling (DAC)	Data Abstraction is a technique of creating new data types suited for an application to be programmed. DAC = number of ADTs defined in a class.	[LI93]
Message Passing Coupling (MPC)	It counts the number of 'send' statements defined in a class.	
Response for a Class (RFC)	It is defined as a set of methods that can be potentially executed in response to a message received by an object of that class. It is given by RFC=|RS|, where RS, the response set of the class, is given by RS = $M_i \cup_{all\ j} \{R_{ij}\}$	[CHID94]
Information flow-based coupling (ICP)	The number of methods invoked in a class, weighted by the number of parameters of the methods invoked.	
Information flow-based inheritance coupling. (IHICP)	Same as ICP, but only counts methods invocations of ancestors of classes.	[LEE95]
Information flow-based non-inheritance coupling (NIHICP)	Same as ICP, but only counts methods invocations of classes not related through inheritance.	
Fan-in	It counts the number of classes that count the given class plus the number of global data elements.	
Fan-out	Count of modules (classes) called by a given module plus the number of global data elements altered by the module (class).	[BINK98]

10.3.2 Cohesion Metrics

Cohesion is a measure of the degree to which the elements of a module are functionally related. The cohesion measure requires information about attribute usage and method invocations within a class. These metrics are summarized in Table 10.2. More cohesiveness is desirable among the methods within a class. In most of the situations, highly cohesive classes are easy to test.

Table 10.2. Cohesion metrics

Metric	Definition	Sources
Lack of Cohesion of Methods (LCOM)	It measures the dissimilarity of methods in a class by looking at the instance variable or attributes used by methods. Consider a class C_1 with n methods $M_1, M_2, ..., M_n$. Let (I_j) = set of all instance variables used by method M_j. There are n such sets $\{I_1\},.......\{I_n\}$. Let $P = \{(I_i, I_j) \| I_i \cap I_j = 0\}$ and $Q = \{((I_i, I_j) \| I_i \cap I_j \neq 0\}$. If all n sets $\{(I_1),.........(I_n)\}$ are 0 then P = 0 LCOM $= \|P\|-\|Q\|$, if $\|P\| > \|Q\|$ = 0 otherwise	[CHID94]
Tight Class Cohesion (TCC)	The measure TCC is defined as the percentage of pairs of public methods of the class with a common attribute usage.	
Loose Class Cohesion (LCC)	In addition to direct attributes, this measure considers attributes indirectly used by a method.	[BEIM95]
Information based Cohesion (ICH)	ICH for a class is defined as the number of invocations of other methods of the same class, weighted by the number of parameters of the invoked method.	[LEE95]

10.3.3 Inheritance Metrics

Inheritance metrics requires information about ancestors and descendants of a class. They also collect information about methods overridden, inherited and added (i.e. neither inherited nor overridden). These metrics are summarized in Table 10.3. If a class has a higher number of children (or sub-classes) more testing may be required in testing the methods of that class. Higher the depth of the inheritance tree, more complex is the design as a larger number of methods and classes are involved. Thus, we may test all the inherited methods of a class and the testing effort will increase accordingly.

Table 10.3. Inheritance metrics

Metric	Definition	Sources
Number of Children (NOC)	The NOC is the number of immediate sub-classes of a class in a hierarchy.	[CHID94]
Depth of Inheritance Tree (DIT)	The depth of a class within the inheritance hierarchy is the maximum number of steps from the class node to the root of the tree and is measured by the number of ancestor classes.	

(Contd.)

(Contd.)

Metric	Definition	Sources
Number of Parents (NOP)	The number of classes that a class directly inherits from (i.e. multiple inheritance).	[LORE94]
Number of Descendants (NOD)	The number of sub-classes (both direct and indirectly inherited) of a class.	
Number of Ancestors (NOA)	The number of super classes (both direct and indirectly inherited) of a class.	[TEGA92]
Number of Methods Overridden (NMO)	When a method in a sub-class has the same name and type signature as in its super class, then the method in the super class is said to be overridden by the method in the sub-class.	
Number of Methods Inherited (NMI)	The number of methods that a class inherits from its super (ancestor) class.	[LORE94]
Number of Methods Added (NMA)	The number of new methods added in a class (neither inherited nor overriding).	

10.3.4 Size Metrics

Size metrics indicate the length of a class in terms of lines of source code and methods used in the class. These metrics are given in Table 10.4. If a class has a larger number of methods with greater complexity, then more test cases will be required to test that class. When a class with a larger number of methods with greater complexity is inherited, it will require more rigorous testing. Similarly, a class with a larger number of public methods will require thorough testing of public methods as they may be used by other classes.

Table 10.4. Size metrics

Metric	Definition	Sources
Number of Attributes per Class (NA)	It counts the total number of attributes defined in a class.	
Number of Methods per Class (NM)	It counts the number of methods defined in a class.	
Weighted Methods per Class (WMC)	The WMC is a count of sum of complexities of all methods in a class. Consider a class K_1, with methods $M_1, \ldots M_n$ that are defined in the class. Let $C_1, \ldots C_n$ be the complexity of the methods. $$WMC = \sum_{i=1}^{n} C_i$$	[CHID94]
Number of public methods (PM)	It counts the number of public methods defined in a class.	
Number of non-public methods (NPM)	It counts the number of private methods defined in a class.	
Lines Of Code (LOC)	It counts the lines in the source code.	

10.4 WHAT SHOULD WE MEASURE DURING TESTING?

We should measure everything (if possible) which we want to control and which may help us to find answers to the questions given in the beginning of this chapter. Test metrics may help us to measure the current performance of any project. The collected data may become historical data for future projects. This data is very important because in the absence of historical data, all estimates are just guesses. Hence, it is essential to record the key information about the current projects. Test metrics may become an important indicator of the effectiveness and efficiency of a software testing process and may also identify risky areas that may need more testing.

10.4.1 Time

We may measure many things during testing with respect to time and some of them are given as:

(i) Time required to run a test case
(ii) Total time required to run a test suite
(iii) Time available for testing
(iv) Time interval between failures
(v) Cumulative failures experienced up to a given time
(vi) Time of failure
(vii) Failures experienced in a time interval

A test case requires some time for its execution. A measurement of this time may help to estimate the total time required to execute a test suite. This is the simplest metric and may estimate the testing effort. We may calculate the time available for testing at any point in time during testing, if we know the total allotted time for testing. Generally a unit of time is seconds, minutes or hours, per test case. The total testing time may be defined in terms of hours. The time needed to execute a planned test suite may also be defined in terms of hours.

When we test a software product, we experience failures. These failures may be recorded in different ways like time of failure, time interval between failures, cumulative failures experienced up to a given time and failures experienced in a time interval. Consider the Table 10.5 and Table 10.6 where time-based failure specification and failure-based failure specification are given:

Table 10.5. Time-based failure specification

S. No. of failure occurrences	Failure time measured in minutes	Failure intervals in minutes
1.	12	12
2.	26	14
3.	35	09
4.	38	03
5.	50	12

(Contd.)

(Contd.)

S. No. of failure occurrences	Failure time measured in minutes	Failure intervals in minutes
6.	70	20
7.	106	36
8.	125	19
9.	155	30
10.	200	45

Table 10.6. Failure-based failure specification

Time in minutes	Cumulative failures	Failures in interval of 20 minutes
20	01	01
40	04	03
60	05	01
80	06	01
100	06	00
120	07	01
140	08	01
160	09	01
180	09	00
200	10	01

These two tables give us an idea about the failure pattern and may help us to define the following:

(i) Time taken to experience 'n' failures
(ii) Number of failures in a particular time interval
(iii) Total number of failures experienced after a specified time
(iv) Maximum / minimum number of failures experienced in any regular time interval.

10.4.2 Quality of Source Code

We may know the quality of the delivered source code after a reasonable time of release using the following formula:

$$QSC = \frac{WD_B + WD_A}{S}$$

Where WD_B: Number of weighted defects found before release
WD_A: Number of weighted defects found after release
S: Size of the source code in terms of KLOC.

The weight for each defect is defined on the basis of defect severity and removal cost. A severity rate is assigned to each defect by testers based on how important or serious the defect is. A lower value of this metric indicates a lower number of errors detected or a lesser number of serious errors detected.

We may also calculate the number of defects per execution test case. This may also be used as an indicator of source code quality as the source code progresses through the series of test activities [STEP03].

10.4.3 Source Code Coverage

We may like to execute every statement of a program at least once before its release to the customer. Hence, the percentage of source code coverage may be calculated as:

$$\% \text{ of source code coverage} = \frac{\text{Number of statements of a source code covered by test suite}}{\text{Total number of statements of a source code}} \times 100$$

Higher the value of this metric, higher the confidence about the effectiveness of a test suite. We should write additional test cases to cover the uncovered portions of the source code.

10.4.4 Test Case Defect Density

This metric may help us to know the efficiency and effectiveness of our test cases.

$$\text{Test case defect density} = \frac{\text{Number of failed test cases}}{\text{Number of executed test cases}} \times 100$$

Where
Failed test case: A test case that when executed, produces an undesired output.
Passed test case: A test case that when executed, produces a desired output.

Higher the value of this metric, higher the efficiency and effectiveness of the test cases because it indicates that they are able to detect a higher number of defects.

10.4.5 Review Efficiency

Review efficiency is a metric that gives an insight on the quality of the review process carried out during verification.

$$\text{Review} = \frac{\text{Total number of defects found during review}}{\text{Total number of project defects}} \times 100$$

Higher the value of this metric, better is the review efficiency.

10.5 SOFTWARE QUALITY ATTRIBUTES PREDICTION MODELS

Software quality is dependent on many attributes like reliability, maintainability, fault proneness, testability, complexity, etc. A number of models are available for the prediction of one or more such attributes of quality. The real benefits of these models are in large scale systems where testing persons are asked to focus their attention and resources on problematic and critical areas of the system.

10.5.1 Reliability Models

Many reliability models for software are available where emphasis is on failures rather than faults. We experience failures during execution of any program. A fault in the program may lead to failure(s) depending upon the input(s) given to a program with the purpose of executing it. Hence, the time of failure and time between failures may help us to find reliability of software. As we all know, software reliability is the probability of failure-free operation of software in a given time under specified conditions. Generally, we consider the calendar time. We may like to know the probability that a given software product will not fail in a time period of one month or one week and so on. However, most of the available models are based on execution time. The execution time is the time for which the computer actually executes the program. Reliability models based on execution time normally give better results than those based on calendar time. In many cases, we have a mapping table that converts execution time to calendar time for the purpose of reliability studies. In order to differentiate both the timings, execution time is represented by τ and calendar time by t.

Most of the reliability models are applicable at system testing level. Whenever the software fails, we note the time of failure and also try to locate and correct the fault that caused the failure. During system testing, the software may not fail at regular intervals and may also not follow a particular pattern. The variation in time between successive failures may be described in terms of following functions:

- $\mu(\tau)$: average number of failures up to time τ
- $\lambda(\tau)$: average number of failures per unit time at time τ and is known as failure intensity function.

It is expected that the reliability of a program increases due to fault detection and correction over time and hence the failure intensity decreases accordingly.

(i) **Basic Execution Time Model**

This is one of the popular models of software reliability assessment and was developed by J.D. MUSA [MUSA79] in 1979. As the name indicates, it is based on execution time (τ). The basic assumption is that failures may occur according to a Non-Homogeneous Poisson Process (NHPP) during testing. Many examples may be given for real world events where poisson processes are used. A few examples are given as:

(i) Number of users using a website in a given period of time
(ii) Number of persons requesting for railway tickets in a given period of time
(iii) Number of e-mails expected in a given period of time

The failures during testing represent a non-homogeneous process and the failure intensity decreases as a function of time. J.D. Musa assumed that the decrease in failure intensity as a function of the number of failures observed is constant and is given as:

$$\lambda(\mu) = \lambda_o \left(1 - \frac{\mu}{V_o}\right)$$

Where
    λ_o: Initial failure intensity at the start of testing
    V_o: Total number of failures experienced up to infinite time
    μ: Number of failures experienced up to a given point in time

Musa [MUSA79] has also given the relationship between failure intensity (λ) and the mean failures experienced (μ) and is given in Figure 10.1.

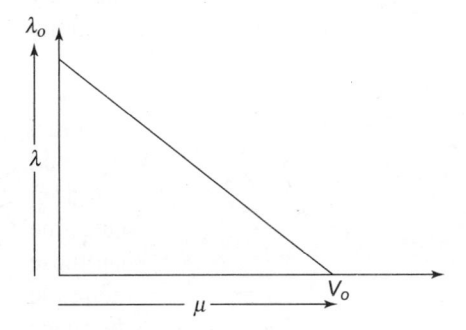

Figure 10.1. λ as a function of μ

If we take the first derivative of the equation given above, we get the slope of the failure intensity as given below:

$$\frac{d\lambda}{d\mu} = -\frac{\lambda_o}{V_o}$$

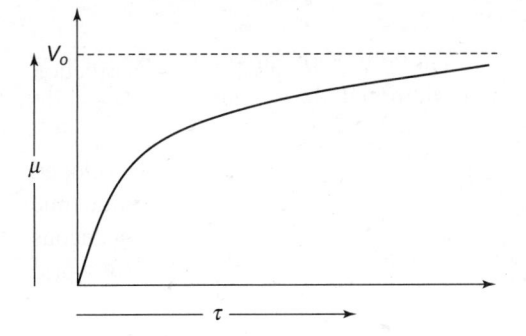

Figure 10.2. Relationship between τ and μ

The negative sign shows that there is a negative slope indicating a decrementing trend in failure intensity.

This model also assumes a uniform failure pattern meaning thereby equal probability of failures due to various faults. The relationship between execution time (τ) and mean failures experienced (μ) is given in Figure 10.2.

The derivation of the relationship of Figure 10.2 may be obtained as:

$$\frac{d\mu(\tau)}{d\tau} = \lambda_o \left(1 - \frac{\mu(\tau)}{V_o}\right)$$

$$\mu(\tau) = V_o \left(1 - \exp\left(-\frac{\lambda_o \tau}{V_o}\right)\right)$$

The failure intensity as a function of time is given in Figure 10.3.

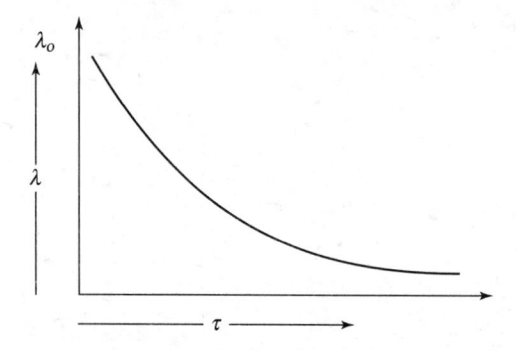

Figure 10.3. Relationship between λ and τ

This relationship is useful for calculating the present failure intensity at any given value of execution time. We may find this relationship as:

$$\lambda(\tau) = \lambda_o \exp\left(-\frac{\lambda_o \tau}{V_o}\right)$$

Two additional equations are given to calculate additional failures required to be experienced ($\Delta\mu$) to reach a failure intensity objective (λ_F) and additional time required to reach the objective ($\Delta\tau$). These equations are given as:

$$\Delta\mu = \frac{V_o}{\lambda_o}(\lambda_P - \lambda_F)$$

$$\Delta\tau = \frac{V_o}{\lambda_o} \ln\left(\frac{\lambda_P}{\lambda_F}\right)$$

Where

$\Delta\mu$: Expected number of additional failures to be experienced to reach failure intensity objective.

$\Delta\tau$: Additional time required to reach the failure intensity objective.

λ_P: Present failure intensity
λ_F: Failure intensity objective

$\Delta\mu$ and $\Delta\tau$ are very interesting metrics to know the additional time and additional failures required to achieve a failure intensity objective.

Example 10.1 A program will experience 100 failures in infinite time. It has now experienced 50 failures. The initial failure intensity is 10 failures/hour. Use the basic execution time model for the following:

(i) Find the present failure intensity.
(ii) Calculate the decrement of failure intensity per failure.
(iii) Determine the failure experienced and failure intensity after 10 and 50 hours of execution.
(iv) Find the additional failures and additional execution time needed to reach the failure intensity objective of 2 failures/hour.

Solution:

(a) The present failure intensity can be calculated using the following equation:

$$\lambda(\mu) = \lambda_O\left(1 - \frac{\mu}{V_O}\right)$$

$V_O = 100$ failures
$\mu = 50$ failures
$\lambda_O = 10$ failures/hour

Hence $\lambda(\mu) = 10\left(1 - \frac{50}{100}\right)$

$= 5$ failures/hour

(b) Decrement of failure intensity per failure can be calculated using the following:

$$\frac{d\lambda}{d\mu} = -\frac{\lambda_O}{V_O}$$

$$= -\frac{10}{100} = -0.1/\text{hour}$$

(c) Failures experienced and failure intensity after 10 and 50 hours of execution can be calculated as:

$$\lambda(\tau) = \lambda_o \exp\left(-\frac{\lambda_o \tau}{V_o}\right)$$

(i) After 10 hours of execution:

$$\mu(\tau) = 100\left(1 - \exp\left(-\frac{10 \times 50}{100}\right)\right)$$

$$= 100(1-\exp(-5))$$
$$= 99 \text{ failures}$$

$$\lambda(\tau) = \lambda_O \exp\left(-\frac{\lambda_O \tau}{V_O}\right)$$
$$= 10 \exp\left(-\frac{10 \times 50}{100}\right)$$
$$= 10 \exp(-5)$$
$$= 0.067 \text{ failures/hour}$$

(ii) After 50 hours of execution:
$$\mu(\tau) = 100\left(1-\exp\left(-\frac{10 \times 10}{100}\right)\right)$$
$$= 100(1-\exp(-1))$$
$$= 63 \text{ failures}$$

$$\lambda(\tau) = \lambda_O \exp\left(-\frac{\lambda_O \tau}{V_O}\right)$$
$$= 10 \exp\left(-\frac{10 \times 10}{100}\right)$$
$$= 10 \exp(-1)$$
$$= 3.68 \text{ failures/hour}$$

(c) $\Delta \mu$ and $\Delta \tau$ with failure intensity objective of 2 failures/hour:

$$\Delta \mu = \frac{V_o}{\lambda_o}(\lambda_P - \lambda_F)$$
$$= \frac{100}{10}(5-2) = 30 \text{ failures}$$

$$\Delta \tau = \frac{V_o}{\lambda_o} \ln\left(\frac{\lambda_P}{\lambda_F}\right)$$
$$= \frac{100}{10}\left(\ln\left(\frac{5}{2}\right)\right) = 9.16 \text{ hours}$$

(iv) **Logarithmic Poisson Execution time model**

With a slight modification in the failure intensity function, Musa presented a logarithmic poisson execution time model. The failure intensity function is given as:

$$\lambda(\mu) = \lambda_o \exp(-\theta \mu)$$

Where
θ: Failure intensity decay parameter which represents the relative change of failure intensity per failure experienced.

The slope of failure intensity is given as:

$$\frac{d\lambda}{d\mu} = -\lambda_o \theta \exp(-\mu\theta)$$

$$\frac{d\lambda}{d\mu} = -\theta\lambda$$

The expected number of failures for this model is always infinite at infinite time. The relation for mean failures experienced is given as:

$$\mu(\tau) = \frac{1}{\theta}\ln(\lambda_o \theta \tau + 1)$$

The expression for failure intensity with respect to time is given as:

$$\lambda(\tau) = \frac{\lambda_o}{(\lambda_o \theta \tau + 1)}$$

The relationship for an additional number of failures and additional execution time are given as:

$$\Delta\mu = \frac{1}{\theta}\ln\left(\frac{\lambda_P}{\lambda_F}\right)$$

$$\Delta\tau = \frac{1}{\theta}\left(\frac{1}{\lambda_F} - \frac{1}{\lambda_P}\right)$$

When execution time is more, the logarithmic poisson model may give larger values of failure intensity than the basic model.

Example 10.2: The initial failure intensity of a program is 10 failures/hour. The program has experienced 50 failures. The failure intensity decay parameter is 0.01/failure. Use the logarithmic poisson execution time model for the following:

(a) Find present failure intensity.
(b) Calculate the decrement of failure intensity per failure.
(c) Determine the failure experienced and failure intensity after 10 and 50 hours of execution.
(d) Find the additional failures and additional failure execution time needed to reach the failure intensity objective of 2 failures/hour.

Solution:

(a) Present failure intensity can be calculated as:

$$\lambda(\mu) = \lambda_o \exp(-\theta\mu)$$

λ_o = 50 failures

μ = 50 failures

θ = 0.01/failures

Hence $\lambda_o(\mu) = 10\exp(-50 \times 0.01)$

$ = 6.06$ failures/hour

(b) Decrement of failure intensity per failure can be calculated as:

$$\frac{d\lambda}{d\mu} = -\theta\lambda$$

$$= -0.01 \times 6.06$$

$$= -0.06$$

(c) Failure experienced and failure intensity after 10 and 50 hours of execution can be calculated as:

$$\mu(\tau) = \frac{1}{\theta}\ln(\lambda_o\theta\tau + 1)$$

$$\lambda(\tau) = \frac{\lambda_o}{(\lambda_o\theta\tau + 1)}$$

(i) After 10 hours of execution:

$$\mu(\tau) = \frac{1}{0.01}\ln(10 \times 0.01 \times 10 + 1)$$

$$= \frac{1}{0.01}\ln(2) = 69 \text{ failures}$$

$$\lambda(\tau) = \frac{10}{(10 \times 0.01 \times 10 + 1)} = \frac{10}{2} = 5 \text{ failures/hour}$$

(ii) After 50 hours of execution:

$$\mu(\tau) = \frac{1}{0.01}\ln(10 \times 0.01 \times 50 + 1)$$

$$= \frac{1}{0.01}\ln(6) = 179 \text{ failures}$$

$$\lambda(\tau) = \frac{10}{(10 \times 0.01 \times 50 + 1)} = \frac{10}{6} = 1.66 \text{ failures/hour}$$

(d) $\Delta\mu$ and $\Delta\tau$ with failure intensity objective of 2 failures/hour:

$$\Delta\mu = \frac{1}{\theta}\ln\left(\frac{\lambda_P}{\lambda_F}\right)$$

$$= \frac{1}{0.01}\ln\left(\frac{6.06}{2}\right) = 110 \text{ failures}$$

$$\Delta\tau = \frac{1}{\theta}\left(\frac{1}{\lambda_F} - \frac{1}{\lambda_P}\right)$$

$$= \frac{1}{0.01}\left(\frac{1}{2} - \frac{1}{6.06}\right) = 33.5 \text{ hours}$$

(iii) The Jelinski – Moranda Model

The Jelinski – Moranda model [JELI72] is the earliest and simplest software reliability model. It proposed a failure intensity function in the form of:

$$\lambda(t) = \phi(N - i + 1)$$

Where ϕ : Constant of proportionality

N : total number of errors present

i : number of errors found by time interval t_i.

This model assumes that all failures have the same failure rate. It means that the failure rate is a step function and there will be an improvement in reliability after fixing an error. Hence, every failure contributes equally to the overall reliability. Here, failure intensity is directly proportional to the number of errors remaining in a software.

Once we know the value of failure intensity function using any reliability model, we may calculate reliability using the equation given below:

$$R(t) = e^{-\lambda t}$$

Where λ is the failure intensity and t is the operating time. Lower the failure intensity, higher is the reliability and vice versa.

Example 10.3: A program may experience 200 failures in infinite time of testing. It has experienced 100 failures. Use Jelinski-Moranda model to calculate failure intensity after the experience of 150 failures.

Solution:

Total expected number of failures (N) = 200
Failures experienced (i) =100
Constant of proportionality (ϕ) = 0.02
We know

$$\lambda(t) = \phi(N - i + 1)$$
$$= 0.02(200 - 100 + 1)$$
$$= 2.02 \text{ failures/hour}$$

After 150 failures:

$$\lambda(t) = 0.02(200 - 150 + 1)$$
$$= 1.02 \text{ failures/hour}$$

Failure intensity will decrease with every additional failure experienced.

10.5.2 An Example of Fault Prediction Model in Practice

It is clear that software metrics can be used to capture the quality of object oriented design and source code. These metrics provide ways to evaluate the quality of software and their use in earlier phases of software development can help organizations in assessing a large software development quickly, at a low cost.

To achieve help for planning and executing testing by focusing resources on the fault-prone parts of the design and source code, the model used to predict faulty classes should be used. The fault prediction model can also be used to identify classes that are prone to have severe faults. One can use this model with respect to high severity of faults to focus the testing on those parts of the system that are likely to cause serious failures. In this section, we describe models used to find relationship between object oriented metrics and fault proneness, and how such models can be of great help in planning and executing testing activities [MALH09, SING10].

In order to perform the analysis, we used public domain KC1 NASA data set [NASA04]. The data set is available on www.mdp.ivv.nasa.gov. The 145 classes in this data were developed using C++ language.

The goal of our analysis is to explore empirically the relationship between object oriented metrics and fault proneness at the class level. Therefore, fault proneness is the binary dependent variable and object oriented metrics (namely WMC, CBO, RFC, LCOM, DIT, NOC and SLOC) are the independent variables. Fault proneness is defined as the probability of fault detection in a class. We first associated defects with each class according to their severities. The value of severity quantifies the impact of the defect on the overall environment with 1 being most severe to 5 being least severe. Faults with severity rating 1 were classified as high severity faults. Faults with severity rating 2 were classified as medium severity faults and faults with severity rating 3, 4 and 5 as low severity faults as at severity rating 4 no class was found to be faulty and at severity rating 5, only one class was faulty. Table 10.7 summarizes the distribution of faults and faulty classes at high, medium and low severity levels in the KC1 NASA data set after pre-processing of faults in the data set.

Table 10.7. Distribution of faults and faulty classes at high, medium and low severity levels

Level of severity	Number of faulty classes	% of faulty classes	Number of faults	% of Distribution of faults
High	23	15.56	48	7.47
Medium	58	40.00	449	69.93
Low	39	26.90	145	22.59

The 'min', 'max', 'mean', 'median', 'std dev', '25% quartile' and '75% quartile' for all metrics in the analysis are shown in Table 10.8.

Table 10.8. Descriptive statistics for metrics

Metric	Min.	Max.	Mean	Median	Std. Dev.	Percentile (25%)	Percentile (75%)
CBO	0	24	8.32	8	6.38	3	14
LCOM	0	100	68.72	84	36.89	56.5	96
NOC	0	5	0.21	0	0.7	0	0
RFC	0	222	34.38	28	36.2	10	44.5
WMC	0	100	17.42	12	17.45	8	22
LOC	0	2313	211.25	108	345.55	8	235.5
DIT	0	6	1	1	1.26	0	1.5

The low values of DIT and NOC indicate that inheritance is not much used in the system. The LCOM metric has high values. Table 10.9 shows the correlation among metrics, which is an important static quantity.

Table 10.9. Correlations among metrics

Metric	CBO	LCOM	NOC	RFC	WMC	LOC	DIT
CBO	1						
LCOM	0.256	1					
NOC	−0.03	−0.028	1				
RFC	0.386	0.334	−0.049	1			
WMC	0.245	0.318	0.035	0.628	1		
LOC	0.572	0.238	−0.039	0.508	0.624	1	
DIT	0.4692	0.256	−0.031	0.654	0.136	0.345	1

The correlation coefficients shown in bold are significant at 0.01 level. WMC, LOC, DIT metrics are correlated with RFC metric. Similarly, the WMC and CBO metrics are correlated with LOC metric. Therefore, it shows that these metrics are not totally independent and represent redundant information.

The next step of our analysis found the combined effect of object oriented metrics on fault proneness of class at various severity levels. We obtained from four multivariate fault prediction models using LR method. The first one is for high severity faults, the second one is for medium severity faults, the third one is for low severity faults and the fourth one is for ungraded severity faults.

We used multivariate logistic regression approach in our analysis. In a multivariate logistic regression model, the coefficient and the significance level of an independent variable represent the net effect of that variable on the dependent variable – in our case fault proneness. Tables 10.10, 10.11, 10.12 and 10.13 provide the coefficient (B), standard error (SE), statistical significance (sig), odds ratio (exp(B)) for metrics included in the model.

Two metrics – CBO and SLOC were included in the multivariate model for predicting high severity faults. CBO, LCOM, NOC, SLOC metrics were included in the multivariate model for predicting medium severity faults. Four metrics – CBO, WMC, RFC and SLOC were included in the model predicted with respect to low severity faults. Similarly, CBO, LCOM, NOC, RFC, SLOC metrics were included in the ungraded severity model.

Table 10.10. High severity faults model statistics

Metric	B	S.E.	Sig.	Exp(B)
CBO	0.102	0.033	0.002	1.107
SLOC	0.001	0.001	0.007	1.001
Constant	−2.541	0.402	0.000	0.079

Table 10.11. Medium severity faults model statistics

Metric	B	S.E.	Sig.	Exp(B)
CBO	0.190	0.038	0.0001	1.209
LCOM	−0.011	0.004	0.009	0.989
NOC	−1.070	0.320	0.001	0.343
SLOC	0.004	0.002	0.006	1.004
Constant	−0.307	0.340	0.367	0.736

Table 10.12. Low severity faults model statistics

Metric	B	S.E.	Sig.	Exp(B)
CBO	0.167	0.041	0.001	1.137
RFC	−0.034	0.010	0.001	0.971
WMC	0.047	0.018	0.028	1.039
SLOC	0.003	0.001	0.001	1.003
Constant	−1.447	0.371	0.005	0.354

Table 10.13. Ungraded severity faults model statistics

Metric	B	S.E.	Sig.	Exp(B)
CBO	0.195	0.040	0.0001	1.216
LCOM	−0.010	0.004	0.007	0.990
NOC	−0.749	0.199	0.0001	0.473
RFC	−0.016	0.006	0.006	0.984
SLOC	0.007	0.002	0.0001	1.007
Constant	0.134	0.326	0.680	1.144

To validate our findings we performed a 10-cross validation of all the models. For the 10-cross validation, the classes were randomly divided into 10 parts of approximately equal size (9 partitions of 15 data points each and one partition of 10 data points).

The performance of binary prediction models is typically evaluated using confusion matrix (see Table 10.14). In order to validate the findings of our analysis, we used the commonly used evaluation measures – sensitivity, specificity, completeness, precision and ROC analysis.

Table 10.14. Confusion matrix

Observed	Predicted	
	1.00 (Fault-Prone)	0.00 (Not Fault-Prone)
1.00 (Fault-Prone)	True Fault Prone (TFP)	False Not Fault Prone (FNFP)
0.00 (Not Fault-Prone)	False Fault Prone (FFP)	True Not Fault Prone (TNFP)

Precision

It is defined as the ratio of number of classes correctly predicted to the total number of classes.

$$\text{Precision} = \frac{TFP + TNFP}{TFP + FNFP + FFP + TNFP}$$

Sensitivity

It is defined as the ratio of the number of classes correctly predicted as fault prone to the total number of classes that are actually fault prone.

$$\text{Recall} = \frac{TFP}{TFP + FNFP}$$

Completeness

Completeness is defined as the number of faults in classes classified fault-prone, divided by the total number of faults in the system.

Receiver Operating Characteristics (ROC) Curve

The performance of the outputs of the predicted models was evaluated using ROC analysis. The ROC curve, which is defined as a plot of sensitivity on the y-co-ordinate versus its 1-specificity on the x co-ordinate, is an effective method of evaluating the quality or performance of predicted models [EMAM99]. While constructing ROC curves, we selected many cut-off points between 0 and 1 and calculated sensitivity and specificity at each cut-off point. The optimal choice of the cut-off point (that maximizes both sensitivity and specificity) can be selected from the ROC curve [EMAM99]. Hence, by using the ROC curve one can easily determine the optimal cut-off point for a model. The area under the ROC Curve (AUC) is a combined measure of sensitivity and specificity. In order to compute the accuracy of the predicted models, we use the area under the ROC curve.

We summarized the results of cross validation of predicted models via the LR approach in Table 10.15.

Table 10.15. Results of 10-cross validation of models

	Model I	Model II	Model III	Model IV
Cutoff	0.25	0.77	0.49	0.37
Sensitivity	64.60	70.70	61.50	69.50
Specificity	66.40	66.70	64.20	68.60
Precision	66.21	68.29	63.48	68.96
Completeness	59.81	74.14	71.96	79.59
AUC	0.686	0.754	0.664	0.753
SE	0.044	0.041	0.053	0.039

The ROC curve for the LR model with respect to the high, medium, low and ungraded severity of faults is shown in Figure 10.4.

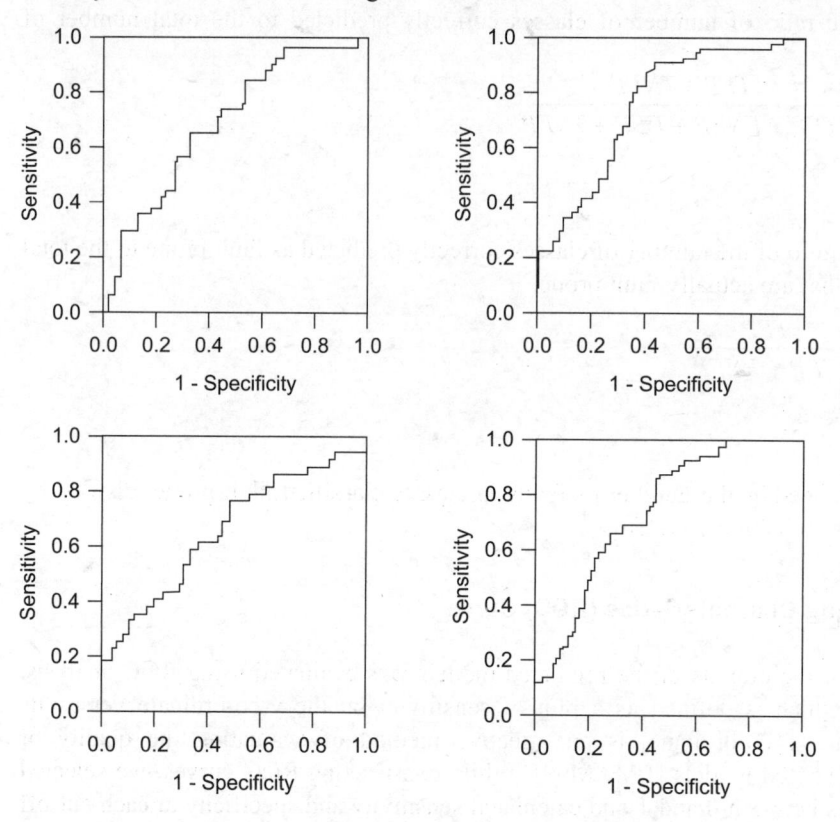

Figure 10.4. ROC curve for (a) Model I (b) Model II (c) Model III (d) Model IV using LR method

Based on the findings from this analysis, we can use the SLOC and CBO metrics in earlier phases of the software development to measure the quality of the systems and predict which classes with higher severity need extra attention. This can help the management focus resources on those classes that are likely to cause serious failures. Also, if required, developers can reconsider design and thus take corrective actions. The models predicted in the previous section could be of great help for planning and executing testing activities. For example, if one has the resources available to inspect 26 percent of the code, one should test 26 percent classes predicted with more severe faults. If these classes are selected for testing, one can expect maximum severe faults to be covered.

10.5.3 Maintenance Effort Prediction Model

The cost of software maintenance is increasing day by day. The development may take 2 to 3 years, but the same software may have to be maintained for another 10 or more years. Hence, maintenance effort is becoming an important factor for software developers. The obvious question is "how should we estimate maintenance effort in early phases of software development life cycle?" The estimation may help us to calculate the cost of software maintenance, which a customer may like to know as early as possible in order to plan the costing of the project.

Maintenance effort is defined as the number of lines of source code added or changed during the maintenance phase. A model has been used to predict maintenance effort using Artificial Neural Network (ANN) [AGGA06, MALH09]. This is a simple model and predictions are quite realistic. In this model, maintenance effort is used as a dependent variable. The independent variables are eight object oriented metrics namely WMC, CBO, RFC, LCOM, DIT, NOC, DAC and NOM. The model is trained and tested on two commercial software products – User Interface Management System (UIMS) and Quality Evaluation System (QUES), which are presented in [LI93]. The UIMS system consists of 39 classes and the QUES system consists of 71 classes.

The ANN network used in model prediction belongs to Multilayer Feed Forward networks and is referred to as M-H-Q network with M source nodes, H nodes in hidden layer and Q nodes in the output layer. The input nodes are connected to every node of the hidden layer but are not directly connected to the output node. Thus, the network does not have any lateral or shortcut connection.

Artificial Neural Network (ANN) repetitively adjusts different weights so that the difference between the desired output from the network and actual output from ANN is minimized. The network learns by finding a vector of connection weights that minimizes the sum of squared errors on the training data set. The summary of ANN used in the model for predicting maintenance effort is shown in Table 10.16.

Table 10.16. ANN summary

Architecture	
Layers	3
Input Units	8
Hidden Units	9
Output Units	1
Training	
Transfer Function	Tansig
Algorithm	Back Propagation
Training Function	TrainBR

The ANN was trained by the standard error back propagation algorithm at a learning rate of 0.005, having the minimum square error as the training stopping criterion.

The main measure used for evaluating model performance is the Mean Absolute Relative Error (MARE). MARE is the preferred error measure for software measurement researchers and is calculated as follows [FINN96]:

$$\text{MARE} = \left(\sum_{i=1}^{n} \left| \frac{estimate - actual}{actual} \right| \right) \div n$$

Where:
- estimate is the predicted output by the network for each observation
- n is the number of observations

To establish whether models are biased and tend to over or under estimate, the Mean Relative Error (MRE) is calculated as follows [FINN96]:

$$MRE = \left(\sum_{i=1}^{n} \frac{estimate - actual}{actual} \right) \div n$$

We use the following steps in model prediction:

(i) The input metrics are normalized using min-max normalization. Min-max normalization performs a linear transformation on the original data. Let's assume that minA and maxA are the minimum and maximum values of an attribute A. It maps value v of A to v' in the range 0 to 1 using the formula:

$$v' = \frac{v - \min_A}{\max_A - \min_A}$$

(ii) Perform principal components (P.C) analysis on the normalized metrics to produce domain metrics.
(iii) We divide data into training, test and validate sets using 3:1:1 ratio.
(iv) Develop ANN model based on training and test data sets.
(v) Apply the ANN model to validate data set in order to evaluate the accuracy of the model.

The P.C. extraction analysis and varimax rotation method is applied on all metrics. The rotated component matrix is given in Table 10.17. Table 10.17 shows the relationship between the original object oriented metrics and the domain metrics. The values above 0.7 (shown in bold in Table 10.17) are the metrics that are used to interpret the PCs. For each PC, we also provide its eigenvalue, variance percent and cumulative percent. The interpretations of PCs are given as follows:

- P1: DAC, LCOM, NOM, RFC and WMC are cohesion, coupling and size metrics. We have size, coupling and cohesion metrics in this dimension. This shows that there are classes with high internal methods (methods defined in the class) and external methods (methods called by the class). This means cohesion and coupling is related to a number of methods and attributes in the class.
- P2: MPC is a coupling metric that counts the number of 'send' statements defined in a class.
- P3: NOC and DIT are inheritance metrics that count the number of children and depth of inheritance tree in a class.

Table 10.17. Rotated principal components

P.C.	P1	P2	P3
Eigenvalue	3.74	1.41	1.14
Variance %	46.76	17.64	14.30

(Contd.)

(Contd.)

P.C.	P1	P2	P3
Cumulative %	46.76	64.40	78.71
DAC	0.796	0.016	0.065
DIT	-0.016	-0.220	-0.85
LCOM	0.820	-0.057	-0.079
MPC	0.094	0.937	0.017
NOC	0.093	-0.445	0.714
NOM	0.967	-0.017	0.049
RFC	0.815	0.509	-0.003
WMC	0.802	0.206	0.184

We employed the ANN technique to predict the maintenance effort of the classes. The inputs to the network were all the domain metrics P1, P2 and P3. The network was trained using the back propagation algorithm. Table 10.16 shows the best architecture, which was experimentally determined. The model is trained using training and test data sets and evaluated on validation data set. Table 10.18 shows the MARE, MRE, r and p-value results of the ANN model evaluated on validation data. The correlation of the predicted change and the observed change is represented by the coefficient of correlation (r). The significant level of a validation is indicated by a p-value. A commonly accepted p-value is 0.05.

Table 10.18. Validation results of ANN model

MARE	0.265
MRE	0.09
r	0.582
p-value	0.004

Table 10.19. Analysis of model evaluation accuracy

ARE Range	Percent
0-10%	50
11-27%	9.09
28-43%	18.18
>44%	22.72

For validation data set, the percentage error smaller than 10 per cent, 27 per cent and 55 per cent is shown in Table 10.19. We conclude that the impact of prediction is valid in the population. Figure 10.5 plots the predicted number of lines added or changed versus the actual number of lines added or changed.

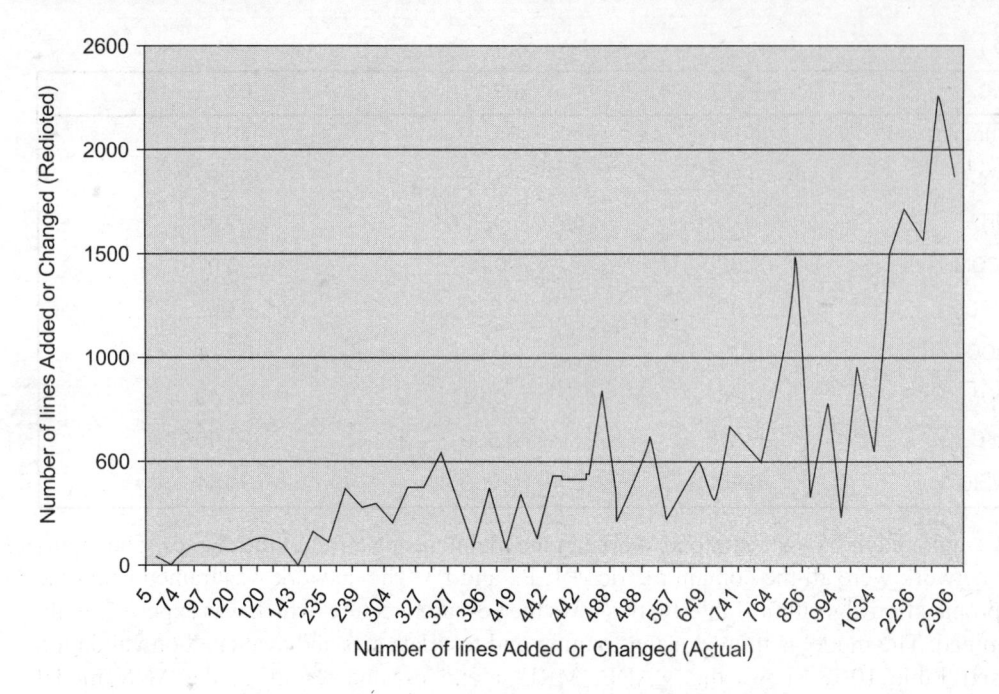

Figure 10.5. Comparison between actual and predicted values for maintenance effort

Software testing metrics are one part of metrics studies that focus on the testing issues of processes and products. Test suite effectiveness, source code coverage, defect density and review efficiency are some of the popular testing metrics. Testing efficiency may also be calculated using size of software tested/resources used. We should also have metrics to provide immediate, real time feedback to testers and project manager on quality of testing during each test phase rather waiting until the release of the software.

There are many schools of thought about the usefulness and applications of software metrics. However, every school of thought accepts the old quote of software engineering i.e. "You cannot improve what you cannot measure; and you cannot control what you cannot measure." In order to control and improve various activities, we should have 'something' to measure such activities. This 'something' differs from one school of thought to another school of thought. Despite different views, most of us feel that software metrics help to improve productivity and quality. Software process metrics are widely used in various standards and models such as Capability Maturity Model for Software (CMM-SW) and ISO9001. Every organization is putting serious efforts to implement these metrics.

MULTIPLE CHOICE QUESTIONS

Note: *Select the most appropriate answer for the following questions.*

10.1 One fault may lead to:
 (a) One failure
 (b) Two failures
 (c) Many failures
 (d) All of the above

10.2 Failure occurrences can be represented as:
   (a) Time to failure
   (b) Time interval between failures
   (c) Failure experienced in a time interval
   (d) All of the above

10.3 What is the maximum value of reliability?
   (a) 0
   (b) 1
   (c) 100
   (d) None of the above

10.4 What is the minimum value of reliability?
   (a) 0
   (b) 1
   (c) 100
   (d) None of the above

10.5 As the failure intensity decreases, reliability:
   (a) Increases
   (b) Decreases
   (c) Has no effect
   (d) None of the above

10.6 Basic and logarithmic execution time models were developed by:
   (a) Victor Baisili
   (b) J.D. Musa
   (c) R. Binder
   (d) B. Littlewood

10.7 Which is not a cohesion metric?
   (a) Lack of cohesion in methods
   (b) Tight class cohesion
   (c) Response for a class
   (d) Information flow based cohesion

10.8 Which is not a size metric?
   (a) Number of attributes per class
   (b) Number of methods per class
   (c) Number of children
   (d) Weighted methods per class

10.9 Choose an inheritance metric:
   (a) Number of children
   (b) Response for a class
   (c) Number of methods per class
   (d) Message passing coupling

10.10 Which is not a coupling metric?
   (a) Coupling between objects
   (b) Data abstraction coupling
   (c) Message passing coupling
   (d) Number of children

10.11 What can be measured with respect to time during testing?
   (a) Time available for testing
   (b) Time to failure
   (c) Time interval between failures
   (d) All of the above

10.12 NHPP stands for
   (a) Non-Homogeneous Poisson Process
   (b) Non-Heterogeneous Poisson Process
   (c) Non-Homogeneous Programming Process
   (d) Non-Hetrogeneous Programming Process

10.13 Which is not a test process metric?
   (a) Number of test cases designed
   (b) Number of test cases executed
   (c) Number of failures experienced in a time interval
   (d) Number of test cases failed

10.14 Which is not a test product metric?
   (a) Time interval between failures
   (b) Time to failure
   (c) Estimated time for testing
   (d) Test case execution time

10.15 Testability is dependent on:
   (a) Characteristics of the representation
   (b) Characteristics of the implementation
   (c) Built in test capabilities
   (d) All of the above

10.16 Which of the following is true?
   (a) Testability is inversely proportional to complexity
   (b) Testability is directly proportional to complexity
   (c) Testability is equal to complexity
   (d) None of the above

10.17 Cyclomatic complexity of source code provides:
   (a) An upper limit for the number of test cases needed for the code coverage criterion
   (b) A lower limit for the number of test cases needed for the code coverage criterion
   (c) A direction for testing
   (d) None of the above

10.18 Higher is the cyclomatic complexity:
   (a) More is the testing effort
   (b) Less is the testing effort
   (c) Infinite is the testing effort
   (d) None of the above

10.19 Which is not the object oriented metric given by Chidamber and Kemerer?
   (a) Coupling between objects
   (b) Lack of cohesion of methods
   (c) Response for a class
   (d) Number of branches in a tree

10.20 Precision is defined as:
   (a) Ratio of number of classes correctly predicted to the total number of classes
   (b) Ratio of number of classes wrongly predicted to the total number of classes
   (c) Ratio of total number of classes to the classes wrongly predicted
   (d) None of the above
10.21 Sensitivity is defined as:
   (a) Ratio of number of classes correctly predicted as fault prone to the total number of classes
   (b) Ratio of number of classes correctly predicted as fault prone to the total number of classes that are actually fault prone
   (c) Ratio of faulty classes to total number of classes
   (d) None of the above
10.22 Reliability is measured with respect to:
   (a) Effort
   (b) Time
   (c) Faults
   (d) Failures
10.23 Choose an event where poisson process is not used:
   (a) Number of users using a website in a given time interval
   (b) Number of persons requesting for railway tickets in a given period of time
   (c) Number of students in a class
   (d) Number of e-mails expected in a given period of time
10.24 Choose a data structure metric:
   (a) Number of live variables
   (b) Variable span
   (c) Module weakness
   (d) All of the above
10.25 Software testing metrics are used to measure:
   (a) Progress of testing
   (b) Reliability of software
   (c) Time spent during testing
   (d) All of the above

EXERCISES

10.1 What is software metric? Why do we need metrics in software? Discuss the areas of applications and problems during implementation of metrics.
10.2 Define the following terms:
   (a) Measure
   (b) Measurement
   (c) Metrics
10.3 (a) What should we measure during testing?
   (b) Discuss things which can be measured with respect to time
   (c) Explain any reliability model where emphasis is on failures rather than faults.

10.4 Describe the following metrics:
   (a) Quality of source code
   (b) Source code coverage
   (c) Test case defect density
   (d) Review efficiency
10.5 (a) What metrics are required to be captured during testing?
   (b) Identify some test process metrics
   (c) Identify some test product metrics
10.6 What is the relationship between testability and complexity? Discuss the factors which affect the software testability.
10.7 Explain the software fault prediction model. List out the metrics used in the analysis of the model. Define precision, sensitivity and completeness. What is the purpose of using Receiver Operating Characteristics (ROC) curve?
10.8 Discuss the basic model of software reliability. How can we calculate $\Delta\mu$ and $\Delta\tau$?
10.9 Explain the logarithmic poisson model and find the values of $\Delta\mu$ and $\Delta\tau$.
10.10 Assume that initial failure intensity is 20 failures / CPU hour. The failure intensity decay parameter is 0.05 / failure. We assume that 50 failures have been experienced. Calculate the current failure intensity.
10.11 Assume that the initial failure intensity is 5 failures / CPU hour. The failure intensity decay parameter is 0.01 / failure. We have experienced 25 failures up to this time. Find the failures experienced and failure intensity after 30 and 60 CPU hours of execution.
10.12 Explain the Jelinski – Moranda model of reliability theory. What is the relationship between 'λ' and 't'?
10.13 A program is expected to have 500 faults. The assumption is that one fault may lead to one failure. The initial failure intensity is 10 failures / CPU hour. The program is released with a failure intensity objective of 6 failures / CPU hour. Calculate the number of failures experienced before release.
10.14 Assume that a program will experience 200 failures in infinite time. It has now experienced 100 failures. The initial failure intensity was 10 failures / CPU hour.
   (a) Determine the present failure intensity
   (b) Calculate failures experienced and failure intensity after 50 and 100 CPU hours of execution.
   Use the basic execution time model for the above calculations.
10.15 What is software reliability? Does it exist? Describe the following terms:
   (i) MTBF
   (ii) MTTF
   (iii) Failure intensity
   (iv) Failures experienced in a time interval

FURTHER READING

An in-depth study of 18 different categories of software complexity metrics was provided by Zuse, where he tried to give the basic definition for metrics in each category:

> H. Zuse, "Software Complexity: Measures and Methods", Walter De Gryter, Berlin 1990.

Fenton's book is a classic and useful reference, and it gives a detailed discussion on measurement and key definition of metrics:

> N. Fenton and S. Pfleeger, "Software Metrics: A rigorous & Practical Approach", PWS Publishing Company, Boston, 1997.

A detailed description on software reliability and contributions from many of the leading researchers may be found in Lyu's book:

> M. Lyu, "Handbook of Software Reliability Engineering", IEEE Computer Press, 1996.

Aggarwal presents a good overview of software reliability models. Musa provides a detailed description particularly on software reliability models:

> J.D. Musa, A. Lannino, and K. Okumoto "Software Reliability: Measurement, Prediction and Applications", Mc Graw Hill, New York, 1987.
>
> K.K. Aggarwal, "Reliability Engineering", Kluwer, New Delhi, India, 1993.

The first significant OO design metrics suite was proposed by Chidamber and Kemerer in 1991. Then came another paper by Chidamber and Kemerer defining and validating metrics suite for OO design in 1994. This metrics suite has received the widest attention in empirical studies:

> S. Chidamber, and C. Kamerer, "A Metrics Suite for Object-Oriented Design", IEEE Transactions on Software Engineering, vol. 20, no. 6, pp. 476–493, 1994.

More detailed accounts on our fault prediction models at various severity levels of faults can be found in:

> Y. Singh, A. Kaur, R. Malhotra, "Empirical Validation of Object-Oriented Metrics for Predicting Fault Proneness Models", Software Quality Journal, vol. 18, no. 1, pp.3–35, 2010.

There are several books on research methodology and statistics with their applications:

> C.R. Kothari, "Research Methodology: Methods and Techniques", New Delhi, New Age International Limited, 2004.
>
> W.G. Hopkins, "A New View of Statistics", Sport science, 2003.

For a detailed account of the statistics needed for model prediction using logistic regression (notably how to compute maximum likelihood estimates, R^2, significance values) see the following text book and research paper:

> D. Hosmer, and S. Lemeshow, "Applied Logistic Regression", New York: John Wiley & Sons, 1989.
>
> V. Basili, L. Briand, and W. Melo, "A Validation of Object-Oriented Design Metrics as Quality Indicators", IEEE Transactions on Software Engineering, vol. 22, no. 10, pp. 751–761, 1996.

Khoshgaftaar et al. introduced the use of the Artificial Neural Networks as a tool for predicting software quality. They presented a large telecommunication system, classifying modules as fault prone or not fault prone:

> T.M. Khoshgaftaar, E.D. Allen, J.P. Hudepohl, S.J. Aud, "Application of Neural Networks to Software Quality Modeling of a Very Large Telecommunications System", IEEE Transactions on Neural Networks, vol. 8, no. 4, pp. 902–909, July 1997.

For full details on ROC analysis and cross validation methods see the publications:

> J. Hanley, BJ. McNeil, "The Meaning and Use of the Area under a Receiver Operating Characteristic ROC Curve", Radiology, vol. 143, pp. 29–36, April 1982.
>
> M. Stone, "Cross-Validatory Choice and Assessment of Statistical Predictions", J. Royal Stat. Soc., vol. 36, pp. 111–147, 1974.

A workshop on Empirical Studies of Software Development and Evolution (ESSDE) was conducted in Los Angeles in May 1999. The authors (well-known and leading researchers) present in this workshop summarized the state of art and future directions regarding empirical studies in object oriented systems:

> L. Briand, E. Arisholm, S. Counsell, F. Houdek, P. Thévenod-Fosse, "Empirical Studies of Object-Oriented Artifacts, Methods, and Processes: State of the Art and Future Directions", *Empirical Software Engineering: An International Journal*, 2000.

Briand and Wüst performed a critical review of existing work on quality models in object-oriented Systems:

> L. Briand and J. Wüst, "Empirical Studies of Quality Models in Object-Oriented Systems", Advances in Computers, 2002.

A recent paper examining the confounding effect of the relationship between Object Oriented metrics and change proneness is published in IEEE Transactions on Software Engineering:

> Y. Zhou, H. Leung and B. Xu, "Examining the Potentially Confounding Effect of Class Size on the Associations between Object-Oriented Metrics and Change-Proneness", IEEE Transactions on Software Engineering, vol. 35, no. 5, pp. 607–623, September/October 2009.

11

Testing Web Applications

Web pages and websites have become an integral part of modern civilization. Everyday a new website for some specific application is hosted and joins the bandwagon of the Internet. We may visit a website and may find a good number of web pages designed for specific applications. The quality of a web application must be assured in terms of response time, ease of use, number of users, ability to handle varied spikes in traffic, provide accurate information, etc. Compromise in any of these parameters may compel the customers to move on to the competitor's site. Testing these web pages is a real challenge because conventional testing techniques may not be directly applicable.

11.1 WHAT IS WEB TESTING?

The main challenge of testing a web application is not only to find common software errors, but also to test associated quality related risks that are specific to a web application. We should know the architecture and key areas of web application to effectively plan and execute the testing.

11.1.1 Web Application versus Client Server Application

In client-server architecture, the client program is installed on each client machine that provides user interface. The clients are connected to a server machine which serves the client by providing requested information. In client-server architecture the functionality of an application is distributed between the client and a server. For example, business logic may reside on a server machine, user interface may reside on the client machine and database may reside on either client machine or the server. Business logic is procedures that are to be followed by an application based on inputs given by the user. This architecture is known as two-tier client-server architecture as shown in Figure 11.1. Any upgrade at the server side would require upgrading of client software that has been installed on all client machines.

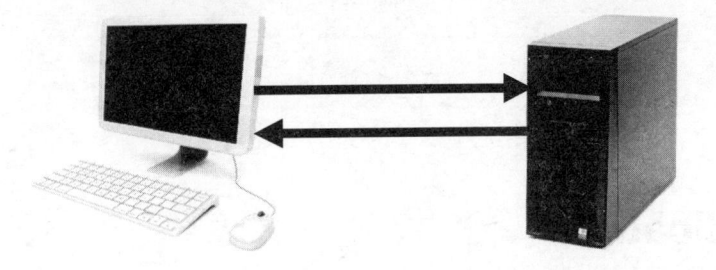

Figure 11.1. Two-tier architecture of client-server application

A web application may consist of multiple web servers and database servers. These applications need only web browser to be installed on the client machine. The web browser is a software programme that retrieves, interprets and presents information to the client in the desirable format. A web application depicts a three-tier architecture shown in Figure 11.2. It comprises of client machines, web server incorporating business logic and database server for handing data storage.

In three-tier architecture, the applications are partitioned into three separate layers; hence changes in one tier do not have any effect on the other tier. The advantages of three-tier architecture include less disk space required at the client machine, automatic up gradation of software and robustness. A comparison between client-server application and web application is given in Table 11.1.

The client application may comprise of many active contents written in Java script, VBscript, DHTML and other technologies. Web servers use dynamic technology (ASP, JSP, Perl, CGI, Python) to render the active content. This may invoke incompatibility issues due to existence of varied browsers.

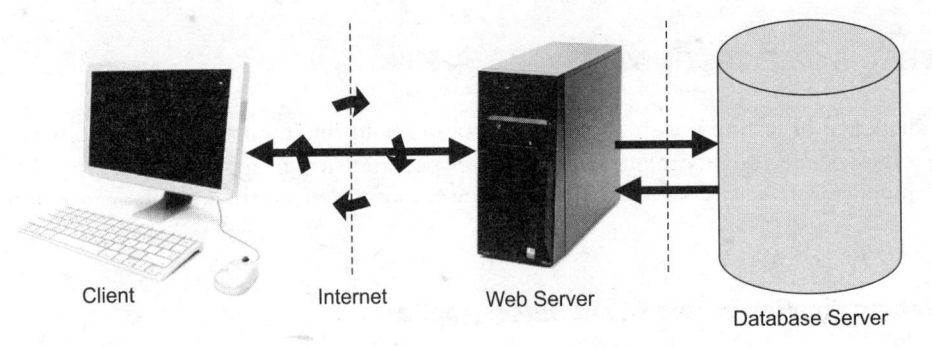

Figure 11.2. Three-tier architecture of web based applications

Table 11.1. Comparison of client/server and web based applications

S. No.	Client/Server Applications	Web based Applications
1.	It is a 2-tier application.	It is a 3-tier application.
2.	Additional software needs to be installed.	No additional software needs to be installed; only a web browser is required.

(Contd.)

(Contd.)

S. No.	Client/Server Applications	Web based Applications
3.	It is an expansive activity.	It is cheaper as compared to client/server application.
4.	It supports a limited number of users.	It supports an unlimited number of users.
5.	Users are well-known.	Any user can login and access the content.
6.	Manageable security issues.	Security issues are critical and complex in nature.
7.	It is less robust as if one server fails, the client request cannot be fulfilled.	It is more robust as compared to client/server application.
8.	More resources are required on the client side.	Fewer resources are needed on the client side.

For example, if a student wants to know his/her final result, the following steps may be followed (see Figure 11.3):

(i) The student requests the client application (with web browser installed).
(ii) The client application sends the request to the web server.
(iii) The web server (incorporating business logic) queries the database server.
(iv) The database server returns the student's marks in all the subjects.
(v) The web server performs all calculations to generate the final marks.
(vi) The web server returns the final marks to the client application.
(vii) The client application displays the final marks to the student.

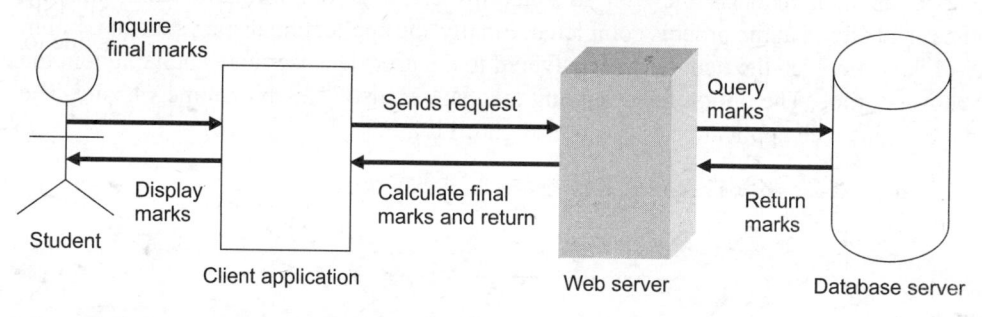

Figure 11.3. Web application process

Popularity of the internet has increased the usage of three-tier architecture. Testing such an application is very important and specialized techniques may be used to ensure the correct operation. Non-functional requirements like usability, performance, compatibility, security, etc. need to be tested thoroughly to ensure the expected quality level of any web application.

11.1.2 Key Areas in Testing Web Applications

What are the key areas that need to be addressed in a web application? Web applications are difficult and complex as compared to traditional client-server applications. They are required to be tested on different browsers and varied platforms. It is important and critical to identify the areas that need special focus while testing a web application. A web application needs to be tested for:

456 Software Testing

(i) Functionality
(ii) Usability
(iii) Browser compatibility
(iv) Security
(v) Load and stress
(vi) Storage and Database

There are numerous issues that need to be considered that are specific to web application, hence, only a sub-set of conventional testing techniques are applicable for testing a web application.

11.2 FUNCTIONAL TESTING

Functional testing involves checking of the specified functionality of a web application. The functional testing techniques are presented in chapter 2. Functional test cases for web applications may be generated using boundary value analysis, equivalence class testing, decision table testing and many other techniques. Table 11.2 presents some sample functional test cases of the order process form of an online shopping website. This example of eCommerce application sells products such as computers, mobile phones, cameras, electronics, etc. For each item it lists the name, quality, price and brief description. It also displays an image of the item. The user may browse through the product and search any product by its name, price or any other descriptive keyword. The user is required to register on the website to obtain access to the online shopping cart (a common tool used by users to place an order online).

The user selects various items and adds them to the shopping cart. After selecting items and adding those to the shopping cart, the user may choose to checkout in order to generate a bill. The application then requests the user to enter his credit card information and shipping preferences and after that the order is completed. Finally, the application displays the maximum number of days in which the item will be delivered to the user. The user may enquire about the order status any time. The option for providing feedback is also available on the website. The home page of this web application is given in Figure 11.4.

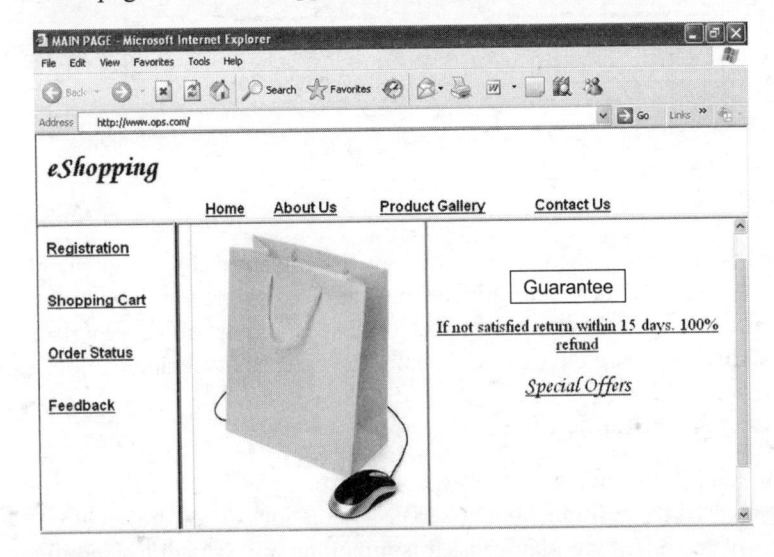

Figure 11.4. Homepage of online shopping web application

In Table 11.2 test cases corresponding to addition, deletion and updation in the online shopping cart are presented.

Table 11.2. Sample functional test cases of order process of an online shopping web application

Test case id	Description (steps followed)	Inputs	Expected output
TC1	1. Search the product gallery to decide which items to purchase.	Search string	List of items searched are displayed.
TC2	1. Register on the website to place an order	Login id, password, confirm password, shipping details (address, city, state, zip code) and billing details (address, city, state, zip code).	If the information entered is valid the user is registered successfully, otherwise an appropriate error message is displayed.
TC3	1. Log into the website.	Login id, password	Item is successfully added in the shopping cart.
	2. Select item to be purchased and its quantity.	Item number, item name, quantity	
	3. Add selected item to the shopping cart.	-	
TC4	1. Log into the website.	Login id, password	Item is not added in the shopping cart.
	2. Select item to be purchased and its quantity.	Item number, item name, quantity	
	3. Do not add selected item to the shopping cart.	-	
TC5	1. Log into the website.	Login id, password	Items are successfully added in the shopping cart.
	2. Select items to be purchased and their quantity.	Item number, item name, quantity	
	3. Add selected items to the shopping cart.	Item number, item name, quantity	
	4. Select some more items and add them to the shopping cart.	Item number, item name, quantity	
TC6	1. Log into the website.	Login id, password	If deletion is confirmed, item is successfully deleted from the shopping cart.
	2. Select two or more items to be purchased and their quantity.	Item number, item name, quantity	
	3. Add selected items to the shopping cart.	Item number, item name, quantity	
	4. Delete one item from the shopping cart.	Item number	
TC7	1. Log into the website.	Login id, password	If updation is confirmed, quantity is successfully updated.
	2. Select item to be purchased and its quantity.	Item number, item name, quantity	
	3. Add selected items to the shopping cart.	Item number, item name, quantity	
	4. Update quantity of the item added to the shopping cart.	Quantity	

(Contd.)

(Contd.)

Test case id	Description (steps followed)	Inputs	Expected output
TC8	1. Log into the website.	Login id, password	User check outs from the shopping cart and total bill of the purchased items is displayed.
	2. Select items to be purchased and their quantities.	Item number, item name, quantity	
	3. Add selected items to the shopping cart.	Item number, item name, quantity	
	4. Checkout	-	
TC9	1. Log into the website.	Login id, password	After authentication, amount is transferred and items are delivered successfully.
	2. Select items to be purchased and their quantities.	Item number, item name, quantity	
	3. Add selected items to the shopping cart.	Item number, item name, quantity	
	4. Checkout	-	
	5. Enter valid credit card information	Bank name, credit card type, credit card number	
TC10	1. Log into the website.	Login id, password,	Appropriate error message is displayed.
	2. Select items to be purchased and their quantities.	Item number, item name, quantity	
	3. Add selected items to the shopping cart.	Item number, item name, quantity	
	4. Checkout	-	
	5. Enter invalid credit card information	Bank name, credit card type, credit card number	

11.3 USER INTERFACE TESTING

User interface testing tests that the user interaction features work correctly. These features include hyperlinks, tables, forms, frames and user interface items such as text fields, radio buttons, check boxes, list boxes, combo boxes, command buttons and dialog boxes.

User interface testing ensures that the application handles mouse and keyboard events correctly and displays hyperlinks, tables, frames, buttons, menus, dialog boxes, error message boxes, and toolbars properly.

11.3.1 Navigation Testing

Navigation testing investigates the proper functioning of all the internal and external links. Navigation testing must ensure that websites provide consistent, well-organized links and should also provide alternative navigation schemes such as search options and site maps. The placement of navigation links on each page must be checked. Search based navigation facility must also be thoroughly tested and search items should be consistent across one page to another. All the combinations of keywords and search criteria must be verified in navigation testing. Table 11.3 presents test cases for navigation testing for an online shopping website as given in Figure 11.4. In Table 11.5, the given user interface testing checklist includes issues on hyperlinks for testers to ensure their proper functioning.

Table 11.3. Navigation testing test cases for online shopping website

Test case id	Description	Inputs	Expected output
TC1	Check all links on each web page.	Link1=Home Link2=About us Link3=Product Gallery Link4=Contact us Link5=Registration Link6=Shopping Cart Link7=Order Status Link8=Feedback	Appropriate web page is opened with respect to each link.
TC2	Click on all links on each web page to test the appearance of content on each web page.	Link1=Home Link2=About us Link3=Product Gallery Link4=Contact us Link5=Registration Link6=Shopping Cart Link7=Order Status Link8=Feedback	Appropriate horizontal and vertical scroll bars are present and the user can view the page contents properly
TC3	Search for items in the available product gallery	Search string	The user is able to navigate across multiple search pages successfully.
TC4	Click on 'back' link present on each page.	-	The appropriate page is displayed.

Manual checking of hyperlinks can be very time consuming. There are various online tools available for checking broken links, accuracy and availability of links and obtaining advice on search engines. Some tools for navigation testing include Performance Technologies' TestLink, W3C's Link checker, Xenu's LinkSleuth, Dead Links' Dead Links, LinkTiger's LinkTiger, Viable Software Alternative's LinkRunner, Elsop's LinkScan, REl Software's Link Validator, UCI's MQMspider and Illumit's WebLight.

11.3.2 Form Based Testing

Websites that include forms need to ensure that all the fields in the form are working properly. Form-based testing involves the following issues:

1. Proper navigation from one field of the form to another using the tab key.
2. Ensures that the data entered in the form is in a valid format.
3. Checks that all the mandatory fields are entered in the form.

Consider the registration form of an online shopping website (web page is given in Figure 11.5). Its inputs include login id, password, repeat password, name, last name, email address, phone number, shipping details (address, city, state, zip code) and billing details (address, city, state, zip code). Its form based test cases are shown in Table 11.4.

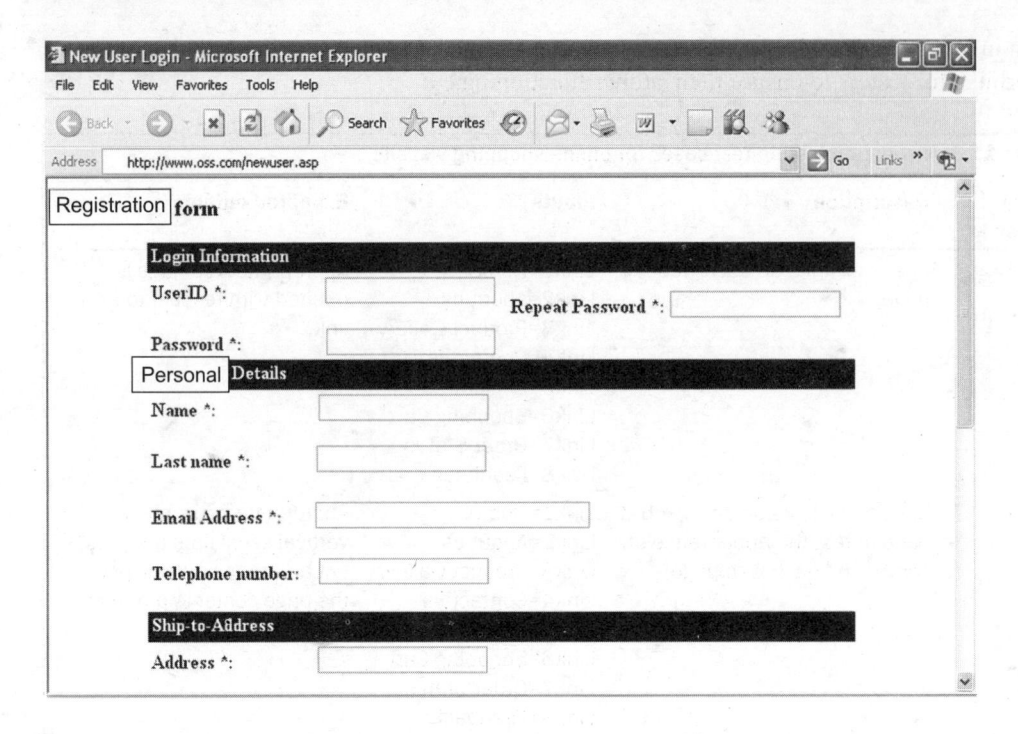

Figure 11.5. Sample online registration form

Table 11.4. Test cases of registration form of an online shopping web application

Test case id	Description	Inputs	Expected output
TC1	Navigate using tab from one field to another in the form	-	The user follows the correct sequence while navigating from one field to another.
TC2	Check maximum and minimum length of all fields in the form (boundary value analysis).	Login id, password, confirm password, shipping details (address, city, state, zip code) and billing details (address, city, state, zip code)	If the characters are entered within the range, the information is added successfully; otherwise an appropriate error message is displayed.
TC3	Check data validations of all fields in the form.	Login id, password, confirm password, shipping details (address, city, state, zip code) and billing details (address, city, state, zip code).	If the characters are valid the information is added successfully, otherwise an appropriate error message is displayed.
TC4	Check whether all the mandatory fields are entered in the form.	Login id, password, confirm password, shipping details (address, city, state, zip code) and billing details (address, city, state, zip code).	If all the required fields are entered the information is added successfully, otherwise an appropriate error message is displayed.

11.3.3 User Interface Testing Checklist

A user interface testing checklist may provide the opportunities for testers to ensure the proper functioning of user interface features such as hyperlinks, tables, frames, forms, buttons, menus, toolbars, dialog boxes and error messages. A checklist may also discipline and organize testing activities and a sample checklist is given in Table 11.5. However organizations and website owners may modify the checklist according to requirements of their web application.

Table 11.5. Checklist for testing user interfaces

S. No.	Description	Yes/No/NA	Remarks
Hyperlinks			
1.	Are the links meaningful?		
2.	Are there any broken links?		
3.	Do all internal links work correctly?		
4.	Do all external links work properly?		
5.	Are all links to external sites in the website tested?		
6.	Are images correctly hyperlinked?		
7.	Can the user navigate using text only?		
8.	Does every hyperlink exist on the site map?		
9.	Are the hyperlinks' colours standard?		
10.	Does the link bring the user to the correct web page?		
Tables			
11.	Are the columns wide enough or the text wraps around the rows?		
12.	Are the row and columns headings of tables appropriate?		
13.	Are the complex tables broken down into simpler ones, wherever required?		
14.	Does the user have to scroll right constantly in order to see the contents in a table?		
15.	Are table captions meaningful?		
Frames			
16.	Is every frame associated with a title?		
17.	Can the user resize the frame?		
18.	Is the frame size appropriate?		
19.	Does the horizontal and vertical scrollbar appear wherever required?		
20.	Does any frame handling mechanism exist for browsers that do not support frames?		
Forms			
21.	Are keyboard shortcuts provided for movement between different fields of forms?		
22.	Does the tabbing feature traverse the appropriate fields in the correct sequence?		

(Contd.)

(Contd.)

S. No.	Description	Yes/No/NA	Remarks
23.	Are the mandatory fields marked clearly?		
24.	Are descriptive labels for all fields provided?		
25.	Is information formatted, wherever required (for example, date format may be in mm/dd/yyyy)		
26.	Are error messages meaningful and appropriate?		
27.	Does the size of text fields give enough room for the user to type?		
28.	Are fields used appropriately?		
29.	Is any information asked more than once in the form? Is the user prevented from entering the same data multiple times?		
30.	Does the form include a 'reset' button to clear its contents?		

Text fields, Buttons, List boxes, Check boxes

S. No.	Description	Yes/No/NA	Remarks
31.	Do the text fields accept invalid characters and special characters?		
32.	Can text be selected using shift + arrow key?		
33.	Is the user able to select any combination of options in check boxes?		
34.	Can the user select more than one option in radio buttons?		
35.	Does the button click trigger the required action?		
36.	Can the user add text in the list boxes?		
37.	Can the user add text in the combo boxes?		
38.	Do the required commands and options exist in each menu?		
39.	Are abbreviations used in list boxes/buttons?		
40.	Are the label names meaningful?		
41.	Are mouse actions consistent across web pages?		
42.	Is red colour used to highlight active items (many users are colour bind)?		
43.	Is all the data inside the list/combo box listed in chronological order?		
44.	Are validation checks for text fields present?		
45.	Do fields with numeric values handle upper and lower range of values appropriately (boundary value analysis)?		
46.	Does the back navigation button work as required?		
47.	Do the text fields accept maximum permissible data?		
48.	Can an alphanumeric character be entered in numeric fields?		
49.	Are the command buttons disabled when they are not in use?		
50.	Is there any spelling or grammatical mistakes in captions or labels?		

11.4 Usability Testing

What makes a web application usable? Usability is one of the quality attributes that a web application must possess. It is important to develop a website that is easy to use. Whenever the user browses an online shopping website, several questions may come to his/her mind. What is the credibility and reputation of the website? Are shipping charges applicable? In how many days a product will be delivered? Is there any guidance on how to place an order? In case of any problem, is there any grievance redressal mechanism? These kinds of usability issues are faced by everyone who tries to purchase an item from an online shopping website.

11.4.1 What is Usability and Usability Testing?

Usability is concerned with the degree to which the software fulfils the user's specifications and expectations. It is the measurement of the amount of satisfaction of the user. It also assesses the extent to which the user finds the software easy to use, learn and understand. Usability can be divided into one or more attributes such as accuracy, efficiency, completeness, learnability, satisfaction, clarity and accuracy of online help and written documentation.

Table 11.6 summarizes the key definitions of these usability attributes.

Table 11.6. Web application usability attributes

Attribute	Definition
Accuracy	It specifies the degree to which the website meets the user's needs with precision and correctness.
Efficiency	It refers to the correctness, easiness and quickness of use of the website by a user. It is generally measured in terms of time.
Completeness	The extent to which a website implements specified functions.
Learnability	It defines the user's ability to effectively perform operations on the website.
Satisfaction	It refers to the user's feeling and opinion about the website. It is usually captured through a questionnaire or survey. Users are more likely to use websites that satisfy their needs as compared to other ones.
Clarity and accuracy of online help and written documentation	The extent to which the online help and documentation is clearly and accurately written.

Usability testing refers to the procedure employed to evaluate the degree to which the software satisfies the specified usability criteria. A systematic approach to usability testing is given in Figure 11.6.

464 Software Testing

```
Identification of participants
          │
          ▼
Development of usability
testing questionnaire
          │
          ▼
Setting up environment for
conducting test
          │
          ▼
Conducting the test
          │
          ▼
Analyze results
and observations
```

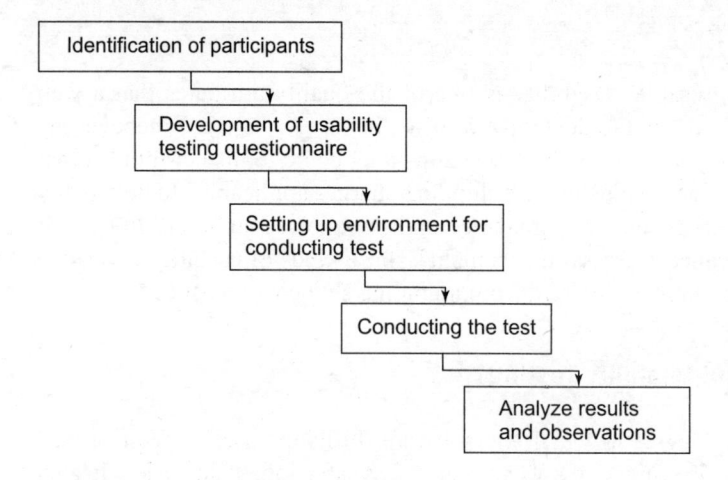

Figure 11.6. Usability testing steps

If all the steps are followed in the given order, we may be able to perform effective and efficient usability testing.

11.4.2 Identification of Participants

Who are the target users of a web application? It is important for an organization to identify the characteristics of the participating users. Such characteristics may include age, gender, profession and application specific experience. An example of participant characteristics for conducting usability tests of an online shopping website is shown in Figure 11.7.

Participant name	
Date	
Age	16-20
	21-30
	31-40
	41-50
	>50
Gender	Male
	Female
Profession	
Education level	Higher secondary
	Graduate
	Post graduate
Customer type	Whole sale purchaser
	Retail purchaser
Shopping experience	
Shopping frequency	

Figure 11.7. Participant characteristics for online shopping website

We must remember two things when identifying the participants, that is, selection of the right number and type of participants. The number of participants depends upon the degree of confidence required, time and resources available, and availability of participants. We must select an appropriate number of participants from different groups of target users as each group of users will use the website with a different purpose. For example, consider the online shopping website, when testing this website, one group of participants may be selected from 'wholesale' purchaser category and other from 'retail' purchaser category.

11.4.3 Development of Usability Testing Questionnaire

This step involves the preparation of a questionnaire for conducting usability testing. A usability testing test plan specifies a pre-defined set of tasks the participants are expected to follow. Preparation of the questionnaire is an important activity and should take into consideration the usability features of the web application. The participant's feedback and reactions are recorded in the questionnaire. The research questions must include the participant's likes and dislikes about the website. Several questions that may be used to perform usability tests for many types of web applications are given in Figure 11.8.

Introduction					
1.	Do all labels and hyperlinks display a meaningful title?	Yes ○	No ○		
2.	Does any internal or external link provide incorrect details?	Yes ○	No ○		
3.	Are appropriate error messages displayed wherever required?	Yes ○	No ○		
4.	Do you frequently encounter problems in the application or not?	Very less ○	Less ○	High ○	Very high ○
5.	At what points mistakes or difficulties were encountered?				
Efficiency					
6.	How easily are features and updates downloadable?	Very easy ○	Easy ○	Difficult ○	Very difficult ○
7.	How easily are common tasks performed?	Very easy ○	Easy ○	Difficult ○	Very difficult ○

(Contd.)

(Contd.)

8.	How frequently are errors encountered while navigating through the web application?	Very less ○	Less ○	High ○	Very high ○
9.	Is the response time a cause of frustration?	Yes ○	No ○		
10.	Are there any major flaws encountered while using the web application? If yes, state them.				
11.	How many pages are accessed to complete a task?	<3 ○	4 to 6 ○	7-15 ○	>15 ○
12.	How quickly does the web application recover from an error?	Very slow ○	Slow ○	Fast ○	Very fast ○
Completeness					
13.	Are some features/topics missing from the web application? If yes, then specify.	Yes ○	No ○	Remarks	
14.	Are any additional controls required?	Yes ○	No ○	Remarks	
15.	To what degree are you satisfied with the application?	Very less ○	Less ○	High ○	Very high ○
16.	Are web pages well designed?	Yes ○	No ○		
17.	Does the online help and documentation provide enough information?	Yes ○	No ○		
Learnability					
18.	How easily is the user able to learn the features (buttons, clicks, hyperlinks) of the web page?	Very easy ○	Easy ○	Difficult ○	Very difficult ○
19.	Are the links, menus and lists easily understandable?	Very easy ○	Easy ○	Difficult ○	Very difficult ○
20.	How often is the search feature used?	Very less ○	Less ○	High ○	Very high ○

(Contd.)

(Contd.)

21.	How easy is it to return to the home page?	Very easy ○	Easy ○	Difficult ○	Very difficult ○
22.	Are the symbols, icons and tables meaningful? If not, which are the problematic ones?				
23.	Can the features be used without any help or assistance?	Yes ○	No ○		
Clarity and Accuracy of Online and Written Documentation					
24.	Is the terminology well understood?	Yes ○	No ○		
25.	How easily are the topics found in the online help?	Very easy ○	Easy ○	Difficult ○	Very difficult ○
26.	What is the most frequent reason for using online help?				
27.	Are the topic contents sufficient in the help?	Yes ○	No ○		
28.	How frequently was the required topic found in the help?	Very less ○	Less ○	High ○	Very high ○
29.	How easily are you able to switch between online help and interface in order to complete a specific task?	Very easy ○	Easy ○	Difficult ○	Very difficult ○
30.	Is online help useful when error messages are encountered?	Very useful ○	Useful ○	Less useful ○	Not useful ○
31.	Do menus, lists, hyperlinks, tool bars and tables operate as stated?	Yes ○	No ○		
32.	Are the steps to compete a task correctly stated?	Yes ○	No ○		
33.	How helpful is the content related to topics?	Very useful ○	Useful ○	Less useful ○	Not useful ○

(Contd.)

(Contd.)

General					
34.	What are your suggestions for improving the web application?				
35.	How easily is the information available in the various sections (such as 'about us', 'contact us')?	Very easy ○	Easy ○	Difficult ○	Very difficult ○
36.	In context to other competitive applications, the given web application was found to be:	Very easy ○	Easy ○	Difficult ○	Very difficult ○
37.	Would you like to use this web application frequently?	Very less ○	Less ○	High ○	Very high ○
38.	Is correcting the mistakes easy or difficult?	Very easy ○	Easy ○	Difficult ○	Very difficult ○
39.	Do you use menu options or shortcut keys?				
40.	How will you overall rate the web application?	Very good ○	Good ○	Bad ○	Very bad ○

Figure 11.8. Usability testing questionnaire

The questionnaire may be modified according to the requirement of the application. Figure 11.9 shows an example of questions from a usability test of an online shopping website.

1. How easily and successfully are you able to register on this website?
2. What paths did you take to complete an order?
3. How closely did the order process meet with your specifications?
4. What problems were encountered while placing an order?
5. How do you feel about the time taken to complete the order process (in terms of time and number of steps)?

Figure 11.9. Sample questions for online shopping website

11.4.4 Setting up Environment for Conducting Test

This step involves deciding and setting up the location for conducting usability tests. The decision of location and setups is based on various factors such as:

(i) Whether the tester's interaction with the user is required or not?
(ii) Whether enough space is available at the developer's/ tester's site in order to conduct usability tests?
(iii) Is the location of the site easily accessible to target participants?
(iv) What equipments will be required for conducting the tests?
(v) How many participants and observers will be required?
(vi) Will the identity of the organization result in biased results?
(vii) What is the availability of the participants?
(viii) Is testing required at multiple geographic locations?

Based on the above issues, different testing setups/environments may be selected.

11.4.5 Conducting the Test

This step consists of the execution of usability testing. The usability tests will be based on the questions prepared in Figure 11.7. These questions may be tailored as per the type of a web application. The initial background details of the web application should not be given to the user. The body language of the observer should not influence the participant.

The execution of usability tests should also involve the observation of reactions of the participants as they perform the intended tasks. The observer must carefully observe the emotions of the participants.

11.4.6 Analyze the Results and Observations

The process of generation of usability testing report involves organizing, summarizing and analyzing the collected data. This report contains a summary of the user's preferences, list of errors and difficulties encountered, identification of customer trends, and analysis of recordings. Finally the observations are statistically analyzed and based on these analysis recommendations are proposed. The tasks that do not meet the desired specifications are identified and prioritized. The goal of usability testing is to improve the quality of the web application as per usability specifications.

11.5 CONFIGURATION AND COMPATIBILITY TESTING

One of the significant challenges of web testing is that it must ensure the proper functioning of a web application on all the supported platforms and suitable environments. In the stand-alone desktop computer environment, testing an application is an easy task, whereas the web application's environment significantly increases the testing effort due to rise in complexity and expectation. The goal of configuration and compatibility testing is to detect faults in the application while it is tested on varied platforms and environments. The performance and system's requirement specifications formed during the start of the project provides a baseline for creating configuration and compatibility test cases.

Configuration testing determines the behaviour of the software with respect to various configurations whereas compatibility testing determines whether the web application behaves as expected with respect to various supported configurations. The configuration and compatibility testing concerns checking web application with difference:

(i) Browsers such as Internet Explorer (IE), Chrome, Opera, Mozilla, etc.
(ii) User interface components such as Java Applets, Active X, etc.
(iii) Operating systems such as Windows (98, NT, XP), Macintosh, Linux, etc.
(iv) Internet connection types such as broadband, Dial-up, leased line, etc.
(v) Hardware devices such as CPU, RAM, CD-ROM, input devices (mouse, keyboard, joystick), output devices (such as printers, plotters) network card, monitor, graphic display card, etc.
(vi) Online services
(vii) Multimedia services such as text, audio, video, etc.
(viii) Database such as MS Access, SQL Server, Oracle, Sybase, etc.
(ix) Mobile devices such as Nokia, Motorola, Samsung, etc.

11.5.1 Browser Testing

There are a large number of browsers available and the behaviour of each of them may vary. Although it is impractical to test the web application with all the browsers, it is necessary to verify the web application with specified and prioritized platforms to ensure its correct functioning.

Browser testing verifies the functioning of web application in terms of text, audio, video and operating system corresponding to different browsers. Browser compatibility matrix may be created to test the web application on different browsers. Table 11.7 presents browser compatibility matrix for testing a web application.

Table 11.7. Browser's compatibility matrix

Browser		IE 6	IE 7	IE 8	Firefox	Navigator	Chrome	Opera	Safari	Lynx
Audio										
Video										
Text										
Platform	Win XP									
	Win 98									
	Win NT									
	Win 2000									
	Mac									
	Linux									
Form										

11.5.2 Guidelines and Checklist for Configuration and Compatibility Testing

The system under test may follow the following guidelines to perform configuration and compatibility testing:

(i) Configuration and compatibility testing must begin after the functional testing is complete, otherwise it will be difficult to determine whether the fault is due to functionality or compatibility.
(ii) Web compatibility matrix must include the most popular browsers that are expected to access the website.
(iii) Compatibility testing must take into account the target audiences.
(iv) Configuration and compatibility test cases must be executed by different tester groups in parallel so that the testing covers a large number of platforms and environments.
(v) The records and results of testing may be kept for future use and predictions.

The checklist given in Table 11.8 addresses the issues of configuration and compatibility testing.

Table 11.8. Configuration and compatibility testing checklist

S. No.	Description	Yes/No/NA	Remarks
1.	Are Java source code/scripts, ActiveX controls, other scripts used by the application?		
2.	Is the application compatible with different peripherals (input and output devices)?		
3.	Is the application compatible with different hardware configurations?		
4.	Is the application compatible with different mobile phones?		
5.	Do text, graphics and animations display properly with browsers under test?		
6.	Are different printers compatible with various web browsers?		
7.	Are web browsers compatible with various user interface items of the web application?		
8.	Are cookies accepted by the web browsers?		
9.	Are different font sizes verified on various web browsers?		
10.	Are the security tools being used?		

11.6 SECURITY TESTING

Security is the procedure used to protect information from various threats. It is very important to protect sensitive and critical information and data while communicating over the network. The user wants implementation of a safeguard to protect personal, sensitive and financial information. We want data to be accurate, reliable and protected against unauthorized access.

Security involves various threats such as unauthorized users, malicious users, message sent to an unintended user, etc. Some of the security threats are shown in Figure 11.10.

472 Software Testing

The primary requirement of security includes:

(i) **Authentication:** Is the information sent from an authenticated user?
(ii) **Access Control:** Is data protected from unauthorized users?
(iii) **Integrity:** Does the user receive exactly what is sent?
(iv) **Delivery:** Is the information delivered to the intended user?
(v) **Reliability:** What is the frequency of a failure? How much time does the network take to recover from a failure? What measures are taken to counter catastrophic failure?
(vi) **Non-repudiation:** Is the receiver able to prove that the data received came from a specific sender?

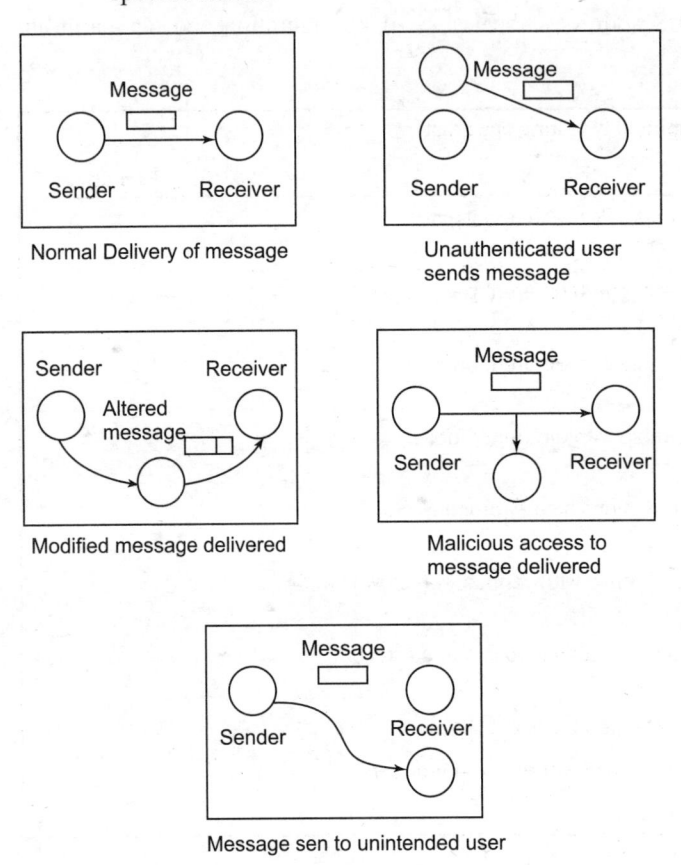

Figure 11.10. Security threats

A web application must fulfil the above mentioned primary security requirements. Testing the threats and vulnerabilities in a web application is an important activity. The tester must check the web application against all known internet threats.

Virus threats are the most sophisticated types of threats to web applications that may enter from the network. A virus is a program that modifies other programs by attaching itself to the program, which may infect the other programs when the host program executes. The virus may perform any function such as deleting files and programs. The goal of testing the web application against virus threats is to verify the methods of virus prevention, detection and removal. Virus testing ensures that:

(i) The antivirus software prevents the virus from entering into the system.
(ii) The antivirus software efficiently detects an infection, removes all traces of that infection from the program and restores the program to its original state.
(iii) Periodical updates and scans are conducted to keep the system updated and prevent new viruses from penetrating into the system.

Computer networks have grown rapidly with the evolution of the internet. Internet connectivity has become a necessity for many organizations. Although the internet provides an organization access to the outside world, it also provides the intruders an opportunity to access the organization's Local Area Network (LAN). If the systems are affected from a security failure, they must be recovered which may consume lots of effort and resources. Firewalls are an effective means of protecting a network from intruders. It is placed between the organization's internal network and the external network (see Figure 11.11). It serves as a security wall between the outside world and the organization's internal network. The aim of this wall is to protect the LAN from the internet-based security threats and it serves as a single point where all security checks are imposed. The firewall may be a single computer or a set of computers may be combined to serve as a firewall [STALL01].

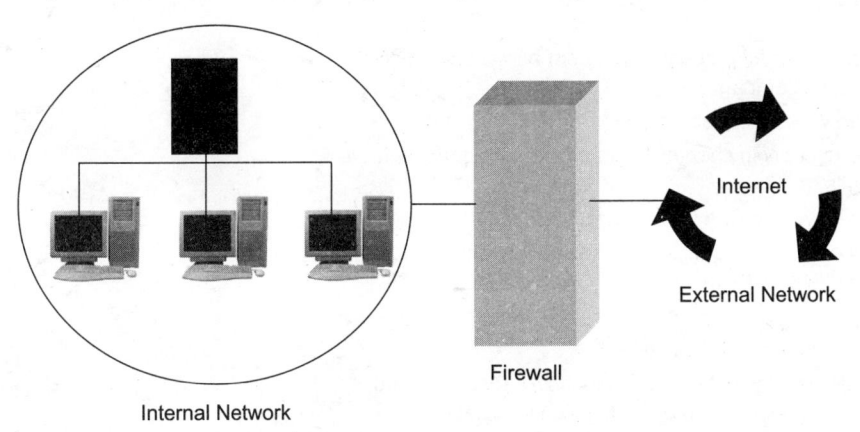

Figure 11.11. Working of a firewall

The idea of firewall testing is to break the system by bypassing the security mechanisms to gain access to the organization's sensitive information. This enables the tester to check the effectiveness of the firewall. Firewall testing ensures that the zones of risks are identified correctly, packet filtering occurs according to the designed rules, penetration within the boundaries established by the firewall is not possible and events are timely logged to keep track of an intruder.

Security testing requires an experienced tester having thorough knowledge of internet related security issues. The security expert needs to check security issues including authentication, unauthorized access, confidentiality, virus, firewalls and recovery from failure. Table 11.9 provides a comprehensive checklist to test an application for security threats and vulnerabilities.

Table 11.9. Security testing checklist

S. No.	Description	Yes/No/NA	Remarks
Authentication, Access Control and privacy			
1.	Are unauthorized users restricted from viewing private data?		
2.	Is sensitive organization information restricted from public access?		
3.	Are users aware of the privacy polices?		
4.	Are legal consequences of policies known to the user?		
5.	Are authentication mechanisms adequate to prevent malicious intrusion to the application?		
6.	Does the web application ask for login id and password?		
7.	Does the web server lock the users who try to access the website multiple times with invalid login ids/passwords?		
8.	Have you tested the combinations of invalid and valid login ids/passwords?		
9.	Is there any provision for forget/change password?		
10.	Are levels of authentication defined?		
Firewall			
11.	Does the firewall properly implement all the security policies of the company?		
12.	Are firewalls' adequacy tested?		
13.	Is the 'security in charge' aware of the known faults in the firewalls?		
14.	Is the location of the firewall effective?		
15.	Is any penetration possible in the security boundaries created by a firewall?		
Data Security			
16.	Are the data validations tested?		
17.	Is sensitive information (such as password, credit card number) displayed in the text field while typing?		
18.	Are privileges to access data enforced?		
19.	Are file download permissions established and tested?		
20.	Is sensitive and important data kept at secure locations?		
Encryption			
21.	Are encryption standards enforced?		
22.	Is there any procedure followed to identify what is to be encrypted?		
23.	Is sensitive and critical information (such as password, credit card number, company's financial sheets) encrypted?		
24.	Is Security Socket Layer (SSL) used to provide encryption of sensitive elements?		

(Contd.)

(Contd.)

S. No.	Description	Yes/No/NA	Remarks
25.	Does the enforcement of encryption standard affect the speed of the web page?		
Virus			
26.	Are mechanisms used to identify and remove viruses?		
27.	Are anti-virus softwares scheduled for periodical updates?		
28.	Does the anti-virus software identify the unprotected sites?		
29.	Are viruses sent for analysis to the anti-virus software company?		
30.	Are users trained for virus prevention and recovery procedures?		
31.	Is the procedure for handling a virus attack adequate?		
32.	Are users alerted from downloading insecure items?		
33.	Is legitimate anti-virus software installed on the client's machine?		
34.	Is virus scan scheduled periodically?		
35.	Is spyware removal software installed and run periodically?		
Failure Management and Recovery			
36.	Are back-ups schedules at defined intervals?		
37.	Does the recovery take a long time?		
38.	In case of site crash, is there any provision to route to another server?		
39.	Have recovery mechanisms been defined and tested?		
40.	Is any criteria followed to ensure the completion and correction of recovery procedures?		
General			
41.	Are any warning messages issued when the user enters or leaves the secured website?		
42.	Is the user allowed to login with the same account from different machines (simultaneously)?		
43.	Are unauthorized external sites identified and screened out?		
44.	Can the previous page be accessed after signing out from the website?		
45.	Is the user able to access restricted pages after the session is timed out?		
46.	Is auditing performed periodically in order to keep a record of all the operations?		
47.	Are all payment methods tested thoroughly?		
48.	Are enough security mechanisms enforced, if customer registration is compulsory on your website?		
49.	Does the application use digital signature to sign a file?		
50.	Does the source code reveal any critical information?		

11.7 PERFORMANCE TESTING

How long does an application take to respond to a user click? We must ensure that the user does not wait for a service for long, otherwise the potential user will move on to the competitor's site. To ensure that the web application can bear the load during the peak hours along with serving the user in a timely and reliable manner, performance tests including load and stress tests need to be conducted.

One of the key advantages of web application is that numerous users can have access to the application simultaneously. Hence, the performance of the application during the peak periods must be tested and monitored carefully. Several factors that may influence performance include:

(i) Response time
(ii) Memory available
(iii) Network bandwidth
(iv) Number of users
(v) User type
(vi) Time to download
(vii) Varied client machine configurations

The goal of performance testing is to evaluate the application's performance with respect to real world scenarios. The following issues must be addressed during performance testing:

(i) Performance of the system during peak hours (response time, reliability and availability).
(ii) Points at which the system performance degrades or system fails.
(iii) Impact of the degraded performance on the customer loyalty, sales and profits.

The above issues require metrics to be applied to the system under test in order to measure the system behaviour with respect to various performance parameters.

11.7.1 Load Testing

Load testing involves testing the web application under real world scenarios by simulating numerous users accessing the web application simultaneously. It tests the web application by providing it maximum load. The development of plans for load testing should begin as early as possible during the software life cycle. Early testing will help in detection of problems prior to deployment of the web application. Load testing may follow the following steps in order to ensure reasonable performance during peak hours:

(i) Defining the environment for a load test
(ii) Defining the testing strategy and determining the number of users
(iii) Identifying potential metrics
(iv) Choosing the right tool and executing the load test
(v) Interpreting the results

Defining environment for a load test

This step involves setting up of a separate testing environment that simulates the production environment. If the attributes of the machine such as speed, memory and configuration are not the same, then it may be very difficult to extrapolate the performance during production. The guideline is to identify the necessary resources in order to establish the lab for conducting load tests. In addition to identification of resources, the load testing team members must be determined to solve specific problems in the following areas:

(i) Team leader: takes charge of the load test activity.
(ii) Database: identifies and removes database problems. Administers database activities.
(iii) Network: sets up the lab, identifies and removes network bottlenecks.
(iv) Business experts: define quality levels of the application.
(v) Performance analyst: analyzes the available measures.
(vi) Quality management: ensures quality testing.

The configuration of environment for load tests include network configuration, setting up server, and database set up, etc.

Defining testing strategy and determining number of users

This step includes writing of test cases focusing on the number of concurrent user requests, synchronization of user requests, system bottlenecks and stability issues. The number of users may be determined by approximating the percentage of users hitting particular areas in the website. The load test team may consult the requirement specification document to collect the specific targets of the user's hitting the website.

Identifying potential metrics

Selection of appropriate metrics enables the practitioner to determine the system performance with respect to the established quality benchmarks. Metrics allow the tester to quantify the results of the load tests. There are various tools available which allow to measure the time of running a test case. The metrics presented in Table 11.10 may be used to monitor the system's performance during load testing.

Table 11.10. Load testing metrics

S. No.	Metric	Description
Scalability and Usage		
1.	Web page views per week	It counts the number of web pages viewed per week.
2.	Web page views per hour	It counts the number of web pages viewed per hour.
3.	Web page views per second	It counts the number of web pages viewed per second.
4.	Web page hits per week	It counts the number of web pages hit per week.
5.	Web page hits per hour	It counts the number of web pages hit per hour.
6.	Web page hits per second	It counts the number of web pages hit per second.
7.	Average hits per web page	It is the ratio of the number of web page hits to the number of web page views
8.	Cycles	It counts the number of times the test is executed.

(Contd.)

(Contd.)

S. No.	Metric	Description
Performance		
9.	Number of concurrent users	It counts the number of simultaneous users accessing a web page within a specified time interval.
10.	Response time	It measures the total time it takes after sending the request till the first response is received.
11.	Wait time	It measures the time between which the request was sent till the first byte is received.
12.	Throughput	It provides the amount of data sent by the application to the virtual users, measured in bytes.
13.	Elapsed time	It measures the time elapsed to complete a transaction, measured in seconds.
14.	Minimum web page run time	It measures the minimum time taken by a web page to execute in seconds.
15.	Maximum web page run time	It measures the maximum time taken by a web page to execute in seconds.
Failure		
16.	Failed hits per second	It counts the number of requests that fail per second.
17.	Connections failed	It counts the total number of connections that could not be established during the test.
18.	Failed cycles per second	It tests the number of rounds that failed per second.
19.	Maximum wait time before failure	It specifies the maximum time the user will wait before abandoning the web site.

Working with the load testing team earlier in the software life cycle is important, as it will help in identifying metrics and will ensure performance of the web site.

Choosing the right tool and executing the load test

To implement the specified testing strategy and perform the established measurements, right load testing tool must be chosen. The selection of tools depends on various factors such as nature and complexity of the web application, technology used in developing the web application and available resources (time, cost and skilled professionals) for testing the web application. For example, Microsoft's Application Center Test (ACT) or Empirix's e-Test tools may be used for testing complex web applications and ACT may be used for testing applications developed in .NET. ACT requires skilled professionals whereas e-Test requires payment of license fees. Some of the load testing tools for web applications include Microsoft's ACT, Neolys' NeoLoad, Radview's WebLoad, Red Gate's ANTS profiler, Yahoo's Yslow, Webperformer's Web Performance Load Tester and Empirix's e-Test.

Execution of load test requires time, effort and commitment in order to perform tests and simulate an actual test environment. The load tests may be executed multiple times (repeatedly) and the measures may be recorded for future evaluations. The metrics corresponding to each change and re-test must be recorded.

Interpreting the Results

The metrics collected by a monitoring tool or manually must be analyzed to check whether the system's performance meets the user expectation. If the system's performance does not meet the specified targets, then corrective action should be taken.

11.7.2 Stress Testing

Stress testing involves execution of a web application with more than maximum and varying loads for long periods. Unlike performance and load testing, stress testing evaluates the response of the system when the system is given a load beyond its specified limits. It is also used to monitor and check the reliability of a web application when available resources are on beyond maximum usage. The behaviour of the system is monitored to determine when the system under stress test fails and how does it recover from the failure. Stress tests may test the web application for the following:

(i)   CPU and memory usage
(ii) Response time
(iii) Backend database
(iv) Different types of users
(v)   Concurrent users

The system performance is expected to degrade when a large number of users hit the web site simultaneously. After the completion of stress tests, the testing team must analyze the noted system's performance degradation points and compare them with the acceptable performance of the system. Risk analysis described in chapter 7 may be used to make decisions of the acceptable level of performance degradation of the system.

11.7.3 Performance Testing Checklist

Table 11.11 shows a list of questions that may be checked while conducting performance tests on the web application.

Table 11.11. Performance testing checklist

S. No.	Description	Yes/No/NA	Remarks
Users			
1.	Have the maximum number of users been identified for the web application?		
2.	Is complexity of the system determined?		
3.	Are peak hours identified?		
4.	Is the duration of session of users analyzed?		
5.	Have the type of users been identified?		
Response Time			
6.	Is the response time calculated?		

(Contd.)

(Contd.)

S. No.	Description	Yes/No/NA	Remarks
7.	Is the maximum response time determined?		
8.	Does the response time meet the established threshold?		
9.	Are break points identified for planning load tests?		
10.	Are the causes of crash at the break points identified?		
Database			
11.	Is the maximum database capacity identified?		
12.	Are the past experiences with the database documented?		
13.	Is load sharing and balancing facility available?		
14.	Does the application read the database content correctly?		
15.	Does the application write the database content correctly?		
Tools			
16.	Are load testing tools identified?		
17.	Are the employees trained?		
18.	Is the load testing tool compatible with the platform?		
19.	Is external support available for the tool?		
General			
20.	Are there any disk space limitations?		
21.	Are people with required skill sets available?		
22.	Has the time and number of iterations required for testing been identified?		
23.	Are rules for concurrency control being followed?		
24.	Is the maximum wait time before failure determined?		
25.	Are memory requirements and disk space usage identified?		

Table 11.11 presents a generic list of performance testing questions that are common to most of the web applications. The performance testing checklist may help to uncover the major performance related problems early in software development process.

11.8 DATABASE TESTING

In web applications, many applications are database driven, for example, e-commerce related websites or business-to-business applications. It is important for these applications to work properly and provide security to the user's sensitive data such as personal details and credit card information.

Testing data-centric web applications is important to ensure their error-free operation and increased customer satisfaction. For example, consider the example for purchasing items from an online store. If the user performs a search based on some keywords and price preferences, a database query is created by the database server. Suppose due to some programming fault in the query, the query does not consider the price preferences given by the customer, this will produce erroneous results. These kinds of faults must be tested and removed during database testing.

Important issues in database testing may include:

(i) Data validation
(ii) Data consistency
(iii) Data integrity
(iv) Concurrency control and recovery
(v) Data manipulation operations such as addition, deletion, updation and retrieval of data.
(vi) Database security

A database must be tested for administrative level operations such as adding, deleting and updating an item in the database, and user operations such as searching an item from the database or providing personal details. In the example of the online shopping website, the most common administrative operations and user operations include:

Administrative operations

(i) Inserting a new item into the database
(ii) Deleting an existing item from the database
(iii) Updating an existing item from the database
(iv) Viewing an existing item from the database

User operations

(i) Searching items from the database
(ii) Registering into the website involves storing the user's personal details
(iii) Placing an order involves storing user preferences and purchase details into the database
(iv) Providing feedback involves storing information in the database
(v) Tracking status of the order placed

In chapter 6, we generated test cases based on administrative operations for testing an application. Table 11.12 shows sample test cases based on a user operation in an online shopping website.

Table 11.12. Sample database test cases

Test case id	Description (steps followed)	Inputs	Expected output
Search an item from the product gallery			
TC1	Search the product gallery to decide which items to purchase.	Search string	List of items searched are correctly displayed from the database that satisfy the search criteria selected by the user.

(Contd.)

(Contd.)

Test case id	Description (steps followed)	Inputs	Expected output
Registering of user on the website			
TC2	Register on the website to place an order	Login id, password, confirm password, shipping details (address, city, state and zip code) and billing details (address, city, state and zip code).	If the information entered is valid, the user information is successfully added into the database.
Providing feedback on the website			
TC3	Enter fields		The information is successfully added to the database.

In database testing, the following aspects of correctness must be ensured:

(i) Are the database operations performed correctly?
(ii) Is concurrent users' access to the database handled correctly?
(iii) Is the database fault tolerant?
(iv) Are the performance requirements such as throughput and response time met?
(v) Are backup and recovery procedures designed and ensure uninterrupted services to the user?
(vi) Does the database restore to a consistent state after crash recovery?
(vii) Does the database have enough space and memory to store records and handle multiple administrative and user operations?

Database testing may include generation of new records, monitoring of system performance and verification of performance of the database processor.

11.9 POST-DEPLOYMENT TESTING

Post-deployment testing may reveal those problems which went undetected before deployment of the web application. Despite all the planning and testing carried out before deployment, obtaining user opinion is important for improvement of a website and it ensures that the website adapts to the needs of the user. User feedback may come in various forms, ranging from reporting of faults to suggestions for improvement of the website.

The effective way to obtain a user's opinion is to get a questionnaire or survey filled by the user. The questionnaire/survey can be used to detect trends and may provide valuable information for improvement of the website. Figure 11.12 presents a survey consisting of general questions which must be asked from the user. The response obtained from this survey may help the developer/owner of the website to improve the website.

S. No.	Description	Overall Rating						
Consistency								
1.	Are the colour schemes consistent across displays?	Bad	1	2	3	4	5	Good
2.	Is the format of display of topics consistent?	Bad	1	2	3	4	5	Good
3.	Is the location of labels consistent?	Bad	1	2	3	4	5	Good
4.	Is the format of labels consistent?	Bad	1	2	3	4	5	Good
5.	Is the orientation (scrolling) of items consistent?	Bad	1	2	3	4	5	Good
Flexibility								
6.	Are the users able to customize windows?	Bad	1	2	3	4	5	Good
7.	Can the user interface items be resized flexibly?	Bad	1	2	3	4	5	Good
8.	Can you enter data flexibly?	Bad	1	2	3	4	5	Good
9.	Can you select data?	Bad	1	2	3	4	5	Good
10.	Can display be expanded by using zooming option?	Bad	1	2	3	4	5	Good
Learnability								
11.	Is the text clearly written and easy to understand?	Bad	1	2	3	4	5	Good
12.	Is data grouping easy to learn?	Bad	1	2	3	4	5	Good
13.	Are the names of user interface items logical?	Bad	1	2	3	4	5	Good
14.	Are the links working correctly?	Bad	1	2	3	4	5	Good
15.	How easy is it to learn various user interfaces in the website?	Bad	1	2	3	4	5	Good
User Guidance								
16.	How helpful were the error messages?	Bad	1	2	3	4	5	Good
17.	Does online help provide useful information?	Bad	1	2	3	4	5	Good
18.	Are error messages informative?	Bad	1	2	3	4	5	Good
19.	Is the 'undo' option available to revert back the user's actions?	Bad	1	2	3	4	5	Good
20.	Can the user navigate easily through the website?	Bad	1	2	3	4	5	Good

(Contd.)

(Contd.)

S. No.	Description	Overall Rating			
21.	Is sufficient information available for the intended audience?	Bad	1 2 3 4 5		Good
22.	Are you able to find the required information you were locking for?	Bad	1 2 3 4 5		Good
23.	Would you recommend this website to other users?	Bad	1 2 3 4 5		Good
24.	How will you overall rate the website?	Bad	1 2 3 4 5		Good
25.	Is website compatible with your browser?	Bad	1 2 3 4 5		Good

Figure 11.12. Post deployment testing questionnaire

Once the user's opinion is obtained, it is important to identify useful fault reporting, suggestions and recommendations. The following criteria can be used to decide which suggestion needs attention:

1. **Frequency of suggestion:** How many users have given the same suggestion or recommendation? If a small number of users are making the same request, then we must think twice before implementing the suggestion.
2. **Source of feedback:** Who is providing the suggestion? It is vital to make sure that suggestions come from regular users and not accidental users.
3. **Cost of implementing the suggestion:** Is the suggested idea worth implementing? The correctness of the proposed change and its impact on the cost and schedule must be analyzed carefully. The benefits of implementing the suggested idea to the business must be determined.
4. **Impact of implementing the suggestion:** Will implementing the suggestion increase complexity of the website? Will the change be compatible with the other functionalities of the website? It is important to obtain the answers to these questions as the results of implementing a change are sometimes unpredictable.

Figure 11.13 shows the typical post deployment testing procedure of a web application.

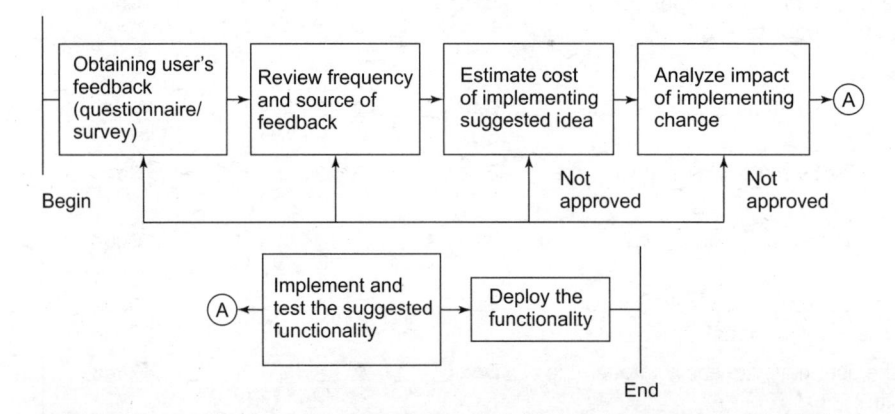

Figure 11.13. Typical post deployment testing procedure of a web application

This procedure is necessary in order to ensure that the suggested functionalities are properly addressed, fixed and closed. If the suggested idea is approved after analyzing its cost and impact, then the suggested functionality is implemented, tested and deployed.

11.10 WEB METRICS

Web page metrics can be effectively used in measuring various attributes of a web page. Table 11.13 provides comprehensive web page measures. There are 41 web page metrics which influence usability. These attributes/metrics can be divided into three categories:-

(i) Page composition metrics
(ii) Page formatting metrics and
(iii) Overall page quality or assessment metrics

Most of the page composition and page formatting metrics can be easily calculated but the attributes that fall in the category 3 i.e. overall page quality or assessment metrics, requires designer and/or user evaluation [MALH10].

Table 11.13. Web metrics

Metric	Description
Page Composition	
Number of words	Total words on a page
Body text words	Words that are body Vs. display text
Link text words	Total words in links
Number of links	Links on a page
Length of link text	Words in the text for a link
Redundant links	Repeated links on a page
Embedded links	Links embedded in text on a page
Wrapped links	Links spanning multiple lines
Within page links	Links to other areas of the same page
Readability	Reading level of text on a page
Number of !'s	Exclamation points on a page
Content percentage	Portion of a page devoted to content
Navigation percentage	Portion of a page devoted to navigation
Page title length	Words in the page title
Number of graphics	Total images on a page
Page size	Total bytes for the page and images
Image size	Number of pixels in an image
Total graphics size	Total bytes of an image
Animated elements	Animated images and scrolling text

(Contd.)

486 Software Testing

(Contd.)

Metric	Description
Page Formatting	
Font styles	Types of fonts
Font point size	Font size employed
Text emphasis	Total emphasized text
Emphasized body text	Total emphasized body text
Number of font sizes	Total font sizes employed
Screen coverage	Total screen area covered
Number of screens	Number of vertical and horizontal scrolls required
Text clustering	Text areas highlighted with colour or bordered region
Text in clusters	Words in text cluster
Text position	Changes in text position from flush, left
Number of lists	List on a page
Number of rules	Vertical and horizontal rules on a page
Number of colours	Total colours employed
Line length	Width of text lines on a page
Leading	Spacing between consecutive text lines on a page
Frames	Use of frames
Number of tables	Number of tables present on a web page
Overall page Quality assessment	
Information quality	Content appropriateness (i.e. relevance, language and tone)
Image quality	Image appropriateness and optimization (size and resolution)
Link quality	Link clarity and relevance
Layout quality	Aesthetics, alignment and balance
Download speed	Time for a page to fully load

Web applications differ from each other in various dimensions such as page content, page size, quality, reliability, screen coverage, etc. The metrics given in Table 11.13 demonstrate quantitative web usability metrics that can provide useful insights into distinguishing features of web pages. These metrics give us some ideas about thoroughness and effectiveness of web testing.

MULTIPLE CHOICE QUESTIONS

Note: *Select the most appropriate answer for the following questions.*

11.1 A client-server application consists of:
    (a) Server application
    (b) Database server
    (c) Application server
    (d) None of the above

11.2 A web application consists of:
   (a) Web server
   (b) Database server
   (c) Client application
   (d) All of the above

11.3 A web application depicts:
   (a) Two-tier architecture
   (b) Three-tier architecture
   (c) N-tier architecture
   (d) Four-tier architecture

11.4 A web server incorporates:
   (a) Business logic
   (b) Database storage
   (c) Web browser
   (d) All of the above

11.5 Key areas in testing web applications do not include:
   (a) Security testing
   (b) Browser testing
   (c) Acceptance testing
   (d) Database testing

11.6 Navigation testing investigates the proper functioning of:
   (a) Forms
   (b) Links
   (c) Tables
   (d) Frames

11.7 Which is not a link testing tool?
   (a) LinkTiger's LinkTiger
   (b) Illumit's WebLight
   (c) Elsop's LinkScan
   (d) Apache's Jmeter

11.8 Form based testing does not check:
   (a) Data validations
   (b) Hyperlinks on each page
   (c) Mandatory fields
   (d) Navigation amongst fields

11.9 Usability does not consist of:
   (a) Accuracy
   (b) Reliability
   (c) Learnability
   (d) Completeness

11.10 In selection of participants we must remember:
   (a) Selection of the right number and type of participants
   (b) Selection of participants with the right type of skills
   (c) Selection of participants of the right age and experience
   (d) None of the above

11.11 The goal of configuration and compatibility testing is:
   (a) To ensure that the web application can handle load during maximum traffic
   (b) To ensure database integrity
   (c) To ensure proper functioning of the web application across varied platforms
   (d) None of the above

11.12 Which of the following is not a browser?
   (a) Internet explorer
   (b) Linux
   (c) Chrome
   (d) Mozilla

11.13 Browser testing does not verify the functioning of the web application in terms of:
   (a) Load
   (b) Operating system compatibility
   (c) Text
   (d) Video

11.14 Compatibility matrix is created in:
   (a) Security testing
   (b) Database testing
   (c) Performance testing
   (d) Browser testing

11.15 The aim of security testing is not:
   (a) To protect the application from unauthorized access
   (b) To protect the application against virus threats
   (c) To ensure proper functioning of user interface items
   (d) To protect the network from intruders

11.16 Architecture of a firewall consists of:
   (a) External network
   (b) Database server
   (c) Router
   (d) Antivirus software

11.17 Virus testing ensures that:
   (a) The network is protected from intruders
   (b) Anti-virus software identifies, detects and removes viruses
   (c) Hyperlinks function properly
   (d) Anti-virus software is installed

11.18 Non-repudiation is:
   (a) The receiver's ability to prove that data came from an unauthenticated user
   (b) The receiver's ability to prove that data is not modified during transit
   (c) The receiver's ability to prove that data came from a specified user
   (d) None of the above

11.19 Access control is:
   (a) Protecting data from virus threats
   (b) Protecting data from unauthorized users
   (c) Recovering the network from failure
   (d) None of the above

11.20 The primary security requirements do not include:
  (a) Reliability
  (b) Authentication
  (c) Delivery
  (d) Performance

11.21 The factors that influence performance include:
  (i) Network bandwidth
  (ii) Reliability
  (iii) Response time
  (iv) Time to market
  (a) (i) and (ii)
  (b) (i) and (iii)
  (c) (i), (iii) and (iv)
  (d) All of the above

11.22 The difference between stress testing and load testing is:
  (a) Stress testing checks performance of the system beyond the specified limits while load testing checks the performance on specified limits
  (b) Load testing checks performance of the system beyond the specified limits while stress testing checks the performance on specified limits
  (c) Load testing consumes more resources than stress testing
  (d) None of the above

11.23 Which one is not a load testing metric?
  (a) Number of concurrent users
  (b) Wait Time
  (c) Total links on a page
  (d) Throughput

11.24 Database testing may not include:
  (a) Data validation
  (b) Virus checking
  (c) Concurrency control
  (d) Recovery from failure

11.25 An effective way to obtain the user's feedback is:
  (a) A questionnaire
  (b) A checklist
  (c) An interview
  (d) None of the above

11.26 Which one is not a web usability metric?
  (a) Total links on a page
  (b) Response time
  (c) Word count
  (d) Number of graphics

11.27 Which is not a load testing tool?
  (a) Empirix's e-Test
  (b) Illumit's WebLight
  (c) Microsoft's ACT
  (d) Radview's WebLoad

11.28 Post-deployment testing is used to:
    (a) Ensure database security
    (b) Ensure proper functioning of user interfaces
    (c) Improve the website and for future evaluations
    (d) Perform stress testing

11.29 Web usability metrics can be divided into:
    (i) Page composition metrics
    (ii) Page formatting metrics
    (iii) Recovery from failure metrics
    (iv) Performance verification metrics
    (a) (i) and (iii)
    (b) (i) and (iv)
    (c) (i), (iii) and (iv)
    (d) (i) and (ii)

11.30 Length of link text metric is used to count:
    (a) Links on a page
    (b) Words in the text for a link
    (c) Total words in links
    (d) Links embedded in the text on a page

EXERCISES

11.1 What is web testing? Differentiate between client/server applications and web application.

11.2 (a) What are the key areas in testing a web application?
    (b) Which conventional testing techniques are applicable in testing a web application?

11.3 What is user interface testing? Explain with the help of an example.

11.4 Consider a web application for registering users in order to create an email account. The registration form includes the following fields:
    (a) User name
    (b) Password
    (c) Re-type password
    (d) First name
    (e) Last name
    (f) Address
    (g) Country
    (h) Date of birth
    (i) Gender
    (j) Security question
    (k) Answer to security question
    Generate test cases using form based testing.

11.5 Explain the significance of navigation testing. List some commercially available tools for link testing.

11.6 Consider the web application given in exercise 11.4. Design test cases using form-based testing. Make the necessary assumptions.

11.7 Define usability. List and explain various attributes of usability.
11.8 (a) What is usability testing? What steps must be followed in usability testing?
(b) What is the purpose of preparing a questionnaire in usability testing?
11.9 What is the purpose of browser testing?
11.10 Describe the procedure to conduct configuration and compatibility testing for a web application.
11.11 What is the most important type of testing which we consider when we test a web application? Justify your answer.
11.12 What factors are considered while performing usability testing?
11.13 Design test cases for testing a search engine such as Google.
11.14 What is security testing? Explain the primary requirements that must be fulfilled by a web application during security testing.
11.15 Explain the significance of virus and firewall testing.
11.16 Define the following terms:
(a) Access control
(b) Authentication
(c) Integrity
(d) Non-repudiation
(e) Virus
(f) Firewall
11.17 What are several factors that influence major components of a performance test report?
11.18 (a) What is load testing? What metrics must be captured during load testing?
(b) What do you understand by the following terms?
(a) Response time
(b) Throughput
(c) Web page views per week
(c) List some commercially available load testing tools.
11.19 Discuss some areas where web testing cannot be performed effectively without the help of a tool.
11.20 Consider the following web page. Design test cases using all kinds of web testing tests.

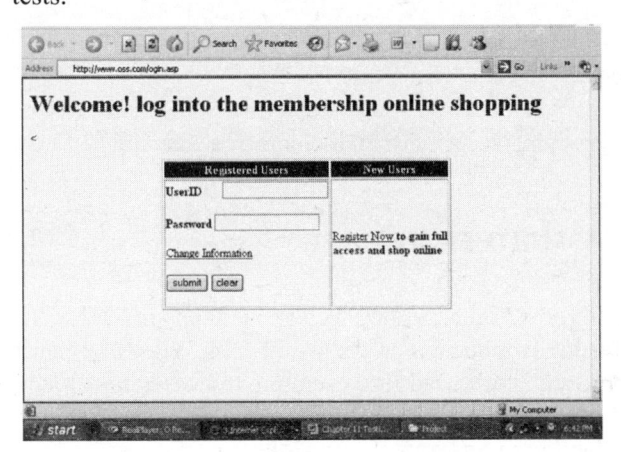

11.21 What is database testing? Identify administrative and user operations of an online purchase of a website.
11.22 What aspects must be covered in order to ensure database correctness in database testing? Explain with the help of an example.
11.23 What is post deployment testing? How are surveys helpful in post deployment testing? Explain the criteria that must be followed for deciding which suggested idea must be implemented.
11.24 (a) Identify major risks in testing a web application.
(b) What issues are considered while constructing test cases during user interface testing?
11.25 Explain three-tier architecture of a web application.
11.26 (a) Which metrics must be captured during web usability testing?
(b) Identify web page composition metrics.
11.27 Explain the significance of stress testing in analyzing the performance of a web application.
11.28 Identify functional and performance test cases of the following web page:

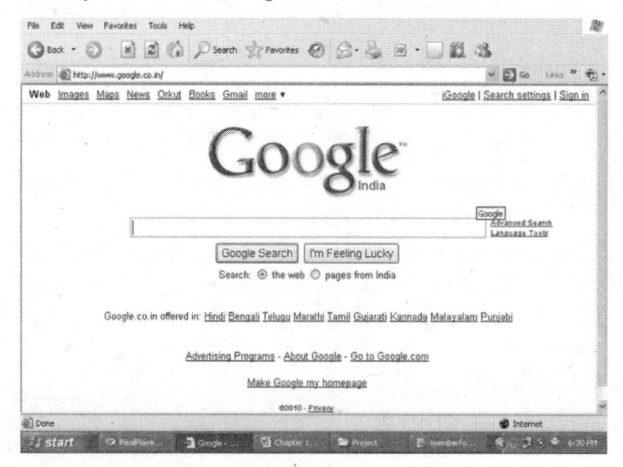

11.29 Describe the following metrics:
(a) Information quality
(b) Link quality
(c) Image quality
(d) Content percentage
(e) Wrapped links
11.30 Prepare a checklist for verifying security of an e-commerce website.

FURTHER READING

Nguyen provides good introduction on testing web applications in the book:
H.Q. Nguyen, "Testing Application on the Web", John Wiley and Sons, 2001.
A practical oriented approach is followed for generating test cases for a website in the book:
L. Tamres, "Introduction to Software Testing", Pearson Education, 2005.

The following link presents a comprehensive list of web testing tools:
> www.softwareqatest.com/qatweb1.html#LOAD.
> Savoia, "The Science and Art of Web Site Load Testing", STOESTAREAST, 2000.
> J. Dunmall and K.Clarke, "Real-World Load Testing Tips to Avoid Bottlenecks when Your App goes Live", MSDN Magazine, January 2003.

The following book is a wonderful guide for practitioners performing usability tests and provides guidelines, report formats and suggestions for conducting these tests:
> J. Rubin, "Handbook of Usability Testing: How to Plan, Design, and Conduct Effective Tests", John Wiley and Sons.

The following link provides links to web test quality assurance testing tools:
> http://www.aptest.com/webresources.html

A comprehensive checklist for testing web applications can be obtained from:
> http://sqa.fyicenter.com/FAQ/Software-Testing-Check-List/

The below survey covers testing of software quality assurance often implemented using web applications:
> Gerardo Canfora and Massimiliano Di Penta, "Service-Oriented Architectures Testing: A Survey", Lecture Notes in Computer Science, vol. 5413, pp. 78–105, 2009.

A detailed description of web metrics and their applications can be found in the following research papers:
> V. Flanders and M. Willis, "Web Pages That Suck: Learn Good design by Looking at bad Design", SYBEX, San Francisco, 1998.
> J. Nielsen, "Designing Web Usability: The Practice of Simplicity", New Riders Publishing Indianapolis, 2000.
> Karen A. Shrive, "Dynamics in Document Design", Wiley Computer Publishing, John Wiley & Sons, Inc, New York, 1997.
> L.D. Stein, "The Rating Game", http://stein.cshl.org/lstein/rater/,1997.
> G.W. Furans, "Effective View Navigation", In proceedings of ACM CHI 97 conference on human factors in computing systems, Information Structures, vol. 1, pp. 367–374, 1997.
> K. Larson and M. Czerwinski, "Web Page Design: Implications of Memory, Structure and Scent for Information Retrieval", In proceedings of ACM CHI 98 Conference on human Factors in Computing Systems, Web Page Design, vol. 1, pp. 25–32, 1998.
> J.M. Spool, Tara Scanlon, Will Schroeder, Carolyn Snyder, and Terri DeAngelo, "Web Site Usability: A Designer's Guide", Margan Kaufmann Publishers, Inc. San Francisco, 1999.
> P. Zaphiris and L.Mtei, "Depth Vs. Breadth in the Arrangement of Web Links", http://www.otal.umd.edu/SHORE/bs04,1997.
> L. Rosenfeld and P. Morville. "Information Architecture for the World Wide Web", O'Reilly & Associates, Sebastopol, CA, 1998.
> Ed H. Chi, P. Pirolli, and J. Pitkow, "The Scent of a Site: A System for Analyzing and Predicting Information Scent, Usage, and Usability of a Website", In Proceedings of ACM CHI00 Conference on Conference on Human Factors in Computing Systems, 2000.
> R. Malhotra and P. Gupta, "Empirical Evaluation of Web Page Metrics", National Conference on Quality Management in Organizations, India, February 2010.

12

Automated Test Data Generation

Is it possible to generate test data automatically? Generating test data requires proper understanding of the SRS document, SDD document and source code of the software. We have discussed a good number of techniques in the previous chapters for writing test cases manually. How can we automate the process of writing test cases? What is the effectiveness of such automatically generated test suite? Is it really beneficial in practice? We may ask such questions wherever and whenever we discuss about the relevance of automated software test data generation. As we all know, testing software is a very expensive activity and adds nothing to the software in terms of functionality. If we are able to automate test data generation, the cost of testing will be reduced significantly.

Automated test data generation is an activity that generates test data automatically for the software under test. The quality and effectiveness of testing is heavily dependent on the generated test data. Hoffman Daniel and others [DANI99] have rightly reported their views as:

> "The assurance of software reliability partially depends on testing. However, it is interesting to note that testing itself also needs to be reliable. Automating the testing process is a sound engineering approach, which can make the testing efficient, cost effective and reliable."

However, test data generation is not an easy and straightforward process. Many methods are available with their proclaimed advantages and limitations, but acceptability of any one of them is quite limited universally.

12.1 WHAT IS AUTOMATED TEST DATA GENERATION?

We require some knowledge of the software for generating test data. This knowledge may be known in terms of functionality and / or internal structure of the software. All techniques given in this book are based on either of the two or any combination of them. We manually write test cases on the basis of selected techniques and execute them to see the correctness of the software. How can we automate the process of generation of test cases / test data? The simplest way is to generate test data randomly, meaning, without considering any internal structure and / or functionality of the software. However, this way may not be an appropriate way to generate test data automatically.

12.1.1 Test Adequacy Criteria

We may generate a large pool of test data randomly or may use any specified technique. This data is used as input(s) for testing the software. We may keep testing the software if we do not know when to stop testing. How would we come to know that enough testing is performed? This is only possible if we define test adequacy criteria. Once we define this, our goal is to generate a test suite that may help us to achieve defined test adequacy criteria. Some of the ways to define test adequacy criteria are given as:

1. Every statement of the source code should be executed at least once (statement coverage).
2. Every branch of the source code should be executed at least once (branch coverage).
3. Every condition should be tested at least once (condition coverage).
4. Every path of the source code should be executed at least once (path coverage).
5. Every independent path of the source code should be executed at least once (independent path coverage).
6. Every stated requirement should be tested at least once.
7. Every possible output of the program should be verified at least once.
8. Every definition use path and definition clear path should be executed at least once.

There may be many such test adequacy criteria. Effectiveness of testing is dependent on the definition of test adequacy criteria because it sets standards to measure the thoroughness of testing. Our thrust will only be to achieve the defined standard and thus, the definition of test adequacy criteria is very important and significant to ensure the correctness of the software. When our test suite fails to meet the defined criteria, we generate another test suite that does satisfy the criteria. Many times, it may be difficult to generate a large number of test data manually to achieve the criteria and automatic test data generation process may be used to satisfy the defined criteria.

12.1.2 Static and Dynamic Test Data Generation

Test data can be generated either by statically evaluating the program or by actual execution of the program. The techniques which are based on static evaluation are called static test data generation techniques. Static test data generation techniques do not require the execution of the program. They generally use symbolic execution to identify constraints on input variables for the particular test adequacy criterion. The program is examined thoroughly and its paths are traversed without executing the program. Static test data generation techniques may not be useful for programs containing a large number of paths. The techniques which are based on the actual execution of the program for the generation of test data are called dynamic test data generation techniques. Test data is generated during the execution of the program. If during execution, a desired path is not executed, the program is traced back to find the statement which has diverted the desired flow of the program. A function minimization technique may be used to correct the input variables in order to select and execute the desired path.

12.2 APPROACHES TO TEST DATA GENERATION

The approaches to test data generation can be divided into two categories i.e. static and dynamic test data generation. One needs execution of the program (dynamic) and other does not need the execution of the program (static). We may automate any functional testing techniques (boundary value, equivalence partitioning) or structural testing techniques (path testing, data flow testing) for the generation of test data. The program will execute automatically and test data will be generated on the basis of the selected technique. The program execution will continue till the desired test adequacy criterion is achieved.

12.2.1 Random Testing

Random testing generates test data arbitrarily and executes the software using that data as inputs. The output of the software is compared with the expected output based on the inputs generated using random testing. It is the simplest and easiest way to generate test data. For a complex test adequacy criterion, it may not be an appropriate technique because it does not consider the internal structure and functionality of the source code. Random testing is not expensive and needs only a random number generator along with the software to make it functional. The disadvantage of this technique is that it may not even generate test data that executes every statement of the source code. For any reasonably sized software, it may be difficult to attain '100% statement coverage' which is one of the easiest test adequacy criteria. It is a fast technique but does not perform well as it merely generates test data based on probability and has low chances of finding semantically small bugs. A semantically small bug is a bug that is only revealed by a small percentage of the program inputs [EDVA99]. Large software or more complex test adequacy criteria may further increase the problems of random test data generators. However, in the absence of any other technique, it is the only popular technique which is commonly used in practice for the automatic generation of test data.

12.2.2 Symbolic Execution

Many early techniques of test data generation used symbolic execution for the generation of test data in which symbolic values are assigned to variables instead of actual values. The purpose is to generate an expression in terms of input variables. Phil McMinn [MCMI04] has explained the concept effectively as:

> "Symbolic execution is not the execution of a program in its true sense, but rather the process of assigning expressions to program variables as a path is followed through the code structure."

We may define a constraint system with the help of input variables which determines the conditions that are necessary for the traversal of a given path [CLAR76, RAMA76, BOYE75]. We have to find a path and then to identify constraints which will force us to traverse that particular path.

We consider a program for determination of the nature of roots of a quadratic equation. The source code and program graph of the program are given Figure 12.1 and 12.2 respectively. We select the path (1-7, 13, 25, 28-32) for the purpose of symbolic execution.

```
#include<stdio.h>
#include<conio.h>
1.   void main()
2.   {
3.       int a,b,c,valid=0,d;
4.       clrscr();
5.       printf("Enter values of a, b and c:\n");
6.       scanf("%d\n %d\n %d",&a,&b,&c);
7.       if((a>=0)&&(a<=100)&&(b>=0)&&(b<=100)&&(c>=0)&&(c<=100)){
8.           valid=1;
9.           if(a==0){
10.              valid=-1;
11.          }
12.      }
13.      if(valid==1){
14.          d=b*b-4*a*c;
15.          if(d==0){
16.              printf("Equal roots");
17.          }
18.          else if(d>0){
19.              printf("Real roots");
20.          }
21.          else{
22.              printf("Imaginary roots");
23.          }
24.      }
25.      else if(valid==-1){
26.          printf("Not quadratic");
27.      }
28.      else {
29.          printf("The inputs are out of range");
30.      }
31.      getch();
32.  }
```

Figure 12.1. Program for determination of nature of roots of a quadratic equation

The input variables a, b and c are assigned the constant variables x, y and z respectively. At statement number 7, we have to select a false branch to transfer control to statement number 13. Hence, the first constraint of the constraint system for this path is:

(i)   (x <= 0 or x > 100 or
      y <= 0 or y > 100 or
      z <= 0 or z > 100)
      and (valid = 0)

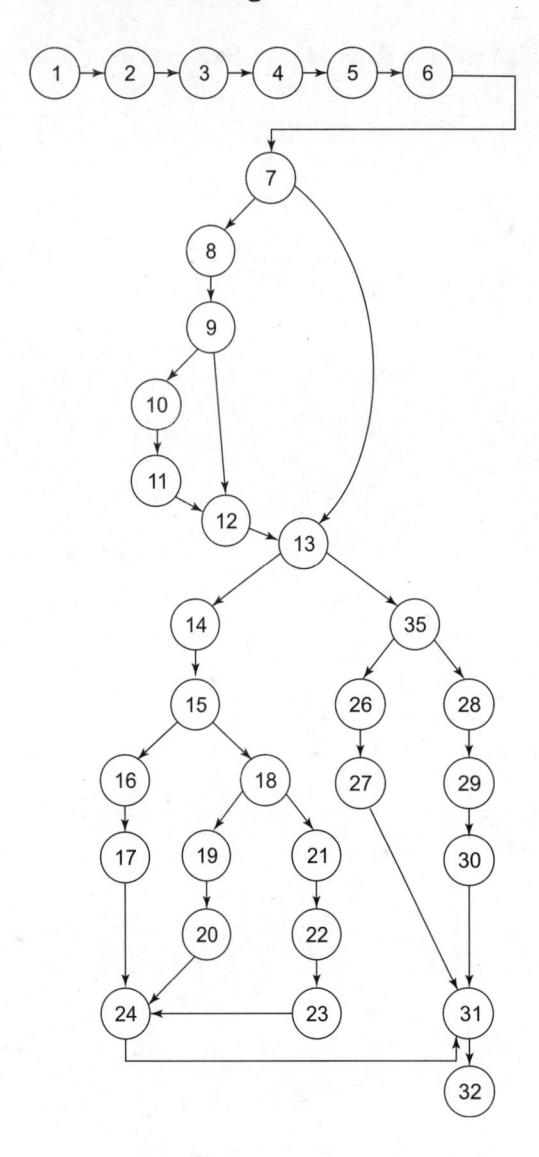

Figure 12.2. Program graph of program given in Figure 12.1

The path needs statement number 13 to become false so that control is transferred to statement number 25. The second constraint of the constraint system for this path is:

(ii) valid != 1

Finally, the path also needs statement number 25 to become false so that control is transferred to statement number 28. Hence, the third constraint of the constraint system for this path is:

(iii) valid != -1

To execute the selected path, all of the above mentioned constraints should be satisfied. One of the test cases that traverse the path (1-7, 13, 25, 28-32) may include the following inputs:

Automated Test Data Generation 499

(x = -1, y = 101, z = 101)

Another set of inputs may be (x = -1, y = 90, z = 60). The same path is traversed with both of the test cases. Similarly, if we select x path (1-7, 13, 25-27, 31, 32), constraints of the system are identified as:

(i) (x <= 0 or x > 100
      y <= 0 or y > 100
      z <= 0 or z > 100)
      and (valid = 0)
(ii) valid != 1
(iii) valid = -1

Clearly constraints (i) and (iii) are contradictory, meaning thereby, infeasibility of path. So path (1-7, 13, 25-27, 31, 32) is not feasible. Table 12.1 shows the constraints and identifies feasible/ unfeasible independent paths of the program given in Figure 12.1. Some paths are not feasible, although shown in the program graph for completion of the graph (see row 2 and row 3 of Table 12.1). Infeasible paths will not have any inputs and expected outputs as shown in Table 12.1.

Table 12.1. Constraints and values of paths (feasible/not feasible) of program given in Figure 12.1

S. No.	x	y	z	Expected Output	Path	Constraints	Feasible?
1.	101	50	50	Input values not in range	1-7, 13, 25, 28-32	(x <= 0 or x > 100 or y <= 0 or y > 100 or z <= 0 or z > 100) and (valid = 0) valid != 1 valid != -1	Yes
2.	-	-	-	-	1-7, 13, 25-27, 31, 32	(x <= 0 or x > 100 y <= 0 or y > 100 z <= 0 or z > 100) and (valid = 0) valid != 1 valid = -1	No
3.	-	-	-	-	1-9, 12, 13, 25, 28-32	(x > 0 and x <= 100 and y > 0 and y <= 100 and z > 0 and z <= 100) and x != 0 and (valid = 1) valid != 1	No
4.	0	50	50	Not quadratic	1-13, 25-27, 31, 32	(x > 0 and x <= 100 and y > 0 and y <= 100 and z > 0 and z <= 100) and x = 0 and (valid = -1) valid != 1 valid = -1	Yes

(Contd.)

(Contd.)

S. No	x	y	z	Expected Output	Path	Constraints	Feasible?
5.	99	0	0	Equal roots	1-9, 12-17, 24, 31, 32	(x > 0 and x <= 100 and y > 0 and y <= 100 and z > 0 and z <= 100) and x != 0 and (valid = 1) valid = 1	Yes
6.	50	50	1	Real roots	1-9, 12-15, 18-20, 24, 31, 32	(x > 0 and x <= 100 and y > 0 and y <= 100 and z > 0 and z <= 100) and x != 0 and (valid = 1) valid = 1	Yes
7.	50	50	50	Imaginary roots	1-9, 12-15, 18, 21-23, 24, 31, 32	(x > 0 and x <= 100 and y > 0 and y <= 100 and z > 0 and z <= 100) and x != 0 and (valid = 1) valid = 1	Yes

Therefore, in symbolic execution, constraints are identified for every predicate node of the selected path. We may generate test data for selected paths automatically using identified constraints.

Christoph. C. Michael [MICH01] and others have discussed some problems of symbolic execution in practice as:

> "One such problem arises in infinite loops, where the number of iterations depends on a non constant expression. To obtain a complete picture of what the program does, it may be necessary to characterize what happens if the loop is never entered, if it iterates once, if it iterates twice, and so on."

We may choose a good number of paths by considering various possibilities in a loop. Thus, it may be a time consuming activity. We may execute the program symbolically for one path at a time. Paths may be selected by a user or by the software using some selection technique.

In addition to loops, there are other constructs which are not easily evaluated symbolically like pointers, linked lists, graphs, trees, etc. There are also problems when the data is referenced indirectly as:

$$x = (y + k[i]) * 2$$

The value of i should be known in advance to decide which element of the array k is being referred to by k[i]. Hence, the use of pointers and arrays may complicate the process of symbolic execution of a program. Another question that arises is how to handle the function calls to modules where there is no access to the source code? Although any program can be written without using pointers, arrays and function calls, but in practice, their usage is quite popular due to the facilities they offer and may also help to reduce the complexity of the source code. The above mentioned limitations may reduce the applicability of symbolic execution to any reasonable size of the program.

12.2.3 Dynamic Test Data Generation

As against symbolic execution, dynamic test data generation techniques require actual execution of the program with some selected input(s). The values of variables are known during execution of the program. We also determine the program flow with such selected input(s). If the desired program flow / path is not executed, we may carefully examine the source code and identify the node where the flow took the wrong direction. We may use different types of search methods to alter the flow by changing the inputs till the desired path is achieved. This process may be very time consuming and may require many trials before a suitable input is identified. When we change the flow at a particular node, some other flows at different nodes may also change accidentally. Christoph. C. Michael and others [MICH01] have given their views about dynamic test data generation as:

> "This paradigm is based on the idea that if some desired test requirement is not satisfied, the data collected during execution can still be used to determine which tests come closest to satisfying the requirement. With the help of this feedback, test inputs are incrementally modified until one of them satisfies the requirement."

We consider a program given in Figure 12.3 in which statement number 8 contains a condition 'if (a >= 10)'. If we want to select the TRUE branch of this condition, we must choose inputs x and y in such a way that the value of 'a' is greater than or equal to 10, when statement number 8 is executed. How do we come to know the value of 'a'? One way is to execute the program up to statement number 8 and note the value of 'a'. The value of 'a' noted at statement number 8, when inputs given to the program are x and y, is represented as $a_8(x, y)$. We define the following function f(x, y) which is minimal when the TRUE branch is executed at statement number 8.

$$f(x, y) = \begin{cases} 10 - a_8(x, y) & \text{if } a_8(x, y) < 10 \\ 0 & \text{otherwise} \end{cases}$$

```
       #include<stdio.h>
       #include<conio.h>
1.  void main()
2.  {
3.     int x,y,a;
4.     clrscr();
5.     printf("Enter values of x and y:\n");
6.     scanf("%d\n %d", &x, &y);
7.     a=x-y;
8.     if(a >= 10)
9.     {
10.        printf("\nx = %d",x);
11.    }
12.    else
13.    {
14.        printf("\ny = %d",y);
15.    }
16.    getch();
17. }
```

Figure 12.3. A typical program

This function is also called objective function and the problem of test data generation is now reduced to only function minimization. To get the expected input (say 'a' for the program given in Figure 12.3), we have to find values of x and y that minimizes f(x,y). The objective function gives an indication to the test generator about its closeness to reaching the goal. The test generator evaluates function f(x, y) to know how close x and y are to satisfy the present test requirement being targeted. The test generator may further change the values of x and y and evaluate the function f(x, y) again to know what changes in x and y bring the input closer to satisfy the requirement. The test generator may keep on making changes in x and y and evaluates function f(x, y) until the requirement is satisfied. Finally, the test generator may find values of x and y that satisfy the targeted requirement. This is a heuristic technique and the objective function definition is dependent on the goal, which is nothing but the satisfaction of a certain test requirement. The program may, at the first time, execute on randomly generated input(s) and its behaviour is used as the basis of a search for a satisfactory input. Hence, using different types of search methods, the flow can be altered by manipulating the input in a way that the intended branch is taken [EDVA99]. It may require many iterations before a suitable input is found. Dynamic test data generation techniques generate a large amount of data during execution of the program to find expected input(s) for a desired path. Based on test adequacy criteria, a search strategy is adopted and the program is executed automatically till the chosen criteria is satisfied.

12.3 TEST DATA GENERATION USING GENETIC ALGORITHM

Evolutionary algorithms provide heuristic search strategy to find a particular solution using operators motivated by genetics and natural selection [MCMI04]. The most popular form of evolutionary algorithm is genetic algorithm in which search is driven by the use of various combinations of input variables in order to satisfy the goal of testing.

Genetic Algorithm (GA) is based on natural genetics and Darwin's principle of the survival of the fittest. It is used to find solutions for searching and optimization problems. A GA is a search procedure with a goal to find a solution in a multidimensional space. GA is generally many times faster than exhaustive search procedure and is a computer model of biological evolution. When GA is used to solve searching and optimization problems, very good results are obtained. With reference to software testing, GA is used to search the domain of input variables and to find those input variables which satisfy the desired goal of testing. GA is loosely based on the concept of genetics by combining samples to achieve new and fitter individuals [JONE96]. Inputs are combined to generate new inputs which are used for further searching of the desired goal. GA does not make incremental changes to a single structure, but maintains a population of structures from which new structures are created using genetic operators. The evolution is based on two primary operators i.e. mutation and crossover. The power of GA is the technique of applying GA operators (crossover and mutation) to a population of individuals. Despite their randomized nature, GA is not a simple random search. It uses the old knowledge held in a parent population to generate new solutions with improved performance. The population undergoes simulated evolution at each generation. Good solutions are retained and relatively bad ones are discarded and are replaced by fitter new members called offsprings. As given by Ali et al., the significant parameters for a genetic algorithm are [ALI10]:

(i) Initial population
(ii) Operators such as mutation and crossover with their values.

(iii) Fitness function created to guide the search procedure.
(iv) Selection strategy for parents.
(v) Stopping criteria.

12.3.1 Initial Population

The initial population comprises a set of individuals generated randomly or heuristically. The selection of the starting generation has a significant effect on the performance of the next generation. Each individual is represented as a chromosome (binary or gray). A binary string representation is most popular to represent a chromosome. The chromosomes are composed of genes and are subjected to modification by means of mutation and crossover. The process is similar to a natural population of biological creatures where successive generations are conceived, born and raised until they themselves are ready to reproduce. Fitness of each individual is calculated for comparing them and to differentiate their performance. An individual who is near an optimum solution gets a higher fitness value than the one who is far away. During reproduction, two members (chromosomes) are chosen from the generation. The evolutionary process is then based on the GA operators (crossover and mutation), which are applied to them to produce two new members (offspring) for the next generation.

12.3.2 Crossover and Mutation

There are two basic GA operators – crossover and mutation, which are commonly used in practice. However, many variants of both are also designed to find efficient solutions to the problem under investigation. Crossover operates at the individual (chromosome) level. Individuals are represented in the binary form. Crossover selects bits from parents (chromosome) and generates two new offsprings. In crossover operation, two members (parents) are selected from the population. A point along the bit string is selected at random, and the tails of the two bit strings are exchanged. This is known as one point crossover [JONE96]. For example, if two parents are $[V_1, V_2, ...V_m]$ and $[W_1, W_2,.......W_m]$, then crossing the chromosomes after the kth gene ($1 \leq k \leq m$) would produce the offsprings as: $[V_1, V_2,.....V_k, W_{k+1}, ...W_m]$ and $[W_1, W_2.....W_k, V_{k+1}....V_m]$. If parents are [11111111] and [00000000] and k = 5, the offsprings (children) after the application of crossover operator are [11111000] and [00000111]. A few examples of one point crossover operator are given in Table 12.2.

Table 12.2. Examples of one point crossover operator

Sr. No.	Parents		Crossover (k)	Offsprings	
	P1	P2		C1	C2
1.	11001100	10011111	4	11001111	10011100
2.	11001100	10011111	6	11001111	10011100
3.	11001100	10011111	2	11011111	10001100
4.	10000000	11111111	4	10001111	11110000
5.	10000000	11111111	6	10000011	11111100

Two point crossover operates by selecting two random genes within the parent strings with subsequent swapping of bits between these two genes. If two parents are $[V_1, V_2....V_m]$ and $[W_1, W_2....W_m]$, and the first randomly chosen point is k with $(1 \leq k \leq m-1)$ and the second random point is n with $(k+1 \leq n \leq m)$ this would produce the offsprings as:
$[(V_1, V_2....V_k), (W_{k+1}....W_n), (V_{n+1}....V_m)]$ and $[(W_1, W_2,....W_k), (V_{k+1}, ...V_n), (W_{n+1}...W_m)]$.
Examples of two point crossover operator is given in Table 12.3.

Table 12.3. Examples of two point crossover operator

Sr. No.	Parents		Crossover points		Offsprings	
	P1	P2	k	n	C1	C2
1.	11001100	10011111	2	6	11011100	10001111
2.	11001100	10011111	1	7	10011110	11001101
3.	11111111	00000000	2	5	11000111	00111000
4.	11111111	00000000	7	8	11111110	00000001
5.	11110000	00001111	2	4	11000000	00110000

Mutation changes random bits in the binary string. In the binary code, this simply means changing the state of a gene from 0 to 1 or vice-versa. Mutation is like a random walk through the search space and is used to maintain diversity in the population and to keep the population from prematurely converging on one (local) solution. Mutation avoids local optima and creates genetic material (say input) that may not be present in the current population. Mutation works by randomly changing the chosen bits from 1 to 0 or from 0 to 1. For example, after crossover, the generated offspring is [10001111] and the same may be mutated as [10011111] by changing the 4th bit from 0 to 1. We may also find optimum mutation probability P_m which is the reciprocal of the chromosome size(s) and is given as: $P_m = 1/5$. It would be unlikely for the code to have on average more than one bit of a chromosome mutated. If the mutation probability is too low, there will be insufficient global sampling to prevent convergence to a local optimum. If the rate of mutation is significantly increased, the location of global optima is delayed. After the crossover and mutation operations, we have the original population of parents and the new population of offspring. The survival of parents and offspring depends on the fitness value of every member of the population and is calculated on the basis of a fitness function.

12.3.3 Fitness Function

GA is used to find the best solution of a problem. This is carried out using a fitness function. The purpose of the fitness function is simply explained by B.F. Jones and others [JONE96] as:

> "Perhaps the most important aspect of using genetic algorithms is the ability to define a suitable fitness function, which is a numeric measure of how close each sample test set is to the goal."

The fitness value is used to compare the individuals and to differentiate their performance. An individual who is near an optimum solution gets a higher fitness value than an individual who is far away. How do we define a fitness function? Every point in the search space is represented by a valid fitness value.

For example, suppose that the function to optimize is $f(A) = A^3$ where $A \varepsilon$ [0,10]. The fitness function here may be the same and is defined as:

Fitness = A^3

Table 12.4 gives the chromosomes with their fitness values calculated by the fitness function.

Table 12.4. Chromosomes with fitness values for initial population

Sr. No.	Chromosome	A1	Fitness (f_i)
1.	C1	2	8
2.	C2	4	64
3.	C3	6	216
4.	C4	1	1

The total fitness of the population is calculated as:

$$\text{Fitness} = \sum_{i=1}^{4} f_i = 289$$

Our objective is to achieve a higher fitness value of individuals which is expected to be closer to the global optimum. In this example, a higher fitness value is achieved when the value of A = 10.

12.3.4 Selection

The selection operator selects two individuals from a generation to become parents for the recombination process (crossover and mutation). This selection may be based on fitness value or could be made randomly. If the fitness value is used, then higher value chromosomes will be selected.

12.3.5 Algorithm for Generating Test Data

1. Genetic algorithm begins with an initial population which is randomly generated where each population is represented as a chromosome.
2. Fitness of each individual is calculated for comparing them and to differentiate their performance.
3. An individual who is near an optimum solution is assigned a higher fitness value.
4. A stopping criterion is decided for stopping the test data generation process. It may be based on coverage criteria, number of iterations or the size of the final population. The following steps are repeated until the criterion is satisfied.
   (a) The genetic operators: crossover and mutation are randomly selected. If the crossover operator is selected the following steps are followed:
      (i) Parents are selected from the initial population on the basis of their fitness value.
      (ii) Crossover is performed to generate offsprings with probably better genes / fitness value.

(a) Otherwise the following steps are followed:
   (i) Each offspring is mutated by occasional random alteration of a bit value with changes in some features with unpredictable consequences.
(a) Data is prepared for the next generation.

The flow chart of the above steps is given in Figure 12.4. The process will iterate until the population has evolved to form an optimum solution of the problems or until a maximum number of iterations have taken place. The GA is an evolutionary algorithm where definition of the fitness function for any search is very important. If the fitness function is effective, desired inputs will be selected early and may help us to traverse the desired path of the program under testing.

GA generates first generation of data randomly (initial population) and then follows the steps of the flow chart given in Figure 12.4 to improve the fitness of individuals. On the basis of fitness value, crossover and mutation operators are used to generate offsprings (2nd generation individuals). This process continues until all individuals reach the maximum fitness. The system performs all operations from initial population to the last generation automatically. It does not require user interference. The automated generated test data may give better results with reduced effort and time [PRAV09].

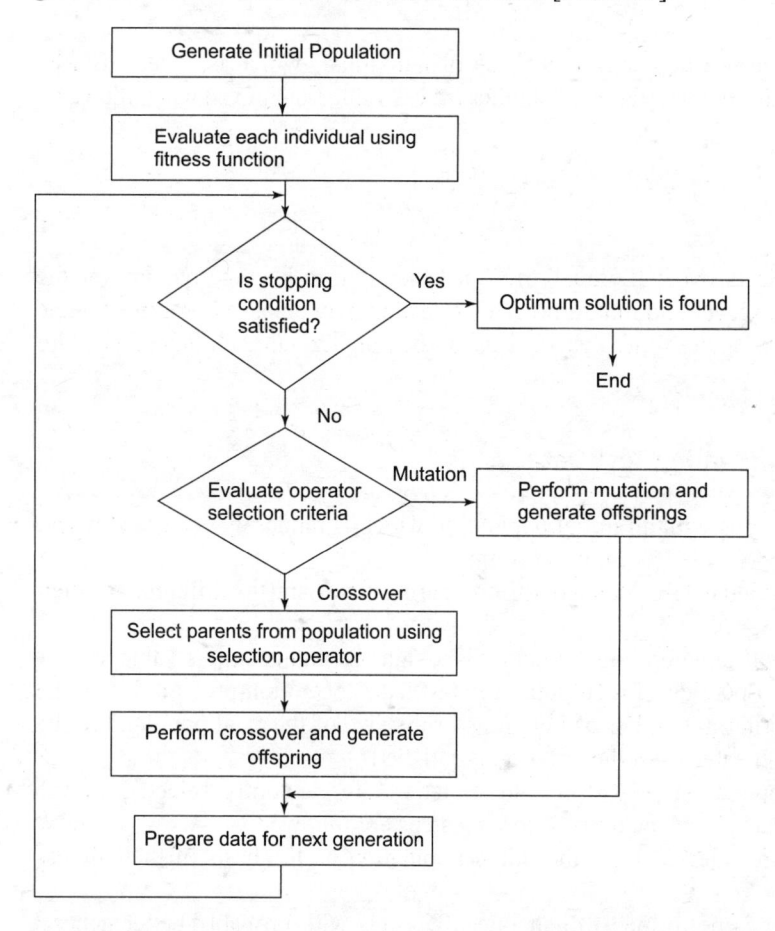

Figure 12.4. Flow chart of various steps of genetic algorithm

Example 12.1: Consider the program to divide two numbers given in Figure 12.5. Generate test data using genetic algorithm.

```
#include<stdio.h>
#include<conio.h>

void main()
{
int a, b, c;
printf("Enter value of a and b");
scanf("%d %d",&a, &b);
if(b==0)
{
    printf("Invalid Data");
}
else
{
c=a/b;
}
printf("\n a/b= %d",c);
getch();
}
```

Figure 12.5. Program to divide two numbers

Solution:

The fitness function is given below:
Fitness function

$$F(x) = \frac{x}{y*100}$$

The criteria for selection of mutation and crossover operators are given below:
If

$F(x) \leq 0.2$, use mutation operator

$0.2 < F(x) < 0.6$, use crossover operator

$F(x) \geq 0.6$, criteria satisfied

The steps for generating test data are given in the following tables. The mutation and crossover (one-point or two-point) bits are randomly selected.

1. First Generation

S. No.	a	b	Operator
1.	5	2	Mutation
2.	100	3	Crossover
3.	80	5	Mutation

a = 5, b=2
00000101 00000010
The 2nd bit is selected randomly for mutation
After mutation
0**1**000101 00000010

a = 100, b=3
01100100 00000011
Two-point crossover is performed. The first randomly chosen point is 4 and the second is 6.
After crossover
0110**0000 0000**0111
a = 80, b=5
01010000 00000101
The 7th bit is selected randomly for mutation
After mutation
010100**1**0 00000101

2. Second Generation

S. No.	a	b	Operator
1.	69	2	Crossover
2.	96	7	Mutation
3.	82	5	Mutation

a = 69, b=2
01000**101** 0000**0010**
One-point crossover is performed with randomly chosen point 5.
After crossover
01000**010** 0000**0101**

a = 96, b=7
0**1**100000 00000111
The 1st bit is selected randomly for mutation
After mutation
11100000 00000111

a = 82, b=5
0**1**010010 00000101
The 1st bit is selected randomly for mutation
After mutation
11010010 00000101

3. Third Generation

S. No.	a	b	Operator
1.	66	5	Mutation
2.	224	7	Crossover
3.	210	5	Crossover

a = 66, b=5
01000010 00000101
The 1st bit is selected randomly for mutation
After mutation
11000010 00000101

a = 224, b=7
1110**0**000 00000**1**11
Two-point crossover is performed. The first randomly chosen point is 4 and the second is 6.
After crossover
1110**0100** 0000001**1**

a = 210, b=5
11010**010** 0000010**1**
Two-point crossover is performed. The first randomly chosen point is 5 and the second is 7.
After crossover
11010**100** 0000001**1**

4. Fourth Generation

S. No.	A	b	Operator
1.	194	5	Crossover
2.	228	3	Criteria satisfied
3.	212	3	Criteria satisfied

a = 194, b=5
11000010 00000101
Two-point crossover is performed. The first randomly chosen point is 5 and the second is 7.
After crossover
11000100 00000011

5. Fifth Generation

S. No.	A	b	Operator
1.	196	3	Criteria satisfied
2.	228	3	Criteria satisfied
3.	212	3	Criteria satisfied

The criteria is satisfied after generating 5th generation population. The testing will be stopped after achieving the defined criteria.

Example 12.2: Consider the program given in Figure 12.1. Generate test data using genetic algorithm.

Solution:

The fitness function is given below:

$$F(x) = (10 - a_g(x, y))/10 \quad \text{if } a_g(x, y) < 10$$

The criteria for selection of mutation and crossover operators are given below:
If
F(x, y) ≤ 0.2, use mutation operator
0.2 < F(x, y) < 0.6, use crossover operator
F(x, y) ≥ 0.6, criteria satisfied
The tables below show the steps for generating test data.

1. First Generation

S. No.	x	y	Operator
1.	10	7	Crossover
2.	19	10	Mutation

x = 10, y=7
00001010 00000111
After crossover
00001011 00000110

x = 19, y=10
00010011 00001010
The 14th bit is selected randomly for mutation
After mutation
00010011 00001110

2. Second Generation

S. No.	x	y	Operator
1.	11	6	Crossover
2.	19	14	Crossover

x = 11, y=6
00001011 00000110
Two-point crossover is performed. The first randomly chosen point is 3 and the second is 6.
After crossover
00000111 00001010

x = 19, y=14
00010011 00001110
One-point crossover is performed with randomly chosen point 6.
After crossover
00010010 00001111

3. Third Generation

S. No.	x	y	Operator
1.	7	10	Criteria satisfied
2.	18	15	Criteria satisfied

After the 3rd generation, the criteria are satisfied. Testing will be stopped at this point.

12.4 TEST DATA GENERATION TOOLS

The use of tools for the generation of test data is still in its infancy, although some software industries have been using their own tools for the generation of test data. The output of such a tool is a set of test data, which include a sequence of inputs to the system under test. Some tools are also available that accept manually created, automatically generated, predefined test sequences and executes the sequences without human intervention and supervision. A few examples of such tools are Mercury's WinRunner, LoadRunner, Rational Robot and Teleogic Tau Tester. The purpose of these tools is to execute already generated test cases and not to generate test data automatically. We should also not confuse this with modeling tools like Rational Rose, Objecteering, Simulink and Autofocus, which are used for modeling various software engineering activities. The automated test generation tools are different and designed for a specific purpose of test data generation.

Some of the popular test generation tools are given in Table 12.5.

Table 12.5. Automated test data generation tools

S. No.	Tool	Language/ platform supported	Description	Remarks
1.	T-VEC	Java/C++	Test cases are generated by applying branch coverage	Easy to use
2.	GS Data Generator	ERP, CRM and data warehouse development	Creates industry specific data for acceptance testing	Focuses on version control and RDBMS repository
3.	MIDOAN	Ada	Used on Ada source code and generates test cases that will be used on branches and decisions.	Product of MIDOAN software engineering solutions for automatic test data generation.
4.	CONFORMIQ	C, C++, Java, Visual Basic	Automates the design of functional tests using black box testing techniques.	It delivers faster test design, higher test quality and better test coverage.
5.	CA DATAMACS test Data Generator (TDG)	Mainframe	Used for mainframe programs	It creates test data from existing files, databases or from scratch.

The software industry is focusing more on the quality of a product instead of increasing functionality. Testing is the most popular and useful way to improve several quality aspects such as reliability, security, correctness, ease of usage, maintainability, etc. If test data is generated automatically, it will reduce the effort and time of testing. Although the process of automated test data generation is still in the early stages, some reasonable success has been achieved in the industry. Further research is needed to develop effective tools and techniques. A special effort is also required to increase the flexibility, user friendliness and ease of use of these tools.

MULTIPLE CHOICE QUESTIONS

Note: *Select the most appropriate answer for the following questions.*

12.1 Automated test data generation is used to generate:
   (a) Test data
   (b) Test cases
   (c) Test suite
   (d) All of the above

12.2 Dynamic test data generation involves:
   (a) Static analysis of the program
   (b) Actual execution of the program
   (c) Verification of requirements
   (d) All of the above

12.3 Symbolic execution is a:
   (a) Black box testing technique
   (b) Gray box testing technique
   (c) Static testing technique
   (d) Dynamic testing technique

12.4 Symbolic execution is based on:
   (a) Variables
   (b) Constraints
   (c) Paths
   (d) Boundary values

12.5 Random testing:
   (a) Generates test data based on constraints
   (b) Generates test data arbitrarily
   (c) Generates test cases based on independent paths
   (d) None of the above

12.6 Symbolic execution is applicable to a:
   (a) Large sized program
   (b) Small sized program
   (c) Medium sized program
   (d) (b) and (c)

12.7 The purpose of objective function is:
   (a) Function minimization
   (b) Function maximization
   (c) Function optimization
   (d) Function execution

12.8 Which one is a popular heuristic search technique?
   (a) Hill climbing
   (b) Simulated annealing
   (c) Genetic algorithm
   (d) Neural network

12.9 Evolutionary algorithms are based on:
   (a) Heuristic search strategy
   (b) Constraint based systems
   (c) Exhaustive search
   (d) None of the above

12.10 Genetic operators are:
   (a) Mutation and addition
   (b) Mutation and subtraction
   (c) Crossover and addition
   (d) Mutation and crossover

12.11 The function of crossover operator is to:
   (a) Mutate a bit
   (b) Transpose a bit
   (c) Generate two new offsprings
   (d) Generate one new offspring

12.12 The function of the mutation operator is to:
   (a) Randomly change bits
   (b) Generate new offsprings
   (c) Reproduce new bits
   (d) None of the above

12.13 Fitness function is used to:
   (a) Verify the effectiveness of variables
   (b) Verify the performance of a test suite
   (c) Measure how close each sample test set is to the goal
   (d) All of the above

12.14 Fitness function is used in:
   (a) Genetic algorithm
   (b) Symbolic execution
   (c) Mutation testing
   (d) Data flow testing

12.15 Which is not a software test data automation tool?
   (a) MIDOAN
   (b) CONFORMIQ
   (c) WINRUNNER
   (d) T-VEC

EXERCISES

12.1 What is symbolic execution? How is it different from random testing?
12.2 Explain the significance of symbolic execution. What are the advantages and limitations of this technique?
12.3 What is random testing? Why is it popular in practice?
12.4 List the advantages of automated test data generation over manual test data generation.
12.5 (a) What is dynamic test data generation?
   (b) Differentiate between static and dynamic test data generation.

12.6 Consider a program to determine the division of a student based on his/her average marks in three subjects. Design test cases and list constraints of each independent path using symbolic execution.

12.7 Explain the use of fitness function. Consider a small program and construct its fitness function.

12.8 What are genetic algorithms? How are they different from traditional exhaustive search based algorithms?

12.9 Write short notes on the following:
   (a) Mutation
   (b) One point crossover
   (c) Two point crossover
   (d) Fitness function

12.10 Explain with the help of a flowchart the functionality of genetic algorithms.

12.11 Consider a program to subtract two numbers. Construct its fitness function and generate test data using genetic algorithm.

12.12 List and explain genetic algorithm operators. Differentiate between one-point and two-point crossover.

12.13 Define the following:
   (a) Genetic algorithm
   (b) Gene
   (c) Chromosomes
   (d) Initial population

12.14 Effective testing is dependent on the definition of test adequacy criteria. Explain and comment.

12.15 List various tools for generating test data. Explain their purpose and applicability.

FURTHER READING

The detailed introduction on search based test data generation techniques is presented in:

> P. McMinn "Search based Software Test Data Generation: A Survey", *Software Testing, Verification and Reliability*, vol. 14, no. 2, pp.105–156, June 2004.

An excellent and detailed survey on search based software engineering including testing and debugging is given in:

> Mark Harman, S. Afshin Mansouri and Yuanyuan Zhang, "Search Based Software Engineering: A Comprehensive Analysis and Review of Trends Techniques and Applications", TR-09-03, April 2009.

A systematic review on automated test data generation techniques can be found at:

> Shshid Mahmood, "A Systematic Review of Automated Test Data Generation Techniques", Master Thesis, MSE-2007:26, School of Engineering, Blekinge Institute of Technology, Ronneby, Sweden, October 2007.

Richard and Offutt provide a new constraint based test data generation technique in:

> R.A. DeMillo and A.J. Offutt, "Constraint Based Automatic Data Generation", IEEE Transactions on Software engineering, vol. 17, no. 9, pp. 900–910, September 1991.

Jones and his colleagues present a good technique for generating test cases using genetic algorithm:

> B.F. Jones, H.H. Sthamer and D.E. Eyres, "Automatic Structural Testing Using Genetic Algorithms", Software Engineering Journal, September, pp. 299–306, 1996.

Few introductory research papers are listed to understand the concepts of automated test data generation:

> D.C. Ince, "The Automatic Generation of Test Adapt", The Computer Journal, vol. 30, no. 1, pp. 63–69, 1987.
>
> Jon Edvardsson, "A Survey on Automatic Test Case Generation", In proceedings of the Second Conference on Computer Science and Engineering in Linkoping, pp. 21–28, ECSEL, October, 1999.
>
> M. Prasanna et al., "A Survey on Automatic Test Case Generation", Academic Open Internet Journal, http://www.acadjournal.com, vol. 15, 2005.
>
> Anastasis A. Sofokleous and Andrew S. Andreou, "Automatic Evolutionary Test Data Generation for Dynamic Software Testing", Journal of Systems and Software, vol. 81, pp. 1883–1898, 2008.
>
> Silivia Regina Vergillo et al., "Constraint Based Structural Testing Criteria", Journal of Systems and Software, vol. 79, pp. 756–771, 2006.

The following research paper presents the use of genetic algorithm for automatic test data generation:

> Christoph C. Michael, Gray McGraw and Michael A. Schatz, "Generating Software Test Data by Evolution", *IEEE Transactions on Software Engineering*, vol. 27, no. 12, 1085–1110, December, 2001.

An excellent introduction on genetic algorithm can be obtained from:

> Goldberg, David E, "Genetic Algorithms in Search, Optimization and Machine Learning", Kluwer Academic Publishers, Boston, MA, 1989.
>
> M. Mitchell, "An Introduction to Genetic Algorithms", MIT Press, Cambridge, MA, 1996.
>
> R. Poli, W.B.. Langdon, N. F McPhee, "A Field Guide to Genetic Programming", www.Lulu.com, 2008,
>
> D. Whitley, "A genetic algorithm tutorial", Statistics and Computing, vol. 4, pp. 65–85, 1994.

A good Ph.D. work on test data generation using genetic algorithms is available in:

> Harman-Hinrich Sthamer, "The Automatic Generation of Software Test Data using Genetic Algorithms", Ph.D. Thesis, University of Glamorgan, U.K., November 1995.

Appendix I

PROBLEM STATEMENT

A university is organized in different teaching schools and each school conducts a variety of programmes. Admissions to the various programmes offered by each school are done through counselling. Admission slips are issued to the admitted students giving their roll numbers, name of the school and name of the programme. Students are registered in various schools manually based on the admission slips. Students are assigned papers (compulsory, elective and practical) depending upon the scheme of the selected programme. Every school is responsible for its registration process and the following are prepared and maintained manually:

  (i) List of students registered in a programme.
  (ii) List of students registered for a particular paper.
  (iii) List of papers offered in a particular semester.
  (iv) List of faculty in a school.
  (v) Personal details of the students.
  (vi) Registration card for every registered student.

The university decides to automate the manual registration process in order to improve the existing system. The proposed system should perform the following functions:

- Issue of login Id and password to the members i.e. students and faculty.
- Maintain the personal details of the students.
- Maintain the details of the faculty.
- Maintain the details of the various papers – theory (compulsory and elective) and practical as per the scheme of the programme.
- Maintain the semester-wise details of each student.
- Issue of registration card to each student every semester.
- List of registered students:
  - Roll number wise
  - Programme wise
  - Semester wise
  - Paper wise

» List of programmes offered by the university.
» List of papers offered in a particular semester for a particular programme.
» List of faculty in a school.

CONTENTS

1. Introdtuction
    1.1 Purpose
    1.2 Scope
    1.3 Definitions, Acronyms and Abbreviations
    1.4 References
    1.5 Overview
2. Overall Description
    2.1 Product Perspective
        2.1.1 System Interfaces
        2.1.2 User Interfaces
        2.1.3 Hardware Interfaces
        2.1.4 Software Interfaces
        2.1.5 Communication Interfaces
        2.1.6 Memory Constraints
        2.1.7 Operations
        2.1.8 Site Adaptation Requirements
    2.2 Product Functions
    2.3 User Characteristics
    2.4 Constraints
    2.5 Assumptions and Dependencies
    2.6 Apportioning of Requirements
3. Specific Requirements
    3.1 External Interface Requirements
        3.1.1 User Interfaces
        3.1.2 Hardware Interfaces
        3.1.3 Software Interfaces
        3.1.4 Communication Interfaces
    3.2 Functional Requirements
        3.2.1 Login
        3.2.2 Maintain School Details
        3.2.3 Maintain Programme Details
        3.2.4 Maintain Scheme Details
        3.2.5 Maintain Paper Details
        3.2.6 Maintain Student Details
        3.2.7 Maintain Faculty Details
        3.2.8 Maintain Student Registration Form
        3.2.9 Generate Reports
        3.2.10 Generate Registration Card

3.3 Performance Requirements
3.4 Design Constraints
3.5 Software System Attributes
3.6 Logical Database Requirements
3.7 Other Requirements

Software Requirements Specification Document for University Registration System

1. Introduction

A university is organized in different teaching schools and each school conducts a variety of programmes. Admissions to the various programmes offered by each school are done through counselling. Admission slips are issued to the admitted students giving their roll numbers, name of the school and the name of the programme.

After admission, every student has to register in the University Registration System (URS) which is open for a specific period at the beginning of the academic session. Every student has to obtain a login Id and password from the 'System Administrator'. After successfully logging on to the system, a student needs to enter his/her personal details in the system. The student also needs to select elective papers of his/her choice as per the programme scheme. Compulsory papers (theory and practical) offered in that semester are then assigned automatically. On submitting the requisite details, a registration card giving the personal information and list of the papers to be studied during the semester is issued to the student.

Faculty members can also access the URS by obtaining the login Id and password from the system administrator. They can view the details of the students who have been registered for various programmes in a school.

1.1 Purpose

The URS maintains information about various papers to be studied by a student in a particular programme. A paper may either be a theory paper or a practical paper. Theory papers may be of two types: compulsory paper or elective paper. Compulsory papers are assigned automatically whereas a student has to select the elective papers of his/her choice in a particular semester.

1.2 Scope

The proposed 'University Registration System' shall perform the following functions:

- Issue of login Id and password to the members i.e. students and faculty.
- Maintain the personal details of the students.
- Maintain the details of the faculty.
- Maintain details of the various papers – theory (compulsory and elective) and practical as per the scheme of the programme.

- Maintain registration details of the students.
- Issue of registration card to each student every semester.
- Generate list of registered students:
  - Roll number wise
  - Programme wise
  - Semester wise
  - Paper wise
» Generate list of programmes offered by the university.
» Generate list of papers offered in a particular semester for a particular programme.
» Generate list of faculty in a school.

1.3 Definitions, Acronyms and Abbreviations

URS: University Registration System
User: Any user (Student, Faculty or Administrator)
LAN: Local Area Network
RAM: Random Access Memory
UG: Undergraduate
PG: Postgraduate
Student: Any candidate admitted in a programme (UG or PG) offered by a school.
Status: Status of the Student – registered or unregistered in URS.
System Administrator/Administrator: User having all the privileges to operate the URS.
Data Entry Operator (DEO): User having privileges to maintain student and faculty details.
Faculty: Teaching staff of the university – Professor, Reader, Lecturer.
School: Academic unit that offers various programmes.
Programme: Degree Programme (UG or PG) as offered by a school.
Semester: Duration for which a student has to study (normally 20 weeks) before appearing for the university examinations. There are two semesters in a year.
Scheme: Details of compulsory and elective papers (including practicals) offered in a semester for a programme.

1.4 References

(a) 'A Practitioner's Guide to Software Test Design' by Lee Copeland, Artech House, 2004.
(b) 'Software Engineering' by K.K. Aggarwal & Yogesh Singh, New Age Publishing House, 3rd Edition, 2008.
(c) IEEE Recommended Practice for Software Requirements Specifications – IEEE Std 830-1998.
(d) IEEE Standard for Software Test Documentation – IEEE Std. 829-1998.

1.5 Overview

The rest of the SRS document describes various system requirements, interfaces, features and functionalities in detail.

2. Overall Description

The URS registers a student for a semester to a programme offered by a school of a university. It is assumed that the student has already been admitted in the university for a specific programme. The system administrator will receive lists of the admitted students (school-wise and programme-wise) from the academic section responsible for counselling. The establishment section will provide the list of the faculty members appointed in the school. Based on this information, the system administrator/Data Entry Operator (DEO) will generate the login Id and password for the faculty and the students.

The user can access URS on the university's LAN. Students are permitted to add, modify and view their information only after they have successfully logged on to the system. After registration, students can print their registration card. Faculty members can make the query about the registered students and view/print the information of the registered students, papers offered in the various programmes, etc. The system administrator is the master user of the URS and will maintain the records of the school, programme, scheme, paper, students and faculty, and generate their login Id and password. The system administrator will also be able to generate the registration card and various reports from the URS. The DEO will be able to maintain the records of students and faculty.

The administrator will have to maintain the following information:

- Login details
- School details
- Programme details
- Scheme details
- Paper details

The administrator/DEO will have to maintain the following information:

- Student details
- Faculty details

The student will be able to add/edit/view the following information:

- Student registration details

The administrator/student requires following reports from the proposed system:

- Registration card

The administrator/faculty will be able to generate the following reports from the system:

- List of registered students
  - Roll number wise
  - Programme wise
  - Semester wise
  - Paper wise
- List of programmes offered by the university.
- List of papers offered in a particular semester of a particular programme.
- List of faculty in a school.

2.1 Product Perspective

The proposed system shall be developed using client/server architecture and be compatible with Microsoft Windows Operating System. The front end of the system will be developed using Visual Basic 6.0 and the backend will be developed using MS SQL Server 2000.

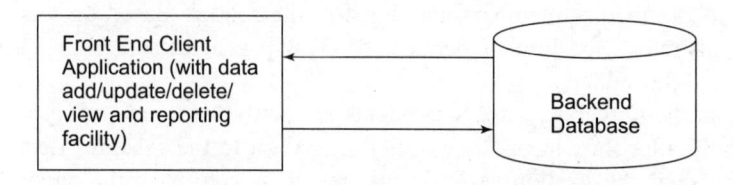

2.1.1 System Interfaces

None

2.1.2 User Interfaces

The URS will have the following user-friendly and menu driven interfaces:

- (a) **Login:** to allow the entry of only authorized users through valid login Id and password.
- (b) **School Details:** to maintain school details.
- (c) **Programme Details:** to maintain programme details.
- (d) **Scheme Details:** to maintain scheme details of a programme.
- (e) **Paper Details:** to maintain paper details of a scheme for a particular programme.
- (f) **Student Details:** to maintain students' details that will include personal information.
- (g) **Faculty Details:** to maintain the faculty members' details.
- (h) **Student Registration Details:** to maintain details about papers to be studied by a student in the current semester.

The software should generate the following viewable and printable reports:

- (a) **Registration Card:** It will contain the roll number, name of the student, school, programme, semester and the papers in which the student is registered. The registration card will be generated after filling the necessary information in the student registration form.
- (b) **List of Students:** It will be generated roll number wise, programme wise, semester wise and paper wise.
- (c) **List of Programmes:** It will give the details of programmes offered by various schools of the university.
- (d) **List of Papers:** It will give the list of papers offered in a particular semester for a particular programme.
- (e) **List of Faculty:** It will give the list of faculty in a school.

2.1.3 Hardware Interfaces

(a) Screen resolution of at least 640 × 480 or above.
(b) Support for printer (dot matrix, deskjet, laserjet).
(c) Computer systems will be in the networked environment as it is a multi-user system.

2.1.4 Software Interfaces

(a) MS-Windows Operating System
(b) Microsoft Visual Basic 6.0 for designing the front-end
(c) MS SQL Server 2000 for the backend

2.1.5 Communication Interfaces

Communication is via Local Area Network (LAN).

2.1.6 Memory Constraints

At least 512 MB RAM and 500 MB space of hard disk will be required to run the software.

2.1.7 Operations

None

2.1.8 Site Adaptation Requirements

The terminal at the client site will have to support the hardware and software interfaces specified in section 2.1.3 and 2.1.4 respectively.

2.2 Product Functions

The URS will allow access only to authorized users with specific roles (system administrator, DEO, faculty and students). Depending upon the user's role, he/she will be able to access only specific modules of the system.
The following is a summary of major functions that the URS will perform:

- A login facility for enabling only authorized access to the system.
- The system administrator will be able to add, modify, delete or view the programme, school, scheme, paper and login information.
- The DEO will be able to add, modify or delete student and faculty information.
- Students will be able to add/modify his/her details and register for papers to be studied in the current semester.

- The system administrator/student will be able to generate student registration card of a particular semester for a particular programme.
- The system administrator/faculty will be able to generate reports.

2.3 User Characteristics

- Qualification: At least matriculation and comfortable with English.
- Experience: Should be well versed/informed about the registration process of the university.
- Technical Experience: Elementary knowledge of computers.

2.4 Constraints

- There will be only one administrator.
- The 'delete' operation is available to the administrator and DEO (can only delete student and faculty records). To reduce the complexity of the system, there is no check on the 'delete' operation. Hence, the administrator/DEO should be very careful before deletion of any record and he/she will be responsible for data consistency.
- The user will not be allowed to update the primary key.

2.5 Assumptions and Dependencies

- The academic section will provide the lists of the admitted students (school-wise and programme-wise).
- The establishment section will provide the list of the faculty members appointed in the school.
- The login Id and password must be created by the system administrator and communicated to the concerned user confidentially to avoid unauthorized access to the system.
- It is assumed that a student registering for the subsequent semester has been promoted to that semester by the university as per rules and has paid the desired university fee.
- The registration process will be open only for a specific duration.

2.6 Apportioning of Requirements

Not Required

Specific Requirements

This section contains the software requirements in detail along with the various forms to be developed.

3.1 External Interface Requirements

3.1.1 User Interfaces

The following user interfaces (or forms) will be provided by the system:

(i) **Login Form**
This will be the first form, which will be displayed. It will allow the user to access different forms based on his/her role.

Various fields available on this form will be:

- *Login Id:* Numeric of 11 digits in length and only digits from 0 to 9 are allowed. Alphabets, special characters and blank spaces are not allowed.
- *Password:* Alphanumeric in the range of 4 to 15 characters in length. Blank spaces are not allowed. However, special characters are allowed.

(ii) **Change Password**
The 'change password' form facilitates the user to change the password. Various fields available on this form will be:

- *Login Id:* Numeric of 11 digits in length and only digits from 0 to 9 are allowed. Alphabets, special characters and blank spaces are not allowed.
- *Old Password:* Alphanumeric in the range of 4 to 15 characters in length. Blank spaces are not allowed. However, special characters are allowed.
- *New Password:* Alphanumeric in the range of 4 to 15 characters in length. Blank spaces are not allowed. However, special characters are allowed.
- *Confirm Password*: Alphanumeric in the range of 4 to 15 characters in length. Blank spaces are not allowed. However, special characters are allowed. The contents of this field must match with the contents of the new password field.

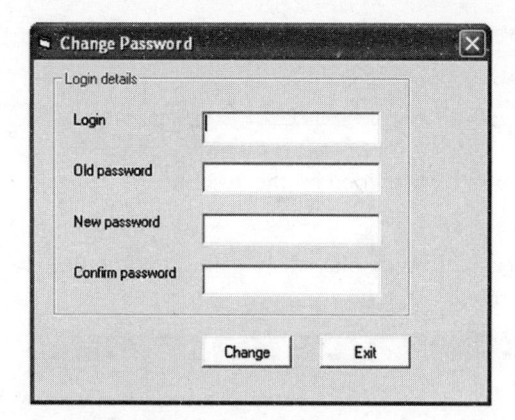

(iii) **School Details**

This form will be accessible only to the system administrator. It will allow him/her to add/edit/delete/view information about new/existing school(s).

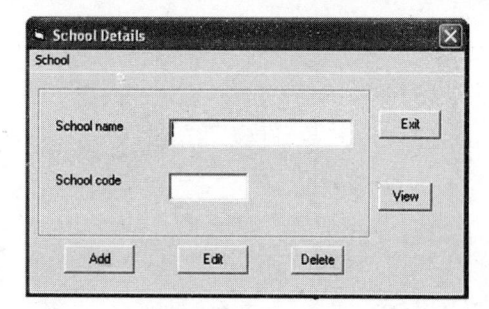

Various fields available on this form will be:

- *School Name:* Alphanumeric of 10 to 100 characters in length. Digits and special characters are not allowed. Blank spaces between characters are allowed.
- *School Code:* Numeric and will have a value from 101 to 199.

(iv) **Programme Details**

This form will be accessible only to the system administrator. It will allow him/her to add/edit/delete/view information about new/existing programme(s) for the school that was selected in the 'Programme Details' form.

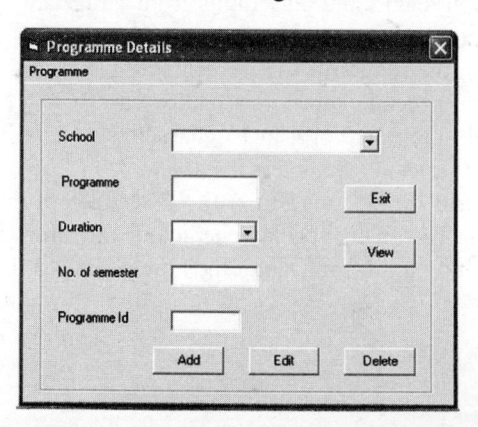

Various fields available on this form will be:

- *School*: will display the name of all the schools.
- *Programme:* Alphanumeric of length 3 to 50 characters. Special characters (except brackets) are not allowed. Numeric data will not be allowed.
- *Duration:* Numeric and can have a value from 1 to 7 years.
- *Number of Semesters :* Numeric and can have a value from 2 to 14 digits.
- *Programme Id:* Numeric and can have a value from 1 to 99.

(v) **Scheme Details**

This form will be accessible only to the system administrator. It will allow him/her to add/edit/delete/view information about new/existing scheme(s) for the school and programmes that were selected in the 'Scheme Details' form. The list of schools and programmes available in that particular school will be displayed.

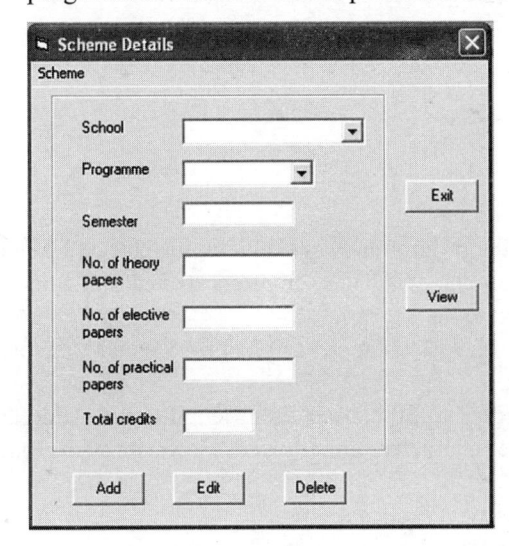

Various fields available on this form will be:

- *School*: will display the name of all the schools.
- *Programme:* will display the name of all the programmes of the selected school.
- *Semester:* will display the current semester of the selected programme. It is a numeric field and can have a value from 1 to 14.
- *Number of Theory (Compulsory) Papers:* It is a numeric field and will have a value from 0 to 10. Compulsory papers in the semester may be 'zero' depending upon the scheme of the programme.
- *Number of Elective Papers:* It is a numeric field and will have a value from 0 to 10. Elective Papers in the semester may be 'zero' depending upon the scheme of the programme.
- *Number of Practical Papers:* It is a numeric field and will have a value from 0 to 10. Practical papers in the semester may be 'zero' depending upon the scheme of the programme.
- *Total Credits:* will display total credits of the current semester. It is a numeric field and will have a value from 5 to 99.

(vi) Paper Details

This form will be accessible only to the system administrator. It will allow him/her to add/edit/delete/view information about new/existing paper(s) for the school, the programme and the semester that were selected in the 'Paper Details' form.

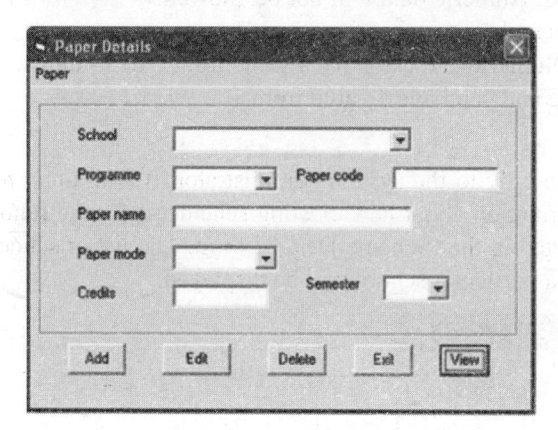

Various fields available on this form will be:

- *School:* will display all the schools.
- *Programme:* will display all the programmes available in the selected school.
- *Semester:* will display the number of all the semesters available in the selected programme.
- *Paper Code:* Alphanumeric of 5 to 7 characters in length. Special characters and blank spaces are not allowed.
- *Paper Name:* Alphanumeric of 3 to 30 characters in length. This field can have only alphabetic letters. Special characters are allowed. However blank spaces are not allowed.
- *Paper Type:* Compulsory/Elective/Practical.
- *Credits:* Numeric and will have a value from 1 to 30.

(vii) Student Details

This form will be accessible to the system administrator/DEO. It will allow them to add/edit/delete/view information about new/existing student(s) for a particular year.

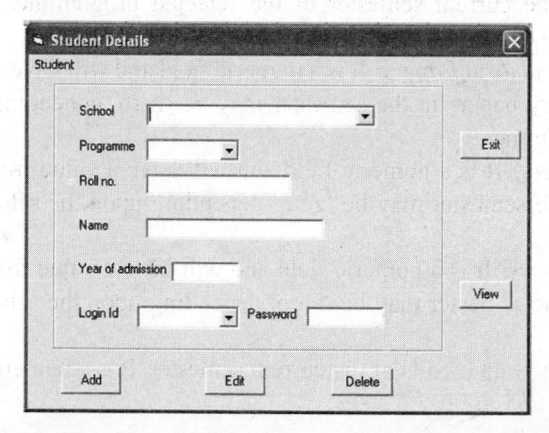

Various fields available on this form will be:

- *School:* will display all the schools.
- *Programme:* will display all the programmes available in the selected school.
- *Roll number:* Alphanumeric of 11 characters in length and only digits from 0 to 9 are allowed. Alphabets, special characters and blank spaces are not allowed.
- *Name:* Alphanumeric of 3 to 50 characters in length. Blank spaces are allowed. Special characters are not allowed.
- *Year of admission:* Numeric of up to 4 digits in length.
- *Login Id:* will be displayed (same as roll number of the student).
- *Password:* Alphanumeric in the range of 4 to 15 characters in length. Blank spaces are not allowed. However, special characters are allowed. Initially it contains 8 digits of a randomly generated number (auto generated).

(viii) Faculty Details

This form will be accessible only to the system administrator/DEO. It will allow him/her to add/edit/delete/view information about new/existing faculty member(s) in a particular school.

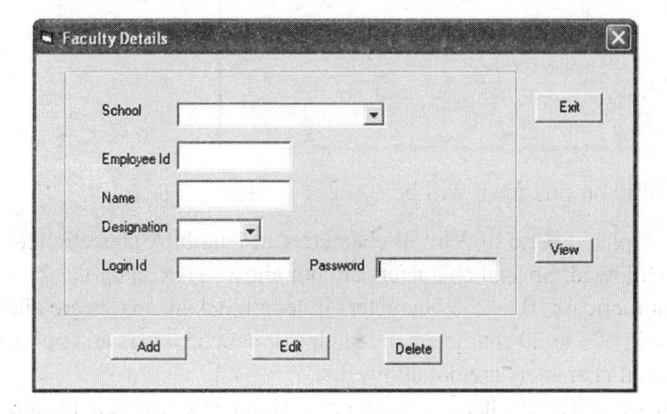

Various fields available on this form will be:

- *School*: will display the name of all the schools.
- *Employee Id:* Alphanumeric of 11 characters in length and only digits from 0 to 9 are allowed. Alphabets, special characters and blank spaces are not allowed.
- *Name:* will have only alphabetic letters and will be of 3 to 50 characters in length. Blank spaces are allowed.
- *Designation:* will have values: Professor, Associate Professor or Assistant Professor.
- *Login Id:* same as employee Id.
- *Password:* Alphanumeric in the range of 4 to 15 characters in length. Blank spaces are not allowed. However, special characters are allowed. Initially it contains 8 digits of a randomly generated number (auto generated).

(ix) Student Registration Details

This form will be accessible to the system administrator and students. It will be available only when registration for a semester is open. It will be filled by the student in order to register himself/herself for the current semester. Every student will fill his/her form only.

[Student Registration Form screenshot]

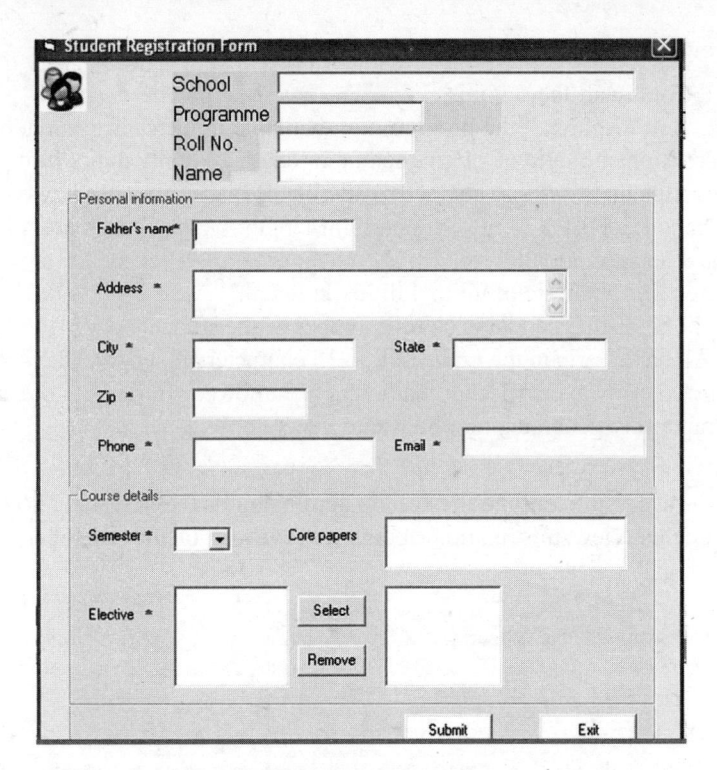

Various fields available on this form will be:

- *Father's Name:* Alphanumeric of 3 to 50 characters in length. Alphabetic letters and blank spaces are allowed. Special characters are not allowed (except'.').
- *Address:* Alphanumeric of 10 to 200 characters in length. Blank spaces are allowed.
- *City:* Alphanumeric of 3 to 20 characters in length. Alphabetic letters and blank spaces are allowed. Special characters are not allowed.
- *State:* Alphanumeric of 3 to 20 characters in length. Alphabetic letters and blank spaces are allowed. Special characters are not allowed.
- *Zip:* Numeric of 6 digits in length.
- *Phone:* Numeric of up to 11 digits in length.
- *Email:* Alphanumeric of up to 50 characters in length. Email must have one '@' and '.' symbol.
- *Semester:* will display the number of all the semesters available in the selected programme.
- *Core:* will display all the core papers in the semester selected by the user.
- *Elective:* will display all the elective papers available in the semester selected by the user.

(x) **Generate Registration Card**

The registration card will be accessible to the system administrator and students. The system will generate student registration card for every student in different semesters.

Name of the University

Semester Registration Card

Name of the Candidate: _____   Roll No.: _____

Name of the School: _____   Course: _____

S. No.	Course Code	Course Title
1.		
2.		
3.		
4.		

(xi) Generate Reports

The reports will be accessible to the system administrator and faculty. The system will generate different reports according to the specified criteria.

(i) List of students roll number wise:

Name of the University		
Roll no. _____		
Name	School	Programme

(ii) List of students programme wise:

Name of the University			
Name of the School			
Name of the Programme			
S. No.	Roll No.	Name	Semester
1.			
2.			
3.			

(iii) List of students semester wise:

Name of the University	
Name of the School	
Name of the Programme	
Name of the Semester	
S. No.	Roll No.	Name
1.		
2.		
3.		

(iv) List of students paper wise:

Name of the University	
Name of the School	
Name of the Programme	
Name of the Semester	
Name of the Paper	
S. No.	Roll No.	Name
1.		
2.		
3.		

(v) List of programmes in a school:

Name of the University	
Name of the School	
S. No.	Programme code	Programme Name
1.		
2.		
3.		

(vi) List of papers in a particular semester:

Name of the University			
Name of the School			
Name of the Programme			
Name of the Semester			
S. No.	Paper code	Paper Name	Paper type
1.			
2.			
3.			

(vii) List of faculty members in a school:

Name of the University		
Name of the School		
S. No.	Faculty name	Designation
1.		
2.		
3.		

3.1.2 Hardware Interfaces

As stated in Section 2.1.3

3.1.3 Software Interfaces

As stated in Section 2.1.4

3.1.4 Communication Interfaces

None

3.2 Functional Requirements

The use cases with their use case descriptions are given in chapter 5 and Appendix II.

3.2.1 Login

A. Validity Checks

(i) Every user will have a unique login Id.
(ii) The login Id cannot be blank.
(iii) The login Id can only have 11 digits.
(iv) The login Id will not accept alphabets, special characters and blank spaces.
(v) The password cannot be blank.
(vi) The length of the password can only be between 4 and 15 digits.
(vii) Alphabets, digits, hyphens and underscore characters are allowed in a password field.
(viii) A password cannot have blank spaces.
(ix) The old password cannot be blank.
(x) The length of the old password can only be between 4 and 15 digits.
(xi) Alphabets, digits, hyphens and underscore characters are allowed in the old password field.
(xii) The old password will not accept blank spaces.
(xiii) The new password cannot be blank.
(xiv) The length of the new password can only be between 4 and 15 digits.
(xv) Alphabets, digits, hyphens and underscore characters are allowed in the new password field.

(xvi) The new password will not accept blank spaces.
(xvii) 'Confirm password' cannot be blank.
(xviii) 'Confirm password' must match with the new password

B. Sequencing information

None

C. Error Handling/Response to Abnormal Situations

If any of the validations' flow does not hold true, an appropriate error message will be prompted to the user for doing the needful.

3.2.2 School Details

A. Validity Checks

(i) Only the administrator will be authorized to access the 'Maintain School Details' module.
(ii) Every school will have a unique school name.
(iii) The school code cannot be blank.
(iv) The school code cannot contain alphanumeric, special and blank characters.
(v) The school code will have only 3 digits.
(vi) The school name cannot be blank.
(vii) The school name will only accept alphabetic characters and blank spaces.
(viii) The school name cannot accept special characters and numeric digits.
(ix) The school name can have between 10 and 50 characters.

B. Sequencing information

None

D. Error Handling/Response to Abnormal Situations

If any of the validations' flow does not hold true, an appropriate error message will be prompted to the user for doing the needful.

3.2.3 Programme Details

A. Validity Checks

(i) Only the administrator will be authorized to access the 'Maintain Programme Details' module.
(ii) Every programme will have a unique programme code and name.
(iii) The school name cannot be blank.
(iv) The programme name cannot be blank.
(v) The programme name can be of 3 to 50 characters in length.
(vi) The programme name can only have alphabets and brackets.
(vii) The programme name cannot have special characters, digits and blank spaces.
(viii) The duration cannot be blank.
(ix) The duration can have a value from 1 to 7.
(x) The number of semesters cannot be blank.

(xi) The number of semesters can have a value from 2 to 14.
(xii) The programme code cannot be blank.
(xiii) The programme code cannot have special characters, digits and blank spaces.
(xiv) The programme code can have only 2 digits.

B. Sequencing information

The school details will have to be entered into the system before any programme details can be entered into the system.

C. Error Handling/Response to Abnormal Situations

If any of the validations'/sequencing flow does not hold true, an appropriate error message will be prompted to the user for doing the needful.

3.2.4 Scheme Details

A. Validity Checks

(i) Only the administrator will be authorized to access the 'Maintain Scheme Details' module.
(ii) Every scheme will have a unique semester.
(iii) The school name cannot be blank.
(iv) The programme name cannot be blank.
(v) The number of theory papers cannot be blank.
(vi) The number of theory papers can have a value between 0 and 10.
(vii) The number of elective papers cannot be blank.
(viii) The number of elective papers can have a value between 0 and 10.
(ix) The number of practical papers cannot be blank.
(x) The number of practical papers can have a value between 0 and 10.
(xi) The semester cannot be blank.
(xii) The semester can have a value only between 1 and 14.
(xiii) The total credit cannot be blank.
(xiv) The total credit can have a value between 5 and 99.

B. Sequencing information

The school and programme details will have to be entered into the system before any scheme details can be entered into the system.

C. Error Handling/Response to Abnormal Situations

If any of the validations'/sequencing flow does not hold true, an appropriate error message will be prompted to the administrator for doing the needful.

3.2.5 Paper Details

A. Validity Checks

(i) Only the administrator will be authorized to access the 'Maintain Paper Details' module.
(ii) A scheme will have more than one paper.

(iii) No two semesters will have the same paper i.e. a paper will be offered only in a particular semester for a given programme.
(iv) The school name cannot be blank.
(v) The programme name cannot be blank.
(vi) The semester cannot be blank.
(vii) The semester can have a value only between 1 and 14.
(viii) The paper code cannot be blank.
(ix) The paper code cannot accept special characters.
(x) The paper code can have both alphabetic and numeric characters.
(xi) The paper code can include blank spaces.
(xii) The paper code can be of 5 to 7 characters in length.
(xiii) The paper name cannot be blank.
(xiv) The paper name can have alphanumeric (alphabets and digits) characters or blank spaces.
(xv) The paper name cannot have special characters.
(xvi) The paper type may be compulsory, elective or practical.
(xvii) The credit cannot be blank.
(xviii) The credit can have a value only between 1 and 30.

B. Sequencing information

School, programme and scheme details will have to be entered into the system before any paper details can be entered into the system.

C. Error Handling/Response to Abnormal Situations

If any of the validations'/sequencing flow does not hold true, an appropriate error message will be prompted to the user for doing the needful.

3.2.6 Student Details

A. Validity Checks

(i) Only the administrator/DEO will be authorized to access the 'Maintain Student Details' module.
(ii) Every student will have a unique roll number.
(iii) The school name cannot be blank.
(iv) The programme name cannot be blank.
(v) The roll number cannot be blank.
(vi) The length of the roll number for any user can only be equal to 11 digits.
(vii) The roll number cannot contain alphabets, special characters and blank spaces.
(viii) The student name cannot be blank.
(ix) The length of the student name can be between 3 and 50 characters.
(x) The student name will only accept alphabetic characters and blank spaces.
(xi) The year of admission cannot be blank.
(xii) The year of admission can have only 4 digits.
(xiii) The password cannot be blank (initially auto generated of 8 digits).
(xiv) The password can be of 4 to 15 characters in length.
(xv) Alphabets, digits and hyphens and underscore characters are allowed in the password field. However, blank spaces are not allowed.
(xvi) The roll number and login Id are the same.

B. Sequencing information

School and programme details will have to be entered into the system before any student details can be entered into the system.

C. Error Handling/Response to Abnormal Situations

If any of the validations'/sequencing flow does not hold true, an appropriate error message will be prompted to the user for doing the needful.

3.2.7 Faculty Details

A. Validity Checks

(i) Only the administrator/DEO will be authorized to access the 'Maintain Faculty Details' module.
(ii) Every faculty member will have a unique employee Id.
(iii) The school name cannot be blank.
(iv) The employee Id cannot be blank.
(v) The length of the employee Id will be equal to 11 digits only.
(vi) The employee Id cannot contain alphabets, special characters and blank spaces.
(vii) The name of the employee cannot be blank.
(viii) The employee name will only accept alphabetic characters and blank spaces. Special characters are not allowed.
(ix) The designation cannot be blank.
(x) The password cannot be blank (initially auto generated of 8 digits).
(xi) The password can be of 4 to 15 characters in length.
(xii) Alphabets, digits, hyphens and underscore characters are allowed in the password field. However blank spaces are not allowed.

B. Sequencing information

The school details should be available in the system.

C. Error Handling/Response to Abnormal Situations

If any of the validations'/sequencing flow does not hold true, an appropriate error message will be prompted to the administrator for doing the needful.

3.2.8 Registration Form

A. Validity Checks

(i) Only the administrator/student will be authorized to access the student registration module.
(ii) The father's name cannot be blank.
(iii) The father's name cannot include special characters and digits, but blank spaces are allowed.
(iv) The father's name can be of 3 to 50 characters in length.
(v) The address cannot be blank.
(vi) The address can be of 10 to 200 characters in length.

(vii) The city cannot be blank.
(viii) The name of the city can be of 3 to 20 characters in length.
(ix) The name of the city cannot include special characters and numeric digits, but blank spaces are allowed.
(x) The state cannot be blank.
(xi) The name of the state can be of 3 to 20 characters in length.
(xii) The name of the state cannot include special characters and numeric digits, but blank spaces are allowed.
(xiii) The zip code cannot be blank.
(xiv) The zip code cannot include alphabets, special characters and blank spaces.
(xv) The zip code can be of 6 digits in length.
(xvi) The phone number cannot be blank.
(xvii) The phone number cannot include alphabets, special characters and blank spaces.
(xviii) The phone number can be up to 11 digits long.
(xix) The email cannot be blank.
(xx) The email can be of up to 50 characters in length.
(xxi) The email should contain one '@' and one '.' character.
(xxii) The email cannot include blank spaces.
(xxiii) The semester should be blank.
(xxiv) A semester may or may not have an elective paper.
(xxv) The student cannot select more than the required elective papers.
(xxvi) The student is required to register within the stipulated registration time.

B. Sequencing information

The student details will have to be entered into the system before any student registration details can be entered into the system.

C. Error Handling/Response to Abnormal Situations

If any of the validations'/sequencing flow does not hold true, an appropriate error message will be prompted to the user for doing the needful.

3.2.9 Generate Report

A. Validity Checks

(i) Only the administrator/faculty will be authorized to access the 'Generate Reports' module.

B. Sequencing information

Reports can be generated only after the school, programme, scheme, paper and student registration details have been entered into the system.

C. Error Handling/Response to Abnormal Situations

If any of the validations'/sequencing flow does not hold true, an appropriate error message will be prompted to the user for doing the needful.

3.2.10 Generate Registration Card

A. Validity Checks

(ii) Only the administrator/student will be authorized to access the 'Generate Registration Card' module.

B. Sequencing information

The registration card can be generated only after the school, programme, scheme, paper and student registration details have been entered into the system for that student for the given semester.

3.3 Performance Requirements

(i) Should run on 500 MHz, 512 MB RAM machine.
(ii) Responses should be within 2 seconds.

3.4 Design Constraints

None

3.5 Software System Attributes

Usability

The application will be user friendly, easy to operate and the functions will be easily understandable.

Reliability

The applications will be available to the students throughout the registration period and have a high degree of fault tolerance.

Security

The application will be password protected. Users will have to enter the correct login Id and password to access the application.

Maintainability

The application will be designed in a maintainable manner. It will be easy to incorporate new requirements in the individual modules.

Portability

The application will be easily portable on any windows-based system that has SQL Server installed.

3.6 Logical Database Requirements

The following information will be placed in a database:

Table Name	Description
Login	Records the login details of the user.
School	Records the details of the various schools in the university.
Programme	Records programmes offered in a school.
Scheme	Stores the details of the schemes of a programme such as number of compulsory (core) papers, number of elective papers in a semester, total number of theory and practical papers offered, etc.
Paper	Stores details of papers offered in a programme.
Student	Records the student details.
Faculty	Records the faculty details.
StudentPaperList	Records semester-wise papers selected by a student.
RegistrationOpen	A student can register only in a semester that is open for a specific duration. If the registration closes, he/she cannot register. The student may not be permitted to register more than once in a semester.

Appendix II

MAINTAIN SCHEME DETAILS

Use Case Description

1. Introduction

Allow administrator to maintain details of scheme of a particular programme. This includes adding, updating, deleting and viewing scheme information.

2. Actors

Administrator

3. Pre-Conditions

The administrator must be logged onto the system. The School and Programme details for which the scheme is to be added/updated/deleted/viewed must be available before this use case begins.

4. Post-Conditions

If the use case is successful, the scheme information is added/updated/deleted/viewed from the system. Otherwise, the system state is unchanged.

5. Basic Flow

This use case starts when administrator wishes to add/modify/edit/delete/view scheme information:

(i) The system requests that the administrator specify the function he/she would like to perform (either Add a scheme, Edit a scheme, Delete a scheme or View a scheme)

(ii) Once the administrator provides the requested information, one of the flows is executed.

(iii) If the administrator selects "Add a Scheme", the **Add a Scheme** flow is executed.
(iv) If the administrator selects "Edit a Scheme", the **Edit a Scheme** flow is executed.
(v) If the administrator selects "Delete a Scheme", the **Delete a Scheme** flow is executed.
(vi) If the administrator selects "View a Scheme", the **View a Scheme** flow is executed.

Basic Flow 1: Add a Scheme

The system requests that the administrator enters the scheme information. This includes:

(i) The system requests the administrator to select school and programme and also enter the following information:
   1. Semester
   2. Number of theory courses
   3. Number of elective courses
   4. Number of practical courses
   5. Total credits

(ii) Once the administrator provides the requested information, scheme is added to the system.

Basic Flow 2: Edit a Scheme

(i) The system requests the administrator to select the school name, programme name and semester.
(ii) The administrator selects the school and programme and also enters the semester. The system retrieves and displays the scheme information.
(iii) The administrator makes the desired changes to the scheme information. This includes any of the information specified in the **Add a Scheme** flow.
(iv) The system prompts the administrator to confirm the updation of the scheme.
(v) After confirming the changes, the system updates the scheme record with the updated information.

Basic Flow 3: Delete a Scheme

(i) The system requests that the administrator specify the school name, programme name and semester.
(ii) The administrator selects the school and programme and also enters the semester. The system retrieves and displays the scheme information.
(iii) The system prompts the administrator to confirm the deletion of the scheme.
(iv) The administrator confirms the deletion.
(v) The system deletes the scheme record.

Basic Flow 4: View a Scheme

(i) The system requests that the administrator specify the school name, programme name and semester.
(ii) The system retrieves and displays the scheme information.

6. Alternative Flows

Alternative Flow 1: Invalid Entry

If in the **Add a Scheme or Edit a Scheme** flows, the actor enters invalid semester/Number of theory papers/number of elective papers/number of practical papers/total credits or leaves the invalid semester/Number of theory papers/number of elective papers/number of practical papers/total credits empty, the system displays an appropriate error message. The actor returns to the basic flow and may reenter the invalid entry.

Alternative Flow 2: Scheme already exist

If in the **Add a Scheme** flow, a scheme with a specified semester already exists, the system displays an error message. The administrator returns to the basic flow and may reenter the scheme.

Alternative Flow 3: Scheme not found

If in the **Edit a Scheme or Delete a Scheme or View a Scheme** flows, the scheme information with the specified school name, programme name and semester does not exist, the system displays an error message. The administrator returns to the basic flow and may reenter the specified school name, programme name or semester.

Alternative Flow 4: Edit cancelled

If in the **Edit a Scheme** flow, the administrator decides not to edit the scheme, the edit is cancelled and the **Basic Flow** is re-started at the beginning.

Alternative Flow 5: Delete cancelled

If in the **Delete a Scheme** flow, the administrator decides not to delete the scheme, the delete is cancelled and the **Basic Flow** is re-started at the beginning.

Alternative Flow 6: Deletion not allowed

If in the **Delete a Scheme** flow, paper details of the semester selected exists then the system displays an error message. The administrator returns to the basic flow and may reenter the specified school, programme or semester.

Alternative Flow 7: User exits

This allows the user to exit at any time during the use case. The use case ends.

7. Special Requirements

None.

8. Associated use case

Login, Maintain School Details, Maintain Programme Details, Maintain Paper Details.

TEST CASES GENERATED FROM USE CASE MAINTAIN SCHEME DETAILS

Table II-1. Scenario matrix for the maintain scheme details use case		
Scenario 1- Add a scheme	Basic Flow 1	
Scenario 2- Add a scheme alternative flow: Invalid Entry	Basic Flow 1	Alternate Flow 1
Scenario 3- Add a scheme alternative flow: Scheme already exists	Basic Flow 1	Alternate Flow 2
Scenario 4- Add a scheme alternative flow: User Exits	Basic Flow 1	Alternate Flow 7
Scenario 5- Edit a scheme	Basic Flow 2	
Scenario 6 - Edit a scheme alternative flow: Invalid Entry	Basic Flow 2	Alternate Flow 1
Scenario 7- Edit a scheme alternative flow: Scheme not found	Basic Flow 2	Alternate Flow 3
Scenario 8- Edit a scheme alternative flow: Edit cancelled	Basic Flow 2	Alternate Flow 4
Scenario 9- Edit a scheme alternative flow: User Exits	Basic Flow 2	Alternate Flow 7
Scenario 10- Delete a scheme	Basic Flow 3	
Scenario 11- Delete a scheme alternative flow: Scheme not found	Basic Flow 3	Alternate Flow 3
Scenario 12- Delete a scheme alternative flow: Deletion cancelled	Basic Flow 3	Alternate Flow 5
Scenario 13- Delete a scheme alternative flow: Deletion not allowed	Basic Flow 3	Alternate Flow 6
Scenario 14- Delete a scheme alternative flow: User Exits	Basic Flow 3	Alternate Flow 7
Scenario 15- View a scheme	Basic Flow 4	
Scenario 16- View a scheme alternative flow: Scheme not found	Basic Flow 4	Alternate Flow 3
Scenario 17- View a scheme alternative flow: User Exits	Basic Flow 4	Alternate Flow 7

For maintain a scheme use case, we identify nine input variables for various basic flows in the use case. There are five input variables namely semester, number of theory papers, No. of elective papers, No. of practical papers, Total credits) and four selection variables (School selected, Programme Selected, edit confirmed, delete confirmed) in this use case. These inputs will be available for the respective flows as specified in the use case.

Table II-2. Test case matrix for the maintain scheme details use case

Test case Id	Scenario Name and description	Input 1 School selected	Input 2 Prog. selected	Input 3 Semester	Input 4 No. of theory papers	Input 5 No. of elective papers	Input 6 No. of practical papers	Input 7 Total credits	Edit confirmed	Delete confirmed	Expected output	Remarks (if any)
TC1	Scenario 1- Add a scheme	Yes	Yes	Valid input	Valid input	Valid input	Valid input	Valid input	n/a	n/a	Scheme is added successfully	--
TC2	Scenario 2- Add a scheme alternative flow: Invalid entry	No	Yes/no	Valid/ invalid input	Valid/ invalid input	Valid/ invalid input	Valid/ invalid input	Valid/ invalid input	n/a	n/a	School not selected	User did not select a school
TC3	--do--	Yes	No	Valid/ invalid input	Valid/ invalid input	Valid/ invalid input	Valid/ invalid input	Valid/ invalid input	n/a	n/a	Programme not selected	User did not select programme
TC4	--do--	Yes	Yes	Invalid input	Valid/ invalid input	Valid/ invalid input	Valid/ invalid input	Valid/ invalid input	n/a	n/a	Invalid Semester	Semester is not in the specified format/range
TC5	--do--	Yes	Yes	Valid input	Invalid input	Valid/ invalid input	Valid/ invalid input	Valid/ invalid input	n/a	n/a	Invalid Number of theory papers	Number of theory papers are not in the specified format/range
TC6	--do--	Yes	Yes	Valid input	Valid input	Invalid input	Valid/ invalid input	Valid/ invalid input	n/a	n/a	Invalid number of elective papers	Number of elective papers are not in the specified format/range
TC7	--do--	Yes	Yes	Valid input	Valid input	Valid input	Invalid input	Valid/ invalid input	n/a	n/a	Invalid number of practical papers	Number of practical papers are not in the specified format/range
TC8	--do--	Yes	Yes	Valid input	Valid input	Valid input	Valid input	Invalid input	n/a	n/a	Invalid total credits	Total credits are not in the specified format/range

(Contd.)

(Contd.)

Test case Id	Scenario Name and description	Input 1 School selected	Input 2 Prog. selected	Input 3 Semester	Input 4 No. of theory papers	Input 5 No. of elective papers	Input 6 No. of practical papers	Input 7 Total credits	Edit confirmed	Delete confirmed	Expected output	Remarks (if any)
TC9	Scenario 3- Add a scheme alternative flow: School already exists	Yes	Yes	Valid input	Valid input	Valid input	Valid input	Valid input	n/a	n/a	Scheme already exits	Scheme with the specified school, programme and semester already exists in the database
TC10	Scenario 4- Add a scheme alternative flow: User exits	Yes/no	Yes/no	Valid / Invalid input	Valid / Invalid input	Valid / Invalid input	Valid / Invalid input	Valid / Invalid input	n/a	n/a	User is allowed to exit and returns to Main menu	—
TC11	Scenario 5- Edit a scheme	Yes	Yes	Valid input	Valid input	Valid input	Valid input	Valid input	Yes	n/a	Scheme is updated successfully	—
TC12	Scenario 6- Edit a scheme alternative flow: Invalid entry	Yes	Yes	Invalid input	Valid/ invalid input	Valid/ invalid input	Valid/ invalid input	Valid/ invalid input	n/a	n/a	Invalid Semester	Semester is not in the specified format/range
TC13	—do—	Yes	Yes	Valid input	Invalid input	Valid/ invalid input	Valid/ invalid input	Valid/ invalid input	n/a	n/a	Invalid Number of theory papers	Number of theory papers are not in the specified format/range
TC14	—do—	Yes	Yes	Valid input	Valid input	Invalid input	Valid/ invalid input	Valid/ invalid input	n/a	n/a	Invalid number of elective papers	Number of elective papers are not in the specified format/range
TC15	—do—	Yes	Yes	Valid input	Valid input	Valid input	Invalid input	Valid/ invalid input	n/a	n/a	Invalid number of practical papers	Number of practical papers are not in the specified format/range
TC16	—do—	Yes	Yes	Valid input	Valid input	Valid input	Valid input	Invalid input	n/a	n/a	Invalid total credits	Total credits are not in the specified format/range

(Contd.)

Appendix II 547

(Contd.)

Test case Id	Scenario Name and description	Input 1 School selected	Input 2 Prog. selected	Input 3 Semester	Input 4 No. of theory papers	Input 5 No. of elective papers	Input 6 No. of practical papers	Input 7 Total credits	Edit confirmed	Delete confirmed	Expected output	Remarks (if any)
TC17	Scenario 7- Edit a scheme alternative flow: Scheme not found	Yes	Yes	Valid input	n/a	n/a	n/a	n/a	n/a	n/a	Scheme not found	Scheme with the specified school, programme and semester does not exist in the database
TC18	Scenario 8- Edit cancelled	Yes	Yes	Valid input	Valid input	Valid input	Valid input	Valid input	No	n/a	Sub menu for scheme details appears	User cancels the edit operation
TC19	Scenario 9- Edit a scheme alternative flow: User exits	Yes/no	Yes/no	Valid / Invalid input	Valid / Invalid input	Valid / Invalid input	Valid / Invalid input	Valid / Invalid input	n/a	n/a	User is allowed to exit and returns to Main menu	—
TC20	Scenario 10- Delete a scheme	Yes	Yes	Valid input	n/a	n/a	n/a	n/a	n/a	Yes	Scheme is deleted successfully	—
TC21	Scenario 11- Delete a scheme alternative flow: Scheme not found	Yes	Yes	Valid input	n/a	n/a	n/a	n/a	n/a	n/a	Scheme not found	Scheme with the specified school, programme and semester does not exist in the database
TC22	Scenario 12- Delete a scheme alternative flow: Deletion cancelled	Yes	Yes	Valid input	n/a	n/a	n/a	n/a	n/a	No	Sub menu for scheme details appears	User cancels the delete operation

(Contd.)

(Contd.)

Test case Id	Scenario Name and description	Input 1 School selected	Input 2 Prog. selected	Input 3 Semester	Input 4 No. of theory papers	Input 5 No. of elective papers	Input 6 No. of practical papers	Input 7 Total credits	Edit confirmed	Delete confirmed	Expected output	Remarks (if any)
TC23	Scenario 13- Delete a scheme alternative flow: Deletion not allowed	Yes	Yes	Valid input	n/a	n/a	n/a	n/a	n/a	n/a	Deletion not allowed	Paper details for the specified scheme exist in the database
TC24	Scenario 14- Delete a scheme alternative flow: User exits	Yes/no	Yes/no	Valid / Invalid input	n/a	n/a	n/a	n/a	n/a	n/a	User is allowed to exit and returns to Main menu	–
TC25	Scenario 15- View a scheme	Yes	Yes	Valid input	n/a	n/a	n/a	n/a	n/a	n/a	Scheme displayed successfully	–
TC26	Scenario 16- View a scheme alternative flow: Scheme not found	Yes	Yes	Valid input	n/a	n/a	n/a	n/a	n/a	n/a	Scheme not found	Paper details for the specified scheme exist in the database
TC27	Scenario 17- View a scheme alternative flow: User exits	Yes/no	Yes/no	Valid / Invalid input	n/a	n/a	n/a	n/a	n/a	n/a	User is allowed to exit and returns to Main menu	–

n/a: option(s) not available for respective scenario

Table II-3. Test case matrix with actual data values for the maintain scheme details use case

Test case Id	Scenario Name and description	School selected	Prog. selected	Semester	No. of theory papers	No. of elective papers	No. of practical papers	Total credits	Edit confirmed	Delete confirmed	Expected output	Remarks (if any)
TC1	Scenario 1- Add a scheme	University School of Information Technology	MCA	1	5	0	2	22	n/a	n/a	Scheme is added successfully	–
TC2	Scenario 2- Add a scheme alternative flow: Invalid entry	*	*	*	*	*	*	*	n/a	n/a	School not selected	User did not select a school
TC3	—do—	University School of Information Technology		*	*	*	*	*	n/a	n/a	Programme name blank	User did not selected programme name
TC4	—do—	University School of Information Technology	MCA	8	*	*	*	*	n/a	n/a	Invalid Semester	Semester exceeds the limit specified in programme details for MCA
TC5	—do—	University School of Information Technology	MCA	1	12	*	*	*	n/a	n/a	Invalid Number of theory papers	Number of theory papers is not in the specified format which should have the value from 0-10
TC6	—do—	University School of Information Technology	MCA	1	5	11	*	*	n/a	n/a	Invalid number of elective papers	Number of elective papers is not in the specified format which should have the value from 0-10
TC7	—do—	University School of Information Technology	MCA	1	5	0	12	*	n/a	n/a	Invalid number of practical papers	Number of practical papers is not in the specified format which should have the value from 0-10
TC8	—do—	University School of Information Technology	MCA	1	5	0	2	4	n/a	n/a	Invalid total credits	Total credits is not in the specified format which should have the value from 5-99

(Contd.)

(Contd.)

Test case Id	Scenario Name and description	School selected	Prog. selected	Semester	No. of theory papers	No. of elective papers	No. of practical papers	Total credits	Edit confirmed	Delete confirmed	Expected output	Remarks (if any)
TC9	Scenario 3- Add a scheme alternative flow: School already exists	University School of Information Technology	MCA	1	5	0	2	22	n/a	n/a	Scheme already exits	Scheme with specified semester already exist in the database
TC10	Scenario 4- Add a scheme alternative flow: User exits	*	*	*	*	*	*	*	n/a	n/a	User is allowed to exit and returns to Main menu	—
TC11	Scenario 5- Edit a scheme	University School of Information Technology	MCA	4	4	2	2	26	Yes	n/a	Scheme is updated successfully	—
TC12	Scenario 6- Edit a scheme alternative flow: Invalid entry	University School of Information Technology	BTech(IT)	18	*	*	*	*	n/a	n/a	Invalid Semester	Semester exceeds the limit specified in programme details for B.Tech
TC13	—do—	University School of Information Technology	BTech(IT)	2	11	*	*	*	n/a	n/a	Invalid Number of theory papers	Number of theory papers is not in the specified format which should have the value from 0-10
TC14	—do—	University School of Information Technology	BTech(IT)	2	5	12	*	*	n/a	n/a	Invalid number of elective papers	Number of elective papers is not in the specified format which should have the value from 0-10
TC15	—do—	University School of Information Technology	BTech(IT)	2	5	0	12	*	n/a	n/a	Invalid number of practical papers	Number of practical papers is not in the specified format which should have the value from 0-10

(Contd.)

Appendix II 551

(Contd.)

Test case Id	Scenario Name and description	School selected	Prog. selected	Semester	No. of theory papers	No. of elective papers	No. of practical papers	Total credits	Edit confirmed	Delete confirmed	Expected output	Remarks (if any)
TC16	—do—	University School of Information Technology	BTech(IT)	2	5	0	2	187	n/a	n/a	Invalid total credits	Total credits is not in the specified format and should have the value from 5-99
TC17	Scenario 7- Edit a scheme alternative flow: Scheme not found	University School of Information Technology	BTech(IT)	2	n/a	n/a	n/a	n/a	n/a	n/a	Scheme not found	Scheme with the specified school, programme and semester does not exist in the database
TC18	Scenario 8- Edit cancelled	University School of Information Technology	BTech(IT)	2	5	0	2	22	No	n/a	Sub menu for scheme details appears	User cancels the edit operation
TC19	Scenario 9- Edit a scheme alternative flow: User exits	*	*	*	*	*	*	*	n/a	n/a	User is allowed to exit and returns to Main menu	User exits from the scheme details use case
TC20	Scenario 10- Delete a scheme	University School of Information Technology	BTech(IT)	2	n/a	n/a	n/a	n/a	n/a	Yes	Scheme is deleted successfully	--
TC21	Scenario 11- Delete a scheme alternative flow: Scheme not found	University School of Information Technology	BTech(IT)	2	n/a	n/a	n/a	n/a	n/a	n/a	Scheme not found	Scheme with the specified school, programme and semester does not exist in the database
TC22	Scenario 12- Delete a scheme alternative-flow: Deletion cancelled	University School of Information Technology	BTech(IT)	2	n/a	n/a	n/a	n/a	n/a	No	Sub menu for scheme details appears	User cancels the delete operation

(Contd.)

Appendix II

(Contd.)

Test case Id	Scenario Name and description	School selected	Prog. selected	Semester	No. of theory papers	No. of elective papers	No. of practical papers	Total credits	Edit confirmed	Delete confirmed	Expected output	Remarks (if any)
TC23	Scenario 13- Delete a scheme alternative flow: Deletion not allowed	University School of Information Technology	BTech(IT)	2	n/a	n/a	n/a	n/a	n/a	n/a	Deletion not allowed	Paper details for the specified scheme exist in the database
TC24	Scenario 14- Delete a scheme alternative flow: User exits	*	*	*	n/a	n/a	n/a	n/a	n/a	n/a	User is allowed to exit and returns to Main menu	User exits from the scheme details use case
TC25	Scenario 15- View a scheme	University School of Information Technology	BTech(IT)	2	n/a	n/a	n/a	n/a	n/a	n/a	Scheme displayed successfully	–
TC26	Scenario 16- View a scheme alternative flow: Scheme not found	University School of Information Technology	BTech(IT)	2	n/a	n/a	n/a	n/a	n/a	n/a	Scheme not found	Scheme with the specified school, programme and semester does not exist in the database
TC27	Scenario 17-View a scheme alternative flow: User exits	*	*	*	n/a	n/a	n/a	n/a	n/a	n/a	User is allowed to exit and returns to Main menu	User exits from the scheme details use case

*: do not care conditions (valid/invalid inputs)
n/a: option(s) not available for respective scenario

MAINTAIN PAPER DETAILS

Use Case Description

1. Introduction

Allow administrator to maintain details of papers of a particular scheme for a programme. This includes adding, updating, deleting and viewing paper information.

2. Actors

Administrator

3. Pre-Conditions

The administrator must be logged onto the system. The school, programme and scheme details to which the papers are to be added/updated/deleted/viewed must be available before this use case begins.

4. Post-Conditions

If the use case is successful, the paper information is added/updated/deleted/viewed from the system. Otherwise, the system state is unchanged.

5. Basic Flow

This use case starts when administrator wishes to add/edit/delete/view paper information
- (i) The system requests that the administrator specify the function he/she would like to perform (either Add a paper, Edit a paper, Delete a paper or View a paper)
- (ii) Once the administrator provides the requested information, one of the flows is executed.
  - If the administrator selects "Add a Paper", the **Add a Paper** flow is executed.
  - If the administrator selects "Edit a Paper", the **Edit a Paper** flow is executed.
  - If the administrator selects "Delete a Paper", the **Delete a Paper** flow is executed.
  - If the administrator selects "View a Paper", the View a Paper flow is executed.

Basic Flow 1: Add a Paper

The system requests that the administrator enter the paper information. This includes:
- (i) The tsytstem requests the administrator to select school, programme, and semester. The system also requests to enter the following:
  1. Paper code
  2. Paper name
  3. Paper type
  4. Credits
- (ii) Once the administrator provides the requested information, the paper is added to the system.

Basic Flow 2: Edit a Paper

- (i) The system requests that the administrator to enter the paper code.
- (ii) The administrator enters the name of the paper code. The system retrieves and displays the paper information.

- (iii) The administrator makes the desired changes to the paper information. This includes any of the information specified in the **Add a Paper** flow.
- (iv) The system prompts the administrator to confirm the updation of the paper.
- (v) After confirming the changes, the system updates the paper record with the updated information.

Basic Flow 3: Delete a Paper

- (i) The system requests that the administrator specify the paper code.
- (ii) The administrator enters the paper code. The system retrieves and displays the paper information.
- (iii) The system prompts the administrator to confirm the deletion of the paper.
- (iv) The administrator confirms the deletion.
- (v) The system deletes the specified paper record.

Basic Flow 4: View a Paper

- (i) The system requests that the administrator specify the paper code.
  - The system retrieves and displays the paper information.

6. Alternative Flows

Alternative Flow 1: Invalid Entry

If in the **Add a Paper or Edit a Paper** flows, the actor enters invalid paper code/paper name/paper type/credits/semester or leaves the paper code/paper name/paper type/credits/semester empty, the system displays an appropriate error message. The actor returns to the basic flow.

Alternative Flow 2: Paper already exist

If in the **Add a Paper** flow, a paper code in a specified semester already exists, the system displays an error message. The administrator returns to the basic flow.

Alternative Flow 3: Paper not found

If in the **Edit a Paper or Delete a Paper or View a Paper** flows, a paper with the specified scheme does not exist, the system displays an error message. The administrator returns to the basic flow.

Alternative Flow 4: Edit cancelled

If in the **Edit a Paper** flow, the administrator decides not to edit the paper, the edit is cancelled and the **Basic Flow** is re-started at the beginning.

Alternative Flow 5: Delete cancelled

If in the **Delete a Paper** flow, the administrator decides not to delete the paper, the delete is cancelled and the **Basic Flow** is re-started at the beginning.

Alternative Flow 6: Deletion not allowed

If in the **Delete a Paper** flow, student registration details of the paper code in a specified semester already exists then the system displays an error message. The administrator returns to the basic flow.

Alternative Flow 7: User exits

This allows the user to quit during the use case. The use case ends.

7. Special Requirements

None.

8. Associated use cases

Login, Maintain School Details, Maintain Programme Details, Maintain Scheme Details, Maintain Student Details, Maintain Student Registration Details.

TEST CASES GENERATED FROM USE CASE MAINTAIN PAPER DETAILS

Table II-4. Scenario matrix for the maintain paper details use case

Scenario	Basic Flow	Alternate Flow
Scenario 1- Add a paper	Basic Flow 1	
Scenario 2- Add a paper alternative flow: Invalid Entry	Basic Flow 1	Alternate Flow 1
Scenario 3- Add a paper alternative flow: Paper already exists	Basic Flow 1	Alternate Flow 2
Scenario 4- Add a paper alternative flow: User Exits	Basic Flow 1	Alternate Flow 7
Scenario 5- Edit a paper	Basic Flow 2	
Scenario 6 - Edit a paper alternative flow: Invalid Entry	Basic Flow 2	Alternate Flow 1
Scenario 7- Edit a paper alternative flow: Paper not found	Basic Flow 2	Alternate Flow 3
Scenario 8- Edit a paper alternative flow: Edit cancelled	Basic Flow 2	Alternate Flow 4
Scenario 9- Edit a paper alternative flow: User Exits	Basic Flow 2	Alternate Flow 7
Scenario 10- Delete a paper	Basic Flow 3	
Scenario 11- Delete a paper alternative flow: Paper not found	Basic Flow 3	Alternate Flow 3
Scenario 12- Delete a paper alternative flow: Deletion cancelled	Basic Flow 3	Alternate Flow 5
Scenario 13- Delete a paper alternative flow: Deletion not allowed	Basic Flow 3	Alternate Flow 6
Scenario 14- Delete a paper alternative flow: User Exits	Basic Flow 3	Alternate Flow 7
Scenario 15- View a paper	Basic Flow 4	
Scenario 16- View a paper alternative flow: Paper not found	Basic Flow 4	Alternate Flow 3
Scenario 17- View a paper alternative flow: User Exits	Basic Flow 4	Alternate Flow 7

For maintain a paper use case, we identify nine input variables for various basic flows in the use case.

556 Appendix II

Table II-5. Test case matrix for the maintain paper details use case

Test case Id	Scenario Name and description	Input 1 School selected	Input 2 Prog. selected	Input 3 Paper code	Input 4 Paper name	Input 5 Paper type selected	Input 6 Credits	Input 7 Semester selected	Edit confirmed	Deletion confirmed	Expected output	Remarks (if any)
TC2	Scenario 2- Add a paper alternative flow: Invalid entry	No	Yes/no	Valid/invalid input	Valid/invalid input	Yes/no	Valid/invalid input	Yes/no	n/a	n/a	School not selected	User did not select a school
TC3	–do–	Yes	No	Valid/invalid input	Valid/invalid input	Yes/no	Valid/invalid input	Yes/no	n/a	n/a	Programme not selected	User did not select programme
TC5	–do–	Yes	Yes	Invalid input	Valid/invalid input	Yes/no	Valid/invalid input	Yes/no	n/a	n/a	Invalid paper code	Paper code is not in the specified format
TC6	–do–	Yes	Yes	Valid input	Invalid input	Yes/no	Valid/invalid input	Yes/no	n/a	n/a	Invalid paper name	Paper name is not in the specified format
TC7	–do–	Yes	Yes	Valid input	Valid input	No	Valid/invalid input	Yes/no	n/a	n/a	Paper type information is required	Paper type is not selected
TC8	–do–	Yes	Yes	Valid input	Valid input	Yes	Invalid input	Yes/no	n/a	n/a	Invalid credits	Credits are not in the specified format/range
TC9	–do–	Yes	Yes	Valid input	Valid input	Yes	Valid input	No	n/a	n/a	Semester not selected	User did not select a semester
TC10	Scenario 3- Add a school alternative flow: School already exists	Yes	Yes	Valid input	Valid input	Yes	Valid input	Yes	n/a	n/a	Paper already exits	Paper with the specified paper code already exist in the database

(Contd.)

Appendix II 557

(Contd.)

Test case Id	Scenario Name and description	Input 1 School selected	Input 2 Prog. selected	Input 3 Paper code	Input 4 Paper name	Input 5 Paper type selected	Input 6 Credits	Input 7 Semester selected	Edit confirmed	Deletion confirmed	Expected output	Remarks (if any)
TC11	Scenario 4- Add a paper alternative flow: User exits	Yes/no	Yes/no	Valid/ invalid input	Valid/ invalid input	Yes/no	Valid/ invalid input	Yes/no	n/a	n/a	User is allowed to exit and returns to Main menu	Users cancels the maintain paper details use case
TC12	Scenario 5- Edit a paper	n/a	n/a	Valid input	Valid input	Yes	Valid input	Yes	Yes	n/a	Paper is updated successfully	—
TC13	Scenario 6- Edit a paper alternative flow: Invalid entry	n/a	n/a	Invalid input	Valid/ invalid input	Yes/no	Valid/ invalid input	Yes/no	n/a	n/a	Invalid paper code	Paper code is not in the specified format
TC14	—do—	n/a	n/a	Valid input	Invalid input	Yes/no	Valid/ invalid input	Yes/no	n/a	n/a	Invalid paper name	Paper name is not in the specified format
TC15	—do—	n/a	n/a	Valid input	Invalid input	Yes/no	Valid/ invalid input	Yes/no	n/a	n/a	Paper type information is required	Paper type is not selected
TC16	—do—	n/a	n/a	Valid input	Valid input	Yes	Invalid input	Yes/No	n/a	n/a	Invalid credits	Credits are not in the specified format/range
TC17	Scenario 7- Edit a paper alternative flow: Paper not found	n/a	n/a	Valid input	n/a	n/a	n/a	n/a	n/a	n/a	Paper not found	Paper with the specified paper code already exist in the database
TC18	Scenario 8- Edit cancelled	n/a	n/a	Valid input	Valid input	Yes	Valid input	Yes	No	n/a	Sub menu for Paper details appears	User does not confirm the edit operation

(Contd.)

558 Appendix II

(Contd.)

Test case Id	Scenario Name and description	Input 1 School selected	Input 2 Prog. selected	Input 3 Paper code	Input 4 Paper name	Input 5 Paper type selected	Input 6 Credits	Input 7 Semester selected	Edit confirmed	Deletion confirmed	Expected output	Remarks (if any)
TC19	Scenario 9- Edit a paper alternative flow: User exits	n/a	n/a	Valid/ invalid input	Valid/ invalid input	Yes/no	Valid/ invalid input	Yes/no	n/a	n/a	User is allowed to exit and returns to Main menu	Users cancels the maintain paper details use case
TC20	Scenario 10- Delete a paper	n/a	n/a	Valid input	n/a	n/a	n/a	n/a	n/a	Yes	Paper is deleted successfully	–
TC21	Scenario 11- Delete a paper alternative flow: Paper not found	n/a	n/a	Valid input	n/a	n/a	n/a	n/a	n/a	n/a	Paper not found	Paper with the specified paper code already exist in the database
TC22	Scenario 12- Delete a paper alternative flow: Deletion cancelled	n/a	n/a	Valid input	n/a	n/a	n/a	n/a	n/a	No	Sub menu for Paper details appears	User does not confirm the delete operation
TC23	Scenario 13- Delete a paper alternative flow: Deletion not allowed	n/a	n/a	Valid input	n/a	n/a	n/a	n/a	n/a	n/a	Deletion not allowed	Students are registered for the specified paper code

(Contd.)

(Contd.)

Test case Id	Scenario Name and description	Input 1 School selected	Input 2 Prog. selected	Input 3 Paper code	Input 4 Paper name	Input 5 Paper type selected	Input 6 Credits	Input 7 Semester selected	Edit confirmed	Deletion confirmed	Expected output	Remarks (if any)
TC24	Scenario 14- Delete a paper alter-native flow: User exits	n/a	n/a	Valid/ invalid input	n/a	n/a	n/a	n/a	n/a	n/a	User is allowed to exit and returns to Main menu	Users cancels the maintain paper details use case
TC25	Scenario 15- View a paper	n/a	n/a	Valid input	n/a	n/a	n/a	n/a	n/a	n/a	Paper displayed success-fully	–
TC26	Scenario 16- View a paper alternative flow: Paper not found	n/a	n/a	Valid input	n/a	n/a	n/a	n/a	n/a	n/a	Paper not found	Paper with the specified paper code already exist in the database
TC27	Scenario 17-View a paper alter-native flow: User exits	n/a	n/a	Valid/ invalid input	n/a	n/a	n/a	n/a	n/a	n/a	User is allowed to exit and returns to Main menu	Users cancels the maintain paper details use case

n/a: option(s) not available for respective scenario

Table II-6. Test case matrix with actual data values for the maintain paper details use case

Test case Id	Scenario Name and description	School selected	Prog. selected	Paper code	Paper name	Paper type selected	Credits	Semester	Edit confirmed	Deletion confirmed	Expected output	Remarks (if any)
TC1	Scenario 1- Add a paper	University School of Information Technology	MCA	BA607	Discrete mathematics	Compulsory	4	1	n/a	n/a	Paper is added successfully	—
TC2	Scenario 2- Add a paper alternative flow: Invalid entry	*	*	*	*	*	*	*	n/a	n/a	School name blank	User did not selected school name
TC3	—do—	University School of Information Technology	MCA	*	*	*	*	*	n/a	n/a	Programme name blank	User did not selected programme name
TC5	—do—	University School of Information Technology	MCA	IT67	*	*	*	*	n/a	n/a	Invalid paper code	Paper code is not in the specified format
TC6	—do—	University School of Information Technology	MCA	BA607	Di	*	*	*	n/a	n/a	Invalid paper name	Paper name is not in the specified format
TC7	—do—	University School of Information Technology	MCA	BA607	Discrete mathematics	*	*	*	n/a	n/a	Paper type information is required	Paper type is not selected
TC8	—do—	University School of Information Technology	MCA	BA607	Discrete mathematics	Compulsory	32	*	n/a	n/a	Invalid credits	Credits are not in the specified format/range

(Contd.)

(Contd.)

Test case Id	Scenario Name and description	School selected	Prog. selected	Paper code	Paper name	Paper type selected	Credits	Semester	Edit confirmed	Deletion confirmed	Expected output	Remarks (if any)
TC9	—do—	University School of Information Technology	MCA	BA607	Discrete mathematics	Compulsory	32	10	n/a	n/a	Invalid semester	Semester does not exist in the specified programme
TC10	Scenario 3- Add a school alternative flow: School already exists	University School of Information Technology	MCA	BA607	Discrete mathematics	Compulsory	4	1	n/a	n/a	Paper already exits	Paper with the specified paper code already exist in the database
TC11	Scenario 4- Add a paper alternative flow: User exits	University School of Information Technology	MCA	BA607	Discrete mathematics	Compulsory	4	1	n/a	n/a	User is allowed to exit and returns to Main menu	Users cancels the maintain paper details use case
TC12	Scenario 5: Edit a paper	*	*	*	*	*	*	*	Yes	n/a	Paper is updated successfully	—
TC13	Scenario 6- Edit a paper alternative flow: Invalid entry	n/a	n/a	B@A	*	*	*	*	n/a	n/a	Invalid paper code	Paper code is not in the specified format
TC14	—do—	n/a	n/a	IT105	Intro12	*	*	*	n/a	n/a	Invalid paper name	Paper name is not in the specified format
TC15	—do—	n/a	n/a	IT105	Introduction to Computers		*	*	n/a	n/a	Paper type information is required	Paper type is not selected
TC16	—do—	n/a	n/a	IT105	Introduction to Computers	Compulsory	0	*	n/a	n/a	Invalid credits	Credits are not in the specified format/range

(Contd.)

(Contd.)

Test case Id	Scenario Name and description	School selected	Prog. selected	Paper code	Paper name	Paper type selected	Credits	Semester	Edit confirmed	Deletion confirmed	Expected output	Remarks (if any)
TC17	Scenario 7- Edit a paper alternative flow: Paper not found	n/a	n/a	IT107	*	*	*	*	n/a	n/a	Paper not found	Paper with the specified paper code already exist in the database
TC18	Scenario 8- Edit cancelled	n/a	n/a	IT105	Introduction to Computers	Compulsory	4	1	No	n/a	Sub menu for Paper details appears	User does not confirm the edit operation
TC19	Scenario 9- Edit a paper alternative flow: User exits	n/a	n/a	IT105	Introduction to Computers	Compulsory	4	1	n/a	n/a	User is allowed to exit and returns to Main menu	Users cancels the maintain paper details use case
TC20	Scenario 10- Delete a paper	n/a	n/a	*	*	*	*	*	n/a	Yes	Paper is deleted successfully	—
TC21	Scenario 11- Delete a paper alternative flow: Paper not found	n/a	n/a	IT107	n/a	n/a	n/a	n/a	n/a	n/a	Paper not found	Paper with the specified paper code already exist in the database
TC22	Scenario 12- Delete a paper alternative flow: Deletion cancelled	n/a	n/a	IT105	n/a	n/a	n/a	n/a	n/a	No	Sub menu for Paper details appears	User does not confirm the delete operation

(Contd.)

(Contd.)

Test case Id	Scenario Name and description	School selected	Prog. selected	Paper code	Paper name	Paper type selected	Credits	Semester	Edit confirmed	Deletion confirmed	Expected output	Remarks (if any)
TC23	Scenario 13- Delete a paper alternative flow: Deletion not allowed	n/a	n/a	IT105	n/a	n/a	n/a	n/a	n/a	n/a	Deletion not allowed	Students are registered for the specified paper code
TC24	Scenario 14- Delete a paper alternative flow: User exits	n/a	n/a	IT105	n/a	n/a	n/a	n/a	n/a	n/a	User is allowed to exit and returns to Main menu	Users cancels the maintain paper details use case
TC25	Scenario 15- View a paper	n/a	n/a	*	n/a	n/a	n/a	n/a	n/a	n/a	Paper displayed successfully	—
TC26	Scenario 16- View a paper alternative flow: Paper not found	n/a	n/a	IT107	n/a	n/a	n/a	n/a	n/a	n/a	Paper not found	Paper with the specified paper code already exist in the database
TC27	Scenario 17-View a paper alternative flow: User exits	n/a	n/a	*	n/a	n/a	n/a	n/a	n/a	n/a	User is allowed to exit and returns to Main menu	Users cancels the maintain paper details use case

*: do not care conditions (valid/invalid inputs)
n/a: option(s) not available for respective scenario

MAINTAIN STUDENT DETAILS

Use Case Description

1. Introduction
Allow administrator/DEO to maintain student details. This includes adding, updating, deleting and viewing student information.

2. Actors
Administrator, DEO

3. Pre-Conditions
The administrator/DEO must be logged onto the system. The school and programme details to which the student is admitted must be available before this use case begins.

4. Post-Conditions
If the use case is successful, the student information is added/updated/deleted/viewed from the system. Otherwise, the system state is unchanged.

5. Basic Flow
This use case starts when administrator/DEO wishes to add/edit/delete/view student information

(i) The system requests that the administrator/DEO specify the function he/she would like to perform (either Add a student, Edit a student, Delete a student or View a student)

(ii) Once the administrator/DEO provides the requested information, one of the flows is executed.

- If the administrator/DEO selects "Add a Student", the **Add a Student** flow is executed.
- If the administrator/DEO selects "Edit a Student", the **Edit a Student** flow is executed.
- If the administrator/DEO selects "Delete a Student", the **Delete a Student** flow is executed.
- If the administrator/DEO selects "View a Student", the **View a Student** flow is executed.

Basic Flow 1: Add a Student

The system requests that the administrator/DEO enter the student information. This includes:

(i) The system requests the administrator/DEO to select school and programme of the student and then enter:

   1. Roll No.
   2. Name
   3. Year of admission

(ii) Once the administrator/DEO provides the requested information, the system checks that roll no. is unique and generates password. The student is added to the system.

Basic Flow 2: Edit a Student

(i) The system requests the administrator/DEO to enter the roll number.
(ii) The administrator/DEO enters the roll no. of the student. The system retrieves and displays the student information.
(iii) The administrator/DEO makes the desired changes to the student information. This includes any of the information specified in the **Add a Student** flow.
(iv) The system prompts the administrator/DEO to confirm the updation of the student.
(v) After confirming the changes, the system updates the student record with the updated information.

Basic Flow 3: Delete a Student

(i) The system requests that the administrator/DEO specify the roll no. of the student
(ii) The administrator/DEO enters the roll no. of the student. The system retrieves and displays the student information.
(iii) The system prompts the administrator/DEO to confirm the deletion of the student.
(iv) The administrator/DEO confirms the deletion.
(v) The system deletes the student record.

Basic Flow 4: View a Student

(i) The system requests that the administrator/DEO specify the roll no. of the student.
(ii) The system retrieves and displays the student information.

6. Alternative Flows

Alternative Flow 1: Invalid Entry

If in the **Add a Student or Edit a Student** flows, the actor enters invalid roll no/ name/ password or roll no/name/password empty, the system displays an appropriate error message. The actor returns to the basic flow and may reenter the invalid entry.

Alternative Flow 2: Roll no. already exist

If in the **Add a Student** flow, a student with a specified roll no. already exists, the system displays an error message. The administrator/DEO returns to the basic flow and may then enter a different roll no.

Alternative Flow 3: Student not found

If in the **Edit a Student or Delete a Student or View a Student** flow, a student with the specified roll no. does not exist, the system displays an error message. The administrator/DEO returns to the basic flow and may then enter a different roll no.

Alternative Flow 4: Edit cancelled

If in the **Edit a Student** flow, the administrator/DEO decides not to edit the student, the edit is cancelled and the **Basic Flow** is re-started at the beginning.

Alternative flow 5: Delete cancelled

If in the **Delete a Student** flow, the administrator/DEO decides not to delete the student, the delete is cancelled and the **Basic Flow** is re-started at the beginning.

Alternative flow 6: Deletion not allowed

If in the **Delete a Student** flow, student registration details of the specified Roll No. already exists then the system displays an error message. The administrator/DEO returns to the basic flow and may then enter a different school name.

Alternative flow 7: User exits

This allows the user to exit at any time during the use case. The use case ends.

7. Special Requirements

None.

8. Associated use cases

Login, Maintain Student Registration Details, Maintain School Details, Maintain Programme Details.

TEST CASES GENERATED FROM USE CASE MAINTAIN STUDENT DETAILS

Table II-7. Scenario matrix for the maintain student details use case

Scenario	Basic Flow	Alternate Flow
Scenario 1- Add a student	Basic Flow 1	
Scenario 2- Add a student alternative flow: Invalid Entry	Basic Flow 1	Alternate Flow 1
Scenario 3- Add a student alternative flow: Roll. No. already exists	Basic Flow 1	Alternate Flow 2
Scenario 4- Add a student alternative flow: User Exits	Basic Flow 1	Alternate Flow 7
Scenario 5- Edit a student	Basic Flow 2	
Scenario 6 - Edit a student alternative flow: Invalid Entry	Basic Flow 2	Alternate Flow 1
Scenario 7- Edit a student alternative flow: Student not found	Basic Flow 2	Alternate Flow 3
Scenario 8- Edit a student alternative flow: Edit cancelled	Basic Flow 2	Alternate Flow 4
Scenario 9- Edit a student alternative flow: User Exits	Basic Flow 2	Alternate Flow 7
Scenario 10- Delete a student	Basic Flow 3	
Scenario 11- Delete a student alternative flow: Student not found	Basic Flow 3	Alternate Flow 3
Scenario 12- Delete a student alternative flow: Deletion cancelled	Basic Flow 3	Alternate Flow 5
Scenario 13- Delete a student alternative flow: Deletion not allowed	Basic Flow 3	Alternate Flow 6
Scenario 14- Delete a student alternative flow: User Exits	Basic Flow 3	Alternate Flow 7
Scenario 15- View a student	Basic Flow 4	
Scenario 16- View a student alternative flow: Student not found	Basic Flow 4	Alternate Flow 3
Scenario 17- View a student alternative flow: User Exits	Basic Flow 4	Alternate Flow 7

For maintain a student use case, we identify eight input variables for various basic flows in the use case. There are four input variables namely roll no., name, year of admission, password and four selection variables (School selected, Programme Selected, edit confirmed, delete confirmed) in this use case. These inputs will be available for the respective flows as specified in the use case.

Table II-8. Test case matrix for the maintain student details use case

Test case Id	Scenario Name and description	Input 1 School selected	Input 2 Programme selected	Input 3 Roll no.	Input 4 Name	Input 5 Year of admission	Input 6 Password	Edit confirmed	Deletion confirmed	Expected output	Remarks (if any)
TC1	Scenario 1- Add a student	Yes	Yes	Valid input	Valid input	Valid input	n/a	n/a	n/a	Student is added successfully	–
TC2	Scenario 2- Add a student alternative flow: Invalid entry	No	Yes/no	Valid/ invalid input	Valid/ invalid input	Valid/ invalid input	n/a	n/a	n/a	School not selected	User did not select a school name
TC3	—do—	Yes	No	Valid/ invalid input	Valid/ invalid input	Valid/ invalid input	n/a	n/a	n/a	Programme not selected	User did not select a programme
TC4	—do—	Yes	Yes	Invalid input	Valid/ invalid input	Valid/ invalid input	n/a	n/a	n/a	Invalid roll no.	Roll no. is not in the specified format
TC5	—do—	Yes	Yes	Valid input	Invalid input	Valid/ invalid input	n/a	n/a	n/a	Invalid Student name	Student name is not in the specified format
TC6	—do—	Yes	Yes	Valid input	Valid input	Invalid input	n/a	n/a	n/a	Invalid year	Year is not in the specified format
TC7	Scenario 3- Add a student alternative flow: Roll No. already exists	Yes	Yes	Valid input	Valid input	Valid input	n/a	n/a	n/a	Roll No. already exists	Student with the given roll no. Is already present in the database

(Contd.)

(Contd.)

Test case Id	Scenario Name and description	Input 1 School selected	Input 2 Programme selected	Input 3 Roll no.	Input 4 Name	Input 5 Year of admission	Input 6 Password	Edit confirmed	Deletion confirmed	Expected output	Remarks (if any)
TC8	Scenario 4- Add a student alternative flow: User Exits	Yes/no	Yes/no	Valid/ invalid input	Valid/ invalid input	Valid/ invalid input	n/a	n/a	n/a	User is allowed to exit and returns to Main menu	—
TC9	Scenario 5- Edit a student	n/a	n/a	Valid input	Valid input	Valid input	Valid input	Yes	n/a	Student is updated successfully	—
TC10	Scenario 6- Edit a student alternative flow: Invalid entry	n/a	n/a	Invalid input	Valid/ invalid input	Valid/ invalid input	Valid/ invalid input	n/a	n/a	Invalid roll no.	Roll no. is not in the specified format
TC11	—do—	n/a	n/a	Valid input	Invalid input	Valid/ invalid input	Valid/ invalid input	n/a	n/a	Invalid Student name	Student name is not in the specified format
TC12	—do—	n/a	n/a	Valid input	Valid input	Invalid input	Valid input	n/a	n/a	Invalid year	Year is not in the specified format
TC13	—do—	n/a	n/a	Valid input	Valid input	Valid input	Invalid input	n/a	n/a	Invalid password	Password is not in the specified format
TC14	Scenario 7- Edit a student alternative flow: Student not found	n/a	n/a	Valid input	n/a	n/a	n/a	n/a	n/a	Student not found	Student with the specified roll no. does not exist in the database

(Contd.)

(Contd.)

Test case Id	Scenario Name and description	Input 1 School selected	Input 2 Programme selected	Input 3 Roll no.	Input 4 Name	Input 5 Year of admission	Input 6 Password	Edit confirmed	Deletion confirmed	Expected output	Remarks (if any)
TC15	Scenario 8- Edit a student alternative flow: Edit Cancelled	n/a	n/a	Valid input	Valid input	Valid input	Valid input	No	n/a	Sub menu for Student details appears	–
TC16	Scenario 9- Edit a student alternative flow: User Exits	n/a	n/a	Valid/ invalid input	Valid/ invalid input	Valid/ invalid input	Valid/ invalid input	n/a	n/a	User is allowed to exit and returns to Main menu	–
TC17	Scenario 10-Delete a student	n/a	n/a	Valid input	n/a	n/a	n/a	n/a	Yes	Student is deleted successfully	–
TC18	Scenario 11-Delete a student: Student not found	n/a	n/a	Valid input	n/a	n/a	n/a	n/a	n/a	Student not found	Student with the specified roll no. does not exist in the database
TC19	Scenario 12-Delete a student alternative flow: Deletion cancelled	n/a	n/a	Valid input	n/a	n/a	n/a	n/a	No	Sub menu for Student details appears	–

(Contd.)

(Contd.)

Test case Id	Scenario Name and description	Input 1 School selected	Input 2 Programme selected	Input 3 Roll no.	Input 4 Name	Input 5 Year of admission	Input 6 Password	Edit confirmed	Deletion confirmed	Expected output	Remarks (if any)
TC20	Scenario 13-Delete a student alternative flow: Deletion not allowed	n/a	n/a	Valid input	n/a	n/a	n/a	n/a	n/a	Deletion not allowed	Registration information exist of the specified student in the database, hence deletion cannot be performed
TC21	Scenario 14-Delete a student alternative flow: User Exits	n/a	n/a	Valid/ invalid input	n/a	n/a	n/a	n/a	n/a	User is allowed to exit and returns to Main menu	–
TC22	Scenario 15- View a student	n/a	n/a	Valid input	n/a	n/a	n/a	n/a	n/a	Student displayed successfully	–
TC23	Scenario 16-View a student alternative flow: Student not found	n/a	n/a	Valid input	n/a	n/a	n/a	n/a	n/a	Student not found	Student with the specified roll no. does not exist in the database
TC24	Scenario 17- View a student alternative flow: User Exits	n/a	n/a	Valid/ invalid input	n/a	n/a	n/a	n/a	n/a	User is allowed to exit and returns to Main menu	–

n/a: option(s) not available for respective scenario

Table II-9. Test case matrix with actual data values for the maintain student details use case

Test case Id	Scenario Name and description	School selected	Programme selected	Roll no.	Name	Year of admission	Password	Edit confirmed	Deletion confirmed	Expected output	Remarks (if any)
TC1	Scenario 1- Add a student	University School of Information Technology	MCA	00616453007	Richa Sharma	2009	n/a	n/a	n/a	Student is added successfully	—
TC2	Scenario 2- Add a student alternative flow: Invalid entry	*	*	*	*	*	*	n/a	n/a	School not selected	User did not select a school name
TC3	—do—	University School of Information Technology	*	*	*	*	*	n/a	n/a	Programme not selected	User did not select a programme
TC4	—do—	University School of Information Technology	MCA	0061645	*	*	n/a	n/a	n/a	Invalid roll no.	Roll no. is not in the specified format and is less than 11 digits
TC5	—do—	University School of Information Technology	MCA	00616453007	Ric123	*	n/a	n/a	n/a	Invalid Student name	Student name is not in the specified format and contains digits
TC6	—do—	University School of Information Technology	MCA	00616453007	Richa Sharma	20009	n/a	n/a	n/a	Invalid year	Year is not in the specified format and exceed the specified length
TC7	Scenario 3- Add a student alternative flow: Roll No. already exists	University School of Information Technology	Valid input	Valid input	Valid input	Valid input	n/a	n/a	n/a	Student already exits	Student with the given roll no. is already present in the database

(Contd.)

(Contd.)

Test case Id	Scenario Name and description	School selected	Programme selected	Roll no.	Name	Year of admission	Password	Edit confirmed	Deletion confirmed	Expected output	Remarks (if any)
TC8	Scenario 4- Add a student alternative flow: User Exits	*	*	*	*	*	n/a	n/a	n/a	User is allowed to exit and returns to Main menu	--
TC9	Scenario 5- Edit a student	n/a	n/a	00616453007	Richa Sharma	2009	Richa123	Yes	n/a	Student is updated successfully	--
TC10	Scenario 6- Edit a student alternative flow: Invalid entry	n/a	n/a	0061645	*	*	*	n/a	n/a	Invalid roll no.	Roll no. is not in the specified format and is less than 11 digits
TC11	—do—	n/a	n/a	00616453007	Ric123	*	*	n/a	n/a	Invalid Student name	Student name is not in the specified format and contains digits
TC12	—do—	n/a	n/a	00616453007	Richa Sharma	20009	*	n/a	n/a	Invalid year	Year is not in the specified format
TC13	—do—	n/a	n/a	00616453007	Richa Sharma	2009	ric	n/a	n/a	Invalid password	Password is not in the specified format
TC14	Scenario 7- Edit a student alternative flow: Student not found	n/a	n/a	00616453007	n/a	n/a	n/a	n/a	n/a	Student not found	Student with the specified roll no. does not exist in the database
TC15	Scenario 8- Edit a student alternative flow: Edit Cancelled	n/a	n/a	00616453007	Richa Sharma	2009	Ric123	No	n/a	Sub menu for Student details appears	--

(Contd.)

Appendix II 573

(Contd.)

Test case Id	Scenario Name and description	School selected	Programme selected	Roll no.	Name	Year of admission	Password	Edit confirmed	Deletion confirmed	Expected output	Remarks (if any)
TC16	Scenario 9- Edit a student alternative flow: User Exits	n/a	n/a	*	*	*	*	n/a	n/a	User is allowed to exit and returns to Main menu	—
TC17	Scenario 10-Delete a student	n/a	n/a	00616453007	n/a	n/a	n/a	n/a	Yes	Student is deleted successfully	—
TC18	Scenario 11-Delete a student alternative flow: Student not found	n/a	n/a	00616453007	n/a	n/a	n/a	n/a	n/a	Student not found	Student with the specified roll no. does not exist in the database
TC19	Scenario 12-Delete a student alternative flow: Deletion cancelled	n/a	n/a	00616453007	n/a	n/a	n/a	n/a	No	Sub menu for Student details appears	—
TC20	Scenario 13-Delete a student alternative flow: Deletion not allowed	n/a	n/a	00616453007	n/a	n/a	n/a	n/a	n/a	Deletion not allowed, returns to deletion screen	Registration information exist of the specified student in the database, hence deletion cannot be performed
TC21	Scenario 14-Delete a student alternative flow: User Exits	n/a	n/a	*	n/a	n/a	n/a	n/a	n/a	User is allowed to exit and returns to Main menu	—

(Contd.)

(Contd.)

Test case Id	Scenario Name and description	School selected	Programme selected	Roll no.	Name	Year of admission	Password	Edit confirmed	Deletion confirmed	Expected output	Remarks (if any)
TC22	Scenario 15- View a student	n/a	n/a	00616453007	n/a	n/a	n/a	n/a	n/a	Student displayed successfully	–
TC23	Scenario 16-View a student alternative flow: Student not found	n/a	n/a	00616453007	n/a	n/a	n/a	n/a	n/a	Student not found	Student with the specified roll no. does not exist in the database
TC24	Scenario 17- View a student alternative flow: User Exits	n/a	n/a	*	n/a	n/a	n/a	n/a	n/a	User is allowed to exit and returns to Main menu	–

*: do not care conditions (valid/invalid inputs)
n/a: option(s) not available for respective scenario

MAINTAIN FACULTY DETAILS

Use Case Description

1. Introduction

Allow administrator/DEO to maintain faculty details. This includes adding, updating, deleting and viewing faculty information.

2. Actors

Administrator/DEO

3. Pre-Conditions

The administrator/DEO must be logged onto the system.

4. Post-Conditions

If the use case is successful, the faculty information is added added/updated/deleted/viewed from the system. Otherwise, the system state is unchanged.

Basic Flow

This use case starts when administrator/DEO wishes to add/edit/delete/view faculty information

(i) The system requests that the administrator/DEO specify the function he/she would like to perform (either Add a faculty, Edit a faculty, Delete a faculty or View a faculty)

(ii) Once the administrator/DEO provides the requested information, one of the flows is executed.

- If the administrator/DEO selects "Add a Faculty", the **Add a Faculty** flow is executed.
- If the administrator/DEO selects "Edit a Faculty", the **Edit a Faculty** flow is executed.
- If the administrator/DEO selects "Delete a Faculty", the **Delete a Faculty** flow is executed.
- If the administrator/DEO selects "View a Faculty", the **View a Faculty** flow is executed.

5.1 Add a Faculty

The system requests that the administrator/DEO enter the faculty information. This includes

(i) The system requests the administrator/DEO to select a school and enter

1. Employee Id
2. Name
3. Designation

(ii) Once the administrator/DEO provides the requested information, the system checks that employee Id is unique and generates password. The faculty is added to the system.

5.2 Edit a Faculty

(i) The system requests that the administrator/DEO enters the employee Id.
(ii) The administrator/DEO enters the employee Id of the faculty. The system retrieves and displays the faculty information.
(iii) The administrator/DEO makes the desired changes to the faculty information. This includes any of the information specified in the **Add a Faculty** flow.
(iv) The system prompts the administrator/DEO to confirm the updation of the faculty.
(v) After confirming the changes, the system updates the faculty record with the updated information.

5.3 Delete a Faculty

(i) The system requests that the administrator/DEO specify the employee Id of the faculty.
(ii) The administrator/DEO enters the employee Id of the faculty. The system retrieves and displays the faculty information.
(iii) The system prompts the administrator/DEO to confirm the deletion of the faculty.
(iv) The administrator/DEO confirms the deletion.
(v) The system deletes the faculty record.

5.4 View a Faculty

(i) The system requests that the administrator/DEO specify the employee Id of the faculty.
(ii) The system retrieves and displays the faculty information.

6. Alternative Flows

Alternative Flow 1: Invalid Entry

If in the **Add a Faculty or Edit a Faculty** flows, the actor enters invalid employee id/ name/ password or employee id/ name/password empty, the system displays an appropriate error message. The actor returns to the basic flow.

Alternative Flow 2: Employee Id already exist

If in the **Add a Faculty** flow, an employee with a specified employee Id already exists, the system displays an error message. The administrator/DEO returns to the basic flow and may then enter a different employee.

Alternative Flow 3: Faculty not found

If in the **Edit a Faculty or Delete a Faculty or View a Faculty** flow, a faculty with the specified employee Id does not exist, the system displays an error message. The administrator/DEO returns to the basic flow and may then enter a different employee Id.

Alternative Flow 4: Edit cancelled

If in the **Edit a Faculty** flow, the administrator/DEO decides not to edit the faculty, the edit is cancelled and the **Basic Flow** is re-started at the beginning.

Appendix II 577

Alternative Flow 5: Delete cancelled

If in the **Delete a Faculty** flow, the administrator/DEO decides not to delete the faculty, the delete is cancelled and the **Basic Flow** is re-started at the beginning.

Alternative flow 6: User exits

This allows the user to quit at any time during the use case. The use case ends.

7. Special Requirements

None.

8. Associated use cases

Login, Maintain School Details.

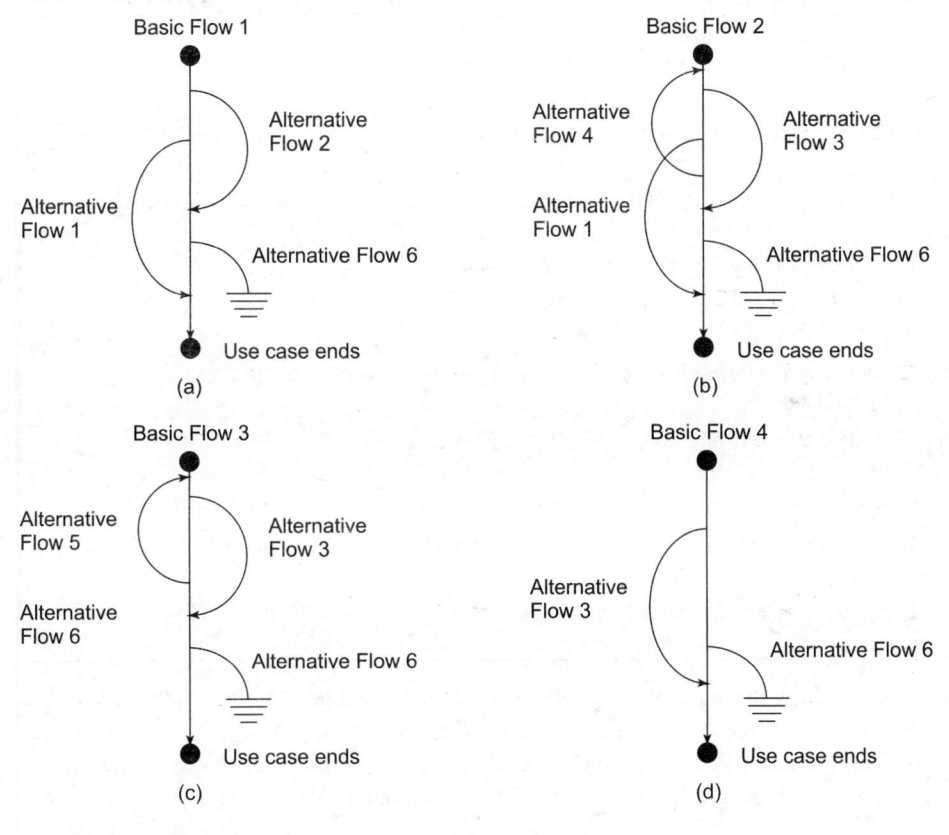

Figure II-1. Basic and alternative flows for maintain faculty details use case (a) Add a faculty (b) Edit a faculty (c) Delete a faculty (d) View a faculty
Alternative Flow 1: Invalid Entry
Alternative Flow 2: Employee Id already exist
Alternative Flow 3: Faculty not found
Alternative Flow 4: Edit cancelled
Alternative Flow 5: Delete cancelled
Alternative Flow 6: User exits

TEST CASES GENERATED FROM USE CASE MAINTAIN FACULTY DETAILS

Table II-10. Scenario matrix for the maintain faculty details use case

Scenario 1- Add a faculty	Basic Flow 1	
Scenario 2- Add a faculty alternative flow: Invalid Entry	Basic Flow 1	Alternate Flow 1
Scenario 3- Add a faculty alternative flow: Employee Id. already exists	Basic Flow 1	Alternate Flow 2
Scenario 4- Add a faculty alternative flow: User Exits	Basic Flow 1	Alternate Flow 6
Scenario 5- Edit a faculty	Basic Flow 2	
Scenario 6 – Edit a faculty alternative flow: Invalid Entry	Basic Flow 2	Alternate Flow 1
Scenario 7- Edit a faculty alternative flow: Faculty not found	Basic Flow 2	Alternate Flow 3
Scenario 8- Edit a faculty alternative flow: Edit cancelled	Basic Flow 2	Alternate Flow 4
Scenario 9- Edit a faculty alternative flow: User Exits	Basic Flow 2	Alternate Flow 6
Scenario 10- Delete a faculty	Basic Flow 3	
Scenario 11- Delete a faculty alternative flow: Faculty not found	Basic Flow 3	Alternate Flow 3
Scenario 12- Delete a faculty alternative flow: Deletion cancelled	Basic Flow 3	Alternate Flow 5
Scenario 13- Delete a faculty alternative flow: User Exits	Basic Flow 3	Alternate Flow 6
Scenario 14- View a faculty	Basic Flow 4	
Scenario 15- View a faculty alternative flow: Faculty not found	Basic Flow 4	Alternate Flow 3
Scenario 16- View a faculty alternative flow: User Exits	Basic Flow 4	Alternate Flow 6

For maintain a faculty use case, we identify seven input variables for various basic flows in the use case. There are three input variables namely employee id, name, password and four selection variables (school selected, designation selected, edit confirmed, delete confirmed) in this use case. These inputs will be available for the respective flows as specified in the use case.

Table II-11. Test case matrix for the maintain faculty details use case

Test case Id	Scenario Name and description	Input 1 School selected	Input 2 Employee Id	Input 3 Name	Input 4 Designation selected	Input 5 Password	Edit confirmed	Deletion confirmed	Expected output	Remarks (If any)
TC1	Scenario 1- Add a faculty	Yes	Valid input	Valid input	Yes	n/a	n/a	n/a	Faculty is added successfully	—
TC2	Scenario 2-Add a faculty alternative flow: Invalid entry	No	Valid/ invalid input	Valid/ invalid input	Yes/no	n/a	n/a	n/a	School not selected	User did not select a school
TC3	—do—	Yes	Invalid input	Valid/ invalid input	Yes/no	n/a	n/a	n/a	Invalid employee id.	Employee id is not in the specified format
TC4	—do—	Yes	Valid input	Invalid input	Yes/no	n/a	n/a	n/a	Invalid Faculty name	Faculty name is not in the specified format
TC5	—do—	Yes	Valid input	Valid input	No	n/a	n/a	n/a	Designation not selected	User did not select a faculty designation
TC6	Scenario 3- Add a faculty alternative flow: Employee already exists	Yes	Valid input	Valid input	Yes	n/a	n/a	n/a	Employee id already exists	Faculty with the given employee id is already present in the database
TC7	Scenario 4- Add a faculty alternative flow: User exits	Yes	Valid input	Valid input	Yes	n/a	n/a	n/a	User is allowed to exit and returns to Main menu	—
TC8	Scenario 5-Edit a faculty	n/a	Valid input	Valid input	Yes	Valid input	Yes	n/a	Faculty information is updated successfully	—

(Contd.)

(Contd.)

Test case Id	Scenario Name and description	Input 1 School selected	Input 2 Employee Id	Input 3 Name	Input 4 Designation selected	Input 5 Password	Edit confirmed	Deletion confirmed	Expected output	Remarks (if any)
TC9	Scenario 6- Edit a faculty alternative flow: Invalid entry	n/a	Invalid input	Valid/ invalid input	Yes/no	Valid/ invalid input	n/a	n/a	Invalid employee id.	Employee id is not in the specified format
TC10	—do—	n/a	Valid input	Invalid input	Yes/no	Valid/ invalid input	n/a	n/a	Invalid Faculty name	Faculty name is not in the specified format
TC11	—do—	n/a	Valid input	Valid input	Yes/no	Invalid input	n/a	n/a	Invalid password	Password is not in the specified format
TC12	—do—	n/a	Valid input	Valid input	No	n/a	n/a	n/a	Designation not selected	User did not select a faculty designation
TC13	Scenario 7: Edit a faculty alternative flow: Faculty not found	n/a	Valid input	n/a	n/a	n/a	n/a	n/a	Faculty not found	Faculty with the given employee id is not present in the database
TC14	Scenario 8: Edit a faculty alternative flow: Edit cancelled	n/a	Valid input	Valid input	Yes	Valid input	No	n/a	Sub menu for Faculty details appears	User chooses to cancel the edit operation
TC15	Scenario 9- Edit a faculty alternative flow: User exits	n/a	Valid/ invalid input	Valid/ invalid input	Yes/no	Valid/ invalid input	n/a	n/a	User is allowed to exit and returns to Main menu	–
TC16	Scenario 10: Delete a faculty	n/a	Valid input	n/a	n/a	n/a	n/a	Yes	Faculty is deleted successfully	–

(Contd.)

(Contd.)

Test case Id	Scenario Name and description	Input 1 School selected	Input 2 Employee Id	Input 3 Name	Input 4 Designation selected	Input 5 Password	Edit confirmed	Deletion confirmed	Expected output	Remarks (if any)
TC17	Scenario 11: Delete a faculty alternative flow: Faculty not found	n/a	Valid input	n/a	n/a	n/a	n/a	n/a	Faculty not found	Faculty with the given employee id is not present in the database
TC18	Scenario 12: Delete a faculty alternative flow: Deletion cancelled	n/a	Valid input	n/a	n/a	n/a	n/a	No	Sub menu for Faculty details appears	User chooses to cancel the delete operation
TC19	Scenario 13: Delete a faculty alternative flow: User exits	n/a	Valid/ invalid input	n/a	n/a	n/a	n/a	n/a	User is allowed to exit and returns to Main menu	–
TC20	Scenario 14: View a faculty	n/a	Valid input	n/a	n/a	n/a	n/a	n/a	Faculty displayed successfully	–
TC21	Scenario 15: View a faculty alternative flow: Faculty not found	n/a	Valid input	n/a	n/a	n/a	n/a	n/a	Faculty not found	Faculty with the given employee id is not present in the database
TC22	Scenario 16: View a faculty alternative flow	n/a	Valid/ invalid input	n/a	n/a	n/a	n/a	n/a	User is allowed to exit and returns to Main menu	–

n/a: option(s) not available for respective scenario

Table II-12. Test case matrix with actual data values for the maintain faculty details use case

Test case Id	Scenario Name and description	School selected	Employee Id	Name	Designation	Password	Edit confirmed	Deletion confirmed	Expected output	Remarks (if any)
TC1	Scenario 1- Add a faculty	University School of Information Technology	194	Arvinder Kaur	Reader	n/a	n/a	n/a	Faculty is added successfully	—
TC2	Scenario 2-Add a faculty alternative flow: Invalid entry	*	*	*	*	*	n/a	n/a	School name information is required	User did not selected school name
TC3	—do—	University School of Information Technology	1	*	*	n/a	n/a	n/a	Invalid employee id.	Employee id is not in the specified length
TC4	—do—	University School of Information Technology	194	12fqw	*	n/a	n/a	n/a	Invalid Faculty name	Faculty name is not in the specified format i.e. it contains digits
TC5	—do—	University School of Information Technology	194	Arvinder Kaur	*	n/a	n/a	n/a	Designation not selected	User did not select a faculty designation
TC6	Scenario 3- Add a faculty alternative flow: Employee is already exists	University School of Information Technology	194	Arvinder Kaur	Reader	n/a	n/a	n/a	Employee id already exists	Faculty with the given employee id is already present in the database
TC7	Scenario 4- Add a faculty alternative flow: User exits	University School of Information Technology	194	Arvinder Kaur	Reader	n/a	n/a	n/a	User is allowed to exit and returns to Main menu	—

(Contd.)

(Contd.)

Test case Id	Scenario Name and description	School selected	Employee Id	Name	Designation	Password	Edit confirmed	Deletion confirmed	Expected output	Remarks (if any)
TC8	Scenario 5-Edit a faculty	n/a	194	Arvinder Kaur	Reader	Arvinder123	Yes	n/a	Faculty information is updated successfully	—
TC9	Scenario 6- Edit a faculty alternative flow: Invalid entry	n/a	196	*	*	*	n/a	n/a	Invalid employee id.	Employee id is not in the specified length
TC10	—do—	n/a	194	12tyr	*	*	n/a	n/a	Invalid Faculty name	Faculty name is not in the specified format i.e. it contains digits
TC11	—do—	n/a	194	Arvinder Kaur	*	Arv	n/a	n/a	Invalid password	Password is not in the specified format
TC12	—do—	n/a	194	Arvinder Kaur	n/a	n/a	n/a	n/a	Designation not selected	User did not select a faculty designation
TC13	Scenario 7: Edit a faculty alternative flow: Faculty not found	n/a	197	n/a	n/a	n/a	n/a	n/a	Faculty not found	Faculty with the given employee id is not present in the database
TC14	Scenario 8: Edit a faculty alternative flow: Edit cancelled	n/a	194	Arvinder Kaur	Reader	Arvinder123	No	n/a	Sub menu for Faculty details appears	User chooses to cancel the edit operation
TC15	Scenario 9- Edit a faculty alternative flow: User exits	n/a	194	Arvinder Kaur	*	Arvinder123	n/a	n/a	User is allowed to exit and returns to Main menu	—
TC16	Scenario 10: Delete a faculty	n/a	194	n/a	n/a	n/a	n/a	Yes	Faculty is deleted successfully	—

(Contd.)

(Contd.)

Test case Id	Scenario Name and description	School selected	Employee Id	Name	Designation	Password	Edit confirmed	Deletion confirmed	Expected output	Remarks (if any)
TC17	Scenario 11: Delete a faculty alternative flow: Faculty not found	n/a	194	n/a	n/a	n/a	n/a	n/a	Faculty not found	Faculty with the given employee id is not present in the database
TC18	Scenario 12: Delete a faculty alternative flow: Deletion cancelled	n/a	194	n/a	n/a	n/a	n/a	No	Sub menu for Faculty details appears	User chooses to cancel the delete operation
TC19	Scenario 13: Delete a faculty alternative flow: User exits	n/a	*	n/a	n/a	n/a	n/a	n/a	User is allowed to exit and returns to Main menu	–
TC20	Scenario 14: View a faculty	n/a	194	n/a	n/a	n/a	n/a	n/a	Faculty displayed successfully	–
TC21	Scenario 15: View a faculty alternative flow: Faculty not found	n/a	194	n/a	n/a	n/a	n/a	n/a	Faculty not found	Faculty with the given employee id is not present in the database
TC22	Scenario 16: View a faculty alternative flow	n/a	*	n/a	n/a	n/a	n/a	n/a	User is allowed to exit and returns to Main menu	–

*: do not care conditions (valid/invalid inputs)
n/a: option(s) not available for respective scenario

MAINTAIN REGISTRATION FORM

Use Case Description

1. Brief Description

This use case allows a student to add/modify his/her information.

2. Actors

Student, Administrator

3. Pre-Conditions

The user must be logged onto the system. The school, programme and student details must be available in the system before this use case begins.

4. Post-Conditions

If the use case is successful, the student information is added/updated/deleted/viewed from the system. Otherwise, the system state is unchanged.

5. Basic Flow

  A. This use case starts when the student/administrator wishes to add or edit student registration from.
  B. The system requests that the student/administrator specify the function he/she would like to perform (either Add student registration details, Edit student registration details, View student registration details)
  C. Once the student/administrator provides the requested information, one of the flows is executed.

  - If the student selects "Add Student Registration Details", the **Add Student Registration Details** flow is executed.
  - If the student/administrator selects "Edit Student Registration Details", the **Edit Student Registration Details** flow is executed.

Basic Flow 1: Add a Student

The system requests that the student enter his/her information. This includes:
  1. Father name
  2. Address
  3. City
  4. State
  5. Zip
  6. Phone
  7. Email
  8. Semester
  9. Elective papers

Once the student provides the requested information, the student is registered to the system.

Basic Flow 2: Edit a Student

A. The system retrieves and displays the student information.
B. The student/administrator makes the desired changes to the student information. This includes any of the information specified in the **Add a Student** sub-flow.
C. Once the student/administrator updates the necessary information, the system updates the student record with the updated information.

6. Alternative Flows

Alternative Flow 1: Invalid mandatory information

If in the **Add Student Registration Details or Edit Student Registration Details** flows, the student enters an invalid value in mandatory fields or leaves the mandatory fields empty, the system displays an error message. The student returns to the basic flow.

Alternative Flow 2: Sufficient number of electives not selected

If in the **Add Student Registration Details or Edit Student Registration Details** flow, a student with does not selects required number of electives, the system displays an error message. The student returns to the basic flow and may then enter the required number of electives.

Alternative Flow 3: Edit cancelled

If in the **Edit Student Registration Details** flow, the student/administrator decides not to edit his/her information, the edit is cancelled and the **Basic Flow** is re-started at the beginning.

Alternative Flow 4: Registration closed

If in the **Add Student Registration Details or Edit Student Registration Details** flow, the registration date is closed, student is not allowed to add/edit registration details. The use case ends

Alternative Flow 5: User Exits

This allows the user to exit during the use case. The use case ends.

7. Special Requirements
None.

8. Associated use cases
Login, Maintain Student Details, Maintain School Details, Maintain Programme Details.

```
Basic Flow 1                        Basic Flow 2
    |                                   |
    |    Alternative         Alternative|    Alternative
    |    Flow 2              Flow 3     |    Flow 3
Alternative                         Alternative
Flow 1                              Flow 1
         Alternative Flow 5                  Alternative Flow 5
    Use case ends                       Use case ends
```

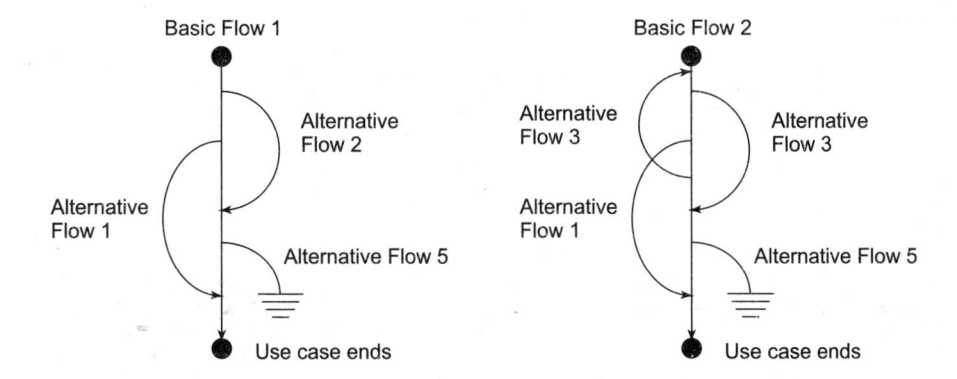

Figure II-12. Basic and alternative flows for maintain registration details use case (a) Add student registration details (b) Edit student registration details
Alternative Flow 1: Invalid Entry
Alternative Flow 2: Insufficient number of electives
Alternative Flow 3: Edit cancelled
Alternative Flow 4: Registration closed
Alternative Flow 5: User exits

C. TEST CASES GENERATED FROM USE CASE MAINTAIN REGISTRATION FORM

Table II-13. Scenario matrix for the maintain registration details use case

Scenario 1- Add a student	Basic Flow 1	
Scenario 2- Add a student alternative flow: Invalid Entry	Basic Flow 1	Alternate Flow 1
Scenario 3- Add a student alternative flow: Insufficient number of electives	Basic Flow 1	Alternate Flow 2
Scenario 4- Add a student alternative flow: Registration closed	Basic Flow 1	Alternate Flow 4
Scenario 5- Add a student alternative flow: User Exits	Basic Flow 1	Alternate Flow 5
Scenario 6- Edit a student	Basic Flow 2	
Scenario 7 - Edit a student alternative flow: Invalid Entry	Basic Flow 2	Alternate Flow 1
Scenario 8- Edit a student alternative flow: Insufficient number of electives	Basic Flow 2	Alternate Flow 2
Scenario 9- Edit a student alternative flow: Edit cancelled	Basic Flow 2	Alternate Flow 3
Scenario 10- Edit a student alternative flow: Registration closed	Basic Flow 2	Alternate Flow 4
Scenario 11- Edit a student alternative flow: User Exits	Basic Flow 2	Alternate Flow 5

For maintain student registration use case, we identify ten input variables for various basic flows in the use case. There are eight input variables namely father's name, address, city, state, zip, phone no., email, electives and one selection variables (Semester selected) in this use case. These inputs will be available for the respective flows as specified in the use case.

Table II-14. Test case matrix for the maintain registration details use case

Test case Id	Scenario Name and description	Input 1 Father's name	Input 2 Address	Input 3 City	Input 4 State	Input 5 Zip	Input 6 Phone no.	Input 7 Email	Input 8 Semester selected	Input 9 Electives	Reg. closed	Expected output	Remarks (if any)
TC1	Scenario 1: Add a student	Valid input	Valid input	Valid input	Valid input	Valid input	Valid input	Valid input	Yes	Valid input	No	Student is registered successfully	—
TC2	Scenario 2: Add a student alternative flow: Invalid entry	Invalid input	Valid/ invalid input	Valid/ invalid input	Valid/ invalid input	Valid/ invalid input	Valid/ invalid input	Valid/ invalid input	Yes/no	Valid/ invalid input	No	Invalid Father's name	Father's name is not in the specified format
TC3	—do—	Valid input	Invalid input	Valid/ invalid input	Valid/ invalid input	Valid/ invalid input	Valid/ invalid input	Valid/ invalid input	Yes/no	Valid/ invalid input	No	Invalid Address	Address is not in the specified format
TC4	—do—	Valid input	Valid input	Invalid input	Valid/ invalid input	Valid/ invalid input	Valid/ invalid input	Valid/ invalid input	Yes/no	Valid/ invalid input	No	Invalid state	State is not in the specified format
TC5	—do—	Valid input	Valid input	Valid input	Invalid input	Valid/ invalid input	Valid/ invalid input	Valid/ invalid input	Yes/no	Valid/ invalid input	No	Invalid city	City is not in the specified format
TC6	—do—	Valid input	Valid input	Valid input	Valid input	Invalid input	Valid/ invalid input	Valid/ invalid input	Yes/no	Valid/ invalid input	No	Invalid zip	Zip is not in the specified format
TC7	—do—	Valid input	Valid input	Valid input	Valid input	Valid input	Invalid input	Valid/ invalid input	Yes/no	Valid/ invalid input	No	Invalid phone no.	Phone no. is not in the specified format
TC8	—do—	Valid input	Valid input	Valid input	Valid input	Valid input	Valid input	Invalid input	Yes/no	Valid/ invalid input	No	Invalid email	Email is not in the specified format
TC9	—do—	Valid input	Valid input	Valid input	Valid input	Valid input	Valid input	Valid input	No	Valid/ invalid input	No	Semester not selected	User did not select a semester
TC10	Scenario 3: Add a student alternative flow: Insufficient numbers of electives	Valid input	Valid input	Valid input	Valid input	Valid input	Valid input	Valid input	Yes	Invalid input	No	Insufficient number of Electives selected	—

(Contd.)

(Contd.)

Test case Id	Scenario Name and description	Input 1 Father's name	Input 2 Address	Input 3 City	Input 4 State	Input 5 Zip	Input 6 Phone no.	Input 7 Email	Input 8 Semester selected	Input 9 Electives	Reg. closed	Expected output	Remarks (if any)
TC11	Scenario 4: Add a student alternative flow: Registration closed	Valid input	Valid input	Valid input	Valid input	Valid input	Valid input	Valid input	Yes	Valid input	Yes	User exits and returns to the main menu	Registration date is closed
TC12	Scenario 5: Add a student alternative flow: User exits	Valid/ invalid input	Valid/ invalid input	Valid/ invalid input	Valid/ invalid input	Valid/ invalid input	Valid/ invalid input	Valid/ invalid input	Yes/no	Valid/ invalid input	No	User is allowed to exit and returns to Main menu	—
TC13	Scenario 6: Edit a student	Valid input	Valid input	Valid input	Valid input	Valid input	Valid input	Valid input	Yes	Valid input	No	Student is updated successfully	—
TC14	Scenario 7 Edit a student alternative flow: Invalid entry	Invalid input	Valid/ invalid input	Valid/ invalid input	Valid/ invalid input	Valid/ invalid input	Valid/ invalid input	Valid/ invalid input	Yes/no	Valid/ invalid input	No	Invalid Father's name	Father's name is not in the specified format
TC15	—do—	Valid input	Invalid input	Valid/ invalid input	Valid/ invalid input	Valid/ invalid input	Valid/ invalid input	Valid/ invalid input	Yes/no	Valid/ invalid input	No	Invalid Address	Address is not in the specified format
TC16	—do—	Valid input	Valid input	Invalid input	Valid/ invalid input	Valid/ invalid input	Valid/ invalid input	Valid/ invalid input	Yes/no	Valid/ invalid input	No	Invalid state	State is not in the specified format
TC17	—do—	Valid input	Valid input	Valid input	Invalid input	Valid/ invalid input	Valid/ invalid input	Valid/ invalid input	Yes/no	Valid/ invalid input	No	Invalid city	City is not in the specified format
TC18	—do—	Valid input	Valid input	Valid input	Valid input	Invalid input	Valid/ invalid input	Valid/ invalid input	Yes/no	Valid/ invalid input	No	Invalid zip	Zip is not in the specified format
TC19	—do—	Valid input	Valid input	Valid input	Valid input	Valid input	Invalid input	Valid/ invalid input	Yes/no	Valid/ invalid input	No	Invalid phone no.	Phone no. is not in the specified format

(Contd.)

(Contd.)

Test case Id	Scenario Name and description	Input 1 Father's name	Input 2 Address	Input 3 City	Input 4 State	Input 5 Zip	Input 6 Phone no.	Input 7 Email	Input 8 Semester selected	Input 9 Electives	Reg. closed	Expected output	Remarks (if any)
TC20	—do—	Valid input	Valid input	Valid input	Valid input	Valid input	Valid input	Invalid input	Yes/no	Valid/invalid input	No	Invalid email	Email is not in the specified format
TC21	—do—	Valid input	Valid input	Valid input	Valid input	Valid input	Valid input	Valid input	No	Valid/invalid input	No	Semester not selected	User did not select a semester
TC22	Scenario 8: Edit a student alternative flow: Insufficient numbers of electives	Valid input	Valid input	Valid input	Valid input	Valid input	Valid input	Valid input	Yes	Invalid input	No	Insufficient number of Electives selected	—
TC23	Scenario 9: Edit a student alternative flow: Edit cancelled	Valid input	Valid input	Valid input	Valid input	Valid input	Valid input	Valid input	Yes	Valid input	No	Student registration form appears	—
TC24	Scenario 10: Edit a student alternative flow: Registration closed	Valid input	Valid input	Valid input	Valid input	Valid input	Valid input	Valid input	Yes	Valid input	Yes	User exits and returns to the main menu	Registration date is closed
TC25	Scenario 11: Edit a student: User exits	Valid/invalid input	Valid/invalid input	Valid/invalid input	Valid/invalid input	Valid/invalid input	Valid/invalid input	Valid/invalid input	Yes/no	Valid/invalid input	No	User is allowed to exit and returns to Main menu	—

n/a: option(s) not available for respective scenario

Appendix II 591

Table II-15. Test case matrix with actual data values for the maintain registration details use case

Test case Id	Scenario Name and description	Father's name	Address	City	State	Zip	Phone no.	Email	Semester selected	Electives	Reg. closed	Expected output	Remarks (if any)
TC1	Scenario 1: Add a student	B.P. Sharma	E92, Kailash Colony	New Delhi	New Delhi	110065	24321322	Ruchika@yahoo.com	3	ITR709 ITR 711	No	Student is registered successfully	—
TC2	Scenario 2: Add a student alternative flow: Invalid entry	Bp123@	*	*	*	*	*	*	*	*	No	Invalid Father's name	Father's name is not in the specified format i.e. it contains digits and special characters
TC3	—do—	B.P. Sharma	12B	*	*	*	*	*	*	*	No	Invalid Address	Address is not in the specified format i.e. it contains digits
TC4	—do—	B.P. Sharma	E92, Kailash Colony	D1	*	*	*	*	*	*	No	Invalid state	State is not in the specified format i.e. it contains digits
TC5	—do—	B.P. Sharma	E92, Kailash Colony	New Delhi	D1	*	*	*	*	*	No	Invalid city	City is not in the specified format i.e. it contains digits
TC6	—do—	B.P. Sharma	E92, Kailash Colony	New Delhi	New Delhi	R110	*	*	*	*	No	Invalid zip	Zip is not in the specified format i.e. it contains alphabets
TC7	—do—	B.P. Sharma	E92, Kailash Colony	New Delhi	New Delhi	110065	234	*	*	*	No	Invalid phone no.	Phone no. is not in the specified length
TC8	—do—	B.P. Sharma	E92, Kailash Colony	New Delhi	New Delhi	110065	24321322	Richayahoo.com	*	*	No	Invalid email	Email is not in the specified format i.e. it does not contain @ sign
TC9	—do—	B.P. Sharma	E92, Kailash Colony	New Delhi	New Delhi	110065	24321322	Ruchika@yahoo.com	*	*	No	Semester not selected	User did not select a semester
TC10	Scenario 3: Add a student alternative flow: Insufficient numbers of electives	B.P. Sharma	E92, Kailash Colony	New Delhi	New Delhi	110065	24321322	Ruchika@yahoo.com	3	ITR709	No	Insufficient number of Electives selected	—

(Contd.)

(Contd.)

Test case Id	Scenario Name and description	Father's name	Address	City	State	Zip	Phone no.	Email	Semester selected	Electives	Reg. closed	Expected output	Remarks (if any)
TC11	Scenario 4: Add a student alternative flow: Registration closed	Valid input	Valid input	Valid input	Valid input	Valid input	Valid input	Valid input	Yes	Valid input	Yes	Yes	User exits and returns to the main menu
TC12	Scenario 5: Add a student alternative flow: User exits	*	*	*	*	*	*	*	*	*	No	User is allowed to exit and returns to Main menu	—
TC13	Scenario 6: Edit a student	B.P. Sharma	E92, Kailash Colony	New Delhi	New Delhi	110065	24321322	Ruchika@ yahoo.com	3	ITR709 ITR 713	No	Student is updated successfully	—
TC14	Scenario 7 Edit a student alternative flow: Invalid entry	Bp123@	*	*	*	*	*	*	*	*	No	Invalid Father's name	Father's name is not in the specified format i.e. it contains digits and special characters
TC15	—do—	B.P. Sharma	12B	*	*	*	*	*	*	*	No	Invalid Address	Address is not in the specified format i.e. it contains digits
TC16	—do—	B.P. Sharma	E92, Kailash Colony	D1	*	*	*	*	*	*	No	Invalid state	State is not in the specified format i.e. it contains digits
TC17	—do—	B.P. Sharma	E92, Kailash Colony	New Delhi	D1	*	*	*	*	*	No	Invalid city	City is not in the specified format i.e. it contains digits
TC18	—do—	B.P. Sharma	E92, Kailash Colony	New Delhi	New Delhi	R110	*	*	*	*	No	Invalid zip	Zip is not in the specified format i.e. it contains alphabets
TC19	—do—	B.P. Sharma	E92, Kailash Colony	New Delhi	New Delhi	110065	234	*	*	*	No	Invalid phone no.	Phone no. is not in the specified length

(Contd.)

(Contd.)

Test case Id	Scenario Name and description	Father's name	Address	City	State	Zip	Phone no.	Email	Semester selected	Electives	Reg. closed	Expected output	Remarks (if any)
TC20	—do—	B.P. Sharma	E92, Kailash Colony	New Delhi	New Delhi	110065	24321322	Richayahoo. com	*	*	No	Invalid email	Email is not in the specified format i.e. it does not contain @ sign
TC21	—do—	B.P. Sharma	E92, Kailash Colony	New Delhi	New Delhi	110065	24321322	Ruchika@ yahoo.com	*	*	No	Semester not selected	User did not select a semester
TC22	Scenario 8: Edit a student alternative flow: Insufficient numbers of electives	B.P. Sharma	E92, Kailash Colony	New Delhi	New Delhi	110065	24321322	Ruchika@ yahoo.com	3	ITR709	No	Insufficient number of Electives selected	—
TC23	Scenario 9: Edit a student alternative flow: Edit cancelled	B.P. Sharma	E92, Kailash Colony	New Delhi	New Delhi	110065	24321322	Ruchika@ yahoo.com	3	ITR709 ITR 711	No	Student registration form appears	—
TC24	Scenario 10: Edit a student alternative flow: Registration closed	Valid input	Valid input	Valid input	Valid input	Valid input	Valid input	Valid input	Yes	Valid input	Yes	Yes	User exits and returns to the main menu
TC25	Scenario 11: Edit a student: User exits	*	*	*	*	*	*	*	*	*	No	User is allowed to exit and returns to Main menu	—

*: do not care conditions (valid/invalid inputs)
n/a: option(s) not available for respective scenario

Appendix III

Case Study: Consider the problem statement of University Registration System (URS). Design the test cases from the validity checks given in SRS.

A. Scheme Details Form

This form will be accessible only to system administrator. It will allow him/her to add/edit/delete/view information about new/existing scheme(s) for the school and programme that were selected in the 'Scheme Details' form. The list of schools and programmes available in that particular school will be displayed. The list of semesters available in that particular programme will also be displayed.

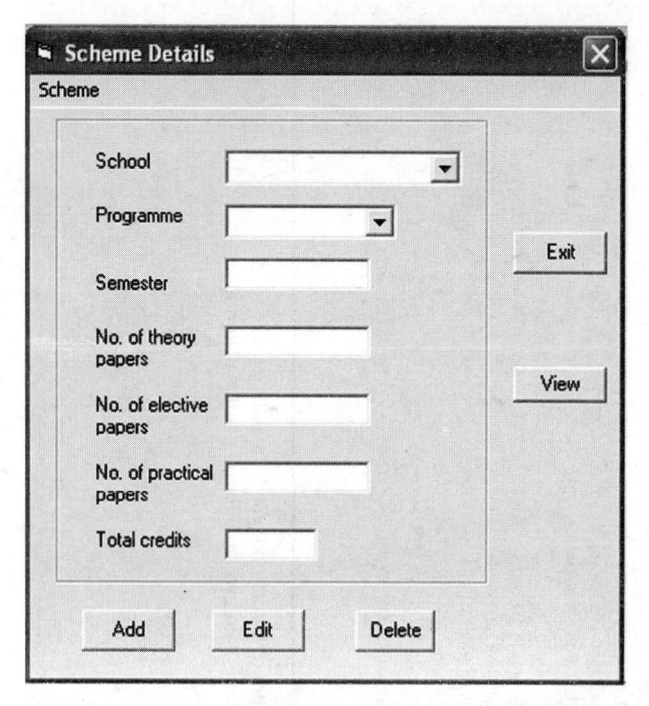

B. Validity Checks

Validity check No.	Description
VC1	Only Administrator will be authorized to access the Maintain Scheme Details module.
VC2	Every scheme will have a unique semester.
VC3	School name cannot be blank.
VC4	Programme name cannot be blank.
VC5	Semester cannot be blank.
VC6	Semester can have value only between 1 to 14.
VC7	No. of theory papers cannot be blank.
VC8	No. of theory papers can have value between 0 to 10.
VC9	No. of elective papers cannot be blank.
VC10	No. of elective papers can have value between 0 to 10.
VC11	No. of practical papers cannot be blank.
VC12	No. of practical papers can have value between 0 to 10.
VC13	Total credit cannot be blank.
VC14	Total credit can have value between 5 to 99.

Figure III-1. Validity checks for scheme form

C. Test cases based on validity checks for scheme form

Test case Id	Validity check No.	School selected	Prog. selected	Semester	No. of theory papers	No. of elective papers	No. of practical papers	Total credits	Expected output	Remarks (if any)
TC1	VC2	University School of Information Technology	MCA	1	5	0	2	22	Scheme is added successfully	—
TC2	VC3		*	*	*	*	*	*	Please select school	User did not select a school
TC3	VC4	University School of Information Technology		*	*	*	*	*	Please select programme	User did not select a programme
TC4	VC5	University School of Information Technology	MCA		*	*	*	*	Please enter semester	Semester cannot be blank
TC5	VC6	University School of Information Technology	MCA	16	*	*	*	*	Invalid semester	Semester should be between 1 to 14
TC6	VC7	University School of Information Technology	MCA	1		*	*	*	Please enter number of theory papers	Number of theory papers cannot be blank
TC7	VC8	University School of Information Technology	MCA	1	11	*	*	*	Invalid number of theory papers	Number of theory papers should be between 0 to 10
TC8	VC9	University School of Information Technology	MCA	1	5				Please enter number of elective papers	Number of elective papers cannot be blank
TC9	VC10	University School of Information Technology	MCA	1	5	11			Invalid number of elective papers	Number of elective papers should be between 0 to 10
TC10	VC11	University School of Information Technology	MCA	1	5	0			Please enter number of practical papers	Number of practical papers cannot be blank

(Contd.)

(Contd.)

Test case Id	Validity check No.	School selected	Prog. selected	Semester	No. of theory papers	No. of elective papers	No. of practical papers	Total credits	Expected output	Remarks (if any)
TC11	VC12	University School of Information Technology	MCA	1	5	0	11		Invalid number of practical papers	Number of practical papers should be between 0 to 10
TC12	VC13	University School of Information Technology	MCA	1	5	0	2		Please enter total credits	Number of theory total credits cannot be blank
TC13	VC14	University School of Information Technology	MCA	1	5	0	2	111	Invalid total credits	Number of theory total credits should be between 5 to 99

*: do not care conditions (valid/invalid inputs)

Figure III-2. Test case with actual data values for the scheme form

A. Paper Details Form

This form will be accessible only to system administrator. It will allow him/her to add/edit/delete/view information about new/existing paper(s) for the school, the programme and the semester that were selected in the 'Paper Details' form.

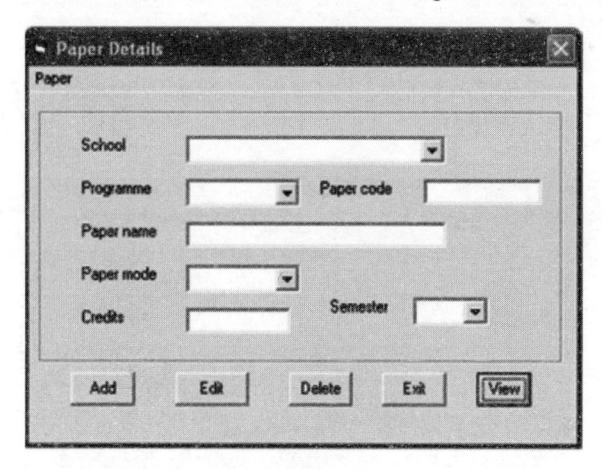

B. Validity Checks

Validity check No.	Description
VC1	Only Administrator will be authorized to access the Maintain Paper Details module.
VC2	A scheme will have more than one paper.
VC3	No two semesters will have same paper i.e. a paper will be offered only in a particular semester for a given programme.
VC4	School name cannot be blank.
VC5	Programme name cannot be blank.
VC6	Semester cannot be blank.
VC7	Semester can have value only between 1 to 14.
VC8	Paper code cannot be blank.
VC9	Paper code cannot accept special characters.
VC10	Paper code can have both alphabetic and numeric characters.
VC11	Paper code can include blank spaces
VC12	Paper code can have length of 5 to 7.
VC13	Paper name cannot be blank.
VC14	Paper name can only have alphanumeric (alphabets and digits) or blank space characters.
VC15	Paper name cannot have special characters.
VC16	Paper type may be compulsory, elective or practical.
VC17	Credit cannot be blank.
VC18	Credit can have value only between 1 to 30.

Figure III-3. Validity checks for paper form

Appendix III 599

C. Test cases based on validity checks for paper form

Test case Id	Validity check No.	School selected	Prog. selected	Semester	Paper code	Paper name	Paper type selected	Credits	Expected output	Remarks (if any)
TC1	VC2	University School of Information Technology	MCA	1	BA607	Discrete mathematics	Compulsory	4	A semester should have more than one paper	–
TC2	VC2	University School of Information Technology	MCA	1	BA609	Mathematics-I	Compulsory	4	–	–
TC3	VC3	University School of Information Technology	MCA	1	BA607	Discrete mathematics	Compulsory	4	Two semesters cannot have same paper	–
TC4	VC3	University School of Information Technology	MCA	2	BA607	Discrete mathematics	Compulsory	4	–	–
TC5	VC4	University School of Information Technology	*	*	*	*	*	*	Please select school	User did not select a school
TC6	VC5	University School of Information Technology	MCA	*	*	*	*	*	Please select programme	User did not select a programme
TC7	VC6	University School of Information Technology	MCA		*	*	*	*	Please enter semester	Semester cannot be blank
TC8	VC7	University School of Information Technology	MCA	16	*	*	*	*	Invalid semester	Semester should be between 1 to 14
TC9	VC8	University School of Information Technology	MCA	*	*	*	*	*	Please enter paper code	Paper code cannot be blank
TC10	VC9	University School of Information Technology	MCA	1	IT_105	*	*	*	Invalid paper code	Paper code cannot contain special characters
TC11	VC10	University School of Information Technology	MCA	1	IT105	*	*	*	–	Alphanumeric and digits can be included

(Contd.)

(Contd.)

Test case Id	Validity check No.	School selected	Prog. selected	Semester	Paper code	Paper name	Paper type selected	Credits	Expected output	Remarks (if any)
TC12	VC11	University School of Information Technology	MCA	1	IT 107	*	*	*	—	Blank spaces can be included
TC13	VC12	University School of Information Technology	MCA	1	IT	*	*	*	Invalid paper code	Paper code should have atleast 5 characters
TC14	VC12	University School of Information Technology	MCA	1	IT123455	*	*	*	Invalid paper code	Paper code cannot have more than 7 characters
TC15	VC13	University School of Information Technology	MCA	1	IT105		*	*	Please enter paper name	Paper name cannot be blank
TC16	VC14	University School of Information Technology	MCA	1	IT105	Introduction to computers	*	*	—	Valid paper name
TC17	VC15	University School of Information Technology	MCA	1	IT109	Data_struct	*	*	Invalid paper name	Paper name cannot contain special characters
TC18	VC16	University School of Information Technology	MCA	1	IT105	Introduction to computers	Compulsory	*	—	Paper type is compulsory
TC19	VC16	University School of Information Technology	MCA	1	IT156	Lab-I	Practical	*	—	Paper type is practical
TC20	VC16	University School of Information Technology	MCA	5	IT111	Software quality management	Elective	*	—	Paper type is elective
TC21	VC17	University School of Information Technology	MCA	1	IT105	Introduction to computers	Compulsory		Please enter credits	Credits cannot be blank
TC22	VC18	University School of Information Technology	MCA	1	IT105	Introduction to computers	Compulsory	32	Invalid credits	Credits should have value between 1 to 30

*: do not care conditions (valid/invalid inputs)

Figure III-4. Test case with actual data values for paper form

A. Student Details Form

This form will be accessible to system administrator and DEO. It will allow them to add/edit/delete/view information about new/existing student (s) for a particular year.

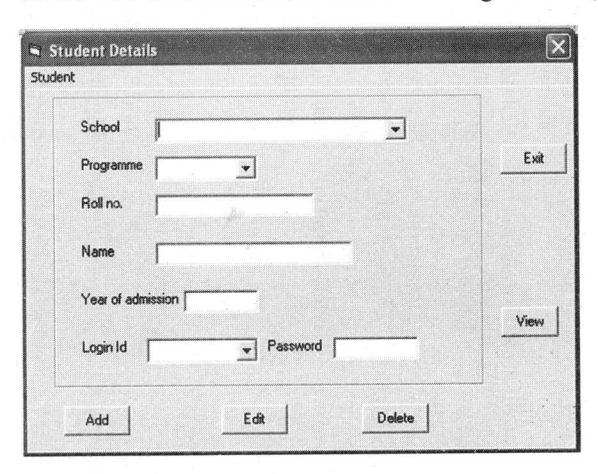

B. Validity Checks

Validity check No.	Description
VC1	Only administrator/DEO will be authorized to access the Maintain Student Details module.
VC2	Every student will have a unique roll number.
VC3	School name cannot be blank.
VC4	Programme name cannot be blank.
VC5	Roll no. cannot be blank.
VC6	Length of Roll no. for any user can only be equal to 11 digits.
VC7	Roll no. cannot contain Alphabets, special characters and blank spaces.
VC8	Student name cannot be blank.
VC9	Length of student name can be of 3 to 50 characters.
VC10	Student name will not accept special characters.
VC11	Year of admission cannot be blank.
VC12	Year of admission can have only 4 digits.
VC13	Password cannot be blank (initially auto generated of 8 digits).
VC14	Password can have length from 4 to 15 characters.
VC15	Alphabets, digits and hyphen & underscore characters are allowed in password field. However blank spaces are not allowed.
VC16	Roll number and login Id are same.

Figure III-5. Validity checks for student form

C. Test cases based on validity checks for student form

Test case Id	Validity check No.	School selected	Programme selected	Roll no.	Name	Year of admission	Password	Expected output	Remarks (if any)
TC1	VC2	University School of Information Technology	MCA	00616453007	Richa Sharma	2009	n/a	Student is added successfully	–
TC2	VC3		*	*	*	*	n/a	School not selected	User did not select a school
TC3	VC4	University School of Information Technology		*	*	*	n/a	Programme not selected	User did not select a programme
TC4	VC5	University School of Information Technology	MCA		*	*	n/a	Roll no. not selected	Roll no. cannot be blank
TC5	VC6	University School of Information Technology	MCA	006164530	*	*	n/a	Invalid roll no.	Length of roll no. should be 11 digits
TC6	VC7	University School of Information Technology	MCA	006tutututu	*	*	n/a	Invalid roll no.	Roll no. cannot contain alphanumeric characters
TC7	VC7	University School of Information Technology	MCA	006_@546467	*	*	n/a	Invalid roll no.	Roll no. cannot contain special characters
TC8	VC7	University School of Information Technology	MCA	00123 567	*	*	n/a	Invalid roll no.	Roll no. cannot contain blank spaces
TC9	VC8	University School of Information Technology	MCA	00616453007		*	n/a	Please enter student name	Student name cannot be blank
TC10	VC9	University School of Information Technology	MCA	00616453007	Ru	*	n/a	Invalid student name	Length of student name cannot be less than 3 characters
TC11	VC9	University School of Information Technology	MCA	00616453007	>50	*	n/a	Invalid student name	Length of student name cannot be more than 50 characters

(Contd.)

(Contd.)

Test case Id	Validity check No.	School selected	Programme selected	Roll no.	Name	Year of admission	Password	Expected output	Remarks (if any)
TC12	VC10	University School of Information Technology	MCA	00616453007	Pooj_a	*	n/a	Invalid student name	Student name cannot contain special characters
TC13	VC11	University School of Information Technology	MCA	00616453007	Pooja sinha		n/a	Invalid year of admission	Year of admission cannot be blank
TC14	VC12	University School of Information Technology	MCA	00616453007		99	n/a	Invalid year of admission	Year of admission cannot be less than 4 characters
TC15	VC13	University School of Information Technology	MCA	00616453007	Richa Sharma	2009		Unable to generate password	Password cannot be blank
TC16	VC14	University School of Information Technology	MCA	00616453007	Richa Sharma	2009	Rj	Invalid password	Length of the password cannot be less than 4 characters
TC17		University School of Information Technology	MCA	00616453007	Richa Sharma	2009	>15	Invalid password	Length of the password cannot be more than 15 characters
TC18	VC15	University School of Information Technology	MCA	00616453007	Richa Sharma	2009	011 67	Invalid password	Password cannot contain blank spaces
TC19	VC16	University School of Information Technology	MCA	00616453007	Richa Sharma	2009	01123456	–	Roll no. should be same as login id

*: do not care conditions (valid/invalid inputs)

Figure III-6. Test case with actual data values for the student form

A. Faculty Details Form

This form will be accessible only to system administrator/DEO. It will allow him/her to add/edit/delete/view information about new/existing faculty(s) in a particular school.

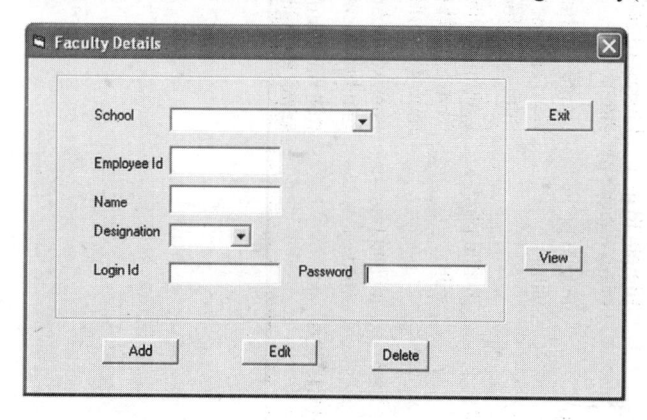

B. Validity Checks

Validity check No.	Description
VC1	Only administrator/DEO will be authorized to access the Maintain Faculty Details module.
VC2	Every faculty will have a unique Employee Id.
VC3	School name cannot be blank.
VC4	Employee Id cannot be blank
VC5	Length of employee Id will be equal to 11 digits only.
VC6	Employee Id cannot contain Alphabets, special characters and blank spaces.
VC7	Faculty name cannot be blank.
VC8	Faculty name will only accept alphabetic characters and blank spaces and not accept special characters.
VC9	Designation cannot be blank.
VC10	Password cannot be blank (initially auto generated of 8 digits).
VC11	Password can have length from 4 to 15 characters.
VC12	Alphabets, digits and hyphen & underscore characters are allowed in password field. However blank spaces are not allowed.

Figure III-7. Validity checks for faculty form

C. Test cases based on validity checks for faculty form

Test case Id	Validity check No.	School selected	Employee Id	Name	Designation	Password	Expected output	Remarks (if any)
TC1	VC1	University School of Information Technology	194	Nisha Gupta	Lecturer	n/a	Faculty is added successfully	—
TC2	VC2		*	*	*	n/a	School not selected	User did not select a school
TC3	VC3	University School of Information Technology		*	*	n/a	Please enter employee id	Employee id cannot be blank
TC4	VC4	University School of Information Technology	011234	*	*	n/a	Invalid employee id	Length of employee id should be 11 digits
TC5	VC5	University School of Information Technology	011rtklmnnq	*	*	n/a	Invalid employee id	Employee id cannot contain alphanumeric characters
TC6	VC5	University School of Information Technology	011@#987678	*	*	n/a	Invalid employee id	Employee id cannot contain special characters
TC7	VC5	University School of Information Technology	011 45 555	*	*	n/a	Invalid employee id	Employee id cannot contain blank spaces
TC8	VC6	University School of Information Technology	01123456789		*	n/a	Please enter faculty name	Faculty name cannot be blank
TC9	VC7	University School of Information Technology	01123456789	Nishar_sh	*	n/a	Invalid faculty name	Faculty name cannot contain special characters
TC10	VC8	University School of Information Technology	194	Neetu Singh		n/a	Designation not selected	User did not select a faculty designation
TC11	VC9	University School of Information Technology	194	Neetu Singh	Lecturer		Unable to generate password	Password cannot be blank
TC12	VC10	University School of Information Technology	194	Neetu Singh	Lecturer	Ggs	Invalid password	Length of the password cannot be less than 4 characters
TC13	VC11	University School of Information Technology	194	Neetu Singh	Lecturer	>15	Invalid password	Length of the password cannot be more than 15 characters
TC14	VC12	University School of Information Technology	194	Neetu Singh	Lecturer	011 67	Invalid password	Password cannot contain blank spaces

*: do not care conditions (valid/invalid inputs)

Figure III-8. Test case with actual data values for the faculty form

A. Student registration form

This form will be accessible to system administrator and students. It will be available only when registration for a semester is open. It will be filled by the student in order to register himself/herself for the current semester. Every student will fill his/her form only.

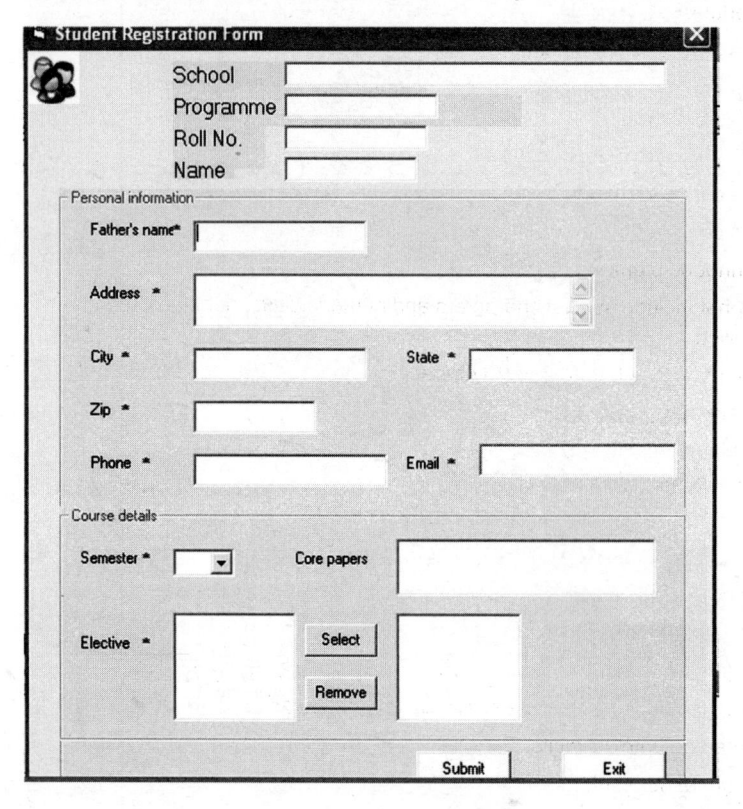

B. Validity Checks

Validity check No.	Description
VC1	Only Administrator/Student will be authorized to access the student registration module.
VC2	Father's name cannot be blank
VC3	Father's name cannot include special characters and digits, but blank spaces are allowed.
VC4	Father's name can have length 3 to 50 characters.
VC5	Address cannot be blank.
VC6	Address can have length upto 10 to 200 characters.
VC7	City cannot be blank
VC8	City cannot include special characters and numeric digits, but blank spaces are allowed.
VC9	City can have length upto 3 to 20 characters.
VC10	State cannot be blank.
VC11	State cannot include special characters and numeric digits, but blank spaces are allowed.
VC12	State can have length upto 3 to 20 characters.
VC13	Zip cannot be blank.
VC14	Zip cannot include alphabets, special characters and blank spaces.
VC15	Zip can have length of 6 digits.
VC16	Phone cannot be blank.
VC17	Phone cannot include alphabets, special characters and blank spaces.
VC18	Phone can be upto 11 digits.
VC19	Email cannot be blank.
VC20	Email can have upto 50 characters.
VC21	Email should contain @ and . character.
VC22	Email cannot include blank spaces.
VC23	Semester should be blank.
VC24	A semester may or may not have an elective paper.
VC25	Student cannot select more than required elective papers.
VC26	Student is required to register within given registration time.

Figure III-9. Validity checks for maintain registration details

C. Test cases based on validity checks for student registration form

Test case id	Validity check No.	Father's name	Address	City	State	Zip	Phone	Email	Semester selected	Electives	Expected output	Remarks (if any)
TC1	VC2		*	*	*	*	*	*	*	*	Please enter father's name	Father's name cannot be blank
TC2	VC3	Hars125	*	*	*	*	*	*	*	*	Invalid father's name	Father's name cannot contain digits
TC3	VC3	Har_ht	*	*	*	*	*	*	*	*	Invalid father's name	Father's name cannot contain special characters
TC4	VC4	Har	*	*	*	*	*	*	*	*	Invalid father's name	Father's name cannot be less than 3 characters
TC5	VC4	>50	*	*	*	*	*	*	*	*	Invalid father's name	Father's name cannot be greater than 50 characters
TC6	VC5	Harsh Gupta		*	*	*	*	*	*	*	Please enter address	Address cannot be blank
TC7	VC6	Harsh Gupta	E-32	*	*	*	*	*	*	*	Invalid address	Address cannot be less than 10 characters
TC8	VC6	Harsh Gupta	>200	*	*	*	*	*	*	*	Invalid address	Address name cannot be greater than 200 characters

(Contd.)

(Contd.)

Test case id	Validity check No.	Father's name	Address	City	State	Zip	Phone	Email	Semester selected	Electives	Expected output	Remarks (if any)
TC9	VC7	Harsh Gupta	E-32, Kailash Colony		*	*	*	*	*	*	Please enter city	City cannot be blank
TC10	VC8	Harsh Gupta	E-32, Kailash Colony	De_!	*	*	*	*	*	*	Invalid city	City cannot contain special characters
TC11	VC8	Harsh Gupta	E-32, Kailash Colony	De12	*	*	*	*	*	*	Invalid city	City cannot contain numeric digits
TC12	VC9	Harsh Gupta	E-32, Kailash Colony	De	*	*	*	*	*	*	Invalid city	City cannot be less than 3 characters
TC13	VC9	Harsh Gupta	E-32, Kailash Colony	>20	*	*	*	*	*	*	Invalid city	City cannot be greater than 20 characters
TC14	VC10	Harsh Gupta	E-32, Kailash Colony	Delhi		*	*	*	*	*	Please enter state	State cannot be blank
TC15	VC11	Harsh Gupta	E-32, Kailash Colony	Delhi	De_!	*	*	*	*	*	Invalid state	State cannot contain special characters
TC16	VC11	Harsh Gupta	E-32, Kailash Colony	Delhi	De12	*	*	*	*	*	Invalid state	State cannot contain numeric digits
TC17	VC12	Harsh Gupta	E-32, Kailash Colony	Delhi	De	*	*	*	*	*	Invalid state	State cannot be less than 3 characters
TC18	VC12	Harsh Gupta	E-32, Kailash Colony	Delhi	>20	*	*	*	*	*	Invalid state	State cannot be greater than 20 characters

(Contd.)

(Contd.)

Test case id	Validity check No.	Father's name	Address	City	State	Zip	Phone	Email	Semester selected	Electives	Expected output	Remarks (if any)
TC19	VC13	Harsh Gupta	E-32, Kailash Colony	Delhi	Delhi		*	*	*	*	Please enter zip	Zip cannot be blank
TC20	VC14	Harsh Gupta	E-32, Kailash Colony	Delhi	Delhi	110ty	*	*	*	*	Invalid zip	Zip cannot contain alphanumeric characters
TC21	VC14	Harsh Gupta	E-32, Kailash Colony	Delhi	Delhi	110,89	*	*	*	*	Invalid zip	Zip cannot contain special characters
TC22	VC15	Harsh Gupta	E-32, Kailash Colony	Delhi	Delhi	1100245	*	*	*	*	Invalid zip	Zip cannot contain length greater than 6 digits
TC23	VC16	Harsh Gupta	E-32, Kailash Colony	Delhi	Delhi	110045		*	*	*	Please enter phone	Phone cannot be blank
TC24	VC17	Harsh Gupta	E-32, Kailash Colony	Delhi	Delhi	110045	981retee	*	*	*	Invalid phone	Phone cannot contain alphanumeric characters
TC25	VC17	Harsh Gupta	E-32, Kailash Colony	Delhi	Delhi	110045	981,yut	*	*	*	Invalid phone	Phone cannot contain special characters
TC26	VC17	Harsh Gupta	E-32, Kailash Colony	Delhi	Delhi	110045	981 435677	*	*	*	Invalid phone	Phone cannot contain blank spaces
TC27	VC18	Harsh Gupta	E-32, Kailash Colony	Delhi	Delhi	110045	911023444534	*	*	*	Invalid phone	Phone cannot contain length greater than 11 digits

(Contd.)

Appendix III 611

(Contd.)

Test case id	Validity check No.	Father's name	Address	City	State	Zip	Phone	Email	Semester selected	Electives	Expected output	Remarks (if any)
TC28	VC19	Harsh Gupta	E-32, Kailash Colony	Delhi	Delhi	110045	26546789		*	*	Please enter email	Email cannot be blank
TC29	VC20	Harsh Gupta	E-32, Kailash Colony	Delhi	Delhi	110045	26546789	>50	*	*	Invalid email	Email cannot be greater than 50 characters
TC30	VC21	Harsh Gupta	E-32, Kailash Colony	Delhi	Delhi	110045	26546789	Ruchyahoo.com	*	*	Invalid email	Email should contain @ character
TC31	VC21	Harsh Gupta	E-32, Kailash Colony	Delhi	Delhi	110045	26546789	Ruch@yahoocom	*	*	Invalid email	Email should contain . character
TC32	VC22	Harsh Gupta	E-32, Kailash Colony	Delhi	Delhi	110045	26546789	Ruch@ yaho o.com	*	*	Invalid email	Email cannot contain blank spaces
TC33	VC23	Harsh Gupta	E-32, Kailash Colony	Delhi	Delhi	110045	26546789	ruchi@yahoo.com		*	Please select semester	Semester is not selected
TC34	VC24	Harsh Gupta	E-32, Kailash Colony	Delhi	Delhi	110045	26546789	ruchi@yahoo.com	2		Student is registered successfully	Semester does no contain a elective paper
TC35	VC25	Harsh Gupta	E-32, Kailash Colony	Delhi	Delhi	110045	26546789	ruchi@yahoo.com	yes	IT 702	Invalid number of electives selected	User selected less number of electives

*: do not care conditions (valid/invalid inputs)

Figure III-10. Test case with actual data values for the student registration form

References

[AGGA06]   K.K. Aggarwal, Yogesh Singh, Arvinder Kaur and Ruchika Malhotra, "Application of Artificial Neural Network for Predicting Maintainability using Object-Oriented Metrics," Transactions on Engineering, Computing and Technology, vol. 15, Oct. 2006.

[AGGA04]   K.K. Aggarwal, Yogesh Singh and Arvinder Kaur, "Code Coverage Based Technique for Prioritizing Test Cases for Regression Testing", ACM SIGSOFT Software Engineering Notes, vol. 29, no. 5, September, 2004.

[AGGA08]   K.K. Aggarwal and Yogesh Singh, "Software Engineering: Programs, Documentation, Operating Procedures", New Age International Publishers, New Delhi, India, 2008.

[ALI10]   Shaukat Ali, Hadi Hemmati, Rajwinder K. Panesar-Walawege, "A Systematic Review of the Application and Empirical Investigation of Search-Based Test Case Generation", IEEE Transactions on Software Engineering, vol. 36, no. 6, pp. 742–762, 2010.

[ANDE98]   Ross J. Anderson, "Information Technology in Medical Practice: Safety and Privacy Lessons from the United Kingdom", University of Cambridge Computer Laboratory, United Kingdom, 1998.

[ANSI91]   ANSI, "Standard Glossary of Software Engineering Terminology", STD – 729–1991, ANSI / IEEE, 1991.

[BACH90]   R. Bache and M. Mullerburg, "Measures of Testability as a Basis for Quality Assurance", Software Engineering Journal, vol. 5, no. 2, pp. 86–92, 1990.

[BALA07]   E. Balagurusamy, "Programming in ANSI C", Tata McGraw Hill Publishing Company Limited, New Delhi, India, 2007.

[BEIZ90]   B. Beizer, "Software Testing Techniques", Van Nostrand Reinhold, New York, 1990.

[BENT04]   J.E. Bentley, "Software Testing Fundamentals: Concepts, Roles and Terminology" pp. 141–30, Wachovia Bank, Charlottes NC, USA, 2004.

[BERT04]   A. Bertolino and E. Marchetti, "A Brief Essay on Software Testing", Technical Report: 2004-TR-36, 2004.

[BEIM95]	J. Bieman, and B. Kang, "Cohesion and Reuse in an Object-Oriented System", ACM SIGSOFT Software Engineering Notes, vol. 20, pp. 259–262, 1995.
[BIND94]	R.V. Binder, "Design for Testability in Object Oriented Systems", Communication of the ACM, vol. 37, no. 9, pp. 87–101, 1994.
[BINK98]	A. Binkley and S.Schach, "Validation of the Coupling Dependency Metric as a risk Predictor", Proceedings in ICSE 98, pp. 452–455, 1998.
[BITT03]	Kurt Bittner and Ian Spence, "Use Case Modeling", Pearson Education, 2003.
[BOGU09]	Robert Bogue, "Effective Code Reviews without Pain", www.developer.com/tech/article.php/3579756, 2009.
[BOYE75]	R.S. Boyer et. al. "A Formal System for Testing and Debugging Programs by Symbolic Execution", In proceedings of the International conference on Reliable Software, pp. 234–244, ACM Press, 1975.
[BRUN06]	M.Bruntink and A.V. Deursen, "An Empirical Study into Class Testability", Journal of System and Software, vol. 79 no. 9, pp. 1219–1232, 2006.
[CHID94]	S. Chidamber, and C. Kamerer, "A Metrics Suite for Object-Oriented Design", IEEE Transactions on Software Engineering, vol. 20, no. 6, pp. 476–493, 1994.
[CLAR76]	L. Clarke, "A System to Generate Test Data and Symbolically Execute Programs", IEEE Transactions on Software Engineering, vol. 2, no. 3, pp. 215–222, 1976.
[COCK01]	Cockburn, "Writing Effective Use Cases", Pearson Education, 2001.
[COPE04]	Lee Copeland, "A Practitioner's Guide to Software Test Design", Artech House, 2004.
[DANI99]	Hoffman Daniel, S. Paul and White Lee, "Boundary Values and Automated Component Testing", Software Testing, Verification and Reliability, vol. 9, pp. 3–26, 1999.
[EDVA99]	J. Edvardsson, " A Survey on Automatic Test Data Generation", In Proceedings of the Second Conference on Computer Science and Engineering in Linkoping, 21–28, ECSEL, October, 1999.
[EDWA06]	Edward Kit, "Software Testing in the Real World", Pearson Education, 2006.
[EMAM99]	K. Emam, S. Benlarbi, N. Goel, and S. Rai, "A Validation of Object-Oriented Metrics", Technical Report ERB-1063, NRC, 1999.
[GOOD93]	Paul Goodman, "Practical Implementation of Software Metrics", McGraw Hill Book Company, UK, 1993.
[FENT04]	N.E. Fenton and S.L. Pfleeger, "Software Metrics", Thomson Books, Singapore, 2004.
[FOUR09]	G. Fournier, "Essential Software Testing – A Use Case Approach", CRC Press, 2009.
[FINK93]	Anthony Finkelstein, "Report of the Inquiry into the London Ambulance Service", University College, London, 1993.
[FINN96]	G. Finnie and G. Witting, "AI Tools for Software Development Effect Estimation", International Conference on Software Engineering Education and Practice, USA, 1996.

References

[HETT01] Hatty Baiz and Nancy Costa, "Project Audit and Review Checklist", Princeton Project Office, Princeton University, New jersey, USA, hetty@princeton.edu, ncosta@princeton.edu, 2001.

[HEUM01] J. Heumann, "Generating Test Cases from Use Cases", Rational Edge, www.therationaledge.com, 2001.

[HUMP02] W.S. Humphrey, "Managing the Software Process", Software Engineering Institute of Carnegie Mellon University, USA, 2002.

[IEEE93] IEEE, "IEEE Guide to Software Requirements Specifications (IEEE Std 830 –1993)", 1993.

[IEEE98a] IEEE, "IEEE Recommended Practice for Software Requirements Specifications (IEEE Std 830–1998)", 1998.

[IEEE98b] IEEE, "IEEE Recommended Practice for Software Design Description (IEEE Std 1016–1998), 1998.

[IEEE98c] IEEE, "IEEE Standard for Test Documentation (IEEE Std 829–1998), 1998.

[IEEE01] IEEE, "Standard Glossary of Software Engineering Terminology", 2001.

[INCE87] D.C. Ince, "The Automatic Generation of Test Data", The Computer Journal, vol. 30, no. 1, pp. 63–69, 1998.

[JACO99] I.V. Jacobson et al., "Object Oriented Software Engineering", Pearson Education, 1999.

[JELI72] Z. Jelinski and P.B. Moranda, "Software Reliability Research in Statistical Computer Performance Evaluation", Academic Press, NY, 1972.

[JONE96] B.F. Jones, H.H. Sthamer and D.E. Eyres, "Automatic Structural Testing using Genetic Algorithms", Software Engineering Journal, September, 299–306, 1996.

[JORG07] P.C. Jorgenson, "Software Testing, A Craftsman's Approach", 3rd edition, Auerbach Publications, USA, 2007.

[JOSH03] Joshi S.D., "Object Oriented Modeling and Design", Tech-Max, 2003.

[KAUR06] Arvinder Kaur, "Development of Techniques for Good Quality Object-Oriented Software", Ph.D. dissertation, Guru Gobind Singh Indraprastha University, Delhi 2006.

[KEIT91] Keith and James, "Using Program Slicing In Software Maintenance", IEEE Transactions on Software Engineering, vol. 17, no. 8, pp. 751–761 August, 1991.

[LEE95] Y. Lee, B. Liang, S. Wu and F. Wang, "Measuring the Coupling and Cohesion of an Object-Oriented program based on Information flow", Proceedings of International Conference on Software Quality, Maribor, Slovenia 1995.

[LI93] W. Li, S. Henry, "Object-Oriented Metrics that Predict Maintainability", Journal of Systems and Software, vol. 23, no. 2, pp. 111–122, 1993.

[LION96] J.L. Lions et al., "Report of the Enquiry Board Constituted by Director – General of ESA for the Identification of the Causes of Failure", www.esrin.esa.it, July 19, Paris, 1996.

[LORE94]   M.Lorenz, and J.Kidd, "Object-Oriented Software Metrics", Prentice-Hall, 1994.
[MACC76]   T.J. McCabe, "A Complexity Metric", IEEE Transactions on Software Engineering, SE–2,4, pp. 308–320, December, 1976.
[MCGR01]   J.D. McGregor and David A. Sykes, "A Practical Guide to Testing Object Oriented Software", Addison Wesley, 2001.
[MALH09]   Ruchika Malhotra, "Empirical Validation of Object Oriented Metrics for Predicting Quality Attributes", Ph.D. Dissertation, Guru Gobind Singh Indraprastha University, Delhi 2009.
[MALH10]   R. Malhotra and P. Gupta, "Empirical Evaluation of Web Page Metrics", National Conference on Quality Management in Organizations, India, February 2010.
[MANN02]   Charles C. Mann, "Why Software is So Bad", Technology Review, www.technologyreview.com, 2002.
[MATH08]   Aditya Mathur, "Foundations of Software Testing", Pearson Education, 2008.
[MCMI04]   Phil McMinn, "Search based Software Test Data Generation: A Survey", Software Testing, Verification and Reliability, vol. 14, no. 2, pp. 105–156, June 2004.
[MICH01]   Christoph C. Michael, Gray McGraw and Michael A. Schatz, "Generating Software Test Data by Evolution", IEEE Transactions on Software Engineering, Vol 27, No. 12, 1085–1110, December, 2001.
[MUSA79]   J.D. Musa, "Validity of the Execution Time Theory of Software Reliability", IEEE Transactions on Reliability, R-28(3), pp. 181–191, 1979.
[MYER04]   G.J. Myers, "The Art of Software Testing", John Wiley and Sons, Inc., 2004.
[NASA04]   NASA, "Metrics Data Repository", www.mdp.ivv.nasa.gov, 2004.
[NORM89]   Norman Parrington et al., "Understanding Software Testing", John Wiley and Sons, 1989.
[PFLE01]   S.L. Pfleeger, "Software Engineering Theory and Practice", Prentice Hall, 2001.
[PRAV09]   Praveen Ranjan Srivastava and others, "Use of Genetic Algorithm in Generation of Feasible Test Data", SIGSOFT, Software Engineering Notes, March, vol. 34, no. 2, 2009.
[PRESS97]   R.S. Pressman, "Software Engineering: A Practitioner's Approach", Tata McGraw Hill, New York, 1997.
[QUAT03]   T. Quatrani, "Visual modeling with Rational Rose 2002 and UML", Pearson Education, 2003.
[RAMA76]   C.V. Ramamoorthy, S.F. Ho and W.T. Chen, "On the Automated Generation of Program Test Data", IEEE transactions on Software Engineering, vol. 2, no. 4, pp. 293–300, 1976.
[SHNE80]   B. Shneiderman, "Software Psychology", Winthrop Publishers, 1980.
[SING10]   Y. Singh, A. Kaur, R. Malhotra, "Empirical Validation of Object-Oriented Metrics for Predicting Fault Proneness Models", Software Quality Journal, vol. 18, no.1, pp. 3–35, 2010.
[STALL01]   W. Stallings, "Network Security Essentials, Pearson Education, India, 2001.

[STEP93]   Stephen Kan, "Metrics and Models in Software Quality Engineering", Pearson Education, 1993.

[TEGA92]   D.Tegarden, S. Sheetz, D.Monarchi, "A Software Complexity Model of Object-Oriented Systems", Decision Support Systems, vol. 13, pp. 241–262, 1992.

[VOAS95]   J. Voas and K. Miller, "Software Testability: The New Verification", IEEE Software, 12: 1728, May, 1995.

[WEIS84]   M. Weiser, "Program Slicing", IEEE Transactions on Software Engineering, vol. SE-10, no. 4, pp. 352–257, July 1984.

[WHIT00]   J.A. Whittaker, "What is Software Testing and Why is it so Hard?", IEEE Software, January / February, pp. 70–77, 2000.

Answers to Multiple Choice Questions

Chapter 1

1.1	(c)	1.11	(a)	1.21	(d)	1.31	(b)	1.41	(c)
1.2	(b)	1.12	(d)	1.22	(a)	1.32	(b)	1.42	(b)
1.3	(c)	1.13	(c)	1.23	(c)	1.33	(a)	1.43	(c)
1.4	(c)	1.14	(d)	1.24	(c)	1.34	(a)	1.44	(d)
1.5	(a)	1.15	(a)	1.25	(d)	1.35	(b)	1.45	(b)
1.6	(b)	1.16	(d)	1.26	(d)	1.36	(a)	1.46	(b)
1.7	(c)	1.17	(a)	1.27	(c)	1.37	(b)	1.47	(a)
1.8	(a)	1.18	(d)	1.28	(c)	1.38	(d)	1.48	(c)
1.9	(a)	1.19	(c)	1.29	(d)	1.39	(a)	1.49	(b)
1.10	(b)	1.20	(b)	1.30	(a)	1.40	(d)	1.50	(a)

Chapter 2

2.1	(b)	2.11	(c)	2.21	(a)
2.2	(a)	2.12	(a)	2.22	(c)
2.3	(c)	2.13	(b)	2.23	(b)
2.4	(c)	2.14	(b)	2.24	(a)
2.5	(d)	2.15	(b)	2.25	(b)
2.6	(b)	2.16	(c)	2.26	(d)
2.7	(a)	2.17	(d)	2.27	(c)
2.8	(c)	2.18	(a)	2.28	(d)
2.9	(d)	2.19	(c)	2.29	(d)
2.10	(a)	2.20	(c)	2.30	(a)

Chapter 3

3.1	(a)	3.11	(c)
3.2	(d)	3.12	(c)
3.3	(a)	3.13	(b)
3.4	(b)	3.14	(a)
3.5	(b)	3.15	(a)
3.6	(a)	3.16	(c)
3.7	(a)	3.17	(d)
3.8	(c)	3.18	(a)
3.9	(a)	3.19	(b)
3.10	(b)	3.20	(b)

Chapter 4

4.1	(d)		4.11	(a)
4.2	(d)		4.12	(d)
4.3	(d)		4.13	(c)
4.4	(a)		4.14	(a)
4.5	(a)		4.15	(a)
4.6	(c)		4.16	(b)
4.7	(c)		4.17	(a)
4.8	(b)		4.18	(d)
4.9	(a)		4.19	(d)
4.10	(a)		4.20	(a)

Chapter 5

5.1	(d)		5.11	(a)		5.21	(b)
5.2	(a)		5.12	(b)		5.22	(c)
5.3	(b)		5.13	(d)		5.23	(d)
5.4	(a)		5.14	(a)		5.24	(c)
5.5	(c)		5.15	(d)		5.25	(c)
5.6	(b)		5.16	(a)		5.26	(d)
5.7	(c)		5.17	(c)		5.27	(c)
5.8	(b)		5.18	(d)		5.28	(c)
5.9	(a)		5.19	(a)		5.29	(a)
5.10	(b)		5.20	(b)		5.30	(d)

Chapter 6

6.1	(d)		6.11	(b)
6.2	(c)		6.12	(d)
6.3	(a)		6.13	(a)
6.4	(d)		6.14	(a)
6.5	(b)		6.15	(b)
6.6	(d)			
6.7	(d)			
6.8	(a)			
6.9	(c)			
6.10	(a)			

Chapter 7

7.1	(b)		7.11	(b)
7.2	(c)		7.12	(b)
7.3	(c)		7.13	(b)
7.4	(d)		7.14	(c)
7.5	(a)		7.15	(a)
7.6	(d)			
7.7	(c)			
7.8	(d)			
7.9	(c)			
7.10	(b)			

Chapter 8

8.1	(c)	8.11	(c)	8.21	(a)
8.2	(b)	8.12	(d)	8.22	(d)
8.3	(d)	8.13	(a)	8.23	(d)
8.4	(b)	8.14	(a)	8.24	(a)
8.5	(a)	8.15	(b)	8.25	(b)
8.6	(d)	8.16	(c)		
8.7	(a)	8.17	(c)		
8.8	(d)	8.18	(d)		
8.9	(d)	8.19	(a)		
8.10	(c)	8.20	(d)		

Chapter 9

9.1	(a)	9.11	(a)
9.2	(b)	9.12	(b)
9.3	(b)	9.13	(a)
9.4	(c)	9.14	(b)
9.5	(c)	9.15	(a)
9.6	(c)	9.16	(c)
9.7	(d)	9.17	(d)
9.8	(c)	9.18	(a)
9.9	(a)	9.19	(b)
9.10	(a)	9.20	(d)

Chapter 10

10.1	(c)	10.11	(d)	10.21	(b)
10.2	(d)	10.12	(a)	10.22	(b)
10.3	(b)	10.13	(c)	10.23	(c)
10.4	(a)	10.14	(d)	10.24	(d)
10.5	(a)	10.15	(d)	10.25	(d)
10.6	(b)	10.16	(a)		
10.7	(c)	10.17	(b)		
10.8	(c)	10.18	(a)		
10.9	(a)	10.19	(d)		
10.10	(d)	10.20	(a)		

Chapter 11

11.1	(a)	11.11	(c)	11.21	(b)
11.2	(d)	11.12	(b)	11.22	(a)
11.3	(b)	11.13	(a)	11.23	(c)
11.4	(a)	11.14	(d)	11.24	(b)
11.5	(c)	11.15	(c)	11.25	(a)
11.6	(b)	11.16	(a)	11.26	(b)
11.7	(d)	11.17	(b)	11.27	(b)
11.8	(b)	11.18	(c)	11.28	(c)
11.9	(b)	11.19	(b)	11.29	(d)
11.10	(a)	11.20	(d)	11.30	(b)

Chapter 12

12.1	(a)	12.11	(c)
12.2	(b)	12.12	(a)
12.3	(c)	12.13	(c)
12.4	(b)	12.14	(a)
12.5	(b)	12.15	(c)
12.6	(d)		
12.7	(a)		
12.8	(c)		
12.9	(a)		
12.10	(d)		

Index

acceptance testing, 22, 373–374
adjacency matrix
    of a directed graph, 115
    of a graph, 114–116
adjacent nodes, 110
alpha testing, 22, 374
alternative flow, 290, 292
Apache's J Meter, 382
artificial neural network (ANN), 443
audit, of software project
    relevance scale, 246
    review checklist, 246–256
    theory and practice on the scale, 246
Autofocus, 511
Automated QA's time, 381
automated test data generation
    approaches, 496–502
    definition, 495–496
    dynamic, 495–496, 501–502
    random testing, 496
    static, 495–496
    symbolic execution for, 496–500
    test adequacy criteria, 495
    tools for, 511
    using genetic algorithm (GA), 502–506
automatic debugger, 379
Auto Tester's Auto Controller, 382

backtracking, 377–378
basic flow, 290, 292
Bertolino, A., 369
beta testing, 22, 374
Bogue, Robert, 241
bottom up integration, 372
boundary value analysis, 38–62
    applicability, 48

robust worst-case testing, 46–47
robustness testing, 43–44
worst-case testing, 44–46
breakpoints, 376
bug, 21

Capability Maturity Model for Software, 446
cause-effect graphing
    applicability, 99
    design of graph, 97
    design of limited entry decision table, 99
    identification of causes and effects, 97
    use of constraints, 97–99
    writing of test cases, 99
chains, 117
checklists
    audit, of software project, 246–256
    software design description (SDD)
        verification, 239–240
    software requirements specification (SRS)
        document verification, 235–238
    source code reviews, 242–243
    user manuals, 244–245
class testing, 411–414
code comprehension tools, 380
code coverage prioritization technique
    deletion algorithm, 352–362
    'modification' algorithm, 347–352
code inspectors, 380–381
compilers, 379
completeness, 441
complexity analysis tools, 380
Comuware's QA Centre, 382
Comuware's QALOAD, 382
connectedness of a graph, 117–119
connection matrix, 114–116

622 Index

control flow testing
    branch coverage, 167
    condition coverage, 167
    path coverage, 167–168
    statement coverage, 166–167
coupling, 370
cycle, 117
cyclomatic complexity, 144
    properties, 144
    value, 145–146
    with P connected components, 146

data flow testing
    advantages, 174
    define/reference anomalies, 174
    defining node for a variable, 174
    definition clear (dc) path for a variable, 175–176
    definition use (du) path for a variable, 175–176
    generation of test cases, 176–179
    identification of du and dc paths, 175
    usage node for a variable, 174
data structure metric, 421
data validity, strategies for, 317–325
database testing, 326–331
debugging, 24
    backtracking method, 377–378
    brute force method, 378
    cause elimination method, 378
    challenges, 374–375
    fixing of a bug, 377
    locating bugs, 376–377
    process, 375–377
    replication of bug, 375
    re-testing activity, 377
    run time debuggers, 379
    tools, 378–379
    trial and error method, 377
    understanding a bug, 375
decision table based testing
    applications, 83
    'do not care' conditions, 82–83
    extended entry decision tables, 82
    impossible conditions, 83
    limited entry decision tables, 82
    parts of decision table, 81–82
    'rule count,' 82–83
    set of conditions and their corresponding actions, 81
Decision to Decision (DD) path graph, 127

deletion algorithm, 352–362
deliverables, 22
directed graph (digraph), 110, 118–119
disconnected graph, 118
distinct edges, 112
documentation manuals, 19
driver, 369
dynamic software testing tools, 381–382
dynamic testing, 24

encapsulation, 394–395
equivalence class testing
    applicability, 65–66
    creation of, 63–65
    graphical representation of inputs, 64

failure intensity, 431–432
failure, definition, 21
failure-based failure specification, 428
Fast Track Courier, 393
fault, definition, 21
flow graph generator tools, 380
flows, 290
Fournier, Greg, 286
functional testing techniques
    boundary value analysis, 38–62
    cause-effect graphing technique, 96–99
    decision table based testing, 81–96
    equivalence class testing, 63–81
    robust worst-case testing, 46–47
    robustness testing, 43–44
    worst-case testing, 44–46

genetic algorithm (GA)
    crossover and mutation, 503–504
    fitness function, 504–505
    initial population, 503
    selection operator, 505
    stopping criteria, 505–506
graph matrix
    of a graph, 115
    of the program graph, 150–153
    Decision to Decision (DD) path graph, 127
    definition of graph, 110–113
    degree of a node, 112–113
    diagrammatical representation, 110–111
    directed (digraph), 110
    generation from a program, 123–127
    identification of independent paths of a program, 144–158
    matrix representation, 113–116

Index

null, 110
paths and independent paths, 116–119
regular, 113
simple, 112
undirected, 110

IBM Rational's Performance Tester, 382
IBM Rational's Robot, 382
IEEE Std 830–1998, 285, 299, 382
incidence matrix of a graph, 114
incident on nodes, 110
independent path, in a graph, 116
inspections, 231–232
integration testing, 370–373
isolated node, 110

Jacobson, Ivar, 285
Jelinski--Moranda model, for reliability estimation, 422, 437

length of the path, 116
limited entry decision tables, 82
logarithmic poisson execution time model, 422, 434–435
logical database requirements, 276–279
loop, 111

Marchetti, E., 369
mean absolute relative error (MARE), 443
mean relative error (MRE), 444
Mercury Interactive's Load Runner, 382, 511
Mercury Interactive's Win Runner, 382, 511
methods, 230–232
    problem statement of a university registration system, 257–258
    software design description (SDD) verification, 231, 239–240
    software requirements specification (SRS) document verification, 231–238
    source code reviews, 241–243
    user manuals, 244–245
milestones, 22
'Minimum' program
    critical/typical situations, 6–8
    inputs and outputs of, 6
    modified, 10–14
    possible reasons of failures, 8–9
modification algorithm, 347–352
multigraph, 112
Musa, J. D., 430–431
    basic execution time model, for reliability estimation, 422
mutant of the original program, 213–215
mutant operators, 216
mutation score, associated with a test suite, 216–217
mutation testing, 212–223
mutation, definition of, 212–215

non-homogeneous Poisson process (NHPP), 430–431
non-replication of a bug, 375
n-regular graph, 113
null graph, 110

object oriented metrics
    cohesion metrics, 424–425
    coupling metrics, 424
    inheritance metrics, 425–426
    size metrics, 426
    test metrics, 427–429
    abstraction concept, 393–394
    class testing, 411–414
    classes and objects, 390–391
    encapsulation, 394–395
    inheritance, 391–393
    levels, 395–396
    messages, 393
    methods, 393
    object orientation, concept of, 389–390
    path testing, 396–401
    polymorphism, 394
    responsibilities, 393
    state based testing, 404–409
    unit testing, 395
objecteering, 511
objective function, 502
operating procedure manuals, 20

parallel edges, 112
Parasoft's Insure++, 381
path testing
    activity diagram, 396–400
    calculation of cyclomatic complexity of a graph, 400–401
    generation of test cases, 401
peer reviews, 231
performance testing tools, 381–382
performance testing, of web application
    checklist, 479–480
    load testing, 476–479
    stress testing, 479
polymorphism, 394

precision, 441
prioritization scheme, 344–346
priority category, 344
'probability of occurrence' value, 344–345
problem statement, of a university registration system, 257–258
process metrics for testing, 423
product metrics for testing, 422–423
program graph, 123–125
program verification, 231
program, definition, 19

quality assurance (QA), 23
quality control, 23
quality evaluation system (QUES), 443
quality of source code, 428–429

Rational Robot, 511
Rational Rose, 511
receiver operating characteristics (ROC) curve, 441–442
regression testing, 377
    definition, 335–336
    process, 336–337
    risk analysis, 342–346
    selection of test cases, 337–340
    test case reduction activity, 340–341
    vs development testing, 336
replication of bug, 375
re-testing activity. see regression testing
review efficiency, 429
risk analysis
    definition, 342
    ranking of risks, 346
    risk matrix, 343–344
    table, 342
robust worst-case testing, 46–47
robustness testing, 43–44
run time debuggers, 379

sandwich integration, 372
scaffolding, 369
Segue Software's Silk Performer, 382
Segue Software's Silktest, 382
sensitivity, 441
simple graph, 112
simple path in a graph, 116
Simulink, 511
slice based testing, 197–212
    creation of program slices, 198–202
    generation of test cases, 202–203
    guidelines, 197–198
    mutant operators, 216
    mutation score associated with a test suite, 216–217
software design description (SDD) verification, 22, 231
    checklist, 239–240
    organization of document, 239
software development life cycle, V shaped model
    graphical representation, 27
    relationship of development and testing parts, 27–28
software development, standards, 285, 299, 382
software failures
    Ariane 5 rocket, 1–2
    financial, 3–4
    London Ambulance Service, 3
    USA 'Star Wars' programme, 3
    USS Yorktown, 3
    Windows XP, 4
    Y2K problem, 2
software maintenance, 335
software metrics
    applications, 421–422
    definition, 420–421
    measurement and measures, 420–421
    process metrics for testing, 423
    product metrics for testing, 422–423
software quality, 23
software quality, attributes prediction model
    example of fault prediction model in practice, 437–442
    Jelinski - Moranda model, 437
    logarithmic poisson execution time model, 434–435
    maintenance effort prediction model, 442–446
    non-homogeneous Poisson process (NHPP), 430–431
    reliability models, 430–433
software reliability, 23
software requirements specification (SRS)
    document verification, 22, 231–232, 421
    characteristics and organization of document, 233–234
    checklist, 235–238
    for university registration system, 259–279
    nature of document, 233
software system attributes
    maintainability, 275
    portability, 276

Index

security, 275
software test plan, 382
software testing
    acceptance testing, 373–374
    integration testing, 370–373
    levels of testing, 368–374
    system testing, 373
    unit testing, 369–370
software testing tools
    code comprehension tools, 380
    code inspectors, 380–381
    complexity analysis tools, 380
    coverage analysis tools, 381
    dynamic, 381–382
    flow graph generator tools, 380
    functional / regression testing tools, 382
    performance testing tools, 381–382
    process management tools, 382
    static, 379–381
    syntax and semantic analysis tools, 380
software testing, guidelines for validity checks
    data range, 316
    data type, 316
    domain specific checks, 316–317
    for university registration system (URS), 594–611
    mandatory data inputs, 316
    special data conditions, 316
    use cases of URS case study, test cases for, 541–593
software, definition, 19
source code coverage, percentage of, 429
source code reviews, 241–243
    checklist, 242–243
    issues related to, 241–242
source code, 376
'standardised' software, 373
state based testing, 404–409
    generation of test cases, 408–409
    state chart diagram, 406–407
    state machines, 404–406
    state transition tables, 407–408
static software testing tools, 379–381
static testing, 23–24
structural testing techniques
    control flow testing, 165–173
    data flow testing, 173–197
    mutation testing, 212–223
    slice based testing, 197–212
stub, 369

syntax and semantic analysis tools, 380
system testing, 373

Telelogic's Logicscope, 381
Teleogic Tau Tester, 511
test case defect density, 429
test case, 21–22
test cases, from use cases
    assigning actual values to variables, 296–299
    creation of use case scenario diagrams, 294–295
    design of test case matrix, 296–298
    generation of scenario diagrams, 293–294
    identification of different input states of a variable, 296
    identification of variables in a use case, 295
    of URS case study, 541–593
test metrics
    quality of source code, 428–429
    review efficiency, 429
    source code coverage, 429
    test case defect density, 429
    time, 427–428
test suite, 22
testing process
    definitions of testing, 6
    difficulty of measuring the progress of, 26
    good, 5
    limitations, 24–26
    need for, 14–15
    of valid and invalid inputs, 16–18
    people involved in, 15–16
    program 'Minimum,' 5–14
time-based failure specification, 427–428
top down integration, 372

undirected graph, 110, 114
Unified Modeling Language (UML), 285
unit testing, 369–370
university registration system (URS)
    assumptions and dependencies, 264
    constraints, 263
    definitions, acronyms, and abbreviations, 260
    functional requirements, 270–275
    hardware interfaces, 262
    logical database requirements, 276–279
    memory constraints, 263
    overview, 260
    performance requirements, 275
    product functions, 263
    product perspective, 261

purpose, 259
references, 260
scope, 259–260
site adaptation requirements, 263
software interfaces, 262
software system attributes, 275–276
SRS document of, 517–540
user characteristics, 263
user interfaces, 262, 264–270
user responsibilities, 261
validity checks, 594–611
use case
generation of test cases from, 292–299
importance of, 286
use case diagram, 285–286
drawing of, 288–289
identification of actors, 286–287
identification of use cases, 287–288
Jacobson's case template, 290
'Login' use case description, 291–292
writing of decription, 290–292
user interface management system (UIMS), 443
user manuals
checklist, 244–245

review process issues, 244
validation, 20, 412
verification, 20, 412
walkthroughs, 231
weakly connected graph, 119
web testing
analysis of results and observations, 469
browser testing, 470
configuration and compatibility testing, 469–471
database testing, 480–482
execution of usability tests, 469
functional testing, 456–458
key areas in, 455–456
performance testing, 476–480
post-deployment testing, 482–485
security testing, 471–475
user interface testing, 458–469
web page metrics, 485–486
web server architecture vs client-server architecture, 453–455
weighted graph, 112
worst-case testing, 44–46